A LIBRARY OF LITERARY CRITICISM

MODERN

Volume I
RUSSIAN LITERATURE

Frederick Ungar Publishing Co., New York

SLAVIC LITERATURES

A Library of Literary Criticism

Compiled and edited by
VASA D. MIHAILOVICH
Associate Professor of Slavic Languages
University of North Carolina

INTRODUCTION

One of the great flowerings of art was the one that took place in literature in nineteenth-century Russia. One need only mention the names of Pushkin, Gogol, Turgenev, Dostoyevski, Tolstoi, and Chekhov to give an immediate indication of the importance of Russian literature and its lasting influence on all of Western literature. This intensely creative activity did not come to an end with the twentieth century. Such major figures as Chekhov and Tolstoi lived and wrote into the twentieth century. New writers, such as Andreyev, Gorki, and Blok, established their reputations in the first two decades of the twentieth century.

Nor did the revolution in 1917 and the triumph of Bolshevism, with its concomitant artistic restraints, mean the end of significant literary creation by Russian writers. On the one hand, many gifted writers left the Soviet Union but continued to develop in emigration, some, like Remizov and Bunin, writing major works abroad. On the other hand, between 1917 and 1932, before Stalin firmly established totalitarian Bolshevism, there was considerable freedom to publish works of a wide variety of forms—including satire. And while it is true that there have been severe limitations on writing since 1932, an actively creative tradition remains in the Soviet Union. In part, the various thaws of the 1950s and 1960s have made it possible for a number of serious, nondoctrinaire works to be published, including previously suppressed works of older writers. Moreover, there is an increasing number of books that are circulated underground and frequently smuggled out and published abroad. Thus, though émigré Russian literature seems to be approaching its natural end—through death and assimilation—writers, from Zamyatin to Solzhenitsyn, largely through works published abroad, have continued the nineteenth-century Russian heritage of artistic excellence.

This book is the first of a two-volume reference work on twentieth-century Slavic literatures in the Library of Literary Criticism series. *Modern Slavic Literatures* follows the format of other volumes in the series (American, British, and German, to name some) in presenting twentieth-century Slavic writers—in Volume I, only Russian—through the eyes of leading critics both at home and abroad. An effort was made to include the earliest reactions to a writer's work as well as more recent criticism.

The critical selections represented here were chosen mainly with the idea of giving a balanced perspective of the authors' achievements and, where appropriate, of including extended remarks on individual works—such as Pasternak's *Doctor Zhivago* and Sholokhov's *The Quiet Don*—as well as overviews of the writers' careers. For the most important writers, a selection focusing on the author's personality is often included; for some writers—most notably Yesenin—the personality is as important as the literary creation, if not more so. The current critical reputation of a writer in the West was the guide for determining space allotted to each writer.

For the purposes of this book, "Russian" means the language, not the country. Excluded are all those writers living in the Soviet Union who do not write in Russian (the two other Soviet Slavic languages—Ukrainian and Byelorussian—are covered in Volume II of *Modern Slavic Literatures*). Included are émigré Russian writers, some of whose work has as yet not appeared in the Soviet Union. The selections on Nabokov, however, cover only his early works, those written in Russian.

Sixty-nine of the most significant Russian authors of the twentieth century are included, from the internationally famous Chekhov and Gorki to such writers as Serafimovich and Pogodin, who are not well known abroad but are important in their own country. One consideration for the selection of authors was the availability of translations of their work, since authors who have been translated into English are those easiest for the interested reader to pursue. Moreover, translation of works, not only into English but into German, French, and so forth, has been a stimulus to critical interest abroad. Almost all the writers included are imaginative, in the sense that they are writers of fiction, poetry, and drama rather than essayists or critics. In Russian literature, however, there is frequently no sharp distinction between imaginative and nonimaginative literature; and the autobiography and the literary reminiscences—whose practitioners include Bunin and Ehrenburg—have a long and respected tradition.

The selections included in this book were chosen from a variety of sources: full-length critical studies, introductions to books, academic periodicals, literary magazines, and book-review sections of major newspapers. Although Western European critics are included, the stress is on American and British critics. Some outstanding imaginative writers are also represented, such as Auden on Voznesenski and D. H. Lawrence on Rozanov. One of the reasons for emphasizing criticism from abroad is that Russian criticism frequently is unreliable because of ideological biases. Nonetheless, Russian criticism is substantially represented. Because so many Russian imaginative writers also write criticism and memoirs, one has the opportunity for the illumination gained from reading the remarks of one major writer about another. Thus, included in this book are the comments of Yevtushenko on Akhmadulina, Tsvetayeva on Pasternak, Pasternak on Tsvetayeva, Tvardovski on Solzhenitsyn, Bunin on Chekhov, as well as numerous appraisals of other authors by Ehrenburg, Fedin, Gorki, Gumilyov, Mandelshtam, and Paustovski.

The history of Russian literary criticism closely parallels that of Russian imaginative literature. At the beginning of the twentieth century, standards of symbolism were dominant in criticism. Such prominent symbolist writers as Belyi and Bryusov also wrote symbolist criticism of other writers. Represented here, for example, are selections by Belyi on Blok, Bryusov, and Sologub, and selections by Bryusov on Annenski, Gumilyov, Merezhkovski, and Sologub.

In the unsettled years from 1917 to 1932 the credos of formalism were dominant in Russian criticism. Formalism insisted on the doctrine of poetry as free creation, of art as divorced from life. In many ways formalism was remarkably close to American New Criticism in its analytical concern for language. Two outstanding formalist critics—Eikhenbaum and Zhirmunski—are represented by several selections apiece.

Since 1932, when the iron hands of Stalin emasculated Soviet literature, Soviet criticism has been reduced, even more so than imaginative literature, to service of the party line. "Socialist realism," formulated at that time, prescribed a standard for literature that criticism was expected to uphold. The notions of socialist realism have been succinctly defined by René Wellek in the *Encyclopedia of World Literature in the 20th Century*: "The term 'socialist realism' is the loose over-all theory which asks the writer, on the one hand, to reproduce reality correctly, accurately, to be a realist in the sense of depicting contemporary society with an insight into its structure; and on the other hand, it asks the writer to be a socialist realist, which in practice means that he is not to reproduce reality accurately, but use his art to spread socialism—that is, communism, the Party spirit, and the Party line."

When in 1946 Andrei Zhdanov made the conception of socialist realism even more binding, and in effect tried to outlaw any writing smacking of individualism or Western influences, Soviet creative literature had either to conform, to be silent, or to go underground. Criticism, which is the intermediary between the artist and the people, was simply reduced to cant or to silence. This political situation explains the minimal representation of postwar Soviet criticism, although parts of the historically important Zhdanov attacks on Akhmatova and Zoshchenko are reproduced. It must be added, however, that the various thaws have helped to unbind Soviet criticism somewhat, and some of the recent Soviet criticism represented here illustrates the movement away from hard-line socialist realism.

For some writers, the gaps in both Soviet and Western criticism often indicate enforced silence. One of the saddest facts of modern Russian literature is that many writers have been subjected, at one time or another, to harassment and persecution, which often led to imprisonment, enforced silence, and even death. Zamyatin, Pilnyak, Babel, Mandelshtam, and Akhmatova were some of the most prominent victims of such persecution.

Many of the selections in this volume have been translated into English for the first time; these are marked with a dagger after the credit line. In new translations, a compromise system of transliterating names and titles was used—one that avoids diacritical marks and still keeps as reasonably close to Russian sounds as possible. However, because the styling of selections previously published in English was left intact, the various transliterations of Russian words as well as the spellings of English words were left intact. The changes in systems of transliterating Russian provides an unexpected interest in that it reflects the increasing knowledge of the Russian language in the English-speaking world.

Titles of works are given in both Russian and English at the first appearance of that title in an author's section. In general, titles of published English translations are given in parentheses. If none exists, a literal translation (neither italicized nor in quotation marks) is given in brackets. Not infrequently, however, the first reference to a title in an English-language selection is in English, in which case the original Russian title is added in brackets as an editorial aid. On a number of occasions, more than one English title appears for the same work. This is because British and American titles frequently differ (indeed, occasionally two different American translations of the same work have different titles). In such instances, the reader is referred back to the original Russian title so that it is clear that it is the same work under discussion. Those interested in an extensive listing of English translations of Russian literature are referred to the series *The Literatures of the World in English Translation,* Volume II: *The Slavic Literatures,* compiled by Richard C. Lewanski and others (New York: The New York Public Library and Frederick Ungar, 1967).

Volume I of *Modern Slavic Literatures* is intended as a reference tool for students, scholars, librarians, and researchers—the first such compendium on Russian literature in any language. It is also hoped that the general reader—or, to use Virginia Woolf's phrase, the "common reader," the interested nonspecialist—will find both a satisfaction of curiosity and a desire to pursue further individual writers and critics.

The editor extends his thanks to all copyright holders who have granted permission to use excerpts from their publications and to the University of North Carolina Research Council for financial assistance to him in preparing this volume.

V.D.M.

AUTHORS INCLUDED

Akhmadulina, Bella
Akhmatova, Anna
Aksyonov, Vasili
Andreyev, Leonid
Annenski, Innokenti
Babel, Isaak
Balmont, Konstantin
Bely, Andrei
Blok, Aleksandr
Bryusov, Valeri
Bulgakov, Mikhail
Bunin, Ivan
Chekhov, Anton
Dudintsev, Vladimir
Ehrenburg, Ilya
Fadeyev, Aleksandr
Fedin, Konstantin
Gladkov, Fyodor
Gorki, Maksim
Gumilyov, Nikolai
Ilf, Ilya
Ivanov, Vsevolod
Ivanov, Vyacheslav
Katayev, Valentin
Kaverin, Venyamin
Kazakov, Yuri
Khlebnikov, Velemir
Korolenko, Vladimir
Kuprin, Aleksandr
Leonov, Leonid
Mandelshtam, Osip
Mayakovski, Vladimir
Merezhkovski, Dmitri
Nabokov, Vladimir
Nagibin, Yuri

Nekrasov, Viktor
Olesha, Yuri
Ostrovski, Nikolai
Panova, Vera
Pasternak, Boris
Paustovski, Konstantin
Petrov, Yevgeni (*See* Ilf, Ilya)
Pilnyak, Boris
Platonov, Andrei
Pogodin, Nikolai
Prishvin, Mikhail
Remizov, Aleksei
Rozanov, Vasili
Serafimovich, Aleksandr
Shklovski, Viktor
Sholokhov, Mikhail
Simonov, Konstantin
Sologub, Fyodor
Solzhenitsyn, Aleksandr
Tendryakov, Vladimir
Tertz, Avram
Tikhonov, Nikolai
Tolstoi, Aleksei
Tolstoi, Lev
Tsvetayeva, Marina
Tvardovski, Aleksandr
Vinokurov, Yevgeni
Virta, Nikolai
Voznesenski, Andrei
Yesenin, Sergei
Yevtushenko, Yevgeni
Zabolotski, Nikolai
Zamyatin, Yevgeni
Zoshchenko, Mikhail

PERIODICALS USED

Where no abbreviation is indicated, the periodical references are listed in full.

ASEER	American Slavic and East European Review (New York)
	Annali: Sezione slava (Naples)
	Apollon (Leningrad)
BA	Books Abroad (Norman, Okla.)
BW	Book Week (Chicago)
	Calendar of Modern Letters (London)
	Canadian Slavic Studies (Montreal)
	Canadian Slavonic Papers (Toronto)
	Christ und Welt (Stuttgart)
	Current Digest of the Soviet Press (Columbus, Ohio)
	Dial (Chicago)
	Encounter (London)
	Epopeya (Berlin)
Harper	Harper's Magazine (New York)
HdR	Hudson Review (New York)
KR	Kenyon Review (Gambier, Ohio)
	Knizhny ugol (Leningrad)
	Krasnaya nov (Moscow, Leningrad)
	Life (New York)
List	Listener (London)
	Literaturnaya gazeta (Moscow)
	Moskva (Moscow)
	Na literaturnom postu (Moscow)
	Nation (New York)
	Neva (Moscow, Leningrad)
NR	New Republic (Washington, D. C.)
NS	New Statesman (London)
NSN	New Statesman and Nation (London)
NY	New Yorker (New York)
NYHT	New York Herald Tribune Book Section (New York)
NYR	New York Review of Books (New York)

NYT	New York Times Book Review (New York)
	Novy mir (Moscow)
	Oktyabr (Moscow)
PLL	Papers on Language and Literature (Edwardsville, Ill.)
PR	Partisan Review (New Brunswick, N. J.)
	Poetry (Chicago)
	Pravda (Moscow)
PC	Problems of Communism (Washington, D. C.)
QR	Quarterly Review (London)
	Rech (Leningrad)
	Rossiya (Moscow)
	Ruski arhiv (Belgrade)
RR	Russian Review (Stanford, Calif.)
	Russkaya mysl (Moscow)
	Russkoe bogatstvo (Leningrad)
	Russkoe iskusstvo (Moscow)
	Satire Newsletter (Oneonta, N. Y.)
SR	Saturday Review (New York)
	Scando-Slavica (Copenhagen)
SwR	Sewanee Review (Sewanee, Tenn.)
SEEJ	Slavic and East European Journal (Madison, Wisc.)
SlR	Slavic Review (Seattle)
SEER	Slavonic and East European Review (London)
SAB	South Atlantic Bulletin (Chapel Hill, N. C.)
SL	Soviet Literature (Moscow)
	Sovremennye zapiski (Paris)
Spec	Spectator (London)
SSF	Studies in Short Fiction (Newberry, S. C.)
	Survey (London)
TLS	Times Literary Supplement (London)
	TriQuarterly (Evanston, Ill.)
	USSR: Soviet Life Today (Moscow)
	Vesna (Moscow)
	Vestnik literatury (Leningrad)
	Vozrozhdenie (Paris)
	Die Welt der Slaven (Wiesbaden)
	Zeitschrift für slavische Philologie (Heidelberg)
	Zeitschrift für Slawistik (Berlin)
	Znamya (Moscow)
	Zvezda (Moscow, Leningrad)

AKHMADULINA, BELLA (1937–   )

Bella Akhmadulina, unlike Yevtushenko, has written hardly any poetry on political themes. Nor does she hold her readers with striking verse forms, play of words, or sharp dissonances as does Andrei Voznesensky. Bella stands closer to tradition in this respect. And yet her clear, lovely measures are so moving, so fresh, that they seem newly discovered, not at all derivative.

Readers are drawn to Akhmadulina's "everyday life" verse, as they are to the work of other new generation poets, because it has something new to say and new and fresh ways to say it.

Feeling is primary in her poetry. Her verses break from her irresistibly, like molten lava. She likes to write about the intricacy of simple things and the simplicity of intricate things. She does not write with cool objectivity. Her lines come straight from a young and impassioned heart. They are spontaneous, moving, fashioned with innate artistry. . . .

Akhmadulina also has her excesses. Infatuated with a "newsy" quality in poetry, she sometimes slips into bookishness. In some of her verses there is an overly fond contemplation of feminine weakness and too much in musical phrases and somewhat tired similes. She then has visions of "roving sails," "an ancient park," "a black swan," "the pilgrim at the gates of a temple," the reckless rider who does not heed the woman crying "Love me!"

It is not without reason, therefore, that the critics have taken Akhmadulina to task for a chamber-music quality, a certain "defenselessness" that threatens to vitiate her poetry.

Evgeni Dvornikov. USSR: Soviet Life Today.
March, 1963, p. 62

We find Bella Akhmadulina's poetry more successful the closer it comes to that profound understatement of pity and faith which is Anna Akhmatova's trademark. Akhmadulina still focuses on the brightness or startling quality of images. . . . [She] has talent, has insight, but, naturally, has not had time yet to be sure of the composition, to elaborate a unifying vision. Such vision, which distinguishes Akhmatova's work, is the substance of poetry's power. A poem that is powerful is always with us; it constantly does its work. It is always becoming contemporary, as the adjustments of our criticism indicate.

F. D. Reeve. KR. Summer, 1964, p. 551

In Bella Akhmadulina's love lyrics, the note of despair, at times verging on anachronism, is coupled with a quite old-fashioned pride. And even though she does not yet write as if a lover were looking over her shoulder all the time, there is at least no representative of the Writer's Union. Her small but distinguished body of work shows that she is one of the most promising poets. . . .

Verbiage spoils Bella Akhmadulina's prenatal autobiography just as glaringly. With her Italo-Tartar lineage, this talented poetess could hardly have failed to do something dashing. Not yet an architect, Akhmadulina works unevenly, untidily in spots, and in this long piece, "My Genealogy" ["Moya rodoslovnaya"], attempts to hang the story of her ancestors on a tricky, false, and unnecessary nail of contingency. But the good outweighs the defects. There is a boisterousness about this uneven poem, a bubbling wonderment about life and self, an innocent incestuousness in her intrusion into the matrimonial beds of her interesting grandparents. The lack of fit between design and detail does not spoil the poem. What does is the pomp and falsehood of the inevitable conversation with the reader.

Vera S. Dunham. SIR. March, 1965, pp. 62, 68

Some poets acquire range first and only later master the formal incarnation. Only in some rare cases do both achievements come together. Bella was too young to have any range in her knowledge of the world. She lacked the personal suffering to feel with her own skin "the tragic essence of the world." Of course, she did feel something instinctively, but that did not blend in her with the intimate experiences of a large-eyed girl, with a Komsomol badge and schoolgirl's plaits. But instead she began seriously to study form. In the instability of her gifted sentimental lines something concrete and concise started to appear. Endowed with an amazing poetic ear, Bella grasped the inner law of freshness of rhyme, resilience of rhythm, and delicacy of epithet, and that is one of the most important components of real poetry. She managed to master in only one year as much as I did in at least ten. She learned the charm of grammatical incorrectness which creates a special air in a poem. She understood that sentimentality and metaphors alone cannot get her very far if there is a lack of tension and compactness in her poems. Out of her sleeves, like an enchantress from a Russian fairy tale, she produced a sparkling shower of epithets, rhymes, intonations, images. Formerly her verses merely rustled. Now they started to ring. However, the compactness of the form, still combined with the poverty of the content, as yet could not command faith in her future in the minds of many serious people, although it did raise some hopes.

Her name became known among readers, but for the sake of honesty one has to admit that this was due not to her poems, but to some kind of promise which was contained in them, as well as to her participation in the general wave of Soviet poetry and to other accompanying circumstances.

Yevgeny Yevtushenko. Introduction to Bella
Akhmadulina, *Fever and Other New Poems*
(New York, William Morrow, 1969), p. 3

AKHMATOVA, ANNA (1889–1966)

The ideology of Anna Akhmatova's *Chetki* [The Rosary] is not clearly thought out. The poetess did not figure herself out, did not, to unite her experiences, place at their center some external fact that does not refer to something understood only by her. In this, she is different from the symbolists. On the other hand, her themes are often not realized within the limits of the given poem. Much in Akhmatova seems unfounded because it is unproven. Moreover, as is the case with the majority of young poets, Anna Akhmatova often utilizes the words "pain," "grief," and "death." This pessimism, so natural and therefore beautiful and youthful, had been until now the property of a "proving pen"; in Akhmatova's poems pessimism has found its place in poetry for the first time. . . .

Akhmatova's book seems exciting and dear to people . . . who are controlled by a deceptive memory and who are wrangling about each stage of the heart they have experienced. It contains the hitherto mute voice of various beings; women who have fallen in love, who are cunning, dreamy, and ecstatic, speak at last in their real and, at the same time, artistically convincing voice. That connection with the world, which I have mentioned before, seems to be the fate of each genuine poet. It is almost attained by Akhmatova because she knows the joy of contemplating the external world and is capable of conveying this joy to us.

Nikolai Gumilyov. *Apollon.* 5, 1914, p. 36[†]

Akhmatova's diction is characterized by a conscious effort toward the simplicity of colloquial speech and everyday words far removed from the narrow circles of lyric poetry; her syntax gravitates toward the freedom of a living word, not a written one. . . . But this colloquial style never lapses into prosaic expressions but always remains artistically effective. It shows Akhmatova's great artistic mastery; her striving for a pristine simplicity of words; her distrust of unjustified poetic exaggerations, excessive metaphors, and worn-out paths; and her clarity and deliberate precision of expression.

One of the most important characteristics of Akhmatova's poetry is its epigrammatic quality. In this, one can see both an affinity with the French poets of the eighteenth century (as well as French classicism) and a sharp distinction from the musical and emotional lyrics of the romanticists and symbolists. A subtlety of observation and correctness of view, an ability to generalize in a short verbal formula, a completeness of verbal expression—these traits, sharply contrasted to the musical lyricism of the old and new romanticists, are indispensable conditions of the epigrammatic style. Yet there is an important difference between Akhmatova and the French; where in the latter there is only a general judgment—antithetically sharpened and expressed in the form of aphorism employed everywhere and on all occasions independent of the conditions that brought it about— in Akhmatova one could hear the personal voice and sense the personal mood even in the most general aphorisms.

Viktor Zhirmunski. *Russkaya mysl.*
Dec., 1916, pp. 34–35[†]

Akhmatova's poetry is a complex lyrical novel. We can trace the treatment of narrative threads forming the novel. We can speak of its composition, down to the relationship between individual characters. Moving from one collection of her poetry to another, we experience the feeling of becoming increasingly interested in the plot and the development of the "novel."

Boris Eikhenbaum. *Vestnik literatury.*
June–July, 1921, p. 8[†]

Akhmatova, employing the purest literary language of her time, applied with utmost determination the traditional forms of the Russian—and the universal—folk song. In her verses there is no psychological fragmentation at all, but rather the typical parallelism of the folk song, with its strong asymmetry of the two adjacent theses, according to the following scheme: "In the kitchen-garden there is an elder-tree, and in Kiev an uncle." Hence a two-leaved stanza, with the unexpected thrust at the end. Her verses resemble the folk song not only in structure but also in essence: they seem invariably to be lamentations. The poet's purely literary vocabulary, muttered through clenched teeth, makes her especially interesting and allows us to divine a peasant woman in a literary Russian lady of the twentieth century.

Osip Mandelshtam. *Russkoe iskusstvo.*
Jan., 1923, p. 79[†]

The subject matter of Anna Akhmatova is feminine, and feminine her attitude towards it. It is almost entirely love, for even when her subject is the absence of love she treats it in terms of love. It is hardly ever happy love, and it is never love in the abstract. It is all occasional; some of her lyrics are so actual, so tangibly personal, that it is impossible to make any comment, for every comment would have to be a revelation of private life. It is all realistic, it has a definite background, and almost every one of her poems may be located. The background, even if it is not described in so many words, is almost invariably recognized as Petersburg, "the granite town of glory and of woe," or Tsarskoe Selo, or a village in North Russia, somewhere between Petersburg and Moscow. It has been said that the success of her poetry among the wide public was mainly due to the fact that each poem of hers is a concentrated novel—a psychological novel compressed to eight or twelve lines. Some of them might be described as dramatic lyrics, a term not irrelevantly suggestive of Browning, the Browning of "Meeting at Night" and "Parting at Morning." It is true that Anna Akhmatova has not anything of the English poet's power of creating an abundance of lifelike men and women. There are practically two actors in her miniature novels: He and She. The men change from time to time, the heroine remains always the same, though the situations vary infinitely. Of course, the full measure of Anna Akhmatova's craftsmanship may be gauged only by one who reads them in the original and may test her "curious felicity" in the choice of words and the happy efficiency of her rhythms. But the narrative or dramatic quality is apparent in a tolerable translation.

TLS. Nov. 20, 1924, p. 746

Akhmatova's subject matter is altogether individualistic. The range of her poetry is limited to squalor; it is the poetry of a frenzied lady, dreaming about the boudoir and the chapel. Basic with her are amorous and erotic motifs, intertwined with motifs of sorrow, yearning, death, mysticism, and doom. The feeling of being doomed, an understandable feeling for the social consciousness of a dying group; the gloomy tones of a deathbed hopelessness; mystical experiences, coupled with eroticism—such is Akhmatova's spiritual world, a splinter from the old culture of nobility, the "good old times of Catherine," which has passed into eternity, never to return. She is not exactly a nun, not exactly a harlot, but rather nun and harlot, with whom harlotry is mixed with prayer. . . .

What has this poetry in common with the interests of our people and state? Exactly nothing. Akhmatova's creative genius is a matter of the distant past; it is alien to the modern Soviet actuality and cannot be tolerated in the pages of our journals. Our literature is not a private enterprise calculated to please the varied tastes of a literary market. We are in no way obliged to provide a place in our literature for tastes and tempers that have nothing in common with the ethics and qualities of Soviet people. What instruction can Akhmatova's works give to our youth? None, besides harm. These works can only sow despondency, low spirits, pessimism, the inclination to turn away from the burning questions of social life and activity for the narrow little world of personal experiences. How is it possible to turn over to her the upbringing of our youth? And yet Akhmatova has been published with great readiness . . . even in separate collections. This is a crude political error.

Andrei Zhdanov. Zvezda.
July–Aug., 1946, pp. 10–13†

Akhmatova's poetry, particularly in *The Rosary*, has also another peculiarity. It is these unexpected but convincing, illogical but fine psychological transitions from words of emotion to words of description, from the soul to nature, from feeling to fact. She assembles artistically the particulars of a given moment which are often unnoticeable to others; she notices everything anew so that her internal world is not merely framed by the external world, but they combine into one solid and organic wholeness of life. "Her poems are her life." She often compares the present with the past, and the recollections of her youth create nostalgic moods. . . .

Akhmatova is essentially an urban poet, a poet of St. Petersburg. The spring's twilight—"the white nights"—with its melancholy and dreaming on the islands, where the Neva rolls her waves into the sea and where calm and serenity reign; the autumn winds round the Winter Palace, when smoke from the chimneys dances a wild witchdance in the air and the steel grey Neva roars with hidden fury, streaming over the parapet into the streets where disaster awaits the citizens of the capital of Peter the Great; or the cold winter brings down masses of snow from the grimy sky, covering the pavements with a white eider-down over which horse-drawn sleighs glide noiselessly—such are the settings of Akhmatova's poetry. But occasionally her muse carries her to the countryside.

Leonid Strakhovsky. ASEER. May, 1947, pp. 6–7

The eternal theme of the poetry of love, when sung by a woman, is the fealty of a loving soul, the loyalty of a passionate heart. Thus the secret of Anna Akhmatova's poetry could be summed up in a single word: fidelity. Fidelity to her man and her passion, as well as to nature and life; above all, fidelity to the glories and miseries of her sex. Hence the strange harmony reconciling the opposite strains of her poetry, made at once of candor and modesty, of spontaneity and discretion, of passion and restraint. All the images employed by this free and capricious lover are feminine in the familiar sense, motherly or housewifely, homespun or domestic, as in the beautiful metaphor by which a smooth liquid surface becomes "the tablecloth of the water." The main theme of her poetry is passion, yet she sings of love in the humble tone of the elegy, rather than in the lofty mode of the hymn. Hers is not the soul of a maenad or a nymph, but of a pious Christian woman, or of a modern, bourgeois lady, simple and direct. She finds love beautiful and terrible for being an all-day reality, an everyday thing: the most intimate of all habits, the daily bread of the soul. The poetess savors the experience of love in all its recurring phases, meeting and separation, distance and absence, desire and longing, jealousy and remorse. Each one of these feelings or events is projected outside, within the visible, objective world and finds forever a local habitation and a name in the place to which it is still connected in the poetess' memory, which turns that place into a kind of private shrine.

Renato Poggioli. *The Poets of Russia*
(Cambridge, Mass., Harvard University Press, 1960),
pp. 231–32

Among many other images in Akhmatova's poetry, three occur particularly often: the willow, Pushkin, and the avenue. The image of the willow is taken from the Russian folk tale and song . . . rather than from the moans of Shakespeare's Desdemona. . . . In many verses throughout the years, Akhmatova presents Pushkin as a symbol of spiritual health and of the dreams of and love for freedom in Russian poetry. With his name are connected Akhmatova's innermost doubts and quests; she thus inherits and preserves the Pushkinian tradition in our poetry. Finally, the image of the avenue in the garden of Tsarskoe Selo, now Pushkinsk, permeated with rich sounds . . . is found in all Akhmatova's verses—from the early ones to the present. If the evolution of these three images, more exactly three image circles, is traced, it would become clear that the simple landscape sketch (often combined with a second motif, amorous and lyrical) of her first books has, in her latest verses, given way to the themes of Russia, its "hour of destiny," and the existence of man and nature.

Lev Ozerov. *Rabota poeta*
(Moscow, Sovetski pisatel, 1963), p. 177†

The difficult atmosphere of a crisis—the sum total of which was [Akhmatova's] *Belaya staya* [The White Flock]—proved painful in light of her own concerns. The search for a new meaning of life; the rejection of deceiving easiness and oppressive idleness; the complex vagaries of private life in conjunction with an alarming, seismologically sharpened feeling of an underground tremor already shaking the abutments of a routine peace and foreboding the end of the criminal Rasputin epoch—all these demanded of a poet a service to the lofty rather than to the tawdry and ephemeral. The complexity of the situation was inherent in her unawareness of the coordinates along which time developed and moved; hence the morbidity and tragicalness of many verses in *Belaya staya*. . . . All who wrote about Akhmatova noticed the tragic intonation of the contents of her books. . . . Contemporaries could not help but feel that deep in Akhmatova's fragile verses, at times decked with haughtiness and coldness, lurk chaos and terror, which in the reader's eyes mercilessly tear asunder the framework of the private love episode to the point of universal tragedy.

A. I. Pavlovski. *Anna Akhmatova*
(Leningrad, Lenizdat, 1966), pp. 38, 54[†]

Akhmatova's poetry above all gives vent to genuine lyric expression, to unaffected feelings and an originality of thought, it is poetry marked by the unusual concentration and exactingness of moral principle, for all its purely earthly and physically tangible basis. It is poetry alien to affectation, to playing at sentiment, to the petty experiences of unsatiated passion, to thoughtless "womanish" jealousy and spiritual egoism. In its domain there is not even a trace of vulgarity—that many-faced and most terrible foe of love lyrics.

The characteristic features of Anna Akhmatova's craftsmanship are, too, determined by a lofty moral code. It is the noble laconicism, the capaciousness of speech which is sparing in the use of words, and due to which behind the sparse lines of a poem a far more complex substance lives and throbs. Her language is by no means a lady's "language of flowers," not a language specially chosen to express "delicate feelings," but one that is living, often colloquial and in ordinary daily use, almost deliberately prosaic.

Aleksandr Tvardovski. *SL*. June, 1966, p. 182

As a poet Anna Akhmatova combines three qualities: classical austerity, lyrical intensity, and a marked gift for precise and concrete language. The combination of these three qualities is rare if not unique in modern Russian poetry.

Classicism is, as a rule, a cold and generalised affair, dealing in allegories and disdainful of the shapeless variety of life. Nor is lyricism necessarily concrete. Blok, for instance, can rarely be pinned down as to the time, location and sequence of events he describes. Again, realism rarely goes hand in hand with classical simplicity. In Akhmatova all three are effectively combined in one powerful, highly idiosyncratic poetic personality.

The epithet "classical" has nothing self-consciously archaic in Akhmatova's case. The language she uses is the ennobled everyday speech of an educated Russian. So, of course, is Pasternak's poetic language. But there is a clear distinction between Akhmatova's speech and that of Pasternak and Tsvetaeva. These two poets reflect the earthy and folksy Moscow ambience. Akhmatova's restraint and reserve are in the Petersburg tradition. On her own testimony her three masters were Derzhavin, Pushkin, and Annensky—three Petersburg poets from three successive centuries. Primeval chaos is as firmly controlled in Akhmatova's poetry as the Neva is by her granite banks. Her diction is austere and distinct. There is a definite Latin sonority about her verse—surprising as this is in the case of a highly feminine poet. Yet this reserve co-exists with great lyrical passion. In fact it requires all Akhmatova's inborn sense of form and proportion to control the passions fighting their way into her lines.

Victor S. Frank. Survey. July, 1966, p. 97

Anna Akhmatova writes about herself, and if her poetry gives us a picture of her country and her epoch, it is through herself that they are seen —an undistorted image, because her vision is clear, her perceptions straight and honest, her sense of actuality very keen. . . . She is her own theme, a Tolstoyan heroine writing of herself, and like a Tolstoyan heroine, responding with tremulous sensitivity to what occurs to her and around her. Her poems are a wonderful self-portrait, drawn from moment to moment, recreating, like a nineteenth-century novel, each scene and event, evoking its atmosphere, and reviving the emotion at its core; but because she is a lyric poet and not a novelist, she is never circumstantial. And she does not distort or exaggerate. In her laconic, understated way, she tells a poignant story of unhappy love, resignation, and profound grief. It is a record of emotions that shape each scene and every event, but are never analyzed or spelled out, never explicitly given but are implicit in details etched on the memory—of a room, an action, a gesture. . . .

Akhmatova has a gift for recreating the painful drama of baffled love, and then of resignation, when her voice strikes a deeper note, and in telling herself that life is easier without love, because insomnia has gone and the pointer that marks the hours on the tower clock is no longer an arrow that threatens death, she is actually underscoring the depth of her loss. Many moods accompany unhappiness, and the love that seemed dead is always there; memory keeps it alive, and there is jealousy, and long, slow, empty days, and the useless question: what did I ever do to have been punished so? Such are Akhmatova's early poems—full of pathos, though not weakness. They are the work of a woman strong enough to be undeceived and of a clear-eyed artist entirely in command of herself, who with a steady hand engraves the image of her unhappiness in lucid, sparse, deep lines.

Helen Muchnic. RR. Jan., 1967, pp. 17–18

The attitude of the prerevolutionary critics toward Akhmatova's poetry differs from that of the critics after the Revolution. Similarly, in the Soviet period the critics looked upon the poet differently before and after

Stalin's death. Outside the Soviet Union the critics, both Russian and foreign, differed sharply with Soviet critics in their evaluation of Akhmatova's contribution to Russian literature. All these differences and changes were brought about not so much by changes in Akhmatova's poetry, of which to be sure there were some, as by the different vantage points of, and changes in, the critics themselves. As is often the case with Soviet writers, their purely literary achievements were accepted or rejected for nonliterary reasons. . . .

While prerevolutionary references to [Akhmatova] are mainly concerned with her new, strong talent and have a relatively easy task because of the single theme of her poetry, later critiques differ sharply in their basic approach. The opponents of the regime tend to see in Akhmatova a victim and a martyr; the proponents of the regime at first reject her, then condescend to accept her into the family. But no matter how all these critics differ in their evaluation of Akhmatova's views or themes, they agree that she is a master of her craft and of the language and that she has decisively contributed to Russian literature. The prerevolutionary critics and those immediately following the Revolution (especially the Formalists) pay much more attention to her purely artistic qualities, while the later critics, both Soviets and émigrés, allow political considerations to govern their judgment and to overshadow their examination and presentation of her works as literary art.

Vasa D. Mihailovich. PLL.
Winter, 1969, pp. 102–3, 110–11

AKSYONOV, VASILI (1932–   )

Slang poses an almost impossible problem to the translator. Alec Brown has done his best with [Aksyonov's] *A Starry Ticket* [*Zvyozdny bilet*], a tale of bright young people in contemporary Moscow. But the result, though nowhere difficult to follow, is not a piece of prose to be savoured for its style. Nevertheless it is a work of the greatest interest, as a picture of the times. In Russia, says the blurb, it caused a stir because of its irreverence and frivolity; though these are redeemed by a sound communist ending. To western readers it is the unspoken assumptions of the author which are really informative. . . .

The atmosphere throughout is that of an old-fashioned prep school. There is even the old antagonism between learning and games. If your soccer is good enough some university will find room for you; but suppose you neglect your studies in favour of football and still don't quite get into the eleven? But it is a prep school with far too many breaks. Any adult is entitled to exhort the young for their own good. Even a barmaid reproaches Dimitri: "Young man, you ought to be studying, not frequenting night restaurants." Arnold's Rugby was Thelema compared to this. The author never sees how appalling is the way of life he depicts.

TLS. June 1, 1962, p. 416

Aksenov in his *Zviozdny bilet* (*Ticket to the Stars*) seems to imitate Salinger in striving to render the speech of the adolescents as realistically as possible. The world in this novel appears as seen through the eyes of its various characters. Even the theme of *Zviozdny bilet* is Salinger-like: the revolt of the Holden Caulfields of Moscow against adults and the life imposed by them upon adolescents. . . .

It is in the struggle against social hypocrisy that the characters of V. Aksenov's *Ticket to the Stars* express and assert themselves; and they see it literally everywhere, from discourses on "morals" to the blaringly optimistic style of official speeches and music. Derision of this style as an attempt to conceal ugly truths behind the facade of lofty words is a constant theme of Aksenov's work. In *Kollegi* (*The Colleagues*), another of his short novels, a character directly links hypocrisy with the most revolting features of Stalinism.

David Burg. *PC*. Sept.–Oct., 1962, pp. 38–39

One of Aksenov's great strengths is his sense of fun—a fascination for the grotesque that suggests a combination of Gogol and a somewhat milder Joseph Heller. He purposely lets things get out of hand. . . . His style of writing is truly arresting (much more so, unfortunately, in Russian than in English translation). It is based, first of all, on a very heavy use of dialogue—brisk, racy, ironical, quarrelsome, tart. Most of his abundant humor, and a great deal of his narrative development, is located in the dialogue. Since Aksenov is also particularly fond of first-person narrative, his dialogue is, more often than not, *reported* dialogue, in which the narrator himself (not the author) has been closely involved, either as a participant or as an interested observer. This method lends an intimacy and warmth, as well as an especially opinionated flavor to the writing. Furthermore, since the narrator is as candid in reporting his own feelings as he is in recounting the utterances of others, there shines through his joking, mocking, sceptical, off-beat language a startling emotional authenticity. . . .

Aksenov's style, however, is more than just a mixture of colorful dialogue and telegraphic authorial statement, for it is full of all kinds of tricks and surprises. Some of these, such as his occasional bizarre experiments with typography, are merely amusing. More interesting and meaningful is the allusiveness of his prose, which is so crammed with topical references that his works constitute a small, though slanted, encyclopedia of contemporary Soviet life. (There are Soviet critics who would deny him this value by arguing that he portrays only a narrow, special, and negligible segment of the Russian scene, but his very popularity among the generation whose life he describes testifies to his relevance.) He cites snatches of songs, current slogans and catchwords, the names of sports greats and movie stars. He parodies the clichés of newspapers and classroom, the cozy advice of parents, and the smug admonitions of the collective. Much of his language is figurative, and it is particularly rich in bold and sprightly metaphors. Interjections and wry rhetorical questions abound. The sentences themselves are short and choppy, enabling the writer to draw attention to the individual word. This is particularly important, for ultimately the most distinctive thing about Aksenov is his vocabulary.

Deming Brown. *TriQuarterly*.
Spring, 1965, pp. 76, 78–79

[Aksyonov] appeals to the Western reader because his work offers fast dialogue and hard-hitting action full of sentiment, combined with plenty of slang, violence, drinking, jazz, and rapid modern transportation. Of course, such a formula is quite generally applicable to almost any Western novel about the younger set; it may even derive from a Remarque novel of thirty years ago. Like Remarque, Aksënov describes in his latest book [*Pora, moi drug, pora (It Is Time, My Friend, It Is Time)*] the uneasy love affair of a movie actress with a tractor-driver. Despite the temptations of extraordinary success, she remains as good as gold, and joins the man she loves in Siberia as his quite ordinary wife. Our hero differs from his he-man comrades on the construction job only in having ambitions as a writer, which he keeps busy pursuing even in his Siberian hut. Though physical labor is idealized at the expense of intellectual achievement, the possibility remains in the end that Tania too may remain true to culture, i.e., the cinematic art, and to her tractor-addict as well. Indeed, an optimistic belief in higher things combined with work differentiates the book somewhat from its archetypes by Remarque or Hemingway: the characters do not drink at every turn, but are sometimes caught turning down a drink for the sake of their usefulness on the morrow's job. Though some abuses of Soviet society are frankly mentioned, essentially the love of country and belief in Communism distinguish Aksënov's people from the pessimists of the lost generation. But, except for its core of ideological belief and a slick surface of technological reference, the book represents a literary lag. However it may intrigue the Western reader to find Siberian geologists preoccupied with Mastroianni, and Alain Delon and a movie crew on location in Estonia relaxing with Dave Brubeck, such delight is merely superficial. Aksënov's novel is not likely to endure as long as the Pushkin poem from which its title comes.

Marjorie L. Hoover. *BA*. Summer, 1966, p. 351

The stories [in *Na polputi k lune* (*Halfway to the Moon*)] are totally un-like each other. In the story entitled "Wild" ["Dikoi"], there are two heroes. One is an old Communist who fought in the Civil War and took an active part in building up the Soviet state. The other is his friend from childhood days, a man who keeps aloof from everything, but de-votes his time to carrying out an impractical idea of constructing a com-plex machine of the "perpetuum mobile" type. These two, who are poles apart, have preserved throughout their lives—each in his own way—their integrity, their dedication to an idea, their ability to serve this idea self-lessly, without thought of reward. True to himself, Aksyonov does not dot his i's or cross his t's. The reader himself, when comparing these two lives, the one—crowded with effort and achievement, the other—fruitless in the end, may draw his own conclusions. This story is undoubtedly one of Aksyonov's genuine literary successes. Here, as in other stories in this collection, the writer is in no hurry to say as much as he can about every-thing on earth (which happened in his novels). Here, he is extremely at-tentive to his characters and takes his time. . . .

The themes vary and so does the author's range of interests, as we see in this collection of stories, but this does not obliterate the quality they have in common, the quality that binds Vasili Aksyonov's book into a single whole: the writer's profound interest in his contemporary.

Felix Svetov. *SL*. March, 1967, pp. 185–86

ANDREYEV, LEONID (1871–1919)

The Man in *Zhizn cheloveka* (*The Life of Man*) is governed by harsh ex-ternal powers. He quickly and unexpectedly changes from rags to riches and gets there by automobile (about which the play so often speaks). Then he loses his riches, and his son is killed by a stone from behind a corner. We see everything that happens to him, but we do not see his own reac-tions. The play has no psychology—the one thing that is needed. In the play everything is disastrous, not just the main sketch. True, Andreyev wants to show that we are toys in the hands of fate, that we are only man-nequins controlled by Someone in Gray. But this in no way vindicates him. Surely Man does not realize that Someone in Gray stands behind his back and that his silent actions become part of our soul. In any case, none of us can remove him. If we are dolls or marionettes, then we are animated dolls with illusions, with rich inner worlds. Wise lips have said long ago that man is a thinking reed; in Andreyev's play there is a reed, but no thought. The unique delicate and inner moment that could deepen An-dreyev's shallow play, but was only mentioned in passing, thrown in by chance, and left undeveloped, is Man's loss of his talent. Here is a true tragedy. But our author quickly passed it by because it is easier and more clever to put a stone in the hands of Someone in Gray and have him strike the head of the Son of Mankind than to show how a living soul dries out and how the inspirational spring of talent stops flowing in it, or to show what role Someone plays in this drying out of the soul.

Yuli Aikhenvald. *Russkaya mysl.*
Jan., 1908, pp. 185–86[†]

No more terrible protest against war has ever been written than Andreev's *Red Laugh* [*Krasny smekh*]. It shows not merely the inexpressible horror of the battlefield and the dull, weary wretchedness of the men on the march, but it follows out the farthest ramifications flowing from the central cause: the constant tragedies in the families, the letters received after the telegraph has announced the death of the writer, the insane wretches who return to the homes they left in normal health, the whole accumulation of woe.

The first two words of the book are "Madness and Horror!" and they might serve as a text for Andreev's complete works. There seems to be some taint in his mind which forces him to dwell forever on the abnormal and diseased. He is not exactly decadent, but he is decidedly pathological. Professor Brückner has said of Andreev's stories, "I do not recall a single one which would not get fearfully on a man's nerves." He has deepened the universal gloom of Russian fiction, not by descending into the slums with Gorki, but by depicting life as seen through the strange light of a decaying mind. He has often been compared, especially among the Germans, with Edgar Allan Poe. But he is really not in the least like Poe. Poe's horrors are nearly all unreal fantasies, that vaguely haunt our minds like the shadow of a dream. Andreev is a realist, like his predecessors and contemporaries. His style is always concrete and definite, always filled with the sense of fact. There is almost something scientific in his collection of incurables.

William Lyon Phelps. *Essays on Russian Novelists*
(New York, Macmillan, 1911), pp. 268–69

Although [Andreyev] possessed a lively and sensitive imagination, he was lazy; he was much fonder of talking about literature than of creating it. The delight of martyr-like work at night in stillness and solitude seated before a white, clean sheet of paper, was almost impossible to him, he valued but little the joy of covering that sheet with the pattern of words. . . .

Leonid was not fond of reading, and himself the maker of books—the creator of miracles—he looked upon old books distrustfully and heedlessly. . . .

Leonid was talented by nature, organically talented; his intuition was astonishingly keen. In all that touched on the dark side of life, the contradictions in the human soul, the rumblings in the domain of the instincts, he had eerie powers of divination. . . .

Leonid regarded thought as a "wicked trick played on man by the devil"; it seemed to him false and hostile. Luring man to the abysses of inexplicable mysteries it deceives him, it leaves him in painful and impotent loneliness in front of all that is mysterious, and itself vanishes.

No less irreconcilably did we differ in our views on man, the source of thought, its furnace. To me man is always the conqueror, even when he is mortally wounded and dying. Splendid is his longing to know himself and to know Nature; and although his life is a torment, he is ever widening its bounds, creating with his thought wise science, marvelous art. I felt that I did sincerely and actively love man—him who is at present alive and working side by side with me, and him, too, the sensible, the good, the strong who will follow after in the future. To Andreyev man appeared poor in spirit, a creature interwoven of irreconcilable contradictions of instinct and intellect, forever deprived of the possibility of attaining inner harmony. All his works are "vanity of vanities," decay, and self-deception. And, above all, he is the slave of death and all his life long he walks dragging its chain. [1919]

Maxim Gorky. Reminiscences of Tolstoy, Chekhov,
and Andreyev (New York, Viking Press, 1959),
pp. 133–34, 136, 143–44

Maxim Gorki and Leonid Andreyev appeared almost simultaneously. . . . The former brought the message of a rebel spirit which forecast a new moral upheaval, a new social protest; the latter appeared clad in the gloom of his time, which he strangely combined with a spirit of almost anarchistic revolt. From the point of view of historical completeness Leonid Andreyev is more representative of the epoch, demonstrating at once two contradictory elements of the Russia of the 'nineties: lack or even absence of faith interwoven with protest and mutiny.

Andreyev is symbolic and romantic. Her Majesty Fate and His Excellency Accident, these are the two dark, unknown, at times brutal forces which dwelt ever before the mind's eye. His symbols are full of horror and at times unbending atrocity. Beginning with his short stories, "In Fog" ["V tumane"], "The Life of Basil of Thebes" ["Zhizn Vasiliya Fiveiskogo"], through his dramas, The Life of Man, and Anathema [Anatema], until his last writings, he saw human beings in the form of ghosts and ghosts in the form of human beings dominating every step, every breath of life. Still his gruesome symbolism, despite his genius for rendering his images in a clear-cut, almost crystalline manner, did not appeal to many of his contemporaries because the dark shroud in which Andreyev enveloped life was impenetrable and at times it was impossible to discern in that gloom the few values which Andreyev still found in life. Leo Tolstoy said once: "Leonid Andreyev tries to frighten me, but I am not afraid."

Gregory Zilboorg. Introduction to Leonid Andreyev,
He Who Gets Slapped (New York, Samuel French,
1921), pp. x–xi

After [the attacks of good spirits] he always became sombre and more often than not would begin one of his monologues on death. It was his favourite theme. He pronounced the word *death* in a special manner—with feeling and emphasis, as some voluptuaries pronounce the word *woman*. In this respect Andreyev possessed a great talent—he knew how to fear death as no one else could. To fear death is no easy matter: many attempt it, but without success. Andreyev succeeded magnificently: here was his real calling—to experience a deathly and terrible horror. This horror is to be discerned in all his books, and I think that his grasping at colour photography, gramophones, painting, constituted attempts to save himself from it. Somehow he had to protect himself from these sickening attacks of despair. In the terrible years after the revolution, when an epidemic of suicide was raging in Russia, Andreyev involuntarily became the leader and apostle of these abandoners of life. They felt him to be one of themselves. I remember his showing me a whole collection of letters addressed to him by suicides before their death. It had evidently become a custom before doing away with oneself to send a letter to Leonid Andreyev.

Sometimes it appeared strange. Sometimes, watching him as he strolled about the yard, among his stables and outhouses, followed by his magnificent hound, Tyucha, or posed, dressed in a velvet coat, in front of some visiting photographer, one could not believe that his man could be carrying within him a tragic consciousness of eternity, non-existence, chaos, worldly desolation. But the spirit bloweth where it listeth, and the whole of Andreyev's life was soaked in this feeling of worldly desolation. It was this feeling which gave to his work a special philosophical colouring, since it is impossible to spend one's whole life meditating on such desolation and not to become in the end a metaphysician. The same thing gave a key also to his personality as a writer: in his books he always handled—well or badly—eternal, metaphysical, and transcendental questions. Other themes failed to move him. The group of writers among which he found himself at the beginning of his literary career; Gorki, Chirikov, Skitalets, Kuprin—was in reality strange to him. They were describers of life, excited by the problems of life, but not by existence itself; and he was the only one among them who was exercized by the eternal and tragic. He was tragic in his very essence and all his ecstatic, affected, theatrical talent, leading as it did to pompousness in style and to traditional and exaggerated forms, was admirably adapted to metaphysically tragic subjects. [1922]

Kornei Chukovski. Dial. Nov., 1923, pp. 471–72

He developed a style of his own—or, to be more precise, two styles, neither of which was quite his own. One of these two styles, and by far the better, was learned from Tolstoy's problem stories, "The Death of Ivan Ilyich" and "The Kreutzer Sonata." The other is a "modernist" concoction of reminiscences from Poe, Maeterlinck, German, Polish, and Scandinavian modernists. The first of these two manners is sober and discreet; the second is shrill, rhetorical, and, to our present taste, ineffective and unpalatable. But it was a novelty in Russian literature, and as Andreev's subjects were intelligible and interesting to the general reader, it had its moment of tremendous success. These two styles may almost seem to belong to two different writers, but the "message" conveyed by the one and the other is the same. It is a message of thorough nihilism and negation— human life, society, morals, culture are all lies—the only reality is death and annihilation, and the only feelings that express human understanding of the truth are "madness and horror."

D. S. Mirsky. Contemporary Russian Literature
(New York, Knopf, 1926), p. 134

Nietzsche's ideas are always transformed after they have gone through the prism of Andreyev's subjective conceptions. However, Andreyev does not stress the exact understanding of the idea as much as the symbol, the metaphor, and the dithyrambic tone with which Nietzsche intoxicated himself. Nietzsche's speech almost always sounds as if it were formed into rhythms. For example, let us take Nietzsche's lines: "Oh, how could I not feel ardor for eternity and for the nuptial ring of rings—the ring of eternal return." Andreyev retains only the metaphor of this quotation when he expresses the mystical engagement of Zhegulyov with his deserted bride in the following manner: "And eternity itself, in its magical circle, became an engagement ring" ["Sasha Zhegulyov"].

Andreyev adheres to Nietzsche's axiom: "Beware so that a narrow creed—a hard, strict madness—does not envelop you in the end! You are tempted and led astray by everything that is narrow and rigid." Chulkov cites his words to us: "I reject life in its present form. I will never come to terms with it, but I don't want to hang out a banner, not even the banner of the revolution" (<i>Kniga ob Andreyeve</i> [<i>Book About Andreyev</i>]). In an argument with Gorki, Andreyev maintains that the power play of life can unfold itself only through an interruption of the equilibrium and that this equilibrium is to be equated with death. He also found an affirmation and justification of his chaos in the words of Nietzsche: "One must still have chaos in himself in order to be able to give birth to a dancing star."

Oswald Burghardt. Zeitschrift für slavische
Philologie. 18, 1942, p. 18†

In "In the Fog" . . . Andreyev tackled the tragedy of awakened sex in a schoolboy who has contracted a venereal disease and eventually murders a prostitute and commits suicide. The story caused much uproar and can serve as a proof of the author's growing hankering for sensational themes, worked out in a dramatic (or melodramatic) manner. This was particularly the case when he came under the spell of Dostoevsky's themes and problems. As the latter were often much bigger than his talent, he tried to make up for it by raising his tone and filling his pages with would-be symbolic *clichés*, designed to surprise, or rather to stun his readers also by means of paradoxical logic. This brought, however, a forced, not to say false note into his writings, and its pretence increased in the ratio in which he abandoned the straightforward realistic method for the sake of stilted pseudo-symbolism. This genre was clearly antici- pated in stories such as "Silence" ["Molchanie"], "The Wall" ["Stena"], "The Tocsin" ["Nabat"], "The Abyss" ["Bezdna"], and "The Thought" ["Mysl"]—all of them written between 1900 and 1902 in a mood of futility. Chekhov's pathetic blind-alley was taken up by Andreyev with relish, but he turned it into a substitute for religion, with its theology of "mystical anarchism," its solemnly hollow rites and incantations, the only genuine element in which was his fear of life. The apotheosis of this fear became Andreyev's "purpose" (one could almost say—moral purpose) which he piously cultivated as the very essence of his own aesthetic modernism.

   Always an individualist, Andreyev was strongly attracted by the heroic pose of a modern anti-philistine. But as he felt more and more the fasci- nation of Dostoevsky's metaphysical rebels, he too became one of them without even believing in metaphysics. He prostrated himself before the principle of negation which he pushed to the verge of grotesqueness. Like some of Dostoevsky's heroes he saw (or forced himself to see) in life only a "vaudeville of the devils"; but instead of searching for something be- yond it, as Dostoevsky did, he derived from the very hopelessness of such a disposition—into which he often worked himself by means of alcohol—a peculiar and almost ecstatic pleasure.

Janko Lavrin. Russian Writers (New York,
Van Nostrand, 1954), pp. 257–58

It is interesting to follow the distortion of form and the "disintegration of realism" in the creative work of Andreyev. He used "realistic," "symbolist," and expressionist styles nearly a decade before the appearance of expressionism in German and other Western European literature. The form of his works, even the language and sentence structure, depends on whether or not at any given moment he believed in the revolution (the so-called "Red myth"). Characteristically, he wrote his best story, the brilliant and realistic "The Seven Who Were Hanged" ["Rasskaz o semi poveshenikh"], at a time when, far from trying to create a masterpiece, he wanted only "to shout as loudly as possible: Don't hang them, you beasts!" as he said in a letter when the revolutionaries of 1905 were to be dealt with by the tsarist regime. The artist's fight gives birth to realism and *fabula*. The artist surrenders and modernism is born. At that instant when words again became a means of communication, the gifted writer Andreyev created a work of genius. [1961]

Mihajlo Mihajlov. Russian Themes (New York,
Farrar, Straus & Giroux, 1968), pp. 278–79

Leonid Andreyev died in Finland in 1919, but he was still a vivid presence in my family when I was a child. I also came to know him through the many photographs we had of him. He was exceptionally handsome in a romantic way—he had dark eyes, somehow cold and yet sensitive. His photographic poses were dramatic, but his portraits never looked affected, although others of that time often do. He appeared plunged in a meditative gloom, which was photogenic, often wearing dashing costumes—evening clothes or traditional Russian shirts and boots or a sea captain's uniform. He had had a passion for the sea and for a while he owned a yacht. In several pictures he wore a black velvet jacket, a favorite garment which gave him a slightly theatrical, medieval air: he resembled the duke out of his own play, *Black Masks* [*Chernye maski*]. There were several photographs of him taken with Maxim Gorki, my father's godfather, who was for a long time Andreyev's very dear friend. These two faces, intent and alive, were part of my childhood world.

Olga Andreyev Carlisle. Voices in the Snow
(New York, Random House, 1962), p. 14

ANNENSKI, INNOKENTI (1856–1909)

It seems to me that Annenski, the author of *Kniga otrazheni* [Book of Reflections], is feeling the first stirrings of an ancient grief; this grief is neither smiled at nor frowned at, but is sighed at with the relief of a man who at last has found his way. With the witchcraft of his own restless thought, he began to summon the shadows of former prophets and kings, in order to speak with them about life. And they disclosed their own hidden faces—so unexpected, yet somehow familiar. There is Heine, tortured by life like the conquistador by the Aztecs, who cries and laughs at the same time. At last Hamlet reveals his fatal secret—his eternal doubt of his own origin. Dostoyevski, the jeweled sun of thought, says that there is neither happiness nor sadness, only the coldness of contemplation. The summoner of shadows looks sharply, accepting nothing on faith, never giving his yes or no to anything.

One must be repelled by Annenski's book to understand it.

In addition to many things that cannot be discussed in a short review, one is pleased in Annenski's books by the rare, purely European mental discipline. He loved the small details of our culture, and he knows how to unite them with the whole. We consider it unimportant to know Hamlet's parentage, to know whether he was killed by a king or a murderess. Annenski carefully grasps the question and finds the threads that unite the fate of the Danish prince with our own.

Working only with [Lermontov's] "Taman," he completely reveals Lermontov, and perhaps not as much Lermontov as that secret, happy hunter of suns—the future man.

He systematically investigates the interdependence of ideas in *Crime and Punishment*, giving his article a plan. But he is always a poet, and every page of his book warms our soul with its authentic flame.

Nikolai Gumilyov. *Rech.* May 11, 1909†

A poet-impressionist, Annenski wished to remain an impressionist in his plays also. At the same time, his love for the world of antiquity and years of translating Euripides drew Annenski to the antique themes. Out of these inclinations grew a quasi-antique drama (*Famira-kifared* [Thamyras Cytharede]) written in the impressionistic manner. Annenski borrowed from his great teachers, the Greek tragedians, not only the internal structure of the play—the unity and compactness of action, the sharpness of the tragic conflict, the idea of catharsis—but also the external forms, among others the participation of the chorus in the acts. However, Annenski changes all that through methods completely foreign to the ancient drama. He not only introduces prose and rhymed verse into the play and adds extensive commentaries, written under the influence of the recent "decadence"; he also makes his heroes feel and speak in a modern way and in a nervous, fractured, sometimes even "neurasthenic" language. . . .

I do not think that such extremism of Annenski enhances the artistic value of his play, for, by itself and independent of the whimsical style, the play is conceived profoundly and constructed beautifully. *Famira-kifared* is without doubt much better than Annenski's previous play,

Laodamia. The antique myth in *Famira-kifared* is subtly treated and psy-
chologically valid. The characters—Famira himself, his mother-nymph,
the old nanny, and others—are drawn distinctly. The action of the play
develops with logical inevitability, and many scenes are permeated with
genuine tragedy. In general, even though one may not agree with Annenski's methods, one reads his play with genuine emotion, as a significant
artistic achievement, and one cannot help but regret once again that the
creativity of this poet was interrupted just at the time when he had reached
his full development.

Valeri Bryusov. *Russkaya mysl.*
July, 1913, pp. 265–66†

Annenski is a representative of heroic Hellenism and militant philology.
His poems and tragedies can be compared to ancient fortresses and towns
erected deep in the steppe by local princes for protection against the
Pechenegs during the Charskoy nights. It is quite astounding that Annenski did not exert any influence either as mediator or translator. With his
original grasp, he grabbed the unknown, and while still in the air, at a
great height, he dropped the prey from his claws, letting it fall alone. And
the eagle of his poetry, more sharp-clawed than Euripides, Mallarmé, or
Leconte de Lisle, brought us nothing more in his clutches than a handful
of dried grass. . . . Gumilyov called Annenski a great European poet. It
seems to me that when Europeans learn of him, after they have humbly
educated their generations on a study of the Russian language, similar to
the way in which former generations educated themselves on the ancient
languages and classic poetry, they will be amazed with the boldness of this
regal plunderer, who stole their dove Eurydice for Russian snows, who
snatched the classic shawl from the shoulders of Phaedra, and who tenderly, as is fitting for a Russian poet, placed the skin of an animal on the
still shivering Ovid.

Osip Mandelshtam. *O prirode slova*
(Kharkov, Istoki, 1922), pp. 16–17†

With as much firmness as Bryusov, Annenski brought historical, objective themes into poetry and psychological constructionism into lyrics.
Burning with desire to study in the West, he did not have teachers worthy
of his own task, and he was therefore forced to feign imitations. Annenski's psychology is neither a caprice nor a flashing of refined sensitivity
but a truly firm theory. There is a direct route from his "Stalnya tsikada"
[Steel Cicada] to Aseyev's "Solovei" [Steel Nightingale]. Annenski learned
to utilize psychological analysis as a working implement in his lyrics. He
was the true forerunner of psychological construction in Russian futurism,
which is more brilliant than the psychological construction headed by

Pasternak. Until now, Annenski has not reached the Russian reader and is known only through the vulgarizations of his methods by Akhmatova. He is one of the most original writers of Russian poetry. *Tikhie pesni* [Quiet Songs] and *Kiparisovy larets* [The Cypress Chest] should be included in their entirety in an anthology.

Osip Mandelshtam. *Russkoe iskusstvo.*
Jan., 1923, p. 79†

Annensky's poetry is in many ways different from that of all his contemporaries. It is not metaphysical, but purely emotional, or perhaps rather nervous. He had no Russian masters. In so far as he had any masters at all, they were Baudelaire, Verlaine, and Mallarmé. But on the whole his lyrical gift is remarkably original. It is a rare case of a very late development. Nor did he at once attain to perfection. *Quiet Songs* is distinctly immature (though written at forty-eight). But in *The Cypress Chest* the majority of the poems are flawlessly perfect jewels. Annensky is a Symbolist, in so far as his poetry is based on a system of "correspondences." But they are purely emotional correspondences. His poems are developed in two interconnected planes—the human soul and the outer world; each of them is an elaborate parallel between a state of mind and the external world. Annensky is akin to Chekhov, for his material is also the pinpricks and infinitesimals of life. His poetry is essentially human and its appeal would be universal, for it deals with the common stuff of humanity. They are constructed with disconcerting and baffling subtleness and precision. They are compressed and laconic—much of the structure has been pulled away and only the essential points remain for the reader to reverse the process and grasp the unity of the poem. Few readers, however, feel themselves capable of the creative effort required. But the work is worth the while. Those who have mastered him usually prefer him to all other poets. For he is unique and always fresh. The extent of his poetry is small, his two books do not contain more than a hundred lyrics all told, and most of them are not over twenty lines long. This makes it comparatively easy to study.

D. S. Mirsky. *Contemporary Russian Literature*
(New York, Knopf, 1926), p. 203

Annenski was an apologist for the Mediterranean world, not only in a general sense (for him, the world began with Homer) but in his relations, for example, with the fate of the Russian language and with questions of versification. He loved neologisms and gallicisms more than any other Russian poet. Very often, his predilection for these disagreeably affects his translations of Euripides (I do not mean to impugn their high quality) and his own tragedies in the classic vein. Gallicisms, even simple bold borrowings of French words, seemed to be an inherent rule of "modernism" (he loved this far-from-distant term, which I employ so often).

At the same time, he was a purist in poetic sounds. He made the most meaningful contribution through the form of his poetry, and, more than anything else, he appreciated the praise of his formal successes. He would often change words in a line by altering a voiced syllable with an unvoiced one, and vice versa. In his criticism of poetry he stressed "a," "u," and "i," which for him contained the magic of expressiveness.

Sergei Makovski. *Portrety sovremennikov*
(New York, Izdatelstvo imeni Chekhova, 1955),
pp. 260–61†

If Annenskij is a Verlaine, he is a Verlaine in a saturnine mood. His voice sounds so intimate and discreet, his tone so unassuming and subdued, that it seems his poetry should be called, as Verlaine named his own, a *chanson grise*. As for the tender musicality of his tunes it is so fluid and vague that his lyrics should be likewise defined with the Verlainian title of *romances sans paroles*. Annenskij himself must have been aware of this, since he entitled the first of his collections *Still [Quiet] Songs*. Yet at second glance that "stillness" reveals the feverish and electric quality of this poet's inspirations, and we discover that the "songs without words" are in reality wordless plaints, that the *chanson grise* is in reality a mournful and wailing chant. Thus, while looking at first like a Russian Verlaine, Annenskij turns out to be the only poet of his nation and time whose temper and vision could be compared, in quality if not in degree, to those of Baudelaire.

Annenskij's landscapes, being *états d'âme* in the most literal sense of the term, cannot be simply interpreted as the emblems of a timid and petty decadence, mirroring itself in the twilights or glimmers of late autumn. As Baudelaire said of himself, Annenskij is a painter working not with light but with darkness. His palette neglects all bright and wholesome colors for vanishing shades or fading hues. Yet it is through such shadows and nuances that he succeeds in depicting the purgatory of life and the hell of the world. Thus in substance all his landscapes are but imaginative projections of the innermost experiences of his psyche; one could say that few modern poets ever turned the pathetic fallacy to a better advantage, by sharing with nature at large the shame of the self and the pain of life. Annenskij resembles Baudelaire also in his tendency to see sin and evil even in the most lovely flowers of the earth. All his poetry is in essence but the pathetic revery or morbid fancy of the sense of being, full of a poignant melancholy intoxicating the soul. Annenskij himself saw the spring of his inspiration in "the subtle poison of remembrance,"

by which he meant a reminiscence mixing loathing and disgust with longing and regret. And it was the poet's awareness of the wicked charm of
his craft that led him to avow that he loved his verses "as only a mother
can adore her sick children."

Renato Poggioli. The Poets of Russia (Cambridge,
Mass., Harvard University Press, 1960), pp. 172–73

As a poet, Annenskij belongs to the "elder Symbolists." This statement
can be found in any history of Russian literature. But as so often is the
case, this literary label does not fit completely and some of his most important characteristics do not correspond to it at all.

There is unquestionably a very strong connection between Annenskij
and French symbolism. Baudelaire, Verlaine, Mallarmé and many minor
symbolist poets influenced him so strongly that he tried to write exactly
as they did. Yet he wrote without giving up his own personality and his
own specific range of metaphysical and literary interests and beliefs. The
result was a poetry that is thoroughly original in spite of its clear literary
genealogy—a kind of paradox which succeeded because the personality
of the poet was great enough to make the contrasts unite on a higher level.

This specific original undercurrent brought Annenskij very close to another literary movement in Russia—Acmeism. The school in between
elder Symbolism and Acmeism—the so-called "younger Symbolism"—
was absolutely foreign to him.

The youngest poets of the first decade of this century, disagreeing with
the mystic development of symbolism, saw in Annenskij an uncompromising champion of pure art. This does not mean a fight for the *l'art pour
l'art* principle, but life transposed into art and intuitively explained and
clarified to the highest possible degree by the transposition.

Annenskij's poetry does not contain hints at a "beyond" which would
imply a religious revelation and therefore be truer than the "here." This
"here" is an emanation of Beauty, but spoiled and degenerated; art
makes the connecting link between Beauty and real life—it is able to
prove their original connection.

To a certain degree this theory might also be termed mysticism, but it
is not a mysticism that requires faith and it does not want to have anything to do with religion. It is an "aesthetic mysticism" which only pre-
supposes a feeling for the creative power of an artist in order to be accepted as a *kind* of solution for the enigma of life.

This last cautious formulation indicates the drop of scepticism which is
constantly present in "aesthetic mysticism" and which is always prepared
to dissolve it into an avowal of complete ignorance. The aesthetic attitude is aware of its own fragility, and its ardent belief in Beauty seems
to be a deliberate turning away from the terrible recognition that the whole

of life is an unexplainable bit of ugly nonsense. The attempt to make life beautiful by transposition is made, and now and again it succeeds very well. But the "unbeautiful" intrudes with a violence which makes one fear that the metaphysical power might be on its side, that evil and ugliness might be victorious at the end.

This feeling of anxiety for the beautiful, the feeling of the constant danger to beauty from "real" life, is the basic motif of Annenskij's poetry. He is not afraid of death itself; he fears the unbeautiful manifestations of death in life—and this is why he fears life and fears for life.

The fear for the beautiful in life results in a second main theme: compassion for life, which might be beautiful in all its stages—starting from a stone and rising up to God. One of the points at which Annenskij and Acmeism converge is this loving interest in the objects of reality, whatever they may be. In Annenskij the accent on pity is much stronger, while the Acmeists try to keep a cooler attitude. Both have a keen interest in things and try to find and to point out what makes them beautiful.

Vsevolod Setchkarev. *Studies in the Life and Works of Innokentij Annenskij* (The Hague, Mouton, 1963), pp. 54–55

A knowledge of Annenski's peculiar and extraordinarily strong tie to the preceding stage in the development of Russian poetry is essential to a correct understanding of the artistic structure of his verse. No matter what the complex, contradictory, and, at times, morbid aspects of contemporary man's consciousness Annenski draws, they are always conveyed in the form of an objective narrative. The situations depicted by Annenski always involve concrete people in concrete surroundings under individually precise circumstances. Annenski exhibits none of the "common" type of lyricism, which any reader is able to take and, with relative freedom, synchronize to his own individual condition as, let us suppose, occurs in perceiving poetry from Pushkin's era. Annenski's action is concrete, while the action itself leads nowhere beyond what is portrayed. They cannot be taken otherwise. Only the method usual in reading prose can be used: originality can and should be extracted only indirectly through the story and through the perception of an incident with concrete characters under spacially and temporally precise conditions. Annenski's verse is a "story in verse," a form unflaggingly sought by the poets of the forties and fifties. However, Annenski bears very little direct resemblance to the older poets of this circle: Grigoriev, Fet, Polonski, and Pavlova. He is closer to the poets of the intermediate stage, to Sluchevski and Apukhtin. Here he does not appear imitative, but, on the contrary, eminently original and incomparably stronger as a poet than these "middlemen" poets. His story in verse is, of course, primarily verse and lyricism; that is, narration here is only a particular means for putting across the primarily lyrical, not some other content.

Pavel Gromov. *Aleksandr Blok:*
Ego predshestvenniki i sovremenniki
(Moscow, Sovetski pisatel, 1966), pp. 224–25[†]

BABEL, ISAAK (1894–1941)

The theme of Babel's work is Man, with a capital letter, Man under the influence of the revolution, awakened among the people of the lower strata. The range of Babel's talent is extremely wide. . . . In our country, as probably everywhere else, writers are divided into national and international writers. Right now our national writers include Pilnyak, Vsevolod Ivanov, Yesenin, Seyfullina, Leonov. . . . Babel is, undoubtedly, an international writer. The nature of his talent is such that he is able to write in America as an American, in Odessa as an Odessan, in the Cavalry Army as a member of the Cavalry Army, and so forth. This quality is rare among Russian writers. . . .

Babel is concrete. He is the kind of writer who does not write about the good old days but who knows well how much the morals and manners in our life are worth. Although the manner of life never becomes the focal point in his works, its "aroma" can be felt everywhere: in Afonka, in Benya, in dialogues, in descriptions, and so forth.

Babel represents a very great hope in contemporary Soviet literature and has already achieved a great success. His talent is extraordinary. We hope that he will be strict enough with himself, that he will not be an easy prey to his first successes. The guarantee for this lies in the fact that he is not only gifted but educated and intelligent. [1924]

A. K. Voronski. *Literaturno-kriticheskie stati*
(Moscow, Sovetski pisatel, 1963), pp. 294–95†

A careful, thoughtful master, Babel is distinguished among the best of our writers by his studied form. In addition to this, he possesses a sharp artistic eye for the details of the external and internal worlds. The path along which the artist can and should move has its own peril—the danger of being trampled on the spot or of freezing his gift in individual aestheticism. It is our firm conviction that aestheticism is Babel's ailment, although it is carefully masked by deliberation and, at times, by the vulgarity of the material chosen by him. Even in his ultrarealistic portrayal of life in *Konarmiya* (*Red Cavalry*), where realism is sharpened to the limit, Babel does not refrain from using naturalism as a means for solving an aesthetic, literary problem. The path of realism is from life to art, but Babel always moves from art to life. Art always takes precedence over life. This is evident in his story "Pervaya lyubov" ("First Love"), saturated with eccentricism and eroticism, which cannot find even an illusory justification in its material, as opposed to the sketches in *Red Cavalry*. We assume that even the material of *Red Cavalry* could have been portrayed in less idiosyncratic and more realistic terms. In asserting this, we do not have in mind silencing the actual excesses; these did take place; consequently, the artist had full right to depict them in all their naked brutality, together with the over-all treatment of life. It seems to us that Babel—undoubtedly a great artist—sooner or later will feel restricted by this armor of aestheticism and eccentricism.

D. Gorbov. *Novy mir*. Dec., 1925, p. 140[†]

I. Babel, one of the younger writers of Soviet Russia, has been compared to Gogol and to Synge; and there is some truth in both comparisons. Cossack life has not had a better interpreter since Gogol wrote *Taras Bulba* and no writer except Synge has shaped colloquial speech to such vigorous poetical forms which for all their deliberate art have the naturalness of life. The word "epic" may, without exaggeration, be applied to his writing, in spite of the fact that his sketches—for externally they are hardly more than that—rarely cover more than five or six pages and on occasions barely more than one or two. For a real inner unity holds them all; and there is the integrity of a continuous narrative, and the completeness and finality which belong to the prose epic. What Babel writes about he has seen, but he has looked not with the eyes of a journalist but of an artist; there are no wasted materials or loose threads in the result. It need not astonish the reader to learn that Babel's output is small, and its future problematical. The fact is, he has used his experience well, but experience is perhaps necessary to him. It remains to be seen what he can do when he has exhausted his material collected in the Ghetto and during his service in the Red Army. Even the enthusiastic Soviet critics express curiosity and doubt on this point; but there can be no question that the present small volume [*Red Cavalry*] is a masterpiece.

TLS. Aug. 2, 1928, p. 566

At a superficial glance [Babel] seems to write crudely, even carelessly. All of his work has a fragmentary quality. And yet it exhibits the nicest precision, alike in the choice of incident and vocabulary. None of his contemporaries can match him for vigor, for speed, for the taut, strained character of his prose, for its lyricism. His style is as terse as algebra, and yet packed with poetry.

Babette Deutsch. *NYHT*. Oct. 27, 1929, p. 4

In the last analysis, Babel evades all his categories, and our own. As Trilling writes, Babel's ambiguous art "was not a dialectic that his Russia could permit," and it seems clear that by the thirties Babel's fiction was unpublishable in the Soviet Union. Yet the signs of inner collapse and regression, the failure of any synthesis or resolution to sustain his vision, are so substantial that we need not look to external censorship to explain his silence. Ultimately Babel was neither so tough as Maupassant nor so shifty as Herschel Ostropolier. Not even his age-old body could contain the tempests of his imagination, let alone any combination of nature and culture, the Jewish community or the Soviet state. In the dozen first-rate stories he left us we have short fictions to rank with any in our time, and in his brief life and work we have perhaps the cautionary tale he saw in Maupassant's, the foreboding of some essential truth.

Stanley Edgar Hyman. *HdR*. Winter, 1956, p. 627

[Babel's] imagination, which is strikingly original, prefers to operate at the level where mere invention can be dispensed with. Despite this, in *Red Cavalry* or elsewhere, he never writes autobiographical pieces in the narrow sense of the term. The character using the first person singular in his tales is more of a spectator than an actor; at any rate, he is never a central figure. That character is often identical with the writer himself, and yet he is not so much a person as a point of view. The vision conveyed through his perspective is often static; what the writer tries to recapture is the tension of being, when time seems to stand still, rather than the ever changing and daily drama of man's life. Many critics misjudged this quality, and this led them to accuse Babel of a lack of psychological depth or complexity. Perhaps they failed to realize that in his chosen medium, a short story as brief as a sketch and as tight as a prose poem, there is room for sudden epiphanies, but not for searching and slowly unfolding insights. We forget all too often that while the novel can be musical, the short story is plastic and visual in essence. And Babel works like a painter, representing on a flat surface and in a small space all the massive and colorful variety of reality. Like an old painter he yields to other figures the center of the scene, while tracing his own self-portrait in one of the corners of the canvas. The immediacy of his vision seems to suggest that he always writes under the shock or impact of the event; yet at second sight we realize that he presents the event itself as if it were detached in both mood and time. In his work rage is controlled by order, and the emotion is recollected in tranquillity. This is why these tales look at first as if they were only vignettes, but this impression is immediately corrected by the sense of their perfection, of their finicky polish and finish, which justifies up to a point the Soviet critic who defined them as miniatures. Yet, although many-colored and vivid, their moral contrast is as simple and elemental as the chromatic one between white and black, and this is why they remind us, more than of anything else, of Goya's engravings about the horrors, and even the splendors, of war.

Renato Poggioli. *The Phoenix and the Spider*
(Cambridge, Mass., Harvard University Press,
1957), p. 236

Babel's prose is poetic in the full sense of the word. His prose was a revelation for those writers beginning a literary career. It exhibited neither the mechanical mixing of styles characteristic of the work of both the prose writer and poet nor the minced rhythmical prose so much the mode in those years. . . .

Convinced that classical literature had served its time and, consequently, little interested in it, our young generation was charmed by the verbal magic possessed by Isaak Babel. The enchantment of his art radiated invisibly from his books. Yet the impression of his work was ever more contradictory. Comparing his stories in *Red Cavalry* with Furmanov's *Chapayev*, we could but note that we encountered, as it were, two different worlds; but we could not understand then that this difference was caused by the difference in views of two artists. We could not disregard Budenny's opinion, expressed with rather coarse frankness, that *Red Cavalry* was an insult to the soldiers of his revolutionary command, and yet we had to agree with Gorki when he defended the book without reservation. . . .

Red Cavalry was an exceedingly complex and contradictory literary phenomenon, inaccessible to our youthful understanding. The problem of the intelligentsia and the revolution, far removed from us, was the essence of the book. Here were the problems of an intellectual and bourgeois humanist: swept into the background by the revolution, but accustomed to considering himself the center of the universe; ready to forsake, under the pressure of history, his principles of "supra class" and "eternal morality," yet still clinging to these principles; ready to renounce his individualism, yet thirsting to save the accustomed ethical norms of universal humanism and intellectual honesty. This suspended state could not help but evoke censure from a writer of Babel's integrity. His indictment assumed an ironic tone toward the hero who narrates the short stories of *Red Cavalry*. But not always, and not in everything.

A. Makarov. *Znamya*. April, 1958, pp. 194–95†

Babel looked less like a writer than anyone I have ever seen. In his story "Nachalo" ("The Beginning") he describes how he rented a room in an engineer's apartment when he first arrived in Petersburg (he was then twenty-two). After taking a good look at his new roomer, the engineer ordered the door leading from Babel's room into the dining room locked and all the overcoats and galoshes removed from the hall. Twenty years later Babel roomed in the house of an old French lady in the Paris suburb of Neuilly. His landlady locked him in at night—afraid he might cut her throat. And yet there was nothing frightening about Babel's appearance; it was just that he puzzled people. Only God knew what kind of man he was and what his occupation might be.

Ilya Ehrenburg. *Novy mir.* Sept., 1961, p. 146[†]

Babel and my father once undertook a motorcycle trip along the Seine, down to Rouen and Le Havre, to see the riverside landscapes described by Maupassant. At the end of their journey they spent long hours in bars in the port at Le Havre, sipping cider and listening to the conversations of seamen. Babel was delighted; he enjoyed watching simple people of any nationality. I remember the pleasure he got from a visit to a colony of Cossacks who had settled on a farm not far from Paris, where they managed to lead a primitive existence similar to the one they had known on the banks of the Dnieper. He told endless tales about those Cossacks, improvising new episodes as he went along. He was a marvelous, lyrical raconteur, but as a writer he was slow and rewrote his stories a great many times, striving for an absolute perfection. Babel's output was considered insufficient. Once, Ilya Ehrenburg had to speak for his friend at a Soviet Writers' Union meeting: "I am myself like a rabbit and can produce books by the litter," said Ehrenburg. "Babel works slowly— like an elephant he carries his baby for two years . . . the result is worth it."

Babel loved Russia and the Russian language above everything. Life abroad was impossible for him, although his wife and daughter lived in Paris. He appreciated the devotion in our family to the Russian language, which had been preserved in its purity over the years, and it disturbed him that his daughter Natasha spoke Russian with a French accent.

Olga Andreyev Carlisle. *Voices in the Snow*
(New York, Random House, 1962), p. 21

[Babel] sacrificed everything to his art, including his relationship with his family, his liberty, and finally even his life.

Like most tormented people, Babel was always vainly seeking the peace he needed for his writing. But the work he did as a journalist obliged him to travel constantly about the Soviet Union observing the industrialization of the country. Whenever possible, he took refuge in the country, but there he was troubled by an even greater sense of estrangement from his family, whose propensity for worry was equal to his. The result of this was an endless series of frantic telegrams.

Babel was convinced that a writer mutilates himself and his work when he leaves his native country. He always refused to emigrate and never once thought of his trips abroad as a means of escape. Moreover, his sense of honor demanded that he stay among his own people.

We know that Babel was well aware of the cruelty of the Stalinist regime, for he talked about it with intimate friends on his trips abroad. Nothing, however, could shatter his feeling that he belonged to Russia and that he had to share the fate of his countrymen. What in so many people would have produced only fear and terror awakened in him a sense of duty and a kind of blind heroism. . . .

I do not know whether one should consider Babel hero or victim. At any rate, life scarcely rewarded him for the sacrifices he imposed upon himself and upon those he loved most. By the cruelest of ironies, almost all of his work done after 1934 seems to have disappeared. So far as I know, he did not read his unpublished writing to anyone. These manuscripts were seized when he was arrested, have vanished, and despite official willingness to locate them have never reappeared. There were, we know, a number of stories which he did not dare publish during the period of the purges, and a novel (or perhaps two novels—there is not enough material to be sure) dealing with the collectivization of the peasants, two chapters of which are published in *The Lonely Years, 1925–1939*.

Nathalie Babel. *KR*. Summer, 1964, pp. 526–27

Babel's overinvestment in violence led him into active personal brutality. "My First Goose" ["Moi pervy gus"] records how he gruesomely slaughtered a bird and upbraided a harmless old peasant woman in order to feel potent and mature and accepted by the Cossacks. Nor should we neglect the fact that Babel later became a member of the Cheka—though no information is available about what he did for it—and that he went along on the infamous grain-collecting expeditions of 1917–1918: on three separate occasions he was somehow associated with the dirtiest work of the Revolution. Mr. Trilling would persuade us that Babel entertained a dialectic which poised the spirituality of the Jews against the carnality, the bodily beauty, of the Cossacks, and in which one criticized and qualified the other. Again this seems to me an error of generosity. Babel's frequent and ingenious juxtapositions seem deliberate and contrived enough, I think, to warrant the supposition that he sensed his overcommitment to the way of violence; and so he called upon objects and sentiments which would have the appearance of compromising his rancor and destructiveness—he sought a dialectic, but this search was essentially strategic. The young Babel was inspired by the negating passions; his one powerful benign impulse was the will to record and understand and convey. This impulse fortified his sense of the need for a dialectic, but it could not alone supply him with one. I do not mean to imply that Babel had no strong affections—indeed he did; nor do I wish to maintain that his use of irony is altogether spurious. But what may appear to be a dialectic in this respect, is, I think, more accurately a duality, in which the spiritual and the fleshly find it politic to appear together in print—like two enemies compelled to associate in public. Actually, I find, Babel's ironies and contradictions often tend to destroy, rather than create, each other.

Steven Marcus. *PR.* Summer, 1965, p. 408

The focal point of [Babel's] letters [*The Lonely Years 1925–1939: Unpublished Stories and Private Correspondence*] is the incessant struggle of their author to create true literature under Soviet conditions. An exacting artist, Babel' looked upon his *Red Cavalry* as a second-rate work belonging to the past and sought new subjects, ideas, and means of expression. His ambitious long-range projects developed simultaneously with his growing passion for creative work and his increasing self-confidence. He claimed in his letters to have become a professional writer at the peak of his power. Yet he showed no appreciable results, for he was constantly diverted from carrying out his plans. His own interests had to be subordinated to those of the state. Most of his time was consumed by semiliterary matters and various "assignments." In addition, he had to produce appropriate work in order to earn trips abroad to see his family. Another equally important reason for the meagerness of Babel''s literary output was his absolute unwillingness to imbue his works with standardized Soviet ideology or to adjust his pen to changes in the Party line. His repeatedly expressed desire was to see the day when he would finish his last work "on order" and devote himself exclusively to "pure art." That day never came, but Babel' nonetheless managed to do some of his own work. He wrote at least several short stories and a small book dear to his heart. There was not much hope that they would be published, yet he was determined to work and try. He wrote on 10 May 1939, in the last letter received by his mother and sister: "I am finishing my last assignment for the movies [a film about Gorky] and will soon devote myself to the final polishing of my true work. I reckon to hand it in to the publishers by the fall." A few days later when brought to Lubjanka prison, he reportedly said only these words: "Ne dali končit' " ["I wasn't allowed to finish!"]. They can serve as an epigraph to his life and work.

The letters are an excellent source for a closer acquaintance with Babel' the writer and man. They contain valuable information on his literary tastes and activity, his nostalgic dream about a quiet country place where he could do his work in peace, his aversion to Moscow, his criticism of Soviet writers who lived in the capital and wrote poorly, his reluctance to move to prestigious Peredelkino for fear of being disturbed there by his fellow writers, his courage in expressing his views on art and in commenting on the undramatic qualities of *How the Steel Was Tempered* in the "black year" of 1937 when his remarks could have been easily interpreted as slander of a masterpiece of socialist realism. The letter of 14 October 1931 sounds a warning not to exaggerate the autobiographical nature of "The Story of My Dovecote" ["Istoriya moei golub-yatni"]. Interesting and at times appalling details are to be found on the privileged position of a writer in Soviet society.

Herman Ermolaev. *SEEJ*. Winter, 1965, p. 460

[Babel's] early stories already have something of the highly formalized manner of the later ones and which bears such a strong resemblance to Hemingway's manner. Since neither could have been influenced by the other we must trace the style of both to a common source, which is certainly Flaubert. Indeed, considering Flaubert's influence on the modern short story, it would not be too much to say that he should be considered among the storytellers. The extraordinary relationship he established between the object and the style is almost unmanageable in anything so long as a novel, but again and again in the short story we see how it serves to delimit the form, establishes the beginning and the end, and heightens the intensity that is so necessary in a story but so embarrassing in a novel, where everything has to have a sort of everyday quality. . . .

I am not confused but confounded by "With Old Man Makhno." In this a Jewish girl is raped by six Russian soldiers in succession. She would have been raped by a seventh except that the rape went by order of seniority, and Kikin, the seventh, realized that in the process she was being raped by another Communist hero reputed to be a syphilitic and, so as not to contract the disease, preferred to nurse a grievance which he expounds to the poor child who has been violated and infected by his comrades. At this point I really want to be vulgar, whip out my notebook and pencil, and ask, "Your point, Comrade Babel, your point? Are you implying that this is a small, inevitable tragic accident such as is bound to occur with Heroes of the Revolution, or do I detect a hint that hanging—as in certain capitalist armies—might best meet the case? Am I in fact speaking to Comrade Babel or Ike Babel?" But Babel, like Hemingway, is being so infernally tough that he leaves me in doubt about a perfectly simple question as to whether I should regard him as a real writer or as a dangerous lunatic.

Frank O'Connor. *The Lonely Voice* (Cleveland,
World Publishing Company, 1965), pp. 189, 192–93

The Babelian short story at its best seems to realize that poetic balance between thought and image, line and color, movement and structure in a way which is characteristic of great lyric poetry. The emphasis is on image, color, and structure, rather than on thought, line, and movement. Ehrenburg is quite right when he calls Babel a poet. Such non-lyrical ingredients as philosophical abstraction, plot, irony, and rhetoric are transformed by him into concrete verbal units, small and light enough to float about in Babel's space of color. Babel also displays a healthy dose of that Goethean "narrowness, enamored of reality," which is proper to the true lyric poet. In many respects Babel's art in *Red Cavalry* resembles that of the acmeist-imaginist school of lyric poetry, in particular that of the great acmeist poet Osip Mandelstamm.

Victor Terras. *SSF*. Winter, 1966, p. 156

In search of a new form, Babel turned not only to prose and to movie scripts but also to the drama. His play *Zakat* (*Sunset*) was followed by his last play *Maria*, which is the story of the disintegration of the aristocratic family Mukovnin in the early years of the revolution. The design of the play is original: the heroine, Maria, for whom the play is named, does not appear in a single scene. She—Mukovnin's oldest daughter—is off at the front as a soldier in a political section of the Red Army. Her name is everywhere; everyone remembers her, talks about her—one with delight, another with jealousy, bitterness, spite. Maria, who figures only behind the scenes, is the embodiment of all that is good, the bearer of the highest revolutionary idea. She is the best criterion for measuring the words and actions of the fallen people of the old order—degenerate nobility, Menshevik speculators, former princes, former cavalry officers, and other has-beens. . . .

The extensive and contradictory literature on Babel both here and abroad compares him with Maupassant, Flaubert, Anatole France, and Rabelais; still others mention Ernest Hemingway. When Babel is compared to other writers, Gogol, Leskov, and, most of all, Gorki are often mentioned. But regardless of the influences he was exposed to and of the universities he attended, his art remains singularly his own.

The prose of Babel is unmistakably identified by its terse sentences, its polish, its rhythmical pattern, the explosive force of his short stories. "A sentence," he wrote, "enters the world both good and bad at the same time. The secret lies in a hardly perceptible twist." This secret of a master artist was attainable to the author of *Red Cavalry*.

L. Polyak. Introduction to Isaak Babel, *Izbrannoe*
(Moscow, Khudozhestvennaya literatura, 1966), p. 22†

As a writer [Babel] was as fastidious as anyone who has ever written prose. He once rewrote a story 26 times and nothing dismayed him more than a manuscript in which "nothing's crossed out." Hemingway himself—never reckless with compliments—admitted that "Babel's style is even more concise than mine. . . ." At the same time Babel was no sheltered esthete. Much as he loved his "craft and sullen art," he loved the human mystery even more. His curiosity about his fellow creatures was incessant, shameless, ruthless, inspired. He could not see a woman's handbag without asking, "Can I see what you've got in there?" He was known to pay strangers for telling him about their first love affairs.

In five or six pages (say, in the uncannily beautiful story called "Odessa"), Babel can convey more of the majesty and menace and sheer inexplicableness of life than any writer I have ever read, except Shakespeare. Like Shakespeare, too, his storytelling line is swift, sudden, supple, unexpected; you can never quite predict what will be said next. And then, on every page, there is Babel's own cachet, a witty, virile, yet somehow abashed wistfulness. The poet is in love with life, but life, for its part, couldn't care less. "What's the use," he once said, "if you have spectacles on your nose and autumn in your heart?"

Robert Phelps. Life. July 18, 1969, p. 10

The subjects of a very large number of Babel's stories are primitive and direct. The war and the expropriations have turned the peasants on the Asiatic border into murderers, looters, and bandits; the new government forces were as ruthless in getting a new regime set up. Babel's prose is sharp and laconic. There is little comment. And yet within the fatalism of the tales there is the unmistakable Jewish humanity, sometimes the Jewish humor and fantasy—what one can only call the irony of recognition: the recognition of the manly or womanly essence of each briefly elicited character. Babel had a master in Gorki, but his deeper masters were Gogol and Maupassant: Gogol for the imaginative richness, Maupassant for detachment, economy, and devilish skill. Eventually Babel was to find Maupassant cold. What I think Babel meant was that the Frenchman was *outside*, whereas all Babel's characters carry some grain of the presence of Russia, the self being a fragment of the land's fatality. One says, as one sees the Kulak kill his horse rather than let it go to the Cheka people when he is turned out, when one sees him become a legend as a bandit, and when he is run to earth and killed in a pit: "Yes, that is how it was. It was the end of an epoch, dreadful." One has seen the rage of a lifetime. . . .

In story after story Babel worked until he hit upon the symbol that turns it from anecdote into five minutes of life. He was not a novelist. By 1937 he was being semi-officially questioned about not writing on a large scale like Tolstoy or the very *bien vue* Sholokhov. It was being insinuated that he was idle and not pulling his weight. Poor devil! Short story writers are poets. Babel could not but be opposed to the clichés of Socialist Realism and particularly to the rhetorical magazine prose it had led to. He was also asked why he wrote of the exceptional rather than the typical, and one knows what Stalinism meant by typical: the middlebrow ideal. He replied with Goethe's simple definition of the *novella:* it is a story about an unusual occurrence. And he went on. . . .

Tolstoy was able to describe what happened to him minute by minute, he remembered it all, whereas I, evidently, only have it in me to describe the most interesting five minutes I've experienced in twenty-four hours.

He was opposed to the short story as a condensed novel. The short story is an insight.

V. S. Pritchett. NYR. July 31, 1969, p. 3

BALMONT, KONSTANTIN (1867–1943)

Although written recently, *Tolko Lyubov* [Only Love] has already become significant work. . . . In my opinion, it best expresses Balmont's talent—as proud as European thought, as beautiful as a tale of our south, and as thoughtful as the Slavic soul. In it, the author appears as Balmont-Arion, who was the ancient tender appellative of a melodious poet. Readers of Balmont's last works (are there many?) will read with sadness this strangely beautiful book refined in thought and feeling. It contains, perhaps, the embryo of the later decay—a corruption of the maiden-like Russian word in the name of its richness. There is something ambiguous in the melodiousness and imagery of these verses, although they are still bashful, like a young girl at the moment of her surrender. Balmont wrote: "If I go to a precipice, I will, glancing at a star, fall without regretting that I am falling on rocks." He approached without hesitation the star of pure poetry, and now he sees the merciless impetuousness of his fall. *Only Love* signifies the end of the brilliant morning of the renaissance of Russian poetry. At that time, the formulas for a new life, literature, and poetry, combined with philosophy and religion, were only outlined as guides of our actions. It was necessary to cross unknown roads, to hide secret worlds in our soul, and to learn to look at the already known with a glance as new and inspired as if it were the first day of creation. Balmont was one of the first of insatiable discoverers, but his thoughts were not directed at a Promised Land, for he enjoyed the charms of the road. Therefore, no hands ever picked such dazzling flowers, and such golden bees never rested on anyone's else's curls. It would seem that his muse was not weighed by the powerful law of gravity. Justly, he is the first of the "decadents" to achieve recognition and love.

Nikolai Gumilyov. *Vesna.* 10, 1908, p. 14[†]

A refusal for "an interlocutor" runs like a thread throughout Balmont's poetry and greatly depreciates its value. In his poems, Balmont constantly slights someone, refers to him carelessly, disrespectfully, and haughtily. This someone is the mysterious interlocutor. Not understood and unacknowledged by Balmont, he is cruelly slandered by him. When we speak, we search for approval and support of our rightness in the personage of this interlocutor. The poet does this even more. The precious cognizance of poetic rightness is often lacking in Balmont, in that he does not have this constant interlocutor. From this shortcoming arise two unpleasant extremes in Balmont's poetry—flattery and impudence. Balmont's impudence is neither true nor original. His need for self-assurance is quite unhealthy. He cannot say "I" in an undertone. He screams out "Me." The screaming individualism of Balmont is unpleasant. It is not the peaceful solipsism of Sologub, which insults no one, but individualism at the expense of somebody else's "I."

Osip Mandelshtam. *Apollon.* Feb., 1913, p. 52[†]

Balmont does not have adequate force to make thought complement his beloved sound. He does not reverberate with thoughts, but with words; or, vice versa, observations reverberate, but the words do not. A complete and internally finished context does not exist in his poetry, nor does a higher inherent quality. His refinement is a secondary derivative; nor is its simplicity original. Neither here nor elsewhere is he entirely natural. Only at times is the scattered structure of his abundant speech restored and a glimmer of truth seen. He could not wisely and quietly expose the indivisibility of thought and sound hidden somewhere in the final depths; nor could he expose their cosmic oneness or the finite unity of what is dear and what strange, what is ordinary and what sought, or what is nature and what culture. However, what he can do is give great joy to the Russian reader. Balmont overvalues himself, but does really possess worth. The music of our poetry will tenderly carry his resounding name into its notes. The treasure house of our subjects, nevertheless, will accept the bright whims of his moods; the shifting from the simple to the refined, from his motherland to exotic places; his art and even his artificiality. Tenderly and frequently, people will listen to this songbird. Although he excites himself, exaggerates, distorts, anesthetizes his soul with some kind of drug—artificial paradise of Baudelaire—even despite all this, a live soul dwells in him, a talented soul; and he, intoxicated with words and enraptured with sounds, sheds words passionately with his singing mouth. He is not strict with himself. The wind that he likens to his poetry will carry away, without a trace, many of his unsuccessful poems and immature ballads. The wind will scatter the weeds from Balmont, and the beauty will remain forever.

Yuli Aikhenvald. *Siluety russkikh pisatelei* (Berlin, Slovo, 1923), p. 113[†]

Balmont was to Russian modernism what Verlaine was to its French counterpart. He elevated Russian poetry to hitherto unattained musical heights. Nor was this his only merit. Like many other symbolist poets, Balmont was well acquainted with Western modernist literature, which he translated for Russian readers. In his translations Balmont emphasized the poetry of the English-speaking peoples. He, more than anyone else, was responsible for popularizing in Russia Oscar Wilde, Walt Whitman, Edgar Allan Poe, and Shelley, to say nothing of Rossetti, Blake, Coleridge, and Tennyson. His translations of Poe are excellent on the whole, for Balmont was able to render much of Poe's musical charm into Russian. His translation of "The Raven," which he did in competition with Bryusov, is particularly deft; in fact, the Russian version of Poe's refrain "quoth the raven—'nevermore!'" (*"kárknul vóron—'nikogdá!'"*) sounds more sinister than the English original; sometimes, however, Balmont translates this line also with *"mólvil vóron—'nikogdá!'"* when a more melodious and less menacing note seemed appropriate. On the other hand, his translations of Shelley show unwarranted liberties with the original. Some wag from the daily press even dubbed him "Shelmont" for his efforts—a pun not only on the surnames of the two poets, but also on the word *shel'ma,* a Russian colloquialism for "rascal." Balmont did not limit himself to the English; his translations include verses from the classical Greeks, the Spanish, and one Italian (Giacomo Leopardi).

Oleg Maslenikov. *The Frenzied Poets* (Berkeley, Calif., University of California Press, 1952), p. 22

The peak of his influence was between 1904 and 1910. He was known and loved much more than were any of his fellow Decadents, and was imitated by many poets. Even those who called him superficial, grandiloquent, raucous, or shallow could not deny his unusual craftsmanship, his musicality, his iridescent imagination, and the great role he played in the rebirth of Russian poetry. Yet his popularity was not lasting, and he was the first victim of the anti-Decadent and anti-Symbolist movements in poetry that sprang up during World War I. Since then, and especially in Soviet Russia, where he was tagged as a White Guard and "reactionary émigré," his name has become a synonym for formalism and frippery in verse.

Probably the only person not to notice the change was Balmont himself. He was very much a poetic Don Quixote, and such trifles as the realities of life did not in the least perturb him in his incessant pursuit of dreams. Even in the 1920's he seemed an anachronism; Bely called him the Russian Troubadour, and he served Poetry with all the devotion of a medieval knight, ready to sacrifice himself (and anyone else at hand) for the sake of his Lady Noble and Fair.

Marc Slonim. *Modern Russian Literature*
(New York, Oxford University Press, 1953), p. 95

Bal'mont was primarily a poet, and his prose, which includes fiction, travel sketches, the critiques collected in the book *Mountain Peaks* [*Gornye vershiny*] (1904), and a few theoretical pieces (the most important of the latter is *Poetry as Magic* [*Poeziya kak volshebstvo*], which appeared in pamphlet form in 1915), has all the defects of his verse but none of its merits. All the collections of poems for which he will be remembered appeared during a brief span of time, that ten- or twelve-year period which formed the only phase of Bal'mont's life marked by creativity, and not by fecundity alone. The production of those years opened with the threefold series of *Under the Northern Sky* [*Pod severnym nebom*] (1894), *In the Boundless* [*V bezbrezhnosti*] (1895), and *Stillness* [*Tishina*] (1898); and closed with another threefold series, *Buildings Afire* [*Goryaschie zdaniya*] (1900), *Let Us Be like the Sun* [*Budem kak solntse*] (1903), and *Nothing but Love* (1903). *Let Us Be like the Sun*, to which the poet gave the subtitle "A Book of Symbols," won the acclaim of the critics as Bal'mont's highest achievement, even though it is merely the most typical, as well as the most popular, of his works. Keener judges feel, however, that Bal'mont's poetry reached its peak in *Nothing but Love*, and already saw a falling off of his powers in *The Liturgy of Beauty* [*Liturgiya krasoty*] (1905), with which Bal'mont's good season came to an end. The many volumes which appeared up to the time of the poet's departure from Russia, and the fewer and slighter ones which he published in the first decade of his exile, are hardly worthy of being mentioned and well deserve the oblivion which was their immediate lot. With rare and random exceptions, the production of the late Bal'mont reveals the decline of his talent into mediocrity and mannerism.

Renato Poggioli. *The Poets of Russia* (Cambridge,
Mass., Harvard University Press, 1960), p. 90

I realize that it is difficult to startle Parisians, but I have more than once seen people turn around and stare after Balmont as he strode along the Boulevard Saint-Germain. In Moscow in 1918 people walked about gloomily with shopping bags, some pulling small sledges. It was cold and people were hungry, yet the passers-by stared at a red-haired eccentric striding in the middle of the street, his head lifted to the grey sky.

In his youth, Balmont attempted suicide by jumping out of a window. He injured a leg and remained slightly lame all his life. For that reason, he walked fast, giving the impression of a hopping bird used to flying rather than walking.

His face was now very pale, now the color of copper. He had green eyes, a small red beard, and red hair that curled down his back. . . . He was proud of his curls. He resembled a tropical bird that has accidentally flown to the wrong latitude.

Ilya Ehrenburg. *Novy mir*. Sept., 1960, p. 104[†]

To take the good things first; Balmont is credited with "musical" quality by almost everyone, including populists and Marxists, who, one suspects, could not be more indifferent to it—especially in a poet who, in their view, failed miserably in such important areas as political verse and folklore. This musicality is sometimes described as "virtuosity in sound," and Balmont is even credited with having discovered alliteration for Russian poetry. The poet himself gave a patronizing nod in the direction of such statements when he said: "I am quietly certain that before me, on the whole, no one in Russia knew how to write sonorous verse (*zvuchnye stikhi*)." Someone should really investigate Balmont's musicality, both in its essence and in the impact it had on his contemporaries (Briusov declared, for example, that "musically, Balmont is superior to Lermontov and Fet"). Few critics are specific when they talk of this "musicality"; even the fact-loving Briusov says merely that Balmont "transformed and recreated [*peresozdal*] meters and instilled them with a new music."

Vladimir Markov. *SlR*. June, 1969, pp. 260–61

BELY, ANDREI   (1880–1934)

We have read the new works of Andrei Bely with deep regret. We pity the author, and it is impossible not to feel truly sorry for him.

Simfoniya [The Symphony], written by him about two years ago . . . had a great success with certain readers. That is, five or six enthusiasts who evaluate art from the point of view of "new" and "old" quickly found faith in Andrei Bely and declared him the true prophet of a new art. Actually, some rare sparks of poetic gift seemed to glimmer in the confusion, roar, and planned affectedness of this "Symphony." The announcement of Andrei Bely as a prophet could not stop there. As a leader, he was required to prophesy.

Now we have this collection of amazing poems—*Zoloto v lazuri* [Gold in Azure]. There is not one living passage here, and the poetry produces an impression of intended confusion and of unnecessary words remaining where they randomly fell among the lines. It can be seen therefore that the "Symphony" has been made with "heroic" strength.

Andrei Bely performed heavy labor. In order to write the *Severnaya simfoniya* [The Northern Symphony], he had slowly and painstakingly to think up all types of complete absurdities; and such thoughts come, of course, only with great difficulty and can cause the author a very painful fatigue. Of course, it might not be too difficult to think up a "giant" who "held a blue cloud on his shoulders, yet strained himself" who forced the author, "seeing his strength, to howl senselessly." Perhaps there would be no difficulty in thinking up a "tree-trunked distance," a "troubador's voice," "the chasuble of a red giant"; but how difficult it would be to imagine and squeeze into a little "Symphony" this deafening collection of most amusing devilries, and even more, to pretend that it is a "terrible mystical element." It is already so terrible that we can not continue to acquaint the reader with the inspiring "goat-magic" of Bely. It is "a global terror," and the author's creation is obviously in "the embraces of gangrene."

Russkaya mysl. Aug., 1904, pp. 243–44†

Andrei Bely represents a sick and negative phenomenon in the life of the Russian language, only because he mercilessly and unceremoniously uses a word to conform completely with the temperament of his own speculative thinking. Choking in his refined verbosity, he can not sacrifice even one nuance, even one fracture of his capricious thought, and he blows up bridges which he is reluctant to cross. As a result, after momentary fireworks, there is a pile of metal, a sad picture of destruction, instead of a full life, an organic whole, and a working stability. The fundamental error of writers like Bely is their disrespect for the Greek element of a word and their ruthless exploitation of it for their own intuitive purpose.

Osip Mandelshtam. *O prirode slova*
(Kharkov, Istoki, 1922), pp. 8–9†

The Silver Dove [*Serebryany golub*] is somewhat less wildly original than his other works. It is closely modelled on the great example of Gogol. It cannot be called an imitative work, for it requires a powerful originality to learn from Gogol without failing piteously. Bely is probably the only Russian writer who has succeeded in doing so. The novel is written in splendid, sustainedly beautiful prose, and this prose is the first thing that strikes the reader in it. It is not so much Bely, however, as Gogol reflected in Bely, but it is always on Gogol's highest level, which is seldom the case with Gogol himself. *The Silver Dove* is somewhat alone also in being the one of Bely's novels which has most human interest in it, where the tragedy is infectious and not merely puckishly ornamental. . . . The novel contains much more narrative interest than most Russian novels do. It has a complicated and excellently disentangled plot. The characters are vivid—like Gogol's, characterized largely by their physical features—the dialogue, alive and expressive. But what is perhaps especially wonderful are the evocations of Nature, full of intense suggestiveness and pregnant poetry. The feeling of the monotonous and endless expanse of the Russian plain pervades the book. All this, together with the splendidly ornamental style, makes *The Silver Dove* one of the works of Russian literature that are most full of the most various riches.

D. S. Mirsky. Contemporary Russian Literature
(New York, Knopf, 1926), pp. 232–33

Of Bely's later works of fiction the most original and remarkable is the autobiographical novel *Kotik Letayev* (begun in 1915, published in 1922), a tale of childhood in which he devises new methods for rendering subconscious emotions and impressions; it is his most daring experiment in the Joyce technique. Much of Bely's later poetry and fiction reflects his infatuation for the anthroposophical doctrine of Dr. Rudolf Steiner, whose disciple he became some time before the war. Bely's sparkling poetical genius has revealed itself once more in his poem, "The First Meeting" ["Pervoe svidanie"], where he restores to us the atmosphere of his youth and that of the intellectual élite of Moscow in the early years of our century; it is a quaint mixture of peculiar realism, of wonderful musical effects and of most abstruse intellectualism—a thing no one but Bely could write. The same atmosphere in a different form is revived in Bely's *Memoirs* [*Vospominaniya*], of which several volumes have appeared under different titles. This, too, is an uneven work; some of its characteristics are excellent; some parts of it, as, for instance, his *Recollections of Alexander Blok* [*Vospominaniya o A. A. Bloke*], are invaluable for the history of Symbolism; but some of it is marred by gratuitous semi-political or anthroposophical reflections verging on foolery.

Bely's attitude to the revolution lacked consistency. In its early stages he was carried away, like Blok and some other poets, by its elemental, Messianic aspect (the outcome was a rather poor poem "Christ is Risen" ["Khristos voskres"]); he identified it with Russia, which he loved passionately; much of his poetry, especially in *Ashes* [*Pepel*], is about Russia, and it is a curious Symbolist interpretation of Nekrasov's themes. Yet in 1922 Bely left Russia and for a time became a virtual émigré, only to go back a year later.

As a literary influence, Bely counted for very much in post-revolutionary Russian literature, especially during its first period. Pilnyak and many

other contemporary writers are inconceivable without Bely. His studies
of the Russian prosody, included together with his philosophical criticism
in the volume entitled *Symbolism [Simvolizm]* (1910), also made a mark
and proved very fruitful.

Gleb Struve. SEER. July, 1934, pp. 184–85

Biely is not and never was a "popular" writer. By nature he is too subjective and esoteric to appeal to a wide public. Only the writers and the
elite among modernist readers could truly appreciate him. Nevertheless,
owing to his brilliance and imagination he influenced Russian literature
to a very great degree. For two decades and more, after the symbolist
movement had begun to retreat, Russian poets from Mayakovsky to
Aseyev reflect Biely's stimulus. The Russian prose of the 1920's also
bears the indelible stamp of Biely's craftsmanship. Even in the field of
literary scholarship, the formalist school undeniably had its roots in
Biely's volume *Symbolism* (1910).

Throughout his life most critics belittled Biely's significance. Only the
modernists praised his earliest works; the others either ignored or ridiculed his "ultradecadent" efforts. . . . For years he was an outcast, obliged
to remain outside the literary pale. Although the Bolshevik revolution of
1917 completely changed the Russian literary scene, the new order soon
created a new obstacle for Biely's recognition. It was the officially accepted materialistic concept of life, a philosophy that was alien, even
hostile, to Biely's spiritual nature. This barrier remained throughout his
lifetime. Only after his death did his peculiar, misfit genius begin to reap
its due, for Biely was the most original and probably the most influential
writer born of the symbolist movement in Russia.

Oleg Maslenikov. The Frenzied Poets (Berkeley, Calif.,
University of California Press, 1952), p. 95

No other Russian writer has experimented so boldly with words as did
Andrei Bely. His narrative prose has no equivalent in Russian literature.
Bely's "stylistic revolution" can be considered a catastrophic failure, but
its considerable significance cannot be denied. The author of *The Silver
Dove* and *Peterburg* (*St. Petersburg*) left no stone unturned in the previous
"literary language." He placed Russian prose on its head, turned the syntax upside down, flooded the vocabulary with a torrent of newly coined
words. Bely's audacious experiments, sometimes bordering on lunacy,
put their stamp on all new Soviet literature. He created a school.

The "word revolution," announced in his lyrical prose *Symphony*, finds
its full expression in *The Silver Dove*. Bely begins by imitating Gogol as
a pupil. He adopts all forms of his style, straining them to an extreme
emotional intensity. . . . The lyricism, irony, grotesqueries, hyperbole,

profusions, contrasts, wordplay, intonations, coloring, and the rhythm of Gogol's prose are shown by Bely as if through a magnifying glass.

Konstantin Mochulski. *Andrei Bely* (Paris, YMCA Press, 1955), p. 157[†]

Naturally, Bely's style is not that of Dostoyevski. New epitaphs, exact phonetic "instrumentation," rhythmic organization—with all these means Bely tips the scales, but nonetheless both images are indicative of a kindred spirit.

Dostoyevski has also directed attention to the grotesque nature of the architectonic embellishment, with which the builders of Petersburg did not economize, an embellishment, which—as it seemed to Bely—fit so little with the northerly skies of Petersburg. . . .

At any rate, an important difference from Dostoyevski must be observed: Bely uses these details purely as artistic vehicles of style, each single detail having its own compository function, while Dostoyevski does not mention these bizarre facades of Petersburg in his novels at all, because he only observes them as a critic of culture. In his novels, Dostoyevski refrains consciously from outer descriptions; they are not important to him even as contrasts. At the most, he incidentally remembers the appearance of a house or a bit of scenery. As leitmotivs, he seldom or never uses such images, since he concentrates totally upon embellishing the inner world, where he is concerned with details.

Johannes Holthusen. *Studien zur Ästhetik und Poetik des russischen Symbolismus* (Göttingen, Vandenhoeck & Ruprecht, 1957), pp. 152–53[†]

Taking into consideration the differences of background and individual character and style, it is possible to establish a parallel between Biely's work and that of James Joyce. Both writers, the Russian and the Irish, born within two years of each other, were to exercise the same tremendous impact on the creative prose of their languages. In places, their verbal innovations are almost identical; in others, their angle of vision and their interests are as remote from each other as the Wall of Hadrian from the Wall of China. They are both immersed in and preoccupied with the problems of memory and the distortion of time. In both writers musical principles are active, but in the work of Biely this is expressed more abstractly and mathematically. Throughout his work, one becomes more and more aware of a structural pattern not only as the whole, but as the part: in the paragraph, the sentence, and the phrase; and it is clear that Biely's pattern, less varied than Joyce's, is based on a principle of verbal point-counterpoint which he discovered and applied with increasing precision throughout his work.

But where Biely and Joyce meet on larger common ground is in their attitude to, and place in, the use of the prose language and the structure of the novel in their respective cultures. In reality, the cultural and historical moment was the same, because both writers were faced with the problems and consequences of the maturity and breakdown of old forms and attitudes—Romanticism, Realism, Naturalism. The novel had reached what seemed to be an apogee in the nineteenth century, but by the 1890's, a new spirit was felt both in Europe and in Russia—of music and of Symbolism. Both Biely and Joyce embody some aspects of this new spirit, and they both use it in varying ways to propound a new esthetic, to explore and enrich the resources of their languages, and to transform the pattern of the novel.

George Reavey. Foreword to Andrey Biely,
St. Petersburg (New York, Grove Press, 1959), p. ix

St. Petersburg has been compared to James Joyce's *Ulysses*, which Biely's novel preceded by several years. Both compress the action of their narratives, both use something of the stream-of-consciousness method, both employ a variety of techniques, both describe sharply divergent characters, present flashbacks and memory associations, newspaper reports, and thoughts and emotions which overlap and interplay. In Joyce's novel it is Dublin; in Biely's, mist-enveloped St. Petersburg, in which people strut about like shadows in a dream-play. There is the impact of middle-class gentry and the proletariat, the impact of metropolitan St. Petersburg on the left bank of the Neva and less impressive, less elegant Vasilyevsky island on the opposite bank, inhabited by the workers, the revolutionaries, and the malcontents, who awakened such horror in the elder Ableukhov, who regarded them as enemies of the Russian people. They were the people who circulated lampoons about him, and cartoons revealing him with oversize ears. The turbulent surface and sublife of the city are reflected in their characters; all in all this novel possesses a many-dimensional quality. The physical scope is infinitely greater than that of *Ulysses*, for the city flings its shadow over all Russia, and, in a more limited measure, offers a critical commentary on Western civilization, of which, in a sense, it is something of a victim.

John Cournos. Introduction to Andrey Biely,
St. Petersburg (New York, Grove Press, 1959),
pp. xv–xvi

[Bely] devoted the best part of the last decade of his life to literary theory and criticism, and, even more, to the composition of his literary reminiscences, as both a continuation and a rewriting of the splendid *Recollections of Aleksandr Blok*, which he had published in the Berlin review *Epopée* in 1922–1923. This rewriting, or rather remaking, was dictated by the sharpening of a chronic resentment, the effect of which was to increase the distortions of the earlier version, and to change them into outright falsifications. The full series of Belyj's memoirs, which he was unable to complete, includes in chronological order the following volumes, the last of which appeared posthumously and in unfinished form: *On the Border of Two Centuries* [*Na rubezhe dvukh stoleti*] (1929), *The Beginning of the Century* [*Nachalo veka*] (1933), and *Between Two Revolutions* [*Mezhdu dvukh revolyutsi*] (1936–1937). It is obvious that these memoirs have less and more than mere documentary importance: biased and inexact as they are, they will remain in Russian literature as a masterful account, always interesting and often appealing, of those strange men and circles, currents and events, which dominated Russian culture from the end of the nineteenth century up to the First World War. . . .

Belyj's criticism too has more than a passing importance. Many of his outstanding contributions in this field belong to the earliest period of his career, and most of them are gathered in the collections entitled *Symbolism* (1910), *The Green Meadow* [*Zelyony lug*] (1910), and *Arabesques* [*Arabeski*] (1911). The first of these is particularly significant, especially in the two essays where Belyj studies Symbolist poetry from the viewpoint of verse and technique. These two essays form a personal and controversial treatise on Russian versification, in which, by distinguishing between "meter," or the abstract verse scheme, and "rhythm," or the actual sound pattern of the line, Belyj anticipates some of the theories of the critical school of the Formalists, concerning what the latter were to call the "melodics" and the "instrumentation" of verse. The most important critical works he wrote in his late years are the monograph *Rhythm as Dialectic and the "Bronze Horseman"* [*Ritm kak dialektika: "Medny sadnik"*] (1929), a splendid metrical analysis of that masterpiece; and *The Craftsmanship of Gogol'* [*Masterstvo Gogolya*] (1929), a complex and often arbitrary study of that master, which influenced the theory and practice of many young Soviet writers.

Renato Poggioli. The Poets of Russia (Cambridge,
Mass., Harvard University Press, 1960), pp. 159–60

The most important progenitor of modern Russian literature is Andrei Bely (pseudonym for Boris N. Bugaev). His novel *Petersburg* marks a crossroads in the history of Russian prose. Bely, which in Russian means white, has a symbolic meaning, for white is the color of the apocalypse. To the sense of alienation and loneliness, which the Russian modernists felt hovering over themselves and over life itself, was joined an awareness of a mysterious force, of the impending apocalyptic end of the world. We take little risk in presuming that this "mysterious force" is really the "wall" of natural law and reason, Hegel's "spirit of objectivity." While the external world still exists in Bely's novel, it continually meshes with an internal world. The second is important and real; the first is unreal, fantastic, grotesque. When the external world intrudes into the internal, the irrationality of the external world provokes the grotesque. Let us not forget that for all "underground people" reason—the "wall"—is the only reality (just as, for the medieval world, *universalia sunt realia*). All the main characters see cogitation as their principal task. In fact, it is their only "proper" life. External events serve only to set internal processes into motion. Bely brilliantly described the sensation of thinking as feeling (entirely of the body) stimulated by certain thoughts. Man's attitude toward the internal world is the same as his attitude toward the external world. [1961]

Mihajlo Mihajlov. *Russian Themes* (New York,
Farrar, Straus & Giroux, 1968), pp. 271–72

Bely was too hermetic, too limited. His scope is comparable to that of chamber music—never greater. If he had really suffered, he might have written the major work of which he was capable. But he never came into contact with real life. . . . Perhaps this fascination with new forms is the fate of writers like Bely who die young. I have never understood those dreams of a new language, of a completely original form of expression. Because of this dream, much of the work of the twenties was merely stylistic experimentation and has ceased to exist. The most extraordinary discoveries are made when the artist is overwhelmed by what he has to say. In his urgency he uses then the old language and the old language is transformed from within. Even in those years one felt a little sorry for Bely because he was so cut off from the immediate, which alone could have helped his genius to blossom.

Boris Pasternak. In Olga Andreyev Carlisle, *Voices in
the Snow* (New York, Random House, 1962), p. 199

BLOK, ALEKSANDR (1880–1921)

From the point of view rejected by Blok and those who are with him, it is not difficult to show that his poetry is all bad, that it is even not poetry at all. . . . In the discordant evaluation of Blok, there will be a few words of praise; the appraisal of his person will be different. For some, he is an impostor and speculator with a fashionable corruption of taste; for others, he is a sick degenerate. He seems to us to be much simpler and more ordinary. In every literary movement there are such mediocre figures, such carriers of unarticulated ideas who cannot control themselves. They grow, but more often they remain in that enigmatic state. It is difficult to judge what they wanted, yet failed, to express. One thing is clear: they lack the power for it. One cannot maintain, however, that they are rare in literature; on the contrary, there is a large group of such literary curiosities.

Russkoe bogatstvo. 12, 1904, pp. 28, 30–31[†]

It is said that Blok is an urban poet. This definition is conditional only. . . . City life on the whole is alien, even hostile to him; he reacts so strongly— I would say painfully—to what are usually considered a sign of city health, so to speak—sounds, movements, the diversity of a city—so much so that he considers these to be an insult to life. . . .

Blok is not a poet of the city as a whole but more or less of sharp and alarming moments of city life. He does not understand the elemental force of a city, or he takes it as being hostile to him; only the arabesque ornaments of a city, its fine and sharp intoxication, touch Blok. A restaurant, the gypsy singing, a suburban walk—these are the themes of Blok's urban poetry. In these he feels some kind of tension, anxiety, power of the moment and of the accident, transience—all that is in tune with the instantaneous, anxious, Blokovian harmony. Only death reconciles him with the city; only a dead city does not insult him, evoking in him calm, beautiful verses permeated with a sacred rhythm.

A. Derman. Russkaya mysl. July, 1913, pp. 61–62[†]

What does the law of personification of Blok's art consist of, and on what is it based?

Even a cursory glance at the enumerated lyrical works can convince us: before our eyes there are familiar, traditional figures; some of them (Hamlet, Carmen) have been exploited to the point of cliché. Such clichés are Harlequin and Columbine, Pierrot and Commendatore—the favorite personages of Blok's lyric narratives. Sometimes it seems that Blok chooses such epigraphs willfully. . . .

He prefers the traditional, even obliterated figures (the walking truths), since in them the old emotionality is preserved; slightly renovated, it is stronger and deeper than the emotionality of the new image, because novelty usually distracts attention from emotionality to objectivity.

That is why Blok, when dealing with symbols, does not avoid the purely allegorical images, which have long been obsolete, metaphors that have already become proverbial. [1921]

Yuri Tynyanov. Arkhaisty i novatory
(Leningrad, Priboi, 1929), pp. 516–17[†]

One cannot admire enough Blok's historical sense. Long before he en-
treated others to listen to the music of the revolution, he listened to the
subterranean music of Russian history at the time when the most attentive ear could discern only a syncopic pause. . . .

Blok was a man of the nineteenth century, and he knew that the days
of his century were numbered. He thirstily widened and deepened his
inner world at the right time, just as a badger burrows in the ground
and builds his home with two exits. . . . Moved by that badger instinct,
he deepened his poetic knowledge of the nineteenth century. For a long
time he was haunted by English and German romanticism, by Novalis's
Blue Flower and Heine's irony, and by an almost Pushkinian thirst to
touch with his burning lips the springs of European folk creations—
English, French, German—pulsating independently in their purity and
variety. Among Blok's creations, there are those directly inspired by the
Anglo-Saxon, Romance, and Germanic genius.

Osip Mandelshtam. Rossiya. 1, 1922, pp. 28–29[†]

A. A. [Blok] was a taciturn, calm person, not in the habit of approaching people himself; he did not make any overtures, as if he expected people to come to him first, so that he could answer them pointedly, directly,
curtly, without ambiguity or pleasing comment, and cut off the jumble
of chattering thought associations with a resolute yes or no. . . .

He gave the impression of a pond in which a large fish was hiding,
seldom swimming to the surface; there was no ripple, no thought, no playing like a small fish and emitting light sprays of paradoxes and sparkling
comparisons, no bubbling. It was a smooth surface, not one theory, not
one playfully glittering idea. He did not seem to be clever, or even rational; for that reason he did not appear remarkable to many "wise"
people. But one sensed his great mind in his tact, in the tone of his gestures—unhurried, sporadic but pointed. Suddenly, the surface of the
pond would rise with a heavy splash of the heaving depth, upset by a
quick movement of some large fish—a great idea with which he had been
pregnant for months, perhaps years.

Andrei Bely. Epopeya. 2, 1922, pp. 71, 75[†]

Blok's genius reached its maturity about 1908. The lyrics written between that date and 1916 are contained in the third volume of his collected poems, which is, together with "The Twelve" ["Dvenadtsat'"], certainly the greatest body of poetry written by a Russian poet since the
middle of the last century. He was a man neither of great brains nor of
great moral strength. Nor was he really a great craftsman. His art is passive and involuntary. He is a recorder of poetical experience rather than
a builder of poetical edifices. What makes him great is the greatness of
the poetical spirit that fills him, coming, as it were from other worlds. He

has himself described his creative process (in "The Artist" ["Khudozh-nik"], 1913) as a purely passive process very much akin to mystical ecstasy as it is described by the great Spanish and German mystics. The ecstasy is preceded by a state of boredom and prostration; then comes the unutterable bliss of a wind from other spheres, to which the poet abandons himself, will-lessly and obediently. But the rapture is inter-fered with by "creative reason," which forces into the fetters of form the "light-winged, benevolent, free bird" of inspiration; and when the work of art is ready, it is dead to the poet, who subsides into his previous state of empty boredom.

> D. S. Mirsky. *Contemporary Russian Literature*
> (New York, Knopf, 1926), pp. 217–18

With Blok begins the decisive freeing of Russian verse from the principle of counting syllables in a metric foot, the abolition of the demand, canon-ized by Tredyakovski and Lomonosov, for the metric regulation of the number and position of unstressed syllables in a verse. In that respect, all of the newest Russian poets have learned from Blok and not from his predecessors. . . . A similar significance of his creativity is found also in the decanonization of exact rhyming that has taken place in recent years. . . . With the appearance of Blok, especially with his second and third collections, the uneven rhyming moves from the stage of theoretical experiments into an organic stylistic feature.

> Viktor Zhirmunski. *Voprosy teorii literatury*
> (Leningrad, Academia, 1928), pp. 256, 258, 262†

Blok is a spokesman of the nobility (the *dvoryanstvo*). He should be re-garded as a scion of the line of the nobility's ideologists and his place is —to extend the metaphor—at the end of that line. With certain reserva-tions he may be considered the last great artist of the Russian nobility.

In so far as his place is at the end of the line of the nobility's historical development, Blok reflects the nadir of its disintegration. Profoundly in-fected by the traditions of the nobility, he is, at the same time, a bearer of anti-bodies. He is charged with hatred for his milieu and for his class. In so far as he finds these in a state of enfeeblement, of disintegration, and is himself a product of such disintegration, Blok is debarred from seeking salvation in that aristocratic nucleus which still, to all appear-ances, formed the acknowledged "establishment" of his society: i.e., in the hard core of reactionary bureaucrats and firmly entrenched landed gentry.

> Anatoli Lunacharski. In Aleksandr Blok, *Sobranie*
> *sochineni* (Leningrad, Sovetski pisatel, 1932),
> Vol. I, p. 12

Blok's articles on the theater are significant not only for their deep concern about the future of dramaturgy close to his literary school. In these articles there is neither narrrow personal interest nor reserved admiration of individual successes. For Blok the theater is the probing stone which "everybody has to touch," as it truly seems to him, for the dramatic art does not allow the poet to remain in the narrow circle of his refined, personal experiences. The theater firmly stands on the threshold of life, and if it is unable to express the demands of reality, it is doomed, no matter how high and intense a lyrical stream is keeping it alive. Blok's merit is his ability to place the problem of the theater in an organic relation to the problem of repertory as well as of the audience, in the broad meaning of the word, that is, in relationship to that fundamental social force which has determined and is determining the fate of this or other literary direction in the theater.

I. Dukor. *Literaturnoe nasledstvo*
(Moscow, Zhurnalno-gazetnoe obedinenie, 1937),
Vols. XXVII–XXVIII, p. 114[†]

Like Mallarmé with his belief in a silent music above the audible, like Rilke with his Orpheus, Blok deduced from the existence of poetry a transcendental order which lay behind art and was responsible for it. He was not concerned merely with art or only to be an artist. The revelation of creative power was more to him than the actual writing of poetry; the inspiration was greater than what it inspired. Nor did he confine his speculations to the regions where this touched poetry. He saw it as a supreme power in life, struggling with those settled habits and forms which he called "civilisation." He felt that his world had lost contact with the Spirit of Music and was caught in the bonds of an obsolete system. With a logic characteristic of himself and of his race, he saw that what mattered most in the creative life was precisely the power to create. It was this that held his own life together and gave a meaning to it. Instead of dismissing it as inexplicable or reducing it to a place among other states of the spirit, he concluded that it was all that mattered for himself and for everyone. It was the only true reality. The old duality which he found between his visions and his sense of fact was solved through this conclusion. What mattered for him was the creative life, the Spirit of Music. He knew this not from theory but from intimate experience. And what was true of himself must naturally be true of others.

C. M. Bowra. *The Heritage of Symbolism*
(London, Macmillan, 1943), p. 164

In 1901 Blok had a revelation of something divine and pure, of a Beautiful Lady, an absolute Good. He felt a great need for faith and assurance.

This was his lofty prayer for an abstract Good. But whether this mysticism could not separate itself from a strong discipline or whether Blok was fundamentally too artistic and sensual to remain in the abstract, the visionary and his vision fell back to earth. Again, the poet perceived and expressed thoughts which were earthly, carnal, and feverish. This was the sad ending of Blok's first mystical experience, which had been an experience of Good.

Evil is the opposite pole of the absolute. The Virgin of Azure changed face and was transformed into a Messenger of Evil. Just as Blok had a revelation of Good in 1901, so in 1905 he experienced a revelation of Violence, Evil, the Demon—all represented by "The Unknown Woman." Now the poet is steeped in his second mystical experience, which is a curve symmetrically opposite to the first. Blok "requests perdition," not for itself but for his hopes that it will raise the last veil in front of him, that it will quench his thirst for the absolute. He remains entirely sincere. He expresses the same quest for Evil as he had for Good, and there is the same rhythm in the ascension of one as there was in the fall of the other. An initial progressing movement carried him beyond Natalia Nikolayevna Volokhova to the abstract Lady of Snows. But this new symbol appears to be just as powerless as "The Beautiful Lady" in holding the poet in his loftiness and rich dreams. Just as the Beautiful Lady was defaced, the Virgin of Snow is also degraded. Fallen to earth, all that remains of her is a gipsy, a serpent with a woman's face. Thus, Blok's second mystical experience, which was an experience of evil, had the same sad ending.

Sophie Bonneau. L'Univers poétique d'Alexandre Blok
(Paris, L'institut d'études Slaves de L'Université de
Paris, 1946), pp. 236–37[†]

Meetings in restaurants, journeys to the islands, incidental encounters, love duels—all this noctural, wanton, and drunken life is necessary to the poet only to make "violins sing" in his soul. How many poems are dedicated to passion and sensuality, and how little of genuine sensuality is in them! Blok is as spiritual as are Dostoyevski's "sensualists." He wallows in lechery and remains incorporeal; he seeks in it not the satisfaction of sensual desire but the agitation of the spirit. Passion, "bitter as a wormwood," assails the strings like a wind—and they begin to sound. This music is his lyrical life, his inspiration, his breathing. When he does not hear the secret inner song, he is dead. But at what terrible price the poetic gift is obtained! What degradation—chance embraces, repulsive rituals, false raptures! No one after Dostoyevski has written such terrible words about the metaphysical baseness of sensuality as did the "lecherous" Blok.

Konstantin Mochulski. Aleksandr Blok
(Paris, YMCA Press, 1948), p. 318[†]

Blok and Biely or Biely and Blok are usually regarded as the youngest pair of the several Siamese twins of the symbolist movement. The mention of either name has come to suggest also the other. Yet Biely was partly justified in insisting that the idyll of Blok and Biely was only imaginary. Although the two poets undeniably shared many characteristics, their dissimilarities are nearly equally basic and deep-rooted. Perhaps one may more correctly say that the two poets mutually complement each other, rather than that they resemble each other. The similarities between the two were great. . . . During their adolescence and youth both became saturated with the mystical currents that floated in the air, and were strongly affected by Vladimir Solovyov's eschatological poetry. Both men were distinct individualists in character, and both were endowed with a remarkable natural sense for rhythm. Both men, moreover, felt uprooted and vainly strove to recover harmonious relations with their surroundings. And, finally, the Russian symbolist movement reached its apex in the writings of the two poets. Their rise in Russian literature was nearly synchronous, and recognition crowned the efforts of both young men as soon as the modernist public discovered their work.

But here the similarity between them ends. Geographically, Blok belonged to urbane, European St. Petersburg, and Biely to patriarchal, colorfully Russian Moscow. Spiritually, the two men were also far apart; the grave, dignified, reticent Blok was surely no mirrored image of the mercurial, garrulous, gyrating Bugayev-Biely. In the life of the Russian literary Bohemia, Blok was a static piece of marble, and Biely a veritable human dynamo of words, actions, and mannerisms. Blok's life was directed almost entirely by intuition; Biely, though by nature perhaps as prone as Blok to let emotions guide his actions, usually tried to subordinate his feelings to reason, or at least to compromise between intuition and intellect.

Oleg Maslenikov. The Frenzied Poets (Berkeley, Calif.,
University of California Press, 1952), pp. 146–47

Blok's theme is not the relationship of an artist to his object, not even the object itself. His themes are only the pictures, the series of metaphors, in which his own mythology is revealed. It is indeed amazing how narrow his range of themes essentially is, when all accidental and situational elements are ignored and these leitmotivs are followed alone. . . .

In his work Blok is so engrossed in his own metaphors that they become his predominant stylistic device. An individual poem loses its concrete theme, the metaphors find their motivation only outside of the given context, and, finally, the images become compositional ornaments only.

Johannes Holthusen. Studien zur Ästhetik und
Poetik des russischen Symbolismus (Göttingen,
Vandenhoeck & Ruprecht, 1957), pp. 88, 95†

As a dramatic work *The Puppet Show* [*Balaganchik*] is open to many criticisms, if the usual theatrical standards are applied to it. It is a lyric in dramatic form, and may be equally appreciated by the reader as by a theatrical audience. Symbolist drama is perhaps a contradiction in terms, or at any rate requires to be judged by other canons, like a morality play. Blok himself did not regard *The Puppet Show* as a play in the accepted sense. It was rather a personal testament, founded, as the poet himself said, on the attacks of doubt and despair which had assailed him even in his youth. If *The Puppet Show* is viewed as a kind of mummer's tale, written with a satiric purpose, it is a telling and incisive work. The mystics with their vapid talk are remorselessly ridiculed and the author himself is reduced to confusion. With ironical reference to the theme of *The Beautiful Lady* [*Stikhi o Prekrasnoi Dame*] the arrival of a mysterious visitor is awaited. It is Columbine, whose curl on her back is taken for a sickle and she herself for Death. Pierrot and Harlequin, the constant "doubles," court her in true pantomimic style. The wounded clown bleeds, but his blood is cranberry juice. Columbine herself turns out to be made of cardboard. The scenery proves to be paper and is torn when Harlequin leaps through the window into the void!

There is much of the former Blok in the play. The figures of the harlequinade themselves recall an earlier lyric. The coming of a mysterious lady is the hope of the mystics. The doubling of Columbine with Death carries out one of Blok's characteristic schemes at the very centre of the play. The actual writing contains some of the poet's most touching and delicate lyrics.

Cecil Kisch. *Alexander Blok: The Prophet of the Revolution* (London, Weidenfeld & Nicolson, 1960), p. 49

There are . . . two Bloks. There is the poet, who, like Eliot, re-created for his generation the language of poetic diction. Blok's whole being was in his poetry. As Sir Cecil says, he was "not a systematic thinker, with a clear cut philosophy," but "a visionary, and at the same time a splendid musical instrument, receiving impulses of many tones and colours and returning them with spontaneous resonance in verses of incredible harmony and infinite variety"; or, to quote Sir Maurice Bowra, he could "re-create in his hearers that almost audible music which he knew when inspiration descended." Music, colour; and I would add a further quality which Pasternak, in a moving cycle of as yet unpublished poems dedicated to Blok, stresses above all—absolute freedom and sincerity of feeling. So long as there are poets writing in Russian, Blok will be studied and honoured. He is indeed still honoured even by the regime which did so much by its inhumanity and lack of imagination to destroy him. . . .

There is also another Blok, the intellectual, the "child of the terrible years" of anticipated catastrophe, of the cataclysm to come which would at once destroy and create anew. Blok was in no sense a politician, but when the Bolsheviks came to power he felt instinctively that he belonged at their side. His vision told him that beneath the ugly exterior shone the light of future joy and justice—that is, after all, the symbolism of Christ at the head of the Red Guards in "The Twelve," which so horrified Blok's friends that it permanently alienated some of them from him. Then come the disillusionment, the despair, the disintegration, and death. A moving account by the poet Ivanov show Blok at the end almost demented by remorse at having written "The Twelve." I think that is too simple as an explanation. Readers of *Dr. Zhivago* will now be better able to understand the love-hate relationship with the Bolsheviks of a sensitive and sincere man, as seen through the eyes of a poet who was himself of Blok's stature.

Leonard Schapiro. List. Jan. 26, 1961, p. 191

The Beautiful Lady is remote, cold, indifferent, and the source of all bliss. She is veiled in an azure, superterrestrial Beyond; she floats like a cloud or melts like the snow. She reveals herself to the poet in the mysterious sound of whispers, of steps, or of voices singing at an immeasurable distance; or she herself is song, or a star, or a planet. The poet has glimpses of her in the gloom or the refulgence of nights or of dawns, on solitary, tangled trails, or on crowded highways. She is an elemental spirit, at home in the distant fog at twilight, in the steppe, in the realm of ghosts and visions, and she will not be lured to the haven of a hearth. She alters her appearance, is "different, faceless, dumb"; she conjures in silence, and he does not know what she will turn into. Or she is young, "golden," walking on a bright path, bathed in sunlight. Sometimes she speaks tenderly, protectively, like a mother. And in her "Beyond" she is nearer than he to the immovable source of life. She is all that is hopeful, all that is light: the song of early spring, the star that shines in daytime, making bright the pavement of the streets; and when she suddenly departs, the poet is in darkness, without God. . . . In the last analysis, in both her worldly and her visionary manifestations, the Beautiful Lady is the embodiment of the poet's necessity to love, and through love to understand the moving principle of life, or at least to find a meaning to his own existence. The eternal, the fathomless, the immortal, the endless, haunt him like promises of bliss and denials of misery; and although the Beyond, by contrast to the here and now, may be a silent, cold, springless, loveless place, it provides rest from earthly passions, while its vastness counteracts the misery of the small and temporary. For the present is a lying dream, and life itself an old fortuneteller, mysteriously whispering forgotten words. The Beautiful Lady alone is Reality. If she changes, the poet will be thrown back into the irreality of his earthly consciousness, of that entangling dream, the world, from which he has tried to escape into Her presence. That is his greatest fear.

Helen Muchnic. *From Gorky to Pasternak*
(New York, Random House, 1961), pp. 111–12

Turning to Blok's critical work, one sees that Blok understood that one does not just put it there, as in pastiche. Blok also understood that to keep the symbols working the poet needs a system. Although he never elaborated a system as powerful as Mallarmé's or as workable as Yeats's, still he moved toward one. That is what all his critical articles are about. Most of his book reviews in magazines or newspapers are only pleasant: they suggest what sort of book they are dealing with and take up a moderate or an enthusiastic tone, depending on Blok's likes or dislikes. But his articles go farther: their subjectivity is not arbitrary response. Their subjectivity follows from a sense of personal obligation to work out adequately a particular kind of poetry. Many of the terms used are conventional or unsatisfactorily abstract, but even these terms seem clearly to work toward a system of real, poetic meaning. One sees in them a further elaboration of that poetics which the French Symbolists introduced, a continuation of the modern revolution in poetry.

F. D. Reeve. *Aleksandr Blok: Between Image and Idea*
(New York, Columbia University Press, 1962), p. 24

Aleksandr Blok, in spite of some attempts to "dethrone" him (it is enough to mention Ivan Bunin's *Memoirs* and, more recently, several essays by the late Sergej Makovskij, the founder and editor of *Apollon*, himself an active participant in, and at the same time a chronicler of, the Russian cultural renascence in the pre-World War I period), is still almost unanimously recognized, both in and out of Russia, as the greatest Russian poet since Tjutčev. The literature about him is vast. Apart from numerous reminiscences and articles and essays discussing various aspects of his personality and work, such book-size studies as Žirmunskij's and Čukovskij's, published in the 1920's, and the more recent ones by P. Medvedev, L. Timofeev, V. Orlov (regarded today as the leading Blok scholar in the Soviet Union), and others, may be mentioned. Outside Russia, K. Močul'skij's book in Russian, S. Bonneau's and N. Berberova's in French, Th. Goodman's in German, and Sir Cecil Kisch's in English—leaving aside numerous shorter studies (such as Sir Maurice Bowra's in his *Heritage of Symbolism*)—testify to the interest aroused by Blok and the attempt to bring him closer to the non-Russian reader.

Gleb Struve. *SEEJ*. Summer, 1963, p. 179

The Fair Lady [*Stikhi o Prekrasnoi Dame*], *The Stranger* [*Neznakomka*], and *The Native Land* [*Rodina*], sequences, held together as each of them is by the unity of the love object, can be said to represent respectively: a) seraphic innocence, b) self-destructive, Dionysian eroticism and, c) an ambivalent, guilt-ridden involvement with Russia's national destiny.

It is essential to note that at each juncture we are dealing with erotic poetry, though the target varies drastically from period to period. The theme of love, or rather of being-in-love remains constant. "Infatuation," a very inadequate English equivalent of *vliublennost'*, is characteristically one of Blok's favorite words. It serves as the title for two poems written during his middle period.

> Victor Erlich. *The Double Image*
> (Baltimore, Johns Hopkins Press, 1964), p. 103

Blok's entire creative and human attention centers on Pushkin. In Blok's diary of the last years of his life, the name of Pushkin appears all the time and in various contexts. A realization of the constant presence of Pushkin's image in Blok's consciousness is extremely important for our understanding of Blok's state of mind and his last thoughts about the fate of the nation, culture, and man. . . . Blok relates Pushkin's destiny to that of his own, to the end of the historically perceptible artistic tension, the "musical rhythm," signifying the tragic sudden change from one period of high culture to another. And the destructive, negative forces in history, which acted against the highest representative of the national culture, had for Blok a purely external significance.

> Pavel Gromov. *Aleksandr Blok: Ego predshestvenniki
> i sovremenniki* (Moscow, Sovetski pisatel, 1966),
> p. 566[†]

The vision of Christ embodying a universal religion and new morality served Blok as a symbol of general rejuvenation of life, and he appeared in such light at the end of "The Twelve." At any rate, in Blok's creative consciousness that symbol did not by itself contradict the revolutionary meaning and tone of the poem; on the contrary, it strengthened them, heralding the idea of the birth of that new world in the name of which the twelve—those unconscious "apostles" of a new justice—carry out a just historical retribution over the forces of the old world. Such was the inner logic of Blok's idea, and it is impossible not to take it into consideration. Thus, Christ appears to be the highest sanction which the poet found in the arsenal of historical and artistic forms of his repertory.

> V. Orlov. *Poema Aleksandra Bloka "Dvenadtsat"*
> (Moscow, Khudozhestvennaya literatura, 1967),
> p. 105[†]

BRYUSOV, VALERI   (1873–1924)

In Bryusov's recently published selected writings the components of his work become distinctly clear. The love of the word itself, and by itself, attains here indescribable beauties. Bryusov was the first Russian poet who could analyze even the smallest elements that compose one's creative work. With the help of slight means, he attains the most subtle effects. In this ability to express, by simple means, the hardly perceptible, the need to preserve his work finds its justification. That is why, when discussing the source of the fascination of his muse, we have to speak about simple shifting of words, about commas and periods. Meanwhile, through these simple means, he permeates the lines of his poems with unprecedented beauty. Bryusov is the first contemporary Russian poet to revive our love of rhyme. Soon after he had lavishly strewn new rhymes in *Urbi et orbi*, his pupils and imitators joined him doing the same. [1907]

Andrei Bely. *Lug zelyony*
(Moscow, Altsion, 1910), pp. 187–88[†]

[In *Ognenny angel* (*The Angel of Fire*)] we find human suffering with all its fatal laws and murderous caprices, the torments of the human soul in pursuit of religious specters . . . There are such movements and seemingly internal drama, such fiery and colorful basic motives in this plan! Add to this the external vicissitudes of the novel! There are the adventures of travels and departures in sixteenth century Germany; an acquaintanceship with the famous contemporary scientist Agrippa von Nettesheim and his students; a meeting with Dr. Faust and Mephistopheles, as they are depicted in documents retaining this legend—and yet with some poetical reflections from the profound concept of Goethe. All these relate the fantastic to psychological and living realism.

Yet, here is the real matter: Bryusov reveals not a creative fantasy but a sober, clear, scientifically refined mind—an unusually sober and cool mind, which dissects even the human soul into its constituent parts, as an anatomist would, and which does not paint a passionate event as an artist would, but depicts it with judiciously chosen words. He always explicates everything to the end, hiding the causative dependence of every spiritual condition from its preceding or accompanying revelation and almost always trying to find some analogy of a subjective experience from our objective life.

L. Y. Gurevich. *Russkaya mysl.*
March, 1910, pp. 148–49[†]

Bryusov's ballads are generally recognized as the center of his work, because they represent a complete and justified source for the oratoric beginning of his poetry, as well as for the solution of picturesque speech problems. They also satisfied the requirement of diversity with what has come out of Bryusov's situation, as the canonizer of symbolism, broadening and quantitatively embracing the thematic field. But if we take Bryusov's ballads to be the genre connected in the nineteenth century with the names of Zhukovski, on one hand, and of Katenin, Pushkin, and Nekrasov, on the other, we are, of course, mistaken. Alongside the clearcut narrative, Bryusov's ballads seem alien; they are static, like a picture, like a sculpture group. From the topical development, one "instant" is taken out; the whole thematic movement is locked in the motionlessness of this "instant." That is why almost all of Bryusov's ballads have the appearance of a monologue; that is why we are unable to find sharp genre demarcation between his ballads and his non-ballads. His poetry is a whole chain of unnoticeable transitions, which makes the very genre general and diffuse. [1924]

Yuri Tynyanov. *Arkhaisty i novatory*
(Leningrad, Priboi, 1929), p. 535†

Artistic prose has never had dominating importance in Bryusov's work. Although there had been such huge proseworks as *The Angel of Fire* and *Altar pobedy* (*The Altar of Victory*), these were, in the first place, isolated, and, secondly, although having indisputable merits, they did not in themselves indicate any new direction in artistic prose. . . .

Thematically, perhaps, they are not new to our society, but they were more than brave in foreseeing a new technique.

When reading Bryusov's fantastic stories today, we find them quite modern. We do not notice that they were written many years ago, because, on the one hand, the problems raised by Bryusov remain vital; on the other hand, these problems are solved by him as they are solved today, as if he had already been acquainted at the time of writing with all the achievements of our modern technology.

The ideas of Tsiolkovski (interplanetary communications), the questions of television, and many others were transformed by Bryusov into artistically attractive, concrete images at the time when these ideas and questions were still only dreams.

Bryusov, thoroughly equipped with knowledge and the broadest scientific view, bravely fought for the themes mentioned above.

Aleksandr Ilinski. *Literaturnoe nasledstvo*
(Moscow, Zhurnalno-gazetnoe obedinenie, 1937),
Vols. XXVII–XXVIII, pp. 471–72†

Bryusov has been accused of opportunism and insincerity in his literary career. The businesslike manner with which he pursued his policies, both literary and personal, and his sudden changes of poetic allegiance, from modernist eccentricity to revolutionary pathos in 1905, to urban realism, to chauvinism, and finally to the exaltation of the proletarian revolution, support this view. After symbolism had disintegrated, Bryusov disclaimed that he had ever had more than a passive interest in or sympathy with the movement. Yet after his essay "Keys to Mystery" ["Klyuchi tain"] and especially after the quotation "and the leader [of symbolism] shall be I! Yes, I!" his claim that "the role of *maître de l'école* of Russian symbolists was forced" on him sounds somewhat grotesque. . . . Bryusov's inconstancy is probably explained not so much by any sinister motives as by a lack of a firm principle other than fear of falling behind times. In such a light his rapid changes of allegiance appear both comprehensible and logical.

Whatever his sins, Bryusov was a vital figure in the development of the symbolist movement in Russia. So long as he chose to remain a part of it, he was an all-important cog in the total mechanism, and when he abandoned symbolism, the movement collapsed.

Oleg Maslenikov. *The Frenzied Poets* (Berkeley, Calif.,
University of California Press, 1952), p. 126

While the erotic theme is totally dissolved in the emotional imagery of Blok's metaphors, Bryusov lets the eroticism attain conceptualization within the metaphor. Bryusov exposes the theme by means of the metaphor, instead of hiding the theme by the metaphor.

In their dynamics, Bryusov's allegories are progressive, since they point to an exemplary reality. On the other hand, Blok's allegories, linked to previous, past feelings, are emotionally regressive. . . .

In a certain sense, Bryusov's metaphors are much more accurately allegorical than Blok's. They truly establish a semantic break with the part to which the comparison refers. The true allegorical metaphor *is* based on the semantic tension of heterogeneous concepts, as Bryusov's allegoric poem "Paris" demonstrates.

Johannes Holthusen. *Studien zur Ästhetik und
Poetik des russischen Symbolismus* (Göttingen,
Vandehoeck & Ruprecht, 1957), pp. 96–97†

The real muse of Brjusov was deliberation itself. Nothing better proves this truth than the lyric where, speaking in the first person, the poet compares himself to a plowman, and addresses his "dream" as his "faithful ox." Man and animal plod abreast along the field, toiling without rest or relief; and when the poet-plowman feels that his oxlike dream is failing in its effort, he incites it with his voice and excites it with his goad. This parable is almost symbolic of Brjusov's art, which is based on strenuous exertion, and on a constant will: a will ruling even over imagination or inspiration, which is what the poet here means by the word "dream." It was this quality of Brjusov's genius that led the critic Julij Ajkhenval'd to compare him to the protagonist of Pushkin's *Mozart and Salieri*, to that Salieri who had sacrificed all, with supreme devotion, to the art of music, and who could not comprehend why God had graced with an effortless creative power such a simple and naïve being as Mozart, unable to take seriously even his divine gift. Yet, precisely because he resembled Salieri, Brjusov felt the overpowering seduction of the Mozart-like wonders of Pushkin's art, up to the point of trying to complete a tale in verse and prose, *The Egyptian Nights*, which Pushkin had left unfinished. Brjusov did not do this to compete with the greatest of all Russian poets, but only to pay a tribute to his greatness, as a token of admiration and a sign of worship. The man who once said of himself, "I would rather not be Valerij Brjusov," sacrificed even his ego for the sake of his art. He never thought of himself as a god of poetry, but as one of its priests; he acted more like the servant than the master of his craft. Posterity may deny him lasting fame, but it will always respect his name at least for what Mallarmé, in his "Toast funèbre" to the memory of Théophile Gautier, called *la gloire ardente du métier*.

Renato Poggioli. The Poets of Russia (Cambridge,
Mass., Harvard University Press, 1960), pp. 104–5

Bryusov was a magnificent organizer. His father had been a cork dealer, and I am sure that if Bryusov had not been exposed in his youth to the poems of Verlaine and Mallarmé, he would have planted huge forests of cork oaks in Russia, as in Estremadura. His capacity for work was complemented by ambition. . . . He organized publishing houses, founded journals, wrote books on the art of poetry, translated from the Latin, carried on debates with recognized authorities, taught the young. He feared one thing only: being left behind by the times. . . .

He has often been called a rationalist, a man of dry reason. Many have tried to convince us that he was never a poet. In my opinion, that is not true: for Bryusov, reason was not common sense but a cult; he exaggerated in his faith in reason. He was a poet even in the most prosaic, narrowminded sense of the word: he lived in an unreal world of frenzied schemes. Vrubel painted a beautiful portrait of him: dry, scorching eyes, and a head as though sliced off at the back.

Ilya Ehrenburg. Novy mir. Jan., 1961, p. 96[†]

Briusov's last years were none too happy. The somewhat grudging official recognition was no substitute for a vital relationship with his fellow writers, which was becoming increasingly difficult if not impossible to maintain. Briusov's loyalty to the Soviets had infuriated those of his former associates who scornfully rejected the November revolution. His bureaucratic mode of collaboration tended to estrange the erstwhile enthusiasts who by 1920 were dispirited and confused. Nor was he getting much aid or comfort from the literary Left. The most vocal and colorful poets in the Bolshevik camp, the Futurists or neo-Futurists, such as Maiakovskii or N. Aseev, insisted that "revolutionary content" presupposed "revolutionary form," that is, *avant-garde* techniques, bold verbal experimentation. They scoffed at Briusov's attempts to pour new wine into old bottles. The idea of celebrating the proletarian revolution in the fairly traditional meters and shopworn imagery of the Symbolist age was adjudged futile and preposterous.

Victor Erlich. *The Double Image*
(Baltimore, Johns Hopkins Press, 1964), p. 95

BULGAKOV, MIKHAIL   (1891–1940)

We are far from seeing the bloody aspect of the counterrevolution stealthily realized or conveyed in Mikhail Bulgakov's works. Bulgakov appears to be ideologically completely unformed and, in the meanwhile, with all his obvious literary gift, preoccupied with his first literary efforts. We see in his "Rokovye yaitsa" ("The Fatal Eggs") such an initial literary effort or, more properly, an arrow sent at random into space without a definite fixed objective. If, as advised by one critic, we should have been ready to deduct some definite thought from the story or some kind of negation of our own building [of socialism], then we were not able to do so, for the thoughts in the novella are too poorly tied together. It is perhaps this latter circumstance, accompanied by an artistic fabric that is both sharp and convincing to the eye, which suggested to one critic that this work is not quite innocent, that it could not be otherwise, and that a tendency is lurking here.

D. Gorbov. *Novy mir*. Dec., 1925, p. 147†

What is the real tragedy of the émigrés? It is that even the few honest people in the White movement went to seed in the surroundings of Paris and Constantinople. These people were reduced to ideologists of trivia who, except for this trivia, had nothing else; the women, in effect, became streetwalkers. Even though superficially, I nevertheless had occasion to become acquainted with the émigrés. I saw the scandalous scenes; I saw the officers fawning in Parisian restaurants, and I talked with them and saw the real degradation of these people. Here is the real tragedy of the émigrés. And if Bulgakov wants to appear a genuine émigré, then he must describe this tragedy, he must describe what these people have come to and what has become of them. But what happens in Bulgakov? Disregarding everything, his émigrés, the most noble of souls, become knights without fear and reproach, and come to a most noble end. This rings false and untrue. Even such a theater as the Khudozhestvenny will be unable to save this piece [*Dni Turbinykh* (*The Days of the Turbins*)]. Even the actors at the Khudozhestvenny will be unable to put across such falsity. If an author does not give an artistic image, then no actor can provide it for him. Bulgakov, regardless of evidence to the contrary, wanted to show the émigrés in every environment as upright, pure, and good. But it is not that way.

I will not speak about other defects in the play, noting only such spots as, for example, a lyrical digression on the dollar or a card game or a cockroach race. This is cheap, this is the limit of banality, this is real buffoonery.

A concluding remark as to who needs this play and whom it will unite. Those who need it and will be united by it are those who would justify the White movement and lay the blame on the allies who deserted the émigrés. The wail of the émigrés, "The dirty English and the dirty French have betrayed us!", resounds in Bulgakov's play.

V. Kirshon. *Na literaturnom postu*. Oct., 1928, p. 18†

Bulgakov did not have a revolutionary approach to life and people, or to the events he depicted—nor could he have had. His works reflect confusion of thought, seeking without finding, questions without answers. But Bulgakov was integrally honest, was a great artist and looked upon his work as service to the people. As a real writer who paid much attention to the technical aspects of dramaturgy, he put the civic duty of an artist above all else. His truthful portrayal of events and characters speaks for itself. . . .

In his works the action unfolds in an outwardly calm, leisurely way. He does not rush to condemn his characters. With some he persistently sympathizes, although they have still not arrived at the point of breaking decisively with the White Guards. But while displaying sympathy for the Turbin family, showing their courage and personal integrity (in *The Days of the Turbins*), he does not want to overstep the bounds of truth beyond which lies deliberate idealization bearing no relation to historical fact. . . .

The Days of the Turbins did not win immediate acclaim. Because Bulgakov portrayed the White Guard camp as it were from within, carefully observing the interplay of thoughts and feelings of his characters, many critics considered that he was defending and idealizing the White Guards. In point of fact he was in no way defending them and was certainly not idealizing them. Although Bulgakov failed to reveal the inner social forces of the Civil War, his play showed the power of the Revolution and the fact that the White Guards were doomed. . . .

In his works Bulgakov treats ancient and modern history in an unextravagant, austere style, obviously preferring the precision of a drawing to the sweeping strokes of a painting. He is sparing of detail, but each one he portrays is highly expressive. Beneath the apparently calm surface of the dialogue there is intensely fierce passion. Bulgakov's plays demand much of the theatre, but they also give much to the theatre, enriching the arts of producing and acting with new discoveries in the sphere Stanislavsky once called "the life of the human spirit."

Aleksandr Karaganov. SL. Sept., 1963, pp. 191–93

Bulgakov was never able to write about what he had not seen, but that did not prevent him from being known as a writer with bold artistic fantasy. Pictures, which appeared in his imagination, although they did recall what he himself had seen in the past, appeared in a form purified and transformed by the strength of his poetic fire.

In his best works, Bulgakov upholds the highest standards of Russian narrative tradition, and especially those of Gogol, Dostoyevski, and Chekhov. From Gogol he inherited the brilliant picturesqueness of the satirical narrative and the ability to present phantasmagorical states; from Dostoyevski, his intense compassion and some of his feverish, captivating, authentically incorrect speech; from Chekhov, lyric intonation and light humor, inseparably fused into one. But, having absorbed these varied styles and influences, Bulgakov seems neither eclectic nor antiquated. He inherited the tradition in a nonepigonic way; his style is contemporary and vital, belonging to him alone and reflecting the fascinating personality of the author himself.

In Bulgakov's prose the visual effects are striking, as is the vividness of detailed settings, costumes, gestures, poses, mimes and expressions—usual attributes of theatrical truth, captured at this time by the storyteller and novelist. Yet, for Bulgakov, art is not a tedious resemblance to living things, taken at random; rather, it is a festival, a feast of imagination, the joy of invention, yet invention in harmony with the laws of psychological truth.

V. Lakshin. Introduction to Mikhail Bulgakov,
Izbrannaya proza (Moscow, Khudozhestvennaya
literatura, 1966), p. 41[†]

Bulgakov's tremendously successful play, The Days of the Turbins (1926), based on his novel The White Guards [Belaya gvardiya], was withdrawn from the repertory of the Moscow Art Theater in 1929. Three other Bulgakov plays were banned in quick succession. The 1930 edition of the

Soviet Literary Encyclopedia called him an unregenerate bourgeois writer, and Stalin himself criticized his play *Flight* [*Beg*].

In 1932 Bulgakov decided to try to follow the example of Zamyatin who had asked Stalin for, and received permission to emigrate. He wrote to Stalin telling him that he was being hounded by the police, that his apartment was frequently searched, and that he would commit suicide if he were not permitted to go abroad. Stalin phoned him, denying him permission to leave but saying that henceforth he would be left in peace and could go on with his work. Stalin then expressed the desire to see *The Days of the Turbins*. This created a frightful commotion at the Art Theater which had to produce the play again on four-day's notice, simply to provide a private performance for Stalin. The play then went back into the repertory.

Several other plays by Bulgakov were later produced, but never again any on contemporary themes. One of these was a biographical play, *Molière*, and a dramatization of *Dead Souls* [*Myortvye dushi*], which is still in the Art Theater repertory. But most of his writings were banned. Out of some 35 plays he wrote, only 11 are known to exist today, and of these six were actually produced in his lifetime. His encounters with censorship, and with terror-stricken directors of Soviet theaters, are described in his *Theatrical Novel* [*Teatralny roman*], which was published for the first time in Russia in 1966. . . . This is a superb satire of the Art Theater in which the figures of Stanislavsky and Nemirovich-Danchenko—old, demoralized and quarrelsome—are only faintly disguised.

During the late 1930's Bulgakov never lost his sense of proportion. Although his work ceased to be performed or published during the great purges, Bulgakov continued to write and to entertain his friends with comic parodies of imagined encounters with Stalin.

Patricia Blake, *NYT*. Oct. 22, 1967, p. 71

The novel's structure [*Master i Margarita (The Master and Margarita)*] is intricate, involving concentric circles of themes whose relations to each other, a bit tenuous in some cases, are not revealed until the end of the story. . . .

Of the several levels on which the novel may be read, the most obvious is that of an expansive story of the amazing adventures of Satan, his aides, and a group of unsuspecting Muscovites. To be sure, the extraordinary effects achieved are made possible and perhaps even easy by the author's extensive use of supernatural devices. . . . The author induces a willing suspension of disbelief in the supernatural by charmingly humanizing his otherworldly characters and by handling these fantastic episodes with the most meticulous attention to realistic detail. That is, Bulgakov manages to create the impression that the natural and supernatural, the moral and immoral are somehow all one and the same.

On another plane one may regard the doings of Satan and his crew as an elaborate satire, at times blunt and at others extremely subtle, of various important features of Soviet life. . . .

More profoundly, the novel may be considered a vast allegory of the struggle between the powers of darkness and the powers of light, with universal implications. The activities of Satan and his associates in Moscow accord with the mission of Mephistopheles indicated in the epigraph to the novel, a quotation from Goethe's *Faust:* "Say at last—who art thou?"/ "That power I serve/ Which wills forever evil/ Yet does forever good." Satan's victims in *The Master and Margarita* are those who have succumbed to evil, and the people he assists belong to the powers of light.

The struggle is the core of the most brilliant and certainly the most serious theme of the novel—Pontius Pilate *vs.* Christ. Though Pilate, who is remarkably portrayed, rejects Christ's belief that "there are no evil people on earth," he is swayed by it as well as by Christ's miraculous knowledge and sense of prophecy. But he lets Him go to His death, in an execution scene which is hauntingly described, because he is too much of a coward to oppose the decision of the high priest and thus risk his own position. And Pilate's conscience gives him no rest, for Christ had declared that cowardice was one of the greatest sins.

Ernest J. Simmons. SR. Nov. 11, 1967, pp. 36, 56

The work which brought Bulgakov virtually overnight success was his play *The Days of the Turbins*, a dramatized version of his own novel *The White Guard*. The theme of both novel and play was the bitter Civil War which raged in Russia for nearly three years after the Bolshevik revolution, fought between the "Whites"—an imprecise generalization covering many shades of political opposition to Bolshevism—and the "Reds." Like all civil wars it was peculiarly savage: the trauma which split and scarred the Russian nation was really the Civil War and its aftermath of chaos and famine rather than the relatively bloodless revolution. The terrible period formed the subject matter of countless stories, novels, poems, plays and films. With one or two outstanding exceptions they all, rather naturally, depicted the Civil War either entirely from the Red viewpoint or in complete sympathy with the Reds.

The most startling fact about Bulgakov's novel-turned-play was that it showed the Civil War wholly from the side of the Whites. This may not strike us as very startling, but it was an extraordinarily daring thing to do in the Soviet Russia of the twenties where the wounds of the struggle had not yet healed and where the government was acutely sensitive to the open conspiracy among White Russian emigrés to discredit and if possible to subvert the Bolshevik regime. What was more, *The Days of the Turbins* implicitly rejected the official Communist Party attitude to the opposing sides in the Civil War by refusing to depict the Whites as bloodthirsty

reactionaries or as evil buffoons of unrelieved villainy and instead showing them as ordinary, honest, rather bewildered people who reacted with
human predictability to the collapse of the world as they had known it.

Yet such was the compelling skill and dramatic power of *The Days of
the Turbins* that it not only survived the Party's initial disapproval of its
political message but remained as one of the best-loved and most successful plays of the Soviet theater's entire repertoire.

> Michael Glenny. Introduction to Mikhail Bulgakov,
> *Black Snow* (New York, Simon & Schuster, 1967), p. 6

The Master and Margarita is a very difficult book. Those reviews I have
seen mostly skirt the critical problem it raises: the reviewers declare it a
splendid novel and a work of spiritual force, all of which is true, but they
do not offer a coherent account of plot, character, and theme. That such
an account can be offered after a first reading I doubt; whether it would
be possible after several readings I am not sure. Bulgakov left the book
in an unfinished state and it is possible that we are dealing with a masterpiece never brought to complete focus. Or perhaps a masterpiece that, like
Ulysses, requires some years of study before it fully reveals itself. I can
only say, at this moment, that while the book yields great pleasures, it does
not yet fall into shape as a coherent work of art. . . .

Meanwhile, however, it is a book to enjoy and ponder: a trophy sal-
vaged from the most terrible decade of twentieth-century life.

> Irving Howe. *Harper*. Jan., 1968, pp. 71–72

It is tempting to think of Bulgakov's ideal and real art theater as a microcosm of Stalin's ideal and real Russia. Good satire emerges out of repres-
sion, as a necessity, and sometimes the best satirists would not have become satirists if it were not for the necessity.

As slight as it is, anecdotal, and of moderate interest as a novel per se,
Black Snow [*Teatralny roman*] is of interest as satire, but also as *roman
à clef*, and as a sketch of artist life in the Moscow of the twenties—how
alike and how different from such life in the West. The book is gentle in
tone if fierce in substance. Bulgakov does not make grandstand plays, and
if you are not listening you may not get the jokes—no demagoguery. One
can almost hear a writer's-congress sort of Soviet writer in the twenties
saying, "Oh, that Bulgakov, he's lazy, vain and arrogant," and adding to
himself, "and besides, he hasn't got the delegates."

Bulgakov is fair-minded. . . . When [he] finds a good trait in someone,
he draws it with an excited hand and a delighted eye. Implicit in his holding up of certain aspects of human behavior to contempt and ridicule is
a set of stubbornly hopeful values so naturally cherished that when he is
confronted by the manifold ugly contradictions to these values he can at

last only react with a frozen passion born of a large pained love, the mastodon bones of which become evident as the glacier recedes. So, by the end of the little book, it is clear that the satirist was not petulantly motivated.

Unlike that famous and able satirist, Molière's misanthrope, one feels Bulgakov never threatened to pick up his marbles and go home when the game wasn't running his way. He continued to write until the end, through blindness, uremia and neglect.

Peter Sourian. *NYT*. Apr. 21, 1968, pp. 4, 23

The appearance of *The Heart of a Dog* [*Sobache serdtse*] (only in English so far; the likelihood of publication in the USSR is remote) firmly establishes Bulgakov as one of the few truly great writers produced by the Soviet Union during the half-century of its existence, and also as that nation's most accomplished satirist. . . .

In *The Heart of a Dog* Bulgakov deals with a problem that disturbed many Soviet writers, Communist and non-Communist alike, in the 1920s: would the Revolution succeed in its bold attempt to create a new man, free from the weaknesses and vices of his forefathers whose psyches, it was claimed, had been mutilated by bourgeois society? Many authors, including such talented novelists as Alexander Fadeyev, answered in the affirmative. Others had serious doubts. Yurii Olesha's *Envy* suggested that the new cult of efficiency might destroy human values and feelings. Essentially similar apprehensions were expressed by Vladimir Mayakovsky in his play *The Bedbug*, where, in the final scene, the audience was left with a choice between a vodka-drinking, guitar-strumming, old-time philistinism and a sterilized, dehumanized society of robots.

Bulgakov's novel, written in 1925 (two years before the publication of Olesha's work and three years before Mayakovsky's), presented a much more frightening vision, and it is clearly for this reason that, unlike the other two, it has not been in print for more than forty years. *The Heart of a Dog* deals with a curiously contemporary subject—the transplantation of organs from one creature into another; and, with effective use of the devices of science fiction, postulates the creation of a hybrid who combines the worst of human and canine features.

Maurice Friedberg. *SR*. July 20, 1968, p. 24

The theme [of *The Master and Margarita*] is a religious one, a new approach to the man Pontius Pilate and to the Crucifixion. But the theme alone is not the reason for the book's success: it is Bulgakov's unique craftsmanship and style, his masterful Russian satirical prose. The ancient struggle between good and evil is treated in an extremely surrealistic manner—yet a manner based, to a great extent, on contemporary Soviet reality. . . .

Bulgakov presents society as being devoid of any moral base. Men of medicine, literature, the theater, and other professions are depicted as weaklings, cowards, or greedy characters. Those who do not wish to compromise with Satan are doomed to impotence, rejected by society, excluded from active life, or simply murdered. All existence becomes desolate. In such a world, with no established norms or moral control, everything is possible. The real becomes unreal, dream becomes reality, the human being is transformed into an animal. Utter horror results.

To portray this chaos, Bulgakov employs a variety of reminiscences and aptly connects the remote with the close at hand. The plethora of surrealistic details demonstrates Bulgakov's high skill in presenting the incomprehensible powers which human beings and their fantasy are capable of.

Victoria A. Babenko. *SEEJ*. Winter, 1968, p. 479

BUNIN, IVAN (1870–1953)

As a descendant of guilty ancestors depicting Russian rural poverty and abandonment, without malice but rather as a martyr, Bunin sorrowfully looks at the past epoch of our history. He looks at the ruined noble houses. He does not consciously pity them, nor does serfdom seem to him idyllic. On the contrary, we already know how he reopens old landowners' wounds and sees scraggy branches and dried-up fruit on his own genealogical tree. More precisely, he feels this tree was never really magnificent, multi-branched, and aristocratic. It never was rich in sap. However, the elegy of an abandoned country estate, the romanticism of silenced clavichords, the worn floorboards of the manor house—all unwittingly evoke melancholy in a sensitive heart and imagination and, if he finds the grave of his forefathers, he will find in it his own refuge and "quietly will lie alongside it." [1908]

Yuli Aikhenvald. *Siluety russkikh pisatelei*
(Berlin, Slovo, 1923), p. 201[†]

In Bunin we are constantly conscious of a disturbance of his vision. He has the authentic power of revelation, but it is not altogether under his control. The pictures he puts before us are like those of a cinema where the camera is old-fashioned; they jump and flicker, they alternate between brilliancy and dullness, and they are sometimes tiring to the eyes. It is as though the control and the unity which are given by a complete aesthetic absorption in the reality were missing, and their place were supplied by another emotion which now reinforces and now retards the act of aesthetic apprehension itself. If we have to give a name to this interfering principle, we can think of nothing better than exasperation. . . .

Whatever its faults "The Gentleman from San Francisco" ["Gospodin iz San Frantsisko"] is certainly one of the most impressive stories of modern times. From the beginning to end the sense of hallucination is maintained with sombre power. As it is, and for what it is, it is perfect. But its effect is as though not a purer light had been cast upon reality, but a violent and lurid one. The illumination does not last after the story is ended. And the cause of this, we suspect, is that Bunin is not wholly engaged in contemplating the reality, but in exposing a passing phase of it. He is indicting the spiritual deadness of modern plutocracy, the soulless and narcotic system which has no place even for death. The artist, as such, has no business with indictment, because the thing which he has to reach is beyond the range of accusation; it simply is, and it will remain long after the hideous garment of plutocracy has been worn out and thrown aside. Nevertheless, it is true that the artist, as such, does not exist save in the world of abstraction: the living artist is a combination of the contemplative and the practical man. If he cannot separate his practical exasperation from his contemplative delight and be the pure artist, then he should choose the way of satire. . . .

It may be that to Bunin the life of the East is in some way more real than the factitious civilization of the West. It does not so appear in his work. Perhaps he himself is more comfortable in a world where non-essential things are not offensively paraded, and death is neither denied nor defied; but the world itself is vague. If his West is a nightmare, his East is a dream; and we are left to wander uneasily between the two. The cumulative effect is lost. Was it Bunin, we wonder, whom Tchechov had in mind when he wrote in his Notebooks, "Of some writers, each work taken separately is brilliant, but taken as a whole they are indefinite; of others, each particular work represents nothing outstanding, but, for all that, taken as a whole they are distinct and brilliant"? Bunin, so far as we can judge, belongs to the former.

TLS. April 20, 1922, p. 256

In . . . this selected group of Bunin's lyrics, between 1900 and 1925, one sees the poet at his best. Though there has been an unmistakable growth of strength, reserve, and sureness of stroke in these twenty-five years of Bunin's poetic output, his essential traits have remained immutable. The uniqueness of Bunin's verse has always defied classification, and has led his critics into a bewildering variety of bogs. Classic in form, reminiscent of Pushkin and Tiutchev at their peaks, Bunin's muse is alarmingly modern, contemporary. Yet the value of his poetry is as untransitory as that of the Psalms of David. Bunin's is a world soul, and its sensitiveness to places and events rises above space and time. His vast travels, his sympathetic sojourn in cities and deserts and islands, East and West, have added an external catholicity to the intrinsic universality of his makeup. What enhances the permanence of his lyrics is their deep religiosity. Whether he contemplates exotic Ceylon or the wilderness of Judea or craggy Brittany or a melancholy village of his homeland, or whether he muses over the catastrophic upheavals in Russia during war and revolution, he invariably dips his pen into the divinity which Carlyle believed to pervade the universe. Beneath and beyond the scenes and things he portrays he envisages a Greater Wisdom, to whose guidance he submits with quiet sadness. In prose, Bunin occasionally hates and curses. But the poet Bunin neither condemns nor scorns, and unlike the Psalmist, he does not stoop to hate even his enemies.

Alexander Kaun. *BA*. Winter, 1930, p. 68

Bunin's all-Russian fame came upon the publication of his first long work—*The Village* [*Derevnya*]. It is not a novel in the conventional accepted sense of the word, and it is not for nothing that Bunin gave it the sub-heading of "a poem." It is a large fresco, a dyptich, picturing Russian village life during the first Revolution (1904–05). In considering the social aspect of Bunin's *Village*, it is necessary to bear always in mind that it gives a picture of pre-revolutionary and revolutionary Russia—I mean, before the Revolution of 1905—of the village as it was before the agrarian reform connected with the name of Stolypin. In *The Village* there is no plot, almost no development; it is a picture of life in a Russian village, painted in dark, sombre colours—the author lays bare before our eyes, on one hand the cruelty and brutality, on the other, the lack of civilisation and the poverty of the Russian peasant. This social aspect of Bunin's work, this "invective" against the peasantry, called forth a fierce controversy in the Press and contributed towards the fame of the work. Gorky proclaimed *The Village* to be the most powerful and true thing that had ever been said about the Russian peasant. The Left wing of Russian journalism and literary criticism became a house divided against itself—the Social-Democrats, who always saw in the Russian peasantry an uncivilised force hampering Russia's political progress, welcomed the book; the Social-Revolutionaries and other "Populists," who were inclined to idealise the peasant, resented it greatly. Among the critics of the modern camp there was no unity either. Some accused Bunin of lack of patriotism, of contempt for his own people. From the purely literary point of view Bunin was blamed for the abnormal development of his outward visual capacity and the lack of psychological insight. Nowadays, after the Russian Revolution of 1917, we are inclined to view many things in Bunin's

Village as prophetic foresight. But, of course, *The Village* was never meant as a complete and exhaustive picture of the Russian peasantry. Cruelty and beastliness were not the only things Bunin saw in it. . . . From the literary point of view *The Village* is, though not a perfect, a powerful and significant work; despite its apparent formlessness, it reveals a great constructive ability; despite all absence of plot and movement— a great inner force and impetus. The style, the language show the same force and firmness—a peculiar blend of realism and poetry. There are scenes where the grotesque and the uncanny intermingle in a kind of Goyesque visions.

Gleb Struve. *SEER*. Jan., 1933, pp. 426–27

Russian literature is a literature of these moods and questions. What then is my life . . . ? Are we not born with a sense of death? If we are not, would we be as fond of life as we are? Or used to be? Who knows? On what problem was my soul intent that afternoon?—so the questions float up and wing away into the immense distances of the steppe, flash and become nothing, like disappearing birds, unanswered and unanswerable. This is their fascination. In a small country of satisfied and closed valleys the questions would never get away; people would stop to answer them; they would soon become metaphysical congestions, the nostalgia would quickly stir up active romanticisations and appease itself with glamour.

Hence the pleasure of Ivan Bunin's *The Well of Days* [*Zhizn Arse-nyeva*], an autobiography sad in its happiness, happy in its sadness, and saved from the lower levels of sentiment and wistfulness by a romantic spiritual austerity. The narrative passes from childhood and youth on a feudal estate by the Don, long before the Revolution which never appears, though the note at the end is, appropriately, exile. It is hard to describe a book which depends so much upon atmosphere, except, perhaps, to note the delicacy of the family portraits. In his father, the young Arseniev has a fine picture of the nobleman whom we have come to regard as typical: reckless, moody, genial, wildly extravagant, artistic, incapable of facing any situation and escaping by way of questions. Who am I? What is happiness? And so on. The contrasted portrait of the bourgeois merchant with whom the youth boards when at the University is equally good and the descriptions of youthful love, its daydreams and idealised ardour van-ishing in some abrupt and simple change of circumstance, are conveyed with the same beauty of feeling. An atmosphere has been recovered and not casually and raggedly, but with a warm, fluid precision.

V. S. Pritchett. *NSN*. Apr. 1, 1933, pp. 419–20

[In *Zhizn Arsenyeva* Bunin] is not half as interesting as he ought to be. Nobel to the contrary, he has a strange, an almost tantalizing lack of

strength, though he writes, as they say, beautifully. He writes, that is, with
everything needful to him save the power of moving and convincing; so
that it begins to seem almost unfair, as one reads on through these pastel
pages, to remember that autobiographies have been written in Russian
by Tolstoy, Aksakov, and Gorki. Such names annihilate a man of whom
the best one can say is that in the original he must possess a very fine style
indeed—fine, and therefore untranslatable.

But there must be another reason than his exquisite prose for the failure
of the present volume to do what might reasonably have been expected of
it, and my guess is this. Bunin has been too conscious of the autobiography
as a literary form. His mind, running in fact wholly to form, has invented
all sorts of irrelevant and intrusive "beauties" which get in the way of our
believing that this is the story of a specific Russian boy who grew up on a
specific estate. He has drawn his life—or Alexey's—in delicate outlines,
and those outlines are never burst through or obliterated by the pressure
of some unconscious truth struggling to express itself. Suavely he makes
his first sketch, smilingly he deliberates as to how he shall adorn it here
and there, and imperturbably he goes on to shade it in with just the right
details. The temptation then is to say that he has used too much art. But
actually he has used too little. Art in an autobiographer consists in his
seeming to forget all art; Bunin seems to remember nothing else. Certainly he has only the thinnest of minor tales to tell—of a sensitive boy
who grew up wondering what the world was about and never, at least by
the end of volume one when he is sixteen years old, finding out anything
more than that he wants to be a poet, that revolutionary groups are full
of shoddy and eccentric people, and that a Grand Duke may have a small,
pointed red beard which curls "firmly and beautifully."

Bunin makes it clear in his later pages that he was not the kind of young
man who could stomach revolution. Nor need he have been; but he also
makes it clear, without of course knowing it, how little energy there was
in the artist who turned aside. There was not enough at any rate for him
to be able to compose, decades later in Paris, an autobiography which
would be anything better than a piece of nostalgic prettiness.

Mark Van Doren. *Nation*. Feb. 14, 1934, p. 192

[Bunin's desire to write on only Russian themes] is a most rare situation,
if not without precedence. It seems that any writer with time reaches natural limits; to go further becomes impossible with the result being a more
or less slow decline. Bunin is nearly the only exception: he writes better
and better. . . . The works which he wrote in Russia must take second
place to those which he has written abroad. However, Bunin has already
written many books abroad. Of them *Zhizn Arsenyeva* (*The Life of Arse-*

nyev) is better than *Mitina lyubov* (*Mitya's Love*), but *Lika* is more nearly perfect than the first volume of *The Life of Arsenyev*.

M. A. Aldanov. *Sovremennye zapiski.*
69, 1939, p. 385†

These recollections [*Vospominaniya* (*Memoirs and Portraits*)] reveal a great deal of the character and personality of Bunin himself. The image is that of a rather shy man with principles, firm ideas, and artistic integrity, but nevertheless a man who nurses a sense of bitterness over unfulfilled hopes and unrealized ambitions. Alexei Tolstoy once told him: "You'll never make a success in practical matters. You have no idea how to sell yourself." And Bunin was often surrounded by Russian artists who knew precisely how to sell themselves, though they also had great talent. In reading this book one has the feeling that the quiet, unobstrusive Bunin, who never really caught the imagination of the crowd, writes of these various authors who did with a certain degree of envy. Perhaps this feeling, as much as his utter loathing for revolutionary Russia and all that the Soviet Union represents, has led him into some misdirected criticism of authors who gave their allegiance to the Soviets, such as Gorky, Blok, and Mayakovsky. For example, one is mildly shocked to read that Blok's great poem, "The Twelve," "is astonishing only by its badness in every respect . . . it is hellishly boring . . ." In spite of these blemishes, one obtains deep pleasure from this evocation of a whole period of Russian letters and art by a writer who was by no means the least of a brilliant group.

Ernest J. Simmons. *SR*. Aug. 11, 1951, p. 12

In "The Gentleman from San Francisco" Bunin has revealed himself as an incomparable master of the Russian language. His choice of words and mode of writing are very impressive: for here we find a fascination which seizes the reader from the very start, and which seems to be brought about by purely verbal means. The adjectives and adverbs are often quite unexpected, yet completely adequate and acceptable in all their unusualness; the nouns offer a mixture of the conventional and the original, while verbs often hit the reader by their sheer force, though without any element of vulgarity. It is a pity that I cannot quote passages here, because even in translation, Bunin's power of expression would survive.

Another facet of Bunin's talent is in evidence in "The Gentleman from San Francisco," an element which has been recognised by other students of his art. It lies in the atmosphere of the story. Not a word has been said which would make the reader think of a fatal ending, and yet he is from the outset haunted by the premonition of an unavoidable catastrophe, of an irreparable tragedy. Consummate art is required for this kind of writing.

The narrative in "The Gentleman from San Francisco" is concentrated and concise, and Bunin's personality is kept well in the background. The word-pictures are drawn outstandingly vividly and cannot fail to make a lasting impression on all who read them. I shall make bold to say that for "The Gentleman from San Francisco" alone Bunin would deserve the name of an outstanding writer. It is appropriate that this work has been translated into many languages.

Andrew Guershoon Colin. *SEER.* Dec., 1955, p. 172

In his post-revolutionary period Bunin began to occupy himself ever increasingly with eternal problems: life, love, death, and religion; and as he did so, he became more preoccupied with the artistic description of himself —his thoughts, his feelings, and his moral and religious convictions. Bunin returned in thought, and consequently in writing, to "historic" Russia, the Russia he knew intimately, at the same time as he turned into himself.

The prime example of this is contained in his last major work, *The Life of Arsen'ev.* This novel is of extreme importance to the student of Bunin, for it presents the reader with a clear and accurate picture not only of provincial Russia during the 70's and 80's of the last century but also of the early life and thoughts of the author himself. It is, none the less, not an autobiographical novel in the accepted sense of the term, nor is it merely a man's fond reminiscences of his youth in a milieu that no longer exists. As K. I. Zaytsev correctly points out, it is not an artistic autobiography so much as the experience, and the realization in words, of a metaphysical transformation in the author himself: "The poet is not constrained by facts—he submits not to biographical, positive truth, but to artistic, metaphysical truth." Consequently, we have an insight into Bunin himself, much more clear and direct than in any of his other works.

C. H. Bedford. *Canadian Slavonic Papers.*
1, 1956, p. 31

Strangely enough, Bunin looks far more like a traditional realist in his verse than in his prose. His poetic production, limited in scope and narrow in range, must have appeared secondary and derivative even to Bunin himself. Description, which is one of the main staples of his fiction, is also one of the mainstays of his poetry, in which, however, it is used with greater taste and discretion. His verse is far more direct and laconic, far less heavy and ornamental than his prose, and this may be the reason why Vladimir Nabokov, an *émigré* author of great distinction, who was destined to become a successful writer in English, once said (perhaps with his tongue in his cheek) that Bunin the poet should be preferred to Bunin the writer of fiction. Short and simple, Bunin's lyrics draw with somber precision lucid landscapes and vivid scenes, which often have the significance of a neat allegory or of a plain parable. It is a pity that Bunin, who went into exile after the Revolution and died in France in 1954, as the grand old man of the Russian literary emigration, did not cultivate more the writing of verse: inferior as they are to his fictional works, the poems of this outstanding storyteller often reveal a good will toward life which is conspicuously absent from the stern and stark world of his prose.

Renato Poggioli. The Poets of Russia (Cambridge,
Mass., Harvard University Press, 1960), p. 115

The peculiar mood and substance of Bunin's prose distinguished him from his contemporaries; the originality and distinctiveness of his prose derived from his own stylistic innovations. His early works in the period from 1892–1903 are, strictly speaking, not short stories at all. They are short, but for the most part tell no story, for they lack both plot and narrative structure. Bunin simply isolated one element, the *paysage,* as it is called in Russian, which is a sketch or description of nature and usually figures as a lyrical digression or setting, and developed it into an independent prose form. Within this form he strove to evoke a particular mood and a myriad of related emotional associations through vivid sensuous imagery and description. The result was a lyrical sketch or an extended mood piece, barely held together by the mood. The narrative is suffused with an overpowering variety of smells, colors, and sounds through which the reader is directly, almost forcibly, drawn into a total sense experience. (In the later, maturer works it is this sensuous perception of the external world which is often blurred and leads to Bunin's highly sensual portrayal of love.)

Thompson Bradley. Introduction to Ivan Bunin,
The Gentleman from San Francisco (New York,
Washington Square Press, 1963), pp. xvi–xvii

I had always admired Bunin for his gloomy, merciless precision, his devotion to Russia and exceptional understanding of the Russians, his quick observation, his intelligent love of beauty in all its forms, and his own particular, clear knowledge that happiness is everywhere, but only for those who know it. I already considered him a master. I knew many of his poems and even some of his prose by heart. The piece I liked best for its depth and its faultless language, was a short story, only a couple of pages long, called "Elijah, the Prophet."

As a result, in Bunin's presence I became speechless, too impressed to open my mouth. I hung my head and listened to his toneless voice, not daring to look up for fear of catching his eye.

Many years later, I read his *Life of Arsenyev.* Some chapters in it

moved me more than any other prose or poetry I know, particularly the
passage where he speaks of his mother's death and, in general, of the
inevitable loss of those we love and the emptiness of surviving them. He
knew how to use simple words. . . .

Konstantin Paustovski. *The Story of a Life*
(New York, Pantheon, 1964), pp. 215–16

Bunin's realistic talent was perhaps most fully revealed in his writings
before the revolution. He himself said: "In those years, I felt my hand
growing stronger from day to day, and the strength which had stored up
in me was ardently and confidently clamouring for outlet. But the war
broke out, and then the Russian revolution."

Bunin was very hostile to the October Revolution and had no intention
of making any sort of "compromise" with the new power. In 1920, he
left the country, never to return. He settled down in Paris, where he joined
the monarchist circles, and in the first few years he never tired of attacking
everything that had anything to do with the young proletarian state. His
negation of the present did not come from outside, from a sudden reap-
praisal of social life in Russia. Social values were gradually shifting to the
plane of "timeless" categories, that was in no way a betrayal of his old
precepts, but merely a sharpening of the tendencies that had already been
present in his outlook and creative approach. It was naturally a shock for
him to find himself separated from his native land, and this lent an especially pessimistic tenor to everything he wrote. . . .

Bunin never understood or accepted the changes that had taken place
at home, and to his dying day he remained true to his out-dated anti-
democratic prejudices. But he was still a Russian patriot, and refused to
collaborate with the nazi invaders, even when he was virtually starving to
death. The time now has come for making an objective and comprehensive
appraisal of Bunin's work. . . .

Bunin, the "turn-of-the-century classic," as Konstantin Fedin called
him, is now being much read and studied. His works are an integral and
organic part of Russia, a part of her national wealth. Bunin's best works
have been given a new lease of life in Russian literature, and in the hearts
of Soviet readers.

O. M. *SL.* July, 1968, pp. 186–87

Bunin, to overcome boredom, sometimes took to reading French novels,
but he didn't like to talk about them and perhaps was unable to do it. He
spoke of himself, of "violet clouds," and of people with whom he met and
lived (accepting them on the domestic plane). He read more of the second-
rate French authors, whom he sometimes praised, sometimes cursed,
praised for their "observation," cursed because the heroine did not marry

the one she should have. Sometimes Aldanov managed to make him talk about his meeting with "Lev Nikolaevich" or a friendly get-together with "Anton Pavlovich"—then he spoke well, in wonderful language, exactly as he wrote of them. And he wrote of them as he spoke.

Both in Merezhkovsky and Remizov one sensed a tremendous nostalgia for Russia, which they both hid. It was constantly hidden, but from time to time it would burst through painfully in a glance, a word, or even a moment of silence in the midst of conversation. In Bunin it was hidden by pride: he tried to convince both himself and others that it was possible to create great things even "after leaving forever the Believsky district." He probably was quite right and indeed he created them. Once, looking at the drawings of Remizov, his papers, his books lying on the desk, his books standing ⸢ shelves, I asked how he could live without Russia when Russia meant so much to him? In a muffled voice he answered, making his grimace of long-suffering:

"Russia has been a dream."

And it seemed to me that in his eyes tears welled up.

Nina Berberova. *The Italics Are Mine* (New York, Harcourt, Brace & World, 1969), pp. 264–65

CHEKHOV, ANTON (1860–1904)

It seems to me that in the presence of Anton Pavlovich everyone felt an unconscious desire to be simpler, more truthful, more himself, and I had many opportunities of observing how people threw off their attire of grand bookish phrases, fashionable expressions, and all the rest of the cheap trifles with which Russians, in their anxiety to appear Europeans, adorn themselves, as savages deck themselves with shells and fishes' teeth. Anton Pavlovich was not fond of fishes' teeth and cocks' feathers; all that is tawdry, tinkling, alien, donned by human beings for the sake of an "imposing appearance," embarrassed him, and I noticed that whenever he met with one of these dressed-up individuals he felt an overmastering impulse to free him from his ponderous and superfluous trappings, distorting the true face and living soul of his interlocutor. All his life Anton Pavlovich lived the life of the soul, was always himself, inwardly free, and took no notice of what some expected and others—less delicate—demanded of Anton Chekhov. He did not like conversations on "lofty" subjects—conversations which Russians, in the simplicity of their hearts, find so amusing, forgetting that it is absurd, and not in the least witty, to talk about the velvet apparel of the future, while not even possessing in the present a decent pair of trousers.

Of a beautiful simplicity himself, he loved all that was simple, real, sincere, and he had a way of his own of making others simple. . . .

Reading the works of Chekhov makes one feel as if it were a sad day in late autumn, when the air is transparent, the bare trees stand out in bold relief against the sky, the houses are huddled together, and people are dim and dreary. Everything is so strange, so lonely, motionless, powerless. The remote distances are blue and void, merging with the pale sky, breathing a dreary cold on the half-frozen mud. But the mind of the author, like the autumn sunshine, lights up the well-trodden roads, the crooked streets, the dirty, cramped houses in which pitiful "little" people gasp out their lives in boredom and idleness, filling their dwellings with a meaningless, drowsy bustle. There goes "the darling," as nervous as a little grey mouse, a sweet, humble woman, who loves so boundlessly and so slavishly. Strike her a blow on the cheek and she will not even dare, meek slave, to cry out. Beside her stands the melancholy Olga from *The Three Sisters* [*Tri sestry*]; she, too, is capable of boundless love and submits patiently to the whims of the depraved, vulgar wife of her faineant

8CHEKHOV, ANTON   81

brother; the lives of her sisters fall in ruins around her and she only cries, incapable of doing anything about it, while not a single living, strong word of protest against vulgarity is formed within her. [1905]

Maksim Gorky. *Literary Portraits* (Moscow, Foreign Language Publishing House, n.d.), pp. 142–43, 155–56

If naturalism had led Russian theater to the use of complicated technique, the theater of Chekhov, the other face of the Art Theater, witnessing to the power of mood on the stage, has creaed something without which the theater of Meininger would have perished long since. Yet naturalistic theater has been unable in the interests of its own further growth to take advantage of this new tone introduced into it by the Chekhovian music. The theater of mood was prompted by the creative work of Chekhov. When the Aleksandrinsky Theater performed *The Seagull* [*Chaika*], they did not catch the mood he had suggested; but his secret does not at all lie in crickets, howling dogs, or real doors. When *The Seagull* was staged in the Hermitage quarters of the Art Theater, the machine had not yet been perfected and technics had not yet spread its tentacles into every corner of the theater.

The secret of Chekhovian mood is hidden in the rhythm of his language, and the actors of the Art Theater heard just this rhythm during the days when they rehearsed the first Chekhov production. They heard it through their affection for the author of *The Seagull*.

Had the Art Theater not caught the rhythm of Chekhov's works, had it been unable to re-create this rhythm on the stage, it never would have acquired this second face which created its reputation as the theater of mood. This was its real face and not a mask borrowed from the Meininger. I am profoundly certain that it was Chekhov himself who helped the Art Theater successfully lodge the theater of mood under the same roof which sheltered naturalistic theater. He helped by his presence at the rehearsals of his plays, and by his personal charm. Through private conversations with the actors, he influenced their taste and their approach to the problems of their art. [1906]

Vsevolod Meyerhold. In *Chekhov: A Collection of Critical Essays*, Robert Louis Jackson, ed. (Englewood Cliffs, N.J., Prentice-Hall, 1967), pp. 67–68

Tchekov's plays are as interesting to read as the work of any first-rate novelist. But in reading them, it is impossible to guess how effective they are on the stage, the delicate succession of subtle shades and half-tones, of hints, of which they are composed, the evocation of certain moods and feelings which it is impossible to define—all this one would think would disappear in the glare of the footlights, but the result is exactly the reverse.

Tchekov's plays are a thousand times more interesting to see on the stage than they are to read. A thousand effects which the reader does not suspect make themselves felt on the boards. The reason of this is that Tchekov's plays realize Goethe's definition of what plays should be. "Everything in a play," Goethe said, "should be symbolical, and should lead to something else." By symbolical, of course, he meant morally symbolical—he did not mean that the play should be full of enigmatic puzzles, but that every event in it should have a meaning and cast a shadow larger than itself.

The atmosphere of Tchekov's plays is laden with gloom, but it is a darkness of the last hour before the dawn begins. His note is not in the least a note of despair: it is a note of invincible trust in the coming day. The burden of his work is this—life is difficult, there is nothing to be done but to work and to continue to work as cheerfully as one can; and his triumph as a playwright is that for the first time he has shown in prose— for the great poets have done little else—behind the footlights, what it is that makes life difficult. Life is too tremendous, too cheerful, and too sad a thing to be condensed into an abstract problem of lines and alphabetical symbols; and those who in writing for the stage attempt to do this, achieve a result which is both artificial and tedious. Tchekov disregarded all theories and all rules which people have hitherto laid down as the indispensable qualities of stage writing; he put on the stage the things which interested him because they were human and true; things great or infinitesimally small; as great as love and as small as a discussion as to what are the best *hors d'œuvres;* and they interest us for the same reason.

Maurice Baring. *Landmarks in Russian Literature*
(London, Methuen, 1910), pp. 184–85

Chekhov is *durch und durch echt russisch:* no one but a Russian would ever have conceived such characters, or reported such conversations. We often wonder that physical exercise and bodily recreation are so conspicuously absent from Russian books. But we should remember that a Russian conversation is one of the most violent forms of physical exercise, as it is among the French and Italians. Although Chekhov belongs to our day, and represents contemporary Russia, he stands in the middle of the highway of Russian fiction, and in his method of art harks back to the great masters. He perhaps resembles Turgenev more than any other of his predecessors, but he is only a faint echo. He is like Turgenev in the delicacy and in the aloofness of his art. He has at times that combination of the absolutely real with the absolutely fantastic that is so characteristic of Gogol: one of his best stories, "The Black Monk" ["Cherny monakh"], might have been written by the author of *The Cloak* and *The Portrait*. He is like Dostoevski in his uncompromising depiction of utter degradation; but he has little of Dostoevski's glowing sympathy and heartpower. He resembles Tolstoi least of all. The two chief features of Tolstoi's work—self-revelation and moral teaching—must have been abhorrent to Chekhov, for his stories tell us almost nothing about himself and his own opinions, and they teach nothing. His art is impersonal, and he is content with mere diagnosis. His only point of contact with Tolstoi is his grim fidelity to detail, the peculiar Russian realism common to every Russian novelist. Tolstoi said that Chekhov resembled Guy de Maupassant. This is entirely wide of the mark. He resembles Guy de Maupassant merely in the fact that, like the Frenchman, he wrote short stories.

William Lyon Phelps. Essays on Russian Novelists
(New York, Macmillan, 1911), pp. 238–39

First of all among Chekhov's teachers is the powerful representative of French naturalism, Guy de Maupassant. . . . The titles of the major works of Maupassant turn up throughout his correspondence. He mentions Bel-Ami and considers Mont-Oriol to be an excellent novel. In conversations with young writers he recognizes Maupassant as the head of a new school in European literature. "Maupassant, as a literary artist, made such tremendous demands, that it became impossible to write in the old fashion any longer," he says to Bunin and to Kuprin.

To begin with, Maupassant's realistic style had a very great impact on Chekhov. It is this special method of depicting life in all its colorlessness, formlessness, and disorder which was equally typical of two other literary models of Chekhov—Tolstoy and Flaubert. But in these writers the art of putting down on paper authentic, everyday life was usually conditioned by the broad dimensions of their works. . . . Rapidly and deftly manipulating his small mirror fragments, Maupassant was able in each of them clearly to reflect a new side of life; he was able to reveal behind the torn lines of the tiny design the broad spaces of receding horizons. . . .

So Maupassant first of all responded to a basic need of Chekhov's temperament as a writer—his love for the miniature. We shall return to Maupassan't role in the creation of the external form of Chekhov's short story. But his role in forming Chekhov's world view was far more significant and important. On this point, the creative works of the two writers are firmly linked. Maupassant suggested to Chekhov, or rather reinforced his convictions about the colorlessness of life, the horror of death, the animal nature of man. Life in its basic nature is much simpler, shallower, and more insignificant than we are accustomed to think it—here is the hard core of Maupassant's work. Our existence is so plain and ordinary that we unquestionably do great honor to that miserable story called life when we expect from it some kind of dazzling joy or quail before its difficult dramas. The first never comes, the second are almost always lived through. Unrealized desires humble themselves before necessity, heavy blows are forgotten with the passing of pain, and the deepest wounds are healed by time. The real horror of life is its colorlessness and insignificance, the dullness of its most festive sensations, the drabness of its most vivid colors, the poverty of its most fanciful forms. "Life is never so frightful, never so beautiful as it seems to us," one of Maupassant's heroines says—and these words might herald all of Chekhov's work. [1914]

Leonid Grossman. In *Chekhov: A Collection of Critical Essays*, Robert Louis Jackson, ed. (Englewood Cliffs, N.J., Prentice-Hall, 1967), pp. 39–40

Chekhov, notwithstanding dry exactnesses like the foregoing, has a fresh and fascinated cordiality of picturing that few realists can muster. He does not furnish, it is true, the filled-full sense of acquaintance that a three-ply Saxon realistic epic lavishes on us; he is not the realist of the itemized account. And he is as little disposed to the accurate, morose baldness, the mere tractarian ripping of decent illusions that Artzibashev practises. His realism is not his theory, really; it is his character, his unflagging native interest. Conditioned always, it is true, by a very article-of-faith reserve, he has, more than most realists, a robust inheritance in the foundation instinct of the natural dramatist: the frank appetite for personality, even abject personality, the gusto for *Sturm und Drang*, even if they are petty, the power of stomach, the zest in acquaintance, the expert interest in everything human. His eyes have seen all with the most absorbed interest, his ears have heard all with the freshest wonder. His perceptions have never gone stale; impressions have formed upon his sensibility inexhaustibly, always full coloured, varied, insistent, real. He may work in the spirit of irony and be as laden with disillusion as Artzibashev, but he writes with a resiliency that Artzibashev, for all his simooms of power and passion, does not know.

Few realists have known so well as Chekhov how to be spellbound. The capital instinct is in him; he is as intent as a fancier when the matter is the items of character and appearance, or the terms of personality, or the set of situation and scene. Through his detachment and against his irony shows something of the robust Pepysian, the thoughtful but eager folklorist, the chimney-cornerer with the gift of vividness. His vision of humanity and its purposes is not intricate, but the consideration of life has never failed to fill his mind and absorb his heart.

Charles K. Trueblood. *Dial.* Feb., 1920, p. 254

Chekhov also used fine detail in describing the elemental souls of children. As we have said earlier, there is something beautiful and touching in the grouping: Chekhov and the child. There are eyes already insulted and wearied by life, shining with the evening light of humor and sorrow; and there are eyes which have just opened upon the morning of life itself and are amazed at and receptive to everything. The writer takes this wondering child gently and lovingly by the hand; he takes this child, Yegorushka or Grisha, and together with him walks through life and explores its burning steppe. Hamlet, with the depth inherent in him, looks into the small heart of his original traveling companion and artistically conveys how the latter perceives this new and fresh reality. In Chekhov we observe not only the child as he seems to us but also ourselves as we seem to the child.

The guardian angel of children leads them glowing with happiness and hope, but he has a face sorrowful and pensive. He knows why the time is hidden from them. In the same manner, Chekhov leads a smiling child by the hand but is himself grave. He knows only too well the fleeting nature of man's smile, even on the lips of a child.

And recent Russian history, which has been oppressive for children and has run them down with its bloodied chariot, has shown that Chekhov, through the incurable sorrow of his own heart, was not able to redeem the children. The quiet, gentle, and sweet life so brightly contemplated by Chekhov's noble soul, not for himself but for others, did not open before the Russian Yegorushkas.

Yuli Aikhenvald. Siluety russkikh pisatelei
(Berlin, Slovo, 1923), pp. 60–61, 73–74†

Astonishing effects achieved by simple means have always been the prerogative of the finest art, but these effects of Tchehov's are different from those attained before him. They do not make the impression of flashes of intuition, and far less of some super-human gift of creation, but of some quite human faculty of knowledge which unfortunately we do not possess. The illumination is so steady and unemphatic that at first it often escapes us altogether; then comes a period when we do notice it and put it down to some sort of deliberate method employed by Tchehov ... finally we are forced to the conclusion that it was a natural function of Tchehov's consciousness and his consciousness a natural function of his being. Tchehov does not insist, but his lack of insistence comes not from a deliberate artistic purpose, but by nature. He is not resisting a temptation—as we feel Flaubert is resisting a temptation in, for instance, "Un Coeur Simple" —he is merely expressing a vision and stating a knowledge which are natural to him. In his world it would be as strange to insist as it would be strange not to forgive.

TLS. Dec. 6, 1923, p. 842

Chekhov's aversion to the mechanical in men is one of the most outstanding characteristics of his stories. There are two types of mechanical characters in Chekhov: those who have sought and have found—not a common thing in Chekhov—and the most prominent example of which is Lopakhin in *The Cherry Orchard* [*Vishnyovy sad*]. He is a man who has worked all his life, and who reaches prosperity and wealth as a result of his perpetual toils and aspirations. It would appear that Lopakhin is the perfect Chekhov hero, the apotheosis to the long series of his characters, the man who at last has shown that the work and aspirations of his predecessors have not proved futile in the end. And yet it is easy to feel, in reading *The Cherry Orchard,* that all the sympathies of Chekhov do not lie with him, but with the "eternal student," Petr Trofimovich and the girl Anya who, full of ideals, love, and futility, go into the wide world to begin their "new life."

The other mechanical type that is a far more frequent one in Chekhov's stories and plays is that of the people who have no aspirations and have never had any, who have no talent and no enthusiasm, people who have never loved anyone or anything, and who merely vegetate in a vicious circle of complete inertia. Torpor is their vice; they are the people that are "unmoved, cold, and to temptation slow," who sleep through their life locked up in a cell of sordid inactivity where no ray of light, no breath of the fresh breeze of life can ever enter. The characters of this type are endless throughout the works of Chekhov, and especially in his first few volumes of short stories, dealing particularly with the class called *meshchanstvo*.

Alexander Werth. SEER. March, 1925, p. 625

Uncle Vanya [*Dyadya Vanya*] exists in order that full-length portraits may be drawn of certain delightful but absurd eccentrics such as only Chekhov's tolerant but unrelenting analysis could make real.... Such company is neither brilliant nor exciting, but when seen through the keen, gentle, and almost passionless eyes of Chekhov it is as interesting as any company could be. He neither admires, nor lectures, nor despises them. He is neither sentimentalist, nor satirist nor cynic. And yet there is something which inspires in him both a profound interest and a complete understanding.

Joseph Wood Krutch. Nation. May 7, 1930, p. 554

After Turgenev, Dostoevsky, Tolstoy, Saltykov-Shchedrin, and Gleb Uspensky, Chekhov's stories seemed to many critics an expression of social indifference and apathy. They began to speak of the "fortuitous" character of Chekhovian themes, of the indifferent collection of facts and incidents, of the absence of a world view. They were amazed that Chekhov only recounted various trifles and explained nothing. "Can it be that all Russia has become so emptied of content," Shelgunov, for example, wrote in astonishment, "that for a thinking man there is nothing in her which he would like to understand and explain?"

This, of course, was a profound error. What seemed a "fortuitous collection of facts" was in fact the realization of one of the basic principles of Chekhov's artistic work—the endeavor to embrace all of Russian life in its various manifestations, and not to describe selected spheres, as was customary before him. The Chekhovian grasp of Russian life is staggering; in this respect, as in many others, he cannot be compared with anyone (partially perhaps only with Leskov). It would seem that there is no profession, no class, no corner of Russian life into which Chekhov has not peered. He set himself the task of giving a picture of all of Russia, because he thought of her and loved her as a whole. A postal official, a district doctor's assistant, and a sexton were just as necessary to him as an engineer, a professor, or an artist. It was important to him to understand the correlation of all that made up Russian life—to understand the very essence of its national character and its possibilities. It was not without reason that he had in mind using the form of *Dead Souls:* putting his narrator in Chichikov's position as a traveler through Russia. Traces of such a scheme remain in several pieces ("Man in a Shell" ["Chelovek v futlyare"], "Gooseberries" ["Kryzhovnik"], "About Love" ["O lyubvi"], —all of 1898). Reproaching Korolenko for never parting from his convicts, Chekhov said: "I have a whole army of people in my head, begging to come out and awaiting the command." If one were to gather together all the people Chekhov portrayed, it almost would turn out to be an army. [1944]

Boris Eikhenbaum. In *Chekhov: A Collection of Critical Essays*, Robert Louis Jackson, ed. (Englewood Cliffs, N.J., Prentice-Hall, 1967), pp. 23–24

"Skripka Rotshilda" ("Rothschild's Fiddle") is the quintessence of Chekhov's style. In it are concentrated, in their strongest manifestations, all basic views of the author as well as the main characteristics of his mastery. . . .

In general, every Chekhov story is so laconic, so consistently concentrated, and its forms are so many-layered, that if someone wanted to comment on any of them, the comment would be much longer than the text. To any fleeting and little-noticed detail, taking up two lines in the text, one would have to devote five to six pages in order to find out, and only partly at that, what idea it contains. And since this idea can be explained only if taken together with other details in the same story, the critical analysis would have to cover not only that isolated detail but all of them, in their complex interweaving and dialectic development and growth.

The dialectics of form, its transformation into opposites and antitheses, is one of Chekhov's favorite methods. This creative method is very clearly evident in the cruel, stupid philistine in "Rothschild's Fiddle," who at the end of the story changes before our eyes into a completely different person. [1945]

Kornei Chukovski. *O Chekhove* (Moscow, Khudozhestvennaya literatura, 1967), 129–30[†]

For a long time Chekhov was never qualified by any epithets other than "gloomy," "morbid," "the singer of twilight moods," a man who looked at everything in life hopelessly and indifferently. Present-day critics have swung to the other extreme: "Chekhovian melancholy, tenderness, warmth . . . ," "Chekhov's love for humanity." . . . I can imagine how he would feel if he could read about his tenderness. And he would be even more shocked at "warmth" and "melancholy."

Speaking of him, even talented people often strike the wrong note. For example, Elpatyevsky wrote: "In Chekhov's house I have met kind and soft, unassuming, unexacting people. He was attracted to them. . . . He always felt an attraction for quiet, misty valleys, for hazy dreams and silent tears. . . ." Korolenko speaks of his talent in such poor words as "simplicity and soulfulness," and attributes to him "a wistfulness for phantoms." One of the best articles about him was written by Leo Shestov, who says that he had "a pitiless talent."

Even in everyday life he used words with precision and economy. He valued words very highly. He could not bear pompous, false, bookish words. His own speech was beautiful—fresh, clear, and to the point. In his way of talking one never heard the writer; he seldom used similes or epithets, and when he did they were usually quite commonplace; he never flaunted or relished a well-chosen word. "Big" words he loathed. A book of memoirs about him contains a noteworthy passage: "I once complained to Anton Pavlovich: 'What am I to do? I am consumed by self-analysis.' And he replied: 'You ought to drink less vodka.' "

It was probably owing to that hatred of the "big" words, the words used in the careless, slapdash manner characteristic of many versifiers, modern ones in particular, that poetry so seldom satisfied him.

Ivan Bunin. *Memories and Portraits* (New York, Doubleday, 1951), pp. 44–45

The many journals left to us by Chekhov can claim a place all their own in literature. He rarely, however, drew upon the matter contained in them for his stories. . . .

Chekhov's being a doctor, in addition to helping him to learn much about people, also affected his style, making his prose analytical, precise and as incisive as a scalpel. Some of his stories (for example, "Ward No. 6" ["Palata No. 6"], "Dull Story" ["Skuchnaya istoriya"], "The Grasshopper" ["Poprigunya"]) are really the skillfully written and extended casehistories of a psychoanalyst.

Compactness and terseness are characteristic of Chekhov's prose. "Delete everything superfluous, all redundant words and hackneyed expressions," Chekhov used to say, "and strive to give a musical quality to each sentence." There were, by the way, many words of foreign origin that Chekhov had an aversion for and avoided using. . . .

Chekhov spent much of his life in trying to better himself. He said that bit by bit he fought to eradicate all elements in his nature which made him a slave to things. And a close chronological examination of his photographs from his youth to the last years of his life will show the gradual disappearance of all vestiges of the middle class from his appearance, his face growing more serene and significant, his attire attaining the true elegance of simplicity. [1955]

Konstantin Paustovski. *The Golden Rose* (Moscow,
Foreign Language Publishing House, n.d.), pp. 188–89

Chekhov's use of literary allusions or echoes represents one of the most striking variations of the playwright's many evocative devices. Such devices, which stand outside the immediate action of his later plays, frequently are of symbolic significance and sometimes have a commentary function similar to that of the Greek chorus. Chekhov's use of literary or folklore allusions in his later plays is usually eclectic and may shift from author to author, folksong to folksong. Quotations from Shakespeare, especially from *Hamlet,* occur in various plays of Chekhov. But in the *Seagull* we find more than incidental background snatches from *Hamlet.* For *Hamlet* appears related to the total structure of the play, and it would seem that the image of *Hamlet* is, in the intent of the playwright, most intimately connected with the situations and characters of the *Seagull.* . . .

What are some of the most striking characteristics of the use of Hamletian themes which permeate the *Seagull?* First the intensity of the Hamlet motif must be noted, in contrast to the incidental use of the theme in the other plays. *Hamlet* sounds, as it were, as a constant background music to the play and references to Shakespeare's tragedy and its characters are contained not only in quotations and brief references, but in broad dramatic situations, as the play within the play, and in some aspects of the dramatic structure of Chekhov's play as well. Secondly, we must note the frequent identification of Chekhovian characters with characters from *Hamlet,* notably Treplev with Hamlet and Arkadina with Gertrude. These identifications grow in intensity as they are presented against a background of other Hamletian themes.

Thomas Winner. *ASEER*. Feb., 1956, pp. 103–5

Chekhov once said, "I write life." Yes, he wrote life. The number and diversity of his heroes are overwhelming. Only the characters born in the imagination of the greatest novelists can equal in abundance and variety those of Chekhov. And just as the greatest novelists capture an entire era through their characters, so Chekhov through his own types and characters has preserved forever the dying image of Russia in the closing quarter of the last century. Indeed, the boundless social diversity represented in Chekhov's art makes it possible to compare him with Balzac.

He lived in a large world and took this world with him to remote places —Aleksin, Melikhov, and Yalta. The great world did not give him peace. But he did not seek peace. He only feigned the little withered old man to hide better from the intrusiveness of everyday life and to work in seclusion: to work, to work, and to work more.

Burning with the idea of going to war, Chekhov decided that he should serve not as a correspondent but as a physician because a physician *can see more*. This was his nature—*a hunger to see more*. [1957]

Konstantin Fedin. *Pisatel, iskusstvo, vremya*
(Moscow, Sovetski pisatel, 1961), p. 28†

Chekhov's early stories are of some interest to the critic only inasmuch as they anticipate the accomplished master, destined to mature a few years later. Otherwise, their importance is slight, although it would be wrong to despise pieces that are still able to amuse and intrigue the reader. They were written in the early eighties, or about seventy years ago; and it is rare for any kind of writing, especially at the popular level, to survive with any effectiveness for such a long interval. This is even truer when one considers that the writing in question was never taken too seriously by the author himself. Both the critic and the reader should never forget that the young Chekhov wrote to entertain, and to add a little to his own income in the bargain.

The periodicals for which Chekhov wrote his early tales wanted to give their public cheap and easy laughter, rather than rare and thoughtful humor, and Chekhov the budding writer readily complied with his editors' demands. He did so without indulging in vulgarity or coarseness; yet at that stage of his career he dealt only with stock situations, to which he gave, half spontaneously and half mechanically, stock responses. In brief, what distinguishes Chekhov's literary beginnings from his mature work is their relative lack of quality—the banality of the stuff, the uncouthness of the style, and the conventionality of the outlook. The ideal of the early Chekhov is the commonplace; the muse of his youth is the muse of commonness. Yet shortly afterwards he was able to grow into a genuine and original writer, and to raise his own inspiration, even within an odd and comical framework, to a level of "high seriousness."

Renato Poggioli. *The Phoenix and the Spider*
(Cambridge, Mass., Harvard University Press,
1957), p. 109

Chekhov took Maupassant as his model. If he had not told us that himself I would never have believed it, for their aims and methods seem to me entirely different. In general, Maupassant sought to make his stories dramatic and in order to do this . . . he was prepared if necessary to sacrifice probability. I am inclined to think that Chekhov deliberately eschewed the dramatic. He dealt with ordinary people leading ordinary lives: "Peoples don't go to the North Pole to fall off icebergs," he wrote in one of his letters. "They go to offices, quarrel with their wives and eat cabbage soup." . . .

Chekhov could give an extraordinary reality to the events he described. You accept what is told you as you would the account of an event described by a trustworthy reporter. But, of course, Chekhov was not merely a reporter; he observed, selected, guessed and combined. As Koteliansky has put it, "In his wonderful objectivity, standing above personal sorrows and joys, Chekhov knew and saw everything. He could be kind and generous without loving; tender and sympathetic without attachment, a benefactor without expecting gratitude."

But this impassivity of Chekhov's was an outrage to many of his fellow writers and he was savagely attacked. The charge against him was his apparent indifference to the events and social conditions of the time. The demand of the intelligentsia was that a Russian writer was under an obligation to deal with them. Chekhov's reply was that the author's business was to narrate the facts and leave it to his readers to decide what should be done about them. He insisted that the artist should not be called upon to solve narrowly specialised problems.

W. Somerset Maugham. *Points of View*
(London, Heinemann, 1958), pp. 171–72

The greatest mistake English and American producers of Chekhov's plays have been making is to accept the view that Chekhov's drama is essentially a drama of frustration. This is only true of his two plays of direct action; of his last four plays the opposite is true: it is a drama of courage and hope. It was Stanislavsky who was mainly responsible for treating Chekhov's plays as plays of frustration and it was he who imposed his view on the rest of the world. But the bitter conflict between Chekhov and Stanislavsky is well known, and the most obvious mistake some producers make is in either overlooking this conflict altogether or drawing the wrong conclusion from it. They all ignore the final aim of the four great plays. Indeed, they usually go so far as to deny that such an aim exists and purposely play down or entirely ignore those parts of the plays which deal with this aim. Hence the spurious "Chekhovian" atmosphere which is laid on so thickly in every production of a Chekhov play.

David Magarshack. *Chekhov the Dramatist*
(New York, Hill and Wang, 1960), p. 42

Against [the] background of careful directions for intonation one understands better why Chekhov sometimes so energetically maintained that it was necessary to follow the author's directions on the stage, that the author really ought to have more to say on the stage than even the producer. On one occasion he was thus able to say that "I really do believe that no play can be set up by even the most talented producer without the author's personal guidance and directions. . . . There are different interpretations, but the author has the right to demand that his play be performed and the parts played wholly according to his own interpretation. . . . It is necessary that the particular atmosphere intended by the author be created."

These intonational directions show how important the emotional key was for Chekhov, but they also show one more important thing: the rhythm of the emotional key. The Chekhov mood was, and perhaps often still is, interpreted as a dominating, all-pervading atmosphere of elegy and despair, an interpretation which threatens to make Chekhov's plays boring and monotonous. But what Chekhov did want was to give an illusion of life on the stage, and life was for him both laughter and tears, both hope and despair, both longing and triviality. It is certainly true that the emotional scale Chekhov works with is of no very broad register. The poles do not lie very far from each other. But in the middle register he uses, Chekhov has been able to capture very subtle nuances. . . .

In this middle register he works with perpetual changes and contrasts. It is as if he were keen that no one key become too dominant or last too long. There must be change and rhythm if his plays are really to give a picture of everyday life. His striving toward this end is most obvious in *The Cherry Orchard*. Here Chekhov marks it very clearly, underlines it, presumably because he thought that insufficient attention had been paid to it in his previous plays. As I said before, there are not many intonational directions in *The Cherry Orchard* that appear more than once. The only ones that occur more often are those that intimate that a line is to be spoken "happily" and "laughingly" or "sorrowfully" and "in tears." In the play there are some fifteen of each type, which in its own way thus shows how he tries to keep a balance between the contrasting keys.

Nils Ake Nilsson. In *Anton Čehov, 1860–1960*,
T. Eekman, ed. (Leiden, E. J. Brill, 1960), pp. 173–74

Chekhov's work comes immediately before the appearance of symbolism; this is not merely a chronological fact. His impressionism, exactly like that of V. Garshin and Fet and some other writers, in a certain sense prepared the way for symbolism. One must not forget that fact when one poses the question of Chekhov's place in the development of Russian literature. There is poor documentation of Chekhov's views on symbolism, and what there is is frequently contradictory. But one can expect no unequivocal opinion about the new literary trends from a writer who always stressed his antipathy toward every "bias." Chekhov's "impartiality," moreover, was one of the reasons for the intense attacks against this allegedly "faceless" and "viewless" writer, the author of "meaningless trifles." However, it must be emphasized in conclusion that Chekhov was, as we have seen, a serious and keen satirist even in his "humoresques." And his later impressionistic style rests on a definite conception of the world and of man, a conception which deserves special attention. . . . But it is still more significant that Chekhov attempts to give his own answers to old questions posed by the great Russian writers. Thus, his story "The Duel" ["Duel"] is an answer to Tolstoy's *Anna Karenina*; alongside that there is an argument with the Russian Darwinists and with Nietzsche— that is, with Nietzsche as he was interpreted (and wrongly) by the Russians. The investigation of such references and direct discussion of ideological problems in Chekhov is a further task for research to which I can here only allude.

Dmitrij Tshiževskij. In Anton Čehov, 1860–1960,
T. Eekman, ed. (Leiden, E. J. Brill, 1960), pp. 309–10

Chekhov began as a Naturalist. His models were Maupassant, Flaubert, Turgenev, Tolstoy. After Maupassant, indeed, he often felt that such high demands had been imposed on the craft of the short-story that it was most difficult to work at all. His scientific approach, his insistence on conciseness, his truthfulness to fact, his clinical exactness when dealing with abnormalities or any physical phenomena, his willingness to pose a problem and leave it at that, his detachment—these are all in harmony with the ideals of naturalism. He is not a Naturalist *pur sang,* however, and it is most interesting to note how he imposes on Naturalism his own personality, and yet how Naturalism crops up repeatedly and often spoils his stories, although it obviously helped him considerably to avoid the evils of sentimentality and cheap romanticism. . . .

There is one thing about him that will specially interest Irish writers. He was Russian in his work, but he was never regionalist in his thought. You may find in his work traces of his life in Taganrog, in Melikhovo, in Saghalien, in the Ukraine—a writer does not invent life!—but the things that were the foundation of his attitude to life, his gospel of normality, was wide as the world: he never concerned himself as an artist with such things as Slavophilism, or with any other kind of "movement." He detested movements. "Labels" or "prejudices" were his words for any kind of "warfare" in literature. He concerned himself only with decency, lies, the frustration of the individual soul, personal freedom, sham, cant, human folly and human virtue in all its oldest forms: he believed in Christianity, much as Balzac did, and made it the framework of his personal idea of what life should be like, though he had no definite creed and did not believe in personal immortality. He had only one conscious aim, to depict life faithfully so as to show how it departed from *the norm*.

Sean O'Faolain. The Short Story
(New York, Devin-Adair, 1964), pp. 85, 100

As Chekhov's own end approached with a growing sense of the brevity and beauty of human life there was also a growing sense of the necessity for grasping it. It is the period of the loveliest of his comedies, *The Cherry Orchard,* and of a half-dozen stories that seem to tremble on the verge of music, so full are they of pure poetry. Here and there there is even an extraordinary sort of romanticism in reverse, romanticism as it might appear to a theologian in an inspired moment. Chekhov does not cease to emphasize the importance of the venial sin, but it is almost as though he were putting in a good word for the mortal sin, the sin that requires character and steadfastness of purpose. It is as though this saintly man, who all his life has been preaching to us to be industrious, respectful to doctors and teachers, considerate to our relatives and friends, were adding despairingly, "But if all this doesn't make you love life better, then for God's sake be bad!" In "About Love," one of the three marvelous stories of 1898, he seems to be defending the mortal sin if in fact it proves to be the only way out of an intolerable existence.

Frank O'Connor. The Lonely Voice (Cleveland,
World Publishing Company, 1965), pp. 95–96

One of the central actions of Chekhov's art in Russian literature and culture was to provide an antidote to the moral and spiritual extremism which is felt so strongly in Dostoevsky and Tolstoy, to reassert (entirely, of course, in his own idiom and form) the strong Pushkin elements of rationality, economy, measure, and sobriety. Pushkin and Chekhov: in both, objectivity and classical restraint are tense with ideas and broad social and philosophical implication. Both, essentially rationalists and of a skeptical turn of mind, react strongly to an overemotional, excited romantic ethos (whether that of a sentimental Karamzin or a late romantic Dostoevsky). Neither Chekhov nor Pushkin makes excessive demands upon man. Man as we find him in Pushkin or Chekhov is revealed in a light that is free of romantic distortion. Lucid realism always blends with a rich but not sentimental or prettifying compassion.

Chekhov's art may be seen, finally, as representing implicitly an arbitration of the gigantic conflicts that split the Russian literary and cultural world into two entities—that of the radical democrats, the revolutionary activists, with their strongly rationalist, materialist, and fundamentally antiaesthetic program, and that of such writers as Turgenev, Tolstoy, Dostoevsky, Leskov, and others who (for all the intensity and diversity in their social and political viewpoints) remain faithful to the artistic vision; in the final analysis, these writers chose to give expression to the entire complex human, social, and historical dilemma imposed upon nineteenth century Russian man. In Chekhov the scientific and rationalist view is reasserted, but freed from that moral utopianism and "rational egoism" which Dostoevsky criticized so sharply in his *Notes from the Underground.*

> Robert Louis Jackson. *Chekhov: A Collection of*
> *Critical Essays* (Englewood Cliffs, N.J., Prentice Hall,
> 1967), p. 6

Critics and biographers are generally in agreement that of all the famous Russian authors Chekhov was personally the most modest and self-effacing. Readers of his short stories and plays know the highly restrained quality of his writing; he detested outbursts of pathos and exhibitionism. Even where these would appear justified—if not, indeed, necessary—Chekhov preferred understatement, soft colors, brevity, and silences. Perhaps it is in these predilections that we should seek clues to Chekhov's decision to produce a dry, factual, socio-historical account. To do otherwise would require a superhuman effort by an artist who could not tolerate melodrama and whose tragic heroes suffer alone, as in "The Bishop" ["Arkhierei"], or conceal their pain with platitudes of society chatter, as in his major plays, or share their grief with a horse, as does the old cabbie in "The Anguish" ["Toska"].

Where reality itself is all too tragic, a writer unwilling to strike a pose of absolute detachment may, in fact, have to soften and hence distort it in order to make it palatable as literature. Chekhov may have believed that his compilation of raw, factual information on Sakhalin would in itself constitute an outcry of conscience more pained and desperate than anything artistic imagination could possibly contrive. Still, *The Island* [*Ostrov Sakhalin*], though seemingly written by Chekhov the citizen, the doctor, and the humanitarian, bears the imprint of the Chekhov we know and love.

> Maurice Friedberg. *SR*. Oct. 7, 1967, p. 36

DUDINTSEV, VLADIMIR (1918–   )

[*Ne khlebom edinym* (*Not by Bread Alone*)] is a good novel by an obviously talented young writer. Certain moods and certain kinds of situation —and these do not imply very nice things about Reality—are conveyed extremely well: the damp hopelessness of waiting in bureaucratic offices and corridors, the arrogance of an official giving orders over the phone, the dreariness of an old apartment building. In short, the novel has the breath of life, without which it would be nothing. Unfortunately, it is a breath which is for many pages still; but it is there.

The plot, if one thinks of it abstractly in outline, is conventional; so much so, that one suspects the author of deliberately mocking the stereotype. . . . Novels not so very different from this one in outline have won Stalin Prizes in the past.

But beneath every turn of the plot there is an undertow which moves it in an unconventional direction. In the stereotyped Soviet novel, it is common for the hero to suffer because certain deeply contaminated persons are out to get him. From the very beginning, these people (they may be enjoying a position of high power and prestige for the moment) intend evil; they are in the pay of a foreign power, they are wreckers or Trotskyites. In Dudintsev's novel, no such villains appear.

Sidney Monas. HdR. Spring, 1958, pp. 104–5

If we consider the sadly sensational novel *Ne khlebom edinym*, it is precisely the falsity and historical deviation of the main dramatic conflict that appear the decisive ideological and artistic weaknesses of the novel. No matter what the reckoning of other critics as to the number of positive and negative heroes in Dudintsev or how many of these there should have been, no matter what sound advice they have at times offered the author about the necessity for mitigating his criticism of negative incidents and for humanizing Lopatkin's image—regardless of this, the novel remains unalterable. His fundamental scheme is discreditable. The conflict of a progressive intellectual with society, the conflict of the individual and the state, unmasked long ago in our literature, have been resurrected anew by Dudintsev's pen. But the artist could not have had and did not have any real material in life for this conflict. The writer was unable to interpret his own observations and to create sound generalizations from them. The errors in principle of the novel's central

conflict are the inevitable result of the very falsity of its subject and all
the rest of its components.

Arkady Elyashevich. Zvezda. Aug., 1958, p. 235†

To unravel the political implications of the tale's [*Novogodnaya skazka
(A New Year's Tale)*] symbolism is not an easy matter. Some of the
interpretations urged by overenthusiastic Western exegetes strike me as
unconvincing and far-fetched. Thus, it seems inconceivable that a leading
Soviet literary journal should consent to publish a story which was likely
to suggest to the reader an analogy between the reformed bandit and
Nikita Khrushchev or between the criminal gang and the party. I find
much more plausible Rufus Mathewson's recent assumption that the
Brotherhood stands for self-perpetuating enclaves of bureaucratic abuse
and corruption "which grow like cancers" within the System. As for the
"dark continent," which through the selfless efforts of Dudintsev's scientist receives the gift of artificial sunlight, the image is an ambiguous one.
Depending on the reader's or critic's ideological bias, it can be made to
represent either an "underdeveloped" area of the Soviet empire or of
Soviet society, still deprived of the benefits of technological or social progress, or else the downtrodden, viz., unenlightened masses of the capitalist
world.

While beyond a certain point speculation about the exact political
significance of the fable's allegorical code becomes sterile and arbitrary, its
fundamental message is clear enough. It is another plea for emotional
spontaneity and personal dedication, a reaffirmation of the author's faith
in the indestructibility of the human spirit and of his revulsion from smug,
self-serving, entrenched organization men. This time, however, the edge
of Dudintsev's attack on bureaucracy is blunted by an indirect mode of
presentation. In fact, it is safe to assume that the allegorical framework of
A New Year's Tale had more to do with the mildness of the official reaction than the alleged mellowing of the Soviet intellectual climate. The fact
that Dudintsev's new work is a fantasy rather than a "realistic" production novel has made it possible for many a Soviet critic to miss the point
or at least pretend to do so.

Victor Erlich. SlR. Oct., 1961, p. 540

Dudintsev's *Not by Bread Alone* is not really a very good novel. The style
is simple, direct, and competent, but it is also undistinguished, and over
long stretches it is flat. We expect mediocrity in Soviet writings of the
postwar period, yet Dudintsev has less verbal power than a number of his
contemporaries: Panova's style has lucidity and charm; both Ehrenburg
and Granin have an ear for the rhythms of contemporary Russian speech.
With the exception of the careerist villain, Drozdov, Dudintsev's charac-

ters do not emerge as visible images, nor can we recognize them by the sound of their voices or the inner movement of their thought and feeling. Lopatkin, the lone inventor who carries on an eight-year fight against "the system," is a fine idea but not a living being, and it is difficult to sympathize with his fanatic devotion to the centrifugal casting and mass production of large-diameter iron drainpipes. The plot has a kind of textbook simplicity; suspense is not maintained; accident or coincidence plays a vital part in the development of the story. Things happen in the novel as the result of the inner needs and purposes not of the characters but of the novelist himself, who has very much to say and manages to say it all honestly and forthrightly.

Edward J. Brown. *Russian Literature Since the Revolution* (New York, Crowell-Collier, 1963), pp. 260–61

Despite the fact that Dudintsev's *Not by Bread Alone* was condemned by official criticism after it had created somewhat of a sensation, it is evident that the most talented among the *shest'desyatniki* have taken exactly the same path chosen by Dudintsev, so that any analysis of his novel is also largely an analysis of the works of the "men of the sixties." A variant of the clash with his environment which Dudintsev's hero, Lopatkin, experiences occurs repeatedly in the creations of the younger authors.

The central idea in *Not by Bread Alone* comes out in a dialogue characterising the essence of what is happening throughout the vast country. One of the novel's main characters, Drozdov, portrayed as a typical intelligent bureaucrat, says to his young wife, who represents the rising generation: "You once told me that I go to extremes. But extremes cannot exist for a man who is building a strong material base. Because this base is what comes first. The more I build it, the stronger our country becomes. This is not Turgenev, my dear." His wife replies: "You're missing the point. The base is the relation of people to matter, not matter itself."

The clash between the builders of the "base" and the young: this is the essential conflict of Russian prose today. One can already maintain that prototypes of both the bureaucrat and his antagonist which have sprung to life in recent Russian prose will live for a long time in Russian literature, just as, throughout the whole of the nineteenth century, Russian writers were developing prototypes created by Fonvizin and Griboedov. [1963]

Mihajlo Mihajlov. *Russian Themes* (New York, Farrar, Straus & Giroux, 1968), pp. 307–8

EHRENBURG, ILYA (1891–1967)

[The characters in *Julio Jurenito* are] queer tools indeed. But their selection is part of the richness of Erenburg's imagination, and through their activities and misadventures he turns society upside down, and sardonically reveals the sham or hollowness of its structure. In the wild parade of quixotic enterprises, amusing hoaxes, paradoxical and Rabelaisian comments of the teacher, there is more than fantasy. More than a futile and querulous jabbing at windmills. Erenburg has the saving grace of humor, sympathy, and that touch of reality which makes him tonic, if bitter. Hurenito is Don Quixote with his tongue in his cheek; he is Bazarov with the last illusion gone.

Hulio Hurenito is a very amusing and a very disturbing book. It is drawn on a large canvas, and the relentless irony of Erenburg leaves untouched little of the social fabric of pre-war, war time, and revolutionary Europe and Russia. It is disillusioning. Compared to Hurenito, the criticisms of Lewis and company appear as pleasant fables for children. It is immoral—or unmoral. Sacrilegious. Rabelaisian. But we must listen to Hurenito. And once we have listened, we shall never escape his questioning smile, though we too return to our safe occupations, smoke our pipes, and assure ourselves that this, at any rate, is reality.

M. Crobaugh. BA. Spring, 1930, p. 166

[*Burya (The Storm)*] covers the whole period of the Second World War. By the rather happy device of having one of his innumerable Soviet characters sent to Paris shortly before the war and giving another an émigré brother who has become a Frenchman, Ehrenburg is able effortlessly to carry his action into France, and indeed as much of it takes place in Paris as in Russia, with a few side excursions into Germany. Curiously, the French characters are the ones which are best drawn; several of them really come to life. The Russians are rather two-dimensional; a stern and high-minded lot, but, for the most part, with little, save formal differences, to distinguish them from one another. The women are particularly unsuccessful. . . . [Ehrenburg] gives them different names into the bargain, and yet the reader is hard put to it to distinguish between them. The point —and the trouble—is that it does not matter too much; what matters is that a young and innocent girl should be brutally put to death, not who that girl is, not what unique and unrepeatable personality is thereby lost to the world. That, I submit, is the difference—or one of the differences, in any case—between the journalistic and the literary approach. . . .

Another curious thing is that—as has been noted in the Russian press —all Ehrenburg's Russian characters come from the educated classes. The peasants and factory workers are forgotten utterly, as though the war had been no concern of theirs; the war, in Ehrenburg's novel, is fought by engineers, doctors, newspaper editors, teachers, and their wives. . . .

Nor can Ehrenburg's descriptions of American newspapermen and officers be considered as accurate reporting; they are vitriolic. More living hatred seems to have gone into them than into the creation of a Gestapo official. The Russian attitude of 1948 is all too plainly visible in scenes taking place in 1945—a serious fault, since the book, if only for the sake of information, will be well worth reading for years to come.

Valentine Snow. BA. Spring, 1949, p. 147

Ehrenburg's talent is undeniable, but most of his works suffer from the rapidity with which they were produced. Too often the journalist is to the fore in him, and some of his novels and stories are clever pamphlets in fictional form. But he knows how to handle a thrilling plot and has undoubtedly learned from Western detective fiction. His caustic intelligence makes his satires witty and pointed. He is good at parody—in *Julio Jurenito* there is some obvious parody of Dostoyevsky and Anatole France. But his characterization is crude and simplified. He is fond of sharp contrasts and often uses stock characters who are either paragons of abstract virtue or unmitigated scoundrels. Although violently denounced by orthodox Communist critics as a typical degenerate bourgeois, a cynic who holds nothing sacred, Ehrenburg enjoyed in the twenties considerable popularity among Soviet readers, which was in no small measure due to the "exoticism" of his non-Russian subject matter and his ability to tell a good story.

Gleb Struve. Soviet Russian Literature 1917–1950
(Norman, Okla., University of Oklahoma Press,
1951), p. 139

Since his youth, Ehrenburg has never deceived himself or sought to deceive the reader with the illusion that capitalism might recover. He told the bourgeoisie then, and he tells it now: you are on your last legs, get off the stage, your painted face has not fooled the world for a long time past!

In Ehrenburg's early books, his scepticism in regard to the moribund society spread, as it were, to the whole of the book, to its whole tone, and to this another element of his talent—irony—was contributory. Ehrenburg's irony seldom has the ring of laughter, there is a challenge lurking in it, it flays no less bitingly than his satire, or it may, as though inadvertently, reveal his genuine attitude to the subject. In one of the stories in *Thirteen Pipes* [*Trinadtsat trubok*], Ehrenburg waxes ironical about himself too, speaking of "the age of supreme illusions . . . when people took . . . cabbage leaves for tobacco and Ehrenburg's books for 'polite literature.' " At first sight, one would think he was simply talking with his tongue in his cheek. Actually, Ehrenburg was declining in all seriousness to have his writing viewed as *belles lettres* in the meaning of the term imbibed from the old school textbooks. There was a whole program behind the irony here, because Ehrenburg was working to produce a new kind of literature—a literature of indignation, and, I would say, efficient ruthlessness towards lies and humbug. We know how much he has accomplished now in this direction.

Konstantin Fedin. *SL*. June, 1951, p. 167

Ehrenburg is more of a journalist than a novelist. Among his Soviet rivals he lacks the profound engagement with life that so wonderfully dignifies the best fiction of Mikhail Sholokhov, nor has he anything of the sensitivity and feeling for human character of Konstantin Fedin, or the psychological density and brilliant language of Leonid Leonov, though at times he is capable of a witty, effective style in fiction. *The Thaw* [*Ottepel*] cannot be compared with the often amusing and competent early tales of Ehrenburg, and it is even inferior to his war and postwar novels, such as *The Fall of Paris* [*Padenie Parizha*], *The Storm,* and *The Ninth Wave* [*Devyaty val*].

Yet *The Thaw* deserves the attention of American readers, for it has become an historical document in the extensive postwar protest against the extremes of Communist Party dictation in the arts. . . . This protest was not initiated by Stalin's death, though it was very much accelerated by that event.

Ernest J. Simmons. *SR*. Oct. 22, 1955, p. 18

Ilya Ehrenburg is rather tall, slightly bent by age, with a mop of hair which was well known in his Montparnasse days (he once had a postcard safely delivered to him at the Rotonde addressed only: "For the man with the uncombed hair.") His hair is now dark gray with white streaks. His eyes are exceedingly sharp yet somehow uncurious. As I stepped into his study I saw a drawing of him on the far wall. It was a pencil portrait, inscribed: *"Pour toi mon ami, Picasso, 29 août 1948."* Brief as this sketch was, it captured Ehrenburg's cold intelligence. A few pencil strokes and everything about Ehrenburg was there: a slightly brooding expression— what the French call *le regard lourd*—with something also of a bird of prey. Picasso had caught him in a moment of concentration. But there is nothing introverted in that concentration; rather, Ehrenburg looks like a haughty old warrior, as one would imagine the chieftain of a Caucasian mountain tribe described by Lermontov.

Olga Andreyev Carlisle. *Voices in the Snow*
(New York, Random House, 1962), p. 113

The ultimate value of [Ehrenburg's] sprawling memoir [*Lyudi, gody, zhizn (People and Life)*] will turn out, I think, to be historic. Travelers' reports and letters from Europe are deep in the Russian literary tradition and have served repeatedly as weapons in the periodic battles to wake Russia out of a deep isolationist sleep and to restore her to the main stream of European cultural evolution. The premise is the same for Ehrenburg in 1963 as it was for Kantemir in the early eighteenth century or Karamzin at the beginning of the nineteenth century: Russia is a European country and becomes culturally sterile whenever it cuts itself off from the center. Ehrenburg expresses a recurrent and powerful longing, one of the strongest rhythms in Russia's history, and, in its service, has hurled himself against the central rationalizations of Soviet power. . . . These memoirs are the record of this man's life—far from completeness, farther from candor—but a self-portrait withal, of a Bohemian Bolshevik, a poet *manqué,* a quick and careless novelist, a sophisticated journalist, an effective literary politician, a man largely untroubled by the life of the mind (there is almost no mention of Marxism, for example), a man whose life takes on its primary meaning through the people he knew and the cafés he sat in. A man, too, with one of the most voluminous memories of modern times, perhaps the greatest *serious* gossip alive.

Rufus Mathewson. *PR*. Spring, 1963, pp. 120–22

Ehrenburg is not simple; and his memoirs are not personal. They are not, though in the beginning he claims they are, "a confession," but rather an apology, a plea, and a course of instruction. They are didactic (that, too, is a Russian tradition) and they are dramatic. . . .

People and Life is not about Ehrenburg, it is about art. Concerning his personal and family life, his politics, his religion, Ehrenburg is extremely reticent except insofar as these open out immediately into his concern for art. Much that many would like to know about his past is not told, or is merely ambiguously and elusively hinted at. Yet art is dramatized in terms of the figures who represented it, who in some way or other played a part in Ehrenburg's life, and with whom he was involved. How deeply or how personally involved is for the most part difficult to judge from the memoirs. There is none of that love of personal detail, that careful building of character from anecdote, that massive following-through that distinguishes the more old-fashioned memoirs of Konstantin Paustovsky. There are brilliantly recollected flashes, dramatic metaphors, connections established between past and present. Many of the characterizations are brilliant. But they are not (with a few notable exceptions) warm; and they are not personal. Ehrenburg seems, in fact, immune to "confession."

Sidney Monas. *HdR*. Spring, 1963, pp. 113, 115

A singular aspect of Ehrenburg's wartime reminiscences [*Lyudi, gody, zhizn*] covered by his last three instalments, is that he looked upon his intense journalistic activity of those years as "wartime service." For Ehrenburg liked above all to look upon himself as a poet, as a novelist, as a literary and art critic, and as a propagandist for modern western art. Even in his war memoirs he continues to campaign for modern art and good poetry; he has a soft spot for generals who show an interest in poetry. . . . The Ehrenburg Memoirs certainly seem to have got under Mr. Khrushchev's skin more than anything else; he makes it clear that Ehrenburg is an "outsider," who took no active part in the Revolution, and merely watched it as an amused observer. According to Mr. Khrushchev "he was once a party member" but then turned his back on the party; for years now he has been No. 1 corrupter of the young with his snarling against Socialist-Realism and his propaganda for western art and for "ideological coexistence"; he even committed the supreme sin of "misrepresenting" Lenin as a man who was ready to admit that he knew nothing about art, and was, if anything, in favour of "the coexistence of different ideological tendencies in Soviet Art."

TLS. May 31, 1963, p. 388

The truth is that Ehrenburg was probably born to be a subversive, but he did not dare to accept this assignment of fate, and he tried—not very fortunately—to become a conformist. Throughout his life he has worn many masks. These are revealed in *The Extraordinary Adventures of Julio Jurenito and His Six Disciples*. . . . Ehrenburg rejects Western mercantile society, but also finds the Russian revolution quite deceitful. Why, he asks, do the Communists tell such nonsense about their defense of freedom, without having the courage to confess that they are building a state of compulsion which will leave intact the old Czarist prisons and only increase the number of bureaucrats?

Julio Jurenito was, undoubtedly, inspired by the French masters of the philosophical novel—Voltaire, Diderot and Anatole France. But Ehrenburg gave a personal twist to this sophisticated kind of literature, according to his own temperament. He wrote his novel in an aphoristic mordant, style; his paradoxes and characterizations were etched in taut, murderous sentences.

Marc Slonim. *NYT*. Jan. 19, 1964, p. 4

A central assumption throughout Ehrenburg's writing career was the primacy of politics in both life and art. No one would deny the great importance of political matters in this century, particularly for a citizen of the Soviet Union. Nor is there any lack of instances in which politics have been made to enter and serve art.

Obviously though, politics is more delible than art or life, and so the writer, if he chooses to deal with political matters, must ingeniously weave them into the fabric of art and life. Unless the writer succeeds in doing this, his novel will yellow faster than last month's newspaper. New generations will turn sooner to histories and good newspapers and journals than to old political novels in order to understand the past. Chatty and chattering though they are, no Ehrenburg novel, not even his first and best one, *Julio Jurenito,* can stand beside political novels like *The Tin Drum, Homage to Catalonia,* or *Man's Fate.*

Ehrenburg wanted, in a formulation that anticipates Truman Capote's famous remark, to give "a new form to the novel," and that new form was simply to be a blending of the individual's fate with "the events which filled the pages of the daily papers." Somehow or other he failed to take note of how close this aim really is to the sort of Soviet novel he affected to disdain. The conclusion must be that a more serious and profound confrontation with political matters simply does not figure in his scheme of things. He survived, and, though he vigorously denies it ("my memories are anything but a dispassionate chronicle"), he deems it sufficient simply to set down his contrived record of what happened.

Andrew Field. *NYT.* Dec. 31, 1967, p. 5

FADEYEV, ALEKSANDR (1901–1956)

Those who expected to see in *Razgrom* (*The Rout*) a monumental work, a heroic epic, or even simply a "sweeping canvas" were disappointed. There is nothing of the monumental here. The scale of the novel is modest—and not only quantitatively. The scene of action is unexalted and constrained. The author cuts down the field of action and limits the number of characters. The masses act comparatively little. The center of gravity is transferred to the psychology of the individual characters. The emphasis is precisely on individual psychology and not on the masses and mass scenes. Likewise, it is impossible to find heroic romanticization here. *The Rout* is written in a very sober, almost naturalistic, strain, without elevation or idealization. . . .

Fadeyev did not discover his own path. It is an extension of that great road carved out long ago by writers in the golden age of Russian literature. This is the road of deep psychological realism. Today realistic art cannot dispense with psychology, which gives it depth, the warmth of life, and persuasiveness. Psychological probing is especially necessary at certain moments as an escape from the shallow and superficial descriptions of life that occupy a substantial part of contemporary literature. Of course, Fadeyev is not the first to have contemplated this escape. But in his *The Rout* he carries psychology to a rare point through consistency and lack of disguise. In this is the significance of the book. It is even more significant when we consider that this attempt to escape a shallow and superficial description of life came from within proletarian literature, where such weakness is especially widespread.

The subject in Fadeyev is simple and acts as mortar linking individual episodes. What is fundamental to the author of *The Rout*, and what he focuses his attention on, is the unfolding of the characters.

Here is the crux of Fadeyev's creativity, in which his merits and shortcomings are interlaced. Here is the focal point where all the beams intersect.

A. Lezhnev. Novy mir. Aug., 1927, pp. 169–71†

The Nineteen [*The Rout*] . . . is the best account of the Russian Civil War, from the point of view of the individuals taking part in it, that we have yet had, and at the same time one of the best of recent war novels. M. Fadeyev seems to be a Soviet sympathizer, but there is no trace in his novel of bias or bitterness. He sets down with faithfulness the adventures, moral and spiritual as well as physical, of a band of "partisans" in Siberia. The chaotic nature of the intervention is reflected in the novel, which is, in fact, a series of episodes in the lives of different members of the company. . . . Into the story of each M. Fadeyev has woven something of the struggle of the revolution and of the futility of the Civil War. When Morozko steals we see the new system at work in the council of his fellow-soldiers which is called to pass judgment on him. In the aimless burning of villages and the commandeering of food from their starving inhabitants we see the effect of the war on those who are not concerned with it. And, finally, we are shown, with a humanity which is neither personal nor partisan, the sufferings, the failures and the hopes of simple people uprooted by a cataclysm greater than any the modern world has known.

TLS. March 13, 1930, p. 210

In a rather intimidating preface [Fadeyev] confesses to the influence of the writings of Marx and Engels on his work [*Posledni iz Udege* (*The Last of the Udeges*)], and does not hesitate to admit that his novel has a purpose. His chief concern is to trace the transition from a primitive tribal communism to a more complex socialist state. Since not even the longest novel could hope to do this chronologically, Fadeev has hit upon the happy idea of setting his story in Eastern Siberia in 1919, when several types of social organization were momentarily thrown into close juxtaposition. As well as fighting the interventionists the Bolshevists are engaged in organizing the Siberian tribes into autonomous republics. The most secret and primitive of these peoples, the Udeges, still preserve a form of clan communism. One of the Bolshevist leaders who had taken refuge with them in the early days of Russian colonization returns to visit them in the intervals of rounding up the local Soviet. He and his companion, the local doctor's son, fall in with the partisan troops. The soldiers go on their way to a strange meeting with a notorious band of Mongolian robbers and the old man and youth go to attend the Bear feast of the Udeges.

There is nothing new in Fadeev's description of partisan warfare; that he portrayed admirably in his first book, translated into English as *The Nineteen*. But even without any pretence to ethnographical accuracy he has handled his new material with refreshing skill. By placing it in the midst of partisan skirmishes, banditry and Soviets, he has, as it were, brought his unique tribe to life.

TLS. Oct. 13, 1932, p. 735

The unity of ethics and esthetics is the basic principle of Fadeyev's novel *The Young Guard* [*Molodaya gvardiya*]. Fadeyev has found the right key with which to unlock the secret of these young souls, still immature in life but already ripe for heroic exploits. In her diary Oulya writes: "every-thing, everything in life must be beautiful." And this brings to mind Zoya Kosmodemyanskaya, the Soviet schoolgirl, who copied into her diary Chekhov's words about Man who must be beautiful and noble in every-thing—in his appearance, in his clothes and in his thoughts. Zoya Kosmo-demyanskaya subsequently went to her death unhesitatingly defending those forms of life which had made the dreams of the Soviet youth about the beautiful, noble human being come true.

The conception about the beauty of life, the understanding of its value are inseparably bound up for these boys and girls with their desire to fulfil their duty to their country. Hence the wish for heroic deeds which are to them the supreme incarnation of their dreams about beauty, the synthe-sis of their moral and esthetic strivings.

It is not by accident that Oulya enters in her diary the words of the well-known Young Communist writer and hero of the Civil War, Nikolai Ostrovsky:

"The dearest thing a person has is life. He has only one life, and must live it so that he should not suffer for his wasted years, so that he should not burn with shame for a contemptible and trivial past. . . ."

Sophia Nels. *SL*. Feb., 1946, p. 51

Commander Levinson in Fadeyev's *The Nineteen*, is . . . utterly devoted to the Revolution. A man of broad theoretical education, he has a pro-found knowledge of life and far-reaching experience of revolutionary work, sees the aim clearly before him and strives passionately towards it. It is not only his actions and sayings that Fadeyev reproduces; he takes the reader into the world of his thoughts and feelings and demonstrates the complete harmony of Communist ideas and the commander's practical work.

There lives in Levinson "a keen desire for the new type of human being, strong, beautiful and good." He loves humanity with all the fervour of his heart. But he is fully aware that the people around him are still far from the desired ideal. They need to be not only loved, but re-educated. An ago-nizing conflict, you will say, between the ideal and the reality. Nothing of the kind! Levinson has resolved that conflict; he knows how noxious are "false tales of pretty birds" and has ruthlessly suppressed the ineffectual saccharine yearning for them. To bring the glorious future closer, he has taught himself to see the present as it is, in order to help change it—has taught himself to exercise an active influence upon surrounding reality, has found the purpose of his existence.

Levinson is an intelligent and farsighted political leader, a competent military leader who appraises the situation with his eyes open and cor-rectly foresees the coming events. . . . He does not allow his subordinates to discover his human failings. While equal with his men in all outward matters (he "ate out of one billycan with them" and would on occasion join in their dancing and tell jokes over the camp fire), he yet maintains a certain distance, which helps to raise his prestige, to strengthen faith in his forces. ". . . No one in the detachment knew that Levinson was ever capable of hesitating, he did not tell anyone what passed in his mind, but produced his 'yes' or 'no' decided and complete. For this reason he seemed to them all . . . a man of a different admirable order."

Fadeyev shows very convincingly how, building up their character, developing new traits, men like Levinson become "capable of controlling events."

They are always at the head of the fighters for the working people's rule and, afterwards, of the builders of Socialism. They are the best of the best in the new society, with which an unbreakable bond unites them.

V. Ozerov. SL. Nov., 1949, pp. 162–63

Soviet critics lost no time in pointing out that both for his method and his style Fadeyev was indebted to Tolstoy. *The Rout* was, indeed, the first Tolstoyan work in Soviet literature, and, significantly enough, it came from a proletarian novelist. Tolstoy's influence was felt in Fadeyev's method of psychological analysis, in his style, in his descriptions of the battle scenes, and in the very structure of his sentences. Some overenthusiastic Soviet critics went so far as to place Fadeyev on a par with Tolstoy. Fadeyev, they said, had mastered Tolstoy's technique while remaining free from Tolstoy's ideological fallacies, thus giving his work the true proletarian orientation. Other Communist critics were more cautious and refused to see in Fadeyev anything more than a gifted disciple of Tolstoy. They were right, of course.

Gleb Struve. Soviet Russian Literature 1917–1950
(Norman, Okla., University of Oklahoma Press, 1951),
pp. 129–30

All of the book *Za tridtsat let* [Over Thirty Years] attests to Fadeyev's sharp feeling for the specific nature of art. Nevertheless, in contradiction to some devotees of the abstract "arts," he understood that art finally demands almost all the vitality and mental stamina of the "vast design" (Pushkin) that lies at the foundation of the creative process.

Therefore, all of Fadeyev's observations on the preservation of form, on the fact that it is impossible to consider the artistic means as isolated from the function they serve, rest concretely on analysis of the writers' work—classical and contemporary.

Not only as a great artist but also as a mature Marxist, Fadeyev understood the functional relationship between "how it is done" and "for what purpose it is being done," and saw beautifully that in other circumstances form itself can become a "leper's coat," that is, the conductor of alien influences and alien ideas.

That is why Fadeyev's rigid demands on himself and others, both as an artist and a master, always originated in the real problems which confronted Soviet literature and which were inseparably joined with the common tasks facing the people and the country. From Soviet writers and from himself, Fadeyev demanded not mere "mastery" but expedient mastery that would assist in giving maximum expression to the living truth of our times and of man in our times.

E. Knipovich. *Znamya.* March, 1958, p. 195†

Fadeyev's insistent emphasis on the portrayal of "living men" in their complex psychological reality was solidly based on Marxist doctrine. Marx and Engels had provided texts suitable for use in the ideological struggle against those relentless "human streams" and romanticized heroes of the early proletarian period. Because Marx, Engels, and Lenin had at times expressed a preference for writers of the realistic school, the words "reality" and "realism" came to be clothed with mystical authority. Fadeyev took upon himself the task of liquidating romanticism. He was an enemy, also, of formalism, stylization, "factography," anything, indeed, that smacked of "modernism." He developed the argument that "realism" is the literary expression of a materialist philosophy and devised a slogan to be used against romantics: "Down with Schiller!"

Edward J. Brown. *Russian Literature Since the Revolution* (New York, Crowell-Collier, 1963), pp. 172–73

FEDIN, KONSTANTIN (1892–   )

It is necessary to say that [in *Goroda i gody* (*Cities and Years*)] Konstantin Fedin overstepped bounds of acceptable subject matter. The subject is satisfying only when it does not distract and burden the reader's span of attention. The subject can be complex, but it must be clear. If the reader must refer back in order to establish, connect, and understand the developing and twisting lines, then the impression of wholeness and the continuity and development of the action is lost and provokes in the reader mere annoyance, unnecessary stress, and a sense of wasting time. True, the proportion between digressions, which appear, as I have said, the foundation of the novel, and the personal fate of the heroes is totally adhered to. However, this does not imply the disruption of time sequence or the artificial mixing of years.

Konstantin Fedin is undoubtedly an interesting stylist. His mastery of the rich and sonorous Volga dialect gives his language beautiful simplicity, lexical richness, terseness and clarity of phrase, and uniqueness of its comparisons and epithets. This is why, in speaking about Fedin as an artist of the word, we must include his style.

Lexical richness gives him the ability to use oral material with sufficient flexibility in the most varied of genres: short novels, tales, lyrical digressions, and statistical descriptions. It seems that he finds the necessary word easily, that it is nearly always appropriate and accurate. The terseness of the chosen word recalls the artistic expressiveness of Bunin, who was distinguished by this quality more in his prose than in his verse.

V. Veshnev. *Novy mir.* Sept., 1925, p. 126[†]

Bitter disagreement has flared up over *Transvaal* (*The Transvaal*). A number of charges have been leveled against Fedin. He has been accused of a neo-bourgeois ideology, while an openly kulak political tendency has been ascribed to *The Transvaal*. Thus, *The Transvaal* was considered a class enemy's conspicuous sortie into fiction. Such formulation of the charge is somewhat superficial. Fedin's own hostility to the figure of Svaaker is very clearly felt. Furthermore, with the general context of Fedin's work, any direct analogy to the kulak is hard to understand. But there remain the irrefutable observations of the critics: that *The Transvaal* draws false social perspectives; that Fedin did not consider the rural forces motivating a socialist path of development; and that the work objectively and subjectively retreats before the kulak, picturing him as the only progressive force in the countryside, its sole industrializer.

A. Selivanovski. *Na literaturnom postu.*
April–May, 1929, p. 29[†]

[*Pervye radosti* (*Early Joys*)] is written in picturesque style, yet with clear-cut precision. Fedin is a leisurely, fastidious artist, who chooses his words lovingly and with almost miserly nicety. Having renounced his former love for ballad-like "narrative" with its surface brilliance, he has achieved the art of presenting psychological portraits, which can only be won by years of painstaking work and observation.

Fedin's portraits as a rule are so precisely drawn and polished that another stroke of the pen, it would seem, would ruin the whole. The composition of this novel is based on the principle to which the author has adhered for a long time: "I seek to distribute the dramatic tension in such a way that enthusiasm should alternate with depression, the exalted with the low, always bearing in mind that in painting there are no 'good' or 'bad' shades but that everything depends upon the art of blending and distributing the colours."

First Joys is the first part of a trilogy planned by the author. Therefore, in reviewing it, we must remember that its plot is not yet complete, the fate of the heroes not yet determined, and the concept of the future still unknown to us. The book is not a long one, but is most comprehensive. It speaks about art and life, struggle and passive non-resistance, love and coercion, petty bourgeois, morality and humaneness. But like rays of light focussed on a central nucleus, all problems lead to one—that of the formation of man and the citizen. Throughout there runs the thought—once so brilliantly expressed by the great Russian critic Belinsky: "Whoever is not a man first of all, is a poor citizen." By "citizen" Belinsky meant a man who had risen to the consciousness of his civic duty, devoting himself to the ideal of truth and freedom.

The heroes of Fedin's novel—Kirill Izvekov and Pyotr Ragozin—are conceived from this point of view.

Israil Mirimski. SL. Feb., 1947, p. 52

Although there is a certain disorder—partly deliberate—about *Cities and Years*, it is a work of considerable originality and undoubted literary merits. In point of time it was the first major work in Soviet literature which tried to answer some questions raised by the Revolution. Fedin does not offer any ready-made solutions; he merely shows us the tragedy of a typical member of the intelligentsia caught in the Revolution and swept aside, after an attempt to adjust himself to it and even to play an active role in it. The general suffering and passive attitude of the intelligentsia is well conveyed in a memorable chapter describing the compulsory digging of trenches outside Petrograd, ordered by Trotsky at the approach of General Yudenich's army. The novel combines many traditional elements, which go back to the Russian classics of the nineteenth century (the general theme, the characters, and in parts the manner, recall Turgenev in particular), with formal innovations, for some of which Fedin was indebted to Andrey Bely, while some were his own. This first full-length novel by a post-Revolutionary author at once set quite a high standard.

Gleb Struve. Soviet Russian Literature 1917–1950
(Norman, Okla., University of Oklahoma Press, 1951),
p. 91

The novel *Bratya* (*The Brothers*) is interesting, above all, because it poses the question of the unity of national and revolutionary art.

In the center of this narrative is the musician Nikita Karev. His music epitomizes "all the great things the revolution has brought us." That is exactly what elevates and makes the novel noble and deeply national. In *Bratya*, Fedin argues with those who are "trying to solve chiefly the formalistic problems" and with those writers "who have alienated themselves from the native soil and have begun to create in a language foreign to us."

In the novel, the author poses a question of the spiritual poverty of the art that has broken away from the national basis and from the revolutionary movement of the masses. . . .

During his work on *Bratya*, Fedin, still not free from "Dostoyevskism," realized that the social optimism and joy of life are an inalienable trait of the Bolshevik character. Arguing with Nikita Karev, with Dostoyevski, and with himself, Fedin affirms the Gorkian joy of life through the characters of the Bolsheviks.

If we compare *Bratya* with his novel *Cities and Years*, we see that the image of the positive hero, the Bolshevik, is drawn here with more vivid, more realistic strokes, containing a definite national coloring, despite the fact that convention and abstraction are by no means overcome in this work either.

B. Brainina. Konstantin Fedin (Moscow,
Khudozhestvennaya literatura, 1951), pp. 118, 128[†]

The window of Fedin's room overlooked the terrace facing the sea. In stormy weather the wicker chairs would be heaped up in front of his window to protect them from splashes. And there would be a pack of hounds sitting on top of them and staring through the window at Fedin who sat writing at his desk. The dogs whined ruefully, longing to be admitted into the warm, bright room.

At first Fedin complained that the sight of the brutes made him shudder. It was indeed terrible to look up from one's writing and meet the glare of a score of canine eyes, all flashing with hatred. They made Fedin feel extremely uncomfortable, perhaps even slightly guilty that he was sitting in a warm cheerful room, engaged in so senseless a business as passing pen over paper. However, in a short time he got used to the dogs. . . .

Fedin had a marvellous capacity for working, if he wished, all day and most of the night. He would say that the roar of the sea helped him to write at night. The silence, on the other hand, made him restless and he could not concentrate. . . .

Fedin was not writing his splendid novel in his usual surroundings. There was something about the whole atmosphere—we were in fact roughing it—that was reminiscent of our young days and was stimulating. Those were the days when a window-sill was just as good as a desk, a wick floating in oil did for a lamp and it was so cold in our unheated rooms that the ink froze in the ink-wells.

By observing Konstantin Fedin at work I learned that he always had a clear picture of what he was going to write before picking up his pen.

He never began a new chapter before the chain of events, the thoughts, the development of the characters, were definitely shaped in his mind and he saw exactly how they would fit in into the whole scheme of his work. He hated any looseness in the plot, any slipshod or hazy delineation of character. Prose, he claimed, must be clad in the granite of integrity and harmony. . . .

Fedin has been able to strike the golden mean in his writing. The critic in him is always alive, but the critic does not get the upper hand over the writer. [1955]

Konstantin Paustovski. The Golden Rose (Moscow,
Foreign Language Publishing House, n.d.), pp. 130–32

[Fedin] adopts in [*Cities and Years*] a somewhat ambiguous attitude towards the hero. In some commentary statements he takes the side of Kurt Wann, but at the same time it is felt that his sympathies are with Starcov, who of all the characters is the one that is best drawn to life and thought out most deeply. The author ascribes Starcov's conflict not only to moral objections, dislike of violence and pity with the enemy, but he points to a deeper metaphysical reason. Starcov is not so much ruined by the treason to the Party as by himself, by his wavering, his incapacity to choose in any situation, because he has not been able to discover "that which is most important of all," the purpose of life. In this respect he is related to the *lišnij čelovek*, portrayed so often in the Russian literature of former times, the superfluous man who also could not find out where he stood in life. A comparison of Starcov and the vacillating intellectual portrayed by the above mentioned communist authors reveals a certain similarity in so far as in both cases the indecision of these figures is represented as a trait of character which is also found in their personal lives. In the works of communist writers this inner uncertainty is determined by class and based on egotistic reasons: the vacillating intellectual turns out to be a coward who feels no pity for the victims of the revolution, only for himself. But Starcov is not depicted as a coward, for ultimately he prefers being killed himself to killing others. Fedin advances motives of a more universal nature to explain his hero's indecision: a metaphysical consciousness of human deficiency which renders the belief in any ideal, also the communist one, impossible for him, and moral objections to the necessity of attaining good with evil.

A. M. Van Der Eng-Liedmeier. Soviet Literary
Characters (The Hague, Mouton, 1959), pp. 53–54

After finishing *The Brothers*, Fedin spent the larger part of the next seven years (1928–34) traveling in Western Europe, and the impact of this experience on the development of his creative art, as well as on his hesitant political and social views, soon became apparent in his fiction. For one thing, his first-hand observations of the depression years in the West inspired the theme of his next novel, a huge, two-volume work, *The Rape of Europe* [*Pokhishchenie Evropy*] (1934–35). His intention was to compare, through the activities of a large group of characters, the deteriorating social and economic upsurge that resulted from the first two Five Year Plans in the Soviet Union. The Dutch family of Van Rossums, importers of lumber, operators of ocean transportation, and owners of a large timber concession in Russia, and their various wealthy connections, stand as the symbols of the material and spiritual decline of the West.

In the first volume of *The Rape of Europe* Fedin's satire and irony were never more effective than in his handling of the big scenes and situations of European life and in the creation of a number of memorable characterizations, such as Philip van Rossum and Klavdia, the beautiful Russian wife of his nephew. Though a Soviet emphasis is apparent in these contrasting scenes drawn from the life of the European rich and poor during the depression years, the total effect is not one of hopelessly biased propaganda. However, when the scene shifts to Russia in the second volume, the answer of Soviet socialism to the economic defeatism of Western capitalism is unconvincing both as a rationale and as an artistically embodied contrast of both ways of life. Somehow Fedin failed to grasp with imaginative power and artistic authenticity the transformed Soviet mentality of Five-Year-Planism, as though he himself were not entirely convinced of either its aims or its necessity. And particularly Ivan Rogov, the socialist ideological opponent of the cynical self-interest of Western capitalism, is hardly the captivating image of the new Soviet intellectual which Fedin obviously intended him to be.

Ernest J. Simmons. Introduction to Konstantin Fedin,
Early Joys (New York, Knopf, 1960), pp. x–xi

Fedin, while he is probably not a "great" writer, does possess in a high degree the talent for communicating the atmosphere of a particular time and place. His best writing is reminiscent re-creation of his own experiences, and his memory is able to select and retain sensuous elements of long-past scenes which render their telling a rich experience. This quality is found in his memories of his youth among the German students and burghers, set forth in *Cities and Years* and *Brothers*, in the recollections of his boyhood contained in *Early Joys* and a number of beautiful short stories, and especially in the pictures of his early manhood among the doomed literary bohemians which one finds in *Gorky among Us* [*Gorki sredi nas*].

Fedin's talent has been one of the casualties of the Soviet epoch, but it has not been a total loss. His career is unique in that it covers the whole span of Soviet literature. He was on intimate terms with the Serapions, but survived all the purges, and, though drawing criticism from time to time, he has never been in serious trouble. His characteristic theme is the tragic dislocation of individual human beings in a time of catastrophic change, but his efforts to deal with this problem have not, as a rule, led him into ideological dispute. While he has paid his due to the demands of the Party for tendentiousness, he has usually succeeded at the same time in maintaining a modicum of literary merit. In short, he has "managed."

Edward J. Brown. *Russian Literature Since the Revolution* (New York, Crowell-Collier, 1963), pp. 130–31

GLADKOV, FYODOR (1883–1958)

Cement [*Tsement*], though an important novel, is not by any means a great novel. The author is woefully addicted to pathos and ornamentation; and not infrequently his pathos degenerates into bathos, and his ornamentation into a heap of obstructing details. His characterizations, too, are not always felicitous: not one of the main heroes is clearly delineated. Many situations are absurdly treated (the Party cleansing is a good example). The two lines along which the story unfolds—the factory and the home— are never welded into an artistically convincing whole.

Joshua Kunitz. Nation. Dec. 4, 1929, p. 695

The Soviet people are mastering the new heights of technics, and the whole country is seized with enthusiasm of construction.

The novel *Energy* [*Energiya*] deals with the construction of the famous water power station on the Dnieper (Dnieproges). The novel gives a broad picture of the working masses, the forty-thousand collective of builders. The author gives a variety of vivid character studies. Not all the men are like-minded, not all of them look at the world through the same eyes, and their past lives had few features of similarity between them. But the majority of them are seized with a single impulse—to go forward and crush all obstacles in their path in order to ensure the speedy victory of Socialism.

Where yesterday the workman had been striving to quickly make good the ruins in order to go on building further, we see him now engaged on the new construction in the process of which he has acquired new qualities. He has grown and developed. He fully appreciates and understands all the complexity of the struggle for the country's socialist industrialization. The character of the Bolshevik worker, the organizer of the masses upon whom the success of the construction depends, is revealed still more profoundly in the course of this struggle. . . .

The character of the hero is revealed in his practical deeds with still greater force in the novel *Energy*. These deeds constitute the sense and substance of his whole life, for the full impact of what men need to make them happy has been clearly apprehended by him and he wishes to win this happiness as quickly as possible.

The author has convincingly shown the new man's vital interest in the destinies of the state, his concern for production matters.

M. Shkerin. SL. Oct., 1949, pp. 149–50

[*Cement*] is an interesting document, reflecting a critical period in the life of the Soviet Union and of the Communist party. The atmosphere of confusion and bewilderment is conveyed with great objectivity, and many of the secondary characters are well portrayed. However, the two heroes, Gleb and Dasha, are much less convincing. They lack individuality. Dasha especially sounds stilted, while many incidents in her life touch on cheap melodrama. The principal defect of the novel lies, however, in its style. It is an incongruous mixture of old-fashioned realism, naturalism, and ill-digested modernism, in which the echoes of Dostoyevsky and of Leonid Andreyev are only too obvious. The diction is often shrill and hysterical, and many of the dialogues—especially of the workers—represent an untenable mixture of coarse, naturalistically reproduced dialect and high-sounding, sophisticated rhetoric. Gladkov lacks all sense of measure. In a later, revised edition he tried to smooth out some of these stylistic incongruities.

Gleb Struve. *Soviet Russian Literature 1917–1950*
(Norman, Okla., University of Oklahoma Press,
1951), p. 127

Cement lacks both verbal artistry and psychological power, yet it had an emotional impact on the Soviet reader, and it became the model and prototype for the vast novels of industrial construction written during the thirties. It was a favorite of Stalin, and as such was circulated in millions of copies. It contained an explicit statement of Marxist philosophy, and in successive editions it quite unsubtly reflected changes in Party policy. Gladkov's fundamental indifference to his novel as a literary product is shown by the ease with which he altered both content and style as times and fashions changed.

Edward J. Brown. *Russian Literature Since the*
Revolution (New York, Crowell-Collier, 1963), p. 168

Cement pretends to be a novel, but is really a romance. Everything passes immediately into action. The love theme comes out of pulp fiction; the reconstruction theme merely renames the clichés of military fiction: the shock troops of industry, commanded by resolute leaders, move out to storm objectives defended by wily enemies. There are no hidden thoughts, no ambiguities. Although the characters take on a semblance of complexity by moving from situation to situation, in themselves they lack depth and consistency. The profusion of subplots and situations, the welter of characters, even the injection of "accused questions" (a man responsible for the death of his brother, the clash of idealism and careerism in Party members, and so on) all provide splendid examples of the uses of retardation in literature. In most cases they have no relevance to the main thrust of the romance, and at the end are left to dangle. *Cement*, then, is a novel only in name. Still, it does stand out as the first novel-length attempt in Soviet fiction at an industrial romanticism that challenges the clinging nostalgia for the Civil War and the gloomy portents for the future by depicting hard work as an exciting adventure and setting it against a surcharged lyrical landscape borrowed from Bunin, Gor'kii, Vsevolod Ivanov, and the Smithy poets.

Robert A. Maguire. Red Virgin Soil (Princeton, N.J.,
Princeton University Press, 1968), p. 322

GORKI, MAKSIM (1868–1936)

Much of Gorki's work is like Swift's poetry, powerful not because of its cerebration or spiritual force, but powerful only from the physical point of view, from its capacity to disgust. It appeals to the nose and the stomach rather than to the mind and the heart. . . . Gorki lacks either the patient industry or else the knowledge necessary to make a good novel. He is seen at his best in short stories, for his power comes in flashes. . . . He is, after all, a student of sensational effect; and the short story is peculiarly adapted to his natural talent. He cannot develop characters, he cannot manage a large group, or handle a progressive series of events. But in a lurid picture of the pit, in a flash-light photograph of an underground den, in a sudden vision of a heap of garbage with unspeakable creatures crawling over it, he is impressive.

William Lyon Phelps. Essays on Russian Novelists
(New York, Macmillan, 1911), pp. 226–27

The most striking and sorrowful peculiarity of Gorki is that while he preached freedom and nature and, in his role as storyteller, rejected culture, he nevertheless deviates far in his own creativity from live immediacy, naïve force, and beauty. No other writer is as stuffy as this lover of air. No other writer is so claustrophobic as this portrayer of space and expanse. The breathing of the Volga, which should have been heard on his pages and which should have freshened them with the strength of its waves, is, as a matter of fact, silenced by the very philosophy and intent that twisted his pen from the onset, a pen that promised freshness and nonartificiality. A moralist and a didactic writer, he rarely relinquishes himself to the carefree wave of free impression. Having entangled himself and the reader in an obvious web of his own intent and design, he presumes to teach others what to do and takes on precisely the mentality and the seaminess of the intelligentsia so damned and hated by him.

Yuli Aikhenvald. Siluety russkikh pisatelei
(Berlin, Slovo, 1923), p. 223†

Gorky is not a pessimist, and if he is, his pessimism has nothing to do with his representation of Russian life, but rather with the chaotic state of his philosophical views, which he has never succeeded in making serve his optimism, in spite of all his efforts in that direction. As it is, Gorky's autobiographical series represents the world as ugly but not unrelieved— the redeeming points, which may and must save humanity, are enlightenment, beauty, and sympathy. . . .

Gorky's last books have met with universal and immediate appreciation. And yet he has not become a living literary influence. His books are read as freshly discovered classics, not as novelties. In spite of his great personal part in the literature of today (innumerable young writers look up to him as their sponsor in the literary world), his work is profoundly unlike all the work of the younger generation; first of all, for his complete lack of interest in style, and, secondly, for his very unmodern interest in human psychology. The retrospective character of all his recent work seems to emphasize the impression that it belongs to a world that is no more ours.

D. S. Mirsky. *Contemporary Russian Literature*
(New York, Knopf, 1926), pp. 118, 120

Gorki is not an irreproachable and straightforward writer, as it is customary to say now. In the story "Karamora," the hero says: "A whole man always resembles an ox, it is boring to be with him. I think that integrity is the result of reservedness born out of self-defense. The man of integrity is, practically speaking, more useful, but the other type is closer to me. Complex people are more interesting." These words can be applied to Gorki as well. He likes complex people, and many contradictions live side by side in him also. In his recent works, these contradictions are unmasked by the author himself with great revelatory zeal and truthfulness. But one should note, especially for the sake of our immoderately monolithic artists and critics, that it is because of the unwholeness and complexity of his nature that Gorki has become a great, honest, and interesting artist. His autobiographical works show the birth, out of the clash of contradictions in the soul and heart, of artistic pathos and aesthetic emotions.

Aleksandr Voronski. *Pravda.* April 7–8, 1926, p. 3[†]

Gorky must be taken, for better or for worse, as a didactic writer. He is always imbued with a social idea, which he is anxious to convey to his readers, and his literary output may be approached with regard to the proportion and intensity of the message preached in each individual work. It hardly need be suggested that the quality of his work is in inverse proportion to the degree and obviousness of its didacticism. Yet one should remember that it was this latter trait that enhanced his value in the eyes of the masses and their fighting vanguard, and lent him the public significance which cannot be discounted by any purely aesthetic considerations.

Alexander Kaun. Maxim Gorky and His Russia
(New York, Harrison Smith, 1931), p. 553

Gorky is truly a great landscape painter and, more important, a passionate landscape lover. He finds it difficult to approach a person, to begin a story of a chapter of a novel without first glancing at the sky to see what the sun, the moon, the stars and the ineffable palette of the heavens with the everchanging magic of the clouds are doing.

In Gorky we find so much of the sea, the mountains, forests and steppes, so many little gardens and hidden nooks of Nature! What unusual words he invents to describe it! He works at it as an objective artist: now as Monet, breaking down its colours for you with his amazing analytical eye and what is probably the most extensive vocabulary in our literature, now, on the contrary, as a syntheticist who produces a general outline and with one hammered phrase can describe an entire panorama. But he is not merely an artist. His approach to Nature is that of a poet. . . .

In order to create Nature's majestic and beautiful orchestrations for his human dramas, Gorky uses most skilfully the frailest similarities and contrasts between human emotions and Nature, which at times are barely discernible. [1932]

Anatoli Lunacharski. On Literature and Art
(Moscow, Progress Publishers, 1965), pp. 222–23

Gorki did not like Dostoyevski. This was not only the result of political and objective hostility toward the author of Diary and The Devils. No, Gorki could not forgive Dostoyevski certain intimate intonations which form the music of a moral philosophy and which color the entire system of the author's emotions. After all, Gorki led a long and complex life without forsaking a maxim that made his youth glorious: "Man—how majestic! It has a proud sound to it!" And how often does literature remember Dostoyevski in connection with another maxim: "Man is a scoundrel: he will get used to anything!" I was astonished to find out that Gorki proposed to consider his Luka simply as a "swindler," like all "conciliators." But then I realized in this an expression of Gorki's cruel consistency. Dostoyevski, by virtue of a different consistency, would certainly not have been as merciless toward Luka.

Konstantin Fedin. Gorki sredi nas
(Moscow, Sovetski pisatel, 1944), p. 109†

Gorky's plays reflect the doctrines of his troubled times; yet they all have more human life in them than the other plays I have mentioned. Gorky is the last of those Russians who produce, without apparent effort, as it were in spite of their creeds and theories, a swarm of living beings. He suffers or perceives, rather than devises, all these human lives and destinies; and he seems to be incapable of violating them in the service of any abstract scheme whatever. I suppose that this Russian gift of sympathy or humility is connected with the fact that their religion never produced a theology; the Russians are true to their feelings, but not to the Law or the concept. However that may be, Gorky shows us, in sharp and violent fragments, the life of the times; but he never really digests it, or works out for it a consistent dramatic form.

Chekov's plays, which Gorky studied and imitated in his earlier work, have a perfection of form which Gorky never attained. Chekov's form would not of course quite do for Gorky's vision and experience. Chekov sees his people at the moment of suffering a fate which they never understand; a Chekov play is a prolonged ensemble pathos. It is not that Chekov deifies Passion or Pathos, like Wagner; Chekov is always natural, never depraved, never a worshipper of nothingness. The pathos of a generation was his subject. He sees much less of human life than the greatest, but what he does see he has digested completely, and can present with the formal perfection of music. Gorky was in a way trying to do more; he felt the simple dynamism of the captains of industry and the revolutionists ("the morality of a Deerslayer equipped with an eighty-ton tank") as well as the pathos of the old regime. But he never digested them together, never saw them as either morally or artistically coherent.

Francis Ferguson. KR. Autumn, 1945, pp. 702–3

[Gorki's] portrait of Tolstoy is a masterpiece, set down in scattered notes that Gorky himself evidently did not mind losing at one time, so much had he revealed of himself in grappling with the fascinating mystery that was Tolstoy. Great in its insight into the "old magician," whom Gorky adored and feared, it reveals more than he realized the liberating effect of Tolstoy's genius. Gorky was a man who gave himself passionately and gratefully to anything which called out his longing for a spiritual hero. He was able to gain from Tolstoy, despite all their differences, an absolute concentration of moral judgment by which to oppose him. That is the curious secret background of their meetings, one not to be guessed from the outward scene. The older writer was exactly forty years older, and at the very top of his influence and massive self-reliance, all the more striking because of the withered and contracted appearance he presented; crushingly direct in all his observations, "beautiful," but with something secretive in him that Gorky disliked, and for all his pleasure in his own genius, curiously baffled by it and following on a road all his own the estrangement he felt from friends and Russian society. The younger writer was awkward and tensely contradictory, full of Western ideas that were like shrill pipings against Tolstoy's Slavic abundance and deep passivity; enthusiastic about culture, science and revolution, and somehow calling up in Tolstoy a curious dislike.

Alfred Kazin. *KR*. Winter, 1947, pp. 134–35

Gorky is a great craftsman, one of the greatest of the Russian short story. He told stories long before he wrote them down, and it is from the point of view of a folk narrator that most of his early stories are written. They are, with few exceptions, simple in plot and composition, centering about two or three characters, with a dialogue or conversation, but always dramatic and intense in action and in theme. . . .

Young Gorky's favorite *genre* was the short story. Some of his short stories . . . are really "short short stories," and others . . . are almost full-length novels. Yet the pattern is that of the modern short story, for it produces a unity of impression, arouses a definite response in the reader, and can be read at one sitting.

The chief weakness of Gorky's early prose style was what Anton Chekhov called "lack of restraint," and Leo Tolstoy, "lack of a sense of proportion."

It is an interesting clue of Gorky's psychology that, unlike Leo Tolstoy, for example, he revised after publication rather than before. As a self-taught man, he was in a great hurry to write and to publish; as an artist, sensitive to form, he suffered from pangs of conscience and spent the rest of his lifetime correcting his verbosity.

Filia Holtzman. *The Young Maxim Gorky 1868–1902*
(New York, Columbia University Press, 1948),
pp. 153, 159

As far as [Gorki's] contribution to Russian literature since the Revolution is concerned, three points are to be noted: (1) Quantitatively speaking, it was not very great and cannot compare with Gorky's pre-Revolutionary output. (2) It was almost entirely retrospective. (3) Its quality was on the whole very high—some of his post-Revolutionary writings will undoubtedly rank among his best. This is true primarily of his nonfiction. . . .

The significant role which Gorky played in Soviet letters in the first years of the Revolution does not mean that, as a writer, he had any real influence on young post-Revolutionary literature, no matter what some of its representatives may say now. Mirsky was on the whole right when he wrote, in 1926, that Gorky's work "is profoundly unlike all the work of the younger generation—first of all, for his complete lack of interest in style, and, secondly, for his very unmodern interest in human psychology." The position, however, was reversed soon after Gorky's return to Russia; not because Gorky himself had changed in the meantime, but because post-Revolutionary Russian literature had moved much closer to Gorky— to his realism tinged with revolutionary romanticism. . . .

Victor Shklovsky wrote once: "Gorky's Bolshevism is ironic Bolshevism which does not believe in man. By Bolshevism I do not mean belonging to a political party: Gorky never belonged to the Party"; and further: "Gorky does not at all believe in mankind. He does not like all men, but those who write well or work well." These "paradoxes" of Shklovsky's are much nearer the truth than the official "icon" of Gorky the humanist, which has been painted all too often. Gorky is still waiting for someone to strip his true face of artificial hagiographic varnish—to do for him what he did for Tolstoy.

Gleb Struve. *Soviet Russian Literature 1917–1950*
(Norman, Okla., University of Oklahoma Press, 1951),
pp. 56, 58–59

When I first met Gorky I was struck by the grace of his person. Even his stoop and the harsh notes of his Volga accent did not diminish this effect. His personality had evidently reached that stage of spiritual fulfilment when inner integrity sets its stamp on the appearance, on gestures, manner of speaking and even dress.

His was a grace combined with great strength of character. It was there in the movement of his broad hands, in the intentness of his gaze, in his gait and in the artistic carelessness with which he wore his loose-fitting garments.

The following incident related to me by a writer who was Gorky's guest in his Crimean home in Tesseli impressed me so much that it helped me to form a mental picture of the great writer.

Early one morning this writer awoke and as he looked out of the window he saw a violent storm raging over the sea. The southern wind whistled in the gardens and rattled the weather-vanes.

Some distance away from the house he caught sight of Gorky standing in front of a majestic poplar. Leaning on his walking stick, he was looking up at the tree, whose thick crown of foliage swayed and filled the air with a murmuring, loud as the strains of a huge organ. For a long time Gorky stood bare-headed, staring up at the tree. Then he muttered something to himself and went farther into the garden, but not without stopping a few times to look back at the poplar.

At supper the writer begged Gorky to tell him what he had said while gazing at the tree.

"So, you've been spying on me," said Gorky laughing. "I don't mind telling you. I said: 'What might!' " [1955]

Konstantin Paustovski. *The Golden Rose* (Moscow, Foreign Language Publishing House, n.d.), pp. 195–96

In *Literaturnye portrety* (*Literary Portraits*), Gorki dwells relatively little on the examination of the works and theories of this or that figure. He strives to engrave the very personality of the writer, illuminating broadly various spheres of life in which the human character is revealed, thereby causing the distinct type of the man to emerge. Gorki's literary portraits are in most cases built on a constant shifting of the angle at which the writer looks at his hero. Gorki, as it were, turns him to the reader from many different sides, changes conditions under which the hero acts, and transfers him from one environment into another in order to reveal more clearly the basic traits of his character in new situations or to uncover other, still unknown traits. Through these constant "switches," one can explain the fragmentary condition of many portraits, which consist of unconnected notes, observations, and remarks. . . .

In the novel *Zhizn Klima Samgina* (*The Life of Klim Samgin*), the problem of individualism and the question of the fate of the bourgeois intelligentsia are solved on a broad historical and social plane. Gorki follows the development of the life in Russia in the course of forty years, unfolds a grandiose panorama of the epoch, and shows all basic phenomena, directions, and processes in the life of the society at the end of the nineteenth and the beginning of the twentieth centuries. . . . The content of the novel is not limited to the tracing of Klim Samgin's life. . . . Connections, mutual relationships, and the destinies of the heroes are motivated not only by Samgin's actions and observations but also by historical events; they are revealed in the light of the general struggle and conditioned by the movement of history.

Andrei Sinyavski. *Istoriya russkoi sovetskoi literatury* (Moscow, Akademiya nauk, 1958), Vol. I, pp. 114, 126, 133†

He preferred to praise rather than pity, and to speak of man's conquests of, rather than his submission to, Nature. Impatient with theory, complexity, "psychologizing," he saw existence in the light of his unambiguous dogma, and, like the solicitous father of very small children, told lies to bolster their morale. All men appeared to him in the guise of the snake and falcon of his fable; he wanted all of them to be falcons, never doubted that they could be, and toward the end of his life had the joy of seeing them so transformed, as he thought. It was an ardent zeal, a generous humanistic faith that, to his mind, was more "loving" than Tolstoy's egotistic passion. . . . He was "engaged" in life, in the French sense of *engagé;* as a writer his business was to "serve," to rouse, to work for improvement, to be actively involved in the moment; unlike Tolstoy, he did not look upon human beings as moral entities but only as social organisms: they either destroyed or built communities, and their role in society determined their value as men.

Helen Muchnic. *From Gorky to Pasternak*
(New York, Random House, 1961), pp. 98–99

It is undeniable that all his work as a playwright made Gorky a most genuine representative of the socio-political drama. He provided Russian repertory with quite a few specimens of this genre yet, by a certain irony of destiny, they became available to large audiences only after the 1917 Revolution when their topical interest was gone and they could be interpreted only as historical documents, in a retrospective fashion. . . . Gorky's plays appear dated and require a tremendous effort of staging and acting for their revival. Today, Gorky is acclaimed as the father of socialist realism and his plays, *post hoc*, are hailed as examples to be followed by Soviet dramatists. Unfortunately, the latter did try to imitate Gorky with definite negative results. None of the plays conceived and executed in Gorky's tradition remained for more than a very few years in the Soviet dramatic repertory.

Marc Slonim. *Russian Theatre: From the Empire to
the Soviets* (New York, Crowell-Collier, 1961),
pp. 153, 157

He concentrated on the sordid details, primarily those of a physical nature: hunger, drunkenness, pain, filth, the lack of all physical essentials. With the exception of Dostoevsky, there is no other Russian writer of the nineteenth century who dealt as much as Gorky did with physical violence and murder. Whatever the psychological explanation may be in terms of Gorky's personality, it would be next to impossible to detect any grin of sadistic pleasure in his gruesome descriptions of wives mangled by their husbands, of vagabonds beaten up by police. From his early childhood he had been deeply affected by all the excesses of violence around him: the fury of blows, the floggings, the madness of drunken brawls. He had become aware of physical violence as a main feature of Russian life, and its exposé remained one of his principal objectives; he denounced it not only as an Asiatic heritage, a survival of the Tartar yoke, but also as a result of ignorance and oppression: the cruelty of the common people was bred by their misery and was a release as well as a compensation for their slavery.

Marc Slonim. *From Chekhov to the Revolution*
(New York, Oxford University Press, 1962), p. 136

His best earlier stories had thrown a highlight on strong and self-reliant characters at loggerheads with their drab environment, by no means only tramps, but also princes, landowners, and legendary figures. . . . While he had neither morally whitewashed nor tried to rationalize their unpredictable, impulsive conduct, he was clearly fascinated by their integrity, by their refusal to be dragged down by convention-bound society. After all these glowing pictures of buoyant energetic men and women, Gorky changed over paradoxically to an apologia for weak or broken individuals. Sometimes they are the same people as before, seen at the later stage of life. The characters in *The Lower Depths* [*Na dne*] have all started boldly, and then been broken on the wheel. But Gorky could more easily start to justify sympathetic but defeated people, because some of his favourite heroes had been men of quite ordinary capacities, struggling to play gigantic roles beyond their strength. It was inevitable that many of his defiant tramps and ultra-individual misfits, if they could not die bravely before their youthful vigour was exhausted, should sink into the dull abasement of the doss-house.

Richard Hare. Maxim Gorky
(London, Oxford University Press, 1962), pp. 60–61

Maxim Gorky was fundamentally a realist, indeed, a determined champion of realism against symbolism, mysticism, naturalism, or excessive verbal experimentation. But as he explained to Chekhov in 1896, Gorky also favored an element of romanticism, the possibility of exaggerating a trait or elevating his subject. As an enemy of pessimism, lethargy, and despair, he vehemently opposed the depressive aspects of the Russian mind and literature. Thus, while Gorky seemed to push his realism to the verge of naturalism, at the same time he rescued it from the naturalistic fact of "raw life" by imparting to it a certain romantic coloration.

Although Gorky—unlike the great Russian writers of the gentry who preceded him or such contemporaries as Chekhov, Bunin, and Leonid Andreyev—came out of the "lower depths," he was no skid-row character. The graph of his life climbed rather than descended. Nor did he write only about outcasts, prostitutes, hoboes, and the "barefoot brigade." He also wrote about artisans, workers, actresses, merchants, self-made millionaires, millionaires' sons, and intellectuals. In fact, Gorky wrote about almost every aspect of Russian life except the court circles, the gentry, and the army.

George Reavey. Foreword to Maxim Gorky,
A Sky-Blue Life and Selected Stories (New York,
New American Library, 1964), p. vii

Lenin thought that Gorky had a great deal to offer the revolutionary movement; the writer's talent, his popularity, his material aid to the

Party were all very important. Gorky thought that Lenin and his Party's program offered him a way to channel his otherwise disorganized cries of social and political protest into effective expression and action. It is not an exaggeration to assert that Lenin gave Gorky his most important example of intellectual backbone, an example which Gorky tried to follow as a model. Throughout his writing on the question, Gorky emphasizes the extent to which he depended on Lenin's agreement and approval, in many ways like a young, admiring son turning to his father.

It is strange for the typical American reader or critic to observe a talented artist almost worshiping a political figure, particularly one who later becomes head of state. . . . While there were and are still undoubtedly among Russian intellectuals many who share our belief in the necessity for skepticism toward leaders, there also remains a much larger proportion of the educated Russian population which would not see anything strange in Gorky's semi-worship of Lenin. In this sense, Gorky may be considered a rather typical example of a large group of the Russian intelligentsia of his time and of the present time. The difference between the Russian and American attitude is as much a function of difference in temperament as it is of differences in political system. . . .

I do not agree with the common critical assertions in the West that Gorky's writing suffered from his deep involvement with revolutionary politics or his deep dependence on Lenin's approval. Just the contrary is true: Gorky apparently needed the kind of guidance and direction that he found in Lenin's personality and program; without it, Gorky would either have had to find some equivalent substitute, or he would not have been able to continue writing at all. Deep political engagement was requisite to the way he wanted to write.

Irwin Weil. Gorky
(New York, Random House, 1966), pp. 18–19

Mother [*Mat*] is proclaimed by Soviet critics as a model of the genre of socialist realism. The only possible justification for such a claim lies in the hatred with which Gorky depicts in it the champions of the old order and the affection which he lavishes upon the revolutionaries. Reality in a work of the school of socialist realism should be portrayed as revolutionary, that is, orientated towards the future when social institutions and human psychology will have assumed new socialist forms. It is difficult to see such a reality in *Mother*.

F. M. Borras. Maxim Gorky the Writer
(London, Oxford University Press, 1967), p. 110

Between Lenin and Gorky yawned an abyss. . . . Gorky had a downright distaste for politics; Lenin was infatuated with it. Despite a weakness for didactic interpolation into his tales and plays and for garrulous sermonizing in his old age, Gorky was all artist. Despite an affectionate memory of the literary classics he had read in his youth, Lenin was all politician. Lenin believed in classes, class struggle, dictatorship, the Party, and himself as the maker and mover of history. Gorky believed in Man, in freedom, in the redeeming power of art and science, in the sacredness of the individual person.

Bertram D. Wolfe. The Bridge and the Abyss
(New York, Frederick A. Praeger, 1967), pp. 3–4

GUMILYOV, NIKOLAI   (1886–1921)

[Gumilyov] is still a fighter for the new, the "ideal" art. His poetry lives in an imaginative and almost spectral world. He somehow avoids the contemporary. He creates countries for himself and populates them with his own creations: people, animals, and demons. In these countries—one could say, in these worlds—things obey not the usual laws of nature but new laws that are ruled by the poet. The people in them do not live and function according to a normal psychology but rather according to strange, inexplicable caprices whispered by the author-prompter. And if in this world we meet names familiar to us from other sources—mythological heroes such as Odysseus, Agamemnon, Romulus; historical personalities such as Tamerlane, Dante, Don Juan, Vasco de Gama; or various geographical locations such as the Gobi Steppe, Castile, and the Andes—they have all been somehow strangely modified, have become new and unrecognizable. . . .

It should be noted that in his new poems he has, to a considerable degree, freed himself from the extremes of his first works and has learned to enclose his fantasies in a more regulated outline. With the years, his visions have acquired a more detailed distinctiveness. Simultaneously his poetry has been strengthened. As a student of Annenski, Vyacheslav Ivanov, and the poet to whom *Pearls* is dedicated [Valeri Bryusov], Gumilyov slowly but surely approaches full mastery over "form." Almost all of his poems are beautifully written in well-planned and sonorously refined verse. Gumilyov did not create a new literary style but borrowed his versification from his predecessors. He knew how to improve, develop, and deepen his style; this we should perhaps recognize as an even greater achievement than a search for a new form that all too often leads to regrettable failures.

Valeri Bryusov. Russkaya mysl. July, 1910, pp. 206–7[†]

The literary activity of Nikolai Gumilyov started back in the epoch of blooming symbolism, long before the particular spiritual mood and the independent poetry of the new school [Acmeism] were formed. But already in the early poems we can recognize those characteristics which made him the leader and theoretician of the new direction. From the other poets represented in *Hyperborey* Gumilyov is distinguished by his active, sincere, and simple masculinity; his intense spiritual energy; his temperament. He himself, in this respect, admits that he stands alone among the young generation. [1916]

> Viktor Zhirmunski. *Voprosy teorii literatury*
> (Leningrad, Academia, 1928), p. 313†

Gumilev's poetry is romantic, he called his first book *Romantic Flowers* [*Romanticheskie tsveti*] and a Romanticist he remained to his end. His poetry is permeated with the spirit of romance, but it has a concrete romanticism, the romanticism of beautiful things, thrilling adventure, and distant country. He called his muse the Muse of distant Travel. He had himself travelled in Africa, and retained a peculiar love for that continent. His poetry is manly, almost boyish. His favourite reading was boys' literature, and much of his poetry will probably become boys' poetry. He was a straightforward, simple, unsophisticated soul, and his religion (which is seldom the case in Russia) is a simple, unquestioning faith. His last books are full of this spirit.

> D. S. Mirsky. *SEER*. June, 1922, p. 221

The last of the conquistadores, a poet-soldier, a poet-cuirassier, with the soul of a Viking, consumed by sorrow in foreign lands, "a discontented lover of foreign skies," Gumilyov is the searcher and discoverer of the exotic. He is singular and unusual and rich in the unexpected. "The orchards of my soul are always patterned," he says of his richly figurative and picturesque soul. His verses are only the dear, the valuable, the rare: verses of pricelessness, verses of pearl. The translator of Theophile Gautier, courtly and clever, he follows in the legacy of his French brother, coining, bending, figuring, and, in addition, like Gautier, not deigning to fight an easy opponent, "not squeezing pliable and soft-clay clods," but gaining brilliant mastery over noble metals and over the marble of Paros or Carrara. He is in fact an Acmeist. He wished only to gain the peaks. It is mainly the feeling of height and the upper limits that forms his unshakable lines. His verse advances courageously and splendidly. Sometimes it is lapidarian, sometimes grandiose, and at times unusually heavy, as in *Shatyor* (*The Tent*); sometimes it carries on its waves a refined figurativeness.

> Yuli Aikhenvald. *Siluety russkikh pisatelei*
> (Berlin, Slovo, 1923), p. 265†

Blok and Gumilyov are opposites in poetry, tastes, philosophy, political viewpoints, and outward appearance—in fact in everything. Blok's poetry is a dark glow; Gumilyov's is an exact, clear, completely regulated poetry. On the one hand stands Blok, a "leftist socialist and revolutionary," who glorfied October in "The Twelve" ("To the grief of the bourgeois, we kindle the world's fire"); on the other hand stands Gumilyov, a "White Guardist" and a "Monarchist." Blok regarded the war [World War I] with disgust, and Gumilyov volunteered to fight. Blok considered the world horrifying, life as absurd, and God as cruel or nonexistent, whereas Gumilyov maintained, in all sincerity, that "the man who loves the world and believes in God contains all within himself." Blok thought all his life that the revolution was a "beautiful inevitability." Gumilyov considered it synonymous with evil and barbarity. Blok was a hater of literary technique, craftsmanship, training, and the very tag "man of letters." . . . Gumilyov called his circle of students "The Guild of Poets," in order to underline the importance and the necessity of studying poetry as a trade. And so it was, even in regard to their outward appearances. Blok was a northern beauty, with his Scandinavian face, wonderful curly hair, velvet jacket, and white shirt with a soft unbuttoned collar. Gumilyov was homely and neatly dressed, had close-cropped hair, and wore a stiff frockcoat.

They were opposed in everything. During their short lives, Blok and Gumilyov fought each other both quietly and openly. Blok's last article, "O dushe" ["About the Soul"], which appeared shortly after his death, is a sharp attack on Gumilyov and his poetics and philosophy. Gumilyov's retort to this article, true to his style—discreet and proper, but just as cutting—was published only after his execution. [1928]

Georgi Ivanov. Peterburgskie zimy (New York,
Izdatelstvo imeni Chekhova, 1952), pp. 200–201[†]

[In the early Gumilyov one] can already feel the influence of the "Parnassians"—Gautier, Leconte de Lisle, and Hérédia—which was to become stronger in later years, although Gumilyov's poetic world is still peopled by romantic images. "Here through a symbolist pattern the true face of Gumilyov is already apparent." His favorite themes still deal with knights in armor, with conquistadors, conquerors, emperors, majestic heroes, the Devil, Satan, Lucifer, the Serpent, the Raven, the Eternal Jew, Ossian, Sindbad the Sailor, Caracalla. They all perform great deeds as a prototype of Gumilyov's own ideal. But side by side there appear some poems of somber wisdom.

It would be an error to think of Gumilyov "who loved life passionately" always as a romantic, sunny poet. He had not only his somber moods, but

moods of depression and despair as well. However, even in his darkest
moments . . . Gumilyov never forgot the force and power of man's will.
Leonid I. Strakhovsky. *SEER*. Oct., 1944, p. 6

Nicholas Gumilyov remains the dominant figure of the group, besides
being a rare phenomenon in Russian literature. His was a positive and
adventurous spirit, allied to a passion for meticulous craftsmanship. His
lust for adventure took him several times to Africa (the African scene is
brilliantly evoked in his volume *Shatyor—The Tent*), and the same
questing spirit led him to explore a vast range of verse forms, from the
sonnet to the Persian ghazali. Proud, intransigent, and openly monarchist
in his sympathies, it is perhaps not to be wondered at that Gumilyov did
not long survive the revolutionary regime. In *Ognenny Stolp* (*Pillar of
Fire*)—published in 1921, and undoubtedly his masterpiece, for in it feeling and technique was perfectly fused—appeared a long and weirdly beautiful poem called "The Trolley Car that Lost its Way" ["Zabludivshisya
tramvai"] in which he seems to foresee his own fate. Soon after the book
appeared, Gumilyov was executed by a firing-squad for participating in a
conspiracy to overthrow the Soviet Government.
TLS. Jan. 20, 1950, p. 37

Although Gumilyov's natural inclinations sought the major key and the
plastic world, his earliest poems were written under the ruling influence of
the Symbolist school. After a brief infatuation for Bal'mont's manner—
it is significant that he was particularly attracted by Bal'mont's slogan
"let us be like the sun"—he gravitated almost inevitably to Bryusov, the
most "heroic" and least typical of contemporary poets and one of the
most conscious craftsmen of the world. *Pearls* [*Zhemchuga*], which Gumilyov dedicated "to my master Bryusov," is a transitional work. If on
the one hand, it still hovers uncertainly between the imagery of Symbolism and a certain attenuated Parnassianism reminiscent of Gautier and
Leconte de Lisle, on the other it anticipates, in the verbal mastery of
"Adam's Dream" ["Son Adama"] and "The Captains" ["Kapitany"], in
the movement of "The Forest Fire" ["Lesnoi pozhar"] and in the beautiful
simplicity of "The Eagle" ["Oryol"], an independence of maturity which
his next volume, *A Foreign Sky* [*Chuzhoe nebo*] (1912), fully justifies.
Here he no longer perceives the world of nature and emotion in terms of
literary tradition and can rightly declare that "in the young world, a young
Adam, I smile at the birds and the fruits." His poetry not only becomes
in the highest sense self-expressive, but continually gains in closeness of
texture and depth of feeling.
This acceptance of some of the features of Symbolism explains certain

elements in Gumilyov's own work. His world of contour, colour and song, peopled with exotic figures, and in which even the bullets that may be carrying his death sing joyously through the air, has been variously compared to the militarism of Kipling and to the return of the masculine Pushkinian strain. But Gumilyov has none of Kipling's limitations of expression or outlook. . . .

Gumilyov's kinship with Pushkin is as obvious as his divergences from him. His sense of harmony with the varied manifestations of life, each alive in its own right, his ability to find poetry in prose and to express the emotion of an idea rather than any depth of thought are as much a part of the Pushkinian tradition as are the bright clarity of his world, his deliberate repetitive word-patterns and his experimentation in form. But he possesses a simple, almost mediaeval piety, which is entirely alien to Pushkin, and behind him lies also the heritage of Lermontov and the Symbolists. In part he cannot but be the visionary Romantic, haunted by the image of the swan and the unicorn and singing in restless anapaests of his unhappy love. He knows the conflicts between flesh and spirit, the yearning after nonexistent golden fields, the bewildering changefulness of personality and the oppressiveness of tradition. Behind the easy conciliation of classical myth and the Bible, exotic nature and skyscrapers, literary language and colloquialism lies a sense of insecurity, a feeling that somewhere, "in the blind corridors of space and time," he has lost his way, and his sun-drenched world with its familiar echoes of firmly grounded traditional beliefs, dear to the Russian reader, is crossed by another world of unfathomable legend and terror.

Nina Brodiansky. SEER. June, 1953, pp. 582–84

The emergence of Gumilev was for Russian poetry an event not too different in kind (although far less in degree) from the earlier appearance in England of Kipling, and in Italy of the martial and patriotic D'Annunzio. Gumilev's sudden rise on the horizon of Russian poetry was viewed at first as a novel miracle, as a wonder of youth. Gumilev came to the fore in the shape of a new David, a gay rogue who relied on his arm and eye no less than on his God, and the weary spirit of the giant, Russian Symbolism, seemed to collapse under the shot from his sling. Gumilev was aware of the novelty, or rather, of the timeliness of his message. He felt that he had come to restore to manliness and health a poetry which had degenerated into the vices opposed to those two virtues. . . . Gumilev refused to explore both the forest of symbols and the cave of our dreams, since the path going through them may lead to what is either too base or too lofty for the heart and the mind of man. He rejected the temptation to wander into the ghostly realms of the metaphysical and the occult, and ventured instead into the material and physical world. His quest was not for Eden or Hell, but for a remote oasis or a lonely island, an unbeaten desert or a virgin continent. What spurred him was not the external urge of literary exoticism, but a romantic and passionate nostalgia for the venturesome discovery of new worlds. The frequence in his poetry of Southern and Eastern landscapes may remind us of the Parnassian predilection for the same distant countries and faraway seas. Yet one must not forget that for the Parnassians those landscapes were hardly more than ornamental frames or decorative backgrounds, while in Gumilev's poetry they are direct illustrations of his states of mind.

Renato Poggioli. *The Poets of Russia* (Cambridge,
Mass., Harvard University Press, 1960), pp. 225–26

Like Xlebnikov, Gumilev seems to be one of those poets who is more talked about than read, perhaps because of the neat way in which his poetic program fits into our construction of literary history. One feels strongly the pressure of this taxonomical tradition even in Struve's Introduction to this volume, entitled *Tvorčeskij put' Gumileva*, in which his poetry is discussed almost entirely in terms of influences and the superficial, movement-oriented criticism of Gumilev's contemporaries: a major issue is, for example, did Gumilev "remain" a Symbolist, or did he "return" to Symbolism? But a poet earns his posterity's interest by outgrowing his ism along with his influences and affectations. Who would now talk about Axmatova and Mandel'štam as Acmeists in any really descriptive sense of that word? Perhaps the label remains stuck to Gumilev because he has been left in his pigeonhole so long. It seems that the habit of not reading this poet began quite early: in his Introduction, Struve expresses doubt as to whether Brjusov had bothered to read *Ognennyj stolp* when he reviewed the book, and the fairness of Blok's famous article of 1921 on Gumilev and the Acmeist Workshop may be questioned on the same grounds.

It seems to me that the question of whether Gumilev remained an Acmeist or became a poet somewhere along the way is very close to the question about how dated he has become, how much he is a creature wholly of his time, to be read as a curiosity or by graduate students as a duty. In his Introduction, Struve, finding a tragic note already in the poem "Discovery of America" ["Otkrytie Ameriki"] (1910), asks if this is not an example of the "humble simplicity" which Èjxenbaum had called upon Gumilev to adopt in place of his loaded words and superficial exotica. While the poet has dispensed with the romantic fustian, and while he requires Columbus to express the tragic aspect of his feat in parabolic terms (a simplification, in a sense), the example—as it points to Gumilev's development—seems to me to be of the sort of complexity that we attribute to the truly tragic vision. It is precisely this greater complexity of the later Gumilev, the chink in the poet-warrior's gaudy armor, that saves him from being superannuated along with his curious ism. It is this which would best support Struve's repeated hints that Gumilev is to be regarded as a poet who was just finding his true voice when death took him.

D. L. Plank. *SEEJ*. Fall, 1966, p. 338

ILF, ILYA (1897–1937) and
PETROV, YEVGENI (1903–1942)

More than the plot, it is the satirical depiction of various negative aspects of Soviet reality that makes *The Little Golden Calf* [*Zolotoi telyonok*] significant—inefficiency, bureaucracy, peculation, petty graft, nepotism, hypocrisy, toadying, cant.

Clearly, Anatole Lunacharsky is altogether wrong when in his Introduction he assures us that "Ilf and Petrov are very gay people . . . not baffled by the sordidness of life." Wrong, too, are the American publishers when they refer to *The Little Golden Calf* as "the book that's too funny to be published in Russia." Under their mask of gayety, superficiality and innocuous buffoonery, Ilf and Petrov have written a very serious book. The authors aim to hit, and hit hard, at the most vulnerable spots. Theirs is more than Bolshevik self-criticism. In places they challenge the basic principles of collectivism and the communist state, a thing the Bolsheviks, who have no pretensions to liberalism, have always frankly refused to tolerate. Certainly, in declining to publish this book, the Soviet authorities were more consistent than was Lunacharsky in recommending it. Yet it may be plausibly suggested that in matters as delicate as creative art consistency is not necessarily the greatest of virtues, especially when it threatens to, and often actually does, degenerate into the application of mechanical formulas. In matters of art, the victorious workers, sustained by their faith in the inspiring and cleansing power of the proletarian revolution, can certainly afford to be more or less indulgent.

Joshua Kunitz. *NR*. Jan. 11, 1933, p. 250

A period of transition invites humor and satire. The Russian revolution has produced a few first-rate writers with an eye for the funny and the vicious in a social order engaged in destroying the old and establishing new human relations. It is safe to predict that the writers in whom robust humor prevails over obvious satire will survive the teeth of time and the passing of the issues involved. Ilf and Petrov are a case in point. Their two novels [*Dvenadtsat stulev* (*The Twelve Chairs*) and *The Little Golden Calf*] are in constant demand, even though the conditions described there have long ceased to be timely. Readers the world over and for ages to come will follow with delight the adventures of that beloved rogue, Oscar Bender, even though his operations are decidedly illegal. Ilf and Petrov are endowed with the divine gift of laughter, which mankind has never been capable of resisting. Is there propaganda?—comes the fearful query of old maids. To be sure! When you close, reluctantly, the story, you cannot help coming to the conclusion that life in the Soviet Union discourages picaresque adventures of Bender's brand, since it offers no outlet for money as a power. The loneliness of a money-seeker and owner, in the midst of a people drunk with the adventure of building a new life, becomes toward the end of the story pathetic. The pathos of this message is quite unobtrusive, however. Hearty laughter over human foibles drowns all other voices.

Alexander Kaun. *BA*. Summer, 1936, p. 362

Readers of *Diamonds to Sit On* [*The Twelve Chairs*] and [*The Little*] *Golden Calf* can hardly imagine that these smoothly written books that are read with breathless interest are the product of long, stubborn and painstaking labour. The writer's labour may be likened to the construction of a railway—just as the speed of the train depends on the care with which the roadbed is made, the ties and rails laid, so the reaction of the reader, his absorption in the book depends on the thoroughness of the plot, the careful choice of words, the ability to discard the superfluous and retain the important. The more polished each line of a short story or book is, the swifter and more spontaneous is the reader's reaction.

Ilf and Petrov knew this, and that is why their books are a great delight to both adults and children the world over.

Will their books live long? Who knows! Humanity may advance so rapidly within the next few years that stories about the trivial doings of money grabbers, blockheads and swindlers, stories about petty creatures who sacrifice to their one passion "to live better," the possibility "to be better," will lose their significance. Already now a good deal about what Ilf and Petrov wrote has ceased to exist in the Soviet Union and much of it has already undergone a cardinal change. But what matter is it if reality has changed, why should that rob their books of their charm?

Georgi Munblit. *SL*. July, 1947, p. 72

To young people with a poor knowledge of Soviet literary history, the late Ilf and Petrov appear as do some monuments, with everything melting together and coated with jubilee bronze—the searching of youth and the gaining of maturity. But we "elders" remember how Ilf and Petrov began their creative journey. We know how complex and winding this path was. It should not be forgotten that Petrov and, particularly, Ilf, like many other members of the Soviet literary intelligentsia, did not arrive at an immediate understanding of the path of development of Soviet society and of the tasks of Soviet writers.

We still remember how the contemporary reader received the first novels of Ilf and Petrov, *The Twelve Chairs* and *The Little Golden Calf.* Even then, readers, our Soviet press, and we ourselves—writers—considered the authors to be little more than the run-of-the-mill person in their novels and, like much of their humor, empty and without principle—humor for humor's sake. Even then, the perspectives in these novels appeared biased, the proportions unbalanced, the power and significance of the Nepman* element exaggerated, and the ordinary mass of Soviet white-collar workers incorrectly pictured. Even then, the central figure of both novels provoked objections—the figure of Ostap Bender, the "sympathetic swindler," in whom the lumpenproletarian of Odessa, the manipulator, the parasite were romanticized and, what is worse from the point of view of the normal Soviet man, rendered poetic. Briefly, new editions, thanks to our crude blundering, are at this very moment doing considerable harm. I have been told there are still young people for whom the ideal hero, not astonishingly, remains Ostap Bender. Obviously, considering the upbringing of these young people, Ostap Bender occupies what for him is an entirely unlikely place. I feel sorry for these poor young people! Happily, such worshipers of Ostap Bender are nevertheless isolated.

Boris Gorbatov. *Novy mir.* Oct., 1949, pp. 215–16†

The hero of *The Twelve Chairs* (and also, it might be added, of *The Little Golden Calf*) is Ostap Bender, "the smooth operator," a resourceful rogue and confidence man. Unlike the nobleman Vorobyaninov and the priest Vostrikov, Bender is not a representative of the *ancien regime.* Only twenty-odd years old, he does not even remember prerevolutionary Russia: at the first meeting of the "Alliance of the Sword and the Plowshare" Bender has some difficulty playing the role of a tsarist officer. Ostap Bender is a Soviet crook, born of Soviet conditions and quite willing to coexist with the Soviet system to which he has no ideological or even economic objections. Ostap Bender's inimitable slangy Russian is heavily spiced with clichés of the Communist jargon. Bender knows the vulnerabilities of Soviet state functionaries and exploits them for his own purposes. He also knows that the Soviet Man is not very different from the Capitalist Man—that he is just as greedy, lazy, snobbish, cowardly, and gullible—and uses these weaknesses to his, Ostap Bender's, advantage. And yet, in spite of Ostap Bender's dishonesty and lack of scruples, we somehow get to like him. Bender is gay, carefree, and clever, and when we

* A derogatory term for private enterpreneurs during the period of partially restored private enterprise, the so-called New Economic Policy (NEP), 1921–28.—Ed.

see him matching his wits with those of Soviet bureaucrats, we hope that he wins.

In the end Ostap Bender and his accomplices lose; yet, strangely enough, the end of the novel seems forced, much like the cliché happy ending of a mediocre Hollywood film. One must understand, however, that even in the comparatively "liberal" 1920's it was difficult for a Soviet author not to supply a happy *Soviet* ending to a book otherwise as aloof from Soviet ideology as *The Twelve Chairs*.

Maurice Friedberg. Introduction to Ilf & Petrov, *The Twelve Chairs* (New York, Random House, 1961), p. xi

At the end of *The Twelve Chairs*, after the twelfth chair has been found with the jewels in it, Bender is killed by Vorobyaninov. But three years later the authors resurrected him, as Rabelais did Epistemon, and sent him out on a new plot for a million rubles. *The Golden Calf* is a sharper and broader book than *The Twelve Chairs*. In the first, Bender is funny, harmless, and bright. Like Chaplin's little guy, he is sympathetic. But he ends up in the second story out on his ear; that is, he gets the cash but loses his adventuresome role. The workaday world passes him by. He no longer fits. He tries to flee. He is turned back; he is unmasked. The joke is over.

The two novels use the devices of comedy with bright success. Like all great comedians, Ilf and Petrov can draw a character with few motions: "Her sagging bosom flopped languidly in her re-dyed blouse." Bender is tagged with the phrase, "The key to the apartment where the money is." The young poetaster Lyapis ("silver nitrate") is addressed as Lyapsus ("a blunder"). In the Columbus Theater, sound effects are by "Galkin, Palkin, Malkin, Chalkin, and Zalkind."

F. D. Reeve. *HdR*. Winter, 1963–64, pp. 614–15

Soon a new notebook would appear. Ilf left many notebooks. Some of them are only half filled with notes, some only a third, a few have only two or three pages written on, the rest are empty or covered with drawings.

In going through them, we found observations relating to his trip to Central Asia in 1925. He was very exacting in matters literary. A writer, he insisted, should be exact, should know how to select observations, striking words, phrases, and names for professional use. His own notes consist of tales told by people he happened to come in contact with on his trips, descriptions of scenes glimpsed through train windows, the colour of the sky or the sea, the form of a tree or an animal. They comprise what we might call the writer's "kitchen." Later on it became our habit to draw up a list of all sorts of observations, themes and ideas before we began writing the book in hand. I have already said that in most cases it is impossible to say which of us contributed what. But Ilf made a habit of using things from his notebooks and insisted that I do the same.

During our last trip to America we bought a typewriter. Ilf was delighted with it. The very first evening he sat down to type out his diary (we were in New York) and made a resolution to do so every day. But we were so exhausted by our many activities that we had neither time nor strength to write diaries.

When we got back to Moscow Ilf was already mortally ill, but he began writing down his observations systematically, not in the form of a diary, but as brief notes. During the last year of his life he wrote about forty pages of notes. In my opinion this, his last, work, is not simply his "kitchen"; it is an outstanding literary effort.

Evgeni Petrov. SL. March, 1967, pp. 162–63

IVANOV, VSEVOLOD (1895–1963)

Ivanov's approach to the muzhik closely resembles those of Gorki, Chekhov, and Bunin. Nonetheless, we must not get carried away by such comparisons for the simple reason that, after all, Ivanov has his own opinion of the muzhiks. By some peculiar warmth, humaneness, and soft, caressing light, he succeeded in depicting the rough, fierce muzhiks with good-naturedness and humor. That is why his partisans do not look like beasts lacking "the image and likeness of God," as they do in Bunin, but like real, suffering, joyful, hungry, and thirsty people. [1922]

A. K. Voronski. Literaturno-kriticheskie stati
(Moscow, Sovetski pisatel, 1963), p. 141[†]

[Ivanov's] stories are distinguished by two essential characteristics: a truthful psychological wholeness and an artistic freshness. Ivanov is not a chance or detached onlooker, and there is no unnecessary tinting in his picture of the revolution. His revolutionary partisanism does not stand on heroic stilts. The peasants struggle for real land to work, for a peaceful and human working life, and for the right to build this life, and not for "great, abstract principles." In the end they go to war because, as a whole, they do not want to fight. Thus the struggle and heroism of Ivanov's partisans is entirely unheroic. . . .

This psychological truthfulness gives Ivanov's heroes an accessibility, a simplicity, and a tangible directness; and his broad outlook gives a rich gallery of types, from the contractor-owner (Yemolin) and the peasant truth seekers (Kallistrat Yefimych and the priest Isodor) to the communist leaders of the partisan movement (Nikitin and Peklevanov).

The artistic images in Ivanov are always fresh and new, expanding the limits of everyday perception. . . . This sensation of freshness also introduces new words—a provincial (Siberian) language, seldom encountered in the city—which unwittingly distract attention and characteristically shade and accentuate a scene.

This *unnecessary* abundance of new and unfamiliar words loses its effect, tires, and makes understanding difficult. Precisely such a change in images will often be incomprehensible. . . . But the main shortcoming is *the lack of a coherent subject.* It is usual in a story for several equally important characters and events to move simultaneously. Attached to this are a great number of accessory scenes so clearly delineated, however, that they begin to assume an independent aspect. This makes reading Ivanov's work burdensome. One's attention cannot encompass such vast and manifold material, such a great number of images, scenes, and episodes.

I. Mashbits-Verov. *Novy mir.* May, 1925, p. 153†

[*Pokhozhdenia fakira* (*The Adventures of a Fakir*)] is part of a fictionalized autobiography. The author's life has been so abundantly adventurous that a plain account of it sounds like fiction, though it is not fictitious. This volume ends on the eve of the World War, and sums up Ivanov's adolescent quests after magic power and control of self and nature. The drab quality of provincial Siberia assumes a fantastic hue under his pen. The foreign reader may wonder indeed, about the probability of such a picture of unrelieved pettiness interwoven with pathology. One recalls, however, that provincial Russia does border on the improbable, when depicted by such deep realists as Gogol, Sologub, or Bunin. Vsevolod Ivanov is such a realist. He is also a humorist, and he does not mind laughing at his own expense. From the first line he makes us aware of his inherited and congenital weakness, "vanity," as he defines the Ivanov family trait of trying to be, or at least to appear, different. All of them, from grandfather down to Vsevolod, refuse to live as mere Ivanovs—the equivalent of the English Jones or Johnson. They prefer the illusory world of their own weave. Actually Vsevolod is a ragged errand-boy or compositor, but he escapes from the dreary environment into make-believe. A Spanish cape, a mask, a dagger—and he holds up a fat merchant and frightens into "religion" his hedonistic Gargantuan aunt. Under the name of Ben Ali Bey he swallows swords, sticks hatpins into his chest and cheeks, and desperately attempts the enchanted life of a Fakir, with India as his ultima Thule. It is the mingling of the actual and fantastic that makes *The Adventures of a Fakir* such grotesque realism.

Alexander Kaun. *BA*. Spring, 1936, pp. 175–76

In the novel *Golubye peski* (*Skyblue Sands*, 1923) we find all the characteristics of Ivanov's early work: the spicy, ornamental language, full of dialecticisms; the jerky narrative, interspersed with lyrical refrains; the animistic attitude toward nature, which is made to participate in human joys and sorrows; the obvious influence of Russian folklore; the stress on the cruel, "bestial" aspect of the Revolution, its "blood and sweat"; and the utter detachment with which most horrible things are related. . . .

Shklovsky has pointed out that Ivanov's story may appear at first trite, that it reminds one of some stories by Bret Harte or Leonid Andreyev or Gorky, but that at the end Ivanov gives it a most unexpected and original twist. It was this *ostranenie* ("making strange"), of which Shklovsky regarded Tolstoy such a superb master, that the Serapions learned from Shklovsky to value as one of the most effective weapons in a writer's arsenal, whether it be in the plot, in description, or in style. In all their early work they were deliberately aiming at this effect of "strangeness" and "freshness," and here there was no difference between the "Westerners," like Luntz and Kaverin, and the "Russians," like Ivanov and Nikitin. In fact, no one sought more these "strange" effects than the last two.

The two novels of Ivanov (*Colored Winds* [*Tsvetnye vetra*] and *Sky-blue Sands*) are novels in name only: they are shapeless, without plot, and full of "ornamental" writing and picturesque local coloring (Siberia, Mongolia)—in fact typical products of the Pilnyak school, but devoid of Pilnyak's intellectualism and free of his historico-philosophical quests. Ivanov is much more genuinely primitive—he has a true pantheistic sense of nature and of man's fusion with it. He brings out forcibly the meaninglessness and aimlessness of life and of human behavior, emphasizing its obscure, inexplicable mainsprings. Characteristic of him is a combination of an instinctive zest for life with a fundamental pessimism. This imparts a somber note to his writings. Like all the Serapions, he is fond of unexpected situations and contrasts, of exoticism, and is given to overnaturalistic descriptions. Life, as Ivanov sees it, is cruel and senseless, and man, a toy manipulated by dark and blind forces. "A man's soul is like a bear's: it don't see its own path," says Ivanov in one of his stories.

Gleb Struve. *Soviet Russian Literature 1917–1950*
(Norman, Okla., University of Oklahoma Press, 1951),
pp. 60–61

Vsevolod Ivanov became the recognized poet of the partisans after the first story written about them. The peculiarity of his unusual talent appeared never again so powerfully as in the partisan stories. In these stories the merciless truth of life foamed, vying with the irrepressible flight of imagination; and the word, which seemed a miracle to the poet, illuminated the foam in many colors. His books are like brewing beer.

Ivanov is a fantast above anything else. Here is his grain, his "little raisin" (as Lev Tolstoi called it). But side by side with turbulent imagination, with the play of dream, with the animation of nature, there lives in Ivanov's books the subtle knowledge of man, with the pains of searching and the limitless joy of discovering and of triumphing. He made the rocks sing, enlivened the aromas, made the winds blossom. For him there was no "dead nature." Furthermore, there were no lifeless people for him. Even the dead are called to life in his books, as his dead partisans were called to life and to fight.

The favorite words of Vsevolod are joy, eternity, and wind.

He was an indefatigable traveler on earth, a drifter who loved the new and undiscovered in the world, the unknown in man.

> Konstantin Fedin. *Literaturnaya gazeta.*
> Aug. 17, 1963, p. 3[†]

His vision angles toward the lower strata of society and comes to rest upon those people who have only the vaguest class ties (like artisans), or who have become *déclassés* altogether (like sailors, circus entertainers, or wanderers). Such people have the greatest mobility; and it is mobility that interests Ivanov. He introduced a new type into Soviet literature: the man who is pulled out of the faceless masses by war, steps over the shards of the old society, and harnesses his energies to the surge of events —a man like Seleznev (*The Guerrillas* [*Partizany*]), the rich peasant become guerrilla leader; or Zapus, the sailor turned revolutionary (*Azure Sands*); or Vershinin, the fisherman converted into Red commander (*Armored Train 14–69* [*Bronepoezd 14–69*]). These were the first heroes of the new literature, the earliest figures in that mythology of Revolution which Soviet writers, in the absence of living models, have been called upon to create. . . . For him, men are hopelessly fragmented creatures, lacking memory, incapable of learning from experiences, and unable to exercise any control over events; they therefore act illogically, irrationally, and inconsistently. If sheer accident appears to play a decisive role in their lives, that is because each new situation presents them with a totally unexpected set of requirements, to which they must hastily adjust or perish. War makes the point brutally clear; perhaps that is why it is Ivanov's most effective setting. Men's only sense of reality, even of existence, hangs on their fidelity to circumstances moment by moment. They are at the beck of necessity.

> Robert A. Maguire. *Red Virgin Soil* (Princeton, N J.,
> Princeton University Press, 1968), pp. 130, 138

IVANOV, VYACHESLAV (1866–1949)

I have said that the images given by Vyacheslav Ivanov are unreal. Actually, they are so complete, all of their parts are so uniformly and exactingly sharp, that the attention of the reader, not being strong enough to encompass the whole, is arrested by particular details, and he can only vaguely guess about the remainder. This causes a feeling of dissatisfaction that forces one to reread the already well-known verses.

Ivanov uses language more like a philologist than a poet. For him, all words are equal, all expressions are good. He has no secret classification dividing words into "his" or "not his," nor does he have deep and often inexplicable sympathies and antipathies. He does not care to know either their age or their origin. For him they are the same as images—simply the clothing for ideas. But his ever-tense thoughts and the distinct knowledge of what he wants to say make the selection of his words so amazingly varied that we are correct to speak of Ivanov's language as being distinct from the language of other poets.

Ivanov has complete control of his verse; it seems as if there is not one complex technique he is unaware of. But technique is not his aid or golden happiness; it is only a means. It is not the verse that inspires Ivanov; on the contrary, it is he who inspires his own verse. This is why he enjoys writing sonnets and *ghazals*, those difficult but important and consummate verses.

Nikolai Gumilyov. *Apollon*. 7, 1911, p. 74[†]

Because Vyacheslav Ivanov was more of a populist, he is more comprehensible than any other Russian symbolist. A considerable part of the charm in his work depends on our philological ignorance. The noise of words and the powerful sound of the bell of native speech, floating and waiting for its turn, rings more clearly in Ivanov than in the other symbolists. A feeling for the past as well as for the future unites him with Khlebnikov. Ivanov's archaism derives not from a choice of themes but from an incapability of thinking relevantly, that is, in step with the time. His Hellenic verse was not written after or with his Greek verse but before it. Not for a minute does he forget his native idiom.

Osip Mandelshtam. *Russkoe iskusstvo.*
Jan., 1923, p. 79[†]

Cor Ardens is the high-water mark of the ornate style in Russian poetry. His verse is saturated with beauty and expressiveness; it is all aglow with jewels and precious metals, it is like a rich Byzantine garment. "Byzantine" and "Alexandrian" are two very suitable epithets for his poetry, for it is all full of the product of past ages, very scholarly, conscious, and quite unspontaneous. Ivanov is the nearest approach in Russian poetry to the conscious and studied splendours of Milton. In his verse every image, every word, every sound, every cadence are part of one admirable planned whole. Everything is carefully weighed and used with elaborate discrimination to the best effect. His language is archaic, and he likes to introduce

Greek idioms. This is in the great tradition of ecclesiastic Russian and adds powerfully to the majesty of his numbers. Most of his poems are metaphysical; he has also written many love lyrics and political poems, but love and politics are always treated *sub specie æternitatis*. His poetry is of course difficult, and hardly accessible to the man in the street, but, for those who can move in his sphere of ideas, there is in his heady and spiced wine an attractively troubling flavour. In his magnificence and his scholarship is hidden the sting of a refined and ecstatic sensuality—the sting of Astarte—rather than that of Dionysos. His poetry may be exclusive, Alexandrian, derivative (in so far as our culture is derivative), but that it is genuine, perhaps great poetry, there can be no doubt. The only objection that can be advanced against it is that it is too much of a good thing.

D. S. Mirsky. *Contemporary Russian Literature*
(New York, Knopf, 1926), pp. 207–8

In Ivanov's conversion to Catholicism one senses the drama of the symbolist mentality and a parallel with Biely's attempt to find an all-explaining way of life first in symbolism, then in Neo-Kantian philosophy, and finally in anthroposophy. Basically yearning to believe in the existence of another world and yet restrained by intellect from doing so, both Biely and Ivanov had sought in symbolist art a *Weltanschauung* that would satisfy their inner craving. Yet symbolism erected no dogmas to uphold its theories. Its intellectual freedom left too much room for doubt and questioning, and therefore failed to overcome the uprootedness of a romantic mentality—the uprootedness which plagued the "children of the lost generation"; children who could not accept the world as their age depicted it, who had to believe in the existence of another world, and yet found themselves organically unable to do so. Disillusioned in his expectations of symbolism, Biely had turned to the dogmatic rationalized mysticism of anthroposophy, which closely paralleled the symbolist ideas, and apparently accepted its main principles. Biely's nature demanded rational explanations for everything, and in anthroposophy, therefore, found a measure of temporary satisfaction. Ivanov, on the other hand, was organically more of a mystic than Biely. Failing to find a satisfactory answer to his questions, Ivanov submitted to the dogmas of the Catholic church like Verlaine, and others, before him. Neither Biely nor Ivanov gave up believing that this world was only a shadow and an echo of another world. But for support of this basic belief Biely was obliged to turn to the rational dogmas of anthroposophy and Ivanov to the authoritarian dogmas of the Roman church.

Oleg Maslenikov. *The Frenzied Poets* (Berkeley, Calif.,
University of California Press, 1952), p. 216

Ivanov bases his aesthetics entirely upon the irrational in art and consequently embarks upon one of the most difficult paths possible. By pro-
ceeding from the concrete and the visible to the "dark areas of essences,"
Ivanov attempts to avoid "associative symbolism," the "stimuli of impressionism," by means of a "stronger and more courageous belief in the
reality of not only the imagined apparitions."

In contrast to "sickly" impressionism, Ivanov places above all the
classical ideal of beauty. His postulates are "compactness and unity of
form, harmony and restraint, simplicity and directness." Decadence, on
the other hand, he characterizes as a short interlude of aestheticism.
Beyond that, he calls it nihilistic in its view of the world, eclectic in its
tastes, sickly in its psychology.

In the demand for greater clarity, Ivanov is in accord with the young
Acmeists and "clearists" (those seeking clarity, among others, Gumilyov,
Gorodetski, and Kuzmin), who voiced their opinions in the *Apollon*. In
the atmosphere of the Petersburg "Tower" (the residence of Ivanov),
these young poets had come strongly under the influence of Ivanov. However, they very soon separated from the master, and with good justification. Despite all his reservations against some symbolists who seek only
effects, Ivanov is entirely bound up with decadence. His old-Slavic,
stylized verses, in their entire mythological ornamentations, were incapable of bringing symbolism upon a new path.

Basically, Ivanov's temperament is completely opposed to classicism.
Even the reverence he accords to the spirit of Goethe cannot cover up this
fact. Ivanov's prediction of a new "organic epoch" of culture is not the
prerequisite of a new classicism; rather, Ivanov sees here (entirely in the
steps of Nietzsche) the return to the organic in the integration of the
"barbaric," in the victory over the "theoretic persons of the criticizing
epoch," in the return to pre-Socratic philosophy.

For Ivanov, symbolistic art is conceivable only in the medium of
romanticism or in the medium of prophecy. Only specifically in these does
art seem (for him) to be sufficiently protected from being "compact in and
of itself, composed, and, in this sense, static." According to Ivanov, art
is not a phenomenon that is capable of existing in itself; art needs mystic
integration in the movement *ab exterioribus ad interiora*.

> Johannes Holthusen. *Studien zur Ästhetik und*
> *Poetik des russischen Symbolismus* (Göttingen,
> Vandenhoeck & Ruprecht, 1957), pp. 44–45†

In spite of the fact that both Ivanov and Herschensohn are, as the former
accuses the latter of being, two "monologists," in spite of the fact that
they stand, as Herschensohn says, "at the opposite ends of a diagonal not
only in our room, but also in the spiritual world," a dialogue between

them is, up to a certain point, still natural and possible, owing to their common decadent background. It is decadent to believe that the only choice left to man lies between cultural traditionalism and religious conservatism on one hand, and revolutionary messianism on the other. It is a symptom of decadent psychology to feel that man's fate at this stage in history offers no alternative but being, as Herschensohn and Ivanov equally are, prisoners in a kind of Platonic cave, which resembles more than they think the corners of those squalid St. Petersburg flats where Dostoevski's heroes—or better, victims—live, suffer, and die. Both in their room and in their minds, like Dostoevski's "underground man," Ivanov and Herschensohn are cornered, as were their younger brothers of the lost generation after the First World War, as are we, too, members of another lost generation, unstable and unsafe survivors of so many social and political floods. Their discarded master, Nietzsche, was more right than they when he prophesied the advent, in a not too distant future, of what he cynically calls "war's classical age." We are even more oppressed and cornered than they are, because we feel more remorse for the past and more fears for the future of man.

This is why we have no right to dismiss either one of them with a curt *medice cura te ipse*. And yet we cannot afford to share the traditional faith, the metaphysical beliefs, the pre-established harmony of Ivanov; nor are we able to indulge in Herschensohn's desire to merge with the present, with those physical bodies which are called parties or masses, or even less, with that mystical body which is called revolution, or what you will. The Western reader is likely to prefer Ivanov's position, or at least to be won over by the greater consistency of his stand. Ivanov has the more powerful intellect of the two, and also the more virile and logical mind, able to avoid the contradictions, paradoxes, and anticlimaxes of the position of Herschensohn—which is that of a man of culture who, by denying it, hopes to save his soul. And if I think that Herschensohn's testimonial is the more important and poignant of the two, it is merely because his illusion is candid and fresh, and also because we have been lucky or unlucky enough to see it shattered before our own eyes.

Renato Poggioli. *The Phoenix and the Spider*
(Cambridge, Mass., Harvard University Press, 1957),
pp. 224–25

Ivanov's threefold concern with the tragic, the mythic, and the mystical suggests his conception of poetry. Poetry is for him essentially a religious search, and he views the poet as, if not a priest, at least an initiate. Ivanov himself, however, was not only a poet, but also a scholar: a seeker of knowledge, as well as of wisdom. This means that he was as attracted by the quaintness and complexity of his own lore as by the truth hidden within it. Thus, like every connoisseur or specialist, he often became a pedant, flaunting his learning and showing off his erudition. He did so by supplying his poems with exegetical notes and bibliographical references, a critical apparatus better suited for a philological paper, as if he were afraid that the complexity of his allusions would escape not only the understanding, but even the attention, of his reader.

Poetry of this kind naturally requires a special idiom. Ivanov's verse may be rightly considered the highest and most extreme manifestation in the history of Russian poetry of both "poetic diction" and "grand style." The very fact that Ivanov is the most typical Russian representative of a type of poetic language which in other literatures is mainly a Renaissance or post-Renaissance phenomenon is a proof of the uniqueness of the development of Russian poetry. Maurice Baring, limiting his consideration to the nineteenth century, and focusing his attention on Pushkin, compared Russian to Greek lyrical poetry, failing to realize that at least in part such eighteenth-century poets as Lomonosov and Derzhavin had indulged in neoclassical fashions and pseudoclassical mannerisms. Yet it is true that, in its main traditions, Russian poetry follows the Wordsworthian ideal of "common speech"; and it is equally true that only such a modern poet as Ivanov fulfills there the task accomplished in other traditions by such figures as Malherbe or Milton. Despite the fact that he was a Greek scholar by trade, Ivanov represents within the poetry of Russia the same tendency that in English literature is often defined by such epithets as "Latinate" and "Italianate." It is not merely coincidental that Lev Shestov gave Ivanov (not without irony) an appellative which was originally given to a great figure of the Italian Renaissance, and called him "Vjacheslav the Magnificent."

Renato Poggioli. *The Poets of Russia* (Cambridge, Mass., Harvard University Press, 1960), pp. 166–67

KATAYEV, VALENTIN (1897–   )

Rastratchiki [*The Embezzlers*] is a mixture of farce, satire and realism. Its theme is the ordinary life of ordinary people in contemporary Russia. . . . Russian fatalism asserts itself—there is nothing [for the characters] to do but accept their fate and go on. Fate has made them criminals against their will; criminals they must be. The indeterminate Russian psychology which is nearly always so surprising and puzzling to a Western European is skillfully presented in this novel. Once again one feels, as so often with Russian novels, that the calamity is harrowing without being tragic, that the "comic relief" is cynical and cruel, and gives none of the release of laughter. Once more the old question, "Who can be happy in Russia?" lugubriously receives the answer, "Nobody." And yet there is a sort of acrid vigour and intensity of life which holds the attention and compels one to read on and to endure this gloom.

TLS. Jan. 3, 1929, p. 10

Valentine Kataev . . . is writing a story of fighting men in a new country. One's first impression of *Time, Forward!* [*Vremya, vperyod!*] is what an easy time the author is having. Kataev is chronicling part of a victory: his technique grows directly out of his story, and he seems to require no philosophy whatever, not even the official Marxianism of his country. His motive for writing is stated briefly: "Let not a single trifle, not even the smallest detail, of our inimitable, heroic days of the first Five Year Plan be forgotten!" And so he chooses one detail of the Plan—the attempt of Ishchenko's brigade at Magnitogorsk to beat the world's record for pouring concrete.

At Kharkov, in the far Ukraine, the workers had poured 306 mixtures in a single eight-hour shift. Can Magnitogorsk make a better showing? All the energies of the people in the book are concentrated on this single problem. There is a host of characters—so many of them, indeed, that the author has to identify them by simple idiosyncrasies: one of them always mispronounces a word, another wears white canvas shoes which are always getting spotted, still another doesn't get anything to eat but gumdrops from one end of the book to the other. All the characters have long confusing Russian names, but no matter—the story moves so quickly that one leaps over the names, leaps over the pages in the hasty desire to learn what is going to happen. And yet what happens is simple;

it can be summarized in a row of figures: Kharkov, 306 mixtures. Kuznetsk, the same day, 402 mixtures (tempos are rising all over the Soviet Union). Ishchenko's brigade at Magnitogorsk, 429 mixtures, breaking the record. And then, next morning at the Chelyaba tractor plant, 504.

But what is the role of destiny in all this? One might say that destiny, for Valentine Kataev, is the Five Year Plan, but that isn't the final answer: after all the Five Year Plan was outlined by men and altered by other men and carried out by still others, some of them wearing white canvas shoes and others munching gumdrops. This Russian novel is somehow more human than the three from Central Europe. From it one gets the idea that in the future destiny may cease to be mysterious fate or the mob in revolt or blind economics—that under communism destiny is men.

Malcolm Cowley. NR. Dec. 20, 1933, p. 173

Katayev's *Vremya, vperyod!* (*Forward, Oh Time!*) is a more genuine Five-Year Plan novel, concerned primarily with production processes, and not with social and individual psychology. Instead of inventing a fictitious setting, Katayev described one of the real industrial projects, the gigantic coke-chemical combine at Magnitogorsk. This element of reality was introduced deliberately—Katayev even called his novel "a chronicle." Where in Pilnyak's *Volga* the wall newspaper was merely a literary trick (similar to those which the *avant-garde* painters before World War I used when they introduced into their pictures three-dimensional objects), the insertion by Katayev of a long article from one of the Soviet papers about the production of high-grade concrete has a different function, and the article is in all probability authentic. Generally speaking, purely technical matter plays a large part in Katayev's novel.

Forward, Oh Time! differs also from Pilnyak's and Leonov's novels in that it is imbued with real enthusiasm for Socialist reconstruction, with that somewhat naïve Americanism, that cult of machinery bordering on fetichism which was characteristic of Russian Communism at the time. While Pilnyak and Leonov were concerned primarily with human beings and their intellectual and emotional problems, in Katayev's novel purely technical problems play the major part in the plot. . . .

The whole novel, with its quick cinematographic tempo, its rapidly shifting scenes, bears traces of the influence of John Dos Passos, who at the time enjoyed great popularity in the Soviet Union and was regarded as a revolutionary, not only ideologically, but also technically speaking. The saboteurs, who had become almost a fixture in the Five-Year Plan literature, are absent from Katayev's novel, and this in itself is a refreshing feature. By comparison with Pilnyak and Leonov, the general tendency of Katayev's theme is much more optimistic. There is no hint of the sharp cleavage between the old and the new in the Soviet Union.

Gleb Struve. *Soviet Russian Literature 1917–1950*
(Norman, Okla., University of Oklahoma Press, 1951),
pp. 232–33

[In *Pochti dnevnik* (Almost a Diary)] Kataev consistently employs the Soviet technique of rewriting history to conform with currently fashionable ideological pronouncements, a methodology which accounts for his failure to discuss some important historical landmarks and for his obvious "retouching" of the historical facts. . . .

The author's claims that he and his State are the true champions of democracy are not surprising to Western readers. Neither is it surprising that he is extremely critical of the English, Americans, and other nations, nor that he accuses them of the very sins committed by the Soviet Union. Kataev, perhaps with justice, is especially hard on the Germans, but often overdoes it. . . .

Počti dnevnik still presents certain interest as a socio-political document. Its shortcomings are in the ideological extravaganzas, the failure to contribute anything original or sincere to a better understanding of the Soviet Union. The book's narrow conformity does not reflect its author's maturity either as a creative artist or a man.

It is with regret that we feel compelled to say that Kataev's truisms, indiscriminate Soviet patriotism, "juggling" with historical facts, and literary style only merit that description which should be termed by history as "Soviet provincialism."

Nonna D. Shaw. *BA*. Winter, 1963, pp. 96–97

Time, Forward! (1932), one of the best of the construction novels, describes the building of the huge metallurgical plant at Magnitogorsk in the Urals. The title of the book was taken from a poem by Mayakovsky, and its theme is the speeding up of time in the Soviet Union where the historical development of a century must be completed in ten years. Katayev devised techniques which convey a vivid impression of time in movement. Objects are shown always in motion: inanimate things are blown by the wind, landscapes are seen through the windows of moving trains or from an airplane circling above. Quick cinematic techniques are used to confuse ideas of space and time: old space and time concepts are made to seem inadequate to the new historical period. And the central event of the story is the successful attempt of a brigade of workmen to break the world's time record for pouring concrete.

Edward J. Brown. *Russian Literature Since the
Revolution* (New York, Crowell-Collier, 1963), p. 133

It is difficult to write about Katayev. This is partly because his latest novel *Trava zabvenya (The Grass of Oblivion)* is so complexly built, with constantly moving and shifting time, where iridescent associations change capriciously in the chain of paradoxical and colorful metaphors. It is also only partly because such figures as Bunin and Mayakovski simply appear, act, and talk, as full-fledged heroes of the story, with the author. But the main difficulty lies in determining the philosophical and lyrical moods that dominate the story. Regardless of the apparent fortuitousness, even chaos, in the choice of episodes, in the appearance of disconnected insertions, isolated meaningful sentences, historical anecdotes and digressions, there is not one word that is accidental in this novel. Into this edifice, each little stone, each little brick, is laid thoughtfully, with special care.

The work is written with such a great power that at times one is under visual hallucination, sympathizing with the author and quarreling with him. Like *Svyatoi kolodets (The Holy Well)*, *The Grass of Oblivion* signals something new in the development of Katayev the prose writer. This novelty is contained in the sharp sensation of the passing of time and in the persistent attempts to move against its flow again and again.

Oleg Mikhailov. Literaturnaya gazeta.
June 21, 1967, p. 6†

With this delightful novel [*The Holy Well*] Katayev has abandoned all the formulas of socialist realism that clearly defeated his imagination for two decades of his career. For these he has substituted what he calls "a new system of signals" to register his apprehension of the confusing and contradictory new era that followed the fierce simplicities of Stalinism. These signals take the form of metaphors, sometimes highly particular, and sometimes extended, in surreal fashion, over several hallucinating spans of space and time. The technique is cinematic, the debt to Fellini explicit. Thus the narrator experiences, in a series of flashbacks and projections, while he is under anesthesia in an operating room, a trans-Atlantic voyage, an evening spent with the late poet Ossip Mandelstam, a tour of the United States and a paradisaical after-life.

Patricia Blake. NYT. Sept. 10, 1967, p. 4

In his latest novel [*The Grass of Oblivion*]—if one may call it that—the seventy-year-old Kataev returns to his youth and to the beginning of his literary career. A mixture of fiction, reminiscences, and contemplations about various subjects, especially about the literary craft, this short work, though unlike everything Kataev has written before except *Svjatoj kolodec*, displays the trademarks that have made him one of the leading

Soviet writers: a lush but uncluttered realism, a penetrating eye and ear, and a remarkable ability to focus on the fine and significant detail. However, the most rewarding aspect of *Trava zabven'ja* is the tribute the author pays to two writers he considers to be his teachers: Bunin and Mayakovsky. . . .

The most remarkable pages in this deliberately plotless, unchronological novel deal with the portraiture of Bunin, both as a man and a writer, with the death of Kataev's father, Mayakovsky's last evening at the author's apartment before the suicide, and a visit with Bunin's widow much later in Paris and her hair-raising account of her husband's death.

Kataev's main intentions here are to write "any way he wants, regardless of anything," and to attempt to arrest time and the fading nature of one's memory. Despite his sad conclusion, inherited from Bunin, that there are some experiences no words could express, he gallantly pursues his not-so-futile effort. His crisp, at times highly lyrical prose and a deeply human understanding colored by mild irony, enable us to share some of his memories which help us to understand better such enigmatic figures as Bunin and Mayakovsky, as well as the author himself. His obsession with the past and with death in this moving, sentimental work, revealing his own main preoccupation at his venerable age of three score and ten, may signify a new, much more mature and meaningful phase in his long and illustrious career.

Vasa D. Mihailovich. BA. Autumn, 1968, pp. 613–14

Katayev is nearing seventy. Like Ehrenburg a survivor, one of those whom Stalin did not destroy. If fire is cold to one's hand it is easy to look down at such men; if not, one can only feel a sense of wonder at man's durability. He has traveled in Europe and America, is a sophisticated, soft-spoken, witty man with large sad eyes and a full head of hair not yet gray. There is nothing parochial, nothing narrowly national about his attitudes, and one of his last books, *The Holy Well*, is a lyrical quest for a lost love in which, as though by-the-way, the mysterious immortality of the idea of human freedom is a leitmotif. Sitting with him on his sunny glassed-in porch, one realizes that at seventy he has lived through the whole agony of the last half-century of Russian history and must have known terrors that reached into the bone, must have wrung rationalizations out of his own mind to justify what he saw, must have died many times. And indeed, he wrote novels which had passages of idolatry for Stalin, passages which he could excise without disturbing the rest of the text, and did so after the Death. Since then he has come forward as a strong defender of writers and liberty and has become a sort of bridge between the younger men and the regime. Perhaps it is my own narrowness, but with all the men of this generation I feel constrained, as though there are large painful areas our conversation must avoid, and yet for all I know he is ready to talk about anything.

Arthur Miller. Harper. Sept., 1969, p. 51

KAVERIN, VENYAMIN (1902–)

The chief characteristic of Mr. Kaverin's new novel [*Dva kapitana (Two Captains)*] is sheer exuberance, a boisterous good nature that romps headlong through the pages. . . . Of course this effervescence has its drawback. Kaverin literally dances upon the surface of his tale. Nothing is examined or probed, we hardly stop to become acquainted with the characters, and the story strings out and multiplies details until we are hard put to it to follow. . . . The lack of focus or emphasis anywhere in the book keeps it from having the unity it needs. Without Sanya as a recognizable constant it would have no form at all, and even Sanya cannot hold it together, being himself so volatile and unreflective a character. For this we are compensated with an atmosphere of wonderful lightness and flow, with gayety unforced and always entertaining. There is news of Russia here, of its mental climate, beyond what we can glean from among the embattled news columns.

R. L. Nathan, SR. April 4, 1942, p. 12

Veniamin Kaverin's *The Unknown Artist* [*Khudozhnik neizvesten*], published in 1931 but apparently written a couple of years earlier, attempts an oddly similar theme [to Olesha's *Envy*] and is also oracular in tone in much the same fashion. But it is, though ingeniously oblique in suggestion, a less satisfactory piece of work, more confused in design and rather more evasive in the moral it points. The doubtful place left for ethics, the romantic impulse, individual liberty and the rest in the Five-Year Plan is here apparent in the margin of the personal contest between the fond and foolish artist Archimedov and the logical saviour of society, the insufferable Shpektorov.

TLS. Aug. 16, 1947, p. 413

The Two Captains cannot be called a novel about the Arctic, the war, or the like. It is simply a novel that tells the story of human passions, gains and losses, hatred and love. Yet the personal life of the heroes is entirely coloured and permeated by their social interests.

The search for the lost Arctic expedition which engages the attention of Sanya Grigoryev, hero of the novel, to the exclusion of all else, is not simply one of the extravagances of romantic youth but a public matter.

The same applies to Pyotr Skovorodnikov's passion for painting, Zhukov's interest in guinea pigs, and so forth. Each one of these boys on growing up shows that his hobby was not simply a fad but a matter necessary and important for the whole country, even in the difficult wartime years. Enthusiasm for their calling, the enthusiasm of public interests pervades the lives of Kaverin's heroes. The person whose strength none attempts to exploit, a personality truly free, thanks to the advanced social system, devotes himself naturally and spontaneously to any given cause, and find in the *common cause* the expression of his own, individual life's work. Hence, the healthy mentality and the pure dislike of affectation, of pretentiousness, of empty and high sounding words.

Yet the simplicity of Kaverin's heroes is by no means a sign of triteness, mental immaturity, or vulgarity. The spiritual world of these young men is full and rich; they are acquainted with the full range of sentiments, emotions and imaginings of a highly-developed human individuality.

The Two Captains speak of the maturity of Soviet culture. As the new Soviet society was formed, as its moral and esthetic principles were more clearly defined, the characters embodying these principles in life were also formed. Problems of the intimate life of his heroes, the intimate relationships, are dealt with in Kaverin's novel. But in these relationships the author finds the same answers as the industrial novels of the thirties discovered in the field of labour, in the matter dealing with Socialist construction. The heroes' personal interests are of a social nature and they understand this, they never think of counterposing their interests and passions for duty. In the hour of the nation's danger, their patriotic duty naturally becomes their overwhelming passion, the supreme need of the individual to the exclusion of all else.

At the same time, the inertia of the novel forces Kaverin to portray the war only insofar as it touches upon the intimate relations of Katya, Sanya, Romashov and Tatarinov with each other. The bounds of a lyrical-intimate novel proved too narrow—in the epoch of a national cataclysm romantic themes, romantic heroes had to give way to the epic in the classic meaning of the word.

Grigory Pomerantsev. *SL*. Aug., 1947, pp. 54–55

Kaverin sees the inevitability of Arkhimedov's defeat in *The Artist Unknown*. Life mercilessly shatters the glasses of reactionary romanticism, and the splinters blind the eyes of the artist and his disciples. Arkhimedov's life is an unending chain of tragic failures. They pursue him on every page of the novel. The illusory world created by him behind the scenes of the student theater collapses with the interference of the administration. The students cast out the "teacher of morals," and puppets become Arkhimedov's only students. The woman whose child the artist has taken away throws herself out of a window. The child turns out not to be his son, and he willingly hands him over to Shpektorov. Arkhimedov is defeated once and for all. But in defeat he paints a picture of genius. He celebrates the triumph of an artist, not in living but in creating, in a higher reality, in the conquest of a lone genius. This concluding thesis of the novel illuminates anew the past life of the artist. His innumerable defeats in the scheme of everyday existence predetermine his artistic triumph. They are indispensable to the creation of a great work by the brush of an obscure artist. "It was necessary to be completely shattered in order to paint this thing": thus the author summarizes the reactionary moral substance of this novel.

This novel shows the degree of dangerous vacillation to which the artistic intelligentsia was subject at the beginning of the period of reconstruction.

The Artist Unknown, in contrast to *Prolog* [Prologue], does not convey the leanings of the bulk of the intelligentsia making the turn toward socialism but rather the attitude of a minority living under the illusion of the independent role of the intelligentsia. The theme of a "higher moral," "true," "honorable" apolitical art, for which the artist strives, expresses a resurrection of the attitudes of the defeated classes that bear malice toward the triumph of socialism.

Appeals to quit the real struggle for a new social structure and return to an art of symbols and shadows, to virtuosity with words, and to formalistic patchworking with pretensions toward half-cracked genius in the field of artistic mastery—all this underlines the bourgeois individualistic aspirations in the novel *The Artist Unknown*.

Nikolai Maslin. Novy mir. April, 1948, pp. 280–81†

During his entire creative life, Kaverin slowly but methodically moved forward, overcoming mistaken opinions on art, trying to draw close to the surrounding reality, to seize the rich material of life. Kaverin strove to be in step with his own times, overcoming his enthusiasm for detective stories; his pursuit of purposeless but sharp-witted plots and exotic life, his infatuation with the disappearing remnants of times past; his search for heroes among the people "at the bottom"; his romantization of murderers, bandits, and robbers; and his despondent psychoanalysis of people trapped, damaged, and crushed by life. Progressively, from book to book, he drew closer to contemporary reality and finally found his hero, worked out his own style, and, in *Two Captains,* was able to handle a taut subject absorbingly and truthfully and to show through the colors of reality the high traits attendant to Soviet man.

In the following novel [*Otkrytaya kniga* (*The Open Book*)], Kaverin retreated from this path, taking a step backward into the past.

We would like to believe that Kaverin, an interesting and original writer, has returned to the path of socialist realism, which he attained with such labor and from which he turned so unexpectedly. Kaverin possesses all the possibilities for overcoming his creative shortcomings.

A. Lozhechko. *Oktyabr.* March, 1950, p. 179[†]

Like *Envy*, Kaverin's novel [*The Artist Unknown*] is unusual in form. It is begun in the third person, but from the second chapter—Kaverin calls his chapters "Encounters," and, in fact, they all center round some crucial encounter—the author himself intervenes, and after that we see Arkhimedov either through his eyes or as described by those who meet him. Shpektorov is portrayed as the author's former school-fellow, and it is through him that the author meets Arkhimedov. The novel is interspersed with frankly autobiographical material, seemingly irrelevant to the story. Kaverin keeps toying with the plot and resorting to what the Formalist school calls "laying bare the device," which results in some original effects. Some of the most important conclusions about Arkhimedov are reached by the author during a performance of Dickens's *Tale of Two Cities;* and in general, the theater plays a significant part in the unfolding of Arkhimedov's story. Some important scenes are laid behind the wings of the School Youth Theater, and here the important motif of Don Quixote is introduced, thus emphasizing the unreal, romantic, quixotic, "theatrical" nature of Arkhimedov's crusade for true art.

Gleb Struve. *Soviet Russian Literature 1917–1950*
(Norman, Okla., University of Oklahoma Press,
1951), p. 111

Kaverin's [*Poiski i nadezhdy (Searches and Hopes)*] is to some extent what the Party envisaged when it encouraged bold criticism, except that it goes much further than the Party wished. Instead of brushing off a few cobwebs, Kaverin made a head-on attack on conditions in science. Science is to him a most important endeavor with great potentialities for removing pain and curing and preventing disease; he is outraged by the usurpation of institutions which he considers sacred in function and unlimited in possibility by men who thwart their aims and abuse them for ends of their own.

Some of the inconsistencies of the book may perhaps be explained by the fact that the latter parts of it were written in the freer atmosphere of the thaw, whereas the earlier parts trace back to days before a substantial relaxation had set in. At any event, while chauvinistically viewed, artificial incidents (such as those cited earlier: triumphs over foreign scientists, the remarks about American profiteering in the manufacture of penicillin) occur in the book, they are contradicted by passages toward the end in which characters who clearly speak for the author condemn the same attitudes which had been favored earlier.

Clear throughout, however, are the author's extremely dark view of the extent to which the summits of Soviet scientific institutions had been penetrated by evil men . . . his relief at the coming of de-Stalinization, and his reluctance to prophesy unequivocally that everything will come out satisfactorily in the end.

George Gibian. *Interval of Freedom* (Minneapolis, University of Minnesota Press, 1960), p. 52

I shall try to circumscribe the discussion of [*The Artist Unknown*] within two sets of problems. First, the novel develops a thematic conflict, a conflict of two distinct characters. This approach brings us to considering the destiny of a Don Quixote. Second, the story reveals, on another level, a conflict in the techniques of representation. This is the conflict between the narrator of the story and an "anti-narrator." Metaphorically speaking, the first conflict forms the warp of the representational texture. The second conflict might be compared to its woof.

The apparent theme of this novel is the cultural lag in the Soviet society of the late twenties and early thirties in connection with the industrialization of the USSR. Will the quality of human values keep pace with the rapid advances in technology? The author dramatizes this question by presenting a philosophical confrontation between the two main characters and opponents: Špektorov, an engineer, and Arximedov, an artist. Both are earnestly dedicated to the welfare of the Soviet society. . . .

Insofar as the thematic level of the novel is concerned, Špektorov and Arximedov, the "two minds," confront each other in ideological conflict. Both fail to measure up to their original expectations. A child and a woman add to this ideological conflict an intensely human, emotional dimension. All this constitutes the "what" of the representation, its "external" dynamics.

On the level of the techniques of representation, another conflict sets in competition with each other the narrator and the "anti-narrator." This conflict involves the "how" of the representation, its "internal" dynamics. Each of them has his own way of viewing and understanding the struggle between Špektorov and Arximedov. Depending on who does the viewing, the representation oscillates between objectivity and distortion, between circumstantial truth and phantasmagoria. The interest of the story lies in this simultaneous conflict both on the thematic level and on the level of the techniques of representation.

Hongor Oulanoff. *SEEJ*. Winter, 1966, pp. 389, 399

KAZAKOV, YURI (1927–   )

Kazakov never stoops to such harping on "morality," but for all that there are amazingly tasteless spots in some of his stories. An example is his short story about a husband and wife on the verge of divorce, who make up on a foggy night; though otherwise excellent, the story ends on an utterly false and saccharine note ("he wanted to see the stars"). On occasion Kazakov turns to social criticism. In the short story, "V gorod" ("Going to Town"), he portrays the almost serf-like position of a collective farmer who is rebuffed when he asks his *kolkhoz* chairman for a passport to move into town. But such themes are at best of minor importance for Kazakov, and they never dominate his stories. In "Going to Town," for instance, he does not hesitate to depict the victim of social injustice as a negative and cruel character.

David Burg. *PC*. Sept.–Oct., 1962, p. 42

There are writers with an individuality so strongly marked that anything to which they have set their hand proclaims their authorship. Yurii Kazakov belongs to this category. His stories could not be mistaken for those of any other author living in Russia today. It is neither any single element of plot, character or setting, nor any one formal, artistic device, which creates the special aura of his stories, but rather a combination of several of them. . . . Kazakov does favour certain kinds of character and motif, which he describes in his own manner, but his stories differ from those of other authors who in some regard resemble him, by being suffused with strong emotion. His characters' reactions to their surroundings are unusually highly charged with feeling. Kazakov is a subtle author; often he leaves his stories without a crisp conclusion. He is a master of the question unanswered, the suggestion allowed to remain equivocal. But above all, his special talent is the gift of conveying, with understatement and restraint, in musical, poetic language, the sense of an intense, private, emotional commitment.

George Gibian. Introduction to Yuri Kazakov, *Selected Short Stories* (Oxford, Pergamon Press, 1963), p. x

The theme in Kazakov's constant search as a writer is happiness—not chance or lighthearted happiness but happiness honestly won. Is this theme readily determined? It is true that happiness is often perceived differently by different people. The happiness of Vasili Pankov in the story "Lyogkaya zhizn" ("An Easy Life") is illusory because he is in essence a man without roots.

The idea of happiness, imaginary and real, permeates in varying measure many stories of Kazakov. One of the characters in the story "Dvoe v dekabre" ("Two In December") ponders this, coming to the conclusion that if happiness readily falls to one's lot, it is not held dear because it is unenviable and acquired at the expense of something more significant. But true happiness is difficult, because work, depth, and the ability to live for the sake of others are its essence.

Kazakov constructs stories so that we, together with the author, continually grope our way. We must contemplate each of the hero's actions, because the writer does not give us ready solutions. Before us, as it were, is life itself, not a book. As in life, we must return to the actions of the heroes, remember the words said by them, and, having compared those words, determine our own relationship to man.

The stories of Kazakov are stories of complex and sober human love, which is inseparable either from radiant happiness or great grief. They are stories of the many-faceted and rich nature of contemporary man. The author strives to understand the complexity of man's character. He can compel the reader to weigh his work, interpret it independently, and re-work it in his own mind. This is a fine gift and makes the new work by Kazakov enjoyable and essential.

A. Chernov. *Znamya.* Jan., 1964, p. 248[†]

The people and animals in Kazakov's stories are always on the move. His heroes wander through forests, go to sea, go skiing, go travelling in trains. And it is while they are on their way, meeting with new people and new experiences, that "revelation" comes to them.

They leave on the road not only the imprints of their footsteps but the imprints of their characters, of their inner selves. But not all of them. Sometimes it is when a person is on the move that his mediocrity, the emptiness of his inner being, becomes more distinctly manifest. Neither new people he meets nor the starry sky seen from a train window move him. He has no solidity yet, is like a feather blown this way and that. Such is Vasili Pankov of the title story "An Easy Life."

The title is ironic, for Vasili's life is not so much easy as empty. A sprightly young man popular with the girls and very much satisfied with himself, he switches from one construction job to another, nowhere leaving any particle of his soul.

At first glance the difference between Vasili and, say, Kudryavtsev, may not seem so very great. The outward circumstances of their life are similar, neither does anything of any importance. Though Vasili goes off to work at a construction site in the city, his roots, like Kudryavtsev's, are in the village. The difference is that Kudryavtsev is a man who has a living soul open to all things beautiful. And though he accomplishes nothing particular in the story, the reader is filled with faith in him as a man of human sensibilities.

Vasili, on the contrary, inspires no faith though the reader knows that he works well at his job and even earns bonuses. In a year or two he will weary of flitting about the country, marry, settle down. But he will remain empty until the day when he is suddenly overwhelmed by a sense of deep inner happiness. Until that happens to him, be where he may and see what he may, he will not see the main thing, the thing that gives meaning to a man's life.

Galina Kornilova. SL. Jan., 1964, pp. 188–89

Kazakov has not only flouted every convention of Soviet literature; he has assailed the great myth of Soviet society which exalts the joys of "collective" living. His preoccupations and sympathies lie with the outcasts, the renegades, the lost souls of the collective. Among his heroes are drunkards, vagabonds, ugly and abandoned women, and, in one of his finest stories, "Adam and Eve" ["Adam i Eva"], an abstract painter whose rejection by society ultimately alienates him from all of human life.

For such stories Kazakov has been consistently denounced for "pessimism," "degeneracy" and an inability to distinguish good from evil. He can, however, scarcely be said to suffer from lack of moral sense; his stories point merely to the fact of human fallibility and its attendant woes. It is this aspect of his work which may seem most naïve to the Western reader. The Soviet reader, assaulted on every side by official optimism, finds in it the deepest sort of recognition.

Patricia Blake. NYT. Jan. 12, 1964, p. 5

Holden Caulfield living in Winesburg-on-the-Volga: this photomontage phrase, for all its seeming breeziness, is the best brief image for conveying the art of Yuri Kazakov to American readers, for indicating his uncanny resemblance to Salinger and Anderson (not via imitation but via a common descent from Turgenev's *Sportsman's Sketches*), and at the same time for extricating him from the various ideological frameworks with which both Russian and American critics distort so much of the post-Stalin flowering. *"Senza ideologia"* (without ideology): so reads a sign in an Italian bookstore announcing Kazakov's first Italian edition. . . . Lots of these sketches could happen anywhere, regardless of social system. The concrete individual is paramount: very human and unheroic, unpoliticized, ungeneralized. The subject matter is the inner private life, especially love and loneliness, and not the outer gregarious public life.

However, if you really want to look for references to current Soviet public disputes, you can find them too.

Peter Viereck. *SR*. Feb. 1, 1964, p. 39

In Iurii Kazakov, this undoctrinaire sense of individuality is coupled with a more finely modulated awareness of the emotional nuance than Aksenov seems capable of achieving. Kazakov's short stories have been compared to Chekhov's. The difference of stature between the two need not be insisted upon. Though possibly the most gifted and skillful among the young Soviet prose writers, Kazakov is a minor figure rather than a budding master. Yet there is something Chekhovian about the blend of sympathy and detachment in Kazakov's narratives and his steadfast refusal to moralize. To the considerable displeasure of the hacks, Kazakov shuns like the plague edifying themes and "positive heroes." The protagonists of his most characteristic tales (e.g., "Adam and Eve," "The Outsider" ["Otshchepenets"]) are loners, deviants, "offbeat" and unadjusted men. Their predicament is epitomized by the sullen and indolent buoy-keeper Egor in "The Outsider," who only in rare moments of shared bliss manages to rise above his usual torpor and break out of his isolation. Kazakov is a poet of brief but fateful personal confrontations, of fleeting yet significant moments. Apparently a faithful disciple of both Chekhov and Turgenev, Kazakov is finely attuned to subtle, barely perceptible shifts in interpersonal relations, to small cues which often make the difference between success and failure, between frustration or fulfillment in a long-awaited, hesitant encounter. This fundamentally un-Soviet sense of the fluidity and complexity of personal emotions goes hand in hand with a lyrical-descriptive evocativeness. Kazakov's protagonists typically have more rapport with nature than with society. The Russian countryside is a compelling presence in these stories, where a sudden radiance of Northern Lights breaks upon an encounter, now to illuminate a moment of shared joy, now to lend a wistful poignancy to the finale of a romance gone awry.

Victor Erlich. *SIR*. Sept., 1964, p. 412

Kazakov's stories are brief, spare and strong. They deal with elemental emotions and have a kind of primitive power and directness, and at the same time a sure sense of people and an artfulness that is reminiscent of Bunin. His people are generally mavericks, oddballs, loners, some perhaps even slightly unsavory. Their milieu is generally out-of-the-way, sometimes even primitive, and he succeeds thus in separating them entirely from the necessity of a socio-moralistic treatment. His style makes us aware of sights, smells, sounds, skin-prickles and wind-currents, longings and desires. He dramatises the animality in their humanity and the

humanity in their animality, but never does he use his people as instances of a particular morality. At his best he takes us, almost as Chekhov
does, to the very source of morality, the human predicament itself.

Sidney Monas. HdR. Winter, 1964–65, pp. 604–5

No recent Soviet writer has so concentrated his creative energies on one
central theme as Jurij Kazakov has; there is hardly a story of his which
does not depict a character who has isolated himself from the normal flow
of life about him, from ordinary social intercourse. In considering Kazakov's stature as a writer, the question one must resolve is whether his stories represent a form of artistic escape or whether the body of his creative
output represents a significant treatment of a major human problem. Do
his characters strive for isolation because it is the *sine qua non* for certain
positive values ordinarily unworthy of serious consideration in Soviet literature, or is the theme of isolation merely an attempt to escape from the
official problems of Soviet literature and life? To be sure, Kazakov is not
the first among even relatively recent Soviet writers who has avoided
large-scale social issues in favor of personal problems. Konstantin Paustovskij, for one, has frequently avoided the larger problems of Soviet life.
But Paustovskij does this through a literary device—the sentimental story.
Kazakov refuses to escape into literary simplification of life; thus, the
problem his fiction poses is whether he is simply rejecting some official
Soviet values—in which case his stories offer a modestly critical view of
Soviet life "through the looking glass of Soviet literature"—or whether he
is on his way toward a serious investigation of man's struggle for personal
emotional fulfillment. . . .

Even Kazakov's genre—the lyric short story—limits itself to the representation of an isolated moment of revelation in a character's life; it
has none of the larger pretensions of the novel. The locale of his stories is
ordinarily the backwoods country or small villages far from the big cities
with their seemingly more direct involvement in the major problems and
institutions of Soviet life. One notable exception to this rule is the story
"Blue and Green" ["Goluboe i zelyonoe"] which is set in Moscow. But
even here the hustle and bustle of the big city is used only to sharpen
through contrast the representation of an adolescent's private emotional
difficulties. His characters are invariably people whose official positions
have no direct relationship to their problems: none of his characters is a
Party member, for example. Thus, the areas of life in which they struggle
inevitably focus on personal needs and shortcomings.

Stylistically, too, there is a desire in Kazakov's work to evade, if not
escape from, a commitment to calling a spade a spade. Adjectives dominate his language, and their effect is to isolate and particularize the things
which he names, to a point where they are removed from ordinary human

experience. In this connection, "Blue and Green" is an especially revealing title for a Kazakov story. Prepositional phrases, whole dependent
clauses, even the nouns frequently take on an adjectival function. . . .

Karl D. Kramer. SEEJ. Spring, 1966, pp. 22–23

Both Soviet and Western critics have noted (although not explored) the
influence of Turgenev and Bunin, among others, on Jurij Kazakov. In
view of Turgenev's use of nature—especially in *Otcy i deti*—to indicate
man's relationship to Self, and of even more complex currents in the works
of Bunin, it is surprising that Kazakov's themes of nature and Self, of
alienation and the overcoming of alienation, have received so little attention by the critics. Few fail to observe that "communion with nature"
seems to be important in Kazakov, or that he seems not to care for the
"larger issues" of the socio-political life of his nation or world, but such
comments, I will argue here, do not touch the most important aspects of
Kazakov's work. . . .

In regards to alienation, transcendence, and city versus country, one
might sum up Kazakov by diagramming the stories discussed above. In
general, the city, the country, and the journey have the following characteristics, although not all will be found in each story: (1) The city is
indifferent or hostile to man and forces the hero to be incomplete. It
creates false values, meaninglessness, and frustration. (2) The journey is
involuntary and leads the hero over water. It leads to a change in character, or a revelation of character. (3) The country is the natural place
for man. It contains the past, water, and Woman. There are graves, and
coldness, and darkness, but the hero can be complete. The heroic, tragic
fulfillment of life is realized. . . .

In his complex and interrelated themes of man, nature, Self, alienation,
death, Kazakov recalls not only Turgenev and Bunin but also more modern writers. In the works of such writers as Zamjatin, Pasternak, and D.
H. Lawrence, emphasis on the natural, the primitive, and the tragic is
closely associated with myth. It will be especially interesting to see if
Kazakov's future works do not reveal a further development of the mythic.

Christopher Collins. SEEJ.
Winter, 1968, pp. 397, 405–6

The tradition in which Yuri Kazakov's art of narration originates is well-
known. At present forty years old, with his world of experience obviously
that of most of his contemporaries, he mentions the great Russian artists
Turgenev, Chekhov, and Bunin as his teachers. Not any less important
is the fact that Kazakov has taken over important characteristics from the
contemporary Soviet prose of Paustovski and Prishvin. Kazakov sees the
greatness of his classical predecessors not only in their mastery of art

but also in their writing about the most important aspects of the individual in the life of a society. . . .

One further aspect of Kazakov's art of narration should be mentioned —the autobiographical element. It plays a prominent role in his entire creative work. His personal experiences often determine the theme— either directly or indirectly—and also the subject matter of his literary production. The author himself has pointed out this fact again and again in numerous utterances: "I travel much, and a story results from each trip—or even two stories—sometimes long after the trip itself." However, we should note that the incidental and accidental experiences of his wanderings do not drive him to writing as much as does the wish to create an existing reality for his attitudes. For this reason, the narratives that should be considered for certain connections with the artist's personality are those in which the first-person point of view is used. Of course, the narrator, acting as a medium, can appear in various ways and have a different function in each story. The fervor for the Russian landscape, hunting, and folk talents, such as we find in the Russian classicists, suits the first-person narrator in the early story "Noch" ("Night"). However, in the story "Pomorka" ("The Old Woman From the Sea") the narrator appears in the role of a reporter who depicts, with utmost respect, the rich working life of a ninety-year-old woman. In both of these stories, the first-person narrator is an observer. Important thoughts and concepts, such as could have been voiced by the real author Kazakov, are not uttered by the first-person narrator but by one of the other characters. Thus, Kazakov's attitude toward creativity is expressed especially beautifully in the tale of the talented youth Semen ("Night"): "A song can be played in many different ways, including a manner in which no one has played it."

Edward Kowalski. *Menschenbild, Weltanschauung, Werkstruktur* (Berlin, Akademie-Verlag, 1969), pp. 125, 136[†]

KHLEBNIKOV, VELEMIR (1885–1922)

Khlebnikov is a visionary. His images are convincing in their absurdity; his thoughts, in their paradoxical nature. It seems that he sees his poems in dreams and writes them later, preserving all their disconnected events. In this connection, one could compare him with Aleksei Remizov writing his own dreams. However, Remizov is a theoretician; he simplifies the outlines, drawing the lines with a thick, black border in order to underline the meaning of the dream logic. Khlebnikov preserves all nuances; therefore, his verses, although losing in literalness, gain in depth. From this technique emanate some of his absolutely incomprehensible neologisms, strained rhythms, and turns of speech, which offend even the most indulgent tastes. Yet, one dreams of everything, and everything in dreams is worthy and meaningful.

Nikolai Gumilyov. Apollon. 5, 1911, p. 77[†]

Futurism put Khlebnikov opposite Blok. What have they to say to each other? Their battle continues in our day, when neither of the two poets is alive. Like Blok, Khlebnikov thought that a language, like a state, does not exist in space, but in time. . . . Khlebnikov does not know what contemporaneousness is. He is a citizen of all history, of all systems of language and poetry. He is a sort of "idiotic" Einstein, not knowing which is closer—a railway bridge or *Slovo o polku Igoreve* (*The Lay of Igor's Campaign*). Khlebnikov's poetry is idiotic in the true, Greek, unoffending meaning of the word. Contemporaries could not and cannot forgive him the absence of even a hint that he was affected by his epoch. How terrible it must have been when this man, who failed to notice his fellow man or could not distinguish his time from others, turned out to be unusually sociable and had bestowed on him, in the highest sense, the purely Pushkinian gift of poetic loquaciousness. Khlebnikov jokes; no one laughs. Khlebnikov makes subtle hints; no one understands. The great part of his writing is nothing but light poetic chattering, as he understood this term. . . . He wrote humorous dramas and tragic buffooneries. He wrote wonderful, exemplary prose, virginal and, like the story of a child, unintelligible in all the flood of images and ideas crowding one another out of our perception. Each of his lines is the beginning of another poem. Every tenth verse has an aphoristic expression which seeks a stone engraving or a copperplate upon which it could rest. Khlebnikov did not write simply verses or poems but a large all-Russian prayer book from which those who are not indolent will draw for centuries.

Osip Mandelshtam. Russkoe iskusstvo.
Jan., 1923, pp. 80–81[†]

Khlebnikov's new view, mingling the little with the big, in a pagan and childish way, discovered that the most basic and intimate things are not best served by the compactness or conciseness of the literary language. This main thing, which was declared to be "incidentality," is at every instant pushed to the side by the weight of our literary language. Thus, the incidental became for Khlebnikov the main element of art. . . .

His theory of language, since it was called "abstruse," has hastily been simplified, and people came to the conclusion that Khlebnikov created an "incomprehensible sound-language." This is not true. The entire essence of his theory is that in his poetry he transferred the center of gravity from the questions of sound to the question of meaning. For him there is no sound that would not be embellished by meaning; the questions of meter and theme are inseparable. "Instrumentation," which is supplied through onomatopoeia, has in his hands become the tool for changing meaning, for making the long-forgotten live again in word relations, and for discovering new relations with foreign words.

Yuri Tynyanov. *Arkhaisty i novatory*
(Leningrad, Priboi, 1929), pp. 588–89†

Victor (renamed by himself "Velemir") Khlebnikov . . . had an intimate knowledge of the Russian language, an inborn feeling for words and their architectonics, and a natural penchant for philological adventures. These qualities he betrayed in his most daring innovations and nonsense-verses, thus differing from most of the futurists, who depended on whim and intuition when taking liberties with grammar and speech. Khlebnikov won his initial fame by a poem in which the word *smyekh*, laughter, was used in an endless variety of derivatives, most of them fantastic, but all marked with an authentic sound, true to the flexibility of Russian words attained through prefixes and suffixes.

The dancing hilarity of Khlebnikov's poem defies transmission into another tongue. . . .

Along with his genuine contributions to linguistic poetics, and his numerous graceful if nonsensical verses, Khlebnikov wrote on occasion with pompous gravity, signing his "Command": "King of Time, Velemir." There is a mixture of the messianic and the megalomaniac in the futurist proclamation "Martian Trumpet."

Alexander Kaun. *SEER*. Dec., 1941, pp. 73–74

In Xlebnikov's work there breathes a kind of pantheistic inspiration *à la* Walt Whitman, but his is an escape pantheism, out of tune with the present, going backward into the past, and trying to find the regained paradise of primitive innocence in the darkness of prehistory. Also from this viewpoint his poetry has little to do with the movement to which he gave his allegiance. One could say that Futurism was in Russia the last and most extreme literary manifestation of the Westernizing tendency, while in the West it was nothing else but an unconscious variation of the Nineteenth Century idea of progress, from which it derived the myth symbolized by the very term "Futurism." But Xlebnikov is perhaps one of the most consistent Slavophiles in the history of Russian poetry: he even anticipates the reactionary ideology, built after the Revolution by a group of émigré historians and geographers, on the belief that Russia and Siberia are an ethnographical and geopolitical unit, forming the sixth continent of Eurasia. Xlebnikov's Utopia is regressive and retrospective: it repudiates our own steel or iron age for a mythical age of gold, even for a stone or wooden age.

Renato Poggioli. *SEEJ*. Spring, 1958, p. 10

In spite of its label, the poetry of Khlebnikov is not Futuristic in the literal sense of the word. This no less true from the standpoint of ideas and feelings than from the standpoint of form and technique. Khlebnikov looked at modern life with a sense of aversion, and worked hard at his experiments and research, while the other Futurists were often satisfied with announcing the most radical innovations in resounding manifestoes, or in rhetorical proclamations. Khlebnikov's indifference toward modern themes, toward the most attractive or repulsive aspects of contemporary existence, is proved by contrast by his deep interest in Slavic mythological lore, which inspired several of his poems; or more generally, by his longing for all those forms of primordial or ancestral life which are the field of study of the archaeologist and the anthropologist.

Renato Poggioli. *The Poets of Russia* (Cambridge, Mass., Harvard University Press, 1960), p. 257

Khlebnikov shows in his works poetic innovation and an acute perception of verse. He is the originator of the "abstruse language." Still, his innovations and his magic over the word are, in many respects, different from the "abstruseness" of Western avant-gardists and abstractionists. Even when experimenting with words, Khlebnikov does not detach them from the meaning. . . .

Khlebnikov's work in no way fits into the framework of futurism. Although he did call himself a futurist, his urge toward the primitive, toward nature, his belligerent rejection of technology, idealization of nomadic Rus and of the Slavs, all of which were expressed with such fervor in the works of these years, show other tendencies. The futurists' ideological and aesthetic nihilism remained alien to him. The slogan "Throw Pushkin, Dostoyevski, Tolstoi, and the rest off the ship of the day"—which was proclaimed in the futurist [manifesto] "The Slap to the Public Taste" (1913)—contradicted Khlebnikov's position in many respects. He remained faithful to the classical principles of poetry even when deforming and destroying them.

N. L. Stepanov. *Annali: Sezione slava.* 10, 1967, pp. 172–73†

The five years Khlebnikov lived under the new Soviet regime were his most prolific and mark his period of greatest creative maturity. Language and time, Utopia, the Orient, rustic life, and Slavic mythology still attracted him; but it was in his poems on civil war and revolution that he achieved a new dimension and showed the rare ability that was his, a direct poetic vision of events and things. After Khlebnikov died of malnutrition somewhere at the edge of a country dirt road, his legend began to grow; his poetic reputation, to flourish; his books, to be published; and his works, to be studied. It is significant that Mayakovsky's group claimed him less wholeheartedly than did some others, and the attitude they manifested toward him was one of respect rather than either of love or of understanding. It has even been suggested that Khlebnikov's *budetlyanstvo* was basically different from what was known as Russian futurism. After the problems of *Nachlass* were more or less settled, Khlebnikov's work went through the stages of textual controversy and of posthumous persecution, and was banned in part for political reasons. At the time of this writing, Khlebnikov is reluctantly accepted as a fact of life by literary officials, but his avant-garde features are diligently de-emphasized. He is adored, however, by many young poets, and interest in him outside Russia is growing.

An assessment of Khlebnikov is still difficult. A few people protect themselves by calling him an idiot. The majority of educated Russians have begun to realize that he was one of the major figures of the Russian prerevolutionary poetic renaissance. Nevertheless, such broad evaluations seem insufficient; Khlebnikov refuses to remain in a pigeonhole, forces one to approach him again and again, and continues to grow in stature with each revaluation. It is quite possible that Russian poetry will be divided someday into the Lomonosov, Lermontov, and Khlebnikov periods.

Vladimir Markov. *Russian Futurism* (Berkeley, Calif., University of California Press, 1968), p. 306

KOROLENKO, VLADIMIR (1853–1921)

Life in the far north, in the deserts of Yakútsk, in a small encampment buried for half the year in the snow, produced upon Korolénko an extremely deep impression, and the little stories which he wrote about Siberian subjects (*The Dream of Makár* [*Son Makara*], *The Man from Sakhalín* [*Sokolinets*], etc.), were so beautiful that he was unanimously recognised as a true heir to Turguéneff. There is in the little stories of Korolénko a force, a sense of proportion, a mastery in depicting the characters, and an artistic finish, which not only distinguish him from most of his young contemporaries, but reveal in him a true artist. *What the Forest Says* [*Chto les shumit*], in which he related a dramatic episode from serfdom times in Lithuania, only further confirmed the high reputation which Korolénko had already won. It is not an imitation of Turguéneff, and yet it at once recalled, by its comprehension of the life of the forest, the great novelist's beautiful sketch, *The Woodlands* [*Polyesie*]. *In Bad*

Society [*V durnom obshchestve*] is evidently taken from the author's childhood, and this idyll among tramps and thieves who concealed themselves in the ruins of some tower is of such beauty, especially in the scenes with children, that everyone found in it a truly "Turguéneff charm." But then Korolénko came to a halt. His *Blind Musician* [*Slepoi muzikant*] was read in all languages, and admired—again for its charm; but it was felt that the over-refined psychology of this novel is hardly correct; and no greater production worthy of the extremely sympathetic and rich talent of Korolénko has appeared since, while his attempts at producing a larger and more elaborate romance were not crowned with success. [1905]

Prince Kropotkin. *Ideals and Realities in Russian
Literature* (New York, Knopf, 1915), pp. 302–3

Korolenko staves off, shirks, and, at the first possibility, hides from tragedy, with such zeal that the force with which he accomplishes this shows how senselessly this aim is desired and how this goal is never achieved.

The tragic world must have complete power over him, because he uses such force to defend himself from it. Does not this strained denial of tragedy itself seem tragic? Indeed, would one who is calm start such a fuss over his own calmness? Why would he have piled up terror on terror, corpse on corpse, despair on despair, and then having done this, destroy it all if he were actually convinced that "the forest rustles," that "the river plays," that all tragedy is solved with freedom, and that a white cross will be raised over every grave? And why did he have to create an ideal if, without and before his efforts, the world already was ideal for him?

Kornei Chukovski. *Russkaya mysl.* Sept., 1908, p. 138[†]

Istoriya moego sovremennika (*The Story of My Contemporary*) is perhaps the best of [its] literary genre. Besides, it is written as if there had been no February or October days or any of the following violent civil war. There is no mention of the burning questions of the present-day reality. Because of this, the gap between the past populism and the present one is emphasized more strongly and has become more noticeable. There was much of the naïve faith, illusions, fetish-like admiration for the people in the revolutionary populism of the seventies. The contemporary theory of revolutionary Marxism is directly opposed to the distinctive idolization of the "people" as well as to the general abstract formulas of the socialism of that day; but while reading Korolenko's book, we, communists, will feel much closer and more familiar to the revolutionary underground of the seventies than many a contemporary epigone of populism acting in Paris, Prague, and Riga. [1921]

A. K. Voronski. *Literaturno-kriticheskie stati*
(Moscow, Sovetski pisatel, 1963), pp. 71–72[†]

My meetings with [Korolenko] were very few, I never observed him unin-
terruptedly, day after day, even for the very shortest period of time.

But every talk I had with him strengthened the impression I had of
V. G. Korolenko as a great humanitarian. I have never met among cultivated Russians anyone with such a thirst for "truth and justice," anyone
feeling so strongly the necessity for embodying truth in life. . . .

I feel certain that the cultural work of V. G. [Korolenko] aroused the
slumbering awareness of truth in a vast number of Russian people. He
gave himself to the cause of justice with an unusual, single-minded intensity in which thought and feeling, harmoniously blended, rise to a
profound religious passion. He seemed to have seen and felt justice,
which, like all man's highest dreams, is a mist created by the spirit of
man, striving towards embodiment in tangible form.

To the detriment of his artistic talent he gave his energies to an incessant, indefatigable struggle against the hydra-headed monster which was
nourished by the fantastic nature of life in Russia.

The austere forms of revolutionary thought and deed perplexed and
tortured his heart—the heart of a man passionately enamoured of beauty
and justice, and seeking to blend them in a single unit. [1923]

Maksim Gorky. Literary Portraits (Moscow, Foreign
Language Publishing House, n.d.), pp. 254–55

In his youth Korolenko was a "fanatical admirer" (his own expression) of
Turgenev, above all as the author of *Fathers and Sons*. For him, Bazarov
was the archetype of the new man; he was a living personality in contrast
with the sketchy "pure souls" of the novels of Mordovtsev and Omulev-
ski. Like Turgenev, Korolenko as a novelist strived for realism, historically correct subject matter, and a lofty style. From his great predecessor,
Korolenko also adopted that consideration for people which characterizes Turgenev's novel. The characters in Turgenev's book appear as per-
sonifications of the historical strengths of the country and people. In the
personal fate of the hero of his novel, Turgenev always saw "the movement of history and the development of the people." Even love is treated
not as an intimate, particular case but as a necessary element of the
cultural and historical characterization of man. Similarly, the psychological analysis of the hero in the novels of Turgenev is not conducted for
the elucidation of the individual psychological peculiarities, or even for
the description of the psychological process—"the dialectics of the soul"
—but rather for the expression of steadfast psychic virtues, once again
"the movement of history and the development of the people." This his-
toricism of Turgenev's novel reappears in Korolenko's novellas.

In prose style, Turgenev's features show up in Korolenko's inclination
for poetic prose and lyrical speech. It is not by chance that one of the

finest of the mature Korolenko's works abounds in Turgenevian lyric prose [*Ogonki* (*The Flames*)].

However, Korolenko exhibits a considerable divergence from Turgenev in the fundamentals of aesthetics, most of all in the place of "beauty" in life and art. Like Turgenev, Korolenko intentionally introduced the element of beauty into his artistic style, but he dealt with it completely differently than did Turgenev. Beauty for Korolenko, unlike for Turgenev, was not a separate and self-sufficient category: the existence of beauty, in Korolenko's mind, was connected with the idea of justice.

G. A. Byalyi. V. G. Korolenko (Moscow,
Khudozhestvennaya literatura, 1949), pp. 310–11†

The descriptive powers of Korolenko's talent and the lack of a profound analytical ability are most clearly evinced in the largely autobiographical *Istoriya moyego sovremennika*. In this work literary elements are almost entirely absent, and the ill-defined borderline between literature and *reportage* becomes increasingly more indeterminate as volume succeeds volume with the record of as much information as can be recollected about as great a number of people as possible. It is tempting to ask why Korolenko veered more and more away from imaginative fiction (grounded as it often was in actual experience) to journalism and non-fictional narrative, why his best short stories were virtually confined to the 1880's and why his exceptionally promising literary career never fully matured. It is not an uncommon phenomenon in Russian literature for poetic inspiration to be subordinated to civic responsibility. . . . There is no doubt that Korolenko with his abnormally sensitive conscience felt impelled to make a more direct contribution to society than was possible by creative literature, but that is not in itself a sufficient explanation. He had not the temperament of a great writer. He reached his full stature early in life and never grew. He was too dispassionate, too cautious, too even in quality. Like himself, his main characters are seldom tempted and never succumb. . . . Korolenko was too honest and too modest to excel in autobiography. His own person remains submerged. He does not draw attention to his individual problems or reveal his innermost thoughts. He is neither self-adulatory nor self-abasing. Nor is he given to touching up his memoirs. . . . It is unfortunate that declining health and considerable physical suffering prevented him from doing justice to the latter sections of his work, for although it lacks the penetration of Tolstoy's autobiographical trilogy and the urbanity of Herzen's memoirs, it can nevertheless, in its early stages, be read with pleasure for its own sake and with profit as a source of period information at all times.

R. F. Christian. SEER. June, 1954, pp. 458–59

KUPRIN, ALEKSANDR (1870–1938)

Apart from the terrible indictment of army life and military organisation that Kuprin has given, the novel *In Honour's Name* is an interesting story with living characters. There is not a single good woman in the book: the officers' wives are licentious, unprincipled, and eaten up with social ambition. The chief female character is a subtle, clever, heartless, diabolical person, who plays on her lover's devotion in the most sinister manner, and eventually brings him to the grave by a device that startles the reader by its cold-blooded, calculating cruelty. Surely no novelists outside of Russia have drawn such evil women. The hero, Romashov, is once more the typical Russian whom we have met in every Russian novelist, a talker, a dreamer, with high ideals, harmlessly sympathetic, and without one grain of resolution or will-power. He spends all his time in aspirations, sighs, and tears—and never by any chance accomplishes anything. The author's mouthpiece in the story is the drunkard Nasanski, who prophesies of the good time of the brotherhood of man far in the future. This is to be brought about, not by the teachings of Tolstoi, which he ridicules, but by self-assertion. This self-assertion points the way to Artsybashev's *Sanin*, although in Kuprin it does not take on the form of absolute selfishness.

William Lyon Phelps. *Essays on Russian Novelists*
(New York, Macmillan, 1911), p. 282

Kuprin . . . is little influenced either by the pessimism or by the mysticism of his fellow-writers. His nature, too, is more simple, more elemental, and he shows a healthy sympathy with life which, if sometimes rather brutally presented, is distinctly refreshing after the soul-probing of the "analysts." Kuprin has had an extremely varied career. He began life as an officer, but his independent nature was ill-suited to military discipline, and he soon left the army to wander at will through Russia in search of whatever living Providence might bring him. From town to town he passed, becoming in turn actor, surveyor, dentist's assistant, and compositor. His experiences, however, stood him in good stead, and before he had reached his thirtieth year he had won his place as a writer both with the public and with the critics. The war with Japan gave him his chance, and, as might be expected from an author who had been an officer himself, his military novel *The Duel* [*Poedinok*] had an enormous success. Although Kuprin has not the same talent as other modern writers for describing complex characters, he has the rare gift of being able to tell a good story. For that reason he is nearly always interesting, even in his crudest creations.

I. d'Auvergne. *RR*. 2, 1914, pp. 153–54

Kuprin is an interesting but very uneven writer. His most ambitious work, in which he displays a taste for mystification, is generally the least successful; his fondness for exotic themes—for secret cults and "mystic orgies," above all—nearly always results in shoddiness. On the other hand, when he is content to draw upon the familiar oddities of Russian life and to describe people and events within the range of his everyday experience, his work has indubitably high merit. "Gambrinus" is one of the best short stories he has written. It invites the reader to enjoy the buffoonery by which a sensitive, melancholy man resigns himself to misfortune. . . . Kuprin is apt to grow theatrical in the excitement of portraying suffering and unhappiness, but for this tale of philosophic clowning he adopts a quiet, humorous method which is ultimately very moving. . . .

Of "Sulamith" it is unnecessary to say more than that if one likes that sort of thing it may be enjoyed. It is Kuprin at his most pretentious, dabbling in the religious mysteries of sensuality. The story recounts in glowing terms the legend of Solomon's love for the lowly maiden of the vineyard. Kuprin has made the legend "colourful" enough, but its very gorgeousness, faithfully reproduced in a good translation, stuns the imagination.

TLS. April 22, 1926, p. 299

Despite the frankness of its propaganda [*Yama (The Pit)*] never loses sight for a moment of the humanity of its unhappy characters, nor attempts to hide the qualities that keep them, in their private lives, affectionate and ordinary human beings. The figures of this huge, gloomy canvas are not caricatures or monsters. They suffer from their environment: they are hysterical, high-pitched, sentimental: they come to miserable ends: but they live, and never fall to be the puppets of a treatise. M. Kuprin has lodged his genius under the Red Light, and left it free to work unprompted. The present reviewer has had to do with many young men and boys. If he were anxious about one of them, he would give him this book.

Spec. Dec. 6, 1930, p. 912

Kuprin . . . chose as his hero the man-in-the-street and depicted everyday life, but even in his early work one discovers a tendency towards the realistic portrayal and interpretation of the essentially important elements of reality. It is thanks to this—although his characters do not act in the broad arena of political struggle, but are shown in the sphere of personal and often extremely intimate experience—that Kuprin's works reflect the protest of the Russian democratic intelligentsia, of ordinary people, against the existing order. . . .

Kuprin clearly perceived the inevitability of the development of capitalism; he also perceived its destructive consequences. But he could not understand—and this is very important if we wish to explain the weak sides of the story—that the forces concentrated at the other social pole were capable of sweeping away the factory-owners. . . .

In his love for all the beauty that is to be found in the world and human nature Kuprin was a great optimist and lover of life. Disbelief in the strength of man, the ideas of the imminent destruction of the world that had seated themselves in the works of the decadents were organically alien to Kuprin's outlook. . . .

In the prime of his artistic growth, which coincided with an upsurge of the revolutionary movement in Russia, Kuprin strove for a deeper understanding of life. He felt the weakness of showing his heroes, for the most part, only concerned with personal conflict and cut off from social clashes.

Side by side with his dispossessed and frustrated characters he begins to show us proud, strong, freedom-loving people, somewhat reminiscent of Gorky's early characters, people with advanced views on society, heroes with great thoughts for the future, who have rejected the false romanticism of the forest retreat that was once Kuprin's ideal.

Lyubov Mikhailova. *SL*. Dec., 1954, pp. 175–77

The world in Kuprin's stories is complex, and his characters are never mere props to bring home the tragedy and isolation of human life without love. . . .

Kuprin's minor characters, however, do not consist of uniformly evil or brutish characters. They are, for the most part, simply limited in their capacity to love. It is not so much that man is a wolf to man; it is that one man is just a lump of wood to another. . . .

Kuprin makes great use of subconscious elements and symbols to present the tragedy of his protagonists. And in his writing, the dreams and daydreams, the hypnotic effects of oft-repeated words, the connections between childhood and adult experience, neurotic worrying which cannot be shaken off until its cause is found, are very different from the textbook illustrations of psychological phenomena that are artificially woven into so many "psychological novels." In Kuprin, these divagations are as alive and real as are the characters in which they occur, and they are, consequently, integrated into the harmonious composition of the story.

Andrew R. MacAndrew. Afterword to Alexander
Kuprin, *The Duel* (New York, New American Library,
1961), pp. 254–55

LEONOV, LEONID (1899–   )

Leonov's path of development is one of long and persistent study. Having begun with the philosophical and fantastic half-fable *Buryga*, which followed closely in the steps of Andreyev, Leonov subsequently published a number of stories. . . . They are all distinguished by an unfailing talent but are admittedly, according to the critics, unfailingly imitative. As a whole, Leonov did not find his own character, although he was a startling master of imitating everyone: Remizov ("Petushikhinski prolom" ["Ferocious Breakthrough"]), Dostoyevski ("Konets melkogo cheloveka" ["The End of a Petty Man"]), and Dostoyevski and Gogol ("Zapis nekotorykh epizodov" ["Notes on Some Happenings"]). In some places the author reaches the pinnacle of imitativeness, verging on the original itself, but all of this, of course, is still in no way properly "Leonov."

Barsuki (*The Badgers*) marks the turning point. There are still many pages, particularly in the first part of the book, which recall the young Gorki's full-blooded and vivid description of the lower merchant class (*Foma Gordeyev*). One can just as well look for (and to a certain extent, find) the influence of Tolstoi. However, taken as a whole, Leonov begins in this novel to reveal his own individual character, his own style. This style is still not entirely clear, still difficult to perceive. But he is undoubtedly traveling along the true and fruitful path of a sound and balanced realism without self-distorted speech (Remizov) and without eccentric, unbalanced "broken" moments (Dostoyevski), which are scarcely capable of communicating our severe and sober times.

Simultaneously, with normal growth, we see in Leonov still another important change—a continuous drawing nearer to our times. . . . *The Badgers*, in this respect, is a work that marks a turning point and is significant. Here Leonov approaches the revolution in earnest, taking in its full magnitude. . . . It is true that there still is not the "revolutionary everyday life"; there is not the restored, already unromantic, life of a country back on the move, that is, not that which counts, so to speak, in the artistic order of the day and which, for example, is given in the most salient novel of our times—Gladkov's *Cement*. And yet, in our revolutionary epoch, the time of our civil war is still far from being exhausted. This novel by Leonov will occupy one of the most distinguished places in our literature.

I. Mashbits-Verov. Novy mir. Oct., 1925, pp. 150–51†

Leonid Leonov, the author of *The Thief* [*Vor*] . . . is still in the early thirties and is one of the most interesting of the novelists who began to write after the Civil War. Two things may be observed of his work: in the first place, he has made no effort to emancipate himself from the older traditions of Russian naturalism, but, on the contrary, although his "ideology" has some quite orthodox Communist features, shows himself markedly susceptible to various literary influences of the past—a fact which has drawn a good deal of hostile criticism upon him; and, secondly, his style, which reveals a constant straining towards originality, is apt to be highly mannered—over-delicate, slightly artificial and marked by an extreme fondness for imagery. He is, however, one of the few novelists in Soviet Russia whose chief concerns is with problems of individual psychology and whose work has an aesthetic quality related to modern standards in the rest of Europe.

This quality is specially pronounced in *The Thief*, which tries to exhibit the interaction of art and life along lines which have been attempted in recent years by several experimental novelists.

TLS. June 25, 1931, p. 506

Leonov, one feels, might achieve a more considerable reputation abroad than the one he has already achieved in Russia. What he is still writing would probably please the European public which venerates Dostoevsky more than a contemporary Russian one which does not. *Skutarevsky*, his latest novel, is far from having so pathological a hero as *The Thief*. The hero is a famous and eccentric physicist, who endeavours to mould his scholarly anarchism into the political discipline demanded by the communist party of all its savants. It is not enough that they should work in their laboratories, they must work with full knowledge of what is happening outside them. Although proletarian by birth, Skutarevsky has developed a capricious and cranky temper which tends to cut him off from an easy understanding of the people he controls. His spiritual isolation is aggravated by a stupid greedy wife with a mania for collecting knick-knacks, and by a weak treacherous son in league with his uncle to ruin the application of his father's discoveries in high-power electricity. Nor are Skutarevsky's shy approaches to his young pupil Cherimov and the girl Zhenka, whom he finds lost and falls in love with, any easier. Finally, however, he comes to feel a kinship with them which, far from distracting him from his work, enhances his joy in it.

Leonov has a masterly touch with psychological abnormalities and emotional conflicts in a character; so, since Skutarevsky is racked by conflict and his unpleasant family tainted by abnormalities, much of the novel makes the most absorbing reading.

TLS. Dec. 28, 1933, p. 918

Skutarevsky, regarded as a novel, is formless and badly planned; but it is an interesting and vivid document of life in the U.S.S.R. . . . The record of events is often obscured throughout the book by a mass of detail and side-issues: but these digressions and the thumbnail portraits of the secondary figures and the vignettes of Soviet life are the best things in the book. The final impression of the book is that of a series of camera-shots, showing a life completely different in some ways, in others quite unchanged from the middle-class Russian life described by Chekhov.

Martin Cooper. *Spec.* May 1, 1936, p. 810

In his presentation of these characters and their relationships [in *Doroga na Okean* (*Road to the Ocean*)] Mr. Leonov exhibits the gifts of a master; even in a translation that sometimes slips into awkward and questionable phrases. It is easy to understand why Maxim Gorky spoke of him in the same breath with Russia's greatest novelists, for he has power and scope and depth, clear sight and sympathy and humor, enormous vitality and an ability to people pages in a way impossible to little writers. Those readers who like the comfort of a straight story line may feel that he makes multiple and confusing claims upon their interest, as he moves from character to character and back and forth through time, but they will surely be impressed and stirred by scene after scene.

B. R. Redman. *NYHT*. Nov. 26, 1944, p. 4

Like Turgeniev, Leonov would probably be surprised to find himself excoriated by the (anti-Stalinist) Left and embraced by the literary Right. American critics seem agreed that this Soviet writer was trying to write a "social" novel on the order of Malraux or Dos Passos—though "it is painful," added some, "to see him working so hard, only to surrender his story to the Soviet formula." But Leonov has no message to offer except the truism that poetry cannot live with politics. It is at once apparent from his tone, containing both irony and humility, and his full comprehension of his people and his special tenderness for the casualties of Revolution, that he will not be content with any political formula. It soon becomes obvious, too, that no social "realism," however grotesquely punctuated, will be able to confine his Gogolian view of life as an illogical comedy, played in the dark by a set of earnest tragedians.

Marjorie Farber. *KR*. Spring, 1945, p. 324

Both dramatically and ideologically speaking, Leonov's plays are inconclusive; there are too many loose ends in them and too little unity of action. But his superiority to such acknowledged Soviet dramatists as Pogodin and Afinogenov is revealed in his characters and his dialogues. His characters may strike one as queer, as too complex and twisted, too

Dostoyevskian, but they are infinitely more interesting, especially in *Untilovsk*, than those of Pogodin and Afinogenov. And Leonov is a great master of Russian: his language is rich and flexible, his dialogues remind one at once of Leskov and Dostoyevsky; however, he sometimes lets these run away with him to the detriment of purely dramatic considerations. His plays also have a great gamut of moods—from tragic pathos to grim humor. In *Polovchanskie sady* (*The Orchards of Polovchansk*, 1936–38) and *Volk* (*The Wolf*, 1938)—the latter also known as *Begstvo Sandukova* (*Sandukov's Flight*)—the dramatic effect is achieved by a close interweaving of family and social conflicts. In both, Leonov comes somewhat closer to the Soviet realities of the day, but his method remains that of symbolic realism. There is an obvious influence of Ibsen and Chekhov, while at least one Soviet critic has noted an affinity between Leonov's plays and the symbolic theater of Maeterlinck.

> Gleb Struve. *Soviet Russian Literature 1917–1950*
> (Norman, Okla., University of Oklahoma Press, 1951),
> p. 291

Leonov's works are concerned primarily with the most acute and topical problems that face his country. As a writer he is fully in the national tradition and has close links with Russian classical literature. His command of language is both masterly and highly individual. Few writers attain his admirable skill in handling a poetic, richly-coloured style that draws deeply from the treasury of popular speech.

In *Russian Forest* [*Russki les*], which appeared in 1953, all his great gifts are provided with ample scope for expression. . . .

On the surface the plot of this novel is Polya's search for the truth about her father. But the justification of a father's character in his daughter's eyes is not the essence of *Russian Forest*. For this we must look to the victory of man's creative forces, forces inspired by the noble aim of harnessing nature for the benefit of mankind. . . .

The characters of this book live on long after one has laid it aside. We feel that Professor Vikhrov must be still alive, raising with his pupils new forests—forests of happiness—on the Russian plains. The pride of a working woman shines in the eyes of Lenochka, the modest, self-effacing participant in a cause which the whole people share. How many daring projects Polya and Rodion have already carried out, how many new dreams cram the daring ambitious minds of these young people! And what a refreshing breeze of creative work and bright hope wafts from the pages of this exciting, inspiring and infinitely moving book!

> Mikhail Kuznetsov. *SL*. June, 1954, pp. 149, 151–52

Leonov's *Road to the Ocean* . . . ventures toward a tragic statement and then withdraws when it approaches the boundary between socialist realism and the larger world of art's undirected possibilities. Leonov is a gifted writer, literate in his craft, and aware of those possibilities which lie just beyond his reach. As a result of his knowledge of forbidden areas, Leonov is forced to expend a great deal of energy devising ingenious compromises between the requirements of the formula and what he might really like to say. Thus the two obligatory situations of the literature of industrialization, the exposure of the hidden wrecker-enemy and the celebration of the achievements of the Communist hero, are both in Leonov's novel, though they are disguised and set in the background. On the other hand, Leonov's pursuit of his genuine interests is clearly evident in the novel, and though he stops short of real tragic revelation, the work is permeated with a sense of the permanence, the dignity, and the value of human suffering.

> Rufus W. Mathewson. *The Positive Hero in Russian Literature* (New York, Columbia University Press, 1958), p. 301

When one lists the characteristics of Gratsiansky [in *Russian Forest*] it is a little difficult to see wherein his fascination lies, yet it is palpably present. He sounds, in summary, like an impossibly complete villain—destructive, connected with non-Soviet, prerevolutionary Russia, son of a professor of theology—a negative character of astonishingly complete negativity. Yet as he lives in Leonov's novel, he is convincing and fascinating. Leonov has him speak in a strange, puzzling, mysterious manner: long sentences, profusions of references to history, vague insinuations, meandering thoughts. There is something uncanny in his style as well as in the content of what he is saying—something hard to put one's finger on, an elusive, elastic quality—dark threats and innuendoes which he withdraws and covers up as soon as a direct question is put to him about them. He is a dark, diabolic character also in his own mysterious fear—the hints of secrets in his own past—which are finally explained as the history of his involvement with Emma and her secret police employers.

Leonov's Gratsiansky, then, is a particularly Satanic, Dostoevskian, and artistically successful villain, despite the fact that in his main traits he corresponds to the Stalinist prescription for a negative character. He is original, curiosity-provoking, shudder-inducing—one of Leonov's best creations.

> George Gibian. *Interval of Freedom* (Minneapolis, University of Minnesota Press, 1960), p. 114

In a literary quarrel with Vakhtangov, [Leonov] defended what was later scornfully referred to as "personal psychologism"; and when in 1927 he was asked by an interviewer: "Whose method, among classical writers, do you consider most appropriate for depicting our contemporary world?"

he answered, "F. M. Dostoevsky's, given sufficient strength and understanding." Three years later, however, on a similar occasion, he replied
that although he himself had learned most from Dostoevsky, "by the
irony of fate" he had "flunked" because of him. Dostoevsky's psychological analysis was "static," he had decided, not suitable for describing the
contemporary world, and his style was "long drawn out, verbose." Between these two opinions had come friendship with and encouragement
from Gorky, and the publication of the Dostoevskian novel which had
"flunked" him, *The Thief*. Now his consciousness became a battleground
on which Dostoevsky and Gorky fought for his allegiance. Gorky scored
an easy victory. For despite his earlier enthusiasm, Dostoevsky had never
been firmly entrenched in his mind. It had been Dostoevsky's trappings
and gestures that had impressed Leonov, not his essence; and just as
from Leskov he had borrowed the form of the *skaz* (i.e., of the extended
anecdote, comically related in semiliterate speech) but not that starkness
of tragedy which makes Leskov's work powerful, and from Gogol the
element of grotesque humor but not his sense of terror, so he had caught
Dostoevsky's fascination with complex and abnormal states of mind but
nothing of his philosophic depth or psychological imaginativeness.

Helen Muchnic. *From Gorky to Pasternak*
(New York, Random House, 1961), pp. 278–79

The plots of Leonov's novels develop from the philosophical meaningfulness of the scheme, from the immensity of generalization. That is why we
find in Leonov such intellectual intensity of narration. To an impatient
reader it may seem that the plot, as in *Russian Forest*, is too sluggish, hin-
dered by meditations and digressions. But this, of course, is an outward
sluggishness; in the novel, the main artistic thought is constantly and intensely developing, that is, the philosophical understanding of life.

Leonov's novels contain enormous aesthetic values, but frequently they
are not on the surface; one has to reconnoiter them. There are readers
who say that much in Leonov's books is difficult and even obscure. . . .

It is not easy to read Leonov, but the efforts offer compensation. His
prose is notable for its semantic compactness; each selected page is fully
saturated with content. Probing into the world of the book, the reader
discovers depths in the phenomena of life, of human philosophy, of the
reality of nature. Leonov's sentence, leading us through the labyrinth of
the author's compact and profound thought, pulsates with vivid expression, glitters with shades of meaning, and captivates us with its intonational expressiveness. Once you comprehend the peculiar beauty of
Leonov's language and style, each reading affords new aesthetic pleasure.

Mikhail Lobanov and Yevgeni Osetrov. *Literaturnaya
gazeta*. Aug. 20, 1963, pp. 2–3[†]

Leonid Leonov's *Evgenia Ivanovna* may be confidently called a philosophical narrative. It is openly problematic. The delineation of characters, the vividness of imagery, and the details of psychological change, in addition to being interesting in themselves, are presented in such a way as to make the thought elicited by them readily apparent to the reader, to show him that all digressions and chance occurrences are governed by the thought about the whole and support the main theme. "The object of art . . . is embodied in the realization of the logic of phenomena. This is achieved by studying its musculature, in searching for a concise formula describing its inception and existence and, consequently, in finding the original scheme. . . . The artist's task is to compact an event into a kernel to make it possible for this kernel to sprout into its previous state, a captivating wonder, once tossed into a living human soul." Judging by the narrative, many of Pickering's thoughts about art are close to those of the author. Leonid Leonov does not relegate the solution of moral problems to dim undercurrents. He lays bare the "sinews of phenomena" with the precision of a surgeon and does not fear the intensity of life when its green tree is concentrated into a kernel.

In contemporary literature the originality of Leonov's books attracts and maintains wide interest. The concern with problems, philosophy, and the social pathos of modern prose requires the ability to see something more in life than imagery and interesting detail.

A. Urban. *Zvezda*. Feb., 1964, p. 208†

Leonov's works are full of people who assemble objects in hopes of creating a three-dimensional world, a world whose solidity withstands the relentless eroding flow of time and gives its maker a kind of immortality, a world whose symmetry shuts out the chaos of the universe and gives its maker an identity by offering him something to touch and name and arrange as he will. . . .

But all have exchanged their freedom and their lives for a terrible kind of immortality: they have created museums of frustrated dreams and futile quests, forever mummified in a dead world of objects. They are Lucifers as well, anxious in their pain and despair to drag down others. . . .

Leonov's point is that all human relations, like physical objects, encumber. He has a cruel view of men as tyrants who lust for domination over one another, with love perhaps the most savage and most powerful weapon they wield. . . . Such love must be cast off, Leonov seems to be telling us, in order that we may be free. Only after man has settled all the claims that are made on his soul can he, like Mitya, attain to an undistracted, unwavering contemplation of himself: naked he stands then, ready to experience rebirth as a whole, vigorous, and unflawed man. The truly free man is the outlaw—not a "circumspect thief," as Mitya contemptuously calls the acquisitive Zavarikhin—but a man beyond all law save a mysterious urge to life that links him with the eternal world of nature, beyond man's defiling touch.

Robert A. Maguire. Red Virgin Soil (Princeton, N.J.,
Princeton University Press, 1968), pp. 350–52

A new humanism was born in the flames of revolution—demanding, revolutionary, active, and, of necessity, sober. Leonov was aware of this even when he wrote The Thief. But he still had to clarify how and at what stage ethical problems, unresolved for a century, were to be incorporated into the new catechism of an emancipated humanity.

The first edition of The Thief was brought to life by such reflections. The acuteness of the crisis was significantly forced by the contradictions of the transitional period through which the country was then passing. The reflections in The Thief express this crisis, and in Untilovsk these reflections torment Raisa with unrelenting pain. Raisa has already begun to detest the suffering of Guga, has already been transformed into a social position, but is still incapable of contenting herself with the simple and exacting truth which regenerates Buslov.

Leonov's failure to understand the historical process then manifesting itself in the transition to NEP has been demonstrably and accurately shown and analyzed many times by the critics. They were much less thorough in examining the philosophical order clouding the mirror of the novel. Leonov's many-tiered and labyrinthine composition is overcomplicated because the intrinsic contradiction of his thought is reflected in it.

E. Surkov. Znamya. Oct., 1968, p. 226[†]

MANDELSHTAM, OSIP (1891–1938)

Kamen (*The Stone*), published some time ago, was Mandelshtam's first book. It contains verses dating from 1909, yet there are only about twenty poems in it. Because the poet switched from the school of symbolism to Acmeism only recently and he regarded his former work with redoubled severity, he has selected only the poems of true value. In this way, his book falls into two sharply delineated sections—the works before 1912, and those after.

The general symbolist merits and insufficiencies are present in the first section, though even here the poet is strong and original. In his first verses there is an abundance of a certain fragility of fully regulated rhythms, a flair for style, and a somewhat ornate composition. In these poems there are those qualities peculiar to all young poets: tiredness, pessimism, and disillusionment. In other men, such qualities create only unnecessary trials of their pen, but, put in Mandelshtam, they crystallize into poetic images, into Music with a capital M. For the sake of a musical idea, he is prepared to give up the world, to renounce nature and even poetry.

But a poet cannot live long with denying the world, and a poet with a warm heart and an active love does not desire images that are not to be looked at or touched by a tender hand. As early as page 14, Mandelshtam makes an important admission: "No, it is not the moon, but the light face of a watch which shines before me." This opens the door of his poetry to all those images of life that exist in time, not only those that last for an eternity or for a second: the casino in the dunes, the parade in Tsarskoe Selo, the restaurant riff-raff, the burial of a Lutheran. With pure southern passion, he fell in love with northern propriety and even simply the severity of ordinary life. He is enraptured with the "secret fear . . . a carriage with the trappings of an aged fraulein returning home" inspired in him. With the same passion he loved "a lawyer who, with a sweeping gesture, wraps his cloak more tightly about him" and Russia, which is "a monster that, like a battle ship at dock, breathes heavily." In the burial of a Lutheran, he liked best of all that "there was a look dulled with decent tears, and a prolonged ringing of a bell." I know of no one else who could so thoroughly extricate romanticism from himself without at the same time affecting his poetic ability.

Mandelshtam also transfers this love for everything living and durable to architecture. He loves buildings as other poets love mountains or the sea. He depicts them in detail, discovers parallels between them and him-self, and makes world theories based on their contours. It seems to me, that this is the most successful approach to the fashionable problem of urbanism.

Nikolai Gumilyov. *Apollon*. 1–2, 1914, p. 128[†]

Going over Mandelstam's poems it is easy to follow the whole path of his development, which led from symbolism to the realization of life and to the poetry of the new school. The early poems of Mandelshtam are characterized by real although very restrained lyricism. The world of his poetic experiences finds its place in a particular domain of feelings, similar to some early representatives of symbolism, especially French symbolism. In his artistic works he perceives the world not as a live, tangible and compact reality, but as the play of shades, as the illusory veil thrown over real life. . . .

Like any poetry in the classical style, Mandelshtam's poetry is the architecture of beautful forms. What have we to do with the "psychol-ogy" of the architect, with his personal, human experiences, when the edifice is being held subject to the laws of artistic equilibrium? Mandel-shtam himself considered himself a poet-architect: He calls his book of verses a "stone" and wants, in his art, to be similar to the anonymous constructors of medieval cathedrals. He is not a lyric poet talking about his intimate spiritual experiences in his poems; he creates as if objective pictures for themes given to the poet but not depending on the poet— short unfinished descriptions, little stories. Like any classical poet, he is a poet-traditionalist. [1916]

Viktor Zhirmunski. *Voprosy teorii literatury*
(Leningrad, Academia, 1928), pp. 302, 327[†]

Contemporary Soviet poetry is developing in a way significantly different from that of Mandelshtam, but just the same it cannot bypass him. . . . His verses are characterized by high mastery and verbal perfection. He is probably one of the most "exacting artists." His poems stand above the petty everyday polemics; they are the model of a great poetic culture that is closely tied to contemporary poetry.

N. L. Stepanov. *Zvezda*. June, 1928, pp. 123–24[†]

The poetry of Mandelshtam is characterized by an attraction for classical examples, by a grandiloquent severity, by the cult of historical themes. . . . There is an imprint upon his poetry of artistic laconism. . . . The October Revolution did not produce any upheavals in Mandelshtam's poetic creation. . . . [He] deliberately denies the novelty of what is hap-pening to him. [In "Nashedshi podkovu" ("The Finder of a Horseshoe")] he proclaimed the principle of inertia as belonging to a "prime-vally eternal" category. . . .

Mandelshtam's work is the artistic expression of the consciousness of the bourgoisie in the interval between two revolutions. . . . His view of the world is characterized by extreme fatalism and the coldness of an inner indifference to all current events. . . . This is simply a highly sublimated and coded ideological perpetuation of capitalism and its culture.

A. Tarasenkov. *Literaturnaya entsiklopediya*
(Moscow-Leningrad, Sovetskaya entsiklopediya, 1932),
Vol. VI, pp. 756–58[†]

Mandelshtam's poetry is not a direct reflection of life but a reflection of its reflection in art. . . . When we reread the works of Mandelshtam, it becomes clear to us that this poet is very much afraid of life, of real people, and of their real conflicts and experiences, and that he obtains relative peace only when he turns from living people to books. The most frightening thing for Mandelshtam is any kind of change in reality. His demand for stability in life and in art is nothing but a demand for their immobility and inertia. He has no social instincts or interests as he says of himself: "No, never was I a contemporary of anyone." . . .

In Mandelshtam's last poems one can sometimes hear a passionate grief, a passionate desire to tear himself out of his circle of old thoughts and habits, in order to align himself with Soviet reality. But this desire is stunted by old memories about the past. He raises the goblet "for the music of the Savoysky pines, the gasoline of the Champs Élysées, the rose inside a Rolls-Royce, the oils of French paintings"; and socialist concreteness becomes covered in a shroud of all those conventions of old books. Thus, in a recent cycle of poems about Armenia, the real Armenia has disappeared; and an improvised landscape is preserved as a pretext for the poet's abstract contemplation. Mandelshtam has remained a poet alien to socialism from the beginning to the end. [1934]

A. Selivanovski. *V literaturnikh boyakh*
(Moscow, Sovetski pisatel, 1959), pp. 278–81[†]

Mandelshtam is continually symbolic. At times, it is impossible to subject this magic to a logical analysis, although it does not seem to be artificial, pretentious, or summarily an expression of mere verbiage—as it is with many symbolists. Mandelshtam's magic is warmed by sincere sentiments. Perhaps this is its most attractive feature. No matter how impersonal or how distant the themes may be, there is never coldness emanating from his lines, which seem to be carved in marble or cast in bronze. This is because these distant subjects are his true love, his suffering, and his happiness. They are the part of his being that has befriended the worlds of his creative imagination, no matter what he dreamed of: the beloved Mediterranean world of the past, legendary Crimea, Scythian barbarity, ancient Moscow with its "five-domed cathedrals," the contemporary Petersburg dying with Isaac . . . or the religious solemnity of noon. The story of these visions is saturated with the raptures of his heart. And, what is more, a living, concrete impression transfers some sort of transcendental essence to his image. Better than anyone else, Mandelshtam understood the lesson of the great French innovators, and he connected Russian verse with the surrealistic insights of the century. But, by their themes and religious accent, these verses stand apart from Russian verse. The great love of the poet for Russian fate and Russian faith is concealed in the very abstractness of these poems.

The religiousness of this "noon" (or "universal liturgy"?) is not only an ecstatically Christian, icon-painted religiousness but also a very Russian one. It is amazing how this could be imbued in a youth who grew up in shallow, Jewish, philistine surroundings and who had received a motley education in Switzerland and Heidelberg.

Sergei Makovski. *Portrety sovremennikov* (New York,
Izdatelstvo imeni Chekhova, 1955), pp. 385–86†

Mandel'shtam's preoccupation with the classical and the Hellenic is not as exclusive and as serious as Ivanov's: generally he prefers to project his philological and archaeological reconstructions into an ironic atmosphere, as if he would place them in the cold and abstract light of a museum. All his learned poems are conversation rather than period pieces, and yet they typically convey the static and abstract quality of Mandel'shtam's vision. Hence the significance of the title of the poet's first collection, *Stone*; hence his predilection, rare in Russian poetry, for composition and architecture, for the "frozen music" of pure design. Thus, even when minuscule in scope, Mandel'shtam's art is monumental in quality, and it tries to transform the historical and the temporary into the untimely and the timeless. The poet once affirmed, paradoxically, that the poetry of the Russian Revolution should be classical in temper, and he saluted its advent with a neo-Pindaric ode, not devoid of an elegiac strain, which he entitled "Liberty's Twilight" ["Sumerki svobody"]. Yet, as we already know and as T. S. Eliot averred, a modern poet can be classical only in tendency. That Mandel'shtam must have been aware of the same truth is shown by his poem on Racine, expressing the poet's impossible longing for an art really able to separate, like a stage curtain, the opposite worlds of imagination and reality, of creation and experience. Beyond that curtain, Racine's heroes and heroines are frozen forever in their inflexible stage attitudes. Mandel'shtam yearns likewise for the absolute perfection of a vibrant, and yet motion-less, pose, for the fixing of passion in a gesture both conventional and unique. For Hegel, the task of Greek art, especially of Greek sculpture, was to express life in the moment of habit, rather than in its instant of tension, or in its exceptional phases. Mandel'shtam's neoclassicism is a similar, all-too-modern, attempt to treat stasis as if it were no less a state of grace than ecstasis itself.

Renato Poggioli. The Poets of Russia (Cambridge,
Mass., Harvard University Press, 1960), p. 311

We were born in the same year, 1891; he was two weeks older than I. Often, as I listened to his poems, I felt that he was many years older and wiser. But in everyday life he looked to me like a child, capricious, touchy, vain. "How intolerable!" I would think for a moment, only to add immediately, "How nice he is!" Concealed under the unstable exterior were kindness, humanity, inspiration.

He was small and frail. He had a habit of throwing back his head with its little tuft of hair. He liked the image of the cock piercing through the night under the walls of the Acropolis with its cry. When he chanted his solemn odes in that little bass of his, he himself looked like a cock.

He would sit on the edge of his chair, and suddenly he would dart away. He dreamed of good dinners, made fantastic plans, charmed editors. Once in Feodosia he gathered some rich "liberals" and told them sternly: "At the Last Judgment you will be asked whether you under-stood the poet Mandelshtam, and you will say no. You will be asked whether you gave him to eat, and if your answer is yes, much shall be forgiven you." At the most tragic moments he would make us laugh with his rhymes. . . .

Those who met Mandelshtam for the first time in an editor's office or a café thought that he was a most lightheaded person, incapable of a thought even for a moment. But Mandelshtam knew how to work. He wrote poetry not at his desk but in the streets of Moscow and Leningrad, in the steppe, in the mountains of the Crimea, in Georgia and Armenia. . . . His poems grew out of a line, a single word. He changed everything hundreds of times. Sometimes a poem that was clear at first would become more complex, almost unintelligible; at other times, however, it would become clearer through revision. He was pregnant with an eight-line poem for a long time—sometimes for months—and he was always struck with wonder at the birth of a poem.

Ilya Ehrenburg. Novy mir. Jan., 1961, p. 142†

Although in *Tristia* Mandel'štam continues the firm verse of *Stone* we can observe certain new features. There are, as Kirill Taranovskij recently pointed out in an interesting paper on Mandel'štam's verse, certain poems from 1922 which are written in a new kind of *dol'niki:* if his earlier *dol'niki* (from 1910–12) are characterized by isosyllabism then the syllabic scheme of the poems is now completely destroyed. Further, the poem beginning with the line *Voz'mi na radost'* has iambic rhythm but no rhymes. And as a third group of experiments there are also a few poems written in free verse; among them "He Who Found a Horseshoe" from 1923 which is one of Mandel'štam's most beautiful; space will not allow me to discuss it here.

With the tension of the words and images becoming increasingly stronger, with the balance shaken, development pointed in the direction of a free verse, a verse close to the general development of European poetry at this time. This seemed a natural line of development for Mandel'štam's poetry but he does not take this step. There are certainly many explanations. One of them is that "time" had a new blow ready for him. Mandel'štam became, as we know, a victim of the literary politics of the thirties. His poems preserved from this period are to be looked upon more as personal documents than as a real continuation of his earlier poetry.

Nils Ake Nilsson. Scando-Slavica. 9, 1963, pp. 51–52

He resembles his exact Western contemporaries, the imagists and the neo-classical poets; his self-imposed discipline derives ultimately from Greek and Roman, French and Italian models. If this conveys the notion of something cold and marmoreal, the impression is misleading. Concentration and intensity of experience, the combination of an exceptionally rich inner life, nourished by a vast literary culture with a clear vision of reality, as agonized and undeluded as Leopardi's, divided him from his more subjective and self-expressive Russian contemporaries. He began of course, as they did, in the shadow of French symbolism, but emancipated himself exceedingly early. Perhaps it was a conscious opposition to everything vague and indeterminate that caused him to cut his cameos so fiercely, to lock his images so firmly, sometimes a shade too firmly, in an exact, unyielding verbal frame. This tendency toward objectivity and his intimate relation to the great classical poets of Europe made him an original and somewhat Western figure in a country educated to confessional literature, and insistence and over-insistence of the social and moral responsibility of the artist. It was this that was described as lack of contact with reality, self-estrangement from the national life and the people, for which he and his fellow Acmeists have been condemned since the early years of the revolution.

Isaiah Berlin. NYR. Dec. 23, 1965, p. 3

Mandelstamm was one of the most brilliant conversationalists. In conversing he didn't listen to himself, nor did he answer himself as almost everyone does today; he was considerate, imaginative, and infinitely varied. I have never heard him repeat himself. Ossip Emilievitch could learn foreign languages with extraordinary ease. He recited by heart in Italian whole pages out of the *Divine Comedy*. Not long before his death, he had asked his wife Nadia to teach him English, which he didn't know at all. He spoke about poetry dazzlingly, often in a prejudiced way, and sometimes he was monstrously unjust—about Blok for example. About Pasternak he said: "I am thinking about him so much that it even makes me feel tired." And also, "I am sure he has never read a single line of mine." About Marina: "I am an anti-Tsvetayevist." He was at home with music and this for a poet is extremely rare. More than anything else, he feared the loss of his poetic voice. When this happened, he rushed around in a state of terror and he invented all sorts of absurd reasons to explain this calamity. A second, frequent cause of distress was his readership. It always seemed to him that he was liked by the wrong readers. He knew well and remembered other poets' poems, sometimes falling in love with a single line. He could memorize with ease poems which were read to him.

Anna Akhmatova. *NYR*. Dec. 23, 1965, p. 8

Mandelstam's novella [*Egipetskaya marka* (*The Egyptian Stamp*)] might serve as a veritable textbook of one of the "devices" of literary art which received its name and formulation in the writings of the Russian Formalist school of criticism: *ostranenie* (making strange). First labeled and analyzed by Viktor Shklovskij, this is a poetic technique for compelling the reader to perceive the familiar external world in a new way. Thus, as Shklovskij pointed out, when Tolstoy in *War and Peace* describes an evening at the opera in the naïve terms of a young girl's vision, without any of the aesthetic sophistication or technical terminology usually associated with such a scene, he renovates our very perception, fatigued by long familiarity, of what we thought we knew.

But Mandelstam's use of *ostranenie* is not that of Tolstoy. Far from presenting the visual world in its primeval state, stripped bare of the accretions of sophisticated terminology, Mandelstam rather increases the complexity and enriches the image of whatever he portrays, "making it strange" by the startling juxtaposition of images from widely different, and usually opposed, areas of life. Thus bast mats are likened to the chasubles of priests; a drawbridge is perceived as a wooden, stone-bound book; the flames of blowtorches are white, shaggy roses; a personified Dawn breaks her colored pencils, which gape like the beaks of nestlings; a page of music is a revolution in an ancient German city. The incongruity of such metaphors, as Berkovskij noted, represents the very essence of Mandelstamian prose style. What Berkovskij did not point out, however, and what it is essential to realize in order to understand the significance of this device for the total meaning of *The Egyptian Stamp*, is that there is a *patterned* selection of the incongruous images that are juxtaposed. Incongruity can be achieved in any number of ways, but Mandelstam achieved it over and over again in only one way, the significance of which must therefore be marked.

Clarence Brown. *The Prose of Osip Mandelstam*
(Princeton, N.J., Princeton University Press, 1965),
pp. 54–55

The "hellenistic" and "classicistic" nature of Mandel'štam's poetry has long been taken for granted. I find little substance in this notion—if it is to mean that Mandel'štam's poetic style resembles that of Greek and Latin poetry in general, or of any individual poets of classical antiquity in particular. Only of some late and very sophisticated ancient poets (such as Ovid) can it be said that their verses are "a quintessence of literature," which is true of the Parnassians, and of Mandel'štam. Yet Mandel'štam goes even further than the Parnassians in eliminating from his poetry all that is "non-poetry" (to use Croce's term). There is little rhetoric to be found in Mandel'štam, but plenty of it in Horace, Ovid, and even Catullus. True, the early Mandel'štam is the typical *doctus poeta*, who likes to shine with his erudition, but this is a trait he shares with many modern but not with all ancient poets. Mandel'štam's tendency to reduce poetry to "pure language" by eliminating the paralinguistic elements of abstract thought and logic, of subjective emotion, of personal involvement, and of actuality, this tendency reminds one of Mallarmé or of Valéry, and not of any ancient poet. Mandel'štam's poems may be called polyphonic verbal compositions with a multidimensional (rhythmic, architectonic, euphonic, synaesthetic, emotional, and intellectual) expressive effect. Such an effect may be found, occasionally and I believe accidentally, in Pindar and the Aeolian poets, but is of course a consciously pursued goal of Mallarmé, Stefan George, or Mandel'štam. It is quite untypical of the bulk of Greek and Latin poetry. . . .

A profound awareness of the continuity and unity of Occidental culture is the most characteristic trait of Mandel'štam's poetry. Hence, the rediscovery of the world of Hellas and Rome must needs be one of his most important poetic projects, if not the most important. He has been eminently successful in realizing it. I believe that Mandel'štam's poetic conquests of "times lost" are due not only to his brilliant intuition but to solid philological erudition as well. As to the latter, Mandel'štam has his equals: Brjusov, Annenskij, Vjačeslav Ivanov. As to intuition, I think that he alone has actually succeeded in leaving the shores of his own age, entering the stream of time, and meeting there the spirits of forgotten ages.

Victor Terras. SEEJ. Fall, 1966, pp. 253, 264

Around this slight, ironical, elusive, witty, physically timid man, a miracle has gathered. He has undergone a second birth. Along with Pasternak and Zabolotsky he has become the inspiration of a whole generation of young poets and intellectuals; and, at the moment, his example is more fruitful than theirs. He is self-consciously surrealist. He throws himself open in a bolder manner to what Freud called "the true reality," that is to say, the unconscious. He is more of an ironist; he not only invites the unconscious, he "entertains" its emissaries with fitting ceremony. . . .

In Mandelstam's prose, especially *The Egyptian Stamp*, sight and sound and touch and smell play upon and transform each other, create new images and smash old ones to release a freshness at the core. . . . Beginnings and ends are played off against each other, time and timelessness; transformations, metamorphoses; through time, from one person to another, from one sense to another, from sound to sight, from smell to sound to image, from low life to high life and back again, the Joycean high-road. . . .

Like Pasternak, Mandelstam was Jewish and became a mystical Christian, but his Jewish background was much closer to him, more of a problem, an unassimilated and provocative fragment—that "Judaic chaos" he wrote about so eloquently in *The Noise of Time* [*Shum vremeni*] and in *The Egyptian Stamp*.

Sidney Monas. HdR. Spring, 1967, pp. 130–31

Of all the curious and sinister encounters of Mandelshtam's life it is one of the most trivial ones that will strike the modern reader of the notes to *Collected Works* as particularly improbable. In what was almost his sole venture into day-by-day journalism Mandelshtam (doubtless because he was hard up) interviewed for *Ogonyok* a young Annamese aristocrat, Nguyen Ai Quoc—the only Annamese in Moscow, and a communist convert. He charmed Mandelshtam with his soft, deep speech, his politeness of manner and his fantasy plans for an international congress in 1947 (the interview took place in 1923). One wonders what impression Ho Chi Minh—for so he later came to call himself—

took away for his part of the shy amateur poet-journalist, one year his
junior.

TLS. May 11, 1967, p. 398

The interest in, and admiration for, Mandelshtam is constantly rising.
It is difficult to foresee any substantial scholarship coming from the
Soviet critics for two reasons: Mandelshtam is irreconcilably alien to the
official Soviet approach to literature; and the Soviet critics avoid dealing
extensively with aesthetic form, an aspect of Mandelshtam's art that
is especially strong and that has great appeal for Western readers and
critics. . . .

The criticism of Mandelshtam's works has been sketchy and unsystematic. Only lately have the critics begun to evaluate him in perspective.
Because of the vicissitudes of his personal life, only during the early
period of his Acmeism and long after his death have the critics been able
to write about him freely. Works on Mandelshtam can be divided into
three groups; those written in Russian before and after the revolution,
and those written abroad. The appraisals vary in each of these areas;
obviously the definitive view of him and his literary achievement is yet
to come.

Vasa D. Mihailovich. *PLL*. Summer, 1970, p. 335

MAYAKOVSKI, VLADIMIR (1893–1930)

Mayakovski never touched a lyre; what was a lyre to him! His hands
would not have known what to do. It would have shattered at his first
touch. It was his nature to thunder. . . . It is held that poetry was made
to be sung and danced—and only then to be spoken. But a time has
come when the poet thinks that he has to cry out his verses with a roar
to a crowd of a thousand faces. What use is it then to consider precise
rhythm, euphony, the conciseness of phrasing, or the exactness of the
rhyme? In the end it is essential that the poet pervade that huge room in
which he imagined himself to be.

This is important. This is revolutionary. A new verse, a new concept
of poetry, a new language—all new. Look! What we used to call poetical rhythm is that no longer. Can't Mayakovski do it? No, he doesn't
want to; he doesn't need this rhythm, but another. Here is a new verse
notation: not by the line, but by the breath, for each word must be
shouted from deep in the chest. . . .

Rhyme in Mayakovski appears only where it is essential, only where
it must be heard. And its nature is new. All of it is concentrated on the
stressed syllable, because only that syllable reaches the threshold of the

farthest listener, and Mayakovski was always before the crowd, never in his study. He rhymes *"gryaz vy"* and *"razve,"* *"naprasno vam"* and *"prazdnovat."* Why can't he? He no longer has any use for the old forms of rhyme. He hurls these stressed vowels at the crowd with a loud challenge; all his dynamic energy is concentrated on them. The other sounds are, at any rate, lost, deadened, confused; it would be singularly pedantic to "distill" these other sounds ad infinitum.

Boris Eikhenbaum. Knizhny ugol. 1, 1918, pp. 4–5[†]

Mayakovski solves the fundamental problem of "poetry for all and not for the chosen few." The extensive broadening of the basis of poetry, of course, takes place at the expense of intensity, flavor, and poetic culture. Splendidly informed about the riches and complexity of world poetry, Mayakovski, in founding his "poetry for all," had to send to the devil all that is not easily understood, that is, everything requiring even the slightest preparation. However, to address in one's verses a poetically totally unprepared listener is as ungrateful a task as is to try to sit down on a stake. The totally unprepared person understands absolutely nothing; thus, poetry, relieved of all culture, ceases to be poetry altogether and, according to a strange characteristic of human nature, becomes accessible to a large number of listeners. Mayakovski writes a very sophisticated poetry; he is a refined showman, whose stanza is broken by a ponderous antithesis, saturated with hyperbolic metaphors, and held back in a brief pause. With this in mind, Mayakovski quite vainly impoverishes himself. He is in danger of becoming a womanish poet, a process which has taken place half way already.

Osip Mandelshtam. Rossiya. 2, 1922, p. 24[†]

Mayakovski renewed the grandiose image, which was lost somewhere in Derzhavin's time. Like Derzhavin, he knew that the secret of this grandiose image lies not in loftiness but only in the extremity of connected planes—high and low—in what was called in the eighteenth century the "closeness of not equally lofty words" and also "the entailment of remote ideas."

His rallying, shouting verse, relying on the resonance of the streets (as Derzhavin's verse was built upon the resonance of the law courts), was not akin to the verse of the nineteenth century; this verse created a peculiar system of poetic meaning. The word occupied a whole poem; it was singled out; therefore, the phrase, also occupying the whole poem and obtaining the same status as the word, shrank. The semantic weight has been rearranged. Here Mayakovski is close to comic poetry (the fable also caused the rearrangement of semantic weight). Mayakovski's verse is always on the edge of the comic and tragic. The street genre, burlesque, has always been a contributing factor as well as a stylistic means of "high poetry," and both high and low steams were uniquely inimical to the poetry of "middle style." [1924]

Yuri Tynyanov. *Arkhaisty i novatory*
(Leningrad, Priboi, 1929), p. 553[†]

There are no images of village life in Mayakovski at all. He does not know what a manor country-house means, what a peasant's courtyard is. There is no nature in his poetry: no landscapes, no birch trees, no park alleys, no poplars, no brooks, no moonlit evenings, no light-blue skies, no gay little clouds—nothing of the marketable trite entourage of acknowledged poetry. There are no living flowers, fish, or animals except for horses and dogs. Peacocks he declared to be Brehm's figment of imagination; and the rose, the invention of idle botanists. If he mentions forget-me-nots, it is a bookish reminiscence; they are the forget-me-nots of his heart. When he speaks of poppies, they are the poppies of the faience teapots. The swans are the "swans of the bellnecks." . . . On the other hand, we find in his poems boulevards and squares, the street diamonds, the gloss of asphalt, sidewalks, crossroads, newspaper stands . . . streetcars, bazaars, streetlights, the ribs of the roofs, the smoke of factories, tunnels, locomotives, automobiles, planes, bridges, trains, and so forth. . . .

In our literature, I do not know of any other writer whose consciousness is so permeated with feeling for the city. Indeed, it is the city that provided Mayakovski with images, epithets, metaphors, and similes.

Vyacheslav Polonski. *Novy mir.* June, 1930, p. 176[†]

See what Mayakovsky himself said of his method of writing poetry. He recalls where and when he found each rhyme: "I was passing Arbat Gates and recalled this rhyme; spent 7–8 days thinking of a way to say it in a few words." Mayakovsky was a hard worker; no improviser he, but a determined, conscientious searcher. Indeed, he has no empty, blank lines, and not only during the years when Shengeli recognised his talent, but during the years when Shengeli ceased to recognise his talent as well. Each line is worth its weight in gold, because each has been discovered, each has been created. Mayakovsky said he was ashamed of those lines which added nothing new. Mayakovsky is poetry's labourer. Obviously, in the simple production process or in industry one can design models and then go on to make innumerable copies. The question here may be of typographical reproduction: when each line has been found, when an article has been written it can be printed in millions of copies, and this is industrial reproduction. But that which the poet creates is always a new model, is always a new sample. Thus did Mayakovsky work. [1931]

Anatoli Lunacharski. On Literature and Art
(Moscow, Progress Publishers, 1965), p. 245

Although one can see at their full height anyone who is walking or standing up, the same circumstance on the appearance of Mayakovsky seemed miraculous, forcing everyone to turn in his direction. In his case the natural appeared supernatural. The reason for this was not his height, but another more general and less obvious peculiarity. To a greater extent than other people he was all in his appearance. He had as much of the expressive and final about him as the majority have little, issuing rarely as they do, and only in cases of exceptional upheavals, from the mists of unfathomable intentions and bankrupt conjectures. It was as if he existed on the day following a terrific spiritual life lived through for use in all subsequent events, and everyone came upon him in the sheaf of its unbending sequences. He sat in a chair as on the saddle of a motor cycle, leant forward, cut and quickly swallowed his *Wiener Schnitzel*, played cards, turned his eyes all ways without turning his head, strolled majestically along the Kuznetsky, intoned hollowly in his nose like fragments of a liturgy particularly significant extracts from his own and other people's stuff, frowned, grew, rode and made public appearances, and in the depths behind all this, as behind the straightness of a skater at full speed, there glimmered always his one day preceding all other days, when this amazing initial take-off was made, straightening him so boldly and independently. Behind his manner of bearing himself, something like decision took one by surprise, decision when it is already put into action and its consequences can no longer be averted. His genius was such a decision, and a meeting with it had once so amazed him that it became his theme's prescription for all times, for the incarnation of which he gave the whole of himself without pity or vacillation. [1931]

Boris Pasternak. Safe Conduct
(New York, New Directions, 1949), pp. 112–13

There was yet one more book which Mayakovsky brought across the ocean—a book well known in America—Carl Sandburg's collected poems *Smoke and Steel* (New York, 1921). . . .

In his American sketches Mayakovsky quotes Sandburg's famous poem about Chicago and compares it with his own fantastic description of Chicago in his poem "One Hundred and Fifty Million" ["150,000,-000"] (1920). Mayakovsky expressed the obvious sympathy he felt for

Sandburg in the course of an interview on the cultural and literary life in America. . . .

In Mayakovsky's minute handwriting we find the Russian translation of single words written between the lines in pencil. . . .

We have every right to be surprised for, with Mayakovsky's exceptionally keen and vivid feeling for language, his active use of words in his poetical works, the phonetics or intonation of any poem must seem to him unreproduceable in any other language system.

Words for him were not just "small change" for his thoughts but individual elements of form emotionally coloured by sounds and intonations. He even took phrases from the common every day speech of France and England and smelted them into his own poems without translating them and without trying to reproduce their rhythmic and phonetical colouring to Russian speech.

Yes, Mayakovsky seriously regarded the translation of poetry so difficult as to be almost impossible, which makes the case of Sandburg all the more interesting.

As far as we know this was the only case—not of translation, for it evidently never came to that—that Mayakovsky considered the work of a foreign poet with idea of translation.

Vasily Katanyan. *SL*. April–May, 1946, p. 66

Mayakovsky's inventions are not so recondite as to be unintelligible. He exploited his own mannerisms, quotations from popular songs and parodies of well-known poems, puns and plays upon words, emphatic repetitions and evocative onomatopoeic noises. With such devices his language is emphatically his own, explosive and expressive. He gave great care to composition and reached his final version of a poem only after several drafts, but in the result there is no sign of labour. All runs with perfect ease as if Mayakovsky were speaking spontaneously.

In recitation metre was no less important. Marinetti had abandoned metre for a staccato prose, and Mayakovsky's fellow Futurist, Khlebnikov, kept a regular verse-structure and rhymes which sometimes interfere with the naturalness of his effect. Mayakovsky found a compromise between the two methods, by keeping a verse-form and rhyme but harmonising them with the natural flow of words. Early in his career he invented a system which combined the freedom of *vers libre* with the harmony added by rhyme. Instead of using regular stanzas of fixed shapes he made the sentence his unit and used rhymes to emphasise the ends of the subordinate clauses and of the whole sentence. . . . At the same time Mayakovsky knew the value of surprise in poetry and secured remarkable effects by peculiar rhymes. His way had been prepared by the Symbolists, but he went much further. He does in Russian what

Browning sometimes does in English but on a larger scale and with less regard for exact correspondence of sounds. Sometimes he uses *la rime riche,* sometimes complex assonances, sometimes mere echoes. The effect of his rhymes is not comic except when he means it to be. They help to maintain his conversational tone and keep the audience waiting to see what will come next. They are an instrument of recitation, of rhetoric, and give a remarkable air of novelty to Mayakovsky's verse.

C. M. Bowra. *The Creative Experiment*
(London, Macmillan, 1949), pp. 100–101

Whatever subject Mayakovsky took on, he filled it with his own vitality, as well as with his sonorous voice, which seemed to be created expressly for the platform and mass meetings. In handling the word as such he certainly had no equal. One of the contemporary Russian critics, Roman Jakobson, goes so far as to say that the "word of Mayakovsky is qualitative and different from anything that preceded him in the Russian verse, and no matter how many genetic links we may try to establish— the pattern of his poetry remains profoundly original and revolutionary." But if so, it is the more interesting to watch how and why he eventually dedicated the whole of his talent to the cause of the working classes and of the Soviet experiment. Not that such a thing happened all at once, or that there was no other side to his being. On the contrary, it is enough to compare his poetry before 1917 with the verses he wrote after the Revolution in order to see that there were at least two Mayakovskys whose interrelations were very much dependent on the peculiar circumstances of his life.

Janko Lavrin. *Russian Writers*
(New York, Van Nostrand, 1954), pp. 312–13

The most striking feature in the style of the poem "Vladimir Ilich Lenin" is the way the poet was able to include, as an organic part, Lenin's language in context, so that, when examining the poem, special collations of the two texts were necessary to establish this or another fact of citation or paraphrasing. But quotation and paraphrasing represent only the most salient examples of the use of Lenin's text. More characteristic of the poem is the reconstruction of Lenin's thought, wrapped in the poet's own words. In this way the grain of thought is exactly preserved along with one or other image of Lenin. . . .

In the poem "Vladimir Ilich Lenin," which rose out of direct deep feeling, a not less important role belongs to the generalizing thought. Proofs of this are to be found in the understanding of the history of the revolution from Lenin's standpoint and the clarification of the role of personality and of the masses in history. But the ideological concept of the poem is expressed by poetic language; that is why the pathos of thought, which permeates the whole artistic fabric of the poem, assumes imaginary form. In its turn, the pathos of thought adds transparent lucidity and strict reasoning to the whole figurative system of the poem.

A. Metchenko. *Tvorchestvo Mayakovskogo*
1917–1924 gg (Moscow, Sovetski pisatel, 1954),
pp. 611, 617[†]

Suprematism appears in Mayakovski's poetry in a still more crystallized form than in Belyi's writing; that is, mechanical suprematism only, for Mayakovski's poetry has nothing in common with cosmic suprematism. Mayakovski did for poetry what Malevich had done for painting. Malevich used cubes, triangles and ellipsoids to render a world in motion. Mayakovski prints his verse in a staggered pattern that gives the same feeling of speed. . . .

Mayakovski was no believer in humility. To him, a poet was a prophet and must break into poetry and life like a rebel, a mutineer. The secret of Mayakovski's popularity and influence lies, above all, in his passionate protest against the enslavement of man. It was his tragedy as an artist and as a thinker that he never resolved the dilemma—present since long before the revolution—between freedom of the individual and collectivism, between the Marxist idea which his reason accepted and Bakunin who appealed to his heart.

Vyacheslav Zavalishin. *Early Soviet Writers*
(New York, Frederick A. Praeger, 1958), pp. 75–76

Much of Mayakovsky's life was squandered in the search for some refuge from the pain that hounded him. He sought it in the absolutes of his time—the Bolshevik revolution and the theology of communism—and these ultimately failing him, in death. During his life he was engaged in a performance which he described in these terms: "I shall plunge head first from the scaffolding of days./Over the abyss I've stretched my soul in a tightrope/and, juggling with words, totter above it." Mass audiences were required for all the parts he assumed in this performance: revolutionist, propagandist, cartoonist, journalist, actor, screenwriter, and, often enough, poet. For nearly fifteen years the most excruciatingly personal of poets traveled from city to city across Russia giving lectures and declaiming his verses.

Inevitably his work reflects this prodigality. He produced some of the most splendid lyrics in Russian poetry and, in the same breath, some of the silliest doggerel in Soviet propaganda history. He wasted his talent drawing posters, and composing thousands of slogans and "agitational" jingles that urged the Soviet people to drink boiled water, put their money in the bank, and patronize state stores. . . . The author of *The Bedbug* [*Klop*] and *The Bathhouse* [*Banya*], two brilliant dramatic satires on the philistinism and bureaucratic idiocies of Soviet society, was also capable of writing, without irony: "I want/a commissar/with a decree/to lean over the thought of the age./ . . . I want/the factory committee/to lock/my lips/when the work is done."

Patricia Blake. Encounter. Aug., 1960, p. 53

What is most striking in Mayakovsky's work is its grotesque anthropomorphism: things appear as people, people as caricatures. Street crowds are a "swift, multicolored cat" that undulates, "enticed by doorways"; "boulevards and city squares do not think it strange" that buildings are "draped in blue togas"; the rain is "crosseyed"; anchors are "earrings in the ears of deaf ships"; "a magician pulls rails out of a tramway's maw"; a fog "chews tasteless people"; the Neva is a two-humped camel wearily driven to the sea; "a bald street lamp lasciviously draws a black stocking off the street," etc. This, of course, is a cartoonist's manner, which reminds one that Mayakovsky was a caricaturist before he became a poet. It is a device that Gogol liked; and indeed Mayakovsky's exaggerated images remind one of Gogol's, for they too are used for both comic and uncanny effects. At bottom, however, they are the reverse of Gogol's, which, as the Formalist critic Yurii Tinyanov has pointed out, are comic through their transformation of people into things and terrifying in their manner of presenting motion as demonic, and in showing all life to be on the threshold of the supernatural, whereas in Mayakovsky's case the opposite is true. With him, things act like people; immobility, not motion, is dreadful; and the horrifying is always human, not supernatural. It has been suggested that this fascination with mobility was generally true of artists at the beginning of the twentieth century and that it reflected the strong impression that science had made on them. But Mayakovsky's work bears a special stamp; with all its humor, his world of animated objects is full of pain.

Helen Muchnic. From Gorky to Pasternak
(New York, Random House, 1961), pp. 195–96

It is tempting to compare Mayakovsky with Kipling. Both poets, for example, express the once fashionable, but now dated, ideology of an imperialist ruling class, and each has become the darling of bliss-was-it-in-that-dawn-to-be-alivers. What Kipling has been to the British Empire and retired colonels of the Indian Army, Mayakovsky is to the early years of the Soviet Empire and to inter-war Communist intellectuals, fellow-travellers and members of the Left Book Club—now, alas, left with their own equivalent of memories of Poona.

Mayakovsky's revolutionary romanticism may be as dated as Kipling's pictures of British India, but that is not the point. The work of both these poets soars far above political fashion and change. One does not have to share their philosophy of life to admire both extravagantly. . . .

Even in those heroic days Mayakovsky stood out from the ruck with his piercing eyes, Mussolini-like jaw and thunderous voice. Scourge of the bourgeoisie and addicted to Russian roulette (which caused his death in 1930), he was nevertheless hypersensitive, and is said to have been capable of fainting at the sight of the blood which, one would have thought from his verse, might flow in rivers for all he cared. Among his qualities as a poet is an uncanny feeling for rhythm. He welded his verse into a magnificent percussion instrument, which can explode into crescendos of syncopated bombination, yet is also capable of whispering. He made the Russian language do things which it had never done before, and Russian poetry has never been the same again since he wrote.

Ronald Hingley. *Spec.* Aug. 20, 1965, p. 239

[Mayakovski's] long poem on Lenin is quite embarrassingly silly, and not to be compared, as a poem about revolution, with Pasternak's "1905," or (in prose) with such things as Isaac Babel's *Cavalry Army.* For example, he claims that Soviet children were asking "What is a police-man?" In this he is merely versifying the cant of an era: the word "policeman" had been abolished, not the thing. (Mayakovsky himself descended to an ode to the OGPU.) He lapses, moreover, into self-righteous nastiness, as when he attacks the Social Revolutionaries, then a suffering remnant in Soviet jails. Perhaps, as the men who had actually gained the suffrages of the great Russian majority, they were an unpleasant reminder to the poet that the "masses" he thought of himself as reaching were an untypical minority. He had cheapened his poetry to reach the people, and he had not reached them. Lenin's comment, "This is quite interesting literature. It's a peculiar kind of Communism, it's hooligan Communism," is very penetrating.

Robert Conquest. *NYT.* Feb. 13, 1966, p. 10

The revolutionary and post-revolutionary periods in which Mayakovsky was active were characterized by material deprivation and cruelty, but also by creative freedom and enthusiasm. Mayakovsky and his "co-Futurists" fervently believed that they were creating new art for a new and better society. Disappointment set in only later. Mayakovsky himself, one of the loudest, most grandiose and egocentric personalities in Russian literature, was eminently fit to represent this period in all its glory and excesses. . . .

Mayakovsky is, admittedly, a very difficult poet because of the complex metaphors which are central to his poetry, the neologisms and the rhymes (the latter often built on word play). It is impossible to reproduce all these features in a translation without sacrifice.

Margaret Dalton. *Nation.* March 7, 1966, p. 271

Mayakovsky, a great master of the art of recitation and declamation, was deeply aware of this problem [the live actor and living spectator] and sensitive to its implications. In the poetic structure of his poetry, in the intonational shifts of key in his longer poems one can see that he was relying on large gestures of the almost theatrical variety to supplement his words, which would be felt even at the back of the stalls, and moulding his verse to suit an almost operatic projection of his voice to make all its modulations carry to the farthest recesses of the gallery. In other words all elements of stylisation and convention without which no speaker addressing the tense (and by no means always favourable) audiences of the day, could dispense, are present in his style. Evidently this perfect pitch of his "ear" for the way his words would sound when delivered to a large audience in "his thunderously rolling bass" was one of Mayakovsky's chief poetic skills. He knew exactly how to pour his verse into the monumental moulds demanded by the revolution.

Yuri Davidov. *The October Revolution and the Arts*
(Moscow, Progress Publishing, 1967), pp. 218–19

Mayakovsky's futurism remains for Soviet scholars an uneasy fact, and they try to dispose of the problem either by declaring it a mistake of his youth, or by insisting that even while belonging to this wicked movement, he was actually alien to it. For any unprejudiced person, however, it is clear that Mayakovsky is a classic example of a futurist before or after the Revolution. He considered himself a futurist all his life and was perhaps more loyal to the main tenets of *A Slap* than any of his friends: the self-oriented word, "standing on the block of the word *we*," a hatred of the past, the urbanism, neologisms, the antiaesthetic and antimetaphysical attitudes, and an enthusiasm for technology remained with him throughout his poetic career, changing shape but not essence; and there is no other label for such a combination than "futurism," even if it is true that Mayakovsky's futurism was of a conservative variety (for instance, he never entered the area of *zaum*).

In exercising leadership over the futurist movement, Mayakovsky differed greatly from Khlebnikov. Khlebnikov merely pointed ways to solutions; Mayakovsky solved the problems, but in his own individual way, because, ironically, he was an artist in the traditional sense: he felt compelled to put a finish on what he did. This trait, incidentally, reduced Mayakovsky's influence and made him less of a *maître*, even during his posthumous deification: it is easy to imitate Mayakovsky, but it is practically impossible to follow him.

Vladimir Markov. *Russian Futurism* (Berkeley, Calif., University of California Press, 1968), p. 317

Majakovskij's Futurism is sincere in all of its stages. It largely coincides with the Russian revolutionaries' secular chiliasm. Majakovskij's Futurist dreams—or nightmares—see man escaping from history, from human existence as we know it, and living in a mechanized world of things which can be manipulated without an exertion of the soul or of the mind. As Stahlberger has pointed out, Majakovskij chose the third of the three alternatives to the human paradox: his ideal was neither God, nor animal, but the superbly efficient machine.

Majakovskij—once again, along with the Party whose propagandist he was—is a lover of technological progress, of the machine, and especially of the flying machine. His poetry stands for everything which even today, decades later, is still considered "modern." It is quite possible that the world of the future seen in *The Bedbug* is fundamentally a positive Utopia, as Party-line critics have asserted all along. S. L. Frank's definition of the revolutionary faith as *"nihilist rationalism,* a combination of atheism and rejection of all objective principles by which human self-will had been checked, with a faith in human initiative which, guided by an inborn striving for happiness and well-being, will easily achieve the latter solely by technological-rational organization of human activity," fits Majakovskij's philosophy only too well. It goes without saying that such faith must abhor the concept of absolute ethic or aesthetic value, that it must be hostile to a conception of history as the creation of such values, and that it must consequently reject the notion of "Time the Creator."

Victor Terras. *SEEJ*. Summer, 1969, p. 155

MEREZHKOVSKI, DMITRI (1865–1941)

Dmitriy Merezhkóvskiy . . . may be taken to illustrate the difficulties which a writer, even when endowed with a by no means ordinary talent, found in reaching his full development under the social and political conditions which prevailed in Russia during the period just mentioned [the end of the nineteenth century]. Leaving aside his poetry—although it is also very characteristic—and taking only his novels and critical articles, we see how, after having started with a certain sympathy, or at least with a certain respect, for those Russian writers of the previous generation who wrote under the inspiration of higher social ideals, Merezhkóvskiy gradually began to suspect these ideals, and finally ended by treating them with contempt. He found that they were of no avail, and he began to speak more and more of "the sovereign rights of the individual," but not in the sense in which they were understood by Godwin and other eighteenth century philosophers, nor in the sense which Písareff attributed to them when he spoke of the "thoughtful realist"; Merezhkóvskiy took them in the sense—desperately vague, and narrow when not vague—attributed to them by Nietzsche. At the same time he began to speak more and more of "Beauty" and "the worship of the Beautiful," but again not in the sense which idealists attributed to such words, but in the limited, erotic sense in which "Beauty" was understood by the "Æsthetics" of the leisured class in the forties. [1905]

> Prince Kropotkin. *Ideals and Realities in Russian
> Literature* (New York, Knopf, 1915), pp. 305–6

Merezhkovski the poet cannot be separated from Merezhkovski the critic and thinker. His novels, plays, and poems speak about the same subjects as do his analyses, articles, and feuilletons. Merezhkovski's poetry is not a series of separate poems prompted by the accidental happenings of life but a growth of definite ideas. Merezhkovski has always been in the forefront of the seekers, and his stated ideas have always quickly become the cherished convictions of a considerable number of people. Following those stages through which Merezhkovski went, a notable part of Russian society experienced the influence of Nietzsche's sermonizing, the renaissance of paganism, an increased interest in questions of world culture, an intensified searching for faith, the influences of Christian eschatology and of Christian mysticism in general. . . .

It is somehow not necessary to speak of Merezhkovski's poetic form. The superfluous rhetoric of his early poems changed to a forced simplicity in his later ones and became a simple, clear, and transparent style in his last works. But Merezhkovski's poems are of the type in which form not only has a definite place but also remains intangible and unnoticed. Reading his poetry, it is necessary not to notice his form; and Merezhkovski is capable of attaining this impression. In those places where he does make a concession to the beauty of form, in places where he actually becomes a virtuoso of prosody (as, for example, in the poem "Lida"), form seems superfluous and almost cumbersome.

> Valeri Bryusov. *Russkaya mysl.*
> Dec., 1910, pp. 397–98†

Merezhkovsky's fame outside Russia is mainly based on his novels. The first of these, *The Death of the Gods* [*or*] *Julian the Apostate* [*Rozhdenie bogov*] (1896), is also the best. Not that it is in any sense a great novel, or even a novel at all in any true sense of the word. It is entirely lacking in creative power. But it is a good work of popularization, an excellent "home university" book which has probably interested more Russian readers in antiquity than any other single book ever did. The same may be said of *Leonardo da Vinci*, but this time with some reservation. In *Julian* the material is kept in hand and the "encyclopaedia" side is not allowed to grow beyond all measure; *Leonardo* is already in danger of being stifled by quotations from sources, and by the historical bric-à-brac which is there only because Merezhkovsky happens to know it. Besides, both these novels are disfigured by the artificiality of the ideas that preside over them, which are of his ordinary crudely antithetic kind. Both *Julian* and *Leonardo* are inferior to Bryusov's *Fire Angel*. . . .

Merezhkovsky's place in literary history is very considerable, for he was the representative man of a very important movement for more than a decade (1893–1905). But as a writer he scarcely survives, and the first part of *Tolstoy and Dostoevsky* [*Tolstoi i Dostoyevski*] remains his only work that will still be read in the next generation.

D. S. Mirsky. *Contemporary Russian Literature*
(New York, Knopf, 1926), pp. 162–63

[The] search for the absolute religious truth was the motivating force of Merezhkovsky's whole life. A man of complex character and a well-developed individualism, he was too original to accept Christianity in any of its historic forms, which he considered to be either a complete denial of life and human values, or at best half-measures in an attempt to reconcile natural human needs and spiritual teachings. At the same time he was not presumptuous enough to preach a new form of Christianity, as did Tolstoy. Mentally torn by the basic duality of his nature which manifested itself in many forms (in his love for Europe and for Russia; in his love for God and for man; in his love for the paganism of Hellas and for the spirituality of Christ), he strove to discover the solution of this duality, which was revealed to him not only in himself but in the world at large.

He sought it first in the populist ideal of service to the people. Yet he knew that he was incapable of following such a path, for his individualism and inability to love mankind in individuals made his service to the people mere hypocrisy. He turned to the other extreme, in which he extolled classical virtues and Nietzschean superhumanity as the highest point of human values. In time he could not but realize that this "religion," which in its very essence denied God, was incomplete, for God was as essential to him as was man. He continued his search in an effort to unite his ideals of man and God and eventually came to the religion of the Trinity, in which all duality would end.

C. H. Bedford. *Canadian Slavonic Papers*. 3, 1958, p. 27

With [his] books, as well as with the periodicals he inspired and the activities he promoted, Merezhkovskij was able to affect the thinking and feeling of his contemporaries in a manner certainly out of proportion to the merits of his ideas and the quality of his work. What he succeeded in creating was but a system of empty generalizations, which impressed the Russian mind, always eager to wrestle with abstract issues, with those which were generally called the "accursed questions" of good and evil, of the Tower of Babel and of the City of God. The influence of the metaphysical problematics of Merezhkovskij decreased gradually but constantly in the years between the first revolution, which he saluted with both enthusiasm and awe, and the second one, which he rejected with revulsion and horror. Many of his writings after October 1917 were vehement anti-Communist tracts, but from the early 1920's, when he settled in Paris, until the time of his death, he repeated and vulgarized for the benefit of his Western readers, in a series of books which were translated into several languages, the same historiosophic doctrines he had preached for more than a quarter of a century in the land of his birth.

Renato Poggioli. The Poets of Russia (Cambridge,
Mass., Harvard University Press, 1960), p. 73

Merežkovskij was firmly grounded in a solid classical education which enabled him to translate Longus' idyl "Daphnis and Chloe" as well as tragedies by Aeschylus, Sophocles, and Euripides. His lifelong preoccupation with classical antiquity and the ancient Near East has left indelible marks on virtually everything he wrote. He, too, was conscious, however, of the melancholy fact that, in the words of Paul Valéry, civilizations are mortal. But reared, like Ibsen, in a Platonic tradition he anxiously looked for an element of abiding force which in a mysterious way sets the mainsprings of cultures in motion—an abiding force which would guarantee ever renewed rebirths, resurrections, and renaissances. He too longed for the advent of a Third Realm which in his younger years he liked to define in terms of a reconciliation between flesh and spirit, and which, the older he grew, he visualized, in apocalyptic terms, as the fulfillment of what was promised by Christ: The Advent of the Paraclete, the Comforter, who will inaugurate the domain of the Spirit in a new Heaven and a new Earth.

It is significant that Merežkovskij, in the footsteps of Ibsen, should also have turned to the Apostate when he planned to embody in artistic form the problems that had begun to trouble his mind and would never cease to do so throughout his whole long life: what is foreshadowed here is his untiring endeavor to glean from the rubble of disintegrated civilizations or the turmoil and travail of times of transition those elements which represent what abides forever.

Heinrich A. Stammler. Die Welt der Slaven.
11, 1966, p. 189

NABOKOV, VLADIMIR (1899–   ).

In the original Russian, young Nabokov has been writing for a number of years under the pen-name of V. Sirin. More than half a dozen volumes have already appeared under his signature, not counting his verse and short stories. The present volume is typical of Sirin-Nabokov's art. *Camera obscura* [*Laughter in the Dark*] is entertaining, clever, urbane. As usual, the author's characters could belong to any country or people, even though they are endowed with certain racial peculiarities (in this story they are German). Sirin-Nabokov is interested in universal human traits, and he projects them with keen psychological insight, carefully avoiding any semblance of gravity. As a result, the story is suggestive of complex issues and problems in human behavior, while yet retaining a lightness and raciness, not devoid of an ironic undertone. The danger lies in the author's extreme facility and cleverness. He is apt to toy with his tools and to spring on the reader a *tour de force*. Refusing to be "serious," Nabokov fails to reflect the social aspect of the life he depicts. His stories, while palpitating with life, seem beyond space and time, as far as contemporary social problems are concerned.

Alexander Kaun. *BA*. Autumn, 1938, p. 523

Upon careful examination, Sirin turns out to be primarily a painter of images and a methodical author. . . . He not only does not conceal his methods, which is something that most authors do and something at which Dostoyevski achieved startling perfection; but on the contrary, Sirin himself reveals them, like a magician who, having startled the spectator, unveils his secrets. Here, it seems to me, is the key to understanding Sirin. His works are full not only of countless real characters but also of countless mannerisms, which, like elves or gnomes, scheme among the characters, working great mischief: they nag, irritate, mess things up. . . . They create the piece of each work, and they themselves turn out to be unavoidably important characters. Therefore, Sirin does not conceal that one of his most important tasks is to show just how these mannerisms operate.

V. F. Khodasevich. *Vozrozhdenie.*
Feb. 13, 1939, p. 7[†]

Nabokov-Sirin's art still awaits thorough analysis. In contemporary Russian literature, as Adamovich has said, he really "is the most original phenomenon." Without any question, he has great talent. But the mainspring of this talent has not yet been fully investigated or dissected. At the base of this dazzlingly brilliant, almost blinding talent, lie a great gift for words, a painfully keen visual perception, and an unusually tenacious memory, the result of which is a secret, almost uncanny merging of the processes of perception and recall.

After 1940, when he moved to America, Nabokov became an American writer. Americans sometimes speak of him as of a second Conrad. However, Conrad was never a Polish author before he became an English author. Time will tell the extent to which Nabokov has been lost to Russian literature. But we should note that, having become an American writer, Nabokov has not completely dropped Russian themes: the hero of his first novel in English [*The Real Life of Sebastian Knight*], Sebastian Knight, is half-Russian, half-English; and Russia is always present in the novel. (The second novel is entitled *Invitation to Execution*, and its action takes place in an imaginary, make-believe country.) For the last two years Nabokov has been publishing a series of stories in *The New Yorker*, united by the presence of the comically portrayed Russian professor at an American university, Timofey Pnin.

Gleb Struve. Russkaya literatura v izgnanii (New York,
Izdatelstvo imeni Chekhova, 1956), pp. 288–90†

Among the novels which Vladimir Nabokov wrote in Russian in the 1920's and 30's and published under the pseudonym of V. Sirin, the novel *Dar* (*The Gift*) occupies a place apart, both because of its unusual form and because of the equally unusual history of its publication and subsequent reputation. . . .

Dar deals with three years in the life of Fëdor Godunov-Čerdyncev, a young Russian *littérateur* who lives in Berlin in the late 1920's. As in some other works of Nabokov in his European period, autobiographical elements are clearly present in the novel. In *Dar* they are always imaginatively transformed and the whole remains at all times a work of fiction. The action develops in three interconnected levels. . . .

Dar serves as a focus for gathering of many of Nabokov's leit-motifs that are known to us from his other writings: butterflies, chess, French literature, *audition colorée*, distant expeditions, and, of course, the solitary, creative individual facing a repulsive, conformist mob. Among Nabokov's later novels written in English, the one that has the closest ties with *Dar* is *Pale Fire* (New York, 1962). The similarities include the use of literary commentary and research as a subject for fiction; the profusion of verse and its importance in both novels; and, oddest of all, the occasional echoes of Černyševskij's patterns of thought in the mentality of the Communist-inspired assassin Gradus.

Simon Karlinsky. *SEEJ*. Fall, 1963, pp. 284–85, 289

This four-volume presentation of one of the world's most attractive poems [*Eugene Onegin*] contains much material which will primarily interest the Pushkinist. The sound and penetrating Appendix on prosody deserves a wider readership—if only because nowadays there is a mass of writing about all aspects of poetry except the one thing which actually defines it as poetry rather than prose, its technique and metric. (It might be supplemented by lines 30–38 of Nabokov's own poem *An Evening of Russian Poetry*). The long Commentary which fills out half this bulky production is full of insights too: for example on "the aphoristic style which was Pushkin's intrinsic concession to the eghteenth century." It is also a regular rodeo of hobbyhorses. Nabokov scoffs at Virgil, Hudibras, Swift, Shchedrin, Béranger. He thinks Coleridge's *The Pains of Sleep* a great poem. He urges the abolition of the Cyrillic alphabet. He sneers at other translations. Odd stuff, but at least individual. As with Yvor Winters preferring Bridges to Hopkins, agreeing or not we must respect this more than a thousand acceptances by rote of current, and probably ephemeral, orthodoxy. Meanwhile, we can note in passing, from Nabokov's extreme rudeness to previous translators, that we would hardly expect any hostile criticisms of himself to be too muted. . . .

It is sad to knock any attempt to bring Pushkin before us. There are long passages without these faults. Nevertheless, on the whole this is too much transposition into Nabokovese, rather than a translation into English.

Robert Conquest. *Poetry*. June, 1965, pp. 236–38

During the past forty years Vladimir Nabokov has published over a dozen novels, several collections of short stories, a number of plays, two volumes of poetry, a memoir, and a study of Gogol. He has also rendered into English some Russian poems, the chief one being Pushkin's verse-narrative, *Eugene Onegin*, to which Nabokov added over two volumes of notes and commentary. Five of the novels, representing his major work since the early nineteen-forties, were written originally in English; of the nine Russian novels, published between 1926 and 1938, all but three have been translated, either by Nabokov himself, his son, or other persons working closely with him. The true character of this achievement, of which the linguistic feat is only a part, is but gradually being recognized, and the following essays will, it is hoped, hasten that recognition. With much of his work either available to or written for the English-speaking reader, there is no reason for Nabokov's reputation to rest on *Lolita* alone, just as there is no reason for not viewing this novel in its true perspective, as an expression of a consistent, subtle artistic vision rather than as an exotic tour de force.

L. S. Dembo, in *Nabokov: The Man and His Work*,
ed. L. S. Dembo (Madison, Wisc., University of
Wisconsin Press, 1967), p. 3

The émigré poet Vladislav Khodasevich, who was Nabokov's best Russian critic, noted very early that in essence Nabokov writes only about artists and artistic problems, but that he does this under various allegorical guises. The early works of Sirin-Nabokov do occasionally, however, confront the figure of the artist directly, and it is most curious that these direct statements concern artists who are failures either in their lives or their art.

The Eye [*Soglyadatai*], which was written in 1930, a year after *The Defense* [*Zashchita Luzhina*], is a slighter work than *The Defense* in most respects including length. It is in fact really a short novella or a long short story which serves as the title story for a 1938 collection of Nabokov's short stories and was only promoted to the rank of a separate novel in its 1965 English translation—but in certain ways it is a more interesting work than *The Defense.* . . .

It is not possible within the confines of an article to demonstrate adequately the many arguments supporting Khodasevich's casual observation that Nabokov really writes only about the artist and art. However it is not really true that Nabokov does this only by way of allegory. As a mature writer Nabokov would make a writer the protagonist of a major novel, *The Gift*, and, as we have seen, he touched directly upon the subject even as a young writer. The infrequency with which this is done in his writing may be related to the fact that the subject of art and the subject of the artist tend to work at cross purposes. *The Eye* is a superb demonstration of the tactical problems of art, but we have only a glimpse of Smurov as *artist*. When the artist is more important than his art, as in the two short stories I have discussed, that is tantamount to saying that he is a false or failed artist. Thus the artist can be best examined as a *person* by putting aside his occupation: in art the shortest distance between two points is sometimes not a straight line.

Andrew Field, in *Nabokov: The Man and His Work*,
ed. L. S. Dembo (Madison, Wisc., University of
Wisconsin Press, 1967), pp. 57, 65

Nevertheless, in the perspective of the past and the future, Nabokov is the answer to all the doubts of the exiled, the persecuted, the insulted and the injured, the "unnoticed" and the "lost"!

Nabokov is the only Russian writer (both within Russia and in emigration) who belongs to the *entire* Western world (or the world in general), not Russia alone. The belonging to one specific nationality for such as he has no meaning and plays no role: native language—for Joyce, Kafka, Beckett, Ionesco, Jorge Luis Borges, and for Nabokov—has ceased to be what it was in the narrow nationalistic sense of eighty or a hundred years ago. Mere language effects related to native parlance and dialectisms that do not rest on other elements of a work are of no paramount interest and value, either for the author himself or for the reader, in modern literature. . . .

But Nabokov does not only *write* in a new manner, we learn from him to *read* in a new way as well. He (like some others) creates a new reader. In modern literature (prose, poetry, drama) he has taught us to identify not with heroes as did our ancestors, but with the author himself, in whatever disguise he may hide from us, in whatever mask he may appear.

Nina Berberova. The Italics Are Mine
(New York, Harcourt, Brace & World, 1969), p. 321

NAGIBIN, YURI (1920–   )

The Russian landscape is a masterfully drawn background against which pass private and social lives of all these people. Nature and man always somewhat compete with each other in the stories, but the unobtrusive human beings invariably manage to assert themselves at the end. Nagibin knows, understands, and respects his countrymen. He admires the wholeness of their personalities, their endurance, courage, unselfishness, and manly idealism. No matter how modest the natural abilities or circumstances of his heroes might be, they are always given a chance to prove their ultimate individual usefulness as members of the society in which they live. Broken down, discouraged, "lonely" types are absent from these stories. By implication, the new collectivist ethics is successful in creating a "new man": Operating through public opinion, it checks an "occasional" egotist, braggart, and a hoarder. The "party line" always lurks in the background of Nagibin's stories, but the people manage always to preserve their humanness. Calm optimism always prevails in Nagibin's stories, and the central ideological message of this collection is unmistakable: the belief of the author in constructive efforts of man directed toward the improvement of his own life and of lives of those around him, within the frame of Soviet ideology. In this, Nagibin feels lies the answer to the general human quest for an aim in life.

Technically, Nagibin contributes nothing new to the art of short story writing. He writes a poetic prose, but is a realist, with many Chekhovian traits. His stories, too, have no dramatic climaxes, no well-made plots, mood often predominates over matter in his stories.

Nonna D. Shaw. BA. Summer, 1962, p. 332

Both Nagibin and Kazakov lately have turned more and more to characters who are "simple," impulsive people not burdened by reflection, who reveal themselves only through emotion—for example, peasants and children. Some of the "perennial topics" that find their way into Kazakov's and, to a lesser extent, Nagibin's writings are the emotional confrontation of passing childhood with coming adulthood; the sudden upsurge of inconsolable grief at the death of a mother, seemingly unloved; the feelings of a man who, because of fatigue, has disregarded the tragedy of another and then—too late—is overcome with shame; the finding of happiness in love. In turning to these subjects that are essentially "neutral," the two authors have openly turned their backs on the neurotic complexity of present-day Soviet existence.

Some of the short stories of Kazakov and Nagibin also display a predilection for paradox: e.g., the wisdom and sensitivity of a dying man versus the blind obtuseness of a strong, living one; the complete rebirth of a dissipated individual as a result of briefly mistaking a "small-time vamp" for a hurt yet forgiving woman; a girl's pure and selfless love given to a village youth who is in love only with himself and thinks mainly of cheap pleasures. These themes suggest the only area of generalization in which the two writers indulge—the conflict between the moral and the natural order of things, between good and reality. Nagibin conveys this idea more frequently and with less subtlety than does Kazakov, and his concept of the good is often stretched to the point of merging with the official credo.

David Burg. *PC*. Sept.–Oct., 1962, p. 42

The title of (*Dreams*) and the cover illustration (two little boys) might suggest a precarious venture for some readers. Salinger, Golding, James, and Cozzens come to mind as creators of children's worlds valuable for their perspective on the authors' adult worlds, but prejudice against stories about children dies hard. The introduction, printed on the inside covers, might cause new trepidation: only the title story deals with imaginary character; "all the others have their prototypes in life." Inspection of the stories themselves justifies a wary approach. . . .

Yury Nagibin's characters are idealized types: little boys are mischievous, but manly; young men are handsome, strong, and uncomplicated—unless they have been corrupted by city life and higher education; women, young and old, cluck affectionately over their husbands, sons, or other charges. Mr. Nagibin is devoted to the simple life. His grown men ideally behave like happy children . . . they are likely to reminisce at some length about their childhood. . . .

In his most ambitious effort among the stories in *Dreams*, Mr. Nagibin never dreams of testing his theme; he simply illustrates it, by putting Chetunov to a test whose results are predictable. Whatever mystery the author sees in life he identifies with nature, from communion with which man may intuitively discover his dependence on others for material and psychological wellbeing. . . . The brotherhood of man is Mr. Nagibin's noble subject. But he treats it as if he were writting *Happiness Is a Warm Puppy*.

Ben Lucow. SSF. Winter, 1966, pp. 272–73

A literary critic said that the dominant feature of Nagibin's writings is the aristocratism of style; this is not artistic flair but aristocratism, for the words, as they are selected, combine into a sentence in such a way as to make it look special, of "blue blood." There is some truth in that observation, but the main characteristic of the author's language is still artistic flair. In his stories Nagibin strives first of all for the most precise presentation of the content, the most responsible reflection of that slice of life that appears in the sphere of his observation, the most precise expression of reality, not the verbal experimentation and refinement that the so-called aristocratism places at the head of that slice.

I. Kozlov. Znamya. Sept., 1968, p. 244[†]

NEKRASOV, VIKTOR (1911–   )

We cannot agree with those who support the Union of Writers' consideration of Nekrasov's novel [*V okopakh Stalingrada (In the Trenches of Stalingrad)*] and explain the poverty of ideas in his writing as a certain literary attitude, the attitude of a former front-line soldier who does not wish to recount the war or people at war as reported in the newspapers. No, there is no question here of a literary pose but of a talented writer, Nekrasov, who reveals in his first work a lack of maturity in his thought and a lack of depth in his penetration of reality. We should not be afraid to talk directly about this young writer who, we trust, will write many good books. I think the best way to hail the young, forceful talent of Nekrasov is with objective and comradely guidance directed toward the defects in his first book, attesting to some narrowness and limitations in the author's ideological horizon and an inability to rise above the material of his observation for the sake of ideological understanding and artistic generalization. Hence, many defects in the composition of the work resemble more the writing of a diary than of a harmonious, artistic whole.

Lev Subotski. Novy mir. March, 1947, pp. 141–42[†]

There is much to be learned from the discussion about the latest novel of Victor Nekrasov, *In the Town of My Birth* [*V rodnom gorode*]. Nekrasov is a modern writer of profoundly human, original and in many ways attractive gifts. He is a master of precise, laconic sketches; a few lines, two or three phrases, suffice him to draw a character or convey a mood. He has a sympathy for decent people who are devoted to their work and their friends. . . .

All the same, one cannot help thinking that the author often stops half-way in his character drawing. The characters of the novel are deciding the problem of their place in life and their share in the common struggle. Their social and personal relations are complicated. Yet the author sometimes simplifies the matter. He at times seems to be hesitating to pass the threshold to the spiritual world of his characters, and as a result their *actions* appear to be more important than their *motives*. He has a habit of cutting short the reflections of his characters, of refusing to penetrate their inner world, of neglecting his right and possibility to describe within the framework of his artistic manner the thoughts and heartsearchings of his characters.

We think that both at the front and in the rear, people were spiritually richer, more conscious and purposeful than Nekrasov describes them. . . .

With his *In the Trenches of Stalingrad* and *In the Town of My Birth* Victor Nekrasov comes out against schematic writing, against the gloss that some writers put on life. But even the first of these books had already prompted the question whether in his anxiety to avoid false beauty, high-sounding phrases and deliberately "effective" situations the author with all his gifts does not overlook true beauty and those fine qualities that raise the hero of Soviet literature above all heroes of the past. For the simple, rank-and-file man is a man of deep feeling and thought. That question arises again in connection with *In the Town of My Birth* whose heroes somehow lack richness of thought. Is it not possible that the "truth" as Victor Nekrasov sees it is something impoverished and cut down, that in his conception life and people are duller than they are in reality?

Boris Rurikov. *SL*. Dec., 1955, pp. 165–67

In the story "Senka," Nekrasov consciously chose an undeveloped, unintellectual man for his hero and one difficult to imagine. This is a man whose reaction to his environment is retarded. He judges his crime totally intuitively, inspired with love for the wounded sergeant who had hero-ically fought against the enemy. In the same dull manner, in essence not understanding the significance of what was taking place, Senka under-takes his heroic effort. If, in reality, the author wanted to describe the spiritual awakening of the soldier and the chance occurrence of the black spot in his biography (and I doubt that this is what entered Nekrasov's mind), he would have had to portray not only Senka's gropings toward consciousness of his crime but also, incomparably more difficult, his evo-lution toward the feat.

Heroic conduct is not encountered every day. All of a man's life with its bright spots and hopes is concentrated in these heroic efforts as in a prism. Moral ideals matured by years, faith in the righteousness of the heroic act, totality of noble ideals and experiences—these are fundamental to the heroic effort. Nevertheless, during the critical moment, Nekrasov's Senka thinks least about any ideals. Again the writer, as in all of his other work, underestimates the ideological-political basis of the heroic in war. Shame and the desire to prove that he is really not a lost individual are the sole factors which control Senka throughout the story. But even if we grant such a doubtful treatment of the image of the common soldier, the "critical point" in the development of the character of the hero remains unmotivated and arbitrary.

The emotional inertia in the final chapter of the story more clearly underlines the falseness of its subject. It sets off the failure of the writer who futilely attempted to show the spiritual rebirth of a man who had marred himself by desertion.

Arkady Elyashevich. *Zvezda*. Oct., 1957, p. 198[†]

Kira Georgievna is a typical story in the neo-naturalistic genre, formally restrained and patterned after a situation well known in Soviet literature: the superficially happy life of the heroine is interrupted by a man who has grown wise through the experience of work and deprivation; under his influence, the once carefree heroine becomes filled with a sense of responsibility to herself and to mankind. But if Nekrasov's story is conventional, his treatment is not. "The man who has grown wise" brings with him the experience not of a builder of communism, as one would expect in orthodox Soviet fiction, but of 20 years innocently spent behind barbed wire. The transgressions of the sculptress Kira are not of the officially fashionable kind, like parasitism or acquisitiveness; they are mindless conformity with officially prescribed values in life and art. Nekrasov, similarly to other "critical realists," has sought to convey new ideas by investing a commonplace literary scheme with unexpected content.

David Burg. *PC*. Sept.–Oct., 1962, p. 37

In distinction to Simonov, who credits the "miracle" of the Stalingrad victory equally to the soldiers and the higher command, Nekrasov cannot [in *In the Trenches of Stalingrad*], even at the hour of victory, forget the mistakes of the military leadership, for which the people paid with so many needlessly lost lives. It is not by chance therefore that in his story of the first day of the Stalingrad offensive (described with remarkable force), Nekrasov gives a great deal of space to the tragic conflict between the regiment's chief of staff Abrosimov and the regimental commander Major Borodin. Borodin issues one order, Abrosimov another; when the officers attempt to show Abrosimov that his order is impossible to carry out, he draws his revolver, threatening to shoot those who oppose him. The officers submit, but many people pay with their lives for Abrosimov's mistake. In the subsequent trial Borodin succeeds in proving Abrosimov's error, and the latter is demoted to a private.

It is probably because of this, as well as the general democratic feeling of the novel, that it did not please the literary powers. Their disapproval was quite transparently expressed in an article by Boris Solovyov, published in *Izvestia* on November 29, 1946, in which the critic tried to prove that Nekrasov's novel, though not devoid of literary merit, was merely the testimony of a "participant in a battle" who had no conception of "the strategy of the war as a whole."

Vera Alexandrova. *A History of Soviet Literature*
(New York, Doubleday, 1963), p. 309

Nekrasov knows very little about either the United States or Italy, nor does he pretend to know much. He uses the occasion of his trip as a way of talking [in *Po obe storony okeana* (*Both Sides of the Ocean*)] about literature, art, architecture, the film, the importance of freer exchanges, and the appalling ignorance among Russians of what is actually going on abroad in the arts, or at least what was until quite recently their ignorance. He writes about the Guggenheim Museum and Corbusier and Frank Lloyd Wright. He himself was trained as an architect and took his degree the year the Stalinist blight descended on that field, when the plans Corbusier submitted to the competition for the Palace of Soviets were rejected in favor of a baroque wedding cake. After that he fought in the war, and later, in 1954, published an interesting novel (translated into French as *La Ville Natale*) which was one of those that marked the beginning of the thaw. Travelling in Europe and the United States, he speculates on the fate of architecture if Wright and Le Corbusier had been given a free hand to plan cities in the Soviet Union as both of them at one time badly wanted to do.

With regard to the film, he talks not only about *La Dolce Vita*, which Russians had not seen, but also about the unreleased Russian film, *Foreposts of Ilyich*, which Khrushchev, emphasizing the very scenes Nekrasov wrote of, later singled out for violent attack, suggesting at the same time that Nekrasov be read out of the Party. The violence of Khrushchev's attack on the one hand, and the fact that nothing seems to have happened to Nekrasov on the other, indicates the curious stalemate of the current situation in the arts.

Sidney Monas. *HdR*. Winter, 1964–65, pp. 605–6

Nekrasov made his debut in literature at a relatively late age, in 1946, with the publication of *In the Trenches of Stalingrad*. This semi-autobiographical war novel, based on his own experience as a combat officer in the Battle of Stalingrad, won him immediate literary success. Deviating completely from orthodox Soviet war writing, this brutally realistic account of day-to-day events on the battlefield introduced a refreshing breeze of truthfulness and a new tone of honesty and sincerity into Russian war literature; it was socialist realism in reverse.

The author avoids the broad dimensions of epic war scenes and, instead, focuses our attention on one narrow segment of the front—his own battalion. It is people that he is mainly concerned with. We are introduced to a vast gallery of officers and soldiers, each portrayed masterfully and standing out clearly as an individual with his heroic endurance and his human weaknesses, as Nekrasov observed them daily in this cruelest of battles. This is why this gripping Stalingrad saga immediately captivated the hearts of so many millions of Russians (it sold close to two million copies). It is a pity that it has not been made available to the American reader.

Herman Carmel. BA. Autumn, 1966, p. 381

OLESHA, YURI (1899–1960)

The sharp expressiveness of Olesha's style is accompanied by its simplicity. The structure of separate forms is simple, be it an image of man or a metaphor. The composition of *Zavist (Envy)* is also simple. In it there is no complex plot, no tying and untying of the threads of the subject matter. The strength of the novel lies in the plasticity of its characters, in the psychological depth of their characterization. *Envy* is a novel of characters or, better, of social types. . . . The two worlds in the novel fight each other. The social irreconcilability of the protagonists is also shown in their philosophical and psychological traits.

The characters are generalized. Strong social coloring is given to individual psychological traits. Behind every character stands a social stratum, a group, or a symbolic generalization. Such structure of forms—both real and symbolic—allows the author to condense and deepen the social and psychological conflict present in the foundation of the novel. Therefore, the analysis of *Envy* must be essentially the analysis of its characters and their actions. [1929]

Vyacheslav Polonski. *Na literarnye temy*
(Moscow, Sovetski pisatel, 1968), p. 303[†]

In our dramaturgy, one can already find the reflection of new relationships between people, of new representations, and of new feelings. In his brilliant play, *Zagovor chuvstv (The Conspiracy of Feelings)*, Yuri Olesha placed the question of old and new feelings on the agenda of the day. Ivan Babichev and Kavalerov, representing and bearing the old feelings, suffer defeat.

However, Yuri Olesha was not successful in portraying the victors. In the play, there is a duel between Ivan Babichev, the "leader of the old feelings," and his brother, Andrei Babichev, a sausage maker and a man devoid of every feeling. Ivan speaks about him: "My brother, Andrei Babichev, a builder of the new world, destroys vanity, love, the family, brutality. . . . There will no longer be lovers, blighters, courageous men, loyal friends, or prodigal children. . . . The powerful human emotions are now avowed insignificant and banal."

Ivan Babichev and Kavalerov are vanquished in the play. The sausage maker uses the razor with which Kavalerov intends to kill Andrei Babichev to cut off a piece of sausage. Can "sausage" replace the old feelings?

Are sausage makers the builders of a new world? Have we no more lovers or courageous men? Is there no place for feelings in our life?

In the play Olesha resolves the question erroneously. Feelings are not destroyed but appear in a different way, and their manifestation little resembles the emotions of the representatives of the old order so talently described by Olesha. In our dramaturgy, one can already see feelings in contrast to those of the old order, resolving in a new way the questions which troubled the subjects of the "king of fools"—Ivan Babichev. [1934]

V. Kirshon. O literature i iskusstve (Moscow, Khudozhestvennaya literatura, 1967), p. 169[†]

One of the most promising essays in Soviet fiction of those years was Yuri Olesha's Envy, which originally appeared in 1927. Like not a few other Soviet writers of the period who did not wholly give themselves up to a communist orthodoxy of sentiment, Olesha has written nothing for many years and has been consigned to outer darkness by the pundits of Soviet criticism. This, no doubt, is very understandable in view of the everyday implications which the theme of Envy has for the questioning Soviet citizen at the present time. What Olesha attempts to do in this short novel is to disclose the moral and emotional shortcomings of the materialist plan of salvation. In the opposition he presents between the brothers Babichev, the one a perfected and eupeptic functionary of the new age, the other an ineffectual arch-romantic, he does not load the dice unfairly. The romantic, with his dream of a "conspiracy of feelings," is also a monster of vulgarity, doomed to defeat; the plea the author enters is not for a dying age but rather for "sentiments that are hallowed by poets and by the muse of history itself." The style of the novel, overladen with imagery and somewhat enervating oracular, is still youthful (it is a difficult book, incidentally, to translate), but there was rich promise here.

TLS. Aug. 16, 1947, p. 413

Olesha's fundamental theme is the same which occupies many searching minds today, especially among former Communists. We find it restated in Arthur Koestler's Darkness at Noon and The Yogi and the Commissar. Andrey Babichev, the "sausage-maker," "the model of masculinity," is an embodiment of Koestler's Commissar type. When Rubashov, the hero of Darkness at Noon, writes down in his diary—"We have thrown overboard all conventions, our sole principle is that of consequent logic; we are sailing without ethical ballast"—he states, in my opinion, the problem which torments Olesha and which leads Ivan Babichev to organize his conspiracy of feelings. What will be the place of personal ethics, of human emotions and human dreams in this new mechanized, planned, totalitarian society which has discarded all ethical ballast and has proclaimed that the end justifies the means. . . . Olesha's romantic rebels are portrayed in all their vulgarity and unattractiveness (one of the merits the Soviet critics saw in it, when they praised the novel on its first appearance, was this showing up of the "enemies of the Soviet regime" in all their naked ugliness). Yet, the unprejudiced reader cannot help being aware that Olesha has a sneaking regard for them—that it is not unintentionally that he endows Kavalerov with talent and imagination; that he sympathizes with his assertion of the worth of the individual and his proud rejection of a fame derived from the manufacture of improved sausages, just as he does with Ivan Babichev for whom "invention is the beloved of reason." For all their vulgarity and meanness the two "negative" characters of *Envy* are human, while the two main spokesmen of the "new world," the world of sausages, machines, and model canteens, are both vulgar *and* inhuman.

Gleb Struve. *Soviet Russian Literature 1917–1950*
(Norman, Okla., University of Oklahoma Press, 1951),
pp. 103–4

Olesha's artistic vision is remarkable. He sees things so minutely and presents them in such a way that even the least significant details become memorable and important. And they are indeed important because they contribute to the character drawing. Here is a case in point in *Envy:*

"I make a hobby of exercising my powers of observation. Have you ever noticed that salt falls off the point of a knife without leaving a trace—the knife gleams spotless; that a pince-nez rides across the bridge of the nose like a bicycle; that every man is surrounded by small inscriptions, an ant-like myriad of tiny inscriptions: on forks, spoons, plates, on the rim of a pince-nez, on buttons and pencils? No one notices them. . . ."

This close-up view of small things gives us a better understanding of Kavalerov as an onlooker. The same sharpness of vision allowed Olesha to take the risk of choosing the relation of mind to being as his poetic theme. His short stories, which might well be called philosophical, are in the nature of an experiment. Only it is not a search for new forms that prompts him. However original are the artistic touches which make a "gem" of the simplest of these stories—"It [a ladybird] detached itself from the highest point of the apple and flew away on wings extracted from somewhere behind as one extracts a handkerchief from under a tailcoat," or: "Lyolya took an apricot from the bag, tore off its small buttocks and threw away the stone,"—similes of a like kind can, of course, be found in the work of authors from other periods of history as well. The difference is that here the author's sharpness of vision serves a profoundly modern purpose: Olesha seeks in his stories to reveal and affirm the material nature of the world, to convey in tangible form the primary nature of being in relation to the mind.

Much in the stories seems incomplete, artificial, unnecessarily complicated. The author set himself a hard task and these stories were as preliminary sketches for a future painting. But in many of them he sought to win through from experimental intricacy to lucid means of depiction, while still preserving the individuality of his style. . . .

Three Fat Men [*Tri tolstyaka*] is a tale beautifully told in the tradition of the French romanticists. Although the scene is laid in an imaginary country and the tone is humorous, Olesha deals with serious matters, helping his young readers to see the victory of the people as the victory of health, beauty and life. The story of the doll that is transformed into the living girl Souok in whose adventures such superbly drawn and fully realistic human characters as Dr. Gaspar Arneri, the dancing teacher One-twothree, the rope-walker Tibul and the gunsmith Prospero become involved quite naturally, captured the fancy of the Moscow Art Theatre. It presented as enchanting a production of the *Three Fat Men* as it did of Maeterlinck's *The Blue Bird*. (Olesha's recent dramatization of Dostoyevsky's *The Idiot* is now in rehearsal at the Vakhtangov Theatre.)

Viktor Pertsov. SL. Nov., 1956, pp. 152–53

Envy, like [Zamyatin's] *We*, contains conscious echoes of Dostoevsky's *Notes from the Underground* as well as of "The Grand Inquisitor." Both novels enter a plea for individual freedom and the autonomy of feelings in opposition to the rationalism of modern mass society. Like Dostoevsky, both novelists rebel against the imagined "Crystal Palace" of the future, where life will respond only to logarithmic tables, and the individual human being, for the sake of happiness, gives up freedom. The principal literary text for Olesha's *Envy* is the passage in *Notes from the Underground* where Dostoevsky lashes out at the "Crystal Palace," the utopian vision of the communist future presented by the socialist critic Chernyshevsky in 1863. Poetry, the human personality, traditional Russian culture are shown in Olesha's farcical fantasy as degraded and discarded. The envious adolescent Kavalerov and the retarded old fool Ivan Babichev, neither of whom has a man's place in the new world, reflect Olesha's pessimistic view as to the fate of the nineteenth-century literary imagination in the twentieth century. Though Kavalerov and Ivan are defeated, Olesha has so contrived the telling of his story that the reader identifies himself with their disreputable human feelings, and never with the Buddha-shaped businessmen in nose spectacles. The bizarre form of the novel conceals a defense of human values which Olesha felt were being trampled upon in the name of building socialism, and a plea for the right to existence of love, a sense of personal honor, and respect for oneself.

Edward J. Brown. *Russian Literature Since the Revolution* (New York, Crowell-Collier, 1963), p. 93

A Stern Youth [*Strogi yunosha*] was an unwitting illustration of Olesha's idea that a theme thrown out of a writer's notebook must, once it was born in his mind, ultimately reappear in another form in one of his future works.

A Stern Youth was never produced; it was Olesha's last major work. Some two years after its publication (in 1934) his name disappeared from Soviet literary journals. It did not reappear until after the war, in the early 1950s, and then mostly over articles, essays, and memoirs. His "Literary Diaries" and the excerpts from his notebooks reveal that, although doomed to silence, Olesha continued to work stubbornly, systematically, and intensively on perfecting his literary form. In a short story, "In the World," Olesha mentions that he had preserved in his old folders three hundred pages of a manuscript, each marked with the numeral "1." They were the three hundred versions of the first page of his novel, *Envy*, none of which was used in the final text.

Vera Alexandrova. *A History of Soviet Literature* (New York, Doubleday, 1963), p. 173

Olesha was conscious of the motifs of castration and sterility he employed in *Envy*. The question is perhaps not quite so relevant as might appear at first sight. Relatively little is known of Olesha's life, but even if more biographical information were available, it might not help us. Such psychic attitudes as fear of sterility or of castration are not necessarily manifested externally, for they are normally not conscious fears. Only a very close, and presumably a long, acquaintance with the author would give us reliable information. But such conflicts are often manifested in symbolic projections, among which imaginative literature falls; it is just to Olesha's writings, then, that we can look for the proper evidence. This is not because we are seeking more information about his life, which is in a sense irrelevant for us, a private fact, but because we are seeking to connect and illuminate the various aspects and planes of the work of fiction we are studying.

Still, two anecdotes from Olesha's memoirs may be of some interest and relevance. Olesha was extremely fond of the circus. Once as a young man he witnessed a performance by three acrobats, two men and a girl. He tells us that he fell in love with the girl, with the way her hair flew in the breeze. Several days later he saw the same two men on the street. With

them, however, was no girl, but a young, unattractive boy of bad com-
plexion who spat, and whom Olesha at first took for an assistant. Suddenly he realized that this was the "girl" with whom he had fallen in
love. And, Olesha adds, he remained in love with her all his life.

In the second anecdote Olesha tells of how, late in life, he handled a
woman's mask, how the hollows of the nose and cheeks reminded him of
a smile, the smile of a young and beautiful face. . . . *Envy* presents us
with a choice of two worlds in conflict, both of which are sterile: the old
order, with its romantic escapism, and the new, with its cult of technology
and contempt for human values.

William E. Harkins. *SlR*. Sept., 1966, pp. 455–57

Olyesha's central concern is a fear for the future of human feelings, both
the noble and the despicable, in a society where worship of technology
is second only to obligatory adulation of a political doctrine. In *Envy* we
observe the clash of two worlds, represented by a pair of intellectuals and
an efficient Communist industrial executive and his two protegés—a young
soccer player and an uncomplicated, healthy female. The intellectuals
are spiteful and dirty, yet it is they who stake their future on a fantastic
machine called Ophelia—"the name of a girl who went mad from love
and despair." Needless to say, Ophelia proves no match for the opposition's weapons: indices of labor productivity (in this case, the manufacture of sausages) and goal scores. American readers who discern a con-
vergence in the problems facing highly industrialized societies irrespective
of their political systems will surely note that this novel, first published
forty years ago, uses an only slightly Slavicized form of a familiar name—
Babichev.

Maurice Friedberg. *SR*. Dec. 23, 1967, p. 31

The talent of Yuri Olyesha is smaller than that of Babel or Pilnyak, but
still very precious. In his best fiction, the short novel *Envy* (which appears
in the volume called *Love* [*Lyubov*]), Olyesha writes, like many of his
contemporaries, about the clash of two worlds, but with a wry, half-
defeated yet touchingly affectionate irony that seems entirely his own.
His subject comes straight out of Turgenev: the plight of "the superfluous man," a figure of hesitation and sensitiveness destroyed by a rationalistic world. His technique resembles that of Charlie Chaplin: the
pathos of slapstick, the heartbreak of horseplay. One hears in Olyesha's
prose something of the trembling irony of Yiddish literature: the grimace,
the shrug of the shoulder, the flick of despair. I have been told the story
of a Yiddish writer who lived as a refugee in wartime Russia and became
friends with Olyesha. The Yiddish writer asked him why he no longer

wrote and Olyesha replied, "I do write—every morning. And every night I tear it up."

Irving Howe. *Harper.* Jan., 1968, pp. 73–74

Envy . . . is a declaration of rebellion against "significance" and "meaning." Reality has no objective value; it is the creation of one individual. We are completely at the mercy of Kavalerov's fantasies, which work in unpredictable ways, and must therefore follow them where they will, taking them, as we do real life itself, on whatever their terms are at any particular moment. We are prisoners of a ruthless present, the world of what is actually happening. There are no accurate interpretations of events, no proper explanations or summing up, few of the trappings of conventional novels. From the viewpoint of traditional fiction, there is a shocking extravagance of means in *Envy* in the pure actions and pure gestures that are absolved from service to the underlying symbol-pattern that unifies the book. On top of this Olesha erects a scaffolding that has all the stark simplicity of a formula plot: two "old" characters (Ivan and Anechka) versus two "new" ones (Volodya, Valya), with Kavalerov and Andrei Babichev providing the bridge. But it is a trap to catch the careless reader, and most critics, hypnotized by the symmetry, have fallen into it, reading the work as a conventional novel of manners, not as the symbolist fantasy it is.

Robert A. Maguire. *Red Virgin Soil* (Princeton, N.J., Princeton University Press, 1968), p. 344

In the summer of 1927 I read *Envy* and received my strongest literary impression for many years. It was and remained for me a great event in Soviet literature, very likely even greater than Pasternak's *Waves*. Before me was a story by a young, original, talented writer, very much alive in his own time, a man who knew how to write and write in a completely modern way as no one in Russia had before him, with a sense of measure and taste, knowing how to interweave drama and irony, pain and joy, and in whom literary devices combined with the inner devices of his personal inversions in an oblique presentation of reality. He depicted people without embracing the rigid laws of "realism," on his own plane, against the background of his own personal vision of the world, with all the freshness of a unique and original sight. I realized that Olesha was one of the few now in Russia who knew what an undercurrent in a text and its role in a prose work were, who had a mastery of prose rhythm, grotesque fantasy, hyperbole, sound effects, and unexpected turns of the imagination. Olesha's consciousness of his goals, and control over achievement of them, and the exquisite balance of the novel were striking. Something had been built or created, linked not to Gladkov's *Cement*, to

Gorky's *Mother* and even to Chernyshevsky's *What Can Be Done?*—but directly linked to Bely's *Petersburg*, to *The Overcoat*, to *Notes from Underground*, the greatest works of our literature.

> Nina Berberova. *The Italics Are Mine* (New York,
> Harcourt, Brace & World, 1969), pp. 318–19

OSTROVSKI, NIKOLAI (1904–1936)

The young author of this largely autobiographical novel [*Kak zakalyalas stal* (*How the Steel Was Tempered*)], who was blind and bedridden before he began writing it, died a few weeks ago, and his death gives a final pathos to the strange story unfolded in these pages. Against the background of war, civil war and the tasks of reconstruction afterwards the author draws a full-length portrait of a youthful hero of the new Russia, Paul Korchagin. The background is vividly realistic, the portrait carries complete conviction. The whole thing is an unmistakable slice of life rendered with vigour, excellent judgment and a sure instinct for what is dramatic. . . . There is an impressive truthfulness of mind and feeling in this extremely vivid life story.

> *TLS.* Jan. 30, 1937, p. 75

[*How the Steel Was Tempered*] has been acclaimed in the Soviet Union with greater enthusiasm than any other first novel ever has. It has a number of glaring defects—clichés, overabundance of casual characters, unevenness of tempo, disproportion of space in describing different periods in the hero's life, occasional lagging of the story, and other flaws. But the book is more than a novel: its title, "How the steel has been forged," suggests the record of the Young Communists who had begun their activity during the civil wars and had gone through all the vicissitudes and upheavals that preceded the present period of more or less peaceful construction. Ostrovsky's novel is documentarily faithful to history. . . .

The uninitiated reader may find the story melodramatic. He may doubt the reality of the youths and girls who show such incredible courage, perseverance, defiance of obstacles and hardships, and steadfast loyalty to the cause. The student of Russian affairs knows, however, that such were the facts. Those Young Communists were not only real; they were typical. This is true even of the main character, Pavel Korchagin. . . .

The Korchagin story might sound unbelievable, were it not for the known fact that it is largely the story of the author. Nikolay Ostrovsky has actually lived through all that. The country is familiar with his fine record as a fighter and with his exertion of will power at the most trying moments. Recently he was decorated by the Government for his past work and for his literary activity today. Ostrovsky and his novel are a living example of heroic, all-conquering youth.

Alexander Kaun. *BA*. Winter, 1937, pp. 52–53

Foreigners visiting the Ostrovski Museum are struck by the writer's classical formulation of the fundamental principles of communist morality: "The most wonderful thing for a man is to serve people with all that you have created, even when you have ceased to exist"; and "A soldier who dies on the front hearing the victorious shout 'hurrah' of his detachment gains a last and somehow higher satisfaction."

The sensation of the joy of struggle, harmoniously merging the individual personality with the collective, is one of those wonderful traits of Pavel Korchagin that make him the antithesis of the romantic heroes of the past, with their contemplative view of life and their fascination with suffering. And when life placed Korchagin in a hopeless position, which any other hero would have resolved with suicide, he made the remarkable comment to himself: "Be able to live life and, even when life has become unbearable, make it useful."

At the same time, Nikolai Ostrovski showed that the fulfillment of a citizen's responsibility in a socialist country, "where each small spark of talent in a man ignites," is connected to the creative unfolding of the individual personality. Korchagin is happy not only because he adds to the common good but because he adds a measure of his own strength and talent to this store. It is primarily the artistically convincing image of Pavel Korchagin that allows those fighting against fascism both here and abroad to see in him a mentor and friend.

Nataliya Tepsi. *Novy mir*. Dec., 1946, pp. 260, 263†

Born of the storm, these newcomers to the historical arena are so much a part of the events which gave them being that the life story of one of them, a boy who became a man, a Young Communist who became a Bolshevik, as told by Ostrovsky in his *How the Steel Was Tempered*, acquired the stature of a novel about the dawn of the Soviet state and the creation of a new world. Few literary works have the power of this book to revive the early period of our Soviet society, to reconstruct our first sense of freedom, while treating of a multitude of issues and problems that will retain their pressing purport for a long time to come.

The late war brought Ostrovsky's Korchagin once again into the limelight. The flower of our youth summoned him at the most trying moments of the struggle and he responded—alive, vital and victorious.

Pavel Korchagin is a young man with a single mind and goal. Dedicating himself to the people, he takes a path which if adhered to ensures a man against both pettiness and half-heartedness; he and his mental powers grow and develop as the revolution grows and develops. Together with the new mode of life the new mode of thinking asserts itself in him. And by actively participating in the building up of better social forms, he finds the key to mankind's eternal questions as well.

We know Korchagin from childhood to the moment he totals up the tally sheet of his life. Although the whole fabric of his life is likened to the process of tempering steel, it would be well to remember that the ascent began at a high point. Pavel Korchagin was only 15 when seven days of torture in a Petlura dungeon failed to wring a single murmur from him. Korchagin's revolutionary activity began with a feat of courage. Hence it is not surprising that the story of his life should end with a victory of the human spirit that makes a bid for immortality.

Abram Gurvich. *SL*. May, 1947, pp. 76–77

Not every figure in the abundant gallery of characters created by Ostrovski is described with such expressiveness as Pavel Korchagin and his comrades in arms. Some scenes from the novel are to a certain degree schematic and lack necessary artistic concreteness. Sometimes the writer does not picture, but only narrates, events. Certain vital characters, such as Ledenev, Zhigireva, and Versenev, never materialize further than the pages of the book, and the reader is left wishing, naturally, to see them vividly and clearly drawn as distinct personalities. The essential continuity of the subject, particularly in the second part of the novel, now and then becomes disordered, interrupted by false episodes essential to the development of the character of Pavel, but poorly linked to the narrative sequence.

In subsequent editions of the novel, deviations in style can still be found here and there as marks of naturalism in the speech of the heroes, from which Ostrovski diligently tried to free himself.

The author himself, conscious of these distinct artistic shortcomings, exaggerated their significance and was forced to check each line of the novel by ear.

Working on the second part of the novel, he even wished himself "to rehash thoroughly" *How the Steel Was Tempered*, but he lacked the physical stamina. "I have sufficient strength"—he wrote to Karavayeva— "only for careful proofreading and clearing up points of confusion in the manuscript."

But these were only partial failures in the details of the young writer's great canvas, specific shortcomings that did not interfere with the artistic conviction of his work or his essential heroic image. The fate of the novel is an irrefutable proof of this.

N. Vengrov. *Oktyabr*. Dec., 1951, pp. 178–79[†]

To counterbalance . . . disenchanted young men of the 1930s, the critics launched, shortly after the assassination of Kirov in 1934, a propaganda campaign for the novel *How Steel Was Tempered*, by a hitherto unknown young Communist, Nikolay Ostrovsky. The novel was autobiographical in character. Nikolay Ostrovsky (1904–36) was born in the family of a poor worker in the Ukraine. He joined the Bolsheviks at an early age, performing, with his friends, a variety of tasks for the party. In 1919 he volunteered for the front without telling his family. A year later he was severely wounded and partially lost his vision. However, he refused to be defeated. In 1926 it was found that he was suffering from polyarthritis, a disease that kept him bedridden for the rest of his life. Three years later Ostrovsky became blind and partially paralyzed. Then he decided to become a writer. He invented a special device with raised lines, which made it possible for him to write, feeling the lines through the paper. He sent the first part of his novel to the magazine *Molodaya Gvardia* (Young Guard) in 1931. A year later he was notified that it had been accepted for publication. The novel was printed serially during 1932, but did not arouse much interest. Nor did the second part attract attention when it appeared in the same magazine from January to May, 1934. It was only after the assassination of Kirov by the young Communist Nikolayev and the discovery of the assassin's diary, voicing the moods of the disenchanted, that Ostrovsky's novel came to the center of attention of the literary world. Wide party and official circles became interested in Ostrovsky's fate; they surrounded him with solicitude and care and tried to save him. A whole brigade of writers was dispatched to help him with his second novel, *Born of the Storm* [*Rozhdennye burei*].

In the meantime his first novel was published in book form, in a considerably edited version. In the version that had earlier been published in *Molodaya Gvardia,* Ostrovsky had described the tense atmosphere of his home, his own suffering when he became an invalid, his relations with his wife, whose mother invited her against him, and their separation. All this disappeared in the later editions of the novel. In its final version the novel was in full conformity with all the rules of "Socialist realism."

Vera Alexandrova. *A History of Soviet Literature* (New York, Doubleday, 1963), pp. 43–44

PANOVA, VERA (1905–   )

Fellow-Travellers [*Sputniki*], though a work of great merit is not without shortcomings. While following the two principal lines along which the writer's concept develops ("not to explain that which is perfectly clear" and "to avoid stereotypes") the reader will find in each some features with which he may rightfully disagree. . . .

What has led to the confusion is obviously Panova's dread to impose "explanations."

Neither the critic nor the reader demand didacticism from the writer. There is no need for the writer to assume the solemn pose of the preacher and judge and read sermons or sit in judgement upon his characters. In her portrait of Danilov, the authoress without in the least digressing from the principle of her method and without resorting to long-winded elucidations might have solved her problem. She could have done it in many ways without direct imposition of her thoughts, by shades of intonation, by the very method of representation.

Though not all the ideas of the novel nor all the artistic lines along which it develops have been consummated and answers have not been given to all the questions posed in its pages, *Fellow-Travellers* is, nonetheless, a talented piece of writing which deals with the recent war, the men and women who won the victory and the new ethical values born out of the moral and political unity of the Soviet people and as such has earned wide popularity among the Soviet reading public.

Vladimir Aleksandrov. SL. Aug., 1947, pp. 58–59, 61

[*Sputniki* (*The Train*)] is a remarkable first novel. You have not read half a page before you realize that you are in the grip of a masterly and masterful craftsman, who knows exactly, to a hair's breadth, where she wants to put you, and who can and does, put you right there on the dot every time. . . . Miss Panova's canvas has a Russian largeness, and she carries on, too, the old Russian classical tradition of writing with a cold objectiveness. . . . But what pleases, particularly, is the never-forgotten contrast between the hopes of the individual and the totally unexpected impact of circumstance upon him.

Julia Strachey. NSN. Jan. 22, 1949, p. 85

Panova's . . . *Kruzhilikha* (1948; the title is the name of a factory) dealt with some problems of transition from wartime to peacetime conditions

in Soviet industry, but Panova's chief concern was again with human beings and their relationships. Though not as good as the earlier work
[*Sputniki*], it had the same quality of detachment and understatement.
Kruzhilikha led to a curious and typical controversy, during which some
critics blamed Panova for this very quality. One of them complained,
with naïve earnestness, that Panova did not "decipher" her characters
enough, that no sooner did the reader come to like a character than he
discovered that the author meant that character to be a "negative" one,
and vice versa, thus "shouldering upon the reader the responsibility for
appraising her characters." . . .

   The Literary Gazette complained that at a critical discussion of *Kruzhilikha* the novel was used by some [Russian] critics "to preach non-
Party spirit in literature." The critic Munblit was quoted as saying that
the principal charm of Panova's novel lay in the fact that "one cannot
tell which character is positive and which negative. . . . I find it interesting to meet such imperfect people who change and toward whom my
attitude changes." This, said *The Literary Gazette*, was the statement
of an aesthete, "aimed at the principle of Party-mindedness in our literature." Although both of Panova's novels were singled out for Stalin
awards, several critics maintained that her "detachment" was incompatible with Socialist realism.

Gleb Struve. *Soviet Russian Literature 1917–1950*
(Norman, Okla., University of Oklahoma Press, 1951),
pp. 362–63

Vera Panova is one of the more gifted and prolific Soviet writers to have
appeared since the last war. She was never a Party writer, nor did she
directly concern herself with major political or social themes. Since the
thaw, she has become increasingly absorbed with the hum-drum, the ordinary, the seemingly trivial and indisputably private events of every
day. This is not easy. Pressure by official critics and state publishing
houses need hardly be described here. But there is another, perhaps new,
probably from the point of view of what it can do to a writer, more dangerous and more subtle pressure. Now that small areas and islands of
private life have been opened for possible habitation, they swarm with
the most intense and sanguine of hopes. There is a large and sympathetic
Soviet reading audience prepared to accept writers who attempt to convey the personal tragedy of a public destiny; but to accept a private life
not directly touched by public affairs as in itself inherently tragic would
be almost more than a Soviet audience could bear. It is an optimism born
of terror, a sincere but distorting necessity, to which Panova unfortunately
cannot resist submitting her judgment as a writer, and which mars the
otherwise excellent little novel *Seriozha* recently translated under the
inappropriately poetic title *Time Walked*.

The book itself (not so much Russian as it is feminine) is presented in terms of the sensibility of an ordinary, sympathetic six year old boy. Delicately, it hangs by a hair. Panova conveys the essential helplessness of a child, and the painful, humorous, touchingly beautiful inner tricks and devices by means of which he tries to make the formidable, incomprehensible world into a world he can manage. Unfortunately, what might otherwise have been a small but flawless jewel is marred by a sentimental, or at least unrealistic ending, in which too much depends on the wisdom, insight, and character of a well-meaning adult, and which shifts attention from the tragic helplessness of the child to the strength of the adult in order to project a falsely optimistic future.

Sidney Monas. *HdR*. Autumn, 1959, pp. 449–50

The novelist Panova is a sensitive woman, whose interests are those of a woman, and whose comments on life have feminine gentleness and tact. She is a "Party writer," but one with sentiment. She wears the "leather jacket," but hers has yellow ribbons on it. Her work is important because she must be credited with having introduced and insisted upon some of the most important themes of the immediate post-Stalin "thaw." Her chief themes are those that have special interest for women: love, the need for human tenderness and consideration, the reality of private emotion, the family, the education of children.

Edward J. Brown. *Russian Literature Since the Revolution* (New York, Crowell-Collier, 1963), p. 245

Panova . . . expressed her ideas about the importance of truthfulness in art, both in big and small things, in the general conception and the details.

"Sometimes," said Panova, "you read a novel, and you don't believe the author on the second page, on the tenth, on the seventeenth. And if there is suddenly a flash of truth on the hundredth page, you suspect even that, for it is buried under all that falsehood. Nothing that compromises artistic truth can be tolerated in art."

Among the new writers who came upon the scene after the war there are some who are more talented than Panova. Her voice is not loud, but she wins the hearts of her readers, not by sharp postulation of contemporary problems, and not even by beauty of style, but by the special warmth of her intonation. Her literary voice is very much like herself, as she appears in numerous photographs. In these portraits we see a woman in her middle years looking at us with small, transparent, very animated eyes. The mobility and even nervousness of the face is revealed by the asymmetry of the eye-brows. The attractive lines of the mouth are enhanced by the soft oval of the chin. But best of all in the face is the smile

—a smile kind to the point of shyness. This smile is felt in her work as well, and it endears Panova to her readers.

Vera Alexandrova. *A History of Soviet Literature*
(New York, Doubleday, 1963), p. 283

PASTERNAK, BORIS   (1890–1960)

There is in his face something of the Arab and his horse: an alertness, an attentiveness, a full readiness to gallop away at any moment . . . a pronounced, also horse-like, wild and shy slant of the eyes. . . . Thus, he imparts the impression that he is always listening to something, with an uninterrupted attention, only to burst suddenly and prematurely into word, as if a rock or an oak tree had spoken. His speech (in conversation) resembles the interruption of a primeval silence. And this is not only in conversation but—I can assure this—his verse, with a much greater authority of experience.

Marina Tsvetayeva. *Epopeya.* Feb., 1922, p. 162[†]

The magnificent native Russian poetry of Pasternak is already old-fashioned. It has no spice because it is immortal; it is without a style because it chokes with banality through the classical rapture of the thrilling nightingale. . . . Reading Pasternak's verses is like purifying the throat, strengthening the breath, rejuvenating the lungs; such verses must cure tuberculosis. We have now no healthier poetry. It is like koumiss after American milk. . . .

Of course, when Gertsen and Ogarev stood on the Sparrow Hills as boys, they experienced physiologically the sacred exaltation of space and bird's flight. Pasternak's poetry told us about those moments; it is a resplendent Nike transferred from the Acropolis to the Sparrow Hills.

Osip Mandelshtam. *Rossiya.* Feb., 1923, p. 29[†]

Boris Leonidovich Pasternak . . . tried to raise himself above the turmoil of the social struggle to the zenith of middle class culture, but all the time a quality of living vitality breaks through the bourgeois-idealist covering of his works. He, therefore, reflects the events of the fight for the dictatorship of the proletariat. . . . P. defends the freedom of his poetic creation in all circumstances and at all times. In the beginning he saw the Revolution as an elementary force of destruction. Finally he accepted it like a pathway to the sacrifice. The thesis of the poet on the incompatibility of art and socialism is bound up with the experience of a single fate, because to P. art is always the expression of the unique character of a single individual. For him socialism is only a cloud of smoke behind the fog of theories, and an epoch in which people "suspect" each other. It is a peculiarity of his lyrical work that he always gives two parallel aspects of a picture, and two parallel motives. His poetry is, as he himself says, a "hypnotic homeland." P.'s great genius has brought him a reputation as an original poet who exerts an influence on Soviet poetry. [1934]

Bolshaya sovetskaya entsiklopediya. Cited in
Gerd Ruge, *Pasternak: A Pictorial Biography*
(London, Thames and Hudson, 1959), p. 66

Pasternak's resemblance to the Imagists was more personal than intellectual. He was not of their number and was too good a craftsman to accept their extreme claims. But, like other modern poets, he saw that the image has a special part to play and that it is almost impossible to express complex states of mind without an adventurous and extensive use of it. It is customary to say that his use of images reflects the world of painting in which he grew up, but though Pasternak's visual sensibility is extremely keen, it does much more than mark and record. It carries with it something which is more than visual. Indeed we might say that his musical training has been quite as important as his knowledge of painting, since it has taught him to give a precise sensuous form to otherwise undefined feelings and to realise what strength can be added to words through combinations of sound. What he sees awakes in him so many remarkable trains of thought and sound that his poetry is packed and complex. It deals with many obscure states which might be material for a musician but are beyond the scope of a painter. Everything that he notices is fraught with mystery and meaning for him. He lives in the real world and observes it intently, but his rapt observation uncovers much more than meets the seeing eye. In the inextricable combination of his senses and emotions he both sees and interprets nature, both marks its manifestations and understands what they mean and what relations they suggest beyond the immediate "given." No doubt the Imagists hoped to do something of this kind through their cult of the image, but they defined its purpose too narrowly. Pasternak, consciously or unconsciously, has picked up their doctrine and shown how it should really be applied.

C. M. Bowra. *The Creative Experiment*
(London, Macmillan, 1949), pp. 131–32

Pasternak's is the consequent position of an idealist and formalist moving in the direction contrary to that of Soviet art. It is not surprising that he is supported by the enemies of the Soviet people. The English professor C. M. Bowra, for example, speaking of Pasternak's poetry, almost chokes with enthusiasm. "Remarkable receptiveness," "a great talent at transmitting the feelings," "a dynamic perception of life," "the powerful poet of Russia"—the article of the highly esteemed professor is replete with such utterances. . . .

Pasternak's artistic work is the most blatant example of rotten decadence. He himself, apparently sensing his alienation from the people, has ceased publishing new poems.

A. Tarasenkov. Znamya. Oct., 1949, p. 163[†]

In this novel [*Doktor Zhivago* (*Doctor Zhivago*)] of a hundred memorable characters there is a third whose significance is central, a woman named Lara Guishar. Among the figures who converge in the opening pages are Pasha Antipov and Lara. When still a schoolgirl she is seduced by a rich lawyer, Komarovsky, a man who was also, by a coincidence, partly responsible for the death of Zhivago's father. It is difficult to speak of Lara without vulgarising the conception. She evades Komarovsky, tries to shoot him at a party where Zhivago (who doesn't yet know her) is also present, and marries Antipov, who later changes his name to Strelnikov. A union between Zhivago and Lara is written into the pattern from the start, and their life together is all hunger, illegality and anonymity, a sort of holist Resistance against revolutionary abstraction. For Lara assumes a vast burden of meaning. She is life, the principle Zhivago worships, and thence she is Russia, betrayed in different ways by the Komarovskys and the Strelnikovs; she has a simple, direct relationship with reality or God, and is capable of a beautiful repentance when her demon is exorcised. Pasternak lovingly enlarges the Magdalen theme. None of this is as crude as I have to make it sound; there is here and elsewhere an element of parable, and Pasternak believes that a story becomes valid only when it acquires the qualities of myth. The wholeness he tries to achieve must carry its own explanations; and he succeeds so far that the terrible history his book contains becomes, like death in tragedy, a part of the complex and irreducible beauty of the whole image.

Frank Kermode. Spec. Sept. 5, 1958, p. 315

The artistic game of Pasternak consists in a sort of balancing act: or in the attempt to fix in a precarious, and yet firm equilibrium, a congeries of heterogeneous objects, of vibrant and labile things. His poetry seems to pass, almost at the same time, through two different and even opposite phases. The first is a moment of eruption and irruption, of frenzy and paroxysm; the second, which often overlaps the first, is the moment when matter seems to harden and freeze. . . . Often the same poem seems to be written now in hot, now in cold blood. This dualism may perhaps be traced in, or symbolized by, the early education of the poet, which was both philosophical and musical. Yet, while his cadence ends in dissonance, and his logic leads to dissent, such a double discordance resolves itself into a harmony of its own. . . .

Many critics have remarked that Pasternak looks at the world with the eyes of the newly born. It would be better to say that he looks at it with *reborn* eyes. As suggested by the title of one of his books, poetry is for him a "second birth," through which man sees again the familiar as strange, and the strange as familiar. Yet, whether strange or familiar, every object is unique. To give the effect of this uniqueness, the poet paints every single thing as if it were a monad, unwilling or unable to escape from the rigid frame of its own contours. Such an effect is primarily achieved through the harshness and hardness of his imagery, through the frequent syncopes of his speech, through the staccato quality of his meter. Rhythmically, he prefers a line heavily hammered, where no stress is blurred, and every beat is pounded as in a heel dance. He fails however to extend this rapid, metallic quality to rhyme, which he treats with the negligence and freedom of Mayakovsky, and which he describes, following Verlaine's famous definition (*"ce bijou d'un sou"*), as a "checkroom ticket."

Though some of his poems, especially the earlier ones, are romantically set against vast exotic backgrounds (for instance against the lofty mountains of the Caucasian landscape), Pasternak usually prefers a restricted, bourgeois, and prosaic scenery, such as a park, an orchard, a garden, or a villa in the suburbs. Yet even "backyards, ponds, palings," are not mere backdrops, but, as the poet says, "categories of passions, hoarded in the human heart." His poetry thus leans towards a highly personal version of the pathetic fallacy, involving in his case not only non-human creatures, such as animals and plants, but also inanimate things or man-made objects. For many of his poems Pasternak chooses, like Mallarmé in his *poèmes d'intérieur*, indoor settings. Yet unlike the French poet, the Russian introduces within the four walls of a room cosmic powers and elemental forces.

Renato Poggioli. PR. Fall, 1958, pp. 545–47

The tumult, the wealth and grandiosity of events are certainly not the essential matter in *Dr. Zivagho*. And even less the depiction of solid, well-rounded characters, the joy of describing life and making it palpitate which fills Tolstoy with such exuberance. In Pasternak, there are on one side the events and the vicissitudes of the individual characters, on the other—as a constant counterpoint—a certain ecstasy of the spirit outside of the immediate reality, an ecstasy found in the vision of universal life and in the effort to understand in human terms that which is happening. There is, more than a religious, a mystical feeling for nature, a powerful and proud "yes" said to life, despite everything. But there is not a single smile, nor a single moment of joy, save for the joy of freedom during the first days of the revolution, and this is an impersonal rapture more than a true joy. The events are narrated in every detail, with bare simplicity; but they seem far-off and muffled, plunged in a kind of twilight; terrible as they are, they occur and pass away in a sort of strange silence and tranquillity, almost as though even their terror cannot disturb that which exists at the bottom of things and of the human spirit. As a result, they give us the feeling of memories which rise to the surface of consciousness, sharp yet insubstantial: shadows which ask to be placated by understanding. And they are shadows which also are characters: almost pure names, with nothing physical about them. What one is told about them is solely the part they play in each other's lives, the way in which they are twisted and beaten by the storm, a few of the essential expressions of their spirit, a few of their thoughts and judgments. Their existences are so disordered and torn to pieces that nothing is left to them (and, in particular, to the protagonist) but the pure distance of the spirit from circumstances, the meditative solitude in which they endure the raging of destiny. At the end, we know that all that has been told was told so as to describe this distance and this solitude: Doctor Zivagho's conscience and how it managed, by resisting death, to remain human.

Nicola Chiaromonte. *PR*. Winter, 1958, p. 129

It is our view that Doctor Zhivago is, in fact, the incarnation of a definite type of Russian intellectual of that day, a man fond of talking about the sufferings of the people and able to discuss them, but unable to cure those sufferings in either the literal or the figurative sense of the word. He is the type of man consumed with a sense of his own singularity, his intrinsic value, a man far removed from the people and ready to betray them in difficult times, to cut himself off from their sufferings and their cause. His is the type of the "highly intellectual" Philistine, tame when left alone but capable in thought as well as in deed of inflicting any wrong whatsoever on the people just as soon as he feels the slightest wrong—real or imagined—has been done to him.

You are no stranger to symbolism, and the death, or rather the passing, of Doctor Zhivago in the late 1920's is for you, we feel, a symbol of the death of the Russian intelligentsia, destroyed by the revolution. Yes, it must be admitted that for the Doctor Zhivago you depicted in the novel the climate of the revolution is deadly. And our disagreement with you is not over this but, as we have already mentioned, over something quite different.

To you, Doctor Zhivago is the peak of the spirit of the Russian intelligentsia.

To us, he is its swamp.

To you, the members of the Russian intelligentsia who took a different path from the one Doctor Zhivago took and who chose the course of serving the people betrayed their true calling, committed spiritual suicide and created nothing of value.

To us they found their true calling on precisely that path and continued to serve the people and to do for the people precisely the things that had been done for them—in laying the groundwork for the revolution—by the best segment of the Russian intelligentsia, which was then, and is today, infinitely remote from that conscious break with the people and ideological renegacy of which your Doctor Zhivago is the bearer.

[The editors of *Literaturnaya gazeta*, in their rejection letter.] *Current Digest of the Soviet Press.* Dec. 3, 1958, pp. 7–8, 11

Unlike the previous work of Boris Pasternak, *Doctor Zhivago* is a straightforward, strictly prose narrative of considerable scope. It has been compared, and not entirely unjustly, to the Russian novels of the nineteenth century. It has their old-fashioned, almost archaic simplicity, their sense of immediacy and spontaneity, and recalls those artful works where the word *zapiski* (variously translated as "notes," "sketches," "diary") seems natural and right in the title. It has also their fine sense of distinction between the human *community*, where men deal with men as human beings on the basis of qualities rooted in nature and in themselves, and the human *collective* where men deal with each other as functions in the machinery of politics or profit. One might even say that Russian literature arose out of the crucial need for this distinction in a country where a European conscience suffered the political yoke of an oriental despotism, and that it culminated in *War and Peace* where the distinction was made most articulate and on the grandest scale.

Pasternak's novel is not, however, a masterpiece in any craftsmanly sense. There are too many clumsy coincidences, too many blank faces, there is too much unabashed philosophizing and too much awkward and unlikely talk. And yet, it moves one to have brought into use again such long-drowsing and nowadays embarrassing phrases as "the meaning of life," "personal integrity," and "tragic wisdom." It moves one for its courageous confrontation of the limitations and the cruelty of politics. The awkwardness seems finally inconsequential, and the courage stands. All this sounds perhaps too solemn. The novel leaves us when we are done with an image not unlike Yeats's Chinamen in the poem "Lapis Lazuli":

> *Their eyes, mid many wrinkles, their eyes,*
> *Their ancient, glittering eyes, are gay.*

Sidney Monas. *HdR*. Winter, 1958–59, p. 612

Pasternak traces back Zhivago's ideas and his Christianity to Alexander Blok. In Blok's *Twelve,* Christ walked at the head of armed workmen, tramps, and prostitutes, leading them, in the blood red dawn of October, towards a greater future. There was a certain artistic and even historic authenticity in this daring symbol. In it were merged the primitive Christianity and the elemental revolutionary élan of the Russia of the muzhiks who, chanting Prayer Book psalms, burned the mansions of the aristocracy. The Christ who blessed that Russia was also the Christ of primitive Christianity, the hope of the enslaved and the oppressed, St. Matthew's Son of Man, who would sooner let the camel go through the eye of a needle than the rich man enter into the Kingdom of God. Pasternak's Christ turns his back on the rough mob he had led in October and parts company with them. He is the pre-revolutionary self-sufficient Russian intellectual, "refined," futile, and full of grudge and resentment at the abomination of a proletarian revolution.

Isaac Deutscher. PR. Spring, 1959, p. 263

[*Detstvo Lyuvers* (*The Childhood of Luvers*)] is a story that has no real plot, a tale of a girl who has just crossed the threshold of puberty, built up from innumerable careful observations, without definite beginning or end. This is a piece of prose which is unique in Russian literature. In method the story is related to the works of Proust. Of *The Childhood of Luvers*, and ideed of all Pasternak's early prose, could be said what Ortega y Gasset said of Marcel Proust, "Proust's characters are without outline: they are unsubstantial wraiths, intellectual images which change constantly in a breath of air or a ray of light. Proust is undoubtedly 'the explorer' of the human soul in the Stendhal tradition." The detailed description of environment, the psychological observation of emotions, is in Pasternak's case never verbose or over-protracted. On the contrary, in the concentrated intensity of his style each word is laden with deep meaning—almost overladen, in fact. This tightly packed method of presentation demands almost too much for the reader. There are no points at which he can relax and digest what he has read; there are no links, no explanations. Pasternak tries to produce in the reader a certain definite sensation, and he omits everything that he considers superfluous to the achievement of this aim. But in spite of all these difficulties, and its strange and unusual style, *The Childhood of Luvers* was to remain, in its pure translucence and gentle charm, his most beautiful and important early work in prose. When this story appeared seven years later in a volume of Pasternak's prose, the critics praised it as one of the most important pieces of prose of the first period of Soviet art.

Gerd Ruge. Pasternak: A Pictorial Biography
(London, Thames & Hudson, 1959), p. 41

Pasternak's translation of Shakespeare was an enriching experience for him, and it ran more or less parallel to his work on his novel. In Shakespeare he has also discovered "the father and the prophet of realism." I shall not be at all surprised if Pasternak next writes a play. . . .

In his translation of the Shakespeare tragedies, Pasternak has stressed both faithfulness in the spirit of the original text and the necessity of free creative interpretation. His method of work, as revealed in the Preface to the Molodaya Gvardia publication of *Hamlet* (1940), was to do a first draft with the assistance of a dictionary and a brief commentary on the text. He then compared his draft with a number of extant translations and did a second version, concentrating this time not so much on the vocabulary as on the spirit and tone behind the various Acts and scenes of the plot. This brought him nearer to the spirit of the play as a whole and removed him somewhat further from a merely literal interpretation of the successive lines. In *Romeo and Juliet*, his second translation, this method was developed even further. . . .

My own reading of Pasternak's *Romeo and Juliet* has convinced me of its quality, of its fluent and natural movement, and of its masterful alternation of colloquial and poetic speech. Pasternak's handling of blank verse, which was already used in Russian by Pushkin and his *Boris Godunov*, is eminently successful and impressive.

George Reavey, ed. Introduction to
The Poetry of Boris Pasternak 1917–1959
(New York, G. P. Putnam's Sons, 1959), pp. 78–82

Dr. Zhivago assuredly is a far-ranging work of the long Russian breath—though not comparable to the vast epic tides of either *War and Peace* or *Anna Karenina*. *War and Peace* is somewhere in the 1800-page range with some 500 characters, we are told by people who count these things. *Anna Karenina* struggles along with less than 200 characters and 1200-odd pages. *Dr. Zhivago* is positively skeletal—some sixty characters in the space of 600 pages. Yet there are unmistakable resemblances to *War and Peace* in structure and viewpoint. There are the characteristic stratified layers and interwoven strands of narrative, pursuing and constantly re-confronting a central nexus of characters. There is a time sweep across three generations, and the painting of a lively, if socially more limited picture of Russian life, just 100 years later, both in the setting and in the writing, than Tolstoj's grandiose, sunny canvas of pre-Napoleonic Russia. Besides the inter-reaction of individual destinies through successive settings in time and circumstance, there is also the device of having one or two characters, the Seekers, carry the philosophical load and the self-identification of the author—all these are features of the Tolstojan signature. These individual destinies are supremely significant in and for themselves, and are not dwarfed into the vagrant atoms of a cosmic revulsion of history. Absent is the notorious "psychological eaves-dropping" of Tolstoj; motives, impressions, psychic processes are externalized in dialogues or inferred through description *not* of the impact itself, but of the scene or image exerting the impact. Tone and technique are reflective and descriptive for the most part, rising to lyric and dramatic intensity in tune with climactic private events and responses.

Walter Arndt. *SAB*. May, 1959, p. 5

It is certainly one of Pasternak's greatest distinctions that as a poet he has never withdrawn from life: he celebrates Lenin and socialism and the victory over Nazi Germany without abandoning his championship of the individual artist or his growing preoccupation with religion and with God. It is no accident that, long before his name was known outside the Russian language, his poems were read and memorized and cherished by Russians in Moscow, in Paris and in New York, men of wholly different political persuasions. . . .

It is not surprising, for a Russian poet, that nature provides most of the themes out of which Pasternak builds the counterpoint of some exceedingly difficult ideas. . . . Rain and wind are the staples of his imagery, raindrops and pools of rain, river beds in flood, thunder claps, snow, a stairway sodden with the damp, rain shuffling at the door. This is especially true of his early poems, those taken from *My Sister Life* [*Sestra moya— zhizn*] which was written in 1917. It is the start of what is a long love affair with the Russian land. Paris and Prague and Egypt are here, but only glancingly; it is Moscow and its suburbs, the Sparrow Hills, Kiev, the Caucasus, the Urals, the Gulf of Finland and the Siberian tundra which move Pasternak. . . .

Other writers are frequently mentioned: Shakespeare, Anna Akhmatova, Tsvetayeva, Balzac. Pasternak singles out four Russians for comment as central to "our Russian contemporaneity, the real and the true, our modern thinking and spiritual consciousness." They are Pushkin, Lermontov, Tolstoy and Chekhov. (He dedicated "My Sister Life" to Lermontov.) These are names one thinks of as one reads the poems, and they belong among the most Russian of all Russian writers. Pasternak, who is himself a linguist and a translator, turns back in his poetry to Russian ideas as he does to the Russian land.

Joseph Barnes. *SwR*. Spring, 1960, pp. 336–37

Pasternak and Mayakovsky admired each other without sharing each other's views. While Mayakovsky, though too un-Pushkinlike for Lenin, fervently attached himself to the Revolution, and employed an "At the Top of my Voice" technique, Pasternak continued on his non-public way,

even eliminating from his style certain resemblances which he and Mayakovsky had noticed. The two poets were not the closest of friends, and
had diverged from each other in the last years of Mayakovsky's life, in
the course of the literary-political quarrels of that time. But such breaches
are not like those between bureaucrats and self-seekers, and did not affect
Pasternak's high, if unsentimental, opinion of the other's poetry.

Yet the solidarity of sincerity and of art between Pasternak and Mayakovsky was deeper in spite of all their differences, than the superficial
ideological solidarity between Mayakovsky and the politicians. Mayakovsky's death affected Pasternak more sincerely than it did the political
authorities. For some time these took the line that Mayakovsky's suicide
was due solely to an unhappy love affair. . . .

Pasternak, on the other hand, has consistenty referred to the tragedy in
moving terms. The scene after Mayakovsky's death is one of the emotional cruxes of his autobiographical *Safe Conduct*, and was later to
reappear as the climax of *Doctor Zhivago*.

Robert Conquest. *Courage of Genius*
(London, Collins & Harvill, 1961), pp. 30–31

On the spur of the moment Pasternak decided to tell me about the plays
he was working on. Quite fascinated, I listened to him and only once or
twice, unsure of some historical or literary point, did I interrupt to ask him
for an explanation. The outline of the plays seemed bewildering at times
because of the wealth of details which Pasternak provided to bring it to
life. But I understood why when I remembered that Pasternak was Shakespeare's and Schiller's translator; clearly he wanted to write the plays with
a German Romantic flavor and Shakespeare's uninhibited scope. He told
me about it in concrete terms. He didn't emphasize the ideas in it but
rather told it as a story, with an occasional gesture of hands emphasizing
some vivid, slightly baroque detail. As he talked, I began to realize that
parts of it were completed, others were still to be filled in. I was hearing
about something which was not yet fully worked out in his mind. Like
Tolstoi, he seemed inclined to give his characters a free hand in writing
up their own destinies. Finally I began to see the underlying ideas. Although Pasternak didn't emphasize it, it appeared to me that he was
absorbed in ideas about art—not in its historical context but as an
element ever present in life.

Olga Andreyev Carlisle. *Voices in the Snow*
(New York, Random House, 1962), pp. 201–2

During the half century of Pasternak's literary creativity, many things
changed and reorganized themselves. But he remained faithful to the end
to a number of ideas, principles, and predilections by which he was

governed during the various periods of his creative life. One such deep
conviction of Pasternak's was that true art is always greater than itself,
for it bears witness to the meaningfulness of being, the grandeur of life,
and the immeasurable value of human existence. This testimony can be
obtained without declarations, profound symbols, and exalted allegories:
the presence of greatness appears in the genuine liveliness of a story, in
the keen awareness and poetic inspiration of the artist, obsessed and astonished by the wonder of reality and telling constantly about one thing—
its important presence—and about life as if he were talking only about
the falling of the snow and the rustling of a forest.

Of course, such evaluation and treatment of artistic creations are applicable in the first place to Pasternak's poetry itself. For him, common
phenomena and signs of existence are characterized by the fantastic presence of life as such and are therefore no less significant than, for example,
the old, primeval chaos in Tiutchev or the global music in Blok.

As always in Pasternak, the loftiest proves in the end to be the simplest
—the all-pervasive and all-exhaustive life. "Poetry," Pasternak spoke,
"will always remain that glorious peak—higher than all the Alps—which
lies in the grass, under our feet, so that one has only to stoop in order to
see it and pick it up from the ground."

Andrei Sinyavski. Introduction to
Boris Pasternak, Stikhotvoreniya i poemy
(Moscow, Sovetski pisatel, 1965), pp. 61–62†

A Christian Zhivago makes sense only if what's meant is a different Christ
from the one we usually have in mind. He has as much to do with anthro-
pology, Hebraicism and historical materialism as with the New Testament.
This is a Christ preoccupied by his destiny and terribly willing to collaborate with it: a supreme victim. . . .

So far as Doctor Zhivago has an underpinning of theory, it seems to
be provided by Yura's uncle, the unfrocked priest. In novelistic terms,
the influence of his ideas on Yura's writing and behaviour is well and
lovingly established. He if anyone could perhaps explain how to reconcile
Christianity with this strong attachment to fatalism. But just what Uncle
Kolya's ideas are, whether they're even intellectually respectable, never
really emerges from their reflection on the page; or only enough to make
one fear the worst. It's a strange thing about this novel that whenever it
refers to the world of the mind—as in Uncle Kolya's ideas or Yura's own
philosophical booklets "of a couple of dozen pages each," and his odd-
sounding theory about "personality as the biological basis of the organism"—or when it produces purely schematised action like that battle-
experience of Yura's—it leaves wide open the possibility that it's pointing
to something merely cranky or absurd. The Christian theme in Doctor

Zhivago is like that. It can't be pinned down as exactly Christian—it's always slipping off into something else: historical determinism or what Professor Davie calls "apocalyptic Marxism," or into that residuary religious emotion in which Symbolists like Pasternak and Rilke tend to indulge.

Robert Taubman. NS. Oct. 1, 1965, p. 485

Unlike most Russian Jews of their generation, Boris Pasternak's father and mother, themselves of Orthodox parentage, brought up their children in the liberal atmosphere enjoyed by assimilated, cultivated Jewry. The writer's father was not averse to using Jewish themes for his canvases, and returned from a visit to Palestine in 1932 with his interest in his own people strengthened; but most of the friends of the household were Christians.

In the poet's early manhood he was steeped in Christian thought. His concern with it is writ largely in *Doctor Zhivago*, and naturally recurs in the poems, purportedly by the doctor, appended to the novel. . . .

The protagonist of the novel is, of course, no surrogate for its author, yet many of the ideas that the former expresses were cherished by Pasternak. Prominent among these is the conviction that man is intent upon exploring the riddle of death, that this search is the source of his inventions and discoveries, and that the spiritual equipment for making them is to be found, in its basic elements, in the Gospels: "What are they? To begin with love of one's neighbor, which is the supreme form of vital energy. . . . And then the two basic ideals of modern man—without them he is unthinkable—the idea of free personality and the idea of life as sacrifice."

In his ignorance of Judaism, Pasternak did not realize that Jesus, as a practicing Jew, may well have taken the substance of the Sermon on the Mount and of other preachments from the Old Testament. This has no place in the Zhivago poems. These, as Donald Davie's comments indicate, have almost as much to do with aspects of sexual love as with lovingkindness.

Babette Deutsch. NYT. Feb. 20, 1966, p. 34

Written and published between 1915 and 1929, Pasternak's short stories have remained the least known and least studied part of his work. At the time of their publication they suffered from the proximity of a highly esteemed poetic output which eclipsed them in the eyes of the Russian public and critics; whereas, on the other hand, the non-Russian reader, by his ignorance of the poetry, has long been deprived of the source of light illuminating their unity. Very different in aim, form, and content, these five stories do not, in fact, appear as a homogeneous and independent whole, but as so many isolated incursions of a poet into the domain of prose. It is mainly from this formal angle that they have been considered till now, the fiction being treated most often as merely an accessory and secondary element, as compared with an original language showing the indisputable freshness of vision of a great poet. It is therefore understandable that critical attention should have been focussed chiefly on *The Childhood of Luvers* which, in fact, is an unfinished novel, where the development of the subject, arbitrarily broken off, counts less than the originality of the means of investigation and description Pasternak employs to follow the paths a child's consciousness takes.

Doctor Zhivago, however, has modified this point of view by showing that these prose experiments are also, and above all, works of imagination whose subjects, situations, and characters already reveal Pasternak's fundamental and permanent novelistic motifs.

Michel Aucouturier. SSF. Winter, 1966, pp. 225–26

By purposive choice of a patron saint, Pasternak is able to suggest the mainspring of a character's motives, as revealed in the saint's life, deeds, and martyrdom. Another rich reservoir for the author lies in the Russian system of patronymics. Each person in *Zhivago* has a patronymic which, in somewhat the manner of Russian folk epics, points to his historical, legendary, or mythological prototype. The finishing touch is conveyed by the descriptive surname—and here a Russian writer has a word-hoard unsurpassed for picturesqueness. By all these means Pasternak has cast his characters in multiple roles, freighting each person's three names with subtle, ever-widening connotations. . . .

Zhivago is the Church Slavonic genitive and accusative form of the adjective *zhivoi* (living, alive)—a perfect one-word description of the Doctor's basic loyalty. *Yuri* is an abbreviated form of *Georgi*, by a process which the intermediate folkloristic *Yegori* makes clear. Yuri's patron saint is therefore St. George, who in history was martyred by Emperor Diocletian, and who in legend slew the dragon (Paganism) and rescued the maiden (Christianity). Incidentally, *Yuryatin*, the name of the city where the Doctor finds himself, means "Yuri's town" or "Georgetown." Zhivago's patronymic, *Andreyevich*, identifies him as the spiritual son of St. Andrew the Apostle who, according to Russian tradition, first brought Christianity to the pagan Slavic tribes along the lower Dnieper River up to the site of present-day Kiev and who was later claimed as patron saint of the nation. If the reader listens to all these overtones sounding together, he must inevitably reach certain conclusions about the harmonic pattern of Yuri Andreyevich Zhivago's life.

Mary F. Rowland and Paul Rowland. Pasternak's
Doctor Zhivago (Carbondale, Ill., Southern Illinois
University Press, 1967), pp. 10–11

PAUSTOVSKI, KONSTANTIN (1892–1968)

Genuine art is always frank, intolerant of any imprint, any routinism and every sort of plagiarism. The heroes of Paustovsky's best works are attractive because of the power of their intellect, their lust for life, their sense of the beautiful. It is as such that we want to see all our contemporaries. And that also is one of the achievements of skill and of no small importance. In his stories there is no bookishness, we are compelled to believe in them to the very last line, for they flow from the evidence of the eyes, from knowledge of life, into which the author peers restlessly and keenly.

The creative style of Paustovsky is peculiar to himself. He loves to portray integral, noble characters, and is attracted by noble emotions. Throughout his story-telling runs a strain of romantic elevation, which is expressed in characterizations, in subject and in particular situations. This method has justified itself and has once again confirmed the truth that within the bounds of the single method of Socialist realism there can be various creative currents, the one represented by the work of Paustovsky among them.

Mikhail Kuznetsov. *SL*. Oct., 1955, p. 138

To my generation, which is now from thirty to thirty-five, Paustovski's books form one of the most vivid memories of our childhood and youth. Our geography teachers will confirm how eagerly we welcomed questions about the eastern coast of the Caspian or the Rion Plain. We could describe these regions as if we had been there ourselves. We had never seen them; we simply knew almost by heart Paustovski's *Kara-Bugaz* and *Colchis*. . . .

The expedition in rowboats along the Desna River was to be led by Paustovski. To the younger ones among us this seemed as fabulous as if they had been told that they would spend three weeks with Jules Verne.

Sergei Lvov. *Konstantin Paustovski*
(Moscow, Detgiz, 1956), p. 40†

Clarity and softness—these two dissimilar qualities are characteristic of Paustovsky's talent. On the eve of 1939 Paustovsky replied to a questionnaire of the *Literary Gazette* with a brief statement of his literary credo. He recalled a winter evening in a seaside town, when "dusk like antique silver hung over the sea," many years ago, when Paustovsky was very young. He had been fond then of visiting a bookseller he knew; the shop, he said, smelled of old books and prints—"a smell reminiscent of carnations." That evening the bookseller spoke about an old engraving of Mozart's portrait, explaining that it was made with a "diamond needle."

The remark reminded Paustovsky of a forgotten story: somewhere in Canada, in a small town, there lived a man who studied the shape of snow crystals; he photographed thousands of snowflakes—melting on "the warm face of a child," settling in the stone folds of a statue in a square. And all of this, thought Paustovsky—the old engravings made with a diamond needle, and the snowflakes—is brought by the literary artist into his work, which must combine the engraver's precision with loving attention to the snowflake melting on a child's face.

Paustovsky's character as a writer is reflected in his face; he looks out of his photograph with keen eyes, and his features are striking in their combination of clear energy with a trace of dreaminess. The Paustovsky family stems from Zaporozhye Cossacks, with an admixture of Turkish and Polish blood. The writer's father was a railroad statistician who died of cancer of the larynx when the writer was in the seventh year of school. It was only much later that Paustovsky understood that his father had been essentially a poet by nature, as was his grandfather, Maxim Grigorievich. It was not by chance that Paustovsky remarked in the first part of his *Story of My Life* [*Povest o zhizni*] that it was partly to his grandfather that he owed his "excessive impressionability and romanticism." "They turned my youth," he wrote, "into a series of clashes with reality. I suffered through this, but I knew that my grandfather was right; a life based on sobriety and common sense may be good, but to me it would be depressing and fruitless." . . .

Paustovsky's books are populated with vast numbers of people, both those who have become a part of history, and simple, ordinary men and women. We meet in his pages Pushkin, Lermontov, Kiprensky, Tchaikovsky, Levitan, Mozart, and Hans Andersen. We find masterfully sketched portraits of modern writers, from the late Arkady Gaydar, with whom the writer had once walked the length and breadth of the remote and desolate Meshchorsky region, down to the literary youth of the 1920s (the so-called Southern-Russian literary school), including Isaac Babel, Eduard Bagritsky, Semyon Gekht, Valentin Katayev, Yury Olesha, and others whom Paustovsky met in Odessa against the background of the Civil War and utter chaos. It was there too that Paustovsky met Bunin shortly before the latter's emigration from Russia.

But most of all, Paustovsky's works are peopled with ordinary folk, lovers of their native regions like the tar-sprayer Vassily and his grandson Tisha, who later becomes the chairman of the local Executive Committee. Although Paustovsky tries to be impartial toward the people he describes, it is easy to see that his warmest feelings are for the "adventurers," like his Uncle Yuzya and his father, who had taught throughout his lifetime that man does not live "by bread alone."

His tireless attention to the details of the life of ordinary people and

the nature of his country brings him into close kinship with his older contemporary, Prishvin. Both came into Russian literature after its greatest
masterworks had already been created, both went through a long period
of torment in search of a theme. And both were helped by the apocryphal
folk legend about the two Adams. Like the second comer, the Landless
Adam, they toiled on a narrow strip of land. But from this narrow strip,
both writers have gathered a rich harvest.

Vera Alexandrova. <i>A History of Soviet Literature</i>
(New York, Doubleday, 1963), pp. 260–61, 271

Dym otechestva (*The Smoke of Fatherland*) is a novel about the native
land, the Russian land, and the nation's art. This is a book about devotion
to what we love. And it is about the all-purifying force of goodness,
before which man bows. Paustovski's people are always good. Evil is
rarely present in his books. And if it appears at all, it is a force which con-
cedes to good. Good invariably has to triumph.

In *The Smoke of Fatherland* Paustovski does not deviate from this
rule. The people live here according to the laws of the good. And they
themselves are good, kind, pleasant. All of them are united by good faith
and by a love of art.

We find ourselves in the usual Paustovskian world, in the world of
unhurried work, of sad dialogues with nature, and of poems, paintings,
glimmering hopes. . . .

The events that upset the world vanish somewhere behind Paustovski's
curtain. They emerge in the novel as the echo of Spanish battles, as the
vaguely audible rumble of the war moving from the West. This rumble
dies out in the deep Russian snow. The winter forest swallows the echo
and sends us back to concentration and peace. Even the heroes behave
peacefully and quietly, as if they were gathering together in the novel to
pay their dues to this silence, to these last prewar days, of which there will
be no more.

This silence makes us spellbound. The melodic speech of Paustovski
captivates us. It flows freely, and we, without noticing it, find ourselves
in its stream, giving ourselves over to its rhythm. It seems to us that somebody is telling us in a kind of low voice a story about the past. The sound
of his voice is close and thrilling; the fascination of his speech is stronger
than what he is telling us about.

Igor Zolotusski. *Literaturnaya gazeta.*
Dec. 19, 1963, p. 3[†]

The Russian landscape into which Pushkin's pale, broody, "literary" Tati-
ana stared from the window of her manor house and which she imbued
with her poetic Arcadian fancies became a haunting and permanent

presence in the Russian literature that followed. The autobiography of Konstantin Paustovsky is full of this landscape and of the "matriotic" literature in which its spirit has lived. . . .

Whereas Ehrenburg's memoirs are a string of sharp, intensely dramatic, carefully selected anecdotes about famous men and exotic places, Paustovsky's are composed like a mosaic, far more lyrical than dramatic, precise and thorough in their recall and dealing for the most part with ordinary people in earthy circumstances, though in the latter volumes (not represented in the English translation) some of the famous writers whom Paustovsky knew well do appear, among them Babel, Bunin and Prishvin, without altering the characteristic tone which is halfway between a documentary chronicle and a fairy-tale for grownups. . . .

Whatever his ultimate stature as a writer, his role in the survival of Russian literature has been of incalculable importance. Not only has he had a hand in the republication of Bunin and Babel, Tsvetaeva and Pasternak, writers more or less of his own generation, he has taught, sponsored and protected a number of the more talented young writers, outstandingly among them, Yuri Kazakov. He also helped to rescue, albeit in a pathetically small edition, the unusual anthology, *Pages From Tarusa*.

Sidney Monas. *HdR*. Winter, 1964–65, pp. 602–3

Though it has many of the strengths of the great Russian masters, *Story of a Life* is not itself a masterpiece of the kind its first chapters led me to hope it might be. About half-way through the book there is a falling-off in its quality, a failure of the disinterestedness which we have by then learned to expect from the author. It comes at a point, in his account of his early adolescence, when his family unexpectedly breaks up. . . . The rest of the memoir being as personal as it is, we cannot help feeling that too much is being held back from us; and, what is more damaging to the book, that the author himself is unaware of how much he is withholding, and of how much his evasiveness here makes other passages appear at times a little forced and sentimental.

Still, this criticism having been made—and one makes it by the standards the book itself has set—*Story of a Life* remains absorbing, full of vivacity and tenderness; an engaging account of an individual boyhood and a remarkable testimony to the continuity of the Russian literary genius. . . .

Ultimately, the best thing one can say about this book is that it manages convincingly to justify the simplicity and breadth of its title.

Dan Jacobson. *Encounter*. Jan., 1965, p. 82

Like *The Story of a Life, Years of Hope* [*Vremya bolshikh ozhidani*] is not a true autobiography but a montage of random memoirs in the tradition of Tolstoy or Gorky, drawn from Paustovsky's adventurous days as a journalist and writer. It deals with his brief sojourn in Odessa from 1920–21 as a refugee from the Russian civil war. In that stimulating, cosmopolitan, and least Russian of cities he experienced in succession White Guard occupation, Red "liberation," and Allied blockade. Plying the only trade he knew, Paustovsky, then nearing thirty, eked out a precarious existence as a journalist on a remarkable newspaper, *The Seaman*, which attracted to its staff some of the brightest young writers of the southern school of Russian literature, including the gifted Isaac Babel.

Paustovsky's recollections of the bitter struggle for survival in the beleaguered city are related in a series of vignettes notable for their poignancy, color, and reportorial fidelity—hallmarks of his distinctive style. But what comes through these short pieces is not history or personal narrative so much as the exquisite artistry of a master storyteller and the nobility of a gentle human being. Partly because such traits were notably lacking in so much contemporary Soviet literature that toed the official line of "socialist realism," they made Paustovsky in his later years one of the most widely read Soviet writers.

Sidney Heitman. *SR*. May 17, 1969, p. 50

PILNYAK, BORIS   (1894–ca. 1938)

Pilnyak is a complex writer and, at first glance, a somewhat ragged one. He dabs and smears at his canvas, by patches and specks, and scatters his lines of fire in all directions, in squares and circles. One cannot guess at once where he is heading and what he is driving at. His path is rough. His affections change irrationally, but with astuteness and calculation. With great deliberation, after much reflection, he changes when he has discovered something better to replace something worse.

He constantly improves his work and improves himself, but not in the accepted sense that one usually speaks about writers, not in the sense that each subsequent work is better than the preceding. He cuts into pieces what he wrote, adding anew to it, and not infrequently his writings appear as merely worked-over, but improved, variations of earlier work, adapted to a new stage in the development of his consciousness. Without literary prejudice, he sorts out what he needs, not only from his own work but from that of others. However, this is far from imitating or adopting the ideas and images of others. On the contrary, everything comes to him as it is needed, everything serves his ends. In this method of work, Pilnyak displays his unique talents as a writer. In this sense, in his own way he completely abrogates the inherent value of literature and then the literature as such. In his creativity, the spirit of our times, the concept of the subservient nature of literature, and a kind of inherent utilitarianism all rule over the interests of the professional dedicated to his art. "My works live with me," he says, "in such absurd fashion that, when I start to write a new piece, I take the old for my material and ruin it in order to make the new better. In part, this is because what I want to say now is much dearer to me than my work, and I sacrifice the old work to the new if it will help me. Another reason for this is that I run low on fantasy. What I (and we) have done is unimportant. What is important is what I (and we) will do. You cannot sum us up yet. Some kind of collective spirit is needed for our work (and was, and is, and will be). I came out of Bely and Bunin; there are writers who do more and better than I, and I consider myself to have the right to take what is better or what I can make better. (Peregudov and Dal, I am not hiding from anyone what I took in this novel from you!) It is not very important to me what will remain of me. But it is our fate to produce Russian literature collectively, and that is a heavy responsibility."

P. S. Kogan. *Novy mir*. Nov., 1925, p. 112[†]

Goli god (*The Bare Year*) is not a "roman" (novel), though called so by its author. It comprises several vivid character sketches, a few colorful descriptions, some charming legends and interesting episodes from folk-life, and a few pictures of the rapidly changing conditions and of the different political parties, along with some lively dialogues representing discussions of a variety of creeds, viewpoints, philosophies, and political theories. The year he calls "bare" is 1919.

Some parts of the book are delightful reading, and can and ought to be included in anthologies and text-books. Other places are so vividly and eloquently realistic and naturalistic in their portrayal of the ugliest sides of human and animal life, that they cause a physical disgust.

On the whole, the book seems to be rather an elaborate notebook of a great writer than a finished literary production: there is material in it for as much as ten novels. It shows a powerful talent at work, one worthy to be compared to that of the great masters.

In his introduction, the author acknowledges the rather unfinished state of his works and explains it by the conditions in which he had written and published them—deprived of the most necessary comforts, constantly changing his mode of living, his place of abode, writing with interruptions, losing manuscripts, etc.

Sophie R. A. Court. *BA*. Spring, 1927, p. 55

Time and again it was pointed out that Pilnyak's passion for journeys and long voyages explains in great measure his lack of subjects and failure to approach contemporary themes. Pilnyak's latest stories are clearly proof of this. In a recent story published in *Novy mir*, a Japanese capitalist receives a concession to raise an English warship, the *Black Prince*, lost at the time of the Crimean War with a cargo of gold, from the bottom of the Black Sea. The capitalist appears as a hero, disinterestedly absorbed in the undertaking and not thinking of the gold at all but of the subjugation of the human will to the forces of nature. For whose edification is such deferential treatment of the concessioner necessary? Who is objectively interested in so calm and placid a regard for a class enemy such as the concessioner? If this story of Pilnyak's can be justified as the result of, let us say, a failure to understand the social implication of his work, then it is impossible to justify the story printed in the second number of *Zvezda*, "The Nizhegorod Slope." The deformed nature of this work is quite evident. This pathological tale about the love of mother and son begins and ends as a so-called Freudian Oedipus complex, blurring the feelings and emotional experiences of the characters and finally rising at the end to the heights of social generalization, to some kind of unique "philosophy of history."

Leopold Averbakh. Na literaturnom postu.
June, 1928, p. 56†

The writer Pilnyak informs his readers that his *Roots* [*Korni yaponskogo solntsa*] (1926) are no good. The writer Pilnyak of 1932 asks his readers to throw out from their shelves the seventh volume of the GIZ edition of his Collected Works. As for the translation of this book, Pilnyak asks that its Japanese translation be destroyed first of all. This must be done out of respect for the author.* [1934]

Boris Pilnyak. Kamni i korni. Cited in Gleb Struve,
Soviet Russian Literature 1917–1950 (Norman, Okla.,
University of Oklahoma Press, 1951), p. 214

[*Mashiny i volki* (*Machines and Wolves*)] is not a pragmatic novel with a plot told systematically. Bulky as Tolstoi's or Dostoevsky's books, it lacks their lucid and firm technique which makes the Russian classics, in spite of their volume, their scores of characters, and the complicated action, so easy and fascinating to read. There is not much action in these scarcely coherent fragments of a story held together by a kind of epic refrain, passages repeated in irregular intervals. The chaos we are plunged into and never get out of till we close the book, is a picture of the Russian revolution which is at the same time the tragic history of man's civilization symbolized in the wolf, the powerful beast of the endless Russian woods, now a prisoner behind bars in the menagerie, pacing restlessly up and down with even, regular motions like a machine.

What there is of vague political theory is set into the all-Russian land-

* Most likely, Pilnyak wrote this with his tongue in his cheek.—Ed.

scape, the vast forests and steppes, wild wolves howling in the night, factories, machines, flaming blast furnaces—irrational and unreal as a whole,
statistics and figures if analyzed, with such characters as the statistician
who is all eye-glasses, moustaches, and figures, or the shepherdess Marja,
overwhelming in her elemental womanhood and animal strength.

The technique of pointillism adjusted to literature produces a somewhat
confused and oscillating picture of a Russian world in the process of
fermentation in the early twenties when the revolution was almost over
but not yet settled. Different types of print, whole pages set in parenthesis,
references, and so on, do not help to make a whole out of the amorphous
parts.

Max Lederer. *BA*. Autumn, 1947, p. 419

Judged by absolute standards, the work of Pilnyak has much in it that is
unsatisfactory: he has little sense of form; his confused composition is
still further obscured by his shallow "philosophy of history" to which
everything in the narrative is subordinated; his efforts at psychological
analysis, especially in the erotic genre, smack of a cheap imitation of
Dostoyevsky; much of his art is of bookish derivation and has a secondhand flavor, certain ready-made patterns being merely cut to post-Revolutionary measure; and his monotonous, shrill diction soon palls on the
reader. But, judged in the general context of Soviet literature, there are
in Pilnyak many valuable elements: his keen sense of the Russian language
and of words in general; his interest in ideas, whatever may be their
intrinsic worth; his deep-seated humanism and sympathy with the suffering, which goes back to the best traditions of Russian literature. His courage and independence were also conspicuous among his contemporaries.
Whatever his later concessions to the demands of those in authority, and
his efforts to adjust himself to the new conditions, he was obviously sincere
in welcoming the Revolution at first. As he put it himself, he saw the
artist's "bitter duty" in being honest with himself and with Russia. Almost
from the outset this attempt at being honest involved him in troubles with
the powers that be. In the twenties he incurred displeasure by his story
"Povest o nepogashennoy lune" ("The Tale of the Unextinguished
Moon," 1927), the subject of which was the death, on the operating table,
of one of the outstanding Communist leaders in the Civil War, Frunze.

Gleb Struve. *Soviet Russian Literature 1917–1950*
(Norman, Okla., University of Oklahoma Press, 1951),
pp. 36–37

Pil'nyak's thinking was strongly influenced by Heraclitian philosophy.
The critic Gurvich once remarked that Pil'nyak's copy of a Russian translation of Heraclitus served as his guide to life.

Throughout his work Pil'nyak's main concern was to distinguish between the essential, which would survive the new times, and the transitory, which would die with them. Everything else was of minor importance. His plots are chaotic, and his characterizations sketchy. The very chaos of his works, however, renders to perfection the catastrophic quality of the times and the impact of catastrophe on the human mind and on individual lives as well as on the life of the nation. Pil'nyak wove terror and disaster into his words and into the structure of his plots. His compulsion to be always in step with the times pushed him in the direction of brilliant reportage rather than imaginative literature.

Pil'nyak once described himself as a follower of Belyi and Bunin. The critics took him at his word and the label stuck. In point of fact, the influence of Aleksei Remizov is more marked in Pil'nyak's best writing. He has been called a master of analytical suprematism in prose, close in spirit and in style to the painter Filonov. Strangely enough, his debt to Vlas Doroshevich and Aleksandr Amfiteatrov, the "kings of reportage" of the old Russian press, is never mentioned.

Vyacheslav Zavalishin. Early Soviet Writers
(New York, Frederick A. Praeger, 1958), p. 195

When he came to Berlin, Pilnyak observed the life in a foreign city with curiosity. He was a talented and woolly-headed man. He knew well what he was writing about, and he startled both Russian and foreign readers both by the cruel details he was describing and by the unusual form of his narrative technique. His books of the 1920s, like those of many of his contemporaries, reflect their period through the combination of crudeness and mannerisms, of hunger and art fetishism, and of enthusiasm for both Leskov and marketplace wrangling. He disappeared in the 1930s, and it is hard to tell what future as a writer he might have had. In Berlin in 1922 he maintained that the Revolution was a peasant and a national revolution, and he accused Peter the Great of "pulling Russia away from Russia." His simplicity revealed an admixture of cunning: he adored *yurodstvo* [this word, it seems, does not have an equivalent in any other European language]—the ancient Russian form of self-defense.

Ilya Ehrenburg. Novy mir. Sept., 1961, p. 97†

The Naked Year [*Goly god*] is a virtuoso performance. It is a symphonic structure of themes and ideas—some of them, the Slavophile idea and the degeneration of the nobility, for instance, traditional in Russian literature and some quite new. Passages of description or cerebration on the part of the author or his characters are packed with ideas both expressed and symbolically suggested. The ideas are not necessarily original or profound, and they may be fantastic or repellent, but Pilnyak has contrived to link them with the troubled characters of his novel in such a way that the reader experiences a kind of aesthetic empathy for each fragment in the philosophic medley. In thus personalizing his ideas Pilnyak is a follower of Dostoevsky.

The book displays an amazing stylistic versatility in the various levels of Russian speech which Pilnyak easily commands: that of the cultivated aristocrat, the radical intelligentsia, the simple peasant. It is a textbook of literary devices, and one from which Pilnyak's contemporaries studied their craft. It is one of the most *literary* novels of the period, in the sense that the author never conceals from the reader his function as a craftsman of words and a dispenser of ideas. The author is present in the narrative *qua* author. He comments on his own work and addresses critical remarks to the reader. The linguistic wealth of the novel is enhanced by the great variety of original documents included in it: records of court decisions, newspaper articles, ancient documents, diaries, and notebooks. One of the first Soviet novels, indeed the first, if we are to believe Pilnyak, *The Naked Year* is also one of the most versatile, and of the novels and stories which deal with the Civil War is the one which, even with all its devices of "estrangement" and "stylization," presents the most immediate, moving, and, if one may be allowed the word, "realistic" account of the period.

Edward J. Brown. *Russian Literature Since the Revolution* (New York, Crowell-Collier, 1963), pp. 108–9

Boris Pilnyak "began" as a writer after the revolution and seemed to many contemporaries to be an artist of the revolution. Furthermore, here was a writer of an obvious modernist bent who wanted to glorify the revolution from the modernist creative position. . . .

The Bare Year contains a cross section of the society agitated by the revolution: the peasantry, workers, the remnants of the past, and the splendid "leather jackets." The novel was sharp and coarse, even to the point of brutality; however, all of this could be interpreted as an expression of the times. . . .

Action and work are the thing that mainly attract and intrigue Pilnyak about the communists. They constitute the new *Rus*. He is mainly concerned with *Rus* and not with Soviet Russia, for the October Revolution to Pilnyak is a phenomenon that is particularly national and deprived of all international connections. . . .

Before us is a writer who does not have an acute and clearly defined world outlook. Disbelief in reason and the laws of the objective development of history is more inherent to him. Pilnyak views the outside world as not subject to reason. *The Bare Year* and his subsequent novels are intentionally chaotic and confused since the objective world is supposed to be equally so. For this reason, the subjective, irrational, subconscious, and physiological always dominate the objective concept of the world in Pilnyak's work. This is the origin of the contradictions in his novels.

Nearly every novel of Pilnyak's describes the countryside and Old *Rus*; however, as was correctly observed in the twenties, he writes about Russia as if he were writing about India. Citations from old manuscripts of the schismatics, descriptions of archaic rites, the rich "life style," over-saturation with folklore—all of this is intricate and at times expressive, but it is not the Russian countryside of 1919–20. It is rather some modernistic "India." Different from Bely, yet similar, Pilnyak's subjective world view dictates everything. In essence, the watershed between the modernist treatment of reality and its representation by artists of socialist realism divides negation and acceptance of the objective regularity of the reflected world. Pilnyak is controversial and inconsistent. Along with the vivid and correctly understood characteristics of the new reality, his novels are at the same time suffused with subjectivity.

M. Kuznetsov. *Novy mir*. Aug., 1963, pp. 226–28†

Pilnyak describes society at the moment when it has no system and is uncertain of its values. He records the inventory of social upheaval, which he neither condemns nor justifies. For the most part his stories are somber, not melancholic; but they have the effect of creating in us an almost unbearable melancholy at the thought of what upheaval meant 50 years ago in Russia and what it would mean again, in another time, in another place.

Not all [Pilnyak's] stories concern the Russian Revolution. Several of the most interesting are set against the revolution in China; the devastating "Story About How Stories Came to Be Written" ["Rasskaz o tom, kak sozdayutsya rasskazy"] is set in a very peaceful Japan. Yet they all turn inevitably on the same themes. People are displaced as though by magic, alienated, plundered, exiled. Times are transformed, values fall into new perspectives. Hope and degradation, for which birth and cannibalism become almost casual symbols, are juxtaposed.

Having delved into Pilnyak's stories, it becomes impossible to resist them: every page insists that we read the next.

Judith K. Davison. *NYT*. Nov. 19, 1967, p. 80

Boris Pil'nyak is one of those writers who miss greatness but who alter the literary history of their country in a decisive way. He lacked a real gift for fiction—an incandescent vision capable of fusing good intentions, prodigious reading, and keen powers of observation into compelling art. He was instead a borrower, an eclectic, the diligent pupil of Belyi, Remizov, and Bunin. Yet his lack of originality determined his importance, for he adapted the techniques and strategies of his teachers to the new themes of Revolution and Civil War. Through him, they took on a respectability that they could no longer command by themselves; and because he was extremely popular and widely imitated during the early twenties, they left a deep and lasting impression on the new literature. . . .

The two-Russias theme—"Asia" or "Europe," village or city, soil or salon—had absorbed intellectuals for a century or more. Pil'nyak's version owed most to the so-called Eurasians: in its contempt for the Russian intelligentsia as products of Western civilization; the rejection of Europe not so much for itself as for its irrelevance to Russian problems; the denial that capitalism (a European invention) could contribute to Russia's development; the interpretation of the Revolution as a cleansing, renewing event; and the assertion that Russians are neither Europeans nor Asians, but a mixture of both, or Eurasians.

Pil'nyak pulled these familiar ideas together into a single view of the world and set them in a new literary context. He rooted the themes of Easternism and primitivism specifically in the peasantry and recast the two-Russias theme in terms of the social conflicts of his time. The result was a version of the revolutionary experience that struck an immediate response in the twenties and has haunted Russian writers ever since. It has taken on the first flesh of myth.

Robert A. Maguire. *Red Virgin Soil* (Princeton, N.J.,
Princeton University Press, 1968), pp. 101, 106

Among the Russian writers of the twenties few can have been more talented than Boris Pilnyak. . . . Though a literary modernist experimenting with abrupt narrative transitions, cryptic philosophical intermezzos, and a style that has been described as a "blizzard of words," Pilnyak also had something in him of the ancient tribal bard. He was a marvelous storyteller, a spellbinder, an enchanted rhetorician. The surface of his fiction deals with revolutionary Russia, but beneath it, like a land buried under lava, there is always traditional sluggish Russia. Pilnyak is a romantic in that he is fascinated by experiences drawn to their breaking point, situations of extreme pressure and revelation; but also a romantic in that he likes to set his stories against a background of peasant timelessness, primitive survivals. He deserves, I think, quite the attention that his contemporary Isaac Babel received in the American literary world about a decade ago.

As a writer Pilnyak is obsessed with the contrasts between the rhythm of a generation trapped in a historical cataclysm and the larger rhythms of the life of an entire people. A man may suppose his life to be driven by conscious purposes, but in reality he is acting out part of a centuries-long national drama. Shattering change is set against flat changelessness. In stories like "The Cheshire Cheese" and "Wormwood" the Revolution is at the stark foreground, but behind it sweeps the anarchic fury of the Russian peasants.

Pilnyak believed that the Revolution, far from being the proletarian uprising that Lenin and Trotsky supposed, was actually an outburst of long-suppressed primitive Russian energies. As it now seems, he was quite as wrong as the Bolsheviks, for in reality neither the peasants nor the proletariat triumphed in Russia. But from a literary perspective it hardly matters that Pilnyak was wrong since his point of view enabled him to dramatize the experience into which he had been thrust. Better than he realized, Pilnyak's stories show the ordeal of a people at a point where tradition has been ruptured, a culture contorted with the agonies of rebirth, and men enslaved to a masquerade of historical consciousness.

Irving Howe. *Harper.* Jan., 1968, p. 72

Plotless and again disjointed, the novella "Mahogany" ["Krasnoe derevo"] is a moving, poetic elegy to the ancient but fast disappearing Russian art of wood-carving and porcelain-making. Set in a small provincial town, "a Russian Bruges and a Muscovite Kamakura," the story is about two brothers who come there from Moscow searching for what remains, after centuries of wars and revolutions, of the labor of unknown and long-forgotten serfs—searching for, in short, the past. Parallel to their quest runs that of two other brothers, elderly men both. One, who has already "outlived" three tzars and Lenin, intends to outlive Soviet power; having lost his sense of time and his fear of life, he is, in a sense, immortal. His brother, a revolutionary Communist who bears more resemblance to the itinerant "soothsayers . . . mendicant chanters, lazars, wanderers from holy place to holy place" than to a rational human being, considers the present state of affairs a "betrayal" of the ideals of "genuine" revolution; for him, too, time had come to a halt. But whether searching for mahogany or past glory the brothers are, in reality, seeking a meaning that can no longer be found, either in the old or the new.

Tamas Aczel. *SR.* Sept. 14, 1968, p. 110

PLATONOV, ANDREI (1899–1951)

When we read Platonov's story "Semya Ivanova" ("The Ivanov Family"), it is as if we observe life in a small stuffy world, isolated from all its surroundings, shut off in its own inner ferment, with absolutely nothing connecting it with a broader life stretching beyond its limits.

The main reason for the severe failure of Andrei Platonov in his attempt to come to grasps with grave moral issues is that he completely wrenched the whole subject of his story away from the concrete life of our country, that in characterizing he did not begin with a realistic representation of people actually existing but merely invented them, enticing imaginary people out of every contact with the world of our Soviet reality and divesting them of the elementary traits of contemporary man. It is as if intentionally, according to some kind of cruel design, the writer created an atmosphere that completely isolates the Ivanov family from all the surroundings. The echoes of the world about them reach the Ivanov family only through the cynical view of a certain invalid who recounts the solution to his own family drama, made all the more terrible by the moral corruption of the speech put into the mouths of children, or through the equally terrible views of the wife who recounts her life without a husband and surrounded by strangers. . . .

What is the philosophy of this story? Is it that man is weak, sinful, brutish, needing forgiveness for his weaknesses? Is it that everything becomes tangled and complex in the encounters within a family, that the only possible solution to the struggle rests in the weak, sinful, brutish urge to continue the race? Only this ancient feeling of concern for one's own posterity can, according to Platonov, solve the terrible drama of the Ivanov family.

A profound disbelief in the organizing strength of social morality dictates such philosophy. This philosophy is the more pernicious as it is expressed in a form both natural and elevated in feeling—as the love for children. But in the love that Sergeant Ivanov shows returning to his family, in this unwanted family servitude, denied by his whole being—in this love nothing is human, and there is only the triumph of instinct.

Lev Subotski. *Novy mir.* March, 1947, p. 151†

Andrei Platonov was one of the most remarkable of Soviet writers, again less because of literary skill than because of moral qualities. Although his stylistically most mature work came along after he had left the *Pereval* organization (he was a member for only a short time and then struck out as a lone wolf), he spoke from the beginning in his own distinctive voice. The germs of his later work, with its intense strain of compassion for luckless, fear-ridden men were already discernible in his first stories and soon invited the disfavor and vilification which he was to suffer throughout his life.

In his prose of the mid-1920's (he began as a poet) Platonov followed in the footsteps of Leskov, although he was also under the influence of Gogol and Remizov. Over and over again the same characters recur in Platonov's stories—the grandsons of Leskov's Levsha, the uncrowned king of self-taught men, the craftsman who shod a mechanical flea. His descendants have come in life and become hoboes, tramps, drunkards, failures and crackpots of all sorts, but have inherited their grandfather's audacity, innate intelligence and conscience. But whereas Levsha made no mistakes and aroused universal admiration by his craftsmanship, his grandsons experience one failure after another and let their work fall from listless hands. Kondrov, eager to help his collective farm, enters into socialist competition with the sun and invents an artificial sun, the only trouble with which is that it gives no light. Makar builds a merry-go-round which is to move by wind power, but the merry-go-round stands still. Levsha's descendants are not stupid or lazy, nor have they lost their skills, but they rebel against dull, senseless labor which calls only for muscular strength without intelligence. They refuse to be an appendage of the machine.

Vyacheslav Zavalishin. Early Soviet Writers
(New York, Frederick A. Praeger, 1958), pp. 245–46

Not long before the second World War, a short story called "The Third Son" ["Treti syn"] by this Russian writer Platonov, who was almost unknown in the West, fell into the hands of Ernest Hemingway, who was already famous. At a meeting with some Soviet journalists, Hemingway spoke with admiration of the pithiness and the expressiveness of Platonov's style. (Hemingway did not know that Platonov had written a brilliant article about his novels *To Have and Have Not* and *A Farewell to Arms*.) To their shame, by no means all of the journalists taking part in this conversation with Hemingway knew the work of their compatriot. Platonov was not spoiled by fame during his life, either at home or abroad. He belongs among the delayed-action writers, whose talent is like a safety fuse which runs many years in length. This fuse smolders unseen but persistent, staying dry even under the drizzle of time, until finally a blinding explosion destroys bridges that had seemed built for eternity.

Yevgeny Yevtushenko. NYR. Jan. 1, 1970, p. 14

Many of the great Russian writers of the past—Turgenev comes most readily to mind—sought to eliminate the discord between Man and Nature. Platonov continues this tradition, but his Nature reflects the changes that took place in Man's natural environment, which in the 1920s and 1930s no longer consisted solely of birch trees, brooks, and birds. By then, Nature had absorbed, as it were, many man-made objects, sounds and smells, and it is with this totality that Platonov seeks to establish a harmonious relationship. As a very young man, he wrote that "besides the fields, the country side, my mother, and the sound of bells ringing, I also loved—and the longer I live, the more I love—steam engines, machines, shrill whistles, and sweaty work."

What set Platonov apart from most of his contemporaries who shared these concerns was his insistence that his protagonists blend with their industrialized environment without surrendering their humanity.

Maurice Friedberg. *SR*. Jan. 10, 1970, p. 44

Indeed, it is difficult to understand why Stalin denounced Platonov personally and why his writings were suppressed as nonconformist. There is very little evidence of irony or skepticism or European sophistication; Platonov obviously wrote to communicate with all readers, and his later works contain only positive references to the authorities, who are "zealous" and work "with great care" and who demonstrate a most admirable brotherhood with non-Party members. Platonov's narratives are unadorned, except for brief "poetic" passages in which nature is honored (though abstractly); there are paragraphs and paragraphs of unashamed rhetoric in praise of man's spirit, which may be fulfilled now for the first time in history as Soviet Russia attempts to work out its fate. . . .

Platonov demonstrates no capacity for—or interest in—commonly held esthetic values of dramatic development, emphasis, or pacing. His characters are often no more than names or attitudes; they are interchangeable, and this would no doubt seem a virtue to their creator, who is concerned with man at the point at which individual personality disappears and the mysterious collective personality emerges. We must take our places in the giant machinery of the State and there we will find happiness, but only there. Our way in to this State is through work, either the work of soldiers or of factory workers or farmers (Platonov's favorite characters).

Joyce Carol Oates. *NYT*. Feb. 1, 1970, p. 42

POGODIN, NIKOLAI (1900–1962)

If we did not already have such a great novel as Fadeyev's *The Young Guard* and if we had to judge the beauty and richness of spirit of the best Soviet people only by mediocre dramatic productions and writing, then we would not have the right to be so exacting in reviewing *Sotvorenie mira (The Creation of the World)*, as long as it remained unique in the serious postwar dramatic production. But we already have an image of the Soviet man in which his attitudes and the nature of his selflessness is artistically perceived. Pogodin arrived earlier than others at the complex task of showing physically and spiritually wounded people under unique conditions, where they once more manifest their own exceptional life force. Perhaps he arrived at this task before postwar motifs had supplanted interest in a war which had not yet terminated; consequently, these motifs could not present the writer with a great quantity of observations from which to select the typical. . . .

We might have asked if there really was a war before *Sotvorenie mira*, so improbably happy are all the outcomes of these seemingly inconsolable dramas, so loftily solemn is the reflection of self-veneration.

But these conclusions cannot compel us to forget entirely the shaken, restless world of the heroes of *Sotvorenie mira*. Despite all their seemingly imaginary misfortunes and senseless suffering evoked by an unhealthy sensitivity, despite the conclusion that all is well and all are good, the stamp of a merciless war is more evident here than in all other postwar plays taken together. It is evident in the tone of *Sotvorenie mira*, in the maturity of its main hero, in the searching of the author seriously reflecting on life, and in his sympathy for man.

Pogodin's persistent, long labor over the burning issues of our life deserves our respect and attention. This noble and poignant, though not exultant, labor gives Pogodin the right to the indignation and sarcasm with which, in recent addresses, he attacked banal and bourgeois drama, which palms off exhibitions of aesthetics, thoughtless significance, and enervating respite onto the man who has lived through war and is tired of it.

A. Gurvich. *Novy mir.* June, 1946, pp. 158–59†

Pogodin's first play written after the 1932 "reform" was *Moy drug (My Friend)*. Written in 1932, it was produced by the Theater of the Revolution in 1934. Largely, it repeats the pattern of his earlier plays—it shows a Soviet plant under construction and the efforts of its director to overcome all sorts of difficulties. But the play is less episodic, less journalistic, and dramatically more compact. There is also an attempt to give a more rounded-off portrait of the central character, Gay, the director of the plant. He is the new Soviet man, the positive hero, one of the builders of Socialism. All the other characters are there merely to set him in relief and are for the most part as conventional as those in Pogodin's earlier plays. This is particularly true of Gay's enemies, those who, guided by various motives, hinder the construction. In the words of one of the leading Soviet dramatic critics, Yuzovsky, who was on the whole quite favorable to Pogodin, "Pogodin's negative characters do not come off. . . . They are mannequins disguised as saboteurs and wandering about the play because one can't dispense with them."

Gleb Struve. *Soviet Russian Literature 1917–1950*
(Norman, Okla., University of Oklahoma Press,
1951), p. 288

[In the play *Aristokraty (Aristocrats)*] Pogodin saw fit to find a comic side to a situation which represented horror, suffering and death for the prisoners directly involved, as well as a constant threat to every person in the country.

The Soviet critic who wrote an introduction to Pogodin's work pointed out that the writer had come to the theater from the newspaper and that he was not accustomed to inventing his subjects: "The fictitious, in the opinion of Pogodin himself, prevents the effect of living reality." For him the thing that is important is the "recording of actuality, the registering of facts." Pogodin is a "playwright of the period of reconstruction. He looks at the world with the loving eyes of a man who is arranging his own life" in his own home, "and thus home is the land of socialism." . . .

To some extent, in regard to his portrayal of the rehabilitation of "nonpolitical criminals," Pogodin's play is based on facts. In his "recording of actuality," however, the author has patently selected only certain facts which contribute to the special purpose of his play, to quiet the widespread unrest caused by the Soviet concentration camp policy. About the typical conditions which were arousing public horror and protest, Pogodin remains silent: the framing of political prisoners or their arrest and exile without being informed of the charge against them, the impossible labor norms, the ragged clothing, the lack of shoes, the beatings, the unsanitary conditions, the primitive medical care, the frightful mortality rate among the convicts, the cruel refusal to allow a prisoner's relatives to know where he was or to correspond with him, even to know whether he was dead or alive. To take these facts into consideration would, of course, preclude the writing of the joyous and cheerful comedy which Pogodin deliberately set out to produce. Whether by design or inadvertence, the Soviet critic who commented on Pogodin's rejection of the fictitious pointed out that nevertheless "it [the fictitious] still appears in his work, particularly in its humorous colors." And it is in this coloring that the playwright sins against the facts.

Peter Yershov. *Comedy in the Soviet Theater*
(New York, Frederick A. Praeger, 1956), pp. 167, 169

One of the fundamental themes of this neo-naturalistic drama is the assertion of the right to love, even in situations that break up families, and the denial of the party's right to interfere with such attachments. This, for example, is the central theme of N. Pogodin's *Sonet Petrarki* (*Sonnet of Petrarch*). Considering the fact that "breaking up a family" is still sufficient cause for expulsion from the Komsomol and the party, Pogodin's play has overtones of social criticism. Yet it is first and foremost a "drama of manners" in the traditional sense. The play traces the development of a relationship between a middle-aged married engineer and a young laboratory technician in an atmosphere of envy and perennial small-town gossip. The important change from the 19th-century plot is that such "illicit love" is persecuted not by the Church or by "public opinion," which at least could be escaped by going to another town, but by the party committee, from which there is no escape. Pogodin, along with the other authors of the genre school, tirelessly affirms his loyalty to the party but actually wants to limit the party's rights, to preserve a special realm of private personal life where a human being is his own master. "I give all my soul to the party; I'd give it my life. But there are private sides to a man's life which he cannot reveal to anybody," says the hero of *Sonnet of Petrarch*.

David Burg. *PC*. Sept.–Oct., 1962, p. 40

Aristocrats [is] a half-serious, half-comical play about the building, by forced labor, of a canal between the White and Baltic seas. Thieves, bandits, and other convicts, the aristocrats of crime, at first do not want to work but gradually become involved in collective action and are transformed and morally regenerated. Kostya the Captain, the main protagonist of the play, even receives official awards for his zeal. This theme of "reforming human character" through toil was current in the thirties, and numerous novels and plays exploited it. By the way, some of them were akin to "miracle plays," the conversion of former villains to Communism being similar to the change of sinners into good Christians. The underlying idea of all the novels and plays on that subject was to prove that Soviet society did create new men and new morality. What redeemed Pogodin's play from becoming an illustration of a thesis were his humor and his technique: *Aristocrats*, like Pogodin's other works, replaced the "trunkline action" of a single plot by a sequence of short episodes or dramatic scenes, each having its own climax and resolution, very much like cinematographic shorts. Excellent dialogues and unity of the main theme tied all these separate skits into a scenic whole. The novelty of this structure attracted directors and actors.

Marc Slonim. *Russian Theatre: From the Empire to the Soviets* (New York, Crowell-Collier, 1962), pp. 337–38

PRISHVIN, MIKHAIL (1873–1954)

Your [Prishvin's] human beings are of the Earth, and on good terms with the Earth. They are more geologically and biologically inclined than those of other writers, they are the most legitimate sons of the Great Mother, truly living particles of the "sacred body of humanity." You remember, always and so profoundly, mankind's painful and miraculous progress from the era of the flint axe to that of the aeroplane.

But what I admire chiefly is that you know how to measure and evaluate human beings by what is good in them, and not by what is bad. This simple wisdom is attained by most people with great difficulty, if at all. We do not wish to understand that the good in man is the most wonderful of all the miracles ever performed by him. After all, human beings really have no reason to be "good," kindness and humanity are not encouraged in them either by the laws of nature, or by the conditions of social existence. And yet you and I know a great many truly good people. [1917]

Maksim Gorky. *Literary Portraits* (Moscow,
Foreign Language Publishing House, n.d.), p. 308

Prishvin's numerous short stories include very few in which man is the leading character, but nevertheless, the human image, even if painted with sparing strokes, is always a finished portrait.

A pathfinder through our world, Prishvin portrays the various national types and local colours with remarkable accuracy and consummate skill, never resorting to false exotics. We are constantly made aware of the "school for the careful treatment of facts." These facts—life, the occupations of man, his world outlook, his dwelling, manners, clothing, speech, the peculiarity of his smile and so forth—are all drawn with sparing and accurate strokes, and are inspired by that same intimate attention which enables the writer to see, behind all the specific national features, those general, human and beautiful traits which are alike common to the northern seamen, Kirghiz, Tatars, and Russians.

The desire for progress, the admiration of lofty human culture, go side by side with the author's respect for the life of men "in the depth of the centuries," his profound interest in all monuments of the past. But in studying and beautifying the past, he never toys with the idea of a return to it; his admiration contains no trace of the tourist's condescension.

Prishvin has studied human character in the light of both national and professional peculiarities. The series of stories *Shoes* [*Bashmaki*] opens up an entire world of shoemakers, the history of their trade, their cities, their life and work. Excellent types of the craftsmen have been drawn, including artists and thieves. Professional pride and the successes of the craftsmen-artists are wonderfully shown.

So we see that Mikhail Prishvin's numerous short stories and sketches about animals and plants, about atmospheric phenomena and the seasons of the year, stories of the most diverse "heroes"—porcupines, mushrooms, thunderstorms, dogs, spiders, chaffinches, streams, nightingales, foxes, and so on—in reality have still another character; we find him in all the books from *Kolobok* to *The Storehouse of the Sun* [*Kladovaya solntsa*]. This hero is man, the master and moulder of life. He is the eyes and the heart, the mouth and the brain of living nature. He sees the world around us, gives it meaning, understands it, tells us about it, having one clear and definite aim—to remake the whole world in such a way that life should be good, happy, just and sensible.

Myra Blinkova. *SL*. March, 1947, pp. 49–50

Mikhail Mikhailovich Prishvin . . . is something of a Russian W. H. Hudson. A trained specialist in agriculture, he first attracted attention in 1907 with *V krayu nepugannykh ptits* (*In the Land of Unscared Birds*), which contained some wonderful descriptions of nature and animal life in the Far North of Russia. A poet of nature, he is also a great master of racy and picturesque Russian. His first important post-Revolutionary work was *Kurymushka* (1924), which he described as his first "real story of a man." It is a novel of obviously autobiographical inspiration, though written in the third person, and describes the hero's childhood with remarkable insight into the inner workings of a child's mind. Further parts of it appeared later under the title *Kashcheyeva tsep* (*Kashchey's Chain*). In Russian folklore Kashchey is the legendary embodiment of evil, and the title symbolizes the fetters of moral and social prejudices from which man must free himself. Prishvin's manner resembles Remizov's, but his outlook of manly and robust optimism marks him off from some of the dominant tendencies of Russian literature. He is a passionate sportsman and at the same time an animal lover, and in many of his stories of the Soviet period he continued to explore the theme of nature. Some of them —for example in the volume *Lesnaya kapel* (*Forest Thaw*, 1945)—are more like short poems in prose, combining descriptions of nature with lyrical meditations.

Gleb Struve. *Soviet Russian Literature 1917–1950*
(Norman, Okla., University of Oklahoma Press, 1951),
pp. 139–40

Prishvin was the kind of writer who needed more than a lifetime to fulfil himself, the kind that could write a whole poem about a single autumn leaf dropping from a tree. And so many of these leaves fall bearing away the writer's unuttered thoughts, thoughts which Prishvin had said may drop as effortlessly upon the world as these self-same leaves. . . .

Prishvin would say that he was a poet sacrificed on the altar of prose. But he was mistaken. His prose is richer in the essence of true poetry than many verses and long poems. . . .

But Prishvin, an amazingly erudite writer, stands in a class by himself for he was able with great skill to organically and unobtrusively incorporate in his prose his extensive knowledge of ethnography, phenology, botany, zoology, agronomy, meteorology, history, folklore, ornithology, geography, regional history and so on. Knowledge lived in his work, enriched by personal experience and observation. Moreover, Prishvin had the happy quality of seeing in scientific phenomena, both large and small, the highest expression of poetry. [1955]

Konstantin Paustovski. *The Golden Rose*
(Moscow, Foreign Language Publishing House, n.d.),
pp. 201–2, 205

Prishvin . . . whose earliest work long antedates the Revolution is perhaps not fully appreciated even in the Soviet Union for the variety, interest, and power of his work, and he is little known elsewhere. His works
are full of knowing observation of wood, field and stream, and they contain, along with the lore of nature, poetic and philosophic reflections at
times reminiscent of Thoreau. His treatment of nature is never divorced
from human activities, and he records ethnographic as well as natural
information.

Edward J. Brown. *Russian Literature Since the*
Revolution (New York, Crowell-Collier, 1963), p. 34

In determining the individualistic qualities of Prishvin's travel sketches,
we must assess the attitude of the writer. The sketch, as a nonfictitious
narrative in which the artist does not need to introduce an outside narrator, renders feasible the closest possible relationship of the author with his
reader. In his sketches and, later, in all of his realistic tales, Prishvin is one
of the most subjective Russian writers. As he later formulated it, writing
was for him *"doroga k drugu,"* the road to a friend. We will not deal here
with the literary and theoretical implications of this thought. Nonetheless,
the author's personality and strong participation in his works is unmistakable both in appraisal of his characters and in his sympathy for his topic.
To be sure, his is again an aesthetic and not a philosophical evaluation:
Prishvin loves the world of the orthodox believers because he likes it,
not because he affirms their view of life. The peculiarity of his manner of
writing derives from his basic emotional attitude. The basis for this is
sympathy, enthusiasm, and finally love for what he has seen and experienced. His emotional attitude creates the pervasive, personally intimate
atmosphere that characterizes Prishvin's style in most of his works. Even
the conversational tone used in *In the Land of the Unscared Birds* is an
expression of this attitude, the expression of satisfaction with experience
that demanded a literary outlet. In addition, there is the loving concern
for details, the imitation of folk expressions that involuntarily create a
comic impression, and—what is especially important—a real humor that
is close to life. For the duration of his life, this humor remained a basic
element in all his writing.

Horst Lampl. *Das Frühwerk Michail Prišvins*
(Vienna, Notring, 1967), pp. 78–79†

REMIZOV, ALEKSEI (1877–1957)

Remizov's variety is astonishing, and even to many of his readers quite disconcerting. Few readers are sufficiently catholic to give an equal appreciation to all the aspects of his work. Add to this a very peculiar and whimsical humour (in the Jonsonian sense) both in his life and in his writings, and an unbending artistic honesty; he has never stooped to popularity or fashion, he has never courted success or curried the favour of either critics or public, he never writes but as his unique and capricious genius impels him to write. All this makes him a peculiarly difficult writer for the public to appraise. And it must be confessed that he is not widely read—he is still a writers' writer. This is, however, due to causes that are rather fortuitous than essential; there is little doubt that his popularity will grow (as it has steadily grown among the "inner circle"), for he has that width of human appeal which makes national classics, and that mastery of form which outlives generations. To the English reader, at least one of Remizov's traits may appeal even more than it does to the Russian: this is his quaint humour and incurable, incalculable whimsicality. England has always produced, and recognized, writers whose characters, as Tristram Shandy has said, "do honour to our climate"; and she would gladly adopt, if he were made presentable to her, one who, in the wilfulness of his whims, outdoes both Sterne and Lamb. The trouble is, of course, the old trouble—*"traduttori traditori."* In the case of Remizov the translation demands particular care and skill. His Russian is unique in its quality, and something of a revelation. It has been said that Russian is the least bookish and the most colloquial of all literary languages, and this is to a great extent true. But Remizov has gone one better. His writings—at least his most characteristic writings—renounce the structure of written language altogether and adopt all the characteristics of colloquial speech; his syntax is based not on logical division but on the variety of spoken intonation, of which he has a marvellous command. He succeeds in producing the impression of actual speech, and those who have once heard his voice are haunted by its intonations from the first sentences, whenever they open one of his books. This gives an uncommonly fresh savour to all he writes. To do him justice in English would require a new school of translators who would be able to preserve his intonations (a thing by no means impossible).

TLS. Feb. 21, 1924, p. 108

"Remizov," says Mr. Cournos, "differs from the author of *Crime and Punishment* chiefly in that he is more conscious of his style"—a statement which would seem to imply that he is a greater Dostoevski. In reality he lacks almost completely the thing which makes the writer with whom he is so casually compared great; namely, his passion. His despair was wrung from him by the bitter results of his heroic efforts, but Remizov takes as a matter of course all that Dostoevski protests against, and he wrings no emotion from his tale because he is so far beyond struggle.

Joseph Wood Krutch. Nation. Feb. 11, 1925, p. 163

Remizov is very largely a man of books and papers; it is not for nothing that he married a palaeographist. No one in Russia has spoken of books with such sincere affection; in no one's mouth does the word *knizhnik* (bookman, lover of books) sound so caressing and laudatory as in Remizov's. A large proportion of his writings are adaptations of folk-lore matter or of ancient legends. One of his books, *Russia in Writ* [*Rossiya v pismenakh*], is a running commentary on certain ancient manuscripts in his possession. He is a very laborious writer, and in more senses than one. Not only is his work at his style as elaborate and patient as was Charles Lamb's (with whom he has certain points of resemblance), but his actual handwriting is a most elaborate and skilful revival of the cursive writing of the seventeenth century.

D. S. Mirsky. Contemporary Russian Literature
(New York, Knopf, 1926), p. 284

In both life and art Remizov is a dreamer. It is easy to label him a surrealist. In his works, as in his dreams, reality and fantasy are intricately and whimsically interwoven. In his art dreams play a large role: his own dreams (real and concocted), the dreams of others, and literary dreams. In the beginning of his émigré period, Remizov depicted the Russian revolution (*Vzvikhrennaya Rus* [Stormy Russia], privately published, 1927) with such interweaving of reality and dream. In recent years he devoted two whole books to dreams: *Ogon veshchei* [The Fire of Prophecy, 1954] about dreams in Russian literature (for example, Gogol's, Pushkin's, Lermontov's, Turgenev's, and Dostoyevski's); and *Martyn Zadeka. Sonnik* [Martin Zadeka: Dreamer, 1954], a collection of his own, often highly intricate, dreams. Authentic? Concocted? It makes no difference. . . .

"Life is a dream"—this is almost always the theme of Remizov's works. Between the world of dreams and the world of reality, seen with "shortened vision" (the title of Remizov's very frank autobiography [*Podstrizhennymi glazami*]), it is difficult to draw a boundary: they almost merge. It is not by chance that Remizov possesses so much of a magical rather than a real nature. Remizov's stories are reminiscent of dreams because of their confusion and freedom from the laws of logic. His dreams are astonishingly similar to his stories. . . .

The question of the influence of Remizov on Russian literature contemporaneous with him is a theme for a future historian. His influence was very great in the early period of Soviet literature. With the change to socialist realism, Remizov found himself out of place. Remizov had little influence on young émigré literature, although in its ranks he had several admirers. Perhaps this explains why young émigré writers have to a great extent lost their intimate tie with the Russian word.

Gleb Struve. Russkaya literatura v izgnanii (New York,
Izdatelstvo imeni Chekhova, 1956), pp. 260, 262[†]

I got to know Remizov in Berlin in 1922. In a lower-middle-class German apartment, in a room cluttered with other people's belongings, sat a small, hunched-up man with a long inquisitive nose and lively, roguish eyes. His wife, Serafima Pavlovna, busily entertained the guests with tea. On the desk I noticed manuscripts written, or rather drawn, by a master calligrapher. All kinds of devils cut out of paper swayed on strings: the domestic and wicked ones, cunning and good-natured as newborn kids. Remizov smiled quietly, for on that day, in addition to his usual toys, he had a new one—Pilnyak, who told fantastic stories about life in Kolomna.

Remizov was exactly the same in Berlin as he was in Moscow or in Petrograd, writing the same kind of stories, playing the same kind of games, and cutting out the same kind of devils. I am saying this now as I read the reminiscences of those who knew him before his departure abroad. Vladimir Lidin says in 1921: "Such little men—Russian, earthy, mouselike—have not yet died out. This Russian man, the king of monkeys, Aleksei Mikhailovich Remizov, still lives in good health, scratching and scratching with his pen at night, in hunger and cold. May God give him a long life."

Ilya Ehrenburg. Novy mir. Sept., 1961, pp. 109–10[†]

Of course, trips to Paris were always special occasions. When I was seven or eight years old I recall Alexei Remizov in his Parisian apartment reading Gogol's "Vii," a story of witchcraft. How menacing it sounded in the dusky room! Remizov and his wife, Seraphima Pavovna, my godmother, rarely went out. We visited them in Auteuil, on Rue Boileau, in a place full of old Russian objects—beadwork, embroidery, icons. Every day Remizov worked until four o'clock in the afternoon. The curtains were usually drawn, and the walls glittered with Remizov's weird, cubistic collages and his drawings of creatures, half-animal, half-human. The house was populated by invisible presences: fairy-tale characters, small bizarre animals, mythical spirits. Alexei Remizov told their stories to his guests; children and adults alike were introduced to his imaginary friends. His intimates were invited to join the "Council of Apes," a fanciful society over which he presided, and to which many well-known Russian writers belonged at one time or another.

My godmother was very religious, and the Remizovs' house was disquieting with its little oil lamps, red and blue, hanging in front of icons. It was all darkness and glitter with the feeling of secret happenings behind closed doors as in an orthodox church. The Remizovs constituted a world in themselves, as profoundly Russian as anything I have ever known. As a writer, Remizov lived in a continual contact with the Russian past, which was his favorite subject matter.

Olga Andreyev Carlisle. *Voices in the Snow*
(New York, Random House, 1962), pp. 18–19

A great deal has been written about an identical scene in [Remizov's *Prud* (*The Pond*) and] Kafka's *The Trial*. But with Remizov this is still a dream; for Kafka, it is reality. Ties to the external world are not yet entirely severed in *The Pond*, and that is why we see more clearly the active crystallization process brought to completion by Kafka. Remizov's principal characters, like all "underground men," "know" that the external world exists but they do not believe in it and that is what makes it unreal and fantastic. In Kafka, Beckett, and other modernists, time is paralyzed, nullified. In Remizov we can still discern how time stopped, because the writer is still trying to write a narrative novel in the classical sense but constantly breaks the thin thread of his story—a thread which serves only as a tie to the external world, just as in Bely—with visions and dreams. For the principal character of the novel the world becomes more and more the internal world, and the powers of the subconscious (or superconscious: we still don't know here which is the master and which the servant) are symbolized in the living persons of two hangmen.

Mihajlo Mihajlov. *Russian Themes* (New York,
Farrar, Straus and Giroux, 1968), pp. 274–75

ROZANOV, VASILI (1856–1919)

Throughout his life Rozanov battled to preserve the bonds *with* the word and *for* a philological culture that solidly stood on the foundation of the Greek nature of Russian language. In his decidedly anarchistic relation to everything and complete befuddlement—whatever that may be—there is one thing he cannot do—live in silence. "I cannot bear separation from words"—that approximates Rozanov's spiritual setup. Thus, even his anarchistic and nihilistic spirit recognized only one power—the magic of the language, the power of the word. . . .

All his life Rozanov fumbled in soft vacuum, trying to discover the walls of Russian culture. Similar to certain other Russian thinkers, such as Chayadayev, Leontyev, and Gershenzon, he could not live without walls, without an acropolis. Everything around him gives way; everything is crumbly, soft, and pliable. Yet he wishes to live historically; within him there is an invincible need to find the hard core of the Kremlin, the Acropolis, no matter whether this kernel is found in the governmental or the public domain. The craving for this kernel, no matter how it is symbolized, determined Rozanov's entire fate and finally removed his guilt feelings about the lack of principles and anarchism.

Osip Mandelshtam. *O prirode slova*
(Kharkov, Istoki, 1922), pp. 11–12[†]

Rozanov's style is of course, more than any other style, untranslatable. In it, it is the *intonation* that matters. He uses various typographical devices to bring it out—inverted commas and brackets—but the effect is changed and lost in another language: so rich is it in emotional shades and overtones, so saturated with the spirit of Russia, and so peculiarly Russian are the intonations. . . . There are people who hate, actively hate, Rozanov, and who think him abominable and disgusting. Strictly Orthodox priests are united in this feeling with men of a very different orthodoxy, like Trotsky. Rozanov is the antipodes of Classicism, of discipline, of everything that is line and will. His genius is feminine; it is naked intuition without a trace of "architecture" in it. It is the apotheosis of "Natural Man," the negation of effort and of discipline.

D. S. Mirsky. *Contemporary Russian Literature*
(New York, Knopf, 1926), pp. 170–71

What is peculiar to Rozanov in "Solitaria" ["Uedinyonnoe"] and the "Fallen Leaves" ["Opavshie listya"] is the literary form his introspection took. The volumes consist of brief notes and fragments in which some thought or observation is set down with terrifying self-consciousness and in a mania of frankness. They were written down at the moment of thought or observation on the back of an envelope, on the soles of his shoes, while walking in the street, while bathing, during hours of examining his coins; and with such an intensity of mental effort that Rozanov could not trust himself to convey his exact shade of meaning save by dressing up half his words in italics or inverted commas. His fury of self-expression often rewards the reader with a flash of enlightenment, but the effect is not that of literature. Reading Rozanov, one catches the tones of a troubled, egoist spirit, of a mind frantically contemplating itself. But one is quite unmoved by his lacerating self-analysis, and often fatigued by its inevitable incoherence.

TLS. Aug. 4, 1927, p. 530

Rozanov had a real man in him, and it is true, what he says of himself, that he did not feel in himself that touch of the criminal which Dostoievsky felt in *himself*. Rozanov was not a criminal. Somewhere, he was integral, and grave, and a seer, a true one, not a *gamin*. We see it all in his *Apocalypse* [*Apokalipsis nashego vremeni*]. He is not really a Dostoievskian. That's only his Russianitis.

The book is an attack on Christianity, and as far as we are given to see there is no canting or recanting in it. It is passionate, and suddenly valid. It is not jibing or criticism or pulling to pieces. It is a real passion. Rozanov has more or less recovered the genuine pagan vision, the phallic vision, and with those eyes he looks, in amazement and consternation, on the mess of Christianity.

For the first time we get what we have got from no Russian, neither Tolstoi nor Dostoievsky nor any of them, a real, positive view on life. It is as if the pagan Russian had wakened up in Rozanov, a kind of Rip van Winkle, and was just staggering at what he saw. His background is the vast old pagan background, the phallic. And in front of this, the tortured complexity of Christian civilisation—what else can we call it?—is a kind of phantasmagoria to him.

He is the first Russian, as far as I am concerned, who has ever said anything to me. And his vision is full of passion, vivid, valid. He is the first to see that immortality is in the vividness of life, not in the loss of life. The butterfly becomes a whole revelation to him: and to us.

D. H. Lawrence. *Calendar of Modern Letters*.
July, 1927, pp. 166–67

If Rozanov is typically Russian in his class psychology and in many of his individual traits, there is no doubt either about the Russian quality of his artistic genius, about the Russian peculiarity of his literary temper. Notwithstanding all the usual and often valid comparisons to be made between him and such Western writers and thinkers as Rousseau, Pascal, and Nietzsche, Rozanov's cultural and artistic ancestors are all Russian. In his somber political obscurantism, his interest in popular religion, even his diction and style, he belongs to a national school of thinking and writing little known in the West, the most extreme representatives of which are perhaps two figures of the late nineteenth century, the philosopher Konstantin Leontiev and the storyteller Nikolay Leskov. In the chain of that tradition he forged a new link, which was to be further strengthened by a few writers of the younger generation, especially the novelist Aleksey Remizov, who considered Rozanov his master, and who defined him as "the most alive of our contemporaries."

In that stream of the Russian literary tradition which is better known in the West, Rozanov naturally belongs, as we have stated before, to the lineage of Gogol and Dostoevski. He possessed not only the deep psychological insight of the latter, but also the former's malicious and indiscreet psychological curiosity. He shared Gogol's idea of literature as a kind of exalted gossip, of the writer as a glorified Peeping Tom: "The postmaster, looking into other people's letters (Gogol's *Inspector*), was a man endowed with excellent literary taste." Yet Rozanov belongs also to the literary tradition of Goncharov and Tolstoy, of *Oblomov* and *War and Peace* (he frequently praises the latter), with their exaltation of patriarchal life, of biological patience, of vitalistic laziness. Among the great Russian masters, only Turgenev and Pushkin (despite Rozanov's frequent praise of the greatest of all Russian poets) are completely alien to him. He must have found both of them either too classical and serene, or too clean and chaste. Yet the only national tradition he fully and scornfully rejects is the tradition of the intelligentsia, with its concern for social service, with its political activism and ideological radicalism: in his enmity toward Belinski and his followers he is even more uncompromising than Dostoevski himself.

Renato Poggioli. *The Phoenix and the Spider*
(Cambridge, Mass., Harvard University Press, 1957),
pp. 179–80

It is a striking coincidence that both Lawrence and Rozanov finished their literary career and their lives in writing an Apocalypse, Rozanov the *Apocalypse of Our Time*, and Lawrence a new evaluation of the last book of the Bible. It could also be argued that with this delving into apocalyptic speculations the creative life circle of both men came to be rounded out. For the first work by which Rozanov had achieved literary fame was an interpretation of Dostoevskij's *Grand Inquisitor* with its many apocalyptic and eschatological overtones, while Lawrence-students, as for instance the German novelist and critic René Schickele, discovered in so early a work as *Sons and Lovers* a sometimes quite dense apocalyptic atmosphere, and the question was raised whether the state of mind of the young Lawrence right before and in the middle of a shattering catastrophe, the War of 1914, which for him meant the downfall of his whole traditional world and environment, does not remind the reader of the twilight of pre-Christian civilization. Also Rozanov's book on the *Legend of the Grand Inquisitor* [*Legenda o velikom Inkvizitore*] contains dark premonitions of the termination of an epoch, a relapse into barbarity, and the exhaustion of the creative substance in Western man. Both authors share a pessimistic outlook as to the manifest and hidden trends of occidental civilization. Modern culture and society appear, in the evaluation of both of them, as a sorry alloy of deadening, abstraction-ridden positivism and a bloodless, hypocritical, quasi-Christian a-cosmism. Both of them denied what the modern age calls "progress" and did not believe in an overall beneficial effect of perfected technological civilization.

Heinrich A. Stammler. *Die Welt der Slaven.*
4, 1959, p. 69

Rozanov has been compared, with varying degrees of accuracy, to Nietzsche, to James Joyce, to Marcel Proust, and to other writers. The Soviet critic Kornej Čukovskij, in comparing Rozanov with Whitman, is surely mistaken: the works of the urbane high-strung Russian lack the raw, natural scent of *Leaves of Grass.* More convincing is an analogy between Rozanov and the forgotten author of *Lavengro* and *The Bible in Spain,* George Borrow (1803–1881). Both are described by the Irish poet, James Stephens, as intimate writers who create the closest and deepest tie with the reader. Some critics have also called Rozanov the Russian Nietzsche, but this exaggerated view is not supported by the facts. The paradoxical immorality of the two differs essentially. Nietzsche glorified strong personalities; Rozanov sympathized with weaklings distinguished only by their rich and strange inner life. Comparisons of Joyce and Proust, on the one hand, and Rozanov, on the other, have more validity, as we shall see below. Nevertheless, it is far better to present Rozanov against a Russian background. . . .

Rozanov was, actually, a new version of Dostoevskij, whose religious and psychological insights he tried to apply to sex. Maksim Gor'kij was correct when he wrote to Rozanov: "Your father is Dostoevskij, a perverted and cruel writer whom I do not like . . ." And Berdjaev linked Rozanov to the hideous and witty Fëdor Karamazov, the father of Mitja, Ivan, and Aleša.

Georg Ivask. *SEEJ.* Summer, 1961, pp. 110–11

[Rozanov] is a writer who cannot be fitted into any one category. . . .

He is a protean figure, full of contradictions. Writing for the semi-official *New Times* he upheld the reactionary policies of the government, praising, for instance, the Holy Synod's excommunication of Tolstoy. But at the same time he contributed, under a pseudonym, to the radical periodical *The Russian Word.* Always emphasizing the importance of sex, of the patriarchal family life, he was yet told by a girl that, "the only masculine thing about you is your trousers." . . .

Rozanov belongs to that other tradition of Russian literature and thought, little known in the West, represented by writers such as Nikolai Leskov and Konstantin Leontyev. He despises the tradition of the intelligentsia, with its liberal ideas and civic themes. "I am not yet such a scoundrel," he writes, "as to think of morality." He is closest of all to Dostoevsky. He wrote about him, married Apollinaria Suslova, his former mistress, shared his prejudices—his anti-semitism, for example. He is the incarnation of Dostoevsky's underground man. Like him, he passionately affirms his belief in the basic illogicality of man; in the importance of the Self and of private life, even in its most trivial and vulgar aspects: "Just sitting at home, and even picking your nose, and looking at the sunset . . . I swear to you: this is more universal than religion." He sees man as an "ahistorical" animal, dominated by the two factors of permanence and inertia. Man cannot be changed by changing society: this is his and Dostoevsky's sobering message to all liberals.

TLS. June 1, 1962, p. 414

SERAFIMOVICH, ALEKSANDR (1863–1949)

The Iron Flood (Zhelezny potok) is metal torn up out of the earth. Well, you might think, what could be better? But just send a bit of that iron to the laboratory and you'll find that it's been gathering rust for a long long time in the cellars of Gorky's Znanie publishing house. And just as one would expect from the tried and true custom of the Znanie writers, for a solid page or two the workers sing: "Thou hast fallen in the brave and fateful struggle." And again according to the Znanie formula, this time inherited from Leonid Andreyev's *Red Laugh*, we find such locutions as: "the mad sun"; "the mother laughs with an inexplicably gay, ringing laughter"; "she wildly kisses her child"; . . . "madly the light trembles"; "above the sky-blue abyss." . . .

But there is something else there, too—something that wasn't in the Gorkyesque [Znanie writer] Serafimovich. When we read: "Toward the windmills there comes out of the throng with an inexplicably red face, with a black mustache just sprouting, in a sailor's cap. . . ." in such a sentence without a subject we sense an unbridled "modern," almost Pshibishevsky. When we find phrases like: "Again among those people who were straining toward salvation there arose an overwhelming astonishment," we must suppose here the beginnings of a kind of instrumentation, almost in the manner of Bely.

And another thing: in Znanie there never was the cheap gilt that one observes in Serafimovich's iron, which he mined "from the Depths." The figure of that "rotten compromiser" Mikheladze is fashioned according to all the rules for gilding. And the gilt is especially thick at the end of the story, with the apotheosis of the hero . . . and the "tears streaming down the windworn faces of the crowd . . . and the young girls' eyes shining with tears."

The ore that Serafimovich used for his *Iron Flood* is so rich that even worked up into operatic stuff it is not completely worthless—we do remember a few scenes. [1924]

Yevgeni Zamyatin. Quoted in Edward J. Brown,
Russian Literature Since the Revolution
(New York, Crowell-Collier, 1963), pp. 158–59

The title (*The Iron Stream*) refers to a dispossessed, dissatisfied horde of men, women and children, with their meager belongings, going, in the

Caucasus, under Kozhukh's iron leadership, to join the Russian communists. Through hostile Cossacks' villages, through well-equipped enemy lines, through inaccessible mountains, over the death-harboring eastern shore of the Black Sea, the "iron stream" makes its progress with tremendous sacrifices in human life and property, in the face of unspeakable fatigue, starvation and danger.

Here and there we find in the book useless insistence on obvious conclusions, repetition of detail, and perhaps too much prominence given to military glory. But there are also beautiful passages of poetic description, stirring scenes and interesting silhouettes of folk-types.

Kozhukh is hardly human; his iron will, his unwavering determination, his fearlessness, vigilance, presence of mind, energy, his quick judgment and endurance make him almost a prodigy of activity, perseverance and leadership.

The author has well seized the mob spirit and the narrow confines of the understanding of the mob-average.

Sophie R. A. Court. *BA*. Autumn, 1927, p. 79

The Iron Flood, unprecedented in the sweeping scope of its portrayal of the uprising masses, also contains one of the earliest portraits of a man who leads their struggle. With consummate skill Serafimovich portrays the relationship between the leader and the mass and shows that Kozhukh, the novel's hero, is wedded indissolubly to the people, that he is part and parcel of them. Kozhukh is typical of the historical period when, as Lenin writes, the workers and peasants bring forth from their midst "unknown heroes who are fused inseparably with the throng and who become ever more deeply imbued with the noble fanaticism of the people's liberation." His personal concerns are subordinated to the common cause, but in this there is no element of sacrifice, for the common cause is indeed his own supreme interest.

Very convincingly the book shows how Kozhukh by his influence over the masses, turns guerilla units into a disciplined army of conscious fighters for the Soviets.

A lofty sense of his personal responsibility, of his duty to the people, helps Kozhukh to develop the specific qualities required of one who marches in the front ranks of the embattled masses.

V. Ozerov. *SL*. Nov., 1949, pp. 161–62

It is quite evident that Serafimovich's legacy cannot be divided mechanically into two unequal parts—before *The Iron Stream* and after *The Iron Stream*—acknowledging him as a proletarian writer only in the latter period. It would be truer to suggest that had he not protested as a socially conscious writer against arbitrary tsarism and capitalist exploitation . . . had he not published stories over the years, particularly in the period between 1905 and 1917, and had there not been his novel *Gorod v stepi* (*City in the Steppe*), then we might have had either no *Iron Stream* at all or another, less clear and convincing version of it.

It is true that the writer's revolutionary universality was not acquired at one stroke. His lack of a direct connection with the developing revolutionary movement, headed by the Bolshevik party, limited the purposefulness of Serafimovich's idealism in his early work. But even then, wrote Volkov, "Serafimovich showed manifoldly how wearying labor in a capitalist society crippled the soul of the worker."

Labor in all its many forms remained Serafimovich's fundamental theme. In his early tales he sketched certain realities of labor in capitalist society—suffering and exploitation—laying bare class conflicts but still not showing the creative basis of labor and its significance as an organized force that holds within itself the inevitability of revolutionary explosion. "And more than that," testifies Volkov, "there is already in the early work of Gorki and Serafimovich that common element which inevitably brought their creative thought closer together. That common element was an undying love for man and an unshakable faith in his high mission and coming emancipation."

B. Volgin. *Oktyabr.* Dec., 1951, pp. 181–82†

Quite apart from its merits or defects as literature, *The Iron Flood* is a significant historical document. It is significant not so much for the events which form the core of its narrative as for the approach and method of the author. *The Iron Flood* has entered into the main arteries of Soviet literary life, and some of its "iron" is still to be found there. Its portrayal of the "mass" as the hero in history; its unconcern with individual personalities; its implacable optimism; its insistence on victory over terrible odds; its tendentiousness—all of these ingredients are to be found in the standard product of socialist realism. That standard product is, however, very inferior to the prototype, for Serafimovich does not shrink from the reality he has chosen to portray. The mixed mob of deserters, mutinous sailors, and Bolsheviks with their women, children, and household goods who marched north from the Taman peninsula, after escaping encirclement by the Whites, is shown as an unruly and bloodthirsty force. Atrocities committed against the enemy are not glossed over.

Edward J. Brown. *Russian Literature Since the Revolution* (New York, Crowell-Collier, 1963), pp. 157–58

SHKLOVSKI, VIKTOR (1893–   )

For the last fifteen years Victor Shklovsky has been one of the most controversial figures in Russian literature. After a striking début as a literary critic in 1914 he became the acknowledged leader of the "Formalists." But for the Revolution this group of critics might have met with a more friendly reception; as it was, by the time the general tumult had subsided sufficiently for them to be fully heard, literature had officially become subservient to politics, and, instead of being regarded as literary revolutionaries, they found themselves accused of political heresy. Shklovsky naturally bore the brunt of Marxian hostility, for as well as being the leader of the group he was obviously the liveliest spirit among them. . . .

Shklovsky's *A Sentimental Journey* [*Sentimentalnoe puteshestvie*] is, perhaps, the most objective record of the early years of the Russian Revolution that has yet been published. The February Revolution found the author acting as technical instructor to a reserve division of armoured cars. In the spring he was sent to bolster up the spirit of the troops on the Galician front. Later, having recovered from a severe wound, he went to Persia to help rid the country of a large Russian force, a legacy of Russian imperialism rendered obsolete by the Revolution. On his return to Petrograd he dabbled in conspiracy, attracted the attention of the Cheka, and was obliged from time to time to take to a new disguise and temporarily to lose himself in the general chaos. In the intervals of lecturing and writing in a famine-stricken and fireless Petrograd he became shoemaker, prisoner of war, vagrant, tumbling in and out of the civil war, lodging in towns which "had suffered sixteen Governments," observing and recording the fantastic tumult of the times. True to his bent, Shklovsky gives us an exact insight into the mechanism of war and revolution. The pathos of his narrative is, however, all the more moving for being purely incidental. Very few war books have achieved so nice a balance between the individual and the historical.

TLS. Nov. 19, 1931, p. 910

Victor Shklovsky's ideas are certainly stimulating, even when they are demonstrably wrong, whimsical, or fantastic. He is a specialist in paradoxes which, while they may shock or amuse, always point to the essence of a problem. When he says, for instance, that "art has always been free of life, and its colors never reflected the colors of the flag waving over the city," or that "new art forms are simply old and inferior genres elevated to the level of art," and that "Pushkin's lyrics come from album verses, Blok's from gypsy songs, Mayakovsky's from comic doggerel," or when he maintains that a literary work is simply the sum of its devices, Shklovsky raises in acute and original form important problems as to the genesis of art, or the succession of genres, or the nature of creative writing.

Shklovsky's propagation of the notion of *ostranenie*, or "estrangement," of reality as a basic function of all literary art, even the realistic variety, had a pronounced influence on the work of Olesha and of many younger fellow travelers. The artist should, according to Shklovsky, break down the habit of automatic reaction to the outside world and force the reader to see and hear it. His own literary style is subjective and impressionistic and, because of the personal and arbitrary movement of his thought, difficult to follow. Clarity is itself a kind of lazy man's vice, he seems to think, and the reader who would follow Shklovsky's turns must work at it all the time.

Edward J. Brown. Russian Literature Since the
Revolution (New York, Crowell-Collier, 1963),
pp. 97–98

Fedin . . . admitted the indispensable role of Šklovskij, whom he considered not just a teacher, but an integral member of the group: "And last but not least, there was Viktor Šklovskij, who spoke of himself as a Serapion and who was indeed the eleventh, or perhaps the first, of the Serapions, owing to the passion which he brought into our lives and the cogent questions which he injected into our debates."

People writing about those hectic years in the House of Arts remember Šklovskij for his feverish activity. Probably the best picture of life in this unlikely dormitory has been left by Ol'ga Forš. In her novel *Sumasšedšij korabl'*, she depicts Šklovskij in the transparent guise of Žukanec, a literary figure who whirled through the House of Arts like a dervish—lecturing, debating, arguing. Vsevolod Roždestvenskij remembers the violent debates between Šklovskij and the Symbolist critic Akim Volynskij. Zoščenko gives a verbal snapshot of Šklovskij totally absorbed in an argument with some adversary.

Šklovskij, with his brilliant, compelling insights, transmitted to the impressionable young students all the esthetic values which he had elaborated in Opojaz. Not only their statements of principle and their impudent autobiographies, but also their creative work showed marked traces of his influence.

This influence sometimes manifested itself in curious ways. Zoščenko achieved fame with his first book, *Rasskazy Nazara Il'iča, gospodina Sinebrjuxova*, a parody of Šklovskij's book *Ėpilog: Konec knigi "Revoljucija i front"* [*Epilogue: The End of the Book "Revolution and Front"*]. Kaverin was indebted to Šklovskij not only for introducing him to the group, but also for discouraging his efforts at poetry.

Richard Sheldon. SEEJ. Spring, 1968, pp. 4–5

Shklovsky at that time (1923) wrote his letter of repentance to the Central Committee of the Communist Party; he was being persecuted as a former S.-R., his wife was in prison as a hostage, he had fled the confines of Russia in February 1922 and now, in torment over his wife, requested his return. Compared to Khodasevich and Bely, Shklovsky was a man from another planet, but for me there always clearly burned in him talent, energy, humor. He felt that his life in Germany was senseless; he could not foresee his future, that he would be "frozen" in the Soviet Union for thirty years (and unfrozen at the end of the fifties). He outlived all his friends, is alive now, but there is but little humor left in him, judging by his writings of the latest period. He never could think systematically and coherently, an academic career was not for him as it turned out to be for his contemporaries—Tynianov, Tomashevsky, Eichenbaum and others. His was the fate of a wasted man, one of the most tragic. In the West, among Slavists, he is known and prized more highly than he is known or prized in Russia.

Shklovsky was a round-headed, smallish, witty man. There was a smile on his face continually, and in this smile one could see the little black roots of his front teeth and clever sparkling eyes. He could be brilliant, he was full of humor and mockery, clever and sometimes impudent, especially when he sensed the presence of an "important person," a "haughty eminence," or people who irritated him by their pedantry, self-assurance, and stupidity. He was a talented inventor, full of ideas, discoveries, and formulations. Life seethed in him, and he loved it. His *Letters Not About Love* [*Pisma ne o lyubvi*] and other books written about himself in these years were a tour de force and a joke; he amused others and amused himself. He never spoke of the future, his own or others', and probably suppressed within himself all premonitions, confident (in any event outwardly) that all would "turn out all right." He would not otherwise have returned, because in the West he was one of the few who could have realized himself fully—Roman Jakobson, a man close to him, of course would have helped him. But the matter of his wife gave him no peace.

Nina Berberova. *The Italics Are Mine* (New York,
Harcourt, Brace & World, 1969), pp. 197–98

One standard by which its [*Zoo*] originality may be measured is provided by Shklovsky in his subtitle: *The Third Héloïse* [*Tretya Eloiza*]. In addition to making a pun on Elsa's name, this title establishes a parallel between Shklovsky's *Zoo* and Jean-Jacques Rousseau's voluminous epistolary novel, *La Nouvelle Héloïse*. Both titles refer obliquely to the famous medieval Héloïse, the ill-fated beloved of Abelard. Their tragic story is preserved in a series of poignant letters.

This intriguing conjunction of three epistolary Héloïses is left hovering by Shklovsky, who never alludes to any of his models in the body of the novel. The similarities suggested by the parallel are quite superficial: all three romances are couched in the epistolary form, and all three end badly, though probably worst of all for Abelard. The contrasts suggested are quite ironic, since both Rousseau and Shklovsky offer diminished versions of the original lovers: the noble, idealistic Héloïse contrasts sharply with Rousseau's sentimental Julie and Shklovsky's self-indulgent Elsa; the heroes, though quite disparate (one would not accuse Shklovsky of being deeply religious), are united by their egocentricity. There are also notable differences between the passionate, stricken love letters of Héloïse to Abelard and the indifferent, but tantalizing, letters of Elsa to Shklovsky. It is an interesting coincidence that Laurence Sterne, whose novels so deeply influenced Shklovsky, also wrote a sort of epistolary novel, highly autobiographical, about his overwhelming love for a woman—a book faithful to Shklovsky's pun in its title, *Journal to Eliza*.

Richard Sheldon. RR. July, 1970, p. 271

SHOLOKHOV, MIKHAIL (1905–   )

Donskie rasskazy (*The Tales of the Don*) will by no means take the last place in literature about the civil war.

As Aleksandr Serafimovich says in the short foreword to this book, "There is a feeling for measure in the decisive moments, and for that reason they are convincing. The author shows great knowledge of the subject matter. He has discriminating, grasping eye, ability to select from among many symptoms the most characteristic ones. . . ."

The stories tell about the collision between the White and the Red cossacks. There is no retouching here: that is the most essential thing. Here, the Reds are truly red, and the Whites are white, and while changing the side the story does not bog down, as is often the case with pot-boiler writers. These stories are also remarkable because, even though they are all about the quiet Don, they do not repeat themselves but, on the contrary, demonstrate their own individuality. . . .

In some stories, it is true, there are shortcomings, manifested mainly in tendentiousness. Such is the case with "Pastukh" ("The Shepherd"), in which the focal position is occupied by a tinsel-gold shepherd, a member of the Communist Youth League, and in which even the last name of one of the communists—Politov—is fully pseudo-classical. Such is also the case in "Kolovert" ("The Whirlpool"), where the White cossack captain is portrayed as an excessively hackneyed villain. Even the pattern of the story reveals some artificiality. The story "Alyoshkino serdtse" ("Alyoshka's Heart") is full of sentimentality, and it is also weak in atmosphere. The end of "Rodinka" ("The Birthmark") turns out to be unexpectedly sentimental because the plot did not lead to such development. . . .

However, all these shortcomings do not mar the general impression of the stories, and it would be too rash to count them as weaknesses of the author. Serafimovich writes, not without reason: "Everything indicates that Sholokhov will develop into a good writer; but he should learn, work on every piece of writing, and take his time."

Viktor Yakerin. Novy mir. May, 1926, p. 187†

[In *Podnyataya tselina* (*Virgin Soil Upturned*), Sholokhov] attacks the all-important subject of the collectivization of the village. On the whole, in the plots, in some of the characters, and in the general atmosphere, this novel, because of the subject matter, is necessarily reminiscent of Panferov's *Brusski,* Zamoyski's *Lapti,* and other novels of this kind. But Sholokhov's book is much less obtrusive propaganda and much more artistic than these other words. This is due partly to the author's unmistakable genius, partly to the fact that the work of collectivization is farther advanced now, and the writer can see it better at this stage than could his predecessors, and partly, no doubt, to the development of self-criticism in Soviet Russia in general. Be this as it may, it is both instructive and esthetically inspiring to read this grandiose portrayal of Soviet village life, the clash of social forces, the truthful delineation of characters, in whom the good and the bad mix as they do in life, whether they are communists, kulaks, or occupy any other position in the struggle. This is only the first volume of the novel, but may be read independently.

Sophie R. A. Court. BA. Autumn, 1933, pp. 431–32

[*Tikhi Don* (*And Quiet Flows the Don*)]* is a work of great vitality, grim and eloquent, sternly realistic, and at the same time steeped in the poetry of Cossack tradition. There are echoes in it of the *byliny* and an inward likeness to Gogol's *Taras Bulba*, whose heroic ardours it recaptures with passion. What in Gogol, however, is of legendary and epic quality savours of barbarism and worse in the modern circumstances of Sholokhov's novel. The praise of the heroic virtues still rings true, but it is of little consequence beside the horrors of war and savagery, the lusts and cruelties, the hardships and violences that Sholokhov describes with relentless integrity. There are not a few passages in the novel for which the reader requires a stout heart and a strong stomach. . . .

* The Russian title is simply *The Quiet Don*. The English translation is in two volumes: *And Quiet Flows the Don* and *The Don Flows Home to the Sea*. —Ed.

The novel is too formless to achieve consistency of effect. These are passages which drag, despite the fire of the author's attack. But the work as a whole is a richly imaginative and eloquent commentary on history. The translator's task has been unusually difficult, requiring an intimate knowledge of Ukrainian terms of speech, and has been carried with fair success.

TLS. April 5, 1934, p. 241

Mr. Sholokhov's novel [*And Quiet Flows the Don*] has no unity of time or place; we follow the Don Cossacks from their village to the front, from the front to Petrograd, and the small recurring sections of natural description (the Don in spring, summer, autumn, winter) is too mechanical a device really to impose on the story a sense of unity. It is a weakness that the incidents we could least happily dispense with . . . touch only in their beginning and their end the fortunes of the Cossack villagers who are Mr. Sholokhov's main theme. There is no obvious reason why this novel should begin or end where it does. There is no lack of economy in the treatment of each incident, but the incidents themselves are too numerous.

Graham Greene. *Spec*. April 6, 1934, p. 551

When the book [*And Quiet Flows the Don*] is not strained it is vivid beyond most books, and when it is not sensational according to the vogue it manages to say a great deal about the Cossacks which must not have been said before and which, since it is said brilliantly, will therefore become part of the permanent record. As a revolutionary novel *Tikhi Don* seems to me a failure; as a novel it seems to me as good as it can be in view of the fact that it was not written by a wiser man for a sounder generation.

Mark Van Doren. *Nation*. July 11, 1934, p. 50

Of the Russian authors I have read, Sholokhov is almost the only one with a highly developed sense of locality. . . .

But besides his sense of locality, he also has a sense of people that is somewhat commoner in Russian fiction, though rare enough in the literature of any country. He writes about them as if he had always known and loved them and wanted the outside world to understand just why they acted as they did. They are of course his own people, the community or nation of the Don Cossacks, and another writer might have a hard time making them seem plausible. They are peasants tied to the soil, and yet until the end of the civil wars they were soldiers wandering over the face of the earth. They are miserly with their wheat but prodigal with their money and their lives; they are heavy drinkers, brawlers, wife beaters and, on occasion, looters and killers, yet they are full of simple kindliness;

they are honest citizens descended from outlaws and ready in any period of disorder to resume the life of their ancestors. Another writer might have insisted on combing the lice from their hair and wiping the blood from their hands before admitting them to his hygienic fiction. Sholokhov pictures them just as they are, without even washing their faces, but without making us feel that he is collecting specimens for an ethnological museum. They are simply people to him; he lives in a Cossack village and these are his neighbors. . . .

Apparently *The Silent Don* is the greatest of all the novels that have been written about the Russian revolution; and I say "apparently" for the one reason that it is hard to tell just how good the book may be in the original. Stephen Garry's translation is by no means the worst that I have read during the past few years; at least he has a feeling for English prose. But to judge from sections of the novel that appeared in *International Literature*, it is far from being complete; and it is full of meaningless expressions and misunderstandings of the Russian text. Not for a single page does it let you forget that it is being translated from a very foreign language.

Malcolm Cowley. NR. Aug. 18, 1941, pp. 225–26

Almost all criticism of *The Quiet Don* notes that one of the distinctive characteristics of the novel is a deep feeling for nature, or, more specifically, a mastery of landscape. Diverse pictures of nature, realistically drawn and majestically beautiful, alternate in the novel in a measured rhythm, defined by the changing seasons of the year and flowing together into one fluid and shimmering panorama of life.

In his novel, Sholokhov confronts man and nature, history—difficult, conflicting, and often bloody—and the land—fertile and indifferent to the grief or joy experienced by those living on it.

Sholokhov loved, felt, and reproduced nature magnificently. He treated it first of all as an artist. Except in a few instances where Sholokhov moralizes, there is nothing abstract in his pictures. The people created by Sholokhov and the natural life reproduced by him are unusually concrete. The heroes of his novel are the Don cossacks; the nature in it is the nature of the Don.

The aesthetic and emotional richness of the natural world of the Don is uncovered by Sholokhov for the first time. It is shown with the force and persuasiveness of a great and distinctive artistic individuality. The painting in Sholokhov is not "tacked onto" the action of the novel. It is not a picturesque digression. In *The Quiet Don* a coherent, artistic environment is created, enveloping both man and nature. Sholokhov conveys the close relationship that has grown over the centuries between the cossack and the natural world of the Don. Looking at the reality he depicts,

Sholokhov is neither condescending nor biased. He does not approach this reality from the outside as either judge or writer, nor does he bring back his material from a "creative assignment." He was submerged in it, recounting it from within and understanding its most concealed movements.

V. Kirpotin. *Oktyabr.* Dec., 1946, pp. 174–75[†]

Sholokhov's novels answer one of the basic requirements of the real epic, that the personal destiny of each character, each participant in the course of events, be interwoven with the destiny of the people and hinge directly on it. The fate of Sholokhov's heroes coincides and forms a single whole with the historical subject.

The role of labour is preeminent in Sholokhov's books, as in the life of the people.

In *And Quiet Flows the Don,* we nearly always see the Cossacks at their tasks. All kinds of farm work are described—ploughing, haymaking, fishing, tending livestock, felling timber.

Together with his songs and thoughts, his labour is the Cossack's boon companion all his life. How the Cossacks love their soil, how they pine for their villages, ploughs and ox teams when they are away at war!

Labour as Sholokhov describes it, is full of that moral inspiration, poetry, struggle, that are possible only in the creation of a new world. It is the key to the character of the man who is building that world, his intelligence, his passions, his temperament, his inmost self.

The creative task Sholokhov set himself in *Virgin Soil Upturned* was a very novel and difficult one. The usual love story of the old novel, with its intrigues and surprises, is missing here. In fact, there are practically no women in the novel, except for the minor characters Lushka Nagulnova and Marina Poyarkova. Neither has it the highly dramatic historical sweep of *And Quiet Flows the Don.* The *Virgin Soil Upturned* reproduces not a whole decade bursting with events and battles, but a few months of 1930. But that was the period of collectivization—words that speak volumes. The content, theme, interest of this novel lie in the rise of a new, Communist attitude towards labour. How much action, how many thrilling events take place in little Gremyachensky village!

I. Lezhnev. *SL.* Aug., 1948, p. 122

In the story "Sudba cheloveka" ("The Fate of a Man"), the epic quality of the action and of the hero are linked with the dramatic quality of situations and with the sincere lyrical tone of the narration. It is not by accident that this emotionally involved tone—if one can express it this way in the given case—is heard both at the end and the beginning of the story and composes, in a way, a lyrical framing of "The Fate of a Man." Even here we become acquainted with the unique lyrical side of the epic gift of the writer. This aspect is familiar to us from the battle scenes and landscapes of *The Quiet Don* and the colorful background of *Virgin Soil Upturned*. These tendencies in the story are characteristic of the development of our postwar prose and are summed up in great narrative manner in Fadeyev's *The Young Guard*.

Sholokhov loves Andrei Sokolov with a great love as only a mother can feel for her child. "More than anything else the writer himself has to transmit the growth of the human spirit," said Sholokhov. "I wanted to tell about this fascination with the man in the person of Gregor Melekhov, but I could not do this to the end. Maybe it will be possible to do this in a novel about those who fought for the fatherland."

Fascination with the man whose soul and mind are emancipated by the revolution and are now dedicated to the great task of building communism—all of Sholokhov's creativity is permeated by this idea. In this lies his pathos. His world-known works, such as *The Quiet Don* and *Virgin Soil Upturned*, speak of the spiritual growth of our people not as a single-faceted movement but as a complex and detailed one. "The Fate of a Man" is also dedicated to this theme.

N. Maslin. *Moskva*. May, 1959, p. 203[†]

There can be no doubt that Sholokhov's gift is genuine and exceptional, neither can his sincerity be called in question. He is perhaps the most wholeheartedly Communist of all Communist writers, and certainly the most popular and honored in the Soviet Union, recipient of the highest awards his country can bestow on artists, deputy to the Supreme Soviet, member of the Academy of Sciences. On the occasion of his fiftieth birthday, the *Literaturnaya Gazetta* announced that in the U.S.S.R. his novels had been published in four hundred and twenty-one editions, totaling twenty million seven hundred and seventy-three thousand copies, and at the Twentieth Party Congress he delivered a major address which, according to reports, was received with rapturous applause. Himself a Don Cossack, he has always been identified with his people; he writes in their language, from their point of view, and he has made them known to the rest of Russia. Nothing of the kind had been done before. Gogol had romanticized the Cossacks in *Taras Bulba*, Tolstoy had written of them from the standpoint of a sophisticated Moscow citizen; in Gorky's work, as in Eisenstein's film *Potemkin*, they appear as the Czar's most reliable tools of oppression. With Sholokhov, they are no longer primitive, fairy-tale heroes nor models of mechanized brutality, but real men and women. Yet Sholokhov's importance lies not so much in his regionalism as in his communism. He has sung the legend of an age. And although his theme of War and Revolution is common among Soviet writers, there is no other work like *The Quiet Don*. Sholokhov's voice is unique. It is a voice that seems to sing unwaveringly of a loved country and a cherished faith; it has the ring of certitude. Nevertheless, in *The Quiet Don* one is disturbed by something like a quaver in this voice, a deep-seated discrepancy between conviction and emotion, which is nowhere openly expressed and of which the author himself is doubtless unaware.

Helen Muchnic. *From Gorky to Pasternak*
(New York, Random House, 1961), pp. 324–25

[Sholokhov] made sweeping statements about the West such as, "All Western literature is effeminate." And it was useless to argue or to invoke writers like Hemingway or the younger generation of American novelists, because he wasn't that interested. But about Russia and Russians he was perceptive and lyrical. It was no affectation; he loved them with an open and irrepressible love. I have seldom encountered a more earthy yet haunting feeling for Russia. Sholokhov's world as a writer and as a man is not intellectual; neither is it spiritual, although it is poetic. No one in Russia in his generation has caught so well the nostalgia of fleeting time. Sholokhov's realm is that of the sentiments and, even more, that of the elusive sensuous perception. The finite nature of the moment as he describes it causes a certain melancholy to pervade his writings. His conversation was full of concrete touches, tangy and yet tender. Through Remizov, I had heard spoken Russian raised to the level of an art. Remizov had a special sense for words and for syntax. But then, he was a medievalist, a man of immense culture and his conversation was often elliptic and even archaic. Sholokhov's was as effective in an entirely different way: free-flowing and yet exact and sharp. Its expressiveness captivated me and I regret my inability to convey it.

Olga Andreyev Carlisle. *Voices in the Snow*
(New York, Random House, 1962), pp. 46–47

The dramatic climaxes of [Sholokhov's] tales derive from the clash of social passions: rich peasants and old influential Cossacks hate the Bolsheviks who threaten to dispossess them of land and authority, while the Communists are equally bloodthirsty toward their "class enemies." On whatever side of the barricade they find themselves, all of Sholokhov's personages move in a nightmare of death and ferocity.

The defects of all these descriptions of blood and cruelty are quite obvious: the stories are constructed of black and white, with generous splashes of red. Some of them are sentimental or unabashedly melodramatic, as for example, the story of an 8-year-old who dies with the name of Lenin on his lips. But it is amazing that at the age of 20 Sholokhov was already such a strong writer, particularly if one considers his lack of literary apprenticeship. His formal education ended when he was 13 and then he had to earn his living and change from one occupation to another—mason, docker, farm hand, clerk and soldier—before becoming a novelist.

Tales of the Don contains all the elements that later made Sholokhov a master of representational narrative; tense dramatic plots, fresh landscape, catching humor and a racy, uninhibited popular idiom. It is true that they are lacking in depth and character portrayal, but these primitive stories about primitive men are interesting as a document of an unsettled time, and they offer revealing material about the origins of an important Soviet writer.

Marc Slonim. NYT. March 4, 1962, p. 4

What has the Red Armyman Makar Nagulnov [in *Virgin Soil Upturned*] found to love in this erring, profligate woman who has maimed his life? He does not love a "bitch," it is not the worst features of her character which endear Lushka to him. What he treasures is what did not become the main part of her character and in the end faded and perished, yet was nevertheless unusually vivid: her captivating beauty, the daring, life-loving force of her character, her striving for independence and freedom, the pride of this Cossack Carmen. "She's got a heart of oak, that cursed woman has!" he says of her with an "ill-concealed note of pride."

These are the feelings dear to Sholokhov, the feelings he strives for. But he knows that it is the daily aims of the Party which lead the masses to the general affirmation of the loftiest humanity. Even from this excerpt it is clear that Sholokhov cannot conceive of life outside these ideals, nor can his main character. However much Makar loves Lushka, he understands very well that: "Why, to keep a woman like that, you'd have to smear your hands with resin, get a good hold on her skirt, shut your eyes tight and forget everything else in the world. . . . Were we to chuck up the revolution and all our everyday Soviet work just for her sake? And club up to buy an accordion? We'd be done for!" The ideal of the future, which the writer has partly revealed to us, is still far from being fully realized. And, while rejecting the extreme of Nagulnov's asceticism, one has at times to make sacrifices for this ideal. The Communist writer and artist shows us the beauty of our aim and enables us to sense also the beauty of the path towards it, the beauty of everyday political interests. These interests deserve to be glorified.

Artyom Dubrovin. SL. Sept., 1963, p. 139

Some writers, let it be said, never succumbed to the utopian outlook. It is this, in my opinion, which accounts for Sholokhov's seeming out of place in the role assigned to him of honorary socialist realist. His basic attitude is that of refusing to be taken in by palliatives, which, in *The Quiet Don*, include a utopian faith. Sholokhov at his best opposes the rosy view—utopian or sentimental. I believe a key to understanding Sholokhov is his recalcitrance in this respect. His fundamental insistence, the bedrock of *The Quiet Don*, is that there are conflicts which one cannot possibly remove, by rephrasing, compromise, or any other way. . . . Sholokhov is similarly tough-minded in the political sphere. He believes the Reds and the Whites are irreconcilable. Gregory Melekhov can never find a cause to which to give allegiance. Atrocities will happen; such is life.

Sholokhov is not oriented toward any utopian future. He is a recalcitrant skeptic who revealed the same temper in his conversations with foreign reporters, sardonically spurning Pasternak or the doctrine of socialist realism. *The Quiet Don* has not changed, but the world around Sholokhov has, and so he looks different to us now. Utopianism has diminished in Soviet writing, and we now look at Sholokhov and see that one of his striking characteristics always was that he was immune to the well-meaning, rosy dreaminess which others lately have also been forsaking.

George Gibian. SIR. Sept., 1964, p. 426

[Sholokhov's] novel *They Fought for the Fatherland* [*Oni srazhalis za rodinu*] in no way enhanced the reputation of this undoubtedly gifted writer. Despite its protracted gestation period, it made a very poor impression. There is no justification, for example, for the opening which deals with an agronomist whose family life is unhappy. The author then jumps from the spring of 1941 to August 1942 and shows the agronomist as an ordinary soldier in a defeated regiment. The theme of the book as a whole is the story of the remnants of this regiment whose numbers are reduced during a fighting retreat in the Don steppes from 170 to 27 men. Battle episodes are described in order to illustrate the valor of Soviet officers and enlisted men, their devotion to their country, etc. A novel can, of course, be built out of such material, but the trouble is that the battle episodes are only incidental. Far more space is devoted to humorous little scenes and inconsequential stories. There are jokes, anecdotes, humorous situations and deliberate caricatures, but there is hardly a page on which the author does not lower the artistry of work by overloading it with clumsy and crude witticisms. . . .

Throughout the book deliberate emphasis is laid on the boorish, leg-pulling relations between one man and another, despite the fact that this little group of men is closely bound by front-line experience, a feeling of solidarity and, may be, sacrifice. Of course it is not difficult to guess that it was the author's intention that the outward boorishness should serve as evidence of an underlying warmth, but he has lost his sense of proportion.

A. Gaev. In *Soviet Literature in the Sixties,*
Max Hayward and Edward L. Crowley, eds.
(New York, Frederick A. Praeger, 1964), pp. 32–33

Šoloxov's objectivity and detachment, qualities for which he has been both praised and blamed by critics, depending whether they were preoccupied with the inclusion or exclusion of ideology in fiction, were probably not conscious devices at first. Rather, they resulted from the straightforward rendering of his own experience during the Revolution. He reproduces what he saw at an age when no comprehensive judgment was possible. His senses were at once innocent and preternaturally acute, hence the accuracy of detail. When his stories fail, the fault will generally be found in some deficiency of language or in an unhappy tendency to adopt formal contrivances such as the accumulation of gruesome trivia. For example, in "The Brat" ["Nakhalyonok"] a boy looks at his father's sabre-slashed face and notes that on "one bulging eye, floating and swaying in blood, was a large green fly."

Insufficiently discriminating in his search for significant detail, Šoloxov will multiply particulars and use four words where one would do better. Anyone who has examined an author's revisions of his early texts (and Šoloxov is no exception) sees at once the marks of an impatient pencil scoring out superfluous verbiage. Pretentious imagery goes next and elegant elaborations close behind, as if directness and simplicity were the final arbiters in every case.

Šoloxov's stories everywhere bear signs of experiment. He was seeking not only an idiom but a perspective from which to render the life he knew.

David H. Stewart. *SEEJ.* Winter, 1965, p. 377

In spite of the genuine emotion of ["The Fate of a Man"] as a whole, it is not hard for the reader to sense a writer in difficulty of a sort that has weakened Sholokhov's prose in the past two decades. There are obviously false touches. The adopting father is no novice at child-raising— yet he instructs the boy to play by floodwaters, without supervision, but not to get his feet wet. With but one exception, all the Russian prisoners of the Nazis act and talk with excessive, unnatural heroism. When the escaping protagonist, in a German uniform, unexpectedly crosses back into Russian lines, he is immediately accepted, without any suspicion, by the Russian front-line soldiers and officers. There is something preventing Sholokhov from capturing the whole, unvarnished experience.

The same holds true for his political statements. The reader is obliged to the original Soviet editor who eliminated Sholokhov's most slavish and fatuous speeches, but even the ones included in this volume embarrass the writer's admirers: the texts are full of half-baked arguments and wobbly exhortations. Nevertheless there is published evidence that he tried to stand up against Stalin himself in the worst days of forced collectivization. And, as his most severe Soviet detractors admit, his works do not lack sympathy for individuals trapped on the losing side.

Irwin Weil. *SR*. June 17, 1967, p. 33

Approximately 10 million peasants were victims of calculated starvation during the years of forced collectivization. It is unknown how many perished in concentration camps. But the main goal, the consolidation of Party rule, was achieved.

It was this process of liquidating a Russian village that Mikhail Sholokhov powerfully and truthfully described in *Seeds of Tomorrow* [*Podnyataya tselina*, II].* No other Soviet novel contains an account as candid as Sholokhov's. Paradoxical as it may seem, the explanation lies in the fact that Sholokhov had been dedicated to the Party heart and soul all his life and was a true believer in Communism, just like the people who crucified Russia, and he could therefore allow himself to depict reality much more truthfully than those who did not share his belief. He described reality honestly because he believed that in spite of all sacrifices the imposed collectivization would benefit Russia in the long run. And we ought to be grateful to him for his candor. For any reader who does *not believe* in Communism, this novel will always provide a key to understanding the evil which dictatorships, be they Communist or Fascist, bring to the world—a total, final evil: death of the soul and then of the body.

Mihajlo Mihajlov. *Russian Themes* (New York, Farrar, Straus and Giroux, 1968), pp. 194–95

SIMONOV, KONSTANTIN (1915–   )

Days and Nights [*Dni i nochi*] will almost certainly be the first work of a Soviet writer to be sold in greater numbers in America than in Russia. . . . This does not mean that *Days and Nights* is a better or more readable book for Americans than it was for Russians. The contrary, in fact, is true. The novel had a far greater influence in the U.S.S.R. than it could possibly have in this country. But it is the best Soviet book so far published here

* This is the second volume of the English translation of *Virgin Soil Upturned*. —Ed.

about what the Russians call "The Great Patriotic War." It is the best, that is, from the point of view of the capacity of a Soviet work to communicate images and moods to Americans. . . . As it stands now—with all hands, heroic and not so heroic, accounted for—*Days and Nights* is assuredly the truest book we have yet had on the Russian war. I think there will eventually be greater and even truer books on the subject, and it is altogether possible that Konstantine Simonov will write them.

John Hersey. *NY*. Nov. 3, 1945, p. 90

Dedicated to the memory of those who died for Stalingrad, Mr. Simonov's novel [*Dni i nochi*] pictures the course of events on a small sector of the front there during the long and all but inconceivably bitter phase of the fighting from the beginning of the actual siege in September, 1942, onwards. The eye-witness quality of many of his descriptions is often arresting, as was only to be expected; as a war correspondent Mr. Simonov has combined graphic documentation with an unfailing heroic emphasis in a more than ordinarily efficient way. There are, in fact, numerous passages in the book which leave a strong impression of truthfulness and hold the imagination by a certain sobriety of dramatic power.

Yet the effect as a whole is less satisfactory than in the best of the author's short pieces of war journalism. As a novel *Days and Nights* is too loosely composed, perhaps too hastily written, to reveal with imaginative justice, even in miniature, the full dimension of the human intensity of the event. It lacks concentration; a great deal of the documentary detail seems discursive and aimless or else seems to be flung together in support of a predetermined thesis. Thus, although there are moments of vivid power in the novel, its cumulative force is dissipated in stretches of featureless observation.

TLS. Nov. 10, 1945, p. 533

Simonov's heroes are men of will power and energy, men with a sense of duty, who give themselves up to the cause heart and soul. Nature and objects are described concretely and tersely in his poetry. He never stops to indulge in the beauty of the landscape, to draw the reader's attention to a rare harmony of colours, to the unexpected appearance of any given object. Simonov is too dynamic for this. He is less interested in nature than in an episode in the life of his contemporaries or his country. His poetry is always full of meaning, movement and action, and frequently bears the accent of the publicist. . . .

What are the objects of Simonov's love lyrics? He does not sing in them the romantically exalted image of his beloved, but the very earthly sensual love of a man, and the desire for the beloved born of this feeling.

Simonov's post-war lyrics were written during his travels abroad.

Wherever his hero wanders he carries with him in his heart the love of the homeland, in foreign lands he yearns for Russia, for Soviet habits and customs. His lyrics are distinguished by a directness of expression. He does not resort to the language of images, but speaks concretely expressing his feelings and thoughts in a way reflecting his own manliness and energy, the sound clarity of his reasoning.

Elena Mikhailovna. *SL*. Aug., 1946, pp. 47, 49

Like his earlier work, Simonov's war poetry is very uneven: now, as in a poem written during the battles on the Voronezh front, at the height of the Russian retreat in 1942, he succeeds in investing his emotions, bordering on despair, with powerful poetic accents; now, as in "Ubey ego!" ("Kill Him!"), a poem inspired by savage hatred for the enemy, he remains cold and prosaic. Too often his poetry is marred by a tendency towards journalism. His best poems are those where the patriotic and the personal notes are mingled. The volume *S toboy i bez tebya* (*With and Without You*, 1944) is composed mostly of purely personal love poetry. Some of these poems, for which Simonov—of all people!—was criticized as an "individualist," are very good, but in the final analysis Simonov seems to lack that indefinable something, that magic which turns merely good poetry into great poetry.

Gleb Struve. *Soviet Russian Literature 1917–1950*
(Norman, Okla., University of Oklahoma Press,
1951), p. 308

[In *Zhivye i myortvye* (*The Living and the Dead*)] as a staunch Communist, and no doubt wishing to avoid the difficulties Fadeev had with his *Young Guard* (which had to be reworked to give party members a greater role), Simonov does not miss an opportunity to assign the most glorious feats of courage and self-sacrifice to card-carrying Red Army men. Indeed, some of them, especially the main hero, "politruk" Sintsov, tend to assume almost superhuman stature. This deprives the work of some of the human element which was characteristic of the author's earlier *Days and Nights*. Nevertheless, the bitterness of the retreat, the tragedy of unequal battle, the suffering and the endurance of the Russian people make this rather artless and at times slow-moving narrative absorbing and even exciting reading.

Emanuel Salgaller. *BA*. Winter, 1962, p. 96

SOLOGUB, FYODOR (1863–1927)

Tvorimaya legenda [*The Created Legend*] is quite unusual. In many respects it is incomprehensible and even morbid. But one thing cannot be denied the author: with good talent and the beauty of rhythmical prose, he somehow strangely unites ornateness with simplicity. *The Created Legend,* not striving to be convincing or realistic, is like an entertaining play of fantasy and reality, in which the world appears as magic. It is shown in various lights because the sun—that Sologubian snake or dragon, which is sometimes flaming and sometimes quiet—looks at it in different ways. In the novel, Sologub's thought is occupied with ideas such as the "fated contradictions" of life, the "inescapable sinning in any world-thought," and the "mystical irony." There, as in the author's re-markable drama *Pobeda smerti* [Victory over Death], where it is more deeply presented, life performs (using the author's own image) in the person of Dulcinea and in the appearance of coarse Aldonsa, whom the author idealized. A highly lyrical spirit of Don Quixote is depicted in Dulcinea. Sologub begins his work with these words: "I take a piece of miserable and coarse life and create a sweet legend from it, for I am a poet. Whether you stagnate in the darkness—gloomy and mundane life —or whether you storm with furious fire, I, the poet, raise above you my created legend about the enchanted and beautiful." Whether the archi-tect has constructed his sweet legend from the substance of life, whether he has accomplished his eternal plan, I repeat, will be possible to judge only when his strange theory is fully revealed in his last lines.

Yuli Aikhenvald. Russkaya mysl. Jan., 1908, p. 190†

No, you can not separate Sologub from the Russian reality. He is one with it in body and soul. Realism in our literature begins with Chekhov and terminates with Sologub. It was Gogol who, out of the depths of sym-bolism, delineated the formula of realism; he is the alpha of it. From the depths of realism Sologub delineated the formula of his own fantasy . . . he is the omega of realism. Chekhov, remaining a realist, turned out to be the inner but secret enemy of realism. . . .

Sologub's style, too, has various characteristics of the Gogolian style: it is distinct, simple, and at the same time complex. But the lyric pathos of Gogol, which produced such lucid pages, becomes transformed in Sologub into the pathos of stern greatness and severity. By no means does Sologub, in his style, always find his own self. In all his novels we can find impure spots as a result of a careless attitude toward literature. Not always are these spots covered with a wordy blanket; there is much dry, trodden stubble and many a wormwood bristling in the snowstorm. Yet, we still carry away to the granary of our literature a very rich crop from other parts of his works. His phrases are often like wheat full of grain. There are no empty words; every word is a heavy grain of his ornate style, mag-nificent in its weight, simple in its structural uniformity. [1908]

Andrei Bely. Lug zelyony
(Moscow, Altsion, 1910), pp. 153–55†

The simplicity of Sologub, like that of Pushkin, has nothing in common with carelessness. Sologub does not wish to admit anything chance or arbitrary into his poetry. All of his words and expressions are well thought out and carefully chosen. Such simplicity appears to be highly refined, because it is a hidden refinement, available only to the sharp and attentive reader.

Although Sologub seldom speaks in the first person, he is still a highly subjective poet. In drawing pictures of nature, telling us his strange ballads, and in repeating ancient myths, he often has but one aim—to expose us to his own viewpoints and metaphysics.

All of the expressions, epithets, and images that he uses are not so much an objective depiction of appearances, happenings, and feelings as they are a subjective interpretation. One must constantly keep in mind the peculiarities of Sologub as an individualist and thinker in order to fully understand his verse. On the whole, Sologub's poetry is a potent hymn in glory of death, of the redeemer from life's burden, and of death's two deputies, illusions and dreams.

Valeri Bryusov. Russkaya mysl.
March, 1910, pp. 53–54[†]

In many respects, Sologub appears to be the most interesting antithesis of Balmont. Several qualities lacking in Balmont are found in abundance in Sologub: love and respect for an interlocutor, and a recognition of his own poetical correctness. These two excellent poetic qualities of Sologub are tightly bound with "the distance of great growth," which he presumes to be between himself and his ideal interlocutor-friend.

Osip Mandelshtam. Apollon. Feb., 1913, pp. 55–56[†]

In the best of Sologub's poetry, there are no "lies." Indeed, it is quite the opposite, for his verses are some of the most truthful in Russian poetry. They are completely truthful, in an artistic and humanitarian sense. The poet's child-like soul is shown in its contents, which are foreign to everything external and showy, and in its chaste clarity.

Recently, Sologub was named a great poet in an answer to a literary questionnaire. This exaggeration is quite understandable. In art, greatness begins with some sort of victory over a fear of life, of which Sologub himself was always a victim. But, of course, he was a poet in the truest and highest sense of the word—not a "man of letters," or a "poet's poet," but one of those who are enumerated in "the Commandments of Bliss." . . .

He died in complete loneliness, poverty, forgotten by all and needed by no one. He had tuberculosis, which does not cause the victim to lose consciousness until the last minute.

Georgi Ivanov. Peterburgskie zimy (New York,
Izdatelstvo imeni Chekhova, 1952), p. 185[†]

Fyodor Sologub, a "highbrow" decadent and symbolist, differed from the rest in so far as he did not cater for popularity. Keeping away from public life, he shut himself in his private ivory tower, where he indulged in an aesthetic or would-be aesthetic cult of death and of weird necromantic phantoms. But even before reaching that stage, he had made—in his novel *A Petty Demon* [*Melki bes*]—a formidable onslaught on that philistine vulgarity, the fight with which was considered almost a duty by every Russian author from Gogol onwards. The hero of Sologub's novel—a paranoiac schoolmaster—outstrips even Gogol's examples of intensified vulgarity and, like the characters in *Dead Souls*, he is symbolic in his realism.

Janko Lavrin. Russian Writers
(New York, Van Nostrand, 1954), p. 255

The Satanism of many other Decadent poets, not excluding Bal'mont and Brjusov, is often hardly more than a pose; and, as such, it is merely the reverse of Romantic sentimentalism. Sologub's Satanism is, however, a genuine reflection of his view of human life. Existence, especially that of modern man, seems to him a kind of nonexistence. Man goes through the limbo of being like a living corpse. Life is demonic not merely because it denies God, but also because God denies life, or, as the poet says, "God does not want life, and life does not want God." By identifying the human and the earthly with the demonic, Sologub lowers the human to the level of the subhuman and sinks the earthly underground. The demonic obsesses Sologub's imagination as much as that of Gogol' and Dostoevskij, yet the evil spirits he conjures resemble more the impish sprites of Gogol' than the black angels of Dostoevskij. . . .

Even more than in the Devil, Sologub believes in black magic. A sorcerer, rather than a wonderworker, he practices his witchcraft in the dim halfway region between death and life, in the no-man's-land of the spirit. . . . It was not the vanity of an aesthete, but a lucid self-criticism, which led him to claim in one of his lyrics that all his sins as a man and as a poet would be remitted and forgiven because of a single merit, which was the purity of his craft. Sologub was right in this expectation: his name will be spared by the judgment of posterity; his poetry will escape that oblivion which is the nemesis of all artists who sin against their calling by bad faith, even more by bad works.

Renato Poggioli. The Poets of Russia
(Cambridge, Mass., Harvard University Press, 1960),
pp. 109–11

I would like to mention the occasion when Sologub came to Paris. There was a literary evening. Sologub explained at length to those present, mostly students, that Dulcinea was different from Aldonza. He looked more like a high school principal than a poet. A sad smile occasionally flickered in his eyes. I realized that before me stood the author of *Melky bes* (*The Petty Demon*). But where did he get that music, those simple words piercing one's heart, those songs that made him akin to Verlaine? He read poetry in a peculiar manner, as if he were storing the words away in various compartments of a large drawer: "The horse—of an enemy—officer—trod—straight to my heart—straight to my heart." I saw him for the last time at the Moscow Press Club in 1920. Some speakers were saying that the era of individualism was over. Sologub nodded his head, obviously agreeing with them. When he spoke his concluding words, he only added that a totality must consist of units, not of zeroes, for if a zero is added to another, the result is not a totality but zero. Later on, he received me cordially, listened to my poems, and talked about music, mystery, and again about Dulcinea.

Ilya Ehrenburg. *Novy mir.* Sept., 1960, p. 96[†]

[Peredonov—the main figure of *The Petty Demon*] . . . is condemned to destruction from the outset, and as "Peredonovism" his very name has become the embodiment in Russian life of everything that is vile, hypocritical, mean, and slimy. The world of reality in this provincial town where Peredonov teaches school has its counterparts in earlier Russian literature. Certain works of Gogol, Dostoevsky, Saltykov-Shchedrin, and even Chekhov have contributed something to its description, its mores, and its inhabitants. However, this world of reality takes on special Sologubian characteristics when seen through the eyes of the demon-ridden Peredonov with his persecution mania. Further, the realism is interpenetrated by an underlying symbolism which suggests that this evil wasteland is only a microcosm of the total evil creation of God. For just as Sologub believes that there is something of Peredonov in all of us, so he also insists on the universality of Peredonov's mad world. Indeed these symbolically suggestive universal implications impart to the novel its mysterious, dark evocative power and elevate it far beyond the level of ordinary fiction.

Perhaps as a counterpoise to the unrelieved tragic gloom of Peredonov, and also as a fulfillment of the author's own perverted vision of life, Sologub introduces into the novel the extensive episode of the seduction of the handsome young schoolboy Sasha by the erotic and sadistically minded *demi-vierge* Ludmila. It is a *Lolita* situation in reverse, and the scenes are wantonly delightful and flecked with humor and not a little satire. But the benignancy of the symbolism is adulterated by the sensuality of the imagery. Satan rules over this idyllic kingdom. Though Ludmila

and Sasha are Sologubian symbols of beauty, they are morbidly devoted
to sex and death.

Ernest J. Simmons. Introduction to
Fyodor Sologub, *The Petty Demon*
(New York, Random House, 1962), p. xii

Fyodor Sologub's personal universe is somber and exitless in comparison
with that of Hippius. If Balmont all his life tried to embrace the world in
all its variety, Sologub's was the most consistent effort to limit himself to a
definite set of symbols and to a consciously colorless vocabulary for a portrayal of the world in which the false and vulgar variety of the surrounding
life, dominated by the evil dragon, the sun, is boldly separated from the
immovable, death-beauty produced by the poet's solipsist imagination.
Sologub's macrocosm, particularly in its satanist aspects, is not likely
to attract many nowadays, but there is grandeur and a peculiar kind of
perverse integrity in his poetry. To compare him with Balmont once more,
here is the limit of romantic subjectivity as against Balmont's extreme
case of romantic objectivity. Unable to leave Russia after the Revolution,
in despair after his wife had committed suicide, Sologub tried to divert
himself by deceptively simple strains about shepherds and shepherdesses,
but ended in complete disgust and depression. Developing one of his
favorite images, the zoo-like captivity on this earth, he comes, in one of
his late poems, to the picture of being surrounded by beasts and having
to eat, without protest, vomit offered him as food.

Vladimir Markov. Introduction to *Modern Russian
Poetry* (Indianapolis, Ind., Bobbs-Merrill, 1966),
pp. lvi–lvii

SOLZHENITSYN, ALEKSANDR (1918–   )

One Day in the Life of Ivan Denisovich [*Odin den Ivana Denisovicha*] is
not a document in the sense of being a memoir, nor is it notes or reminiscences of the author's personal experiences, although only such personal experiences could lend this story its sense of genuine authenticity.
This is a work of art and it is by virtue of the artistic interpretation of this
material from life that it is a witness of special value, a document of an
art which up to now had seemed to have few possibilities.

The reader will not find in A. Solzhenitsyn's story an all-encompassing
portrayal of that historic period which is particularly marked by the bitter
memory of the year 1937. The content of *One Day* is naturally limited
in time and place of action and the horizons of the main hero of the story.
But in the writing of A. Solzhenitsyn, who here enters the literary scene

for the first time, one day in the life of the camp prisoner, Ivan Denisovich Shukhov, develops into a picture which gives extraordinary vitality
and fidelity to the truthfulness of its human characters. Herein above all
lies the uncommon power of the work to impress. The reader can visual-
ize for himself many of the people depicted here in the tragic role of
camp inmates in other situations—at the front or at postwar construction
sites. They are the same people who by the will of circumstance have
been put to severe physical and moral tests under special and extreme
conditions.

In this story there is no deliberate concentration of terrible facts of the
cruelty and arbitrariness that were the result of the violation of Soviet
legality. The author chose instead to portray only one of the most ordinary
of days in the life at camp from reveille to retreat. Nevertheless this "ordinary" day cannot but arouse in the heart of the reader a bitter feeling
of pain for the fate of the people who, from the pages of this story, rise
up before us so alive and so near. Yet the unquestionable victory of the
artist lies in the fact that the bitterness and the pain have nothing in common with a feeling of hopeless depression. On the contrary, the impression left by this work is so extraordinary in its unvarnished and difficult
truth that it somehow frees the soul of the burden of things unsaid that
needed to be said and at the same time it strengthens one's manly and
lofty feelings.

This is a grim story—still another example of the fact that there are
no areas or facts of reality that can be excluded from the sphere of the
Soviet artist in our days or that are beyond truthful portrayal. Everything
depends on the capabilities of the artist himself. [1962]

Alexander Tvardovsky. Foreword to Alexander
Solzhenitsyn, *One Day in the Life of Ivan Denisovich*
(New York, E. P. Dutton, 1963), pp. 13–15

The science of joy is an inseparable quality of our literature, an expression of its deepest optimism. It is true, it seems to me, that recently there
have been appearing on the pages of our journals too many "querulous"
stories and tales. . . . I must confess that I experienced a feeling of deep
spiritual pain when I read in *Novy mir* the story "Matryona's Home"
["Matryonin dvor"] by A. Solzhenitsyn, who has written such a remarkable work as *One Day in the Life of Ivan Denisovich*. It seems to me
that "Matryona's Home" was written by its author when he was still in a
state of mind in which he could not with any depth understand the life of
the people, the movement and real perspectives of that life. In the first
post-war years, such people as Matryona really did harness the plough to
themselves in villages desolated by the Germans. The Soviet peasantry
performed a great feat in those circumstances and gave bread to the peo-

ple, fed the country. This alone must evoke a feeling of reverence and delight. To draw the Soviet village as Bunin's village of our day is historically
incorrect. Solzhenitsyn's story convinces one over and over again: without a vision of historical truth, of its essence, there can be no full truth,
no matter what the talent. [1963]

> Vadim Kozhevnikov. In *Soviet Literature in the*
> *Sixties*, Max Hayward and Edward L. Cowley, eds.
> (New York, Frederick A. Praeger, 1964), pp. 94–95

[*One Day in the Life of Ivan Denisovich* is] not just a new book, a good
book, a great book. Anyway, these adjectives have been dulled for us by
soap ads and by political slogans. This book is as important as Dostoevsky's first book. It not only marks the emergence of an unknown and
major literary craftsman but it also revives and reshapes the language and
culture to which it belongs. Solzhenitsyn's great trick, like Dostoevsky's
before him, is that he identifies the motions of awareness so accurately
that they take on, in a world in which awareness is death (what else is a
political prisoner but a man incarcerated for too much reliance on his
own awareness?), all the meaning of symbolic acts. The smallest gesture
in the compound—Shukhov's standing patiently in front of Caesar, hoping for a drag—is equally the profoundest affirmation of human value and
human dignity. In this book, an "average" man in inhuman surroundings
is studied to the depths. His story is presented as the catalogue of his moti-
vations as he proceeds through the physical and moral odyssey of one
day in his life. And "all" he wanted was to get to the end, to get home, to
be himself. The brilliance of the book is that he does become himself,
though he has none of the tools which for thousands of years we have
said a man must have. This book tells us how great a thing a man's life is.

> F. D. Reeve. *KR*. Spring, 1963, p. 357

Alexander Solzhenitsyn's work [*One Day in the Life of Ivan Denisovich*]
is a significant event in Soviet literature. But it would be naïve to think it
arose on bare ground. From a political viewpoint the novel is a good
sign of the substantial changes taking place in Soviet society which has
resolutely broken with the dark inheritance of the cult of personality.
From an artistic viewpoint it is a logical continuation of the best traditions
of Russian classical and Soviet literature, traditions which even during the
period of the cult of Stalin never vanished below ground. Even in the
darkest times, the truth of life triumphed, for without it art cannot exist
at all. There is no need to enumerate here the works of Soviet writers
which portrayed the life of the people with authentic truthfulness. That a
number of books sometimes painted crude pictures of well-being instead
of portraying life, is another matter. Such books have been discarded,
never to return, along with the cult of Stalin. The art of socialist realism,

whose development was undoubtedly retarded in period of the cult of personality, has now gained full freedom. In this sense Solzhenitsyn's novel is a crushing blow to those who still doubt the vitality of socialist realism. The novel is one of the latest testimonials to the force of realism. Permeated with love for the people and profoundly truthful, it has a unique form dictated by the author's desire to express the truth of life as accurately as possible. It lacks any formalistic devices. Any such devices would seem blasphemous and greatly impair its artistic quality. It is a small work but one "weightier than many volumes."

Aleksei Kondratovich. *SL.* April, 1963, p. 171

Perhaps we would not talk about Solzhenitsyn's failures in "Dlya polzy dela" ("For the Good of the Cause") if the mistakes in that story were not similar to those the critics had already pointed out in "Matryona's Home." The mistakes consist of the author's attempts to solve the most complex ideological and moral problems, to judge people and their actions outside the real-life relationships, and to deal with abstract categories void of concrete social content. . . .

It would seem to us that "For the Good of the Cause" is the most modern of Solzhenitsyn's stories. But if we analyze it, if we disregard such outward signs as the palms on the shirts, the crew cuts, the "supermodern" judgments of children about literature, it would seem that the writer's view on life and his position remained as unmodern (in many respects even archaic) as in "Matryona's Home." We could not recognize here the "new," "modern" Solzhenitsyn. . . .

But there is no doubt that before us is a great and honest talent, whose originality lies in the acute sensitivity to any manifestation of evil, untruth, and injustice. This can mean great power, but only when combined with the knowledge and profound understanding of laws governing our lives and with the capability to see clearly the direction of these laws.

Yuri Barabash. *Literaturnaya gazeta.*
Aug. 31, 1963, p. 3[†]

One Day in the Life of Ivan Denisovich possesses a peculiar power. It is not written in the offended tone of "about this I cannot keep silent." It is contained by a detached, workmanlike narrative manner that comes from the concentration of its energy on the most meticulously minute description of the details involved in getting through the single day of prison life, from reveille to lights-out, it covers. In places it reads almost like a kind of manual, a book of instructions on how to survive hunger and cold and the sadistic ferocity of the guards—the three elements against which Ivan Denisovich and his mates must wage their daily battle in order, literally, to live another day. . . .

One Day in the Life of Ivan Denisovich is not a cry of pain; it does not pile on horrors. The shattering impact of this story is produced precisely by its restrained, objective manner; the suppressed force of that matter-of-fact appraisal of a bread crust's superiority over a spoon is sprung by the reader's imagination, and how slight a movement of it is needed to understand how hungry a man can be. Solzhenitsyn's prose style contributes powerfully to the story's effect. In keeping with Shukov's village speech, it is frequently ungrammatical, composed in rich variety of the colloquialisms of the uneducated folk and the semi-obscene, harsh argot of the camp. It has a jagged texture. Frequent ellipsis and the staccato brevity of thoughts and observations reported on the run, broken down into the most simple primitive statements. It is a coarse style, completely adequate to the unbeautiful material it governs, capable of striking with a kinetic immediacy at the reader's perception.

Solzhenitsyn's laconicism frequently moves into aphorism—a special, macabre variety of aphorism, again, appropriate to his material. . . .

From a purely artistic point of view, in its language, style and in the nobility of its author's vision, *One Day in the Life of Ivan Denisovich* was the most excitingly fresh work to have appeared in Soviet literature in many years; Solzhenitsyn earned the praise he received. But, of course, there was at least an equal measure of politics in the enthusiasm of Solzhenitsyn's reviewers, and this, at the time, was its most significant aspect.

Burton Rubin. In *Soviet Literature in the Sixties*,
Max Hayward and Edward L. Crowley, eds.
(New York, Frederick A. Praeger, 1964), pp. 90–91

The majority of Soviet critics stress Shukhov's attitude toward work as the most laudable feature of his character. Shukhov works well and with a will, as we see from the way he constructs a building with his squad. On a prisoner's fulfillment of his quota depends his food, his very existence. One of the basic criteria on which a person is assessed in Soviet society is his attitude toward work; *ergo*, prisoners who do not work well are not good people.

None of the critics, however, notices that work—i.e., building—is not the same for Shukhov as for Captain Buinovsky or for any other of the camp inmates. At home, too, Shukhov had done some building, although only with wood; for him, therefore, this work represents in some measure his life outside, work is a function of his freedom. For Buinovsky, on the other hand, who "was fading away under your very eyes," hard work in the camp is not a function of freedom but, on the contrary, one more shackle—and the heaviest one at that. Consequently, a positive attitude toward work cannot in this case be expected from Buinovsky. [1964]

Mihajlo Mihajlov. *Russian Themes* (New York,
Farrar, Straus & Giroux, 1968), pp. 104–5

I don't know about others, but as I was reading the story, I was persistently plagued by one question: what was I doing then, what was my life like? . . . At that time, thirteen years ago, in the month of January our newspapers were discussing the progress of works on the Volga-Don Canal; the speeding up of the steel-casting process; the enlargement of kolkhozys; the transplanting of several varieties of Georgian tea in the northern regions; the approaching elections; the Korean War; the Alisher Navoi jubilee, the Hockey Cup finals. . . . But how was it I was told nothing of Ivan Denisovich? Can it really be I was not aware that on that silent, bitterly cold morning he and thousands of others were marched out by guards with dogs through the main gate of that camp and across snow-covered fields to their work assignments? . . . It is most difficult not to be obsessed with this thought. . . .

One Day in the Life of Ivan Denisovich is only one year old. Yet it has provoked more argument, interpretation, and polemic than any other book published in the past several years. This book will not suffer the fate of those flash-in-the-pan sensations that flare into controversy and are then forgotten. On the contrary, the longer this book lives in our literature, the clearer its importance to that literature will become and the more fully will we understand how necessary its appearance was. This story will live a long time. [1964]

> V. Lakshin. Quoted in Mihajlo Mihajlov, *Russian*
> *Themes* (New York, Farrar, Straus & Giroux, 1968),
> pp. 318–19

Solzhenitsyn's keen ear for the leisurely rhythms of the Russian folk speech and his thoroughly un-Soviet affinity for Alesha Karamazov-like meekness are writ large in what is perhaps his most accomplished work to date, "Matryona's Home." The narrator of the story, who, not unlike its author, is a former political prisoner and a teacher, decides to "cut loose and get lost in the innermost heart of Russia, if there is any such thing." The phrase seems to suggest a hankering for some traditional Russian ambiance. In fact, both the language and the moral climate of "Matryona's Home" have a strikingly old-fashioned quality. The central figure in the story, a selfless, gentle, pure-of-heart peasant woman, makes one think of the quiet radiance of that chastened village belle Lukeria in Turgenev's "The Living Relics." When Matryona dies, a victim, symbolically, to her neighbor's brutal, unthinking acquisitiveness, the narrator is moved to comment: "We all lived beside her and never understood that she was the righteous one, without whom no village can stand nor any city. Nor our homeland."

None of this was likely to please the official critics. Owing to Khrushchev's personal imprimatur, *One Day* enjoyed, at least until recently, a measure of immunity. But "Matryona's Home" was fair game. The story was promptly attacked for offering a distorted picture of the Soviet village. The implication that such "capitalistic" attitudes as competitiveness and greed were still rampant in the Soviet countryside was bound to be resented. Nor was Solzhenitsyn's positive message—his emphasis on personal "righteousness," on unaggressive goodness, so clearly at odds with the "struggle"-oriented and stridently public Soviet ethos—any less objectionable.

Victor Erlich. *SlR*. Sept., 1964, p. 411

The martyred hero of Solzhenitsyn's novel [*One Day in the Life of Ivan Denisovich*], "crucified" by the Stalin system, has the Everyman name of Ivan. So far as we know, no Soviet or western critic has noted the concealed symbolism in the fact that Ivan, like the first of all Christian martyrs, is by profession a carpenter. Perhaps we may draw an analogy in part with Faulkner's victimized Joe Christmas, another symbolic name. Despite the propensity for narrow political interpretations (pro or anti-Communism) on both sides of the cold war, neither *One Day* nor the author's subsequent stories are the short-run realistic journalism they may seem. They are long-run works of art whose theme is not local Russian politics (any more than Faulkner's theme was local Mississippi reportage) but universal good and evil. The best of them, "Matryona's House" (*Novy mir*, 1963), has a heroine who is, in effect, a medieval Christian saint.

Solzhenitsyn's avowed masters are not the Zola-style realists, despite his use of labor-camp documentation, but the symbolist poets Pasternak and Akhmatova. Solzhenitsyn himself is the author of some beautiful prose poems. . . . To resume his carpenter theme: like his novel, these poems contain implicit, never-articulated hints of religious symbolism, not to mention an ironic reference to Soviet Moscow as the Greek Orthodox "Third Rome." The Soviet censorship being what it is, the western reader must be alert for such hints. But not over-alert: often the westerner reads into Soviet texts a rebellious double meaning that is not there. Leonov and Solzhenitsyn are the two authors who most lend themselves to this, for both are completely sincere Communists who yet use or seem to use a Christian symbolism of redemption through suffering, and it may be that in both cases our above interpretations are misinterpretations.

Peter Viereck. *TriQuarterly*. Spring, 1965, pp. 35–36

Disregarding the political implications involved, Solzhenitsyn's interest in verbal experiments, his predilection for popular (sometimes regional) speech, his skillful employment of *skaz*, link him with the great tradition of the past and mark him as the heir of N. Leskov.

The most striking feature of Solzhenitsyn's version of *skaz* (especially in *One Day*) is his masterful fusion of two separate elements of speech: of popular expressions and the Soviet prison-camp slang. A singular attention to peculiarities, local and individual, of the spoken language results in the creation of a unique idiom, characteristic of a particular social group. In succeeding works Solzhenitsyn resorts to *skaz* only occasionally, more so in "Matryona's House" than in the rest. And it is precisely in these two stories that Solzhenitsyn is at his best as the "interpreter of the 'popular' mind." In both stories the chief protagonists are of peasant stock —one more link in the long chain of peasants peopling the pages of Russian nineteenth-century fiction. Significantly, one could hardly call either of them a *kolkhoznik*. In the case of Matryona especially it is possible to pinpoint her origin with some degree of accuracy: she is a spiritual offspring of the heroine of one of Leskov's less famous stories, "Malania—golova barania" [Malania, the Muttonhead].

Ludmila Koehler. RR. Spring, 1967, p. 177

There is a truly important novelist in Russia today . . . Solzhenitzin has fire, but he also has absolute professionalism. I have never met a more hard-working, better-organized writer in all my life. When in Moscow he frequently stays with me. He works right here, behind this glass partition. . . .

Solzhenitzin is in full control of his literary means, and also of the difficult social and political situation that has been his since his stand against censorship at the Writers' Congress last May. As a man, as a writer, he has a clear vision of the responsibilities. He has to tell the truth about the heroism and the shortcomings of the Russian people in recent years. No one I know has a stronger, more exclusive love for his country. But in the best Russian Revolutionary tradition, his is not a complacent love. This is the secret of his tremendous prestige as a writer: he has revived something very important out of the past—a search for truth through literature.

Kornei Chukovski. NYT. May 26, 1968, p. 40

As a medical novel, *The Cancer Ward* [*Rakovy korpus*] offers a fair and quite interesting picture of medicine as practiced in a Central Asian city in 1955. The author himself was cast up in Tashkent, sick with cancer, at about the same period, after spending eight years in prisons and camps. Still in exile—he was not "rehabilitated" until 1957—he entered a hospital where his cancer, never clearly diagnosed as malignant, was arrested. As Solzhenitsyn is the ultimate realist writer, whose life story is indistinguishable from his fiction, it can be assumed that the cancer ward he describes is much as he observed it.

In spite of Solzhenitsyn's clinical preoccupations, the reader must strain hard to read this novel as a book about cancer. What are we to make of this question posed by the author: "A man sprouts a tumor and dies—how then can a country live that has sprouted camps and exile?" Again and again Solzhenitsyn is compelled to return, perhaps despite himself, to his great theme. Who are his cancer-ridden patients? Exiles, an ex-prisoner, a concentration-camp guard, and a secret-police bureaucrat whose denunciations have sent dozens of people to prison. As *One Day* stands for the agony of all Russia under Stalin, so *The Cancer Ward* irresistibly conveys an image of the immediate post-Stalin period when both victims and executioners were confined, all equally mutilated, in the cancer ward of the nation.

Patricia Blake. *NYT*. Oct. 27, 1968, p. 50

The publisher's foreword attempts to draw a parallel between Solzhenitsyn and Dostoevsky, and there are, indeed, a number of remarkable coincidences in the two men's biographies. The parallel is, however, a misleading one. Nothing in Solzhenitsyn's life and work suggests that he might follow in his predecessor's footsteps and ultimately become a champion of political reaction and submission to authority. For, in spite of his outward preoccupation with politics, Solzhenitsyn's basic concerns are really moral and ethical, though in a nonreligious sense; the master in whose tradition he follows is Chekhov. *The Cancer Ward* is in many respects reminiscent of Chekhov's *Ward No. 6*, a frightening story of muffled horror that had, in the years following its appearance, gradually grown into a symbol of everything that was cruel and evil in Imperial Russia.

Maurice Friedberg. *SR*. Nov. 9, 1968, pp. 43–44

[Solzhenitsyn] has extracted from his experiences a distinctive philosophy of life, which is closely modelled on that of his acknowledged master, Lev Tolstoy.

Like *War and Peace, The First Circle* [*V kruge pervom*] rests heavily on the dialogue of two main characters, both of them inmates of the prison, and both of them in a sense embodiments of two different facets of the author's personality. Gleb Vikentich Nerzhin is Solzhenitsyn's Pierre, Lev Grigoryevich Rubin his André. Whereas Rubin believes passionately that history will eventually sort out the anomalies of the Stalinist system and put communism back on to its proper, gloriously constructive path, Nerzhin prefers to take refuge in quietist philosophy. The books of the Sankhya tell him consolingly that "For those who understand, human happiness is suffering." . . .

Solzhenitsyn has expertly—and heroically—presented Soviet life in the late 1940s in all its complex variety. Where he is weak is in accounting for its superstructure, for the political machine that is fundamentally responsible for each of his individual tragedies. The portrait of Stalin himself in this novel—very much like Tolstoy's portrait of Napoleon in *War and Peace*, with which it invites comparison—is too grotesquely satirical to be effective.

It is impossible to judge the qualities of this book dispassionately because it is impossible to forget that whatever faults it might have *The First Circle* does provide authentic evidence of a time and society for which most of the evidence has been suppressed, and that to write it was an act of heroism. Solzhenitsyn certainly manages to keep his reader deeply absorbed in a world that is sad and unpleasant to contemplate, a world where one character's "need to conceal his thoughts, to repress his sense of justice, had etched deep lines round his mouth and given him a disagreeable expression and a stoop."

Solzhenitsyn spent a great deal of time rewriting and pruning *A Day in the Life of Ivan Denisovich* before it was published, but both *Cancer Ward* and *The First Circle* suffer from being often loose and rambling, the consequence, perhaps, of having been written at excessive speed in a cultural vacuum.

TLS. Nov. 21, 1968, p. 1301

Solzhenitsyn's lack of self-consciousness about being judged is part of his strange distinction. His choice of willing alienation from the business of life, from any of the projects of life, his commitment to contemplation, this is the only consistency in him, and it shows up just as clearly, though much less powerfully and interestingly, in *The Cancer Ward*, the subject of which my reader can by now predict for himself. What I keep trying not to imply is that Solzhenitsyn's naïvely simple-minded view of life is valuable just because it is so decidedly his own, but I wonder why it should be so wrong to say that. It's a rare enough thing to meet in anybody past a certain age. And that's the other point: Solzhenitsyn isn't, on any page of this novel, sophomoric: he isn't callow, cocksure; he isn't under the illusion that he's bringing you news, he doesn't shout or wave his arms. It's merely that every word he writes is guaranteed by his own experience. One can see that it's his unaggressive but unshakable individualism, together with his lack of interest in politics and his interest in a church-less and dogma-less religious contemplation, that alarmed the Russian censors; and one can understand, too, the American reviews that were also alarmed by these strange qualities and then helplessly took their clue from this sort of thing in the publisher's blurb: "It is a sublime hymn of praise to man, an outpouring of love and pride, a celebration of nobility, courage, selflessness, honor." Let me take my clue from James' wonderful sentence about Mrs. Capadose in "The Liar": "she had no imagination and only the simpler feelings, but several of these had grown up to full size." If Solzhenitsyn were a good novelist he might be a great one; in any case, he is a human being grown up to full size.

Robert Garis, *HdR*. Spring, 1969, p. 154

Solzhenitsyn's book [*The First Circle*] comes out of a world of almost unrestricted tyranny and oppression, of unexampled human misery, and of a more perfect system of the exploitation of man by man than history has ever previously known. Indeed, if one had any doubt about the accuracy of this description of the U.S.S.R., one would only have to read *The First Circle* to recognise its truth. For it is, I think, a very great book, which itself verifies the truth which it tries to convey, in the same way that the greatest novels of the past, of Stendhal, or Dickens, of Balzac, or Tolstoy or Dostoevsky, are the evidence of their own truth, and perhaps for this reason in reading Solzhenitsyn it is to such models that one's mind instinctively recurs. . . .

Indeed, one could say with every confidence that it would be quite impossible for any Western novelist to write such a book today; not so much because of the particular experiences and environment which it embodies, but because of the intellectual and spiritual standards by which they are judged. For despite all his imagination, his capacity for sympathy and understanding, Solzhenitsyn retains the faculty of judgment and that is not a quality which we any longer look to literature for in the West today. Moreover, though he writes of experiences which to us are infinitely unfamiliar except by hearsay, we instinctively trust his judgment because it is based on standards which are universally acceptable and intelligible, and are such indeed as any ordinary man might understand. He writes indeed as a human being might write if he also possessed the highest degree of literary talent, and this also is something which for many years now we have been unaccustomed to meet in the West.

R. *Encounter*. May, 1970, p. 48

The full force of Solzhenitsyn's moral concerns undoubtedly comes over in all his stories, though it would be wrong to suggest that these are all of the same high standard. It would be enlightening to discover the author's own opinion of his stories. One feels he would agree that "For the Good of the Cause" is the least successful, if only because it has a mundane quality, a Dudintsev-like feasibility which deprives it of the atmosphere and power of "The Right Hand" ["Pravaya ruka"] and "Matryona's House." More than anywhere else, it is in the character of Matryona that Solzhenitsyn upholds the value of the *pravednik*, the pious or righteous person whom Leskov and Tolstoy portrayed. Matryona is the repository of the prized Tolstoyan ethic in the era of the *kolkhoz*, "without whom, in the words of the proverb, neither hamlet, nor town, nor our whole land can survive."

As with Pasternak and his "Zhivago Poems," Solzhenitsyn's so-called "prose poems"—variously referred to elsewhere as *krokhotki* (tiny stories) or *études*—are vital to a deeper understanding of him as a writer and thinker. No foreign language can do them justice, and people who have had the privilege of hearing Solzhenitsyn read "The Ashes of a Poet" ["Prakh poeta"] and "Lake Segden" ["Ozero Segden"] will agree that their author expresses in these studies—the musical analogy is very appropriate—all the intensity of his attachment to Russia and to nature, to honesty about the past and the present, to the Russian cultural tradition. They show the origins of his humility, and also his black irony. They demonstrate effectively his profound religious belief in a God who, as he has said in another context, is "the supreme creative force in the universe." Like an *étude*, they are a series in different keys, each with a twist, a moral, a *pointe*. Any translation of them, no matter how accurate and painstaking, tends to sound rather like Chopin played on a cinema organ.

TLS. July 2, 1971, p. 752

August 1914 [*Avgust chetyrnadtsatogo*] consists of more than 60 short untitled chapters. It aims to portray with complete factual accuracy the defeat of General Samsonov's Second Army by the Germans at the battle of Tannenberg at the beginning of the First World War. The time scale it covers is the 11 days from August 10–21, 1914, and in this way it is reminiscent of the Aristotelian three days described in *The First Circle* or the fortnight in *The Cancer Ward*. Otherwise his Tolstoyan fascination for men in a microcosmic setting is reinforced by a meticulous attention to historical detail, to the minutiae of military strategy and the structure of the command hierarchy.

Where Tolstoy took Borodino and Austerlitz, Kutuzov and Napoleon, as the basis for a study and a philosophy of history, Solzhenitsyn tries to catch the flow of events stripped bare of metaphysics. To achieve this end he has adopted a number of technical innovations which, though pale by comparison with Joyce or Burroughs, hark back to Eisenstein, or the Constructivists of the 1920s. Between narrative chapters he inserts review chapters to summarise events, documents are quoted at length in the manner of Pil'nyak's novel *The Naked Year*, scraps of newspaper advertisements and headlines are presented in montage, and there are a number of what the author terms "cinematic" (*kinoekrannyi*) episodes, which read like the shooting script for scenes from a film. All this is conveyed in a language which is highly innovatory, lilting and lapidary. At times broadly idiomatic, at others richly poetic, Solzhenitsyn more than ever before draws on and expands the great 19th-century tradition of Tolstoy and Chekhov.

The crucial fact about *August 1914*, and one which will probably prevent its publication in the Soviet Union at any time, is that it invites comparison of the First World War with the Red Army debacle in 1941. It demands an honest appraisal of facts, without *lakirovka* or "varnishing," without glib hindsight. It is as yet unclear what other crucial areas Solzhenitsyn will touch on in future volumes: 1917, the Civil War, collectivisation, the siege of Leningrad, the battle of Stalingrad? Whatever he chooses, it is certain that he will be pursuing his own particular brand of truth. As he says at the end of *August 1914*: "The lie did not commence with us, and it will not end with us."

N. J. Anning. *NS*. July 9, 1971, p. 55

TENDRYAKOV, VLADIMIR (1923–)

Vladimir Tendryakov, who is just making his first steps on the literary arena . . . has the keen eye and the sharp sensitivity of the realist artist. Here, for instance, is how he sees nature:

"On a hot noon towards the end of July the woods are generally silent if there's no wind. The trees droop their branches wearily and the birds hide themselves. Only occasionally a cone will drop from an upper branch of a fir-tree, stripping the dead needles from wasted branches on its way down."

This is more than a descriptive passage. It is an essential part of the story, because on that hot noon its "hero," secretary Glukharyov, was resting on an uprooted tree in the silent woods while his chauffeur repaired their car. Glukharyov, the same callous careerist who in the spring ordered the seeds to be cast in the water, now sits thinking of the evil days ahead of him. A "dead needle from a wasted branch" could just as well be said of him, and he is vaguely aware of it. "Glukharyov suddenly recognized the spot. Here in the spring, during a thunderstorm, he had seen a birch struck down by lightning. That was the tree he was resting on. A rotten tree . . . it wasn't the lightning that struck it down; no, the elements were not to blame. Had it been sound, it might have been scorched, its crown might have been sliced off, but it would have weathered the storm. The trouble with this birch is dry rot. . . ." That is the trouble with Glukharyov too.

Least of all can Tendryakov be described as a publicist. He has the make-up of a realistic psychologist. And although he calls his stories "sketches," they are not really so. Never could he have written as Ovechkin did at the conclusion of his *Daily Round:* "This sketch has no continuation as yet because it is written almost from the life . . . we must wait for the further development of events." Tendryakov also writes "almost from the life," but he seeks to give his tales of life the complete, rounded form of a story. And he is eminently successful in the effort. Best of all, he does not impose his literary inventions and whims of plot structure upon real life. His stories do, indeed, preserve the full authenticity of a sketch.

Daniel Danin. *SL.* July, 1954, pp. 145–46

Tendryakov [is] an author who stands somewhat apart. His *contes philosophiques* combine social criticism with an interest in moral paradoxes and human emotions. Tendryakov's first notable work stressed social criticism, depicting the impoverishment of the collective-farm village. In his latest novels, however, moral paradoxes have come to the fore. Most of all, he is haunted by the inevitability of evil. Why is evil attractive? What makes it so powerful that it cannot be defeated except by another evil, by killing? These are the central issues in his novelette *Valet, dama, korol* (Jack, Queen, King). They are not resolved, but the very posing of them challenges belief in a Communist reign of benevolence which is supposed to result from the reshaping of social relations. For Tendryakov, it is not the vestiges of capitalism that account for evil, but something very deep-rooted in man himself—something that has no definition in the author's atheistic and at the same time pre-Freudian vocabulary. General moral issues, however, do not completely overshadow either Tendryakov's naturalistic description of the hard life of workers engaged in timber-floating (not accidentally, his story was published in *Novyi mir*) or his dynamic treatment of relationships between people. His novels are rich; they combine philosophic ponderings with realistic yet imaginative description, placing Tendryakov in a category by himself among Soviet literary libertarians.

David Burg. *PC*. Sept.–Oct., 1962, pp. 42–43

We might call the art of the talanted young writer Vladimir Tendryakov a kind of "neo-realism" similar to the technique employed in postwar Italian films. In the story that brought him acclaim, "Three, Seven, Ace" ["Troika, semyorka, tuz"], Tendryakov starkly describes conflict among a few simple individuals in a primitive part of modern Russia. The basic idea is that changes in the social order by no means solve all human problems. [1963]

Mihajlo Mihajlov. *Russian Themes* (New York, Farrar, Straus and Giroux, 1968), p. 309

When [Tendryakov] is not tendencious, he is masterful. He knows how to depict the individual in all his human frailty. He creates authentic characters which have a universal quality recognizable under any system of government because Tendriakov enters fully into their lives and problems. The literary merit of his works is somewhat uneven. At times he becomes didactic, and the reader can readily predict whether the character will develop into a "good" or "bad" character. The good are always altruistic, stern, wise, and self-sacrificing for the advancement of the Soviet collective welfare. The "bad" are bad.

Most of his writings are concerned with moral questions, and the human conscience is often the punitive force. His language is rich in texture, direct, colloquial, and expressive. His description of nature, the forests, the rivers is abundantly rich. . . .

Few of Tendriakov's stories end on a happy note. They do not fit the narrow prescriptions of socialist realism. His method is psychological realism. It may be said that his stories are vignettes of life. They speak of tragedy and failures, of weakness and strength, of joy and gloom. The Soviet writer says as many before him have said: "There is no harsher judge than your own conscience."

Fan Parker. BA. Winter, 1965, pp. 36–37

Judging by his fictional works, one of Tendrjakov's main concerns is moral behavior and, by extension, the moral vacuum that has existed in his country. He places his characters in extraordinary situations and then examines their reactions. The behavior of his characters when faced with a difficult decision allows the author to comment on his society. When we come to his most recent stories we see that although he has retained his interest in morality, Tendrjakov has attempted to conceal this interest and broaden his scope. In "The Trial" ["Sud"] and "Three, Seven, Ace" it seems to me that he has succeeded, with the result that the application of what happens in them to Soviet society is not nearly so obvious, nor indeed is it the main point of the works. Tendrjakov is more interested in the irony of character and situation, in the living out of philosophical credos. The most refreshing feature of his recent work is that it can be read as literature without reference to Marxist aesthetics or to the Party line in domestic affairs. It is in this separation of literature from politics that I see the significance of Tendrjakov's stories.

In 1962 in a rare statement on literary matters Tendrjakov wrote in answer to a question posed by the editors of *Voprosy literatury* that when an author is writing a work, "it is the logic of life which takes control, that logic which a writer tries to bring into his work; he obeys it and tries to avoid coercing it." He did not elaborate. We can only make a guess as to what he meant by the "logic of life." Taking his own prose as an indication of his beliefs, I think we are on safe ground in assuming that Tendrjakov feels a writer should try to portray people and events as he sees them, not as he would wish them to be. This submission to the "logic of life" is diametrically opposed to the approach of the Soviet Marxist, who believes he knows the laws that govern life and can alter it as he wishes.

J. G. Garrard. SEEJ. Spring, 1965, pp. 15–16

Like all Tendrjakov's stories, [*Svidanie s Nefertiti* (A Meeting with Nefertiti)] too has a Čexovian "open end"; only thinly does he assist the reader to decide for himself about the outcome, aiming thus at restoring to Russian prose the modern conscience of free choice and independent thinking. Nonetheless, one closes the book with a certain feeling of having been cheated out of a great deal—that the author would have done more justice to this novel if he had divided it into a trilogy, each book more elaborate in action and well rounded in time, instead of into these four loosely connected parts. His expertise of concentration, unmatched in the short story, is detrimental here where wider backdrop and dimensions are of the essence. The regrettable lapses of time and gaps in plot are poorly bridged even by the sharply focused flashbacks and masterful stylistic devices.

These shortcomings, however, do not to a great degree diminish the excellence of the book as a whole. It is written with deep human understanding and fine humor; the narrative is interspersed with delightful descriptions of nature and interesting discourses on art. (The author also painted the pictures that illustrate the text.) The novel captivates with its vivid, truthful portrayal of protagonists, both good and bad, who behave like mortals without any of the artifices of "socialist realism" heroes. Although set safely in the Stalin era (it concludes symbolically with Stalin's funeral), it is obvious that Tendrjakov refers to present conditions. This is why *Svidanie s Nefertiti* aroused the bitter anger of the philistine dogmatists on the one hand, but on the other it stirred the hearts of millions of Soviet readers with the hope of justice and rectification.

Herman Carmel. *BA*. Summer, 1966, pp. 352–53

TERTZ, AVRAM (1925–   )

Tertz, a remarkably independent thinker, desires neither to return to prerevolutionary ways nor to embrace (and be embraced by) Western democracies. He looks back with nostalgia to the Revolution, but is heterodox in relation to various essential features of Soviet life and thought. He makes references showing a broad background of Russian culture and reveals close acquaintance with the works of early Soviet literary and art critics.

Dudintsev's *Novogodnaia skazka* and, to a greater degree, Tertz's own *Fantasticheskie povesti* [*Fantastic Stories*] (if authentic), and *Est-li zhizn na Marse* [*Is There Life on Mars?*] (published in France under the pseudonym Ivanov) exemplify in practice what the present essay demands in theory. *On Socialist Realism* [*Chto takoe solsialisticheski realizm*] has already become a minor classic within the genre of Soviet writings smuggled out of the USSR and published abroad. It deserves close study not only by students of Soviet literature but by all those interested in Russian intellectual developments.

George Gibian. *SIR*. Sept., 1962, pp. 571–72

[Tertz] is certainly no realist, socialist or otherwise, though he is deeply engaged with both illusion and reality and with the areas of experience where they appear to conjoin. It would be both fatuous and misleading to describe him as a rebel, except in the sense in which all serious writers are such. Surrealist (a word which has been used by one of his excellent translators, Mr. Max Hayward) is a suggestive but still somewhat inaccurate way to describe him. His publishers do him certainly no service in describing him as a Soviet "angry young man."

Mr. Tertz has an imagination like that of Leskov: fantastic, generous in its comedy, tart, bitter even, but not embittered. He has been quoted in *Encounter* (where both *The Icicle* [*Gololeditsa*] and *The Trial Begins* [*Sud idyot*] first appeared) putting his "hope in a phantasmagoric art, with hypotheses instead of a purpose, an art in which the grotesque will replace descriptions of ordinary life. Such an art," he said, "would correspond best to the spirit of our time." . . .

It would be wrong to suggest that all who are interested in Soviet writing should read *The Icicle*: all who are interested in serious comic writing, wherever it comes from, should do so.

TLS. June 28, 1963, p. 473

The stories composing *The Icicle* (the volume was smuggled out of Russia) are all about losing, or exchanging, one's identity; and whereas the material of several of them (the paranoiac civil servant at supper at a colleague's house, imagining the latter's wife is, as part of a conspiracy against him, a man in disguise) is psycho-pathological, these materials are not put to "psychological" use. The heroes' fantasies are granted full rights; they are given autonomy. . . .

Tertz shifts imperceptibly from this most airy kind of fun into bitter political satire. In the title-story the same kind of fantastic comic hypotheses are made—the hero becomes gifted with clairvoyance, and at the same time with an inability to see the faces of his fellow-humans for the crowd of past and future incarnations jostling for room in them. . . . This allegory of the writer vis-à-vis the Stalinist autocracy is sprung on us obliquely and with marvellous cleverness—I have singled out only one thread of its tangle of straight-faced ironies. And though in his piling-up of logical absurdities Tertz certainly comes out [of] Gogol's overcoat, he is, in certain precise and technical respects, a more contemporary writer than Greene.

P. N. Furbank. *Encounter*. Oct., 1963, pp. 83–84

Free from official censorship and from the compulsory aesthetics of Socialist Realism, Tertz and others are able to describe the hypocrisy and the sense of unreality that arise from the contrast between the official Soviet image and the harsher aspects of everyday Soviet life. In addition to satire, the literary device most frequently employed by these writers is fantasy, which is in itself a form of literary protest, the miraculous and the supernatural being strictly banned by Socialist Realism. The mixture of the grotesque, the satirical, and the supernatural in the work of Tertz has led certain Western critics to speak of it as "Socialist Surrealism."

Ljubimov [*Makepeace*], the latest novel by this author, is a story of an idealistic but semi-literate Soviet youth who acquires the power of mental telepathy and uses it to seize control of a provincial town in present-day Soviet Union. The hero's attempts to run the city of Lubimov in accordance with Leninist precepts brings him into sharp conflict with the ruling party philistines who see subversion everywhere and think only in slogans and stereotypes.

The experimental use to which Tertz occasionally puts the contemporary Soviet idiom (including the Party jargon) is not devoid of linguistic inventiveness. Yet, by and large, the novel does not rise above the level of a competent piece of writing of the type found in one of the popular American magazines devoted to fantasy and science fiction. Its interest as a political satire aside, *Ljubimov* could have easily appeared in, say, *Galaxy*, where it would be enjoyed by the regular readers and attract no special attention.

Simon Karlinsky. *BA*. Winter, 1965, p. 102

I belong to those writers who, like all Soviet people, are proud to be a small part of a great and noble people . . . we call our Soviet Motherland our mother. We are all members of one great family. How then are we to react to the behavior of traitors who have raised their hands against everything we hold most dear? The Russian proverb notes bitterly that "no family is without its monster." But there are different kinds of monstrosity. I think everybody understands that there is nothing more blasphemous and disgusting than to tell lies about one's mother, to insult her, to raise one's hand against her. . . . I am ashamed for those who have told lies about our Motherland and bespattered with mud everything that is most bright to us. They are amoral. I am ashamed for those who have tried and are trying to defend them, whatever their motive for defending them may be. I am doubly ashamed for those who offer their good offices as guarantors of the condemned renegades [this is an interesting detail: evidently some pleas to the authorities have suggested that they be released on the understanding that they will be responsible for their future behavior to their fellow writers]. . . . Some people, using phrases about humanism, moan about the severity of the sentence. I see here delegates from the party organization of our dear Soviet Army. What would they have done if traitors had appeared in one of their units? Nobody knows better than our soldiers that humanism is not slobbering soft-heartedness. . . . If these scoundrels with their black conscience had been found out in the memorable days of the twenties, when judgments were carried out without reference to strictly defined articles of the criminal code, but "in accordance with revolutionary justice," then, my goodness, these turn-coats would have received a very different punishment! But now, if you please, there is all this talk about the "severity" of the sentence.

Mikhail Sholokhov. In *On Trial*, Max Hayward, ed.
(New York, Harper & Row, 1966), pp. 31–32

Since the conversion of water into champagne [in *Lyubimov*] occurs on the occasion of Tikhomirov's marriage, one could equally well interpret the episode as a parody of the wedding feast at Cana.

This is of some significance, since there is evidence from Sinyavsky-Tertz's work—particularly at the end of *Lyubimov* and in *Unguarded Thoughts* [*Mysli vrasplokh*]—that, apart from having some personal religious creed (no doubt rooted, like Pasternak's, in Russian Orthodoxy), he certainly has respect for religious belief and for the Christian faith. Yet he nevertheless does not hesitate to introduce images or scenes which, theoretically, would appear blasphemous to many Christians (a similar example is the scene involving a monk and necrophilia in "The Icicle." At his trial Sinyavsky countered the prosecution's allegations that he had uttered blasphemies about Lenin by saying that things said about Lenin by his characters, or the mention of Lenin's name in certain contexts, could not be taken as evidence of his, Sinyavsky's, lack of respect for Lenin as a person and founder of the Soviet state. The sincerity of this assurance—though he did not himself make the point—is borne out by the fact that he also writes in a "sacrilegious" tone of religious matters with regard to which there can be doubt of his respect.

Max Hayward, ed. Introduction to *On Trial*
(New York, Harper & Row, 1966), p. 15

Tertz's *The Trial Begins* is written in the vein of his phantasmagoric art, in which the bizarre supplants the ordinary. The book will be of special interest to the contemporary reader who may be unacquainted with famous masters of the grotesque, in whose writings the absurd and the fantastic reign supreme. As in Tertz's *Fantastic Stories*, underlying the pronounced surrealistic element in *The Trial Begins* are sober thoughts and apprehensions of man's possible future misfortunes. The narrative also abounds in witty observations of incongruous scenes and situations in the life of Soviet higher officials and their women. Yet *The Trial Begins* strikes a serious tone each time the author portrays their petty bourgeois way of living, their shallow thinking, and their fundamental inability to form normal relationships with husbands, wives, and children. The people depicted in the story cannot rise above ordinary pursuits in a world which "lacks perspective" and which is weighed down by the absolute power of the Master, who is a deity and a devil at the same time. Like Tertz's other works, *The Trial Begins* reveals the author's vivid artistic imagination, his boldness of style and surrealistic imagery, his superb sense of humor, and above all his moral soundness and honesty, qualities which place him among the best contemporary writers.

Temira Pachmuss. Canadian Slavic Studies.
Fall, 1967, p. 507

To contemplate life as a whole, one must stand beyond it. To contemplate time as a whole, one must stand beyond it. Tertz in some way is always "outside the reality of the moment," like Camus's "Stranger," like the Jews. Shestov and Berdyaev, who come closest to Tertz in spirit, are émigrés, people also thrown out of everyday reality; Dostoevsky was wrenched out of life into ten years of hard labor. Thrown out of time, out of the "reality of the moment," they discovered things which Shestov and Berdyaev described in terms of philosophy and Dostoevsky and Tertz through their art: that this is not the final, last world, that another reality and another life exist, and that man had no reason to fear death or the horror of material reality because faith liberates the human soul and opens that path to eternal life.

The difference between Tertz on the one hand and Kafka and Orwell on the other is great. Kafka's *The Trial*, Orwell's *1984*, Tertz's *The Trial Begins* are the children of one spirit, but Kafka, like Orwell, was unable to shatter the test tube and to the end of his life remained in the clutches of an inescapable reality. *The Trial Begins* was only the beginning for Tertz. He broke through the test tube and fled into life. Kafka did not succeed in saving himself from the horror of reality in this life, not even in spirit, as Tertz did.

The "new realism" of Tertz can be compared with the creative achievement of Dostoevsky, with the paintings of Hieronymus Bosch, with European surrealist painting, with the philosophy of the "absurd," with the writings of Shestov, Rozanov, Berdyaev, and especially with the work of the young and gifted Belgrade painter Leonidas Sejka, whose paintings might well illustrate Tertz's stories. Tertz is a man of the new era, the era soon to come, the "new Middle Ages." He is close, of course, only to those who were driven by the reality of *The Trial, The Trial Begins*, and *1984* and by their unlimited thirst for life to break out of the test tube of reason, out of the walled world of "final reality," into the limitless space of eternal life.

Mihajlo Mihajlov. *Russian Themes* (New York,
Farrar, Straus and Giroux, 1968), pp. 70–71

TIKHONOV, NIKOLAI (1896–   )

Tikhonov's verse illustrates to the basic motifs of his work: he is dry, tense, short, terse (sometimes to the point of hoarseness), strong, firm. There is no sentimentalism, no slackness in him, nor does he play with words complacently or finically. The poet knows how to bring the poem to the end and give it the final shape, strongly and unexpectedly saying with the last two words what is necessary, summing it up.

His verse has a plot. Tikhonov has a preference for ballads, even when, at first glance, it seems that he is creating a lyric. He is a narrator in his poem, and this is good because, frankly speaking, the pure lyrics of our time have become thoroughly insipid; after reading them, there remains only a vague emptiness. [1923]

A. K. Voronski. *Literaturno-kriticheskie stati*
(Moscow, Sovetski pisatel, 1963), p. 165[†]

The ballad can be created on the basis of an exact word that is almost prosaically honest; not without reason has Tikhonov become a prose writer. The word in his balladic verse has lost almost all of the poetic color in order to be the pillar of the plot, its focal point. The plot's drum beats out the roll of precise words, as if one were counting them. . . .

The impression made by Tikhonov's ballads was great. No one before had put the question of the genre so earnestly or had used the poetic word as a focal point of the plot movement. In his ballads Tikhonov developed to the limits that trend of the poetic word which can be called Gumilyovian, thereby revealing the genre for which it was striving. [1924]

Yuri Tynyanov. *Archaisty i novatory*
(Leningrad, Priboi, 1929), p. 575[†]

While speaking of many and varied subjects, Tikhonov always remains true to himself. This individuality of style is not based on a special "manner," or "motif" repeated continually but on the integrity and scope of the poet's point of view.

The poet is both a direct participant in the events and their witness and observer. He takes part in the action and at the same time analyzes and watches.

This "second sight" persists in seemingly quite simple and obvious poems about the mountains and the hill people, poems written by Tikhonov just before the war and forming a part of the cycles *The Mountains* [*Gory*] and *The Wondrous Alarum* [*Chudesnaya trevoga*]. The poet is drawn to "the strong characters that are like avalanches, steeds rushing down precipices, the unreserved passions." But this integrity, "unreservedness of passions" are seen through the shrewd, analytical eyes of an advanced man of our epoch.

Tikhonov adheres to the same principles in his prose writings. His narrative is restrained and calm, but strong characters clash in it and passions rage. At the same time, Tikhonov is not afraid to write of the most prosaic subjects because he possesses the ability of revealing their hidden drama. Tikhonov formulates his view on the relations between art and life as follows: ". . . There are two truths in the world. The truth of existence, of life. A human being can be described with all his habits and customs, preserving photographic accuracy. The second truth is the artistic conception which becomes a fine art—to transform existence in such a way that it leaves the limits of an individual case and becomes general, multiplane and of all times. Such is the task of the writer."

Joseph Grinberg. *SL*. Sept., 1946, p. 50

Nikolay Tikhonov's development in the late twenties was complex and devious. Constantly on the lookout for new forms, he fell under a strong influence of Khlebnikov, Mayakovsky, and Pasternak. At the same time he tried to move closer to Soviet realities. Temperamentally romantic, he fell in love with the Soviet East, and many of his poems of this period have for their setting the Caucasus and central Asia. He was attracted both by their exoticism and by the pioneering efforts to bring modern civilization to Lermontov's "drowsy East." The old Orient satisfied his romantic craving for the picturesque, while the work of the new Soviet "Kulturträgers" appealed to his innate desire for adventure. Even when he voiced orthodox Communist sentiments and glorified the civilizing mission of the Soviets, he romanticized and hyperbolized the reality. . . .

Tikhonov's style is in keeping with his romantic realism: it is compact, robust, and picturesque; in its wise economy one feels the influence of his poetic training, of his Acmeist heritage. He is also in no small degree indebted to Kipling, both in the technique of his stories and in the spirit of romantic realism which pervades them. Like Kipling's, many of his stories deal with military life, and often their action is set on the eastern fringes of Russia. His characters also have a Kiplingesque touch.

Gleb Struve. *Soviet Russian Literature 1917–1950*
(Norman, Okla., University of Oklahoma Press, 1951),
pp. 179, 180–81

If I had to name the most complete individual I have met in the genera-tions of Soviet writers, I would have to name Nikolai Tikhonov. The marvel of his internal stability is reflected in the very countenance of this man. Since as far back as twenty years ago, he has looked the same: lean, light, gray-haired, with eyes flashing in the quick movement of the coarse, strong muscles on his face. The hollow bursts of Tikhonov's laughter echoed in our arguments at every meeting, and there was in them something militarily sudden, delighting, and irrevocable—like shots.

There was something military also in the way he read his poems to us. His short lines exploded steeply and terribly, resounding with the rumble deep in his rapidly breathing chest. Reading poetry, he always hurried, as if running and struggling toward the end, and, having finished, he glanced quickly at us, smiling and asking everyone impulsively, "Well?" If he himself found in his poems imperfection and failure, he was the first to laugh loudly, giving the tone to all of us, as if to say, "This is only an exercise; wait, I'll write it tomorrow for real!"

He flew forward precipitously, to newer and newer conquests, annihi-lating and swallowing a tremendous amount of the most varied material, so that the heaps of his observations, books, and experiences—the moun-tains of written-out paper—would be enough for an entire poetic school.

Konstantin Fedin. *Pisatel, iskusstvo, vremya*
(Moscow, Sovetski pisatel, 1957), pp. 216–17[†]

TOLSTOI, ALEKSEI (1883–1945)

The most salient feature in the personality of A. N. Tolstoy is a very curious combination of very great natural gifts and a complete absence of brains. As long as he simply and confidently surrenders to the flow of his natural creative force, he is a charming and unique writer; the moment he tries to express ideas, he becomes piteous. As he very seldom com-pletely refrains from ideas, very few of his writings are above censure. But for natural verve and for spontaneous force, he has few equals among contemporary writers, and is second perhaps to Andrey Bely alone. One of his best qualities is admirable, racy, unbookish Russian, learned in his

Samara home, and not so much influenced as let loose by the example of Remizov.

D. S. Mirsky. Contemporary Russian Literature
(New York, Knopf, 1926), p. 293

Tolstoi is the portrayer of the morals and manners not only of the land-owners in the Volga region but also of our intellectual society. Besides his short stories, he wrote novels about the intelligentsia on the eve of the revolution. His novel *Khozhdenie po mukam* (*Road to Calvary*), the greatest of all his works, is an objective, expressive artistic document of that epoch. The main characters of the novel are in part connected with the noblemen's manner of living but more with the new bourgeois city life. They are representatives of the well-to-do layers of the intelligentsia. The signs of decline and spiritual impoverishment are also present here. The people are living as if in a haze, not knowing what to do with themselves or what to expect from tomorrow. Grief, boredom, depression, the lack of ideas, the realization of their uselessness, naked individualism, the dead-end street feeling, the vague foreboding of the approaching end—these are their basic moods. The war infects them with chauvinism. They are looking for a way out of the war, but the passion for the war is not sincere in some and not lasting in others. The egoistic estate society, with its vices, perversions, neurasthenia, spicy banalities, and joyless existence, is depicted by the writer with expert mastery and knowledge. Tolstoi was less successful with the days of February and October, and his attempts to descend into the revolutionary underground seem quite unsuccessful to us. These chapters of the novel are rewritten in the new Soviet edition. . . .

Tolstoi approaches our Soviet way of life with the greatest circumspection and care. This caution is the proof of how hard it is for the writer of the old stock to reflect on and express the revolutionary present. Not without reason and not by accident does one find fantasy, adventure, relativity in his latest works, *Aelita, Bunt mashin* (*The Riot of Machines*), *Soyuz pyati* (*The Union Five*), and *Giperboloid inzhenera Garina* (*Hyperboloid*). [1926]

A. K. Voronsky. Literaturno-kriticheskie stati
(Moscow, Sovetski pisatel, 1963), pp. 386–87†

In some respects one gets [in *Khmuroe utro* (*Darkness and Dawn*)] a panoramic experience from this book, which is plainly written out of first-hand information concerning the scenes and people it describes. It is a book which gives some effect of size and very often some effect of life and movement. On the other hand, it cannot overcome a disposition to sprawl, which lessens its unity; and to clot, which lessens its vividness. . . .

[The author] has conveyed stress and chaos in literary terms, and though one will look in vain for the richness and vitality which makes Sholem Asch's *Three Cities* a much finer book on a subject much the same, *Darkness and Dawn* is still not negligible. Its impassioned subject-matter will not let it be.

Louis Kronenberger. NYT. March 29, 1936, p. 6

[*Pyotr Pervy* (*Peter the Great*)] has met with universal approbation, even on the part of Russian émigré critics. As a historical novel, laid in the early part of the eighteenth century, the story is less likely to provoke partisan prejudices. The personality of Peter the Great cannot help but arouse admiration and wonderment, with all his occasional coarseness and brutality. Perhaps only the last Mohicans of the Slavophils may still resent Peter's enforced westernization of Russia as a calamity and violation of the natural process of history. Merezhkovsky, in *Peter and Alexis*, gave a profoundly keen portrait of Peter, with his customary penchant for drawing parallels and contradictions. Tolstoy's Peter is not so neat an "arrangement." His Peter is hewed large and raw, a giant in stature, a savage child in his emotions, indomitable of will and impatient of contradictions, a statesman of vision tinkering at times with petty details, a crowned revolutionist forging his country ahead with utter contempt for slow evolution, for tradition and sentiment, for human life, his own life especially. But Tolstoy is a Soviet author, adhering to the platform of Socialist Realism. Consequently, the dominant figure of Peter is drawn against his social background, and is thus made more understandable, less of a violent freak of history. The keynote of the novel is struck at the outset, with the portrayal of the conditions of the serfs and the petty gentry. Throughout, one does not lose sight of the people, their economic and social misery. The policy of Peter is no longer regarded as a whim of a tyrant, but is a manifestation of his intuitive wisdom in attempting to civilize and industrialize Byzantine-Tartar Muscovy. Tolstoy's talent has steadily matured in the last ten years, and is in a position to cope with the complex task of reviving the age of Peter individually and collectively.

Alexander Kaun. BA. Summer, 1936, pp. 362–63

It took Tolstoy a long time to find a real place for himself in Soviet literature. He was always at his best in describing real life, especially the life he knew well. His pictures of the decaying gentry in *Khromoy barin* (*The Lame Squire*), and in numerous pre-Revolutionary stories and plays, were his best work. His post-Revolutionary work was handicapped, for a long time, by his inability to hit upon a congenial theme. Fundamentally a man of the past, a cross between a country gentleman and a literary bohemian, he felt lost in the melting pot of post-Revolutionary Russia.

As a former *émigré* he had to tread warily. Reluctant to draw upon the recent past, he wisely abstained at first from portraying and interpreting the unfamiliar present. Hence his escapes into the realm of fantasy and attempts to clothe fantastic plots with revolutionary ideas. In *Aelita* (1922), a combination of a Wellsian scientific romance with a Russian psychological novel, the plot revolves round the arrival of a Soviet scientific expedition on Mars and an attempt to start a social revolution there. Upon this social fantasy are superimposed two other themes: of love being stronger than death or than any sense of revolutionary duty, and of elemental, irrational revolt.

> Gleb Struve. *Soviet Russian Literature 1917–1950*
> (Norman, Okla., University of Oklahoma Press,
> 1951), p. 135

All writers know how intractable their characters can get. "Right in the middle of my writing I never know what my characters will do or say the next minute and I watch them with amazement," Alexei Tolstoi used to say. . . .

Alexei Tolstoi had to have a ream of good-quality paper lying on his desk before he could settle down to write. And he usually began writing a story with nothing but one little detail in his mind. That detail would set him off on a train of events—it was like the unravelling of a magic ball of thread.

As I have already said, he possessed great powers of improvisation, his thoughts running ahead of his words and flowing so fast that he had a hard time keeping up with them. If he ever had to strain himself to write, he ceased writing at once. [1955]

> Konstantin Paustovski. *The Golden Rose* (Moscow,
> Foreign Language Publishing House, n.d.), pp. 60, 137

When Tolstoi was still working on his novel [*The Road to Calvary*], he was involved in a controversy about the epic principles of his work. The editor of the magazine *Novy mir* concluded from the first parts of the novel that the author was still in the "Camp of the Whites" and that he was thus not capable of depicting the heroism of the civil war objectively. In his answer, Tolstoi defends his right to depict the historical occurrences objectively. He writes: "We know that the Revolution was victorious. You, however, write that I should show the fanfare and the defeated army from the very beginning. I refuse to write the novel according to such a plan. That would only create one more of the numerous posters, which don't convince anyone anymore, above all, certainly not the youth. You want to start the novel with the conclusion."

In writing the novel, Tolstoi had to consider the inner laws governing the creation of an epic—this besides the historical occurrences of the year 1918. In the letter mentioned above, Tolstoi also points to the following prerequisite: "Comments regarding the style and the spirit of the novel. The author is on the side of the proletariat; consequently, he must always view the pathos—the final victory, the Leninistic conception of the events, the total objectivity of the individual parts, that is, the texture of the novel, the texture of tragedy—in the participating persons. He may never simply watch from the side." The author emphasizes here that he never forgets the protagonists and that he sees everything with their eyes whenever he creates any scene or detail. Although Tolstoi was concerned with depicting a complete picture of the most important events of 1918 in his novel *Vosemnadtsaty god* (*The Year 1918*), the plot is nonetheless determined by the fates of the main characters. Thus, the historical events always occur in their significance to the characters.

Harri Jünger. *Zeitschrift für Slawistik*.
Fall, 1958, p. 574†

The publication, section by section, of Alexei Tolstoy's *The Road to Calvary* spans the full era between the wars; the first volume appeared in 1920, the last in 1940. For this reason it is a laboratory specimen of the important changes in Soviet writing, most notably in the matter of the writer's control over his material. It may be that Alexei Tolstoy simply changed his mind, but it must be pointed out, also, that in doing so he has betrayed the vital interests of his profession and capitulated to the political invaders.

The novel has no hard center of moral purpose, nor any strong inner necessity of development. The mass of material might have been shaped to many ends; individual destinies, since they are not closely interlocked, might have been worked out in a number of ways. Only one thing is certain: the final solution Tolstoy did impose on the novel is extremely questionable, because it is introduced in the last third of the book in total disregard of what has gone before.

Despite its shortcomings, in its first two-thirds the work exhibits a number of the traditional attributes of the novel as an independent comment on experience. Tolstoy's interest in his material seems largely documentary. Thus, Part I stands as a vivid sketch of the St. Petersburg intelligentsia on the eve of the revolution; Part II is an attempt, like many others, to reflect the chaos of civil war itself. In his investigation on this not too profound level, Tolstoy has assembled a large group of sharply individualized characters, who embody, among other things, a number of contrasting attitudes toward the revolution.

Rufus W. Mathewson. *The Positive Hero in Russian*
Literature (New York, Columbia University Press,
1958), pp. 310–11

Tolstoi worked not like an architect but like a sculptor. He abandoned planning his novels or stories very early in his career. When he began, he often was not sure how he would continue. Many times he told me that he did not yet know how his hero would end up or what would happen on the next page. His characters came to life slowly, were developed along with the plot, and imposed the story on the author. (This refers to Tolstoi's late period.)

There are writers who are thinkers; Tolstoy as a writer was a painter. . . . He had a remarkable talent for saying what he wanted to say by images, narratives, pictures, but he could not think abstractly. He always failed when he tried to imbue his novels or stories with a universal idea. He could not be separated from the element of art, just as a fish cannot live without water. His best works—*Zavolzhe* (*Beyond the Volga*), *Detstvo Nikity* (*Nikita's Childhood*), and, above all, *Pyotr Pervy*—possess an inner freedom. The author is not limited by a plot; he narrates. He is particularly powerful when his tale is rooted either in his own childhood or in Russian history, where he felt himself at home and as confident as in the room of a house in which he lived.

Ilya Ehrenburg. Novy mir. Sept., 1960, p. 125[†]

Tolstoy secured a place for himself with Stalin through conforming to the dictator's literary tastes and prejudices, and he made no effort to defend himself or other writers against the insane persecutions of the thirties. Ehrenburg tells of Tolstoy's behavior when in 1936 the sudden onset of a campaign against "formalist distortions" and "cynicism" created tortured consternation in the whole writers' community. Tolstoy's reaction was one of decisive and complete acquiescence in the charges and ready repentance for having himself written a "formalistic" play. Ehrenburg explains that Tolstoy wanted only "peace and quiet," and implies that Tolstoy would go to great lengths to achieve them. . . . How far he would go became clear in 1937 when, as insurance against the purge, he produced the novel *Bread* [*Khleb*], which falsified history in order to present Stalin as the heroic defender of Tsaritsin (Stalingrad) during the Civil War. Stalin's successors have stigmatized this work as shameless flattery, and they have even changed the name of the city.

Edward J. Brown. Russian Literature Since the
Revolution (New York, Crowell-Collier, 1963),
pp. 256–57

TOLSTOI, LEV   (1828–1910)

Leo Tolstoi's recent volume on Art closes significantly the series of his arraignments of what we have been pleased to call civilisation. Like all his later works, whether treatise or play or novel or parable, this volume on art shows Tolstoi in his character of lay prophet, with all its powers and all its weaknesses. For it would seem—we notice it in two other great lay prophets, Carlyle and Ruskin—that the gift of seeing through the accepted falsehoods of the present, and foretelling the improbable realities of the future, can arise only in creatures too far overpowered by their own magnificent nature to understand other men's ways of being and thinking; in minds so bent upon how things should be as to lose sight of how things are and how things came to be. While Carlyle, embodying his passionate instincts in historical narrative, was moderated at least by his knowledge of the past and of the consequent origin and necessity of the present; while Ruskin, accepting the whole moral and religious training of his times, was in so far in touch with his contemporaries; Tolstoi has broken equally with everything, if ever he had really much to break with. Destitute of all historic sense, impervious to any form of science, and accepting the Gospel only as the nominal text for a religion of his own making, he has become incapable of admitting more than one side to any question, more than one solution to any difficulty, more than one factor in any phenomenon. He is destitute of all sense of cause and effect, all acquiescence in necessity, and all real trustfulness in the ways of the universe. For him most things are wrong, wholly, utterly wrong; their wrongness has never originated in any right, and never will be transformed into right until—well, until mankind be converted to Tolstoi's theory and practice. Economic and domestic arrangements, laws, politics, religion, all wrong; and now, art also.

Vernon Lee. *QR*. April, 1900, p. 359

In all literature there is no writer equal to Tolstoy in depicting the human body. Though he misuses repetitions, he usually attains what he needs by them, and he never suffers from the *longueurs* so common to other vigorous masters. He is accurate, simple, and as short as possible, selecting only the few, small, unnoticed facial or personal features and producing them, not all at once, but gradually and one by one, distributing them over the whole course of the story, weaving them into the living web of the action. Thus at the first appearance of old Prince Bolkonski we get only a fleeting sketch, in four or five lines, "the short figure of the old man with the powdered wig, small *dry hands* and grey, overhanging brows that sometimes, when he was roused, dimmed the flash of the clever youthful eyes." When he sits down to the lathe "by the movement of his small foot, the firm pressure of his thin veined hand" (we already know his hands are dry, but Tolstoy loves to go back to the hands of his heroes), "you could still see in the Prince the obstinate and long-enduring force of hale old age." When he talks to his daughter, Princess Maria, "he shows in a cold smile, his strong but yellowish teeth." When he sits at the table and bends over her, beginning the usual lesson in geometry, she "feels herself surrounded with the snuffy, old-age, acrid savour of her father," which had long been a sign to her. There he is all before us as if alive, height, build, hands, feet, eyes, gestures, brows, even the peculiar savour belonging to each man. . . .

Tolstoy is the greatest depictor of this physico-spiritual region in the natural man; that side of the flesh which approaches the spirit, and that side of the spirit which approaches the flesh, the mysterious border-region where the struggle between the animal and the God in man takes place. Therein lies the struggle and the tragedy of his own life. He is a "man of the senses," half-heathen, half-Christian; neither to the full.

In proportion as he recedes from this neutral ground in either direction, it matters not whether towards the region of the cold "pre-animal" Nature, that region which *seems* inorganic, insentient, inanimate, "material" (the terrible and beatific calm of which Turgeniev and Pushkin have told so well); or as he essays the opposite region; human spirituality, almost set free from the body, released from animal nature, the region of pure thought (the passionate workings of which are so well embodied by Dostoevsky and Tiutchev) the power of artistic delineation in Tolstoy decreases, and in the end collapses, so that there are limits which are for him wholly unattainable. But within the limits of the purely natural man he is the supreme artist of the world.

In other provinces of Art, for instance the painting of the Italian Renaissance and the sculpture of the ancient Greeks, there have been artists who with greater completeness than Tolstoy depicted the bodily man. The music of the present day, and in part the literature, penetrate us more deeply. But nowhere, and at no time, has the "natural man" appeared with such startling truth and nakedness as he appears in the creations of Tolstoy.

Dmitri Merezhkovski. *Tolstoi as Man and Artist,*
With an Essay on Dostoievski (New York,
G. P. Putnam's Sons, 1902), pp. 174–75, 187–88

Tolstoy is to be congratulated on the vigorous way in which he clears the ground at the beginning of *What is Art?* [*Chto takoe iskusstvo*]. We were more than weary of a hundred different kinds of "beauty," of "ideals" and "theories" and "manners." Consequently it was refreshing to come across a simple definition, viz. that art is the expression of human feelings with a view to infect others with like feelings,—the feelings themselves being good, bad, or indifferent. There is little to quarrel with, so far; but when Tolstoy begins to expound his position, we soon find cause to dissent. How are we to distinguish good art from bad art? By "religious perception," which signifies an understanding of the meaning of life; in other words, a knowledge of the highest good. Any picture, poem, or statue that fails to minister to this end is bad art. Perhaps so, but much depends on the accuracy of the words as here used. The "meaning of life" and the "highest good" are elastic terms, and novels which to our mind minister to both would be condemned by Tolstoy. The plain truth is that with him good art is an exploitation of the sense of brotherhood and mutual helpfulness, and all else is bad art. If a man has a feeling to transmit to his fellows, he is bound by the law of the greatest number, that is, he must simplify his feeling and rob it of every trace of personality so as to make it plain to those who are most numerous,—the working classes. In itself the aim is morally commendable, but it is impossible of accomplishment, and for that reason is absurd. An art whose sole advantage lies in its being appreciated by the greatest number of people is not an art that is likely to live; it is against facts as we know them. Moreover, it is hardly the kind of doctrine that should come from a man who elsewhere speaks of "the narrow-minded people who compose the multitude." And if these people are the best critics, where is there one among their number who can write an analysis like Tolstoy's *Guy de Maupassant?*

T. S. Knowlson. *Leo Tolstoy*
(New York, Frederick Warne, 1904), p. 142

In *War and Peace* [*Voina i mir*] we are conscious that Tolstoy's proud nature, the "Lucifer" type in him, is searching for another ideal; and that in the character of Pierre Bezuhov he is already setting up before us the ideal of Ivan Durak as the model which we should seek to imitate. And in Pierre Bezuhov we feel that there is something of Tolstoy himself. Manners change but man, faced by the problem of life, is the same throughout all ages; and, whether consciously or unconsciously, Tolstoy proves this in writing *Anna Karenina.* Here again, on a large canvas, we see unrolled before us the contemporary life of the upper classes in Russia, in St. Petersburg, and in the country, with the same sharpness of vision, which seizes every outward detail, and reveals every recess of the heart and mind. Nearly all characters in all fiction seem bookish beside those of Tolstoy. His men and women are so real and so true that, even if his psychological analysis of them may sometimes err and go wrong from its oversubtlety and its desire to explain too much, the characters themselves seem to correct this automatically, as though they were independent of their creator. He creates a character and gives it life. He may theorize on a character, just as he might theorize on a person in real life; and he may theorize wrong, simply because sometimes no theorizing is necessary, and the very fact of a theory being set down in words may give a false impression; but, as soon as the character speaks and acts, it speaks and acts in the manner which is true to itself, and corrects the false impression of the theory, just as though it were an independent person over whom the author had no control.

Maurice Baring. *Landmarks in Russian Literature*
(London, Methuen, 1910), p. 57

"The Kreuzer Sonata" ["Kreitserova sonata"] shows no diminution of Tolstoi's realistic power: the opening scenes on the train, the analysis of the hero's mind during the early years of his married life, and especially the murder, all betray the familiar power of simplicity and fidelity to detail. The passage of the blade through the corset and then into something soft has that sensual realism so characteristic of all Tolstoi's descriptions of bodily sensations. The book is a work of art, and contains many reflections and bitter accusations against society that are founded on the truth.

The moral significance of the story is perfectly clear—that men who are constantly immoral before marriage need not expect happiness in married life. It is a great pity that Tolstoi did not let the powerful little novel speak for itself, and that he allowed himself to be goaded into an explanatory and defensive commentary by the thousands of enquiring letters from foolish readers. Much of the commentary contains sound advice, but it leads off into that *reductio ad absurdum* so characteristic of Russian thought.

Many of the tracts and parables that Tolstoi wrote are true works of art, with a Biblical directness and simplicity of style. Their effect outside of Russia is caused fully as much by their literary style as by their teaching. I remember an undergraduate, who, reading "Where Love is there God is Also" ["Gde lyubov tam i Bog"], said that he was tremendously excited when the old shoemaker lost his spectacles, and had no peace of mind till he found them again. This is unconscious testimony to Tolstoi's power of making trivial events seem real.

The long novel, *Resurrection* [*Voskresene*], is, as Mr. Maude, the English translator, shows, not merely a story, but a general summary of all the final conclusions about life reached by its author. The English volume actually has an *Index to Social Questions, Types*, etc., giving the pages where the author's views on all such topics are expressed in the book. Apart from the great transformation wrought in the character of the hero, which is the motive of the work, there are countless passages which show the genius of the author, still burning brightly in his old age. The difference between the Easter kiss and the kiss of lust is one of the most powerful instances of analysis, and may be taken as a symbol of the whole work. And the depiction of the sportsman's feelings when he brings down a wounded bird, half shame and half rage, will startle and impress every man who has carried a gun.

William Lyon Phelps. *Essays on Russian Novelists*
(New York, Macmillan, 1911), pp. 212–13

[Tolstoi] spoke marvellously about the past, and best of all about Turgenev. Fet, he always mentioned with a good-humoured chuckle, always remembered something comic about him; of Nekrasov he spoke coldly, sceptically, but he spoke about writers in general as if they were his children, and he a father who knew all their shortcomings, but was defiantly determined to make more of the bad in them than of the good. And whenever he spoke derogatorily about anyone I always felt as if he were bestowing alms upon his hearers; it was disconcerting to listen to his criticisms, one lowered one's eyes involuntarily beneath his keen smile —and nothing remained in one's memory. . . .

The inexpressible individual charm of his speech, so incorrect on the surface, with such incessant repetitions of certain words, so saturated with a peasant-like simplicity, could only be understood by those who watched him talk. The force of his words lay not only in his intonations and in the liveliness of his features, but in the play and gleam of his eyes, the most eloquent eyes I have ever seen anywhere. L. N. had a thousand eyes in one pair. [1919]

Maksim Gorky. *Literary Portraits* (Moscow, Foreign
Language Publishing House, n.d.), pp. 75, 79

Tolstoy began as the liquidator of Romantic poetics and the destroyer of established canons. He changed the matter, the devices, and the form of art. In place of a refined metaphoric style, in place of emphatic musical syntax, Tolstoy used a plain but complex, almost awkward sentence; in place of a rambling stream of feelings and emotionally colored descriptions, the detailed description of minutiae and the analysis and exfoliation of spiritual life; in place of complex plots, the parallelism of several lines, barely connected but not intertwined.

From the very beginning Tolstoy was conscious of himself against a background of disintegrating romantic art. Bypassing the generation of the fathers, he went back to the grandfathers, to the eighteenth century. His mentors and inspirers were Sterne, Rousseau, Bernadin de Saint-Pierre, Franklin, Buffon, and Goldsmith. *Childhood* [*Detstvo*] reflects the influence of Töpfer, brought up during that very eighteenth century; in the *Sevastopol Sketches* [*Sevastopolskie rasskazy*] Tolstoy follows in the wake of Stendhal—"the last man of the eighteenth century." A great deal of Tolstoy is determined by the battle with romantic clichés. "Realism" is only a motivation for that battle. It is a motto continually repeated when literary schools change, and continually changing its meaning. Tolstoy wanted to write in a way different from that of his fathers. [1924]

B. M. Eikhenbaum. In *Tolstoy: A Collection of*
Critical Essays, Ralph E. Matlaw, ed.
(Englewood Cliffs, N.J., Prentice-Hall, 1967), p. 52

What about *War and Peace*? That is certainly great, that likewise empha- sizes the effects of time and the waxing and waning of a generation. Tol- stoy, like Bennett, has the courage to show us people getting old—the partial decay of Nicolay and Natasha is really more sinister than the com- plete decay of Constance and Sophia: more of our own youth seems to have perished in it. Then why is *War and Peace* not depressing? Probably because it has extended over space as well as over time, and the sense of space until it terrifies us is exhilarating, and leaves behind it an effect like music. After one has read *War and Peace* for a bit, great chords be- gin to sound, and we cannot say exactly what struck them. They do not arise from the story, though Tolstoy is quite as interested in what comes next as Scott, and quite as sincere as Bennett. They do not come from the episodes nor yet from the characters. They come from the immense area of Russia, over which episodes and characters have been scattered, from the sum-total of bridges and frozen rivers, forests, roads, gardens, fields, which accumulate grandeur and sonority after we have passed them. Many novelists have the feeling for place—Five Towns, Auld Reekie, and so on. Very few have the sense of space, and the possession of it ranks high in Tolstoy's divine equipment. Space is the lord of *War and Peace*, not time.

E. M. Forster. *Aspects of the Novel* (New York,
Harcourt, Brace & World, 1927), pp. 57–58

Tolstoi remains true to himself to the end. The internal world of the aris- tocrat was always in the center of his attention. For him, the peasantry is not a social category. It is not an independent world. He penetrates its nature independently of his own circle. He sees the peasantry only in relationship to the lord. One thinks that the peasant is only important and of value to him because he serves to correct the lord. He is a salutary force for the depraved and fashionable world. Even fifty years ago, Tkachev, a precursor of Marxist criticism, though in an overexaggerated and biting form, in essence noted correctly this characteristic in the work of Tolstoi: "All of the heroes of Tolstoi's novel *Anna Karenina*—the Levins, the Vronskis, the Oblonskis, the Karenins—are people who are insured with material adequacy and sufficiently limited in their moral and mental de- velopment, who are exclusively taken up with their personal interests and who live outside the common movement of life, who do not feel on their own moral and intellectual level any of the effects of time; if they do sense these, they attempt to relate to these effects as if they were nonsense, without any essential significance." One of the most beloved of Tolstoi's heroes, the gentleman farmer Levin, is dedicated to the cares of agriculture, but these heeds are "not particularly difficult for him, and it seems they serve more as entertainment than as labor essential for living." The running of the estate is not work that Levin must fulfill in order to maintain his existence. Work for him is a pleasant way of spending time, unsteady, unsystematic, having in itself the fascination of aesthetic sensations.

Despite the biting form of the criticism and the failure to see the positive values in Tolstoi, Tkachev in essence is correct. The simplified heroes of Tolstoi are not peasants and cannot become peasants, for they are materially secure. Peasant labor, for them, does not represent vital necessity. The tide of events proved a long time ago the bankruptcy of Tolstoi's social ideals. History did not heed his direction. The Russian people did not seek to learn from the Karatayevs and Akins. No humility; no submissive fulfillment of any kind of vital task regardless of what the task may be—these are slogans of our day. The decade following the death of Tolstoi developed other slogans. The inexorable struggle for the rebuilding of life, the forced overthrow of the capitalist order built on exploitation, and the actual transfer of the land and means of production to the workers—these were slogans which the proletarians brought forth.

P. S. Kogan. *Novy mir*. Sept., 1928, pp. 190–91[†]

[Tolstoi's] seekers are pitiable. Clumsy, verbose, inconsequential. That young *alter ego* of Tolstoy, Olenin—what a pale, flaccid, futile dullard, by the side of the robust Cossacks! How pitiful the would-be-Christian, Olenin, face to face with the magnificent Pagan, Eroshka! Pierre Bezukhov is lovable as an awkward, near-sighted, stooping bear, but how tedious when he has been infected with the Tolstoyan virus and waxes introspective. Compared with the splendid animal, Count Vronsky, the Tolstoyan Levin is a depressing bore. The chapters on his tortuous quest and conversion form the most anaemic part of Anna Karénin. As to Nekhludov, in *Resurrection*, he is a *débâcle*. One must be naïve not to realize the irony and the bitterness in the title of this novel, the last to appear in its author's lifetime. Nekhludov's efforts to be Tolstoyan makes him ridiculous and repellant not only to the convicted prostitute, Katyusha Maslova. In his unfinished play, *Light Shineth in Darkness* [*I svet vo tme svetit*], Tolstoy exhibits without pity for himself the baneful effect of his conversion on all who come near him. Bernard Shaw sees in the plot "the transfiguration of the great prophet into a clumsy mischievous cruel fool."

Potent contradictions. How much nearer and more precious he is to us because of his failure to attain perfection. Because of the indecisive battle between Dionysus and Christ, perpetually waged in the arena of his fearless mind. Because of the frequent triumph of his sense of proportion over his sense of righteousness. Because of the immeasurable superiority of Tolstoy the artist over Tolstoy the preacher.

Alexander Kaun. *Dial.* Sept., 1928, p. 233

The Homeric, the typically-epic, was perhaps more marked in Tolstoy than in any other man of genius. In his work is the heaving might and rhythmic uniformity of the sea, its pristine vigour, its native pungency, imperishable health, and deathless realism. For surely it is permissible to see and feel these things as one, health and realism—the world of plastic form, of instinct, of high kinship with nature on the one hand, contrasting with, as I once tried to suggest in a more comprehensive way, the world of hyper-susceptibility and mental aristocracy, Schiller's world of the ideal, Dostoevsky's apocalyptic world of shadows. Goethe and Tolstoy —when their names were first linked together in criticism, surprise and doubt were aroused; but recent psychological studies have enabled us to take such comparisons for granted. To elaborate the parallel beyond the generically-typical would be pedantic caprice. We need not dwell upon the too obvious and predetermined differences of mind, country, or period. As soon as we advert to culture—that formula which implies nature's groping after mind and the inevitable impulse of mind towards nature— we must abandon the too facile analogy. We ought to be honest enough to admit that to those who possess Goethe, Tolstoy's absurd, naïvely tragic reaching after culture must present the spectacle at once pathetic and sublime, of a child-like barbarian's noble but futile striving towards what is true and human.

Nevertheless, this very Titanic helplessness, recalling the swollen, straining muscles of one of Michael Angelo's tortured creations, lends tremendous moral force to him as an artist. As a story-teller he is without equal; his art, even when he no longer had use for it, except as a means of furthering a dubious and depressing kind of moralizing, affords to any receptive talent (there can be no other) unfailing strength, refreshment, and elemental joy. Not at all with a view to imitating, for who could imitate? He has no following which could accurately be termed a school. Tolstoy's influence, indeed, whether on the spirit or form of a work, makes itself felt in very different ways, and above all, in writings quite unrelated to his own. But even as he, an Antaeus, received fresh creative strength from each contact with earth, so the world of his mighty art is to us, earth and nature—a reincarnation of itself. To reread him, to let that preternaturally sharp gaze of the lower animals cast its spell on us, the force of his imagery, and limpid clarity of style untinctured with mysticism, again so reminiscent of Goethe, is to find release from every phase of artificiality and useless frivolity, a return to what in each of us is fundamentally wholesome.

Thomas Mann. *Dial*. Dec., 1928, pp. 454–55

The delight of Tolstoy's plays is in their refusal to allow any discussion of them to be imprisoned by the walls of the theatre. They are a perpetual reminder of the truth, to which the routine of playgoing often gives the appearance of a lie, that the drama is not a domestic slave of greed and cowardly thinking, but a companion of philosophy whom it is no dishonour to serve. So Tolstoy regarded it. He was not a "man of the theatre," a worshipper of a life within life, a twister of puppets into emotional positions which can be enjoyed only by gross insensitiveness or by a special sophistication. To him the drama was a means of expressing spiritual truths which could not otherwise be so completely or forcefully expressed; he demanded of it the particular justification by which alone, in his view, could any art be justified. . . .

Criticism of Tolstoy cannot rest on a contemporary theatrical basis; every attempt to make it do so ends in disaster to the critic. There were for him, as Mr. Granville-Barker says [in his introduction], "three necessary virtues, and three only, in artistic conception and expression—individuality, clarity, and sincerity." In *The Light Shines in Darkness* [*I svet vo tme svetit*]—and judgment of his dramatic theory stands or falls by judgment of this play—the first and the last qualities were abundantly present; and the second, clarity, was lacking only where Tolstoy's own view of the duty of Man was not yet clear. By his own standard, then, the piece, though its last act was never written, is indeed a masterpiece. But is it a "great play"? Mr. Granville-Barker says "No"—the characters do not "get hold" of him; that is his standard and the standard of us all when we visit the theatre as it is; and it is true that to our minds, long accustomed to dramatists whose whole purpose is to create an intimate, human illusion, Nicholas Ivanovich is "aloof," as Matrëna and Nikita in the earlier play are not. But does not his aloofness spring from the same qualities in the play and the same distortion in ourselves which make the figures of Greek tragedy seem remote from a modern audience? Are we because of it to condemn the play and Tolstoy's reversionary theory of religious art? It is better to condemn, to say frankly that the play does not "get hold" of us, than to twist it beyond recognition and then call it a masterpiece; but the wiser course is to recognize Tolstoy's affinity with the religious and philosophical dramatists of the past, and to estimate his greatness, so far as may now be possible, by their standard rather than by our own.

TLS. Jan. 10, 1929, p. 25

Eight years after "The Death of Ivan Ilych" ["Smert Ivana Ilicha"], Tolstoy wrote "Master and Man" ["Khozyain i rabotnik"]. These two stories
are, in spite of their surface dissimilarity, so intimately connected with one
another that they seem to be only variations on a single theme. Since Tolstoy had been forced out of the common way by the terrors which he had
described to us in "The Diary of a Madman" ["Zapiski sumasshedshego"],
one single thought, one single problem pursued and obsessed him. If Plato
is right in saying philosophers "concern themselves with nothing but dying
and death" . . . then we must admit that few of our contemporaries have
so wholly devoted themselves to philosophy as Tolstoy. Tolstoy begins
by describing to us, in these two stories, a man in the ordinary circumstances of existence, circumstances which are well known and universally
admitted. Then suddenly, in "Master and Man" (the catastrophe is even
less prepared than in "The Death of Ivan Ilych"), he transports his characters to that solitude which could not have been more complete in the
bowels of the earth or in the depths of the sea. . . .

The end of "Master and Man" turned out to be a prophecy. Leo Nico-
laievich Tolstoy also ended his days on the steppe, in the midst of storms
and tempests. Thus destiny will end. The glory of Tolstoy was spread
abroad throughout the whole world while he still lived. And yet, in spite
of that, soon after his eightieth birthday, which was celebrated in the
four quarters of the globe, in every language—an honour which no one before his day had enjoyed—he yet left all and fled from his home one
dark night, not knowing whither or wherefore. His works, his glory, all
these were a misery to him, a burden too heavy for him to bear. He
seems, with trembling, impatient hand, to be tearing off the marks of the
sage, the master, the honoured teacher. That he might present himself
before the Supreme Judge with unweighted soul, he had to forget and
renounce all his magnificent past.

Leo Shestov. *In Job's Balances*
(London, J. M. Dent and Sons, 1932), pp. 64–65

When in 1898 Tolstoy resumed "artistic" work with the writing of *Resurrection*, the entire family—and even several of the guests—were pressed
into the work of copying and re-copying the manuscript. Tolstoy would
emerge from his study to give instructions, would retire, the family would
copy for dear life—and the next morning the copying would have to be
done afresh. The Countess Alexandra was too young at this time to
share in "the common work," as she calls it, and had to content herself
with manipulating a screw press to make copies of her father's letters.
Her opportunity came later, when one of his recurring dangerous illnesses
attacked him and she accompanied him to the Crimea. From that point
onwards she did not spare herself in her devotion to him. The copying

of his manuscripts, never an easy task, became increasingly difficult as time went on; he began to write less and less legibly, in unfinished words and without punctuation, making use of scraps of paper torn from letters, cutting the sheets into strips whenever he wished to transpose sentences, and revising endlessly. The copyist herself was forced to use scissors and paste, but, "if he had written a long article, I used to work all the evening, part of the night, and early the following morning, to have it ready to return to him for his next day's session."

TLS. July 13, 1933, p. 473

In the four-and-fiftieth year of a life that was exercising a worldwide influence, Tolstoy for the first time perceived this great Nothing, its recognition being his share in the universal human lot. Thenceforward to the day of his death, he continued to stare unceasingly into the vacancy, the impalpable void that lies behind existence. But even when facing that awesome prospect, the vision of Tolstoy was unclouded; it was still the vision of a man who for wisdom and spirituality was unmatched in our day. His titanic energy was unrivalled in the struggle with the unnamable, in the contest with the primal terror of mortal man; never did anyone more resolutely than he contrapose to the question which destiny asks of man, the question which man asks of destiny. No one ever suffered more intensely than he from the empty and soul-cramping prospect of the Beyond; no one endured the suffering with more splendid fortitude, since in him the clear and bold and determined observation of the artist was sustained by a virile consciousness which enabled him to look into the black vacancy undismayed. Leo Tolstoy was the most vigilant, the most sincere, the most incorruptible personality in modern art and literature; and never for a moment did he blench as he faced the tragedy of existence. Nothing could have been more heroic than his endeavour to give form and meaning to the incomprehensible, and to discover a core of truth in the unavoidable. [1935]

Stefan Zweig. Master Builders
(New York, Viking Press, 1939), p. 762

To call War and Peace an historical novel of the classical type shows how important it is not to interpret this term in a narrow literary-historical or formal-artistic sense. In contrast to important writers like Pushkin, Manzoni or Balzac, no direct, literary influence of Scott is traceable in Tolstoy. Nor as far as I know did Tolstoy ever study Scott very thoroughly. He created an historical novel of a unique kind out of the real conditions of life in this transitional period, and only in terms of the *most general and ultimate* creative principles does it constitute a brilliant renewal and development of Scott's classical type of historical novel. This unifying, ultimate principle is that of *popular character*. Apart from Balzac and Stendhal, Tolstoy also had a very high regard for Flaubert and Maupassant as writers. But the real and decisive features of his art go back to the classical period of bourgeois realism, for the social and ideological spring of his personality draw their strength from a deep bond with the central problems of national life during a great transitional period and his art still has the contradictorily progressive character of this period as its central theme.

War and Peace is the modern epopee of popular life even more decisively than the work of Scott or Manzoni. The depiction of popular life is broader, more colourful, richer in characters. The emphasis on popular life as the real basis of historical happenings is more conscious. Indeed, this manner of presentation acquires a polemical accent in Tolstoy which it did not and could not have in the first classics of the historical novel. The latter portrayed above all the *connection;* the historical events emerged as the crowning peaks of the contradictory, vying forces in popular life. (It is a consequence of the special development of Italy that certain historical events were presented by Manzoni in a purely negative way, as disturbances of popular life.) At the heart of Tolstoy is the contradicition between the protagonists of history and the living forces of popular life. He shows that those who despite the great events in the forefront of history, go on living their normal, private and egoistic lives are really furthering the true (unconscious, unknown) development, while the consciously acting "heroes" of history are ludicrous and harmful puppets.

This basic conception of history determines the greatness and limitation of Tolstoy's work. The individual lives of the characters unfold with a richness and liveliness scarcely equalled before in world literature. But while they are aroused, while their sympathies may be excited by the events in the foreground, they are never wholly absorbed by these events. The historical concreteness of feelings and thoughts, the historical genuineness of the peculiar quality of reaction, in sufferings and deeds, to the outer world—all this is on a magnificent level. But the basic Tolstoyan idea—that these individual strivings, spontaneous in their operation, unconscious of their significance and consequences, which together constitute popular forces, equally spontaneous in their operation, that these strivings really motivate the course of history—this idea remains problematic. [1937]

Georg Lukacs. The Historical Novel
(London, Merlin Press, 1962), pp. 86–87

If there is one notion which represents what Tolstoy is up to in his novels —emphatically in *Anna Karenina* and *War and Peace*—it is this: He exposes his created men and women to the "terrible ambiguity of an immediate experience" (Jung's phrase in his *Psychology and Religion*), and then, by the mimetic power of his imagination, expresses their reactions and responses to that experience. Some reactions are merely protective and make false responses; some reactions are so deep as to amount to a change in the phase of being and make honest responses. The reactions are mechanical or instinctive, the responses personal or spiritual. But both the reactions and the responses have to do with that force greater than ourselves, outside ourselves, and working on ourselves, which whether we call it God or Nature is the force of life, what is shaped or misshaped, construed or misconstrued, in the process of living. Both each individual life and also that life in fellowship which we call society are so to speak partial incarnations of that force; but neither is ever complete; thus the great human struggle, for the individual or for the society, is so to react and so to respond to "the terrible ambiguity of an immediate experience" as to approach the conditions of rebirth, the change of heart, or even the fresh start. Tragedy comes about from the failure to apprehend the character or the direction of that force, either by an exaggeration of the self alone or of the self in society. That is why in Tolstoy the peasants, the simple family people, and the good-natured wastrels furnish the background and the foils for the tragedy, for these move according to the momentum of things, and although they are by no means complete incarnations of the force behind the momentum are yet in an equal, rough relation to it. The others, the tragic figures, move rather, by their own mighty effort, in relation, reaction, response to that force, some with its momentum, some against it; some falsifying it in themselves, some falsifying it in society, but each a special incarnation of it; some cutting their losses; some consolidating their gains; some balancing, some teetering, in a permanent labor of rebirth. There is thus at work in the novels of Tolstoy a kind of dialectic of incarnation: the bodying forth in aesthetic form by contrasted human spirits of "the terrible ambiguity of an immediate experience" through their reactions and responses to it. It is this dialectic which gives buoyancy and sanity to Tolstoy's novels. [1950]

R. P. Blackmur. *Eleven Essays in the European Novel*
(New York, Harcourt, Brace & World, 1964), pp. 3–4

No author who has ever lived has shown such power of insight into the variety of life—the differences, the contrasts, the collisions of persons and things and situations, each apprehended in its absolute uniqueness and conveyed with a degree of directness and a precision of concrete imagery to be found in no other writer. No one has ever excelled Tolstoy in expressing the specific flavour, the exact quality of a feeling—the degree of its "oscillation," the ebb and flow, the minute movements (which Turgenev mocked as a mere trick on his part)—the inner and outer texture and "feel" of a look, a thought, a pang of sentiment, no less than that of the specific pattern of a situation, or an entire period, continuous segments of lives of individuals, families, communities, entire nations. The celebrated life-likeness of every object and every person in his world derives from this astonishing capacity of presenting every ingredient of it in its fullest individual essence, in all its many dimensions, as it were; never as a mere datum, however vivid, within some stream of consciousness, with blurred edges, an outline, a shadow, an impressionistic representation: nor yet calling for, and dependent on, some process of reasoning in the mind of the reader; but always as a solid object, seen simultaneously from near and far, in natural, unaltering daylight from all possible angles of vision, set in an absolutely specific context in time and space—an event fully present to the senses or the imagination in all its facets, with every nuance sharply and firmly articulated.

Isaiah Berlin. The Hedgehog and the Fox
(New York, Simon and Schuster, 1953), pp. 39–40

When a visitor to Tolstoi's home in Yasnaya Polyana told the great writer that he had been cruel to make the lovely Anna Karenina throw herself under a moving train, he replied: "What you say reminds me of a story told about Pushkin. The poet once said to a friend of his: 'Just think what a trick Tatyana has played on me. She's gone and got married. Never expected it of her.' I can say the same about Anna Karenina. My characters sometimes do things I don't in the least want them to do. In fact they do the things that are done in life, and not what I intend them to do." [1955]

Konstantin Paustovski. The Golden Rose (Moscow,
Foreign Language Publishing House, n.d.), pp. 59–60

Tolstoy is one of those rare figures who represent a cultural span far greater than that of their age. Like Goethe, whom Friedrich Schlegel defined as both the Shakespeare and the Voltaire of his own nation and time, Tolstoy was a child of both the enlightenment and the nineteenth century. He was one of the few great men of his generation who was deeply rooted, and felt always at home, in the culture of *le siècle des lumières*. The cultural hero of *le siècle des lumières* had been the man of letters, understood not as a magician of words (like the poet for the romantics), or as a craftsman of style (as the novelist for Flaubertian realisms), but as a critic and a teacher of life, as a shaper of thought and as a spreader of truth. Nothing conveys such a conception as fully as the names of *philosophe* and *Aufklärer*, by which the great masters of the eighteenth century chose to label themselves. Besides being a modern literary artist, Tolstoy was also a *philosophe* or an *Aufklärer* in the old-fashioned sense of those terms. This justifies the traditional parallel between him and Rousseau on historical, as well as on psychological, grounds. Yet Rousseau was not the whole of eighteenth-century thought. As for Tolstoy, he was not only the Rousseau of his age, but the Voltaire too.

Renato Poggioli. *The Phoenix and the Spider*
(Cambridge, Mass., Harvard University Press,
1957), p. 95

Are Tolstoy and Dostoevsky, in fact, comparable? Is it more than a critic's fable to imagine their minds engaged in dialogue and mutual awareness? The principal obstacles to such types of comparison are lack of material and disparities in magnitude. . . . But the documentation on Tolstoy and Dostoevsky is abundant. We know in what manner they regarded each other and what *Anna Karenina* signified to the author of *The Idiot*. I suspect, moreover, that there is in one of Dostoevsky's novels a prophetic allegory of the spiritual encounter between himself and Tolstoy. There is between them no discordance of stature; they were titans both. . . .

There was common ground between them. Their images of God, their proposals of action, are ultimately irreconcilable. But they wrote in the same language and at the same decisive moment in history. There were a number of occasions on which they came very near to meeting; each time they drew back out of some tenacious premonition. Merezhkovsky, an erratic, untrustworthy, and yet illuminating witness, termed Tolstoy and Dostoevsky the most contrary of writers. . . .

On reflection, it becomes evident that for both Tolstoy and Dostoevsky plenitude was an essential freedom. It characterized their lives and persons as well as their view of the art of the novel. Tolstoy composed on a vast canvas commensurate to the breadth of his being and suggestive of the links between the time structure of the novel and the flow of time through history. The massiveness of Dostoevsky mirrors fidelity to detail and an encompassing grasp of the countless particularities of gesture and thought that accumulate towards the moment of drama.

The more we consider the two novelists, the more we come to realize that they and their works were hewn to the same scale.

Tolstoy's gigantic vitality, his bearish strength and feats of nervous endurance, the excess in him of every life-force are notorious. His contemporaries, such as Gorky, pictured him as a titan roaming the earth in antique majesty. There was something fantastical and obscurely blasphemous about his old age. He passed into his ninth decade every inch a king. He laboured to the end, unbent, pugnacious, rejoicing in his autocracy. Tolstoy's energies were such that he could neither imagine nor create in small dimensions. Whenever he entered into a room or a literary form he conveyed the impression of a giant stooping under a door built for ordinary men. One of his plays has six acts. There is appropriateness in the fact that the Dukhobors, a religious group whose emigration from Russia to Canada was financed by the royalties on Tolstoy's *Resurrection*, should parade naked in blizzards and burn down barns in exuberant defiance.

Georg Steiner. *Tolstoy or Dostoevsky*
(New York, Knopf, 1959), pp. 11–12, 14–15

Tolstoy's world, for all its breadth, is no less single in its moral outlook. It is a truism that the greater the novelist the more sweeping his vision. We tend to combine the persuasive universality of the moral abstraction with the wide scope of the major novelist and attribute to Tolstoy a representation of all life. This ascription, praiseworthy as a tribute to the commanding imagination of a superb writer, has the pernicious critical result of disarming in advance the attempt to define the theme of *War and Peace*. Even so responsible a critic as Forster (in *Aspects of the Novel*) seems almost captiously, and at the same time indolently, content merely to gape at the masterpiece, leaving unchallenged Lubbock's equally imperceptive assertion of thematic disunity in the novel. . . .

Reality in some strange way seems to have broken Tolstoy as he turns from moral insight to moral program in his insane last years. His penchant to substitute shallow abstraction for deep perception is prefigured by *War and Peace*'s disjunct disquisitions on a meaning already commandingly present in the analyses of the narrative itself. This tendency to disrupt fiction for tendentious theorizing is held in abeyance by the formal finish of *Anna Karenina*. But it breaks out shortly in Tolstoy's abandonment of art for the half-lights of nightmare abstraction. Sex, mastered in the vision of *Anna Karenina*, has become an obsession in those conversations Gorky records; in his writing it becomes either a platitude in *Resurrection* or an obsession with the extreme and narrow force of *The Kreutzer Sonata*, itself a gargoyle on the cathedral of *Anna Karenina*.

A novel must fully realize its center of moral insight in order to characterize its people fully and consistently, as Tolstoy does. His people are inward, and they grow in process, lucidly enunciated, into whole selves. But they exist in society, and their psychology, however inward, is defined through the consistent social insight which a moral idea implies, into a world widely coordinated in its relations and its temporal process.

Albert Cook. *The Meaning of Fiction* (Detroit, Wayne
State University Press, 1960), pp. 179–80, 200–201

On July 22, 1910, when Tolstoy was in the midst of what was to be his final crisis, he went into the woods with three friends to copy and sign the testament that had been drawn up according to his instructions, hoping thereby to settle both the tormenting spiritual problems and the distasteful bickering with his wife and family that the disposition of his property and rights induced. As Tolstoy began to copy the document he misspelled "twenty," started to correct it and to reach for a fresh sheet of paper, but then smiled and said, "All right, let it be thought that I was illiterate," adding "I will put the numeral next to it so that there will be no possibility of doubt." The remark may be taken as emblematic of Tolstoy's concern for craftsmanship and precision, just as the sylvan setting might be an emblem for the deep communion with nature that informs the crucial moments of his characters' lives. For few writers, particularly in the nineteenth century, have been so much and so consistently aware of the relationship between form and content, the irreducibility of a work of art to other terms, and the technical possibilities available to the professional writer; and few writers have expressed themselves quite so fully on the topic. Yet this awareness is an aspect of Tolstoy's art that has been little investigated in the West, particularly in English, a surprising fact considering the modern critical temperament and its penchant for analyzing techniques of fiction, structure, symbols, tensions, and the like.

The reasons are not difficult to find. It is not only the sheer size (at least of the two major novels) that makes such an approach unwieldy, but also some special quality that engages the reader's imagination and leads to critical speculations of another sort. That quality is summed up in Matthew Arnold's unfortunate dictum, intended as the ultimate compliment, that *Anna Karenina* was not to be taken as a work of art but as a piece of life.

Ralph E. Matlaw. *Tolstoy: A Collection of Critical Essays* (Englewood Cliffs, N.J., Prentice-Hall, 1967), p. 1

Anna Karenina one of the great European novels?—it is, surely, *the* European novel. The completeness with which Tolstoy, with his genius, was a Russian of his time made him an incomparably representative European, and made the book into which his whole experience, his most comprehensive "relatedness," went what it is for us: the great novel of modern— of our—civilization. The backwardness of Russia meant that the transcendent genius experienced to the full, taking their significances with personal intensity, the changes that have produced our modern world. In a country in which serfdom has been recently abolished, the characters of *Anna Karenina* travel as a matter of course by railway between the two capitals. The patriarchal landowner participates in a cosmopolitan culture, and, using French and English in intercourse with members of his own class, is intellectually nourished on the contemporary literature and thought of the West. Anna herself, having had at the outset of the book the shock of the fatal accident that marks her arrival at Moscow, ends her life under the iron wheels. The apparition of the little peasant with the sack who horrifies her, and is so oddly associated with the wheels and the rails, acts on our imagination as a pregnant symbol and a sinister augury (he is seen, too, later in a nightmare by Vronsky). The disharmonies, contrasts, and contradictions are challenging in a way that makes the optimisms of Progress impossible for Tolstoy—as the inability of Levin, the earnest and public-spirited, to see a duty in Zemstvo-attendance very characteristically intimates. *Anna Karenina*, in its human centrality, gives us modern man; Tolstoy's essential problems, moral and spiritual, are ours.

F. R. Leavis. *Anna Karenina and Other Essays*
(London, Chatto & Windus, 1967), p. 32

TSVETAYEVA, MARINA (1892–1941)

Marina Tsvetayeva (in the book *Vecherni albom* [*Evening Album*)] is innately talented and innately original. Although her book is dedicated to "the brilliant memory of Maria Bashkirtseva"—an epigraph taken from Rostand—the word "mama" is on almost every page. This leads to thoughts about the poetess's youth, thoughts that are confirmed by her own words of admission. There is a good deal new in this work: a new, brave (almost excessive) intimacy; new themes—a child's love, for example; a new spontaneous, mad predilection for the trifles of life. And, as is to be expected, here the main laws of poetry are instinctively guessed, so that this book is not only a book of a young girl's confessions but also a book of excellent poetry.

Nikolai Gumilyov. *Apollon.* 5, 1911, p. 78[†]

Tsvetayeva's poems are very well conceived and polished. She is a great master of the word, with a predilection for poetic effects. First of all, she endeavors to give her verse a conciseness approaching aphorism. She wraps thought and infinity in a form polished and concise to the limits. She speaks almost in formulas, in sharp sentences. What is called "darkness" in Tsvetayeva's poetry is in fact concentration, lightning speed, which sometimes requires decoding. In Tsvetayeva, every word carries meaning and does not fail to evoke an image or thought. Perhaps that is why it is not easy to read her, even her best works, such as "Poema gory" ("The Mountain Poem") or "Poema kontsa" ("The Poem About the End"); it is necessary to follow her every word with the greatest attention. . . . Tsvetayeva's images are only hinted at: she never elaborates them, so that even here her sharpened precision is like the piercing of a knife.

Tsvetayeva's interrupted, nervous verse is verse in flight, in motion. Hence its dynamism, its pathos, its avoidance of the superfluous. As in Akhmatova, in Tsvetayeva's poems the expression and the poetic punctuation are more important than the melody of sound. But while Akhmatova is inclined toward the common speech, to what is known as "vulgarization of the poetic diction," Tsvetayeva's words are rich in sound and playful. Her poems reflect literary richness and the brilliant and capricious manner of people's speech, unexpectedly accompanied by witticisms, of which every average man is capable.

Marc Slonim. *Ruski arhiv.* 4, 1929, p. 108[†]

She belonged neither to the Pushkin nor to the Lermontov school of Russian poetry, although in view of her romanticism, Pushkin had to be (and was) closer to her than Lermontov, whom . . . many of the Parisian émigré poets were attracted to. . . . Pushkin's poetic style is not reflected in Tsvetayeva's: in the realm of poetry they had nothing in common. Nevertheless, Tsvetayeva's poetic tastes were in some sense eclectic. Perhaps it should be said that she could be unselfishly and enthusiastically carried away by any authentic poetry she found: in Blok, Bely, Balmont, Bryusov, Akhmatova (Tsvetayeva's verses to Akhmatova are full of unexpected tenderness, revealing their closeness in some mystic Russian depths), Voloshin, Mandelshtam, Pasternak, Mayakovski. She speaks of them all both in prose and in verse with truly poetic generosity (I don't recollect her speaking of Gumilyov). Tsvetayeva has little in common with other women poets in Russian literature, such as Akhmatova, Zinaida Hippius, Carolina, or Pavlova. Contrary to Adamovich's judgment of her "decadent female egocentrism," in her verse there is little specific femininity, and insofar as there is femininity, it is of different gender from theirs, not decadent but hearkening back to folk laments. Here, perhaps, can be found a secret, deep kinship with Akhmatova.

Gleb Struve. *Russkaya literatura v izgnanii* (New York, Izdatelstvo imeni Chekhova, 1956), p. 151[†]

Marina Tsvetaeva learned her *métier* (we have seen that she took a Russian synonym of this term as the title of one of her books) from two very different sources. One was the "grand style" of the eighteenth century, as exemplified by Derzhavin, with his lofty rhetorics and weighty archaisms. The other was the popular tradition of the heroic or lyric folk song. Yet she learned also from her contemporaries, for instance Khlebnikov, whose example perhaps she followed when she freely reinterpreted in *King-Maiden* ancient Russian myths and old folk motifs. But the poet of her time who taught her most was the early Pasternak, whom Tsvetaeva resembles in her romantic temper, as well as in her expressionistic technique. As in Pasternak's case, the marks of her style are a tight syntaxis and an elliptic imagery, a discordant sound pattern and a rigid metrical design.

Tsvetaeva's poetry is deeply feminine, but of a femininity which is neither soft nor weak. Unlike Akhmatova, who cannot express her experience except personally and directly, by means of poems which read like fragments from a private diary, Tsvetaeva is often able to convey her vision of life through historical or legendary "masks." It is from the Biblical and the Christian tradition, as well as from mythological and literary lore, that she takes all the exalted figures of saints and knights, lovers and poets, heroes and heroines whom she turns into objects of praise: David and Saint George, Phaedra and Hippolytus, Don Juan and *Manon Lescaut's* Chevalier des Grieux, Pushkin and Byron, Napoleon and Marina Mniszek, the Polish princess who married the Pseudo-Dmitrij to seize with him the Russian crown. Tsvetaeva does not hesitate, however, to seek her idols or *personae* even among the women and men of her circle, paying her homage in verse to Anna Akhmatova or Aleksandr Blok. To the latter she consecrated a lyrical cycle full of loving admiration and of lucid psychological insight.

Renato Poggioli. The Poets of Russia (Cambridge,
Mass., Harvard University Press, 1960), p. 314

I do not believe that in my life I have met a more tragic figure than Marina. Everything in her life history is vacillating and illusory: political ideas, critical opinions, personal dramas—everything except poetry. There are few people still alive who knew Marina, but her poetry is only now beginning to become familiar to many people.

From her childhood until death she was lonely, and this alienation was connected with her constant rejection of her environment. . . . She liked many things just because they were "out of place": she applauded when those around her did not, stared alone at the lowered curtain, walked out of the auditorium during a performance, and wept in a dark, empty corridor.

In her youth Marina had admired *L'Aiglon* and the conventional romanticism of Rostand. Later, her enthusiasms went deeper: Goethe, Hamlet, *Phèdre*. Sometimes she wrote poems in French and German. Yet she felt a foreigner everywhere but in Russia. Her whole being was closely connected with her native landscape, from the "hot rowan" of her youth to the final elder tree stained with blood. Love, death, and art were the basic themes of her poetry, and she resolved them in a Russian manner.

Ilya Ehrenburg. Novy mir. Jan., 1961, pp. 100–101[†]

I place Tsvetayeva highest; she was a formed poet from her very beginning. In an age of affectations she had her own voice—human, classical. She was a woman with a man's soul. Here struggle with everyday life was what gave her strength. She strived for and reached perfect clarity. She is a greater poet than Akhmatova, whose simplicity and lyricism I have always admired. Tsvetayeva's death was one of the great sadnesses of my life.

Boris Pasternak. In Olga Andreyev Carlisle, Voices in the Snow (New York, Random House, 1962), p. 199

Tsvetaeva is in essence a religious poet, an appellation which should be taken as a necessary but by no means a limiting or sufficient description. The religious current in her poetry is particularly evident in her cycle (and sixth book) of poems, *Poems to Blok [Stikhi k Bloku]*, one of Tsvetaeva's major achievements and an outstanding monument of modern Russian poetry.

First, a brief description of the structure of the work. The natural analogy and the probable model for the cycle was, of course, Aleksandr Blok's own famous early volume of Symbolist poetry, *Poems on the Beautiful Lady* (1901–1902). The cycle consists of three parts, the first of which is almost as long as the other two combined. It is also divided in time—the first part was written in 1916 (except for its conclusion, written in 1920), while the two shorter sections were written in 1921, presumably on the occasion of Blok's death. As then might be expected, there is a marked difference in tone between the parts. In the first portion the "high and lofty" language which has been frequently noted in Tsvetaeva—it is worth noting that one of her favorite Russian poets was the 18th century poet Derzhavin—sounds most clearly. The second part is a threnody to Blok in the folk manner: the theme "in which cradle do you lie?" recurs continually, and such motifs as "a prince without a country" and "a friend without friends" bear a distinct folk imprint. The third part is an apostrophe to Russia symbolized as the grieving Virgin; it combines the disparate styles of the first two sections in an intense and stirring counterpoint of imagery and language. There is a valid question, it should be said, as to whether or not *Poems to Blok* ought to be read as a unified work rather than merely a book of poems, but the thematic order and progression of the poems lend great weight to the former reading—it might be best to say that Tsvetaeva, like Eliot, took individual poems on a single theme and "at some point" decided to use them as the basis for a larger whole work. . . .

Marina Tsvetaeva may best be characterized as a Mayakovsky of the Middle Ages, a heretic in an age of non-believers. Her *Poems to Blok* are a living liturgy of Russia and the Russian language.

Peter Viereck. TriQuarterly. Spring, 1965, pp. 58, 61

The deliberate stylistic mixture in *Fedra [Phaedra]* was received by the émigré critics with a veritable howl of outrage. Xodasevič wrote of an "inexcusable and tasteless confusion of styles." Adamovič wrote that *Fedra* is "howled and screamed rather than written," and Vladimir Vejdle complained of a "total absence of feeling for words as responsible and meaningful *logos*." The critics compared *Fedra* to Racine's tragedy and to *Penthesilea* by Kleist and found Cvetaeva verbose, inelegant, and incoherent by comparison. The reception of *Fedra* by the émigré criticism is the most obvious example of a condemnation on the basis of irrelevant comparisons and inapplicable criteria. Even as astute a critic as Xodasevič failed to see that the essential intention of Cvetaeva was considerably different from either classical or romantic poets and that the unfamiliar "mixed" style was adequate for conveying her conception of the myth. The reception of *Fedra* demonstrates how the tyranny of what is considered the current good taste can serously impede a comprehension of valid forms of artistic expression which happen to be outside such current definition.

We know of no attempt to produce any of Cvetaeva's dramatic works on the stage. With the possible exception of *Konec Kazanovy* [*The End of Casanova*], they would offer considerable difficulties both in terms of staging and interpretation. In her preface to *Konec Kazanovy*, Cvetaeva pointed out that anything she might write for the theater should be considered a poem in dramatic form rather than a play. Read as poems, many of her plays make exciting and rewarding reading. "Fortuna," the best of the early plays, is an elegant piece of ripe romanticism, while "Tezej" is not only a magnificent poetic accomplishment but an impressive philosophical conception as well. On the whole, Cvetaeva's plays, while not being the striking and unique contributions to Russian literature that her lyric poetry and *poèmy* are, remain a significant and respectable part of her total literary accomplishment.

Simon Karlinsky. Marina Cvetaeva (Berkeley, Calif.,
University of California Press, 1966), pp. 264–65

Now and then, in reading the early verse of Tsvetayeva, one is struck with the feeling that here a character has jumped out of the *dramatis personae* of Blok and that his elemental traits have been developed with particularly sharp expression. In this case, I do not mean at all to deny the distinctive originality inherent in the poetry of Tsvetayeva. It is important, however, even in so sharp, sometimes whimsically expressed a manner as her own to see the general peculiarities of the times, a general line of development in Russian poetry of which the most significant innovations are Blok's. Tsvetayeva, with the expressive directness so peculiar to her, sometimes even demonstratably underscores her own longing to express the national feminine character. . . .

Everything in the poetry of Tsvetayeva is as if woven from contrasts and contradictions. Here is the contrast between naturalness and bookishness. Naturalness should stress the dismissal of broad social relationships and the historical perspective. The characters in Tsvetayeva are really possessed of enormous emotional power. Of all the poets of the "Blok school," Tsvetayeva is the most organically given to elementality, to an explosive strength of the poetic temperament. It often happens that a great poet's perspective of historical movement, instead of disappearing, strives to enter into a character, as if to feel at home in it. In this instance, bookish conventionality becomes not so much a reminder of the finished model as the particular method for great poetic generalization. If, let us say, Tsvetayeva stylized her character according to the prose of Leskov or Dostoyevski, then as a result there would appear not only stylization but the disclosing of certain traits in the national feminine character. Bookishness becomes the means of broadening the possibilities of the poetic image. The vitality of Tsvetayeva contrasts to the conventionality of social relationships. But Tsvetayeva expresses this contrast between vitality and conventionality only through generality carried to the extreme and only through characters almost theatrically contrived.

Pavel Gromov. *Aleksandr Blok: Ego predshestvenniki i sovremenniki* (Moscow, Sovetski pisatel, 1966), pp. 453–55[†]

She gave the impression of a woman, full of creative inventions, who had put off her problems, but a woman who did not look into herself, who did not know her vital (and feminine) possibilities, who had not matured towards a consciousness of her present and future reactions. The part of a misfit, which she adopted and about which she wrote beautifully in the poem "Roland's Horn" ["Rolandov rog"], after many years betrayed her immaturity: being a fish out of water is not, as was once thought, a sign of originality in a human being who stands *above* others, but is the misfortune—both psychological and ontological—of a man who has not matured to the point of uniting with the world, of fusing with it and his time, that is with history and other people. Her involvement with the White Army was foolish; it was to a certain degree the outcome of her attachment to her husband, Sergey Efron, to whom she "promised a son." Thus she said to me: "I will have a son, I have sworn to Serezha that I will give him a son." She had a certain faith in dreams, she trusted in certain fantasies. In Marina this maladjustment was the more tragic in that with the years she began to seek fusion, that her built-up peculiarity gradually began to oppress her; she outlived it and nothing arose in its place. She matured slowly, like the majority of Russian poets of our century (in contrast with the preceding one). But having understood, perhaps in the last years of her life, that man cannot all his life remain an outcast, and that if he does the blame rests with him and not with his surroundings, she did not achieve maturity; her conflict was aggravated in that, as a poet in emigration, she had no readers, there was no reaction to what she wrote, and perhaps she had no friends of her stature. The poet carrying his gift like a hunchback his hump, the poet on an uninhabited island or descending into catacombs, the poet in his tower (of ivory, brick, or whatever), the poet on an iceberg in the ocean—all these are tempting images, but they hide a romantic essence that is sterile and dangerous in its deadliness. You might insert these images in immortal or simply good verse, and someone undoubtedly will react to them inwardly, but they will bear with them one of the most insidious elements of art—escapism, which, if it embellishes the poem, destroys the poet. The Prague isolation of Marina, her role of outcast in Paris, could only lead her to silence in Moscow and tragedy in Elabuga. In her own personality, in the character of her relation to people and the world, this end was already masked: it was foretold in all those lines where she cried to us that she was not like everyone else, that she was proud that she was not like us, that she never wanted to be like us.

She yielded to the old decadent temptation of inventing a new self: the poet as a monster deformity, unrecognized and misunderstood; the mother of her children and the wife of her husband; the lover of a young ephebus; a heroine of a glorious past; a bard, singing the doom of an army; a young disciple; a partner in a passionate friendship. From these (and other) "personality images" she made verse—great verse of our time. But she had no power over herself, did not create herself, did not even know herself (and cultivated this ignorance). She was defenseless, reckless, and unhappy, enclosed by a "nest" and lonely: she found and lost and erred without letup.

Nina Berberova, *The Italics Are Mine* (New York,
Harcourt, Brace & World, 1969), pp. 204–6

TVARDOVSKI, ALEKSANDR (1910–1971)

Tvardovsky followed his collective farm poem *The Land of Muravia* [*Strana Muraviya*] by a book about the soldier *Vassili Terkin* which won greater and more immediate popularity with the Soviet reader than his first poem. The book, in reality, has no plot. It consists of separate battle episodes in all of which the invulnerable Vassili Terkin, a rank-and-file soldier and hero, takes part. These episodes are taken from the road of battle travelled by the Red Army from the Volga to Berlin, and reveal the heroism of the Soviet people. There is a certain element of chance in the composition and hence apparently in the very creation of *Vassili Terkin*. It seems that in beginning work on this new poem the author had not yet plumbed all the depths, measured the full scope of this happily chosen theme. Hence the abundance of deviations, of commentaries given by the author to his living, expressive sketches which without the support of these, lyrical yet wise comments would have remained only thumbnail sketches (of which there are not a few in Tvardovsky's front-line note-books).

In the end the author succeeded in subordinating all the chapters and lines of *Vassili Terkin* to a certain unity of plot and form, in turning the very element of chance into something essential and logical, something organic and noteworthy, almost philosophical, which determined the nature of the poem. It seems that every accidental episode, conversation and joke is connected by invisible threads to the very soul of the life of the people. We do not know whether this was the original concept of *Vassili Terkin* and it does not matter. The important fact is that this is how the book was finished, this is how Tvardovsky worked on it, with a constant understanding of the profound, not the superficial, of the im-portance to the whole nation of the events taking place; he expresses ecstatic joy at the fact that the true meaning and everlasting rock-bottom of the life of the people are so clearly shown in any external movement of this life.

Vassili Terkin is a book for and about the people. It is not only written for the people but was created in living cooperation with them. In other words it is permeated by those "improvisations" (to quote the term used by the well-known Russian novelist Leskov) which the Russian people always favoured.

Nikolai William-Wilmont. SL. Oct., 1946, p. 37

The political moral of [*The Land of Muravia*] is . . . quite orthodox. But it is not a propaganda poem. The author has an understanding for, and sympathy with, the personal proprietary instincts of the average Russian peasant personified in Morgunok. The scene of the carousing, dispos-sessed peasants has a tragic accent. One of them sings a song about a little bird which refuses to eat or sing and asks for its cage to be opened. The charm of the poem lies in its blend of realism and whimsical fancy, of spicy satire and gentle humor. It is a modern counterpart of *Who Lives Happily in Russia?*, Nekrasov's great epic of peasant life; like the latter it is satu-rated with the genuine spirit of folk poetry. Tvardovsky not only uses the racy peasant speech which fits naturally into his easy-flowing verse, but also handles skillfully various folklore devices and especially the motifs and meters of the *chastushka* (village ditty). Folklore motifs are worked, for instance, into the imaginary speech which Morgunok addresses to Stalin, asking the latter to be allowed to keep for a while his holding and promising to join the *kolkhoz* later.

Gleb Struve. *Soviet Russian Literature 1917–1950*
(Norman, Okla., University of Oklahoma Press,
1951), p. 296

[A] natural, wholehearted expression of Communist ideas is to be found in the work of Alexander Tvardovsky, possibly the greatest poetic talent in the Soviet Union today. Many of Tvardovsky's works bear the stamp of the mature master and are marked by a limpidity that may well be likened to Pushkin's. And for all the difference between his manner and Mayakovsky's, he has deep kinship with Mayakovsky's revolutionary tradition. His language is very much the language of the people; he writes in a natural, conversational style—and what a wealth of implied meaning there is in his lines! The deep appeal of his verse lies in his warm love for the common man and his sensitive sympathy with the people in their joys and sorrows. A humour sly and sad by turns, a gift of intimate understanding, an unwavering faith in all that is best in man, a deep insight into the Russian national character—these fine attributes of the great Russian 19th-century poets are to be found again—as they were in Mayakovsky— in Tvardovsky's major works of the 'forties—*Vasili Tyorkin* and *The House by the Road* [*Dom u dorogi*].

The form of Tvardovsky's verse is so perfectly suited to the meaning that for the most part one is scarcely aware of it as such. The metre, the rhyming, the imagery are always made to serve the idea to be conveyed. And that idea centres invariably around the common man.

V. Ognev. *SL*. Dec., 1953, pp. 132–33

Tvardovski's masterfulness and his positive attitude toward the word and the verse are evident in his new "Tyorkin." As always, the poet's art originates not secondhand but from the primary sources of life and poetry.

Tvardovski's poetic language is very simple. It contains not a trace of the various refined and intolerably strained comparisons, metaphors, and similes, which some poets, especially those who are not too sure of themselves, overuse. Tvardovski's language shows that supreme simplicity which comes from mature and subtle mastery, void of any dry pedantism or petty snobbism. His poetic word, as a rule, is straightforward, precise, laden with meaning, and perceptible. . . .

In the domain of poetic language and imagery, Tvardovski shows enviable freedom. For him, there are no conventional categories and norms, no insurmountable boundaries between the high and low, the ridiculous and serious. His language contains the richness of conversational speech.

V. Orlov. *Literaturnaya gazeta*. Sept. 12, 1963, p. 3[†]

Aleksandr Tvardovski's place in Soviet cultural life can, without exaggeration, he called unique. It could be compared with that of Gorki, if their points of departures had not been so fundamentally different. However, it can be explained, as with Gorki, by Tvardovski's double function as a writer and committed politician of culture. Consequently, Tvardovski's life falls into two phases, into two epochs: the time of his relatively unproblematic activity as a lyricist; and the period after Stalin, the period of the cultural and political war of taking sides, in which his name as editor of the prominent literary magazine *Novy mir* was supposed to be taken as the showpiece of Soviet liberalism. . . .

The Land of Muravia, a verse narrative of over two thousand lines, remains Tvardovski's most original work. It is at the same time poetry of agitation and true folk poetry, a Soviet paraphrase of Nekrasov's great peasant epic, *Who Lives Happily in Russia?* It retains its tragic concept despite the happy end. This is due to its success in depicting, with an absolute certainty, the inner trauma of the Russian peasant on the threshold of a changing epoch.

Helen von Ssachno. *Christ und Welt.*
Dec. 27, 1963, p. 21†

In Poland I saw the 1954 first edition of Tvardovsky's *Hills Beyond Hills* [*Za dalyu dal*]; that edition is now withdrawn and unobtainable; almost no one seems to know of it. It contains passages, later superseded and reversed by Tvardovsky's more considered judgment, of an embarrassingly gushy adoration for Stalin as the sacred lost father-image. This is the kind of thing Kremlinologists can make too much of; though of psychological interest, it does not really discredit either the political or literary integrity of Tvardovsky. Every case is individual; westerners must bear in mind what it meant to live under continuous totalitarian pressure; and every authority you talk to in Russia, on both the thaw and deep-freeze sides, agrees that Tvardovsky is honest and sincere and that he is also the most effective liberalizer (though often compromising with circumstances) on Russia's ruling Central Committee.

Peter Viereck. *TriQuarterly.* Spring, 1965, p. 37

Aleksandr Tvardovski's *Stikhi iz zapisnoi knizhki* (*Verses From A Notebook*) should not come as a surprise to the reader. They continue the inward theme of nearly the whole of the poet's postwar creativity. The narrative verse of Tvardovski is rooted in the Nekrasov tradition, while, at the same time, it represents the emergence of a new form. From *The Land of Muravia* to *Vasili Tyorkin* and *The House by the Road*, the poet transformed the narrative poem by the ever-increasing introduction of a perceptible lyrical basis, arriving at a lyrical genre, the traveling diary, and the poem *Hills Beyond Hills*. . . .

A deepening of reflections and their concentration on the very concrete gives the new verse of Tvardovski the weight of true knowledge. The assiduous experience of the poetry is reflected in its unhurried nature, I should even risk saying, in a certain mildness of intonation that conforms with the character of the development of the lyrical subject. Tvardovski avoids, even in the smallest degree, imposing his own impressions and thoughts on the reader. He leads the reader along a road of doubt and anxiety, along a road of spiritual experience; how it will be perceived and how it will affect the heart are not his concern.

It has never been necessary to reproach Tvardovski for seeking a reader. The traditions of classical verse were for him the measure of harmony, the measure of beauty, the measure of observing the "worth of form," and, on the whole, the measure of the essence and depth of the content. The lyrical scenes composing the cycle *Verses From A Notebook* are melancholy meditations on everyday human existence, not very simple and full of deep meaning. This is the gaze turned inward, the absorbed introspection.

A. Mikhailov. *Znamya*. Sept., 1968, pp. 209–10†

VINOKUROV, YEVGENI (1925–   )

Evgenij Vinokurov is relatively young. In one of his poems, "Vot snimok moj" ["My Portrait"] he pictures himself. See my photograph, he says: a man from the twentieth century and the year 1945. He participated in Russia's last great war, carrying his verses all over the frozen ways in autumn and winter. He is one who has happened to cross over what he calls "the depths," the abyss of things and matters, which means to him heavy earnestness in his conception of life and man. Poetry is his vocation, to which he must be true in the same way as he was true to his country during war. The first part of his lyrics is consecrated to duty in war. Then follow the reminiscences from sunny childhood in his native Moscow where he understood for the first time that true poetry springs out from the glitter of ice hanging down from the frozen roof of his home. Still there remains on all his fresh and sunny poetry the imprint of seriousness, the shadow of death and nothingness always present. He has mastered the various forms of his verse perfectly and may therefore be considered one of the very best living Soviet lyric poets.

Maria Widnäs. BA. Autumn, 1962, p. 450

Vinokurov pays much less attention than Voznesensky to experiments with form; from time to time, it is true, he finds good alliterations. . . . But these phonetic preoccupations are of secondary importance to him; he is interested above all in *rapidity of rhythm* and exactitude of *concrete detail*. He excels in the evocation of an object, a moment, a memory, a person, in a few words: he does not allow the evocation to extend into description or dissertation; he does not develop it. Like Voznesensky, he leaves part of his poem to the reader's guesswork. . . . That is why Vinokurov sometimes gives the impression that he is slightly out of breath. It is a method which, in the same piece, mixes . . . commonplace images . . . with fine, new images. . . . Vinokurov's qualities are less striking than those of Voznesensky and Evtushenko; his words are less exalted, there is less brio and glitter; he has neither Voznesensky's mastery of words nor the eloquence and lyrical elevation of Evtushenko. He nevertheless occupies an important place in contemporary Soviet poetry. Like Evtushenko, with less noise but certainly with more penetration and sensibility, he has helped to restore a personal quality to lyric poetry, and to bring the "I" back into poetry.

Pierre Forgues. In *Literature and Revolution in Soviet Russia 1917–1962*, Max Hayward and Leopold Labedz, eds. (London, Oxford University Press, 1963), pp. 190–91

Vinokurov's poem "Monuments" ["Pamyatniki"] is both serious and colloquial, informal and profound. In ordinary turns of speech, he reports his humility before the grandeur of artistic, or symmetrical, creation, and his feeling that he has an obligation to enact the ideals of his craft. . . . If you put this poem against Pushkin's version of Horace's "Exegi monumentum," you can see how the young poet, contemporary to us, has simplified the syntax and made his message not personal but interpretive: any "I" will fit it. Of course, poetry of this sort runs the risk of deteriorating into a series of explicatory phrases. Pushkin asserted the right to proclaim the value of his service. Vinokurov assumes that his "I," the first-person protagonist in the poem, stands for any other man's emotional impact. Vinokurov does not mean that he, personally and alone, is guilty for having failed to accomplish his ideals; rather every man is guilty, or "at fault," to the extent that he fails himself. There is a nice turn here, one that is not easily got at. I mean this: the more we, in our world, assert the uniqueness of our individuality, the more, paradoxically, we assert that that individuality is representative, almost symbolic, of everybody else's. Pushkin never entertained such a notion.

F. D. Reeve. *KR*. Summer, 1964, pp. 539–40

The verse of Vinokurov is not musical. This is neither fault nor merit: it is simply its nature. It is sober and sincere, written with the intonation of our everyday speech. Some poetry captivates the listener with the sweetness of lyrical speech; in Vinokurov this speech is tattered, sometimes consisting of short phrases whose rhythm recalls the laconic shouts of city streets. Or, in contrast, they assume a complex and ramiform syntactical structure in which the poet tries as accurately as possible to grasp some aspect of life. The phrases do not fit within the restriction of stanza and are generally hampered by the many limitations of traditional versification; the poet then turns to free verse.

The thought that "not everything in the world is really so simple and dull" varies from poem to poem. This is abundantly clear in itself, but in Vinokurov it is not mechanically adopted sententiousness. The poet felt and experienced fully the complexity of the world. One understands this when reading carefully his poems on youth, war, and love.

The hero of Vinokurov's poetry is the man of independent thinking.

A warm, human personality appears in his poetry, one without false sentiment. Man in Vinokurov's poetry is candid and courageous. He knows how to stand up for himself, his work, and his love; he is wise and direct in his feelings. And by this he commands respect.

Anatoli Aleksandrov. Zvezda. Dec., 1964, p. 214[†]

Evtushenko characterized Vinokurov's poems with the words "manliness and tenderness." This manliness sometimes becomes bravado. . . . And as for the tenderness, the poet does speak of his feelings, but in the few poems in which love or sex plays a role he is extremely reserved and prudish. He gives evidence of a vivid imagination, an animated inner life, but his thoughts are never extremely deep or elevated. Sometimes he writes ordinary little scenes from life in which the poetic element is very weak . . . or mere trifles. . . . The already mentioned notion of the tragic appears in several poems. . . .

As for their form, it is always striking to note how the most modern Russian poetry resembles the poetry Pushkin wrote one hundred fifty years ago: the vocabulary remains almost the same, and even the youngest and boldest poets carefully polish their meter and maintain rhyme (only a few of Vinokurov's poems are in blank verse without rhythm); the only innovation is that since Mayakovsky assonance rhyme is allowed and even fashionable and the verses are sometimes expanded in steps over several lines. By these ties the Russian poet is bound, more than modern Western poets, and his art requires more craftsmanship. But this involves the danger that pure poetry may be superseded by virtuosity, the rhyme word being used for the sake of the effect; and this danger is not altogether avoided in Vinokurov's poems.

Tom Eekman. BA. Spring, 1965, p. 232

VIRTA, NIKOLAI (1906–   )

Virta is a rising star on the Soviet firmament. . . . *Aloneness* [*Odinochestvo*] describes an episode during the civil war, laid in Central Russia, the province of Tambov. Here the war against the Bolsheviks was instigated not by tsarist generals backed by landowners, manufacturers, and such foreign statesmen as Clemenceau or Lloyd George. The mass of the peasantry on the rich soil of Tambov eagerly followed one out of their own midst, Antonov, a member of the Socialist-Revolutionary Party, in his uprising against the Communists. . . .

Virta, a native of Tambov who lived through the civil war in the province, treats his subject with an intimate understanding. He is free from the clichés of villainous *kulaks* and valiant commissars. He takes you into the huts and secret dens of the rebels, into Antonov's headquarters and into the minds of individual leaders and rank-and-filers, and he makes you see and feel and think as the others do. Virta concentrates on Storozhev, a leading peasant rebel. His dominant passion, greed for land, dictates his actions and explains his cruelty and unscrupulousness. He remains unreconciled, even after the defeat of Antonov and the return of the peasants to peaceful husbandry. Alone, Storozhev hides in marshes and forests, reverts to savagery, and nurtures his hatred for the victors and for his former allies who have laid down their arms. He steals up to his village, greedily observes his former possessions and those he had hoped to acquire, and watches with resentment the reconstruction activities. After a number of attacks and murders he is finally caught and imprisoned by his brother. On the eve of his probable execution he kills his guard and escapes, into aloneness and hatred.

Alexander Kaun. *BA*. Summer, 1937, pp. 314–15

The Conspiracy of the Doomed [*Zagovor obrechennykh*] by N. Virta was particularly popular among the plays on international themes.

The play is a well-aimed blow at the incendiaries of war, at the reactionaries who stop at nothing in the realization of their base misanthropic plans for a new imperialist war.

In one of the People's Democracies (hence the subtitle: *In a Certain Country*) reactionaries, directly instructed by the imperialist tycoons of the U.S.A., are getting ready to overthrow the government. Unconcealed intervention is one of their objectives. These traitors to their country will go to any length in order to strangle liberty.

But the people, steadfast, watchful and intrepid, emerge victorious from this struggle.

The play is a vivid account of the people's liberation struggle that is being waged in our day. Its heroes are the leaders of this movement—charming, fearless, inspired men and women.

Several Moscow theatres staged this play.

Y. Kalashnikov. *SL*. Dec., 1949, p. 123

Virta's second novel (the third part of the trilogy was never published) was, as far as I know, the first important Soviet work of fiction to deal with the background of the wreckers' and opposition trials that swept the country in the late thirties. It is very interesting since it shows the variety of the characters involved in anti-Soviet activities and especially the diversity and complexity of the motives ascribed to them. It is true that Virta does his best to show Lev Kagarde—this miniature caricature of Trotsky and embryonic "Führer"—in all his repulsiveness. But some of Kagarde's victims, willing and unwilling, are very attractive. The picture painted by Virta is on the whole objective but, of course, is far from complete. Some of the riddles presented by the famous "trials" are left unsolved; and certain aspects of the affair are completely ignored. The moral of the tale, as the author sees it, is given in the purely political epilogue....

Virta's novel may be regarded as a good specimen of what is expected of Socialist realism, for it combined edifying purpose with a sufficiently detached portrayal of realities.

Gleb Struve. *Soviet Russian Literature 1917–1950*
(Norman, Okla., University of Oklahoma Press, 1951),
pp. 284–85

In his new play *Dali-dalnie, neoglyadnye* [Expansive Distances] . . . Virta endeavors to show truthfully the processes taking place not only in the economic life of the present-day village but also in the consciousness of the people. Virta has made a huge advance from his novel *Krutye gory* [Steep Mountains], according to whose motifs the play was written.

With a thorough knowledge of, and feeling for, life, Virta tells about the everyday life in the kolkhoz "Honest Work," where the old elements are still in opposition, unwilling to retreat under the pressure of the emerging and growing forces of the new. But no matter how persistent the old is, the fresh new forces, like springs, strike new paths and remove from their roads everything that hampers their forward movement. . . .

Virta constructs his play in such a way that the author does all relating of the story. This interesting device lends the play an emotional saturation and a journalistic tone. With the passionate involvement of a witness, the author tells about the kolkhoz chairman Khiznyakov, trying to make the reader and spectator empathize with the chairman's fate, show interest in, think about, and be excited by it. . . .

Some carelessnesses and errors of the playwright are annoying, but they do not spoil the impression one gets from the play. *Dali-dalnie, neoglyadnye* excels in the rich and expressive language of the characters and in a number of beautifully described scenes.

V. Mironova. *Zvezda.* June, 1958, pp. 209–10[†]

VOZNESENSKI, ANDREI (1933–   )

Andrei Voznesenski's popularity among young Russians is second only to Evtushenko's, while he often ranks first with connoisseurs. His verse is full of youthfulness and talent—youth is his main theme as it is Evtushenko's; in Voznesenski, however, it is never coquettish. Technically Voznesenski has learned from Pasternak and Tsvetayeva, but he has a completely personal sense of both rhythm and visual imagery; he loves and understands painting and finds inspiration in Rubens, Renoir and Goya. He was trained as an architect and has been publishing his poems only for the past three years, but his rise was meteoric.

He is a compelling, very young man with a childlike face and blue eyes. Slight, quick, he wears a snap-brim cap and looks like a student. Besides his outstanding poetic powers, he has a light-heartedness both as a person and as a poet which is characteristic of the new Soviet generation. His amused and tender love for the Russian way of life, for both its good and less good aspects, is in contrast with the high-mindedness of a Pasternak or a Tsvetayeva.

Olga Andreyev Carlisle. *Voices in the Snow*
(New York, Random House, 1962), p. 90

Voznesensky, a friend and initially a protégé of Yevtushenko's is a poet of an entirely different type. Being more bookish and more clearly conscious of his particular literary forebears, Voznesensky perpetuates (probably consciously) one specific trend in Russian poetry—the school of futurism, represented by Khlebnikov and Mayakovsky, Tsvetayeva, and Pasternak. But within the framework of this movement, Voznesensky is no mere imitator; he is a creator, as unlike any other as Tsvetayeva is unlike Mayakovsky. His chief preoccupation is maximum dynamic expressiveness. Everything in his verse is subordinated to this end—the frequent unexpected changes of his rhythm, the daring intensity of his imagery, which often surprises "common sense" but is strikingly precise and profound poetically. (One of his most-quoted passages is: "And the Century roars mightily—/a cross between ape/and jet engine.") In search of expressiveness Voznesensky does not hesitate to "shock the party functionary." In his "Ballada raboty" ("Ballad of Work") he has the "belly" of Rubens "dangling like a furry turnip," and in "Poslednaia elektrika" ("The Last Streetcar") a prostitute, suddenly gripped by the force of art, "whispers obscenely the purest of words." Of all the Soviet avant-garde writers who have managed to penetrate into published literature, Voznesensky is probably the most "leftist" in his esthetics, although there are, of course, many underground poets who are much more extreme.

David Burg. *PC*. Sept.–Oct., 1962, p. 38

In the 1962 Moscow *Day of Poetry* [*Den poezii*] and also in his latest book, Voznesensky has included his "Polish Poem," a deliberately fitful concatenation of images and puns, emotions and tricks. The poem, written in expressionist style, is designed to liberate Voznesensky from his impression of Poland—that is, to convey to the reader an essence without making either a definition or a formal declaration. Voznesensky seems to me to have a skill superior to most of the other young poets in the group, especially in this: he knows how to get out from inside himself, so to speak, by verbal devices, by conventional puns, by clichéd rhymes. This is one of the ways Pushkin defines his difference, his separateness, from Evgeny.

F. D. Reeve. *KR*. Summer, 1964, p. 542

Rublyov, the old Russian icon painter; Goya; Gauguin; Miró—this eclectic roll-call of painters is heard in Voznesensky's poems, and a sense of freedom and liberation in the worlds of shapes and color, combined with the "inward vision" of a Paul Klee, will be found in [Voznesenski's poems]. Also, indications of influences by the great classics of modern European poetry, Apollinaire with his Cubist mind-jumps and juxtapositions, Mayakovsky, Pasternak, and Federico Garcia Lorca: the visionary clarity and sharpness of his images. . . . To him, Voznesensky pays moving homage, in "Lover of Lorca": this section of prose gives greater insight into the mind that is Andrei Voznesensky than any amount of analytical or descriptive wordage could, and I would like to end this introductory note by quoting a paragraph from it here: "Poetry always means revolution. The hypocrite jailers of the New Inquisition recognized it in the songs of Lorca: he was all freedom inside, abandon and wildness. A tulip, growing at the foot of a concrete bulwark: it is like a shout of rebellion."

Anselm Hollo, ed. Introduction to
Selected Poems of Andrei Voznesensky
(New York, Grove Press, 1964), pp. 11–12

What Voznesenskij is hinting at with this title ["Parabolicheskaya ballada" ("The Parabola")] is a combination of several things. One is a topic which during the last forty years has perhaps been the most controversial in the Soviet literary discussion: the way of poetry to its reader, the relationship between the poet and his public. At first glance this does not seem to be a problem too difficult to solve. If we should make a geometrical approach—why not the straight line? The shortest distance between two points—is not that the simplest and at the same time the most natural path of a verbal message from sender to receiver? It may be so as regards everyday communication, or the languages of science and logic. But does it also have reference to poetry? . . .

Socialist realism, as we know, solved the problem in its own way. The demand for mass-communication completely drowned all lyricism. The straight line was victorious, quite in accordance with what Evgenij Zamjatin had once predicted in his novel *We:* "The line of the united state is the straight line. The divine, exact, wise straight line, the wisest of all lines." For this reason it is easy to understand that after Stalin's death young poets have taken up this question again, trying to solve it from a new point of view.

It is, I think, against this background that Voznesenskij's title gets its first meaning. To stress this interpretation he wrote a poem called "Parabolic Ballad" ("Paraboličeskaja ballada"). It has the distinct character of a manifesto.

Nils Ake Nilsson. Scando-Slavica. 10, 1964, pp. 49–50

The name of Voznesensky in Soviet poetry often becomes the centre of heated discussion. The young poet leaves nobody indifferent. Widely differing estimations are given to his poetry—some call him a daring innovator, others a cold rhymester.

Even his supporters among critics admit that sometimes his good qualities turn into their own opposites—the intricacy of his verse becomes an intentional complexity, his unconventional manner of expression becomes an effort to be original and his attempt to give an all-embracing treatment of his theme leads to fragmentation and lack of unity. When theoreticians write about Voznesensky, who claims that his teachers were Mayakovsky, Pasternak and Tsvetayeva, they invariably ask themselves a question: how can he unite in his poetry such different schools, outlooks and styles? Perhaps Voznesensky is an eclectic? Moreover, though each of the above-mentioned poets has his own style, and his own, personal destiny, all of them reflect the epoch in which they lived and worked. Does Voznesensky's complicated, "tattered" poetry reflect *his* day too? . . .

For Voznesensky lyrical digressions and the thread of the plot are merely a starting point of his composition. His thought branches out, the form follows his reflections which are at times rather vague, tense, full of contrasts and contradictions. Then suddenly the verse is interrupted by a prose-passage—a piece of information from a theoretical book on physics —then a quotation from Mayakovsky, then a historian's conception of the "age-reversal" of humanity. Then commentaries on the plot are introduced (sometimes, for example, in the form of notes in the margins of the forgotten notebook, written by a commonplace character, a physicist who knew nothing outside of his science). Then comes the theme of the poet's grotesque introductions in which a serious idea is ridiculed by presenting it in rhythms suggesting classical translations of Edgar Poe. The tension of atomic catastrophe is debunked by introducing trite, popular-song refrains about the vanity of earthly existence.

> *Progress becomes reactionary*
> *If Man crumbles under its onslaught.*

That is his credo. He sees the humanistic value of progress in the integrity of personality, in the individual's natural and harmonious relation-

ship to the world he lives in. That is why we may state that in his best
works Voznesensky reflects his time. That is why we find it only natural
that contemporary Soviet literature should produce—among others—
also such a poet as Andrei Voznesensky.

Vladimir Ognev. SL. Oct., 1965, pp. 196–98

Here, at least, is a poet who knows that, whatever else it may be, a poem
is a verbal artifact which must be as skillfully and solidly constructed as
a table or a motor-bicycle. Whatever effects can be secured in Russian
by rhythm, rhyme, assonance, and contrasts of diction, he clearly knows
all about. . . .

Effects like the introduction of a slang word for nose in the middle of
more conventional diction can be reproduced more or less in another language, but Mr. Voznesensky's metrical effects must make any translator
despair. Russian verse seems to be predominantly trochaic or dactylic,
whereas English falls naturally into iambic or anapaestic patterns.

Obvious, too, at a glance is the wide range of subject matter by which
Mr. Voznesensky is imaginatively excited—he is equally interested in
animals and airports, native and alien landscapes—and the variety of
tones, elegiac, comic, grotesque, quiet, rebellious, etc., which he can
command.

Lastly, every word he writes, even when he is criticizing, reveals a profound love for his native land and its traditions. I wish to stress this
strongly because, given the existing political climate, there is a danger
that we shall misunderstand him by looking for ideological clues instead
of reading his poems as one would read any poet who is a fellow-country-
man.

W. H. Auden. NYR. April 14, 1966, p. 3

Voznesensky is exciting to hear even if his voice is distant and muffled by
translation. He writes about war, nature, hatred, love, cruelty, clerks,
airports, bicycles, computers; he writes about man dehumanized by objects and man humanizing objects. He is contemporary in his imagery,
subject matter, and cacophonous rhythms; and he is Russian in his insistence on being human. He communicates shock and wonder before a
world that grows stranger every day, and confidence and hope in his attempts lyrically, tenderly, outrageously, and whimsically to make it familiar. I think, to judge from his poems, he likes America, and America,
too, will like him.

Edward Wasiolek. BW. May 22, 1966, p. 2

In poetry—Voznesensky asserts in a note—"the best tradition is novelty."
And he pursues it sometimes with notable effect as in "New York Airport
at Night" ["Nochnoi aeroport v Nyu-Iorke"], which is well translated

in both collections. Here the poet boldly identifies himself with the huge glass structure which in the end inspires an outpouring of almost mystical transports. Arresting, too, is the long poem "The Masters" ["Mastera"], on the building of St. Basil's Cathedral. . . . To appreciate the novelty of the poem, one must read the conclusion with its amazing fusion of the craftsman of the time of Ivan the Terrible with those of the Soviet Union, with whom Voznesensky symbolically identifies himself in celebrating his country's progress.

Equally impressive in its novelty is "The Skull Ballad" ["Lobnaya ballada"], in which the decapitated head of Peter the Great's unfaithful mistress speaks out in defense of her conduct to the Czar, who is present at the execution. . . .

Some of the poems, and their translations in these collections, reach the reader readily enough, such as "I Am Goya" ["Goiya"], "The Cashier" ["Kassirsha"], "My Achilles Heart" ["Akhillesovo serdtse"], "Dead Still" ["Zamerli"], "Hunting a Hare" ["Okhota na zaitsa"]—brilliantly rendered by Auden—and "First Frost" ["Pervy lyod"] which is wonderfully effective in its simplicity. But other poems seem banal or as naïve and ambiguous in their communication as a child's smudged finger paintings.

Nor, after perusing the originals, can one always agree with the assertion of the editors of *Antiworlds* that Voznesensky's modernist use of language is always disciplined and devoid of the tendency of lesser poets to flaunt their emancipation in this respect. Though he no doubt possesses a mastery of his medium, Voznesensky's employment of scientific and technological terms is excessive, and his effects in language in general and in poetic devices are at times overdone and patently contrived. But there can be no question of his talent or that his poetry—as Auden puts it—has much to say to foreign readers as well as to Russians.

Ernest J. Simmons. *NYT*. June 19, 1966, p. 7

The youthful and brilliant Andrei Voznesensky descends as much from Mandelstam, whom he never mentions, as he does from Pasternak and Lorca, to whom he pays eloquent tribute. He is strong (as he needs to be under the circumstances), talented, and in his reach and ambition, capacious. Perhaps this makes him sound too solemn; his work also has about it a touch of Marcel Duchamp, dada, and the Beatles. . . .

At these readings [in the United States], how terribly young, how awkward, how altogether "homey" and out of place this homely, tall young man appeared—until he began to read. It was broadly dramatic in the Russian manner; but there was also irony about the Russian manner, a nimble humor that was at the same time tense and confident. He contrasted with his older and professionally practiced translators there on the platform with him, who, though some read their translations quite well, seemed to place themselves deliberately out of place, as though they meant to apologize for a poet's appearing in public at all. "An artist true-born . . . is both tribune and trouble-maker," Voznesensky has written. He not only carried the role on-stage, he projected a sense of the cost and the suffering, but also of the delights of the play and the possibility of a real creativity in that very tension.

His poems are the dynamic asides of a very private person in a very public place. Who is the audience? Who is the poet? They become one; they incorporate each other. Worlds are energized by their antiworlds. The poet has his counterpart in Bukashkin (Buggins-Parnok-Akaky), the withered and dehumanized clerk, and even in his socialist-realist critic who grows "an anti-head." The self-affirmed genius Andrei Voznesensky looks back and tries not to let go of "Andriusha"; he cries from the platform of a train to a receding feminine figure "Save me!" The poet is an airport, a center of world-communication, into and through which the outcasts of the world must pass and be transformed. Poetry is a severed head in the hands of power, speaking not only to the drama-stricken multitude that watches, but in bubbles of blood to the very hands of power that dangle it. Worlds and antiworlds are ineluctably interlocked and in their high-tension become each other: "If you live, you burn!"

Sidney Monas. *HdR*. Spring, 1967, pp. 132–33

As the years pass, Voznesenski's wish is to gain the limelight more often. Examples of this are "Lonzhyumo" and "Oza" and his lyrics of recent years. . . .

For Voznesenski himself, the concept of the poem "Lonzhyumo" rests in his own convictions about the life force and the contemporary meaning of the ideals of the revolution. Because the poem about Lenin turned out to be so personal and lyrically exciting, it seems the poet came to this thing as if to a confession and communion. The spiritual contact with Lenin and with his ideas opened for the poet the prospective of a deeper understanding of the present era.

The poem "Oza" is the epicenter of the book *Akhillesovo serdtse* [Achilles Heart], and all parts of the book are related to this poem and permeated with its ideals. "Oza" synthesized in a single artistic organism all that had been stored up from various sources of perception and every-thing that sought and found an outlet in the concrete and in generalized pictures and images. The overall human theme of protecting the person-ality from the despiritualization of robotization and the theme of love and its true freedom in an age of cruel shocks are freely and organically embodied in this poem. The numerous branchings of the general theme of the work deepen the poetic conception of man—a free man in a free world who makes subservient to himself the blessings of progress and civilization.

In "Oza" Voznesenski explicitly shows the danger that technical progress hides within itself to be used for the suppression of man's personality. The poet leads a man to the edge of disaster to give him a feeling of the chill of nonexistence. A similar idea of opposition is that every man should think about the forestallment of the possible catastrophe. The lyrical hero of the work enters a path where his eyes begin to open, a path along which every man must travel. When he thinks about his loved one, he thinks about all mankind.

A. Mikhailov. *Moskva.* June, 1967, p. 204†

A notable, and in the end not quite satisfactory, long poem, "Oza," written in alternations of verse and prose, and in a fine variety of metres which at one point parodies Poe's "The Raven," explores the feelings of an artist in a world of science. In one delicate and moving section, already famous, the central theme of protecting gentle and intuitional human values against the encroachments of cybernetics is floated into the image of a pair of woman's slippers, empty but still warm from the feet, lying askew and helpless "like doves perched in the path of a tank." Voznesensky can say "I love Dubna" (the atomic research centre), yet remain deeply suspicious of the research his scientific friends are engaged in; the fragmented body of the poem reflects divisions and uncertainties in his own mind. Is one wrong to be disappointed that such a fine sensibility as his should seem to be adding his voice to the anti-science brigade? He refers to Russia as the land "of Rublev, Blok, and Lenin," which brings together art, poetry, and politics. But Russia is also Lomonosov, Mendeleyev, and Gagarin, and there is nothing to be ashamed of in that.

TLS. Nov. 2, 1967, p. 1039

[Voznesensky] is acutely aware of himself, of his own body and embarrassed by the sense of being yet another object in a world of valueless objects, a world at times oppressive in its heaviness and density and at times frightening in its fugitive fragmentariness. This is his sense of fallenness, his metaphysical doubt. But Voznesensky does not rest there. As an artist, he is able to attack the world and affirm himself. The seen becomes the seer. The object becomes the triumphant subject. He volatilises the density of the world and lightens its darkness so that in the luminosity of what has been made transparent true existence becomes apparent. And he gives shape and life to a drifting fragmentary universe by his dynamic curves and parabolas.

Voznesensky is also a civic poet who has written a number of poems on the theme of Lenin. What is interesting in these poems is to see how Lenin is placed firmly within the general topography of Voznesensky's poetry. . . . Lenin appears in these poems not in any social or historical situation, but within that condition of metaphysical doubt felt by the objectified person. . . .

Brittleness, brashness, technical brilliance are not merely qualities of Voznesensky's verse but an integral part of what he has to say about his existence. Face to face with a world in which existence may appear gratuitous and obscene, Voznesensky on the one hand gives acute expression to this human predicament while simultaneously wrestling with it and attempting to bring his world to a tense, dynamic equilibrium. In this he evokes the aid of artists, and, more boldly, Lenin who is less of an historical than an existential Lenin set firmly within the topography of Voznesensky's poetical universe.

W. Gareth Jones. *SEER*. Jan., 1968, pp. 86–87, 90

Like Yevtushenko, Voznesensky seems to be writing too fast, spurred on perhaps by the thought of the large hungry audiences at his public readings, but unlike Yevtushenko's, the poems on the page nearly always manage to suggest the firm tones of an individual voice, even in translation. He is liable to be sentimental about girls weeping in telephone boxes or about women having to live without men and his moralising often seems facile, but he largely redeems himself by the speed of his gearchanges and the rich mixture of scenes and images. Technically he is very canny, swathing rough subject matter in smooth prosody (as in "Ballad of a Skull") and using his almost metaphysical wit to make the dreariest of objects into springboards for his energetic imagination. . . .

When he finally tries to put everything—including the poem and himself—into perspective, Voznesensky sounds a bit like one of Chekhov's characters speculating about what the world will be like without them and what difference, if any, their lives will have made. But, saying goodbye to Zoya-Oza-Life, the predominant feeling is positive because it was so well worth while knowing her, even if the struggle to keep her was bound to end in defeat.

Ronald Hayman. *Encounter*. July, 1968, pp. 69–70

Semantic shift, excessive alliteration, a predilection for technical terms and foreign words, frequent use of near rhymes and striking metaphors, and a large variety of stanzaic patterns are characteristic of Voznesenskij's poetry, and yet fail to characterize it. Voznesenskij employs the semantic shift brilliantly, but often reverts to conventional rhyme, assonance, and alliteration. Many of his metaphors are striking; many are strained. His near rhymes would be more impressive were one oblivious to Majakovskij's genius for rhyme. His stanzaic patterns are sometimes perfect, sometimes ordinary, and sometimes the sole feature which rescues his words from becoming prose.

Voznesenskij's themes occasionally are as elusive as his formal technique ("Sketch for a Poem" ["Eskiz poemy"]), which makes the editors' task of arranging the poems according to theme and content a difficult one indeed. In the last analysis, however, his best poems are unified both in theme and in the consistent application of formal devices (e.g., "I am Goya" and "Autumn in Sigulda" ["Osen v Sigulde"]. The long, vari-structured poem "Oza" (1964) contains his most intense "love song" to date.

Daniel Bures. *SEEJ*. Fall, 1968, pp. 366–67

YESENIN, SERGEI (1895–1925)

Yesenin's previous lyrics were deeply traditional. They proceeded both from Fet and the conventional poetic populism as well as from the primitively understood populism of Klyuev and Blok. Essentially, Yesenin was never really a strong innovator, a leftist, or an independent spirit. The least convincing is his relationship with the imagists, who, to be sure, were neither particularly new nor independent; it is not even certain that they really existed at all. Yesenin's lyrics had a strong emotional tone. The naïve, sincere, and therefore unusual vital emotionality of his poems—this is what Yesenin is leaning upon. His main concern in poetry is the incessant search for the embellishment of this naked emotion: first the old church slavonicisms, the painstakingly maintained rural coating, and the very traditional "muzhik Christ"; then the selected diction from the repertory of the imagists, which meant essentially the same embellishment for Yesenin's emotionality as the old church slavonicisms. [1924]

Yuri Tynyanov. *Arkhaisty i novatory*
(Leningrad, Priboi, 1929), pp. 544–45†

Yesenin's career, closed for the present with poems about the tavern Moscow, is very indicative. It demonstrates that in our era [Yesenin's earlier, peasant-extolling works], in some form or other, lost their positive meaning long ago, outgrew themselves, and became extinct. . . . The muzhik-*Inoniya* has led one of the greatest poets to the tavern, to café hooliganism. There is nothing accidental about this; on the contrary, it is a symbol, the sign of the times, its ruthless logic. . . .

Yesenin's gift manifests itself in the world of concrete, rural figures; his force, in the ability to make them real to the point of tangibility. He has the formalistic ability to bring into our poetry simplicity, strength, and succulence wrought out of folklore, the epic, the songs, and so forth. He is one of the most delicate and fine lyric poets of our time. However, a "studied aberration" sidetracked the poet away from these direct aims; and the inner disintegration of his poetical personality, along with the elements of ideological decomposition, threaten him with destruction. Yesenin has a few followers and imitators. Suffice it to say that Vsevolod Ivanov's prose is very akin to the "inutterable animalism" and figurativeness of Yesenin. Yesenin is read a lot. Is it not possible that he may, in fact, enter our great epoch mainly as the author of *Moskva kabatskaya* (*The Tavern Moscow*)? At the present, he "is spreading around himself the space" in that direction. [1924]

A. K. Voronski. *Literaturno-kriticheskie stati* (Moscow, Sovetski pisatel, 1963), pp. 264–65, 269†

Yesenin accepted the revolution as Blok did. He did not understand the revolution's momentous significance for the countryside and peasantry. Its power was a drum roll hailing the collapse of the old order. The old order bent down in the face of the revolution.

His mystical "Tovarishch" ("Comrade"), in which Christ descends from the icon and goes to the barricades and dies there, differs little from Blok's *The Twelve*, not withstanding that it was written earlier. Yesenin hailed the revolutionary storm, writing still more poems glorifying it. But on the whole, the revolutionary upsurge bypassed him, for the social movements which he represented were not standing in its mainstream. At this time a new period of creativity began for him, a new illness. This period was to link his work with the imagists.

V. Kirshon. *Krasnaya nov.* Dec., 1925, p. 47†

We have lost Esenin—such a fine poet, so fresh and real. And we have lost him so tragically. He left of his own accord, bidding farewell with his own blood to an undesignated friend, maybe to all of us. Startling for their tenderness and softness are these his last lines. He left life without a clamorous insult, without a pose of protest—not slamming the door, but quietly closing it with his blood-soaked hand. In this gesture the poetic and human image of Esenin has blazed forth in an unforgettable farewell light.

Esenin composed the sharp songs of a *hooligan* and added his inimitable Esenin melodiousness to the naughty sounds of coarse Moscow. He frequently plumed himself with an insolent gesture, with a rude word. But above all this quivered the quite special tenderness of an unprotected, undefended soul. With half-superficial coarseness Esenin sought refuge from the stern time into which he was born; he sought refuge, but did not find it. . . .

Our time is a stern time, maybe the sternest in the history of so-called civilized mankind. The revolutionary born for these decades is possessed by the violent patriotism of his epoch—his fatherland in time. Esenin was not a revolutionary. The author of "Pugachev" and "The Ballad of the Twenty-Six" ["Ballada o dvadtsati shesti"] was a most intimate lyric poet. Our epoch is not lyrical. In this lies the *main* reason why self-

willfully and prematurely Sergei Esenin left us and his epoch. [1926]
Leon Trotsky. Quoted in *RR*. April, 1967, pp. 142–43

Yesenin was a broken man. He was spoiled by success and by exaggerated attention—the unavoidable tribute which the inadequate cultural environment pays to its favorites. He possessed many traits that made for complexity in his character: an unusual faith in himself and a shy, sometimes transparent, insecurity; a brash audacity and timidity; a rigid coarseness of the heart along with tender lyricism. All these spoke of duality of his character. But as a poet, he was of one piece, poured out of good, though fragile, glass. He lived no dual life: his poems were his real existence, though a torturing and dissatisfying one. In contrast to many contemporary poets, he did not write poetry in order to live: he lived in order to write poetry. And his true portrait, the one that will remain in history, is contained in the pages of his slender booklets. The key to his drama can be found in the close connection between poetry and the inner life, in the lyrical disposition of his soul. Life is "the prison of emotions," and the poet is condemned "to turn the grindstones of poems." Such is the fate of a poet caught in the narrow circle of lyricism. Yesenin could not find an exit from this circle, although he was searching for it anxiously and untiringly. . . .

Is there any wonder that this romanticist of the grandfather's village life avoided city motifs? They were incompatible with his poetic consciousness. The city entered the scene only when an elemental danger threatening the village appeared in the poet's view. In Yesenin's lexical richness, full of precious stones, and in his entire poetic worldview, there appeared only one image by which he fully expressed his feelings about the city— "the iron guest," resembling "the martial god" from a painting of a German romanticist, steps gloomily and slowly forward, leaving in his wake a dead strip. With that dreary and lifeless image, Yesenin examined nothing in the city up close. Roaming through the world, sailing twice across the ocean on an iron ship, having experienced the ecstasy of a flight on the iron bird, having availed himself of all achievements of an industrial culture, and colliding on every step with its power, he was still not influenced by any of these achievements. He sang, humorously at that, only about a wildly glittering hat and polished boots. Alien to the city, he remained deaf to the city's culture; for him, it confined itself to iron-cement and the multicolored lanterns of the cafés. It is strange: after traveling through Western Europe, he went to America, where he saw and heard many remarkable things—after all, America and the West represent everything mankind has achieved in its cultural history. Yet, foreign travels were not reflected either in his poetry or in his thinking, just as if they never existed. He returned across the ocean in the same frame of mind as when he went there, only his voice became more hollow and he began to drink more often and more despairingly. There was nothing in Europe and America that could draw his attention or exert an influence on him, either in a small or a big way.

Vyacheslav Polonski. *Novy mir.*
Jan., 1926, pp. 158–59†

Esenin is probably to-day, of all contemporary Russian poets, the most sincerely appreciated. His appeal has been wide and many-sided. The principal reasons for his popularity are, in the first place, an unquestionable spontaneous gift of song, in which he has few equals; in the second place, an essential "conservativeness" of his poetry. It is thoroughly "nineteenth-century" and emotional, quite free both from the unexpectedness that makes the poetry of Pasternak and Marina Tsvetayeva so disconcerting, and from the deliberate crudeness that makes Mayakovsky's so unpalatable to the reader whose taste has been educated on 19th century standards. Both the revolutionary mysticism of Esenin's poems of 1917–1918, and the elaborate conceits of his imaginistic period were only skin-deep. The essence of his genius is a wistful melancholy, dashed through occasionally by a daredevil "hooliganism" (one of his most characteristic poems is entitled "The Confession of a Hooligan" ["Ispoved khuligana"]), which makes him profoundly akin both to the Russian folk-song and to the poetry of the age of Turgenev.

D. S. Mirsky. *SEER.* March, 1926, pp. 706–7

Some time later, one afternoon when Isadora sat in her room with some callers Esenin came again to demand his bust. He demanded it loudly and instantly, and finally forced his drunken way into the room. The bust, which Konienkov had genially hacked out of a huge block of wood, stood atop a high bric-a-brac cabinet in one corner of the room. When Isadora refused to give him the bust and asked him to come back again some time when he was more fit to carry it away, he dragged a chair over to the corner and with shaky legs mounted it. As he reached the bust with feverish hands and clasped it, its weight proved too much for him. He staggered and fell from the chair, rolling head over heels on the floor, still clasping tightly to his breast his wooden image. Sullenly and shakily he rose to his feet; and then reeled out of the room to wander later about the byways of Moscow and lose the encumbering bust in some gutter. That was the last view Isadora Duncan had of her poet and her husband, Sergey Alexandrovich Esenin.

Irma Duncan and Allan Ross Macdougall.
Isadora Duncan's Russian Days
(New York, Covici, Friede, 1929), pp. 226–27

There was his separation from Isadora and the lonely return to Moscow. There was a new marriage and a new separation. In passing, there were many more love meetings and separations. There was a trip to Persia and his "forced rest" . . . in the mental hospital. There was his last and very sad trip to the country, where everything charmed him. There were, at the end, new drinking bouts and debaucheries, which were different from the former ones in that they invariably ended in anti-Soviet and anti-Semitic pranks. Almost every night the drunk Yesenin would scream out in a restaurant or in Red Square, "Kill the Communists! Save Russia!" and other similar things. Of course, anyone else but Yesenin would have been executed. But the perplexed powers-that-be did not know how to handle the "first peasant poet." They tried to appeal to his conscience—without result. They tried to frighten him by putting him under "public trial" in the "House of Printing"; this didn't help either. In the end, oddly enough, the Bolsheviks gave in. The Moscow police were ordered to take the scandalizing Yesenin to the police station until he became sober, and "to pay no further attention to the matter." Soon, the Moscow police force knew Yesenin by sight.

Yesenin is significant in that he appeared at the time of the Russian people's realization of "Russia's horrible years," he was with them to the end, and he became a symbol of Russia's fall and her striving to be reborn. In this, the Pushkin-like indispensability of Yesenin, his sinful life and imperfect poems, turned into a source of light and goodness. Therefore, wthout exaggerating, we can say that Yesenin is Pushkin's successor in our days.

Georgi Ivanov. *Peterburgskie zimy* (New York,
Izdatelstvo imeni Chekhova, 1952), pp. 238, 240†

[Yesenin] on the one hand, and Mayakovsky on the other, are the two dominant figures among the crop of the poets who came into their own during the first decade of the Soviet regime. Yet what a contrast between these two gifted youths, both of whom ended eventually by suicide! While Mayakovsky became the poetic voice of the rising proletarians, Esenin preferred to turn his enormous gift into a lament for the old peasant Russia, and he could hardly have made any other choice. Born and brought up in the depths of rural Russia (the district of Ryazan), Esenin was so much steeped in the soil and the peasant lore that he was never able to detach himself from them, not even when he did his best to fit into the life of the capital, or into the spirit of the Revolution. It would be a mistake, though, to regard his rural poetry from the angle of mere village folk-lore or local color. It goes deeper. In a way it could be defined as poetic self-assertion of the "eternal peasant" against the encroaching machine and the mentality of the industrial town. The village in its primeval quintessence, sifted through his individual temperament, found in Esenin's verse one of the most poignant expressions in modern poetry. It was and remained the basic and perhaps the only source of his inspiration.

Janko Lavrin. *Russian Writers*
(New York, Van Nostrand, 1954), pp. 290–91

Both the early revolutionary pieces, which are the weakest part of his work, and the later autobiographical poems may all too often seem to a foreign reader the most important fruits of this poet's talent. Certainly, nobody can deny their significance as human and social documents. Yet the most genuine of Esenin's masterpieces are to be found among his shortest and less ambitious lyrics, written in the pure and simple modes of the elegy and the idyll, devoid of any rhetorical and anecdotical structure, and lightly woven as a cobweb of transparent words around the cluster of a few bright and striking images. Each one of these songs may be reduced to a landscape and to the mood it evokes within the soul of the poet. Although the narrative element is lacking, or hardly present, the poems partake of the magic aura of the legend and the fairy tale. They recreate a private and intimate universe, domestic and rustic, where all things are humanized by a naïve animism, by a pathetic anthropomorphism. The ingenuousness of Esenin's vision is evident in the central image of each one of such poems, defining its object by a kind of childish puzzle that follows or accompanies its name.

It is from the same simplicity of outlook that Esenin derives his gusto for the colorful, the vivid, the picturesque. His favorite color is the color of the sky, in all its shades, and he loves it so much as to attribute it to his native land, to his "blue Russia." But his poems are equally full of white and yellow patches, so enameled as to give the effect of gold and silver, and to remind us of icon and miniature painting, of Byzantine mosaics and of popular prints or cuts. This chromatism is not merely a decorative, but rather a compositional element, and intensifies the stylization of the poet's vision, so evident in the stillness of the landscapes, with their motionless figures and timeless moods. But almost always this stillness is broken by a sudden burst of song, by a hidden stream of music, changing the stasis into ecstasy, and flooding the entire scene with a melodic grief which makes a vibrant chord of every fiber.

Renato Poggioli. *SEEJ*. Spring, 1958, pp. 18–19

In subsequent poems, Yesenin uses and develops the same images. Terrestrial truth is the embodiment of celestial truth, and terrestrial is as holy as celestial.

In his poems, Yesenin will use Christian myth and Christian terminology, which have been familiar to him since his childhood, all the while breathing into them a content and meaning entirely his own. In this way, the old peasant image of the earth equals a cow; the harvest, a calf. Yesenin simply enlivens and makes frequent use of this because it is well suited to his own conception of the world.

Here is how this pseudo-Christian terminology can be deciphered: the Virgin = the earth = a cow = peasant Russia; God the father = the sky = truth; Christ = the son of sky and earth = a harvest = a calf = the incarnation of celestial truth = the future Russia. He understands this Russia to be a terrestrial paradise, the result of a mystical revolution.

Sophie Lafitte. *Serge Essénine—une étude*
(Paris, P. Seghers, 1959), p. 99†

Above all, Yesenin was a poet. Historical events, love, friendship—all these retreated before poetry. He had a rare gift for a song. . . . No one can explain why we are moved by many of his poems. . . . Yesenin wrote poetry simply because he had been born a poet. . . . Deep sadness was an inherent characteristic of Yesenin's poetic voice. This sadness cannot be blamed on the epoch. . . . He himself knew that no one was to blame for his loneliness and his misery. . . .

In life he was gentle and touching but at the same time, in the furry of his inner conflict, intolerable. I have seen him tender, calm, and attentive, but also in a state bordering on madness. . . . In Berlin I saw him several times with Isadora Duncan. She realized that he was going through a terrible ordeal, wanted to help him, but could not. She was almost twice as old as he was and possessed not only great talent but humanity, tenderness, and tact. But he was a nomadic gypsy. Nothing frightened him so much as the thought of being emotionally settled.

He was always surrounded by fellow nomads: imagists, Kusikov with his guitar, and the "peasant poets" who looked as if they had stepped off the lacquered lids of Palekh boxes. The poets were simply elbowed out by drunks happy to be allowed at the table of a famous man.

Ilya Ehrenburg. *Novy mir.* Feb., 1961, pp. 103–4†

YEVTUSHENKO, YEVGENI (1933–   )

Evtushenko's career has depended partly on his remarkable facility as a poet. He said that he was able to go to the *Literary Gazette*'s offices—he contributes regularly to this newspaper—and write a poem on a given theme in a few hours. Thus his poems are uneven, sometimes brash, with a journalistic stamp on them, but they are always individual. Evtushenko has a certain tone all his own. At best, his poems are tender, yet virile. He is frequently compared to Mayakovsky, and his mixture of declarative matter-of-factness and subjectivity is reminiscent of that great revolutionary poet. Evtushenko is, of course, a lesser poet than Mayakovsky, but as an individual he too has created an image of the poet as a Communist participating in public affairs. Paradoxically, in a society in which all poets have been expected to voice their adherence to Communist ideals and to participate in politics, those two almost alone have created such a public image. Every other outstanding Russian poet of our time—Akhmatova, Mandelstam, Martinov—emphasizes the individual rather than the social role of man.

In fact, Evtushenko's tone as a poet is deceptively simple and it is misleading to compare him to some other poet. Without being a poetic genius, he has created a lyric style which is the mark of a generation in the USSR. He has asserted and sung his own spontaneity, his optimism, his youth. Youth proved a powerful force against the monolithic official ways.

Youth is Evtushenko's principal theme, or rather his consistent point of view.

Olga Andreyev Carlisle. *Voices in the Snow*
(New York, Random House, 1962), pp. 82–83

Yevtushenko's heroes are those who through honesty and strength of character stand up for the truth as they see it, regardless of their unpopularity and the spite of less men: no poem expresses this better than does "Kar'era" ["Career"], and in several others it is a fundamental theme. . . . He strives in such a direction himself—though with a strong consciousness of his own shortcomings. He admires women for their mental and physical toughness and fixity of purpose. Not surprisingly Hemingway—tough, solitary, uncompromising—is an admired figure. . . . In fact the people Yevtushenko admires are not confined to any one class or country or system of belief. He sees a nation of good people stretching across the world; also a nation of the philistines, a nation of the bureaucrats, a nation of the blinkered, the out-of-date. Yevtushenko is very much a man of his generation; he has more fellow-feeling with the young writers of modern America than with those of his compatriots who cannot move with the times. He is a citizen of the world, hungry for new experience and new human contact . . . yet of course more than anywhere he loves Russia . . . its efforts to build a new society, its past heroism which is thrown into all the sharper relief by manifestations of philistinism or vulgarity.

R. Milner-Gulland. Introduction to Yevgeny
Yevtushenko, *Selected Poetry*, ed. R. Milner-Gulland
(Oxford, Pergamon Press, 1963), p. xviii

Evtushenko is very strongly attached to and proud of his rugged Siberian ancestry, a feeling which does not tend to make him a defender of the Western way of life, traditionally considered by Russians as spoiled and soft. . . . Judged on the basis of the poems in *Wave of the Hand* [*Vzmakh ruki*], Evtushenko is neither pro-Western nor anti-Soviet. Expressed bluntly, *he knows where his bread is buttered*. He remains consistently apolitical; when commissioned to produce a few pro-Soviet or anti-Western propaganda items, he discreetly intersperses them among his lines, as . . . in his "Verses on Foreign Lands" ["Stikhi o zagranitse"].

Evtushenko's anger is of a subtle, general, and abstract nature; it springs from his keen sympathy for the underdog (perhaps reminiscent of Victor Hugo's angry romantic outcry: "I love the spider and the nettle, because they are hated!"), as well as from a devastating contempt for mediocrity and hypocrisy.

Max Oppenheimer, Jr. *SAB*. May, 1963, p. 3

Deprived of the benefit of its author's delivery and reduced to a printed page, Yevtushenko's poetry produces a frankly disappointing impression. He is by no means the important and original Russian poet that his current international publicity would lead one to believe.

Yevtushenko is predominantly a civic poet. As such, he voices, in versified editorials and within certain prescribed limits, the aspirations of the Soviet younger generation. Abroad, his poems are often read as a sort of political barometer. Both at home and abroad his popularity seems to be due to extra-literary reasons. His more orthodox pieces, such as the protestations of fealty to the Revolution or the odes in honor of Fidel Castro, are not very different from the sort of thing Soviet poets wrote under Stalin, except possibly for the "Yevtushenko rhyme." (The method of rhyming in which the first rather than the last syllable of the final word in a line is rhymed, with an assonance in the stressed syllable where the rhymed syllable is unstressed, was introduced in Russian poetry at the turn of the century, evidently by Zinaida Hippius and was later used by Gumilev in *Zavodi*. It is at present very popular with the younger Soviet poets and Yevtushenko is usually credited with having invented it.)

Yevtushenko also writes more personal poetry in which he comes close to the kind of verse Igor Severyanin used to write around 1912. This resemblance is evident both in Yevtushenko's bouncy and facile enthusiasm and in his attempts to achieve elegance by using a "refined" foreign vocabulary. . . .

For all that, the sheer fact of Yevtushenko's popularity may yet lead to new and salutary developments in Russian poetry. Despite the orthodox tone of much of what he has to say, he does make a conscious effort to bring the Russian verse back into the twentieth century from the limbo of the Soviet neo-Victorianism to which it was relegated under Stalin. Above all, there is in his work an open concern for problems of technique and versification. In the work of Yevtushenko's more talented contemporaries

(Voznesensky, Akhmadulina, Novella Matveeva), his example has already
led to some fresh and promising poetic departures.

                                   Simon Karlinsky. *BA*. Summer, 1963, p. 355

This book, one might conclude, is shaped by strategy, which makes it full
of intellectual banality and political piety—a work of little intrinsic interest to the student of modern culture. In this sense, the rebel would seem
to be tainted by the world he would transform. But if one sees Evtushenko
in relation to the situation in Russia, it is possible to read the book through
the euphemisms, as it were, as a daring polemic, a personal statement by
a courageous, embattled and fragile man. There is no place where literature—as exemplified by a militant few—is engaged more fully in the
cause of humanism. The record of Evtushenko's collisions with the cultural bosses—the time-serving editors, the poet-bureaucrats of the Writers'
Union—not only testifies to his courage, but also indicates the terms of
the cultural war. It should be remembered, too, that one of the cruellest
risks he runs is estrangement from the purists of his own group, who may
denounce him as a bad poet, a crowd-pleaser, an international clown. If
he is able to maintain his public position and to endure as a person and
to grow as a poet, he will at least have served the cause he stands for.

                                   Rufus Mathewson. *PR*. Fall, 1963, p. 440

Evtushenko both suits and discomfits his age. He has adopted a striking
posture within a sentimental context—"When I was too unhappy and
lonely, the example of my friends gave me strength"—and he has been
aware of the temptation to pander—"There was of course the danger of
falling into rhetoric." He declared war on the Establishment, and he
catered to the desires of the young and the hopeful for stridency and no-
toriety. The fact that thereby he himself became notorious, and especially
the fact that he was touted in the West as a poet of protest, caused puri-
tanical, middle-class Russians to disavow him and his work. A prepon-
derant segment of poetry readers became hostile to Evtushenko for what
they considered provocative writing, avant-garde posing, and a sensation-
making personal life. A small group of genuine, dedicated, anti-Stalinist
intellectuals felt that Evtushenko, important as he was, had substituted
politics for poetry and betrayed both his own promise and the proper
future of Russian poetry. Like a number of intellectuals in the West, they
found that Evtushenko was turning out only inferior verse, that he had
become a poetaster, and they felt that he was allowing himself to be
used by the Establishment as a spokesman for the younger generation. I
suspect that Evtushenko was deeply affected by this judgment. All his
public triumphs could not overcome the gnawing awareness that his

poetry was essentially expedient. He had haplessly to push his luck farther. That is what this "autobiography" is.

F. D. Reeve. *HdR*. Winter, 1963–64, p. 612

Westerners do Yevtushenko a disservice by exclusively praising his political contribution. The old Irish freedom-fighter O'Leary once remarked to Yeats that you may be permitted almost any crime for the sake of your country except bad verse. Most of Yevtushenko's political poems are bad verse in a good cause. Meanwhile, what gets lost in the shuffle is Yevtushenko's excellent non-political love poetry. At heart he is not so much the tribune of "revisionism" as the troubadour of the "conspiracy of feelings." When I asked his ally, Ilya Ehrenburg, why the Young Communist League temporarily expelled Yevtushenko in the 1950's, Ehrenburg replied: "Puritanism is the curse of the Soviet arts. Yevtushenko's love poetry was guilty of revealing the State secret that men are physically different from women." . . .

Fundamentally Yevtushenko is not a political animal at all, though like his hero Mayakovsky he tries to be one. Yevtushenko is in the tradition of the magnetic, self-dramatizing Byronism of Lermontov, with just enough narcissistic hamminess to annoy his more serious friends when he exploits personality for the crowds but with enough real poetic genius to make them gladly forgive him and deeply believe in him. What makes it so painful to predict his future candidly is the fact that this Russian Byronizing tradition has an undercurrent of unconscious self-destructiveness, constantly oscillating between would-be folk hero and would-be martyr, between matinee idol and Grand Pariah.

Peter Viereck. *TriQuarterly*. Spring, 1965, pp. 25–26

Much of what appears in his autobiography would have been anticipated from a reading of Evtušenko's poetry. His disillusionment with the Stalin regime especially in the fields of literature and the arts leaves no doubt. In this period, he states, "Many Soviet writers failed to write about their personal thoughts, about their own complexities or conflicts, and needless to say, about the conflicts and complexities of others." As a rule in order for their poetry to be published they were forced to write a few lines devoted to Stalin. Evtušenko questions this and labels it as evil. . . .

In his *Avtobiografija* [*Autobiography*] he promotes Communistic views. He is a staunch believer in the Communist revolution and when he talks about his belief in the brotherhood of man, he means the brotherhood of man, Soviet-style. Throughout his poetry his beliefs are orthodox and there is no trace of disillusionment in Communism as was often reported in the West. His views are liberal and different from the dogmatic approach to life of Stalinists. But they are still Communistic and Russian. He glorifies the Russian people, Russian culture and Russian patience in the struggle for Communistic ideals.

His tragedy is in the fact that he was naïve enough to believe that the forces dominating the Soviet Union after Stalin's death would allow him to publish abroad his unauthorized life story without being subjected to punishment.

W. T. Zyla. BA. Autumn, 1965, pp. 474–75

The driving force of Yevtushenko's poetry was the passionate thirst for assertion, not only self-assertion but the assertion of the vitalizing force of the revolution, of faith in the spiritual force of the country, in justice, in the rights of man, and in the civic role of art.

The capacity to respond effectively with poetic passion to the questions troubling the reader, with emotion and clarity—these are the characteristics of his personal gift that played no small role in his popularity. Happily, in handling the evil of the day, he evaded the complexities of a temperamental Andrei Voznesenski and the rationality of a clever Robert Rozhdestvenski. The openness to which Yevtushenko was prone disposed him to confess courageously the confused state of his own spiritual world, clearly echoing a note of dissatisfaction with himself in his own poetry. . . .

The poem "Bratskaya GES" ("The Bratsk Hydroelectric Station") sums up these confessions: in general, the poem for the poet is always the summation of experience and long reflection. But such lines are not written for the sake of repentance and the confession of one's own weaknesses. Acknowledging that he was thrown "at times into the inflated uselessness of odes, into the false practicality of feuilletons," the poet hardly repents but rather calls out implacably. . . .

Being a summation, "The Bratsk Hydroelectric Station," like any real summation, is a serious step forward from the particular to the general and is done with the categorical manner and sweep peculiar to Yevtushenko. The lively aspect of the poet is reflected in the poem, together with everything that constitutes his qualities and, not without foundation, contributes to his deficiencies. But it is precisely that which is priceless and alive!

A. Makarov. Znamya. Oct., 1965, p. 230[†]

Yevtushenko is neither a modernist nor a strict adherent to tradition. When a somewhat hectic and not unattractive narcissistic self-examination is expressed through his favorite devices, he comes into his own. He is a narrative poet whether his pieces are long or short, and as a narrator and reciter he plays skillfully with language. Within conventional limits, he exploits frequent repetition, near rhymes, sustained and sonorous echoes.

Punning is an important device for him, as it is for most good young poets, and he revels in the game of verbal association which, until not so long ago, was almost illicit in Soviet poetry. Yevtushenko's dactylic rhymes do more than mark the ends of his lines. They bind and mirror associations.

Vera S. Dunham. NYT. Dec. 26, 1965, p. 17

If Mayakovsky was the poet of the Revolution, Yevtushenko occupies a similar position in the post-Stalin thaw. Something of Mayakovsky's personal dynamism and public appeal is present, though to a weaker degree, in Yevtushenko. In tone, language and form, Yevtushenko is at times very close to Mayakovsky. This is especially the case in his rhetorical poetry, declaimed "at the top of the voice" and addressed to the masses rather than to the "chosen few." . . .

Like Mayakovsky, Yevtushenko is primarily a "civic" poet (though not to the exclusion of personal, lyric poetry), involved in contemporary issues and committed to the ideology of the Communist regime. Yet the dissimilarities which become apparent at closer scrutiny—caused by different political and intellectual climates and by differing poetical personalities—may possibly be more fundamental and decisive than are the points of contact. . . . Yevtushenko is representative of those young poets who were slowly groping their way toward more individual and less prescribed art; but they were hardly daring innovators: they looked back to poets like Mayakovsky, just as they looked back to the Revolution as a distant ideal which had been darkened and corrupted.

Compared to Mayakovsky, Yevtushenko is more restrained, more narrow in his emotional scale and, possibly, more lyrical. Although he will avoid the "lapses" and vulgarity of Mayakovsky, his tendency at overt moralizing strikes at times an unpleasantly pedantic note as compared to Mayakovsky's expansiveness. Despite the fact that Yevtushenko is still developing, it seems fairly certain that he will never approach the linguistic genius and emotional élan of Mayakovsky.

Margaret Dalton. Nation. March 7, 1966, p. 271

Evtushenko's verse is subtle and responsive. The rhythm is catchingly regular; the rhymes are elusive and deep, not so much clipping together the ends of the lines as breathing freely through the whole complex of a verse. You are plunged into a shifting sea of meditation which can be transformed from one minute to the next into highly-strung dramatics or into semisoporific self-contemplation. Evtushenko is essentially a mixture of incompatibles, he unites extremes, yielding utterly to everything which succeeds in catching his strung-up sensibility.

The theme of youth which brought Evtushenko such wide popularity is now exhausted, and he knows it. He is on the look-out for new themes. The result is a long poem, "The Bratsk Hydroelectric Station" (1965), in which he unites scattered impressions of his journeys with flash-backs on the history of Russia.

Evtushenko prefaces this poem with a kind of auto-review: "To tell the truth, it may not even be a poem at all, but simply my own thoughts united round the argument of two themes, the theme of scepticism expressed in the monologue of the pyramid, and the theme of faith." The poem really is far from the traditional pattern of carefully constructed narrative verse. It is rather an aggregate than an organism. What holds together this huge aggregate which we have called a narrative poem? What makes it tick? What kind of personality provides the filter through which we are shown the flow of history, what does he select to draw up for us from that vast flow, what is going on in his own heart? Evtushenko conceived the plan of showing us thousands of years of history as a logical line of development justified by the final result. No historian would have had the courage to attempt so bold a plan—it could only have occurred to a poet. The conception of Evtushenko the historian is the direct product of the constant, below-the-surface agonies of Evtushenko the poet.

He is agonized by the tragedy of human history. In this poet's pain, in the profound, half-conscious implications of the poem, lie hidden the poet's compassion for people, kindness and fellow-feeling. Possibly it is this painful quality of his thought which goes to form the most precious truth of his perception. Perhaps, indeed, there would be no poet Evgeni Evtushenko were it not for the efforts to resolve the head-on clashes of these two currents within himself.

Lev Anninski. SL. Jan., 1967, p. 129

A main feature of the two Yevtushenko books is his long poem "The Bratsk Station." This very uneven, large-scale work, partly epic and partly philosophical in its intentions, uses the building of a massive new Siberian hydro-electric station as a focus for thoughts, beliefs, and feelings about human destiny. It is very much, in Pound's phrase, a "poem containing history," but naturally with a different conception of the progressive forces and movements that give history meaning. . . . The poem is rather lacking in basic structure, since it consists mainly of a series of moralized scenes and incidents—from Stenka Razin's execution in the seventeenth century to Auschwitz and the Twentieth Party Congress. . . .

The device of using the Egyptian Pyramid as a cynical spokesman from the past is the weakest part of the poem. It is unreflecting, and unconvincing, to equate the Pyramid merely with slavery, blood and priestly oppression and to equate Bratsk with the optimistic labours of free men.

No doubt one would rather be a Siberian electrician than one of Pharaoh's fellahin, but that is not the whole story and Yevtushenko—by nature as well as by his Soviet upbringing—draws back from any profound consideration of the mystery of human ambitions and aspirations.

TLS. Nov. 2, 1967, p. 1039

ZABOLOTSKI, NIKOLAI (1903–1958)

Zabolotski loved poetry since he was a boy. The first poet who impressed him and whom he learned by heart was Aleksei Konstantinovich Tolstoi. . . . Later, he became disenchanted with him. He began to be truly acquainted with Russian poetry as an adult in Leningrad. Here he fell under the influence of Kharms and Vvedenski, and he discovered Khlebnikov; for a long time, Khlebnikov overshadowed all other poetry. Zabolotski approached Khlebnikov differently from all his other followers. He liked the fact that Khlebnikov did not resemble any of the preceding poets, of whom Zabolotski was tired. He also fell in love with Khlebnikov's poetry because it was the first genuine poetry he had met. He mastered Russian classical poetry later, in his mature years, and it put its stamp on his entire later creativity. This was a unique, unusual development—from Khlebnikov to Tyutchev. Zabolotski traveled this road laboriously and thoroughly, because he was an independent sage who did not trust the opinions of others. He also tried to solve for himself, with his own mind, the two greatest riddles preoccupying him—death and love.

Nikolai Chukovski. Neva. Sept., 1965, pp. 189–90†

Zabolotski is, above all, a poet-philosopher. He belongs to those artists who, in Belinski's words, "do not understand the pleasure of presenting reality truthfully just for the sake of presenting it truthfully. . . . For them, the importance lies not in the object but in the meaning of the object." In that sense, Zabolotski continues the poetic line begun and developed especially by Baratynski, Tyutchev, and Bryusov. At the same time, Zabolotski, a deeply original artist-thinker, is not only unlike any of his predecessors but strongly in disagreement with them, mainly with Tyutchev. He can be related to Tyutchev in their common delight over the beauty and grandeur of nature, but their understanding of nature is entirely different. The Bryusovian principle in Zabolotski's work consists of his ability to look at the world from the lofty elevation of the knowledge of natural sciences, but unlike the propagandist and founder of "scientific poetry," as Bryusov is known in our poetry, Zabolotski never limited himself to the role of an illustrator of scientific facts: the thought in his verses, especially in the later ones, contains at the same time a strong, self-obliterating, all-pervasive emotion. Moreover, as a poet, he was, it seems, apprehensive of the burden of knowledge, which weighs excessively upon the modern man, marching self-confidently and hurriedly toward the eternal secrets of life.

A. Pavlovski. *Poety-sovremenniki* (Moscow and Leningrad, Sovetski pisatel, 1966), pp. 171–72[†]

Zabolockij's wide poetic range—including modernistic, Futurist practices in the early period, and the adherence to "classical" traditions of Russian eighteenth- and nineteenth-century poetry in his later period—was less the result of a specific artistic development than of political pressures and persecutions which marked Zabolockij's whole life. Nevertheless, the fact that Zabolockij could express himself through such divergent poetic forms testifies to his creative powers and his acute sense for language.

Zabolockij's early manner is most clearly manifested in *Stolbcy*, a collection of poems deceptively simple and even primitive at first glance, but laden with complexity and density of imagery and meaning. *Stolbcy* earned Zabolockij his literary reputation among poets, and the permanent enmity of Party functionaries. Following the example of Xlebnikov, his acknowledged master, Zabolockij concentrated on verbal play rather than on metrical experimentation and startled the reader by the unexpectedness of his images, his grotesque comparisons, and incompatible combinations of diverse lexical and logical elements. . . .

Zabolockij's vision of the large modern city in *Stolbcy* is grotesque and nightmarish: people appear in it as marionettes manipulated by an unseen hand, while inanimate objects become independent of their usual associations and acquire a life of their own—much as Gogol''s "Nose" paraded around St. Petersburg in the uniform of a state councilor. Zabolockij's connection with Gogol' in portraying a topsy-turvy world with strange mechanical prostitutes and puppet-like Ivanovs on the one hand, and animated cupboards, couches, and lamps on the other, was immediately recognized. It became equally obvious, however, that under the guise of the temporal Zabolockij, like Gogol', was presenting the "eternal" themes of mediocrity, stupidity, and *pošlost'*, which were as current in 1930 as they had been a hundred years earlier.

Margaret Dalton. *SEEJ*. Summer, 1966, pp. 215–16

Zabolotski was a natural master of the grand style. . . . He loved to write with accuracy and detail, to sketch a poetical image. The poet's narratives met those standards traditionally demanded in the writing of epics. Zabolotski considered it binding that the poet be an artist, and it is more than chance that his verses recall the picturesque. In his own time, the poet learned from the gifted master painter Filonov.

The poet loved to develop a theme, to outline its limits, to fill it out with novel strokes. Certain of his early poems give the impression of beginning in the middle, as if they were pages torn from a book. This principle of infinite duration, when a poem fits a given minute or hour, a slice of existence without conclusion, was adopted by Zabolotski from Khlebnikov. But Zabolotski soon changed to a concise and orderly verse structure with its own exposition, culmination, and conclusion. With time, each construction in which his analytical gift appeared seemed even rational. But on the whole, Zabolotski is far from schematic rationalism.

A tendency to analyze and a rare ability to paint with words—these traits of genius guided Zabolotski in his poetry.

Anatoli Aleksandrov. *Zvezda*. Oct., 1966, p. 214[†]

Although he started writing in disgusted protest, not unlike Mayakovsky's, against the greedy pettiness of the NEP period, and although the poem which was the primary cause of his arrest had to do with collectivization, [Zabolotski's] work is essentially nonpolitical. He writes for the most part about nature, death, and immortality, sometimes about reason and art, sometimes about individual human beings. And whether in its early "futurist" phase or in its later "classical" one, his poetry is technically masterful. He is a great virtuoso, a master of the grotesque and "the last of the Russian surrealists," as Vladimir Markov calls him. But to speak of him, as Mr. Markov does, as "one of the world's poetic discoveries" seems to me extravagant. He has an important place in Russian letters, of course, but he is not equal to the greatest in poetic grandeur, emotional depth, or philosophical insight. His utterance is so original that critics are at pains to explain him by means of analogies. Emmanuel Rais finds him Dostoevskian in his pity, and in his feeling for nature, like all the poets in the main current of Russian poetry from Derzhavin to Fet; Boris Filipoff speaks of him as having heaved the whole weight of Russian culture on to his shoulders and of resembling especially the Gogol of "The Petersburg Tales" and the Dostoevsky of "The Double." But it is to pictorial artists he is most readily compared: to Hieronymus Bosch by Boris Filipoff, to Henri Rousseau by Vladimir Markov and Emmanuel Rais, and to both of these and many more by Aleksis Rannit, who seeks to define him as an Expressionist, finds similarities between him and Chagall, Maurice Vlaminck and Georg Grosz, among others, and believed that he achieved the impossible, a synthesis of two contrasting themes, "the bacchanal and the pastoral . . . Van Gogh and Matisse." There is perhaps some exaggeration in all this, but it is undeniable that his work is a brilliant combination of classic formalism and wild fantasy, that it can set into an elegant eighteenth-century frame the kind of bizarre, absurd and devastating images to which we have become accustomed in the work of Surrealists, Expressionists, and Dadaists. And as with the other inner émigrés, his highly original work is a moving example of that invincible freedom of the artistic imagination which is able to build "out of the very material of exile, a tranquil world of its own."

Helen Muchnic. *RR*. Jan., 1967, pp. 24–25

[Zabolotski's] later poems are formally unexciting by the side of *Stolbtsy* —yet they have their own riches, and the transition from the one manner to the other can no longer be held to be abrupt, or to have done violence to the poet's inspiration. Indeed, the most satisfying part of his output may well be that which dates from the mid-1930's, having something of the virtues of both manners: smoothness of form and imagery, wide scope, together with a tension in the language and sudden strangenesses of perception which are a legacy from his early days as an experimentalist. Above all Zabolotsky is seen to have been from first to last one of the more notable philosophic poets of our time. In *Stolbtsy* and related poems the arbitrary, tragicomic jumble of the world (specifically Leningrad under NEP), mirrored in language itself, continually affronts the poet's rational powers. From his earliest period onwards, however, Zabolotsky extends this vision of chaos to the whole of nature, impassively giving life and taking it away—in all his remaining work he is basically attempting to order man's place within this beautiful, haphazard and ruthless environment. This feeling is sharpened by the continued apprehension of death, justifiable only as a stage in the metamorphosis between living beings which is the incessant rule of natural existence.

TLS. May 11, 1967, p. 398

Zabolotski's new method of depicting nature is, of course, closely connected with the entire socialist lyric poetry. In part, we find in the landscape lyrics of Marshak, Pasternak, Rylenkov, and Tvardovski . . . much that is similar to Zabolotski's. However, he stands apart in his unique feeling for the "brilliance of colors" in nature, its profound and enormous contradictions, its meditations and frenzy, and the dynamism of its metamorphoses. Zabolotski's landscapes, despite all the common basic premises and tendencies, differ, for example, from Tvardovski's multivoiced nature, rich in hues and shades and close to the steady and attentive gaze of the observer. . . . It differs also from the transparent, modest, and intimate beauty of the birches in Rylenkov's "lavish, although seemingly meager" Smolensk region. Finally, it differs from the deep warmth, simplicity, and clear wisdom of Marshak's comradely encounters with nature. Zabolotski's nature is more luxuriant, complex, contradictory: now "fantastic," now less limpid, but always very deep and full of movement, dynamic contrasts, and impulses.

A. Makedonov. *Nikolai Zabolotski*
(Leningrad, Sovetski pisatel, 1968), pp. 334–35[†]

ZAMYATIN, YEVGENI (1884–1937)

Zamyatin's example serves as an excellent affirmation of the truth that talent and intellect, no matter how well endowed the writer is with them, are not sufficient if the contact with the epoch is lost, if the inner feeling has changed and the artist or thinker feels himself, in the midst of contemporaneity, like a passenger or tourist on a boat, hostilely and cheerlessly looking around. . . .

From the artistic point of view *My* (*We*) is excellent. Zamyatin attained here his full maturity, so much the worse, since all this has come to serve an evil cause. . . .

Zamyatin's influence on contemporary artistic life is undoubtedly significant. It is sufficient to say that Zamyatin determined in many respects the character and the direction of the circle called Serapion Brothers. And although the Serapions claim that they gathered simply on the principle of working together in concord, that they do not have even a trace of unity in artistic methods, and, it seems, that they also have "no relation whatsoever with Zamyatin," we still have serious doubts about this. They have Zamyatin's passion for words, for mastery, for form. According to Zamyatin, things are not written about: they are made. From Zamyatin come stylization, experiment pushed to the extremes, passion for *skaz*, the tenseness of characters, their halfway-imagery. Zamyatin views the revolution contemplatively, from the outside. I do not want to say that their relationship to the revolution is the same, although even here in some of them we can feel the Zamyatin savor. And if among the Serapions there is a tendency for the artist, like the biblical Jehovah, to create for himself—and these views are not accidental among Serapions at all—it also comes from Zamyatin. Perhaps here the coincidence is greater than the influence, but it is an amazing coincidence. [1922]

A. K. Voronski. *Literaturno-kriticheskie stati*
(Moscow, Sovetski pisatel, 1963), pp. 85, 109, 110–11[†]

We is, as Zamiatin himself calls it, the most jocular and the most earnest thing he has written thus far. It is a novel that puts before every thoughtful reader with great poignance and earnestness the most difficult problem that exists today in the civilized world—the problem of the preservation of the independent, original, creative personality. . . .

A few words should be said about the method by which Zamiatin tries to drive home his main ideas to the reader. It is the method of "laughter through tears," to use an old expression of Gogol's. It is the form that is dictated by a profound love for humanity, mixed with pity for and hatred of those factors which are the cause of the disindividualization of man today. It is the old emotion of ancient Catullus: *"Odi et amo."* Zamiatin laughs in order to hide his tears; hence amusing as *We* may seem and really is, it barely conceals a profound human tragedy which is universal today.

Gregory Zilboorg. Foreword to Eugene Zamiatin, *We*
(New York, E. P. Dutton, 1924), pp. xiv–xv

We is a kind of bomb boldly thrown at "standardization," "rationalization," "socialization" and other slogans fashionable at the present time. Philosophical as Plato's *The Republic*, interesting as the best Utopias of H. G. Wells, cold as a muzzle of a loaded revolver, and sarcastic as *Gulliver's Travels, We* is a powerful challenge to all Socialist Utopias. It is natural that the book should have come out of Russia. Only a man of talent who, as Zamiatin, has been and still is amidst the greatest experiment in the "standardization" and "communization" of human beings, could write this Utopia of an absolutely standardized and socialized society. This does not mean that *We* is a propagandist book ridiculing Communist Russia. Not a bit. The Communist experiment gave only the first patterns necessary for a start. The rest is the creation of the thought and fantasy of the author.

Pitirim Sorokin. *SR*. Feb. 7, 1925, p. 507

[*We*] is saved from the dullness of a tract by the skill with which the author has introduced the elements of "heart-interest" and suspense, and by the peculiar, rapid, disjointed quality of the style. It is a pity that the translation is somewhat stilted and inexact, for Zamiatin's method is an original one.

The man himself suggests the Anglo-Saxon rather than the Russian. He is tall, straight, blond, and clean-shaven except for a little moustache; his blue eyes are lit with fragmentary smiles, like the jerk of an electric bulb in a flashed advertisement; and his crisp manner is less that of the littérateur than of the naval engineer.

He has brought his mathematical bent into his writing; his images are frequently drawn from calculus; and his contributions to a recent symposium on modern Russian art expressed the conviction that it is the business of the author to import technology and to work with the synthetic image of the elliptic Syntax, to clip the phrase and speed up the action, if it is to reflect the life of our time.

The novel under review, while less moving and less amusing than certain of his short stories, is valuable as a document for social historians. The order that Zamiatin asks us to laugh at is, I think, less likely to eventuate in Russia than in countries further west, geographically and spiritually. But it is sufficiently in the minds and desires of men to afford material for both satirist and student.

Babette Deutsch. NR. March 18, 1925, pp. 104–5

Zamyatin's early stories go back to Russian traditions, to Gogol and Leskov, both directly and through the intermediary of Remizov. From them he has inherited his predilection for verbal effects, for stylistic elaborateness, for ornamentalism of speech. His early manner may be described as Realism with a touch of the grotesque. Later on he developed a style of his own, a peculiar blend of Realism with Symbolism and Imagism, which D. S. Mirsky has aptly compared to Cubism in painting (his mathematical studies . . . may have had something to do with this "geometrical" tendency). Zamyatin himself described his method as Neo-Realism. In one of his critical articles he came forward as an advocate of a broken narrative conducted simultaneously on several planes. He applied this method most thoroughly in one of his most difficult and "obscure" stories—"The Story about What Matters Most" ("Rasskaz o samom glavnom") which has been denounced by Communist critics as fundamentally anti-revolutionary. There is, however, more continuity and direct simplicity in what is one of Zamyatin's best stories, "The Flood" ["Navodnenie"] (1926), a tragic story of love, jealousy and murder, told against the background of a flood in Leningrad.

By nature Zamyatin was a rebel, a heretic, quite unable to toe any line. In 1921, during a period when certain freedom of opinion was allowed in Soviet Russia, Zamyatin expressed the view that Communist Russia would not produce real literature. His reason for thinking so was very typical: "Real literature," he said, "can exist only where it is produced by madmen, hermits, heretics, dreamers, rebels and sceptics, and not by painstaking and well-intentioned officials." It was equally characteristic of Zamyatin that he used to be a Bolshevik before the Revolution of 1917 and ceased to be one when Bolshevism came to power.

Gleb Struve. SEER. April, 1938, p. 702

Zamyatin remarked in Herbert Wells that Russian literature had a meager tradition of social and scientific fantasy and singled out the utopian novels of the nineteenth-century writer V. F. Odoyevski as rare examples of the genre. Certainly if Zamyatin is to be considered in relation to the Odoyevski "tradition," the label "incorrigible pessimist" is appropriate. To the extent that Odoyevski saw apathy as the most deadly danger of future generations and maintained that imagination and suffering went hand in hand and were liberating and constructive forces, Zamyatin agreed with him. In We the mathematically worked out happiness of the citizens of the new world is an illusion. What they call happiness is nothing but inertia and habit. . . .

Stylistically, Zamyatin was a many-faceted writer. In his pre-revolutionary work he owed much to Leskov and Remizov and frequently employed the *skaz* form, in which the plot is related in the speech, usually vernacular, of the narrator. At the same time he often conducted the narrative on several planes, retaining the plane of the author himself, with his subtle psychological analysis.

Vyacheslav Zavalishin. *Early Soviet Writers* (New
York, Frederick A. Praeger, 1958), pp. 183, 185

The prophetic scope of *We* has not been fully exhausted. Totalitarianism has shown that Zamiatin's state was right about the practicability of intensive regimentation over long periods of time; however, there has been no broad proving ground for the theory on which Zamiatin's state is built, the theory that most men believe their freedom to be more than a fair exchange for a high level of materialistic happiness. It appears, though, that this theory will be put to a final test in the future. If the present rapid rate of technological development continues, both totalitarian and democratic societies will be involved in this test. When the material wants of the Soviet people are satisfied, will many of them continue to resent regimentation? As we ourselves pursue even higher goals of materialistic happiness, the complexity of our technological society will increase and exert even more intense pressures for efficiency through the regulation of our lives. What decision will we make under those circumstances? Mankind is rushing toward a final proof or refutation of Zamiatin's prophecy?

Peter Rudy. Introduction to Eugene Zamiatin, *We*
(New York, E. P. Dutton, 1959), pp. ix–x

Zamyatin is a self-conscious mirror of a world in violent process, and therefore his prose tends to the grotesque in both form and content. His art, to use his own phrase, portrays the world as it might be seen in a storm from the mast of a ship listing at a forty-five-degree angle "when the green jaws of the sea are gaping, and the ship itself is cracking." At such times it is impossible to present land- and sea-scapes of settled Euclidean dimensions.

Zamyatin's writings—his novels and stories as well as his essays—are a systematic defense of heresy as a way of life. . . .

Zamyatin in *Islanders* [*Ostrovityane*] not only provides a preview of the main themes of *We*, but practices the literary tricks and devices that he would later use in that novel to such good effect. Characters are identified by the device of the repeated metaphor: Campbell is regularly a "lumbering truck," then "a truck out of control." Or they are repeatedly associated with objects that typify them for the reader: for instance Mrs. Dooley's "basic organ" is her pince-nez. Vivid, impressionistic pictures are provided by a few simple line strokes: the "two brows of a face raised to form a triangle." The narration moves in a brisk staccato, with swift ellipses and insistent repetition of key visual images. The "eye" of Zamyatin's camera moves abruptly from one scene to another. Zamyatin is a mannered literary artist whose style belongs to the school of Remizov and Bely, and to that style Zamyatin has given the fillip of his own preoccupation with modern mathematics, which no doubt suggested to him the systematic distortion of visual images based on the old-fashion geometry.

Islanders is an important event in Russian literary history, for the novel places in clear focus the real nature of Zamyatin's rebellion against the machine and mechanized civilization. The novel *Islanders* was obviously not inspired by an apocalyptic vision of a future society governed by the proletarian mass; rather it describes an industrial society of the present dominated by a smug and conformist middle class.

> Edward J. Brown. *Russian Literature Since the*
> *Revolution* (New York, Crowell-Collier, 1963),
> pp. 69, 72–73

We is an example of a novel used as a weapon against us, against our order, and against our literature. Marxist critics openly attacked this work. Gorki's correspondence deals with this novel (of course Gorki had a critically negative attitude toward this novel, considering it harmful in thought and antiartistic in nature). In essence, the whole of young Soviet literature rejected what *We* portrayed. Finally, it is quite natural that this novel was and is being praised by modern American archreactionaries among literary critics.

We contains neither fabricated words, the ingenious design of the ironic tale, the influx of the subconscious, nor pure invention. It was not written for a small group of aesthetes, as was the case with some of Zamyatin's other stories, but as reading for the general public. *We* is a rectilinear, spitefully clear, and rationalistic piece of agitation propaganda. "The pure experimenter" (as Zamyatin was known in the Serapion group) changed into a desperate political figure when the subject of discussion turned to whether or not bourgeois individualism was or was not close to his heart. The writer changed painlessly from the laboratory search for new forms of storytelling to the lampoon novel, or more precisely the slander novel. . . .

Zamyatin thought that he had written a lampoon on socialism. That was a profound error! The picture he draws has nothing in common with

Marxist socialism. His descriptions more likely depict the Prussian bar-racks or the government of the subservient so ably described by Heinrich Mann. Marxists never agreed with the primitive concept of equality de-fined as the depersonalization of the individual. On the contrary, Marx-ism always fought against this most reactionary notion about socialism! The "Ant-Hill Concept," the inhuman effacement of personality, the ex-termination of freedom, and the discipline (nearly Jesuit in nature, where the individual is a corpse in the hands of his superiors) that kills free-dom—all of these are the delirious ideas of archreactionary, bourgeois politicians.

It is also characteristic that the novel *We* is lacking any kind of Soviet Russian color. Everything in it is Central European, as if it consisted of quotes from a utopian novel like Wells's *The Time Machine.*

The critics of the twenties were profoundly correct when they wrote that "Zamyatin wrote a lampoon which did not refer to communism but to the Bismarckian, reactionary, Richterist socialism."

M. Kuznetsov. *Novy mir.* Aug., 1963, pp. 231–32[†]

The modernistic imagery used in Zamjatin's *We* often seems senseless and chaotic. The diarist, D–503, undergoes a mental crisis while he is keeping his record; from a narrative point of view his own inner turmoil justifies, to a large extent, the disconnected nature of the diary entries and the rapidly shifting focus of attention within each entry. Because he has been educated in the Single State, his ability to describe his personal life clearly and methodically has never developed; he can think only in terms of straight lines, uncomplicated geometrical figures, and mathematical formulae. This does not suffice for treating the new and strange mental events which overpower him, and for this reason his record often becomes chaotic, almost incoherent. He falls in love, is introduced to life beyond the Green Wall, and is drawn into a revolutionary plot; all this is too much for him to endure without confusion, especially since he is trying to resist all these new influences.

Many strange images appear in his diary, images which seem to be senseless products of his own agitation and confusion: yellow dresses jump into his mind, water drips on a stone, sap pours from a brass Buddha, fiery golden suns blind him, beasts' eyes stare at him, the eyelids of I-330 become curtains, secrets seem to hide in the opaque dwelling of the head, under its crust the earth seems to be on fire, fires leap up behind I-330's eyes. These and other images recur constantly, seemingly with no pattern and no meaning.

Yet in all the apparent chaos, these images do fall into a coherent pat-tern and have important bearing on the theme of the novel.

Carl R. Proffer. *SEEJ.* Fall, 1963, p. 269

The many archetypal images and patterns [in *We*] lead the reader, consciously or unconsciously, to recognize the entire novel as a myth.

If the central trope in Gogol''s style is termed the downward-directed metaphor, so might *Dead Souls* be read as a sort of downward-directed myth of the Holy Grail. And Čexov, whose work Zamjatin also admired, places many of his stories within the framework of classical and literary myths, but proves them in character and situation banally inferior. If Gogol''s myth is grotesque and Čexov's banal, Zamjatin's is horrific. His myth is peopled with strong, serious figures engaged in a deadly archetypal struggle. But the myth does not have the ending we expect—the maternal monster survives, the *anima* dies, Perseus does not slay the Medusa and save Andromeda, and a false Self triumphs. Not only does psychic wholeness remain unachieved, but the protagonist, a representative of modern man, loses what little human qualities and possibilities he possessed in the beginning. The impact felt at the novel's end derives from the violent denial of the expectation of the eventual victory of the true Self that myth encourages.

Christopher Collins. SEEJ. Summer, 1966, p. 132

Two other famous utopian novels, *Brave New World* (1932) and *1984* (1948), are clearly far less powerful works than *We*. Unlike Huxley's rather comic and homely brave new world, Zamyatin's single state is described in coolly abstract, universal terms that greatly heighten the impression of horror. Orwell, who acknowledged his debt to *We,* is closer to Zamyatin in his vision of totalitarianism, but it should be recalled that by 1948, Orwell could pick and choose from among any number of past or present features of Franco's Spain, Mussolini's Italy, Hitler's Germany and Stalin's Russia.

What makes *We* a great novel is the perfect fusion of subject and artist. Zamyatin's choice of subject was scarcely accidental; they belong together, absolutely. The realization of such a union constitutes what Kierkegaard called (writing of Mozart and Don Juan) "the fortunate in the historical process." With such a subject, Zamyatin's faults become virtues. If the stage machinery creaks a bit in his writing, so indeed does the machinery of terror. His contrivances of language are ideally suited to render the diction of tyranny. Here, ideas and fantasy merge in a fiction that is at once phantasmagoric and manifestly real.

It is scarcely surprising that *We* has never been published in the Soviet Union.

Patricia Blake. NYT. Feb. 26, 1967, p. 33

The prerequisite to a real appreciation of Zamyatin's talent and contribution to Russian literature and to *belles-lettres* in general is a careful perusal of the works of Gogol and Dostoevsky. The latter's well-known comment, "We have all come out of Gogol's 'Overcoat,' " applies equally to Zamyatin. His stories are in many respects a continuation and at times an emulation of the works of Gogol and Dostoevsky.

As with Gogol's "The Revizor," many of Zamyatin's stories contain not a single redeeming character. His emphasis on the seamy side of Russian and Soviet life may have stemmed from his belief that "true literature can exist only where it is produced by madmen, hermits, heretics, visionaries, rebels, and skeptics"—in other words, by conscious or unconscious nonconformists. Although dissenters and nonconformists are indispensable to society and to literature, there is danger to both when extremists take control of the state and the arts.

Ivar Spector. SR. April 1, 1967, p. 36

Zamjatin's literary works of both the early and the middle periods reflect his conception of life as tragic and his belief in irony as the best means of overcoming this tragedy. Basic to both periods is a broad humanism and a firm belief in man's capabilities and in human progress. Whereas the early works are essentially satires on non-human, provincial bestiality, the middle works attack the automated philistinism of the large city. In either case, what is at stake is the preservation of the individual personality. In the middle works passionate love became associated with the rebellion of the individual against the philistine conformity and dogmatism of society. The shift in thematics was reflected by changes in setting and style. Provincial Russia was replaced by population centers: England, Petersburg, the Single State. Correspondingly, the *skaz* narrative with its regional and dialectal expressions was modified in favor of a condensed, staccato, and elliptical narrative that nonetheless was based on a contemporary conversational style. The tendency to brevity, already apparent in the early works, was continued. The impressionistic imagery of the early works was systematically extended and developed to such an extent that in many instances it became a dominant organizing principle; in some short stories it even relegated plot and psychology to secondary positions. With the intensification and primacy of the image system, visual and acoustical elements assumed much greater importance: the rhythmic and musical qualities of prose were intensified, and a semi-symbolic color system relating to the central images was developed. Conceived as an expression of the new age with its tempestuous headlong rush forward, Zamjatin's elliptical, staccato prose aimed at conveying only the bare essence of his vision by using impressionistic images.

Alex M. Shane. The Life and Works of Evgenij
Zamjatin (Berkeley, Calif., University of California
Press, 1968), pp. 166–67

It is no exaggeration to say that Zamyatin's influence on Soviet literature to come will be enormous, equaling perhaps that of Gogol on nineteenth-century Russian literature. Zamyatin is not only the creator of a
highly original satirical-grotesque style with pronouncedly expressionist
attributes, not only a writer whose flow of language has an elastic, almost tactile quality with restless, disharmonic, inverted clauses that
seem to mirror the spirit of our age. He is also a superb artist-technician,
which is not as unimportant as it usually seems to be. His choice of
words and metaphors is that of an engineer, a technician of today, and
thus foreshadows the "technical" terminology becoming more and more
current in popular speech and thought. For this reason Zamyatin should
appeal to present-day readers. While he does not accept realism in his
art, neither does he permit decadent symbolism. He believes in movement from reality to an inner world, and vice versa, and the greatness
of his art is the skillful transition across the frontier between them. . . .

Zamyatin's novels are the literary counterpart of Chagall's paintings.
People fly in the air, flow about the room and collide with objects; small
animals leap from people's eyes; there are endless such effects.

Mihajlo Mihajlov. *Russian Themes* (New York,
Farrar, Straus and Giroux, 1968), pp. 291, 295

ZOSHCHENKO, MIKHAIL (1895–1958)

The path of the humorist (if he is a sincere writer) can be outlined briefly:
the first period is the period of cheerful laughter, lighthearted fun, and
youthful mocking, but the second period is a period of bitter, dampened
thought. This path was traveled by Gogol and Chekhov and many other
humorists, irrespective of the nature of their gift. It is clear that Zoshchenko likewise travels this path. With his new collection [*O chem pel
solovei* (*What the Nightingale Sings About*)] he enters the second phase;
these are no longer the little biting and cheerful tales of his *Uvazhaemye
grazhdane* (*Esteemed Citizens*). The humor of his *Rasskazy* (*Tales*) is
shaded and toned down by the author's honest bitterness (sometimes skillfully disguised) and by his melancholy sympathy for the mental and material squalor of everyday life.

But here Zoshchenko runs into serious trouble. Indeed, the foundation
of his unquestionable talent is the individual syntax which accurately reflects the new speech of the postrevolutionary city, of its common stratum.
But in these stories the center of gravity is transferred to plot and psychological analysis. Here beginning to shine through Zoshchenko's style
is the familiar aspect of that powerful influence which speaks so clearly
in Leonov's *Kovyakin's Notes* and Nikitin's *Oboyan Tales* and in much of

young Soviet literature. I am talking about the author of *Mirgorod* [Gogol]. A province, a Soviet province, described by Zoshchenko in his *Tales* very much recalls *Mirgorod*. . . . Not infrequently, Zoshchenko rings like an echo of Gogol. . . . Still, it is possible to talk about influence but not about imitation. This influence (in particular, stylistic) apparently is sensed by the author himself, perhaps instinctively.

There are in these stories a quieting tenderness, a skeptical mildness, and an absence of malicious irony, all of which signify a transition from lighthearted youth to creative maturity.

A. R. Palei. *Novy mir*. June, 1927, p. 205[†]

Zoshchenko has distinguished himself as a satirist, poking fun at Soviet citizens, or rather at universal and ubiquitous philistinism. In the present volume, *Youth Restored* [*Vozvrashchennaya molodost*], he attempts a departure in *genre* and style, mixing fiction with informal causerie of a semi-scientific nature. The book is obviously the result of his personal efforts at combating the lassitude of middle-age. The professor of his story succeeds, temporarily at least, in throwing off his physical and mental decrepitude by dint of simply "making up his mind." His affair with a vulgar flapper barely misses turning tragic, but he is saved in time, none the worse for the shakeup. If not taken seriously the book makes pleasurable summer reading.

Alexander Kaun. *BA*. Autumn, 1935, p. 467

The simple public loved Zoshchenko because he made them laugh; it took him for an extraordinarily funny fellow and felt stricken at finding unhappy themes in happy books. No, the reader says, it's not his business to be taken up with that—he's a humorist. In essence this means: I don't want to bother weighing things; I just want to laugh. A valid wish. But Zoshchenko does not give it much consideration.

With time, the critics, having recognized him as a satirist, turned their attention to what they would not like to see in his satire. One decided that Zoshchenko's sarcasm lashes out at the remnants of the past—the petite bourgeoisie inherited by the revolution from the past and still not eradicated by it. According to their opinion, Zoshchenko exaggerated the presence of these vestiges in our day-to-day existence, and it was not worth the while wasting strength battling windmills.

Others held that satire is not Zoshchenko's intent because the ridiculed hero does not exist. There is no place for him in a new society devoid of the deformity and ugliness for which the writer wishes to provide reality. A third group went further and claimed that Zoshchenko himself is the pedestrian individual in whose name he weaves his tales, that he looks at the world through the eyes of a petit bourgeois, that he is a Philistine.

I suppose, if controversy is possible, if an object of satire exists, then, evidently, satire too exists, and that either it is not understood or people do not want to see it. In arguments over Zoshchenko, a historically traditional attitude on the part of society toward its own satirists is evident: it calls into question what the satirist claims. Society is very content to cry, "Well, look how he lays *them* out!" But, in the same instance, one cannot expect it to cry with glee, "Well, he lays *me* out!"

And as a matter of fact, Zoshchenko precisely does "lay out" me, us, the people of our times, and our society, that is, a part of it that is inseparable from it. Perhaps no other writer has given such abundant artistic and, it seems, true proof of his understanding of the private side of our national character as Zoshchenko. [1943]

Konstantin Fedin. *Pisatel, vremya, iskusstvo*
(Moscow, Sovetski pisatel, 1961), p. 242[†]

Zoshchenko takes absolutely no interest in the labor of the Soviet people, their exertions and heroism, their high social and moral qualities. With him this theme is always absent. Zoshchenko, like the philistine and vulgarian that he is, chose as his permanent theme the analysis of the basest and pettiest sides of life. This digging in the trivialities of life is not accidental. It is characteristic of all vulgar philistine writers, and hence of Zoshchenko. . . . It is known that since the time of his return to Leningrad from evacuation Zoshchenko has written several things characterized by the fact that he is incapable of finding in the life of the Soviet people one positive phenomenon, one positive type. As in the "Adventures of a Monkey" ["Priklyucheniya obezyany"] Zoshchenko is accustomed to mock at Soviet life, Soviet ways, Soviet people, covering this mockery with a mask of vacuous diversion and pointless humor.

It would be hard to find in our literature anything more repulsive than the "moral" preached by Zoshchenko in *Before Sunrise* [*Pered voskhodom solntsa*], which depicts people and himself as vile, lewd beasts without shame or conscience. And this moral he presented to Soviet readers in that period when our people were pouring out their blood in a war of unheard-of difficulty. [1946]

Andrei Zhdanov. *On Literature, Music & Arts* (New
York, International Publishers, 1950), pp. 16–17

Perhaps Zoshchenko did not know the "secret of humor" and the "magic of laughter," or was not "initiated"? He did not know and did not want to know the truth about life: he slandered our reality, made our Soviet people appear foolish and stupid, and—pay attention—his writing was not only stupid and ideologically defective but artistically repugnant. More than that, his writing was not even humorous: it was gloomy, dejected. If this was humor, then it was hypocritical and misanthropic humor, and the reader contemptuously throws away this gloomy concoction.

Boris Gorbatov. *Novy mir.* Oct., 1949, p. 215†

Although Zoshchenko's situations are often improbable and grotesque, the label of "everyday-life writer" suits him more than it does anyone else. He gives a true picture of Soviet weekdays, stripped of all romantic and heroic varnish, of all pretension and make-believe. Some of the orthodox Soviet critics were from the outset at a loss what to make of Zoshchenko. In turn they praised him for exposing so mercilessly the petty-bourgeois weaknesses of the average Soviet citizen—the spirit of *embourgeoisement* invading large circles of Communist society, including the Party itself— and denounced him as a vulgar "bourgeois," identifying him with his own characters. . . .

At his best Zoshchenko reminds one simultaneously of two great masters of Russian literature, so dissimilar on the whole, but so alike in one thing—in their keen vision of the mean vulgarity and insipidity of life: Gogol and Chekhov. It is the pettiness, the vulgarity of life, the essential incomprehensibility of one man to another, that forms the keynote of Zoshchenko's stories. In some of the best—in "Wisdom" ["Mudrost"], for instance—one can sense a deep feeling of tragedy beneath and beyond the humorous and grotesque presentation of a humdrum, vulgar life. The most hilarious of modern Russian writers is at heart a thorough pessimist, and for a discerning reader his comic stories must inevitably leave an aftertaste of sadness. Often one feels that Zoshchenko is speaking with his tongue in his cheek, and it is not surprising that Communist critics were baffled by him.

Gleb Struve. *Soviet Russian Literature 1917–1950*
(Norman, Okla., University of Oklahoma Press, 1951),
pp. 150–51

On the face of it, by the end of the thirties, Zoshchenko and the Soviet powers, like the author's first hero and his bosom friend, appeared to sit "hugging each other all day." The fictional character had been driven to refuge in his friend's home and embrace as "hired man": there was nowhere else to go. All doors were closed to him. He could not come to terms with life. Zoshchenko, too, had contrived a place for himself, one which he occupied with considerable uneasiness and ambivalence.

He had attempted to comply with the demands of the Communist Party by writing *Story of One Life* [*Istoriya odnoi zhizni*], "Retribution" ["Vozmezdie"], "The Black Prince" ["Cherny prints"], "Inglorious End" ["Besslavny konets"], the biographic sketches of Taras Shevchenko, and the "Stories about Lenin" ["Rasskazy o Lenine"]. With them he had won the plaudits of the Party-oriented critics as a serious writer of literature possessing moral and educational value for the new society. By any criteria other than those applied by Soviet critics at the moment, these stories belong to Zoshchenko's weakest works, and demonstrate his inability to go successfully beyond his own genre, the genre of a satirist, and to deny the dictates, conscious or subconscious, of his own esthetic imperatives. In response to demand, he had tried to do what one or two of the more forbearing critics had protested must not be asked of him: to interlard his satire with the "positive," in the manner of a layer cake. The result was invariably flat and insipid. The vision of life as it should be, as it *must* be under Communist guidance, was not his forte. As ever, his eye lighted on human foibles and the shortcomings of Soviet life as they were, and, despite critical adjuration, they evoked in him no cheerful laughter nor cheerful certainty that there would soon be an end to all these "negative" things. When, as in his conformist pieces, he forced an expression of certainty, there was no laughter; and when the laughter came, there was no certainty, even of his meaning, as in *Youth Restored* and *Blue Book* [*Golubaya kniga*].

> Rebecca A. Domar. In *Through the Glass of Soviet*
> *Literature*, Ernest J. Simmons, ed. (New York,
> Columbia University Press, 1953), p. 233

Zoshchenko's moods and techniques often bear the mark of his enjoyment of the performances of the well-known circus clown Vasili Gushchinski, his personal friend. Another influence is that of Charlie Chaplin's films.

The lonely misfit of Zoshchenko's stories is a typical Soviet citizen. The Bolshevik regime has made man into a grotesque reflection of himself in a distorting mirror, inwardly and outwardly a caricature of a human being. Zoshchenko's heroes are either such distorted creatures or extremely stupid, primitive, animal-like characters. The best illustrations to his stories were done by the cartoonists Malyutin, Malakhovski and Radlov in an overstated "primitivist manner"; the people in their drawings look like animated blocks of wood.

Zoshchenko's later stories often have a moral tacked on at the end, and the moral often reveals a revulsion for the primitivism imposed on life. . . .

Zoshchenko differs from other Soviet satirists, in particular from Mayakovski, in that his stories center not on an ideological premise but on the common man, the plain, unremarkable character who takes no interest in politics but is trapped in politics against his will.

> Vyacheslav Zavalishin. *Early Soviet Writers* (New
> York, Frederick A. Praeger, 1958), pp. 341–42

Zoshchenko uses careless language carefully. His narrators are not illiterate peasants, but they are usually not far removed from that condition. Their talk is anything but folksy. It is a weird mixture of peasant
idiom, misunderstood highfalutin phrases, rhetorical flourishes, explanatory asides that are anything but explanatory, repetitions, omissions,
propaganda jargon absurdly adapted to homey usage, instructional pseu-
doscientific words, foreign phrases, and proverbial clichés joined to the
latest party slogans. For his diction and syntax, even more than for the
situations in which they occur, Zoshchenko was charged with "caricature." In his autobiography, however, Zoshchenko insists that he merely
records the language of the streets, arranging and selecting, it is true, but
not exaggerating.

The struggle between nature and history, backwardness and revolution, produces the kind of anomalous situation that Zoshchenko delights
in, and he swoops like a hawk on those peculiarities of the Russian
language and its usage which reflect that struggle. His verbal "soup," the
words he chooses for his palette, are often themselves the product of the
kind of situation he is writing about.

Sidney Monas. Introduction to Mikhail Zoshchenko,
Scenes from the Bathhouse (Ann Arbor, Mich.,
University of Michigan Press, 1961), pp. viii–ix

Even in its unfinished state [*Before Sunrise*] is his most elaborate exercise
of humor. In his ironic search through the well of recollection, aided by
modern tools of psychological analysis, for the one single thing that had
caused his melancholy, Zoshchenko has laid before us a texture of consciousness that is all woven of normal human melancholy. Perhaps that
is what he discovered—that the melancholy he experienced was a general
human condition and not peculiar to himself. Perhaps that is what he
meant when he said in the Introduction to *Before Sunrise* that "he had
become a happy man." His stories are evidenced that he was so sensitive
to the incongruities of the human predicament that he had no recourse
but good-natured and sympathetic laughter.

Edward J. Brown. *Russian Literature Since the
Revolution* (New York, Crowell-Collier, 1963), p. 234

Comedy has always been conspicuously successful in times when there
existed a powerful literary tradition, men of literary excellence, a clear
and common set of standards, and an experience of moral degeneration.
All of Zoshchenko's stories depend on the dichotomy between the preva-
lence of old, pre-revolutionary cultural values and the effort of the newly
liberated proletariat to adopt those values, in the attempt debasing both
the old values and the freshly acclaimed communist ideals.

Zoshchenko is a bitter comedian, not a jokester. Ilf and Petrov are funny; Zoshchenko ridicules. Ilf and Petrov were criticized in reviews; Zoshchenko was publicly denounced. . . . Zoshchenko wrote "miniature" stories, but their scope reveals all the madness of our reason, the "matter and impertinency mix'd." They are the work of a great writer. . . .

Zoshchenko, who is five years dead now, comes to us more loudly every day; he has a high, special, subtle, personal style; his private melancholy and hypochondria are, in his fiction, overcome by his consciousness of vitality, by his compassion for the vitality of others. He comes across easily and trenchantly on this side of the ocean, as if he were one of us. The story behind his stories is the autobiography of our world.

F. D. Reeve. *HdR*. Winter, 1963–64, pp. 616–17

Zoshchenko's technique is in essence the technique of Wodehouse or Damon Runyon—a particular colloquial speech-pattern stylised to the point of self-parody. The colloquial idiom he starts with is what one might call working-class Sovietese. He cuts it like a clown's suit, at once too short and too baggy—monosyllabic where it ought to be expansive ("And on the way the general over-ate, and died of dysentery"), heavily paddled with euphemisms and so-to-speaks where it should be terse ("On the one hand, sometimes it would seem more advantageous for us not to be alive. But on the other hand, so to speak, no, thank you very much"). He exaggerates that curious Russian obliquity and inconsequentiality which lend such an indissoluble air of Russianness to even the best translations of Russian novels, and he laces the mixture with misapplied scientific terminology and plonking Party clichés. Armed with this superbly inappropriate piece of linguistic equipment he sets out to describe love, birth, and death, and to elucidate the finer points of Soviet manners. It's like a clown performing a surgical operation with a giant collapsible rubber knife and fork, and a lot of the pleasure comes from watching the delicacy and ingenuity with which he wields his preposterous instruments.

Is he a satirist, though? Well, he makes fun of the shortcomings in Soviet bath-house administration and the supply of electric light bulbs. So do the writers in *Krokodil*. The staff of *Krokodil* do it because they want inefficient bath-house personnel to mend their ways. Zoshchenko does it because he thinks it's funny that human beings who aspire to run an ideal state cannot even run a bath-house properly. Again and again he slyly measures the grandiose pretensions of political optimism against the scale of man—and a small man at that. In all his stories he reminds us that men are moved by greed, hampered by idleness and fate, bound by the squalor of their circumstances, preoccupied with the trivia of daily living. He remarks on these things ostensibly to help bring reality into line with the ideal, in fact to cut the ideal down to the size of reality. His superficial ambiguity is both part of his comic technique and his political protection. In the long run, of course, it was not ambiguous at all, and he was silenced.

Michael Frayn. *Encounter*. Jan., 1964, p. 70

"Adventures of a Monkey" was labeled by many critics, even by the Western ones, as an innocuous story meant primarily for children. . . . Scholars seem to agree that "Adventures of a Monkey," being basically an innocent and simple story, certainly did not warrant the severity of Zhdanov's wrath. True, the plot is a marvel of simplicity geared, most likely deliberately, to a child's level of comprehension. . . . The question is, however, whether the story is what Zhdanov claims it to be. It must be kept in mind that Zoshchenko never was an innocuous writer. To maintain that he wanted nothing else but to write an innocent story for children would be to underrate him as a writer. On the other hand, to accuse him in Zhdanov's fashion would be casting him in an even more incongruous role—that of a stealthy denigrator of his own people. Indeed, even his most innocent sketches are concealed barbs at the rulers of the people through the alleged shortcomings of the people themselves. In addition, the time when the story was written—immediately after or perhaps even during the terrible war—was certainly not conducive to innocent writing. The very fact that Zhdanov found it necessary to castigate Zoshchenko in public for this story gives it a weight far exceeding the framework of a simple, humorous children's story.

There is, therefore, a distinct temptation to interpret this story as an allegory. . . .

[Such interpretation] best explains the motives behind Zhdanov's wrath and the real meaning of his accusations. A loyal servant of the system and the state, he could not overlook the implications of Zoshchenko's devastating words that "it's better to live in the zoo than at liberty." Not willing to admit publicly to the sting of Zoshchenko's allegory, he assailed it at its face value. Those who are acquainted with Zoshchenko's tribulations at the hands of the authorities on account of his boldness and independent spirit are inclined to see in all his works a running argument with an all-powerful, all-usurping agency—hostile to the best in himself and to the welfare of the people around him.

Vasa D. Mihailovich. *Satire Newsletter*. Spring, 1967, pp. 84–86, 88–89

Pered vosxodom solnca is a work in which patriotic rhetoric plays only an insignificant part and the pieties of the Method none at all. It is crisp and clean in style, completely free of Communist clichés and jargon. It is deviant in ideology, resurrecting, if not openly advocating, some long-forbidden ideas of Freudian psychoanalysis. And most of all, it is a genuine work of art, by comparison with which the dutifully spurious products of the Method are revealed all too starkly as the time-serving potboilers they are. Like any genuine work of art, it is intrinsically "subversive," since it has an integrity of its own which refuses to fit the prescriptions and *idées reçues* of any official system. And like many very original works, its stature has not readily been recognized, even by people who need not tremble before any Soviet taboos. It is not only unconventional, but uncomfortable—uncomfortably honest.

No wonder the Stalinist culture bosses were shocked when they got around to looking into those issues of *Oktjabr'*, whose exteriors appeared so safely gray and respectable. Further publication of *Pered vosxodom solnca* was stopped; the "critics" were mobilized for a Stalin-style campaign of vilification; and Zoščenko was, as it were, earmarked as the obvious victim for the much more vicious campaign of ideological reconditioning to be launched by Andrej Ždanov after the war.

Since Stalin's death Zoščenko has been vouchsafed a partial (very partial) rehabilitation. Volumes of his works, carefully selected and occasionally touched up to suit current ideological requirements, such as anti-Americanism, have been published several times since 1956. In none of these, however, has there been any sign of *Pered vosxodom solnca,* nor of any unpublished works written during the long years of silence. That there are such works is evident from the memoirs of Veniamin Kaverin, who says of Zoščenko: "He worked every day. He wrote plays, he wrote *feuilletons*, which were returned to the author with polite or impolite replies. He wrote letters to Stalin in which he demanded justice. He wrote, but he got no answer."

Hugh McLean. *SEEJ*. Winter, 1968, p. 475

The heroes of his early stories hardly understand what is going on around them and in the country in general. As a result they cannot find their place in life, in the general break-up of social conditions. They have no clearly expressed, active attitude either to one or the other side of the social conflict. . . .

The inimitable features of Zoshchenko's hero possess a far wider significance for the writer and his creative progress than might have appeared at first glance. With particular force and decisiveness he poses the question of the "man-in-the-street's" loss of individuality and spirituality in the old society; he is doomed by the overpowering force of various, seemingly fortuitous and trifling circumstances. According to Zoshchenko, even epoch-making historical events lack the power to rouse this type of faceless man, deprived of individuality, out of his state of complete vacuity; they carry their spiritual emptiness all through the revolution and into a new epoch. It is characteristic of Zoshchenko's creative interest that he pays little attention to revolutionary events and the Civil War in their relation to the individual.

Like many other writers in the initial years of Soviet literature, Zoshchenko entrusted the narration to his hero; owing to the literary inexperience and quaintness of his heroes' perceptions, the narrative assumes the shape of a sort of folk tale. The more exotic and colourful his tale, the scarcer the actual and individual spiritual colours. The hero's speech reveals his lack of individuality. These early stories are filled to the utmost with this "folk-tale" element, the author is totally absent, things are seen through the eyes of his characters alone, perceived "at their level." . . .

In the twenties and thirties, a salient feature of Zoshchenko's views and writings was his negative attitude to the role and significance of mental activity, of intellectualism in the old society. It afforded the writer scope for scathing criticism of the use of intellectualism as a camouflage for concealing bourgeois essence. Nevertheless, a certain underestimation of "intellectuality" is extended by the writer to the new social conditions.

One-sidedness of this kind or even—to put it more plainly—oversimplification in the interpretation of the spiritual aspect of people's lives, their individual and social behaviour, the tendency to negate "intellectuality" in toto is connected with the writer's general literary standpoint and his artistic credo. Throughout the twenties, and more definitely in the thirties Zoshchenko often proclaimed that he could not accept psychological approach as a means in the literary presentation of a man of the bourgeois or the gentry type, and, in particular, of the bourgeois intellectual. According to Zoshchenko, the psychological approach to the images of the new people, living in new and totally different conditions, was anomalous and it was not true art.

A deep-seated contradiction made itself felt in Zoshchenko's work in the thirties. The problem of the day was the social training and re-education of the individual. This Zoshchenko resolved to treat after his own fashion in his work. He proved very consistent in defending his own creative principles, and out of this came the inevitable collisions. The question was: would his hero, while remaining within the bounds of the usual Zoshchenko situations, prove capable of being guided by other, broader, spiritually more profound motives? The evolution of this writer shows that by the end of the twenties and particularly in the thirties this problem assumed the greatest importance for him.

Pavel Gromov. SL. April, 1969, pp. 188–91

COPYRIGHT ACKNOWLEDGMENTS

INDEX TO CRITICS

Names of critics are cited on the pages given.